TWAYNE'S
FILMMAKERS SERIES

Frank Beaver, Editor

THE MEN WHO
MADE THE MONSTERS

THE MEN WHO
MADE THE MONSTERS

Paul M. Jensen

TWAYNE PUBLISHERS
An Imprint of Simon & Schuster Macmillan
New York
PRENTICE HALL INTERNATIONAL
London • Mexico City • New Delhi • Singapore • Sydney • Toronto

Twayne's Filmmakers Series, Frank Beaver, General Editor

The Men Who Made the Monsters
Paul M. Jensen

Twayne Publishers
An Imprint of Simon & Schuster Macmillan
1633 Broadway
New York, NY 10019

Library of Congress Cataloging-in-Publication Data

Jensen, Paul M.
     The men who made the monsters / Paul M. Jensen.
         p.   cm. — (Twayne's filmmakers series)
     Filmography: p.
     Includes bibliographical references and index.
     ISBN 0-8057-9338-0 (pbk.)
     1. Horror films—History and criticism.   2. Motion picture producers and directors—
United States—Biography.   3. Motion picture producers and directors—Great Britain—
Biography.   I. Title.   II. Series.
     PN1995.9.H6J46   1996
     791.43'616—dc20   96-27582
                                                                                    CIP

10 9 8 7 6 5 4 3 2 1 (pbk)

Printed in the United States of America.

CONTENTS

FOREWORD

Of all the contemporary arts, the motion picture is particularly timely and diverse as a popular culture enterprise. This lively art form cleverly combines storytelling with photography to achieve what has been a quintessential twentieth-century phenomenon. Individual as well as national and cultural interests have made the medium an unusually varied one for artistic expression and analysis. Films have been exploited for commercial gain, for political purposes, for experimentation, and for self-exploration. The various responses to the motion picture have given rise to different labels for both the fun and the seriousness with which this art form has been received, ranging from "the movies" to "cinema." These labels hint at both the theoretical and sociological parameters of the film medium.

A collective art, the motion picture has nevertheless allowed individual genius to flourish in all its artistic and technical areas: directing, screenwriting, cinematography, acting, editing. The medium also encompasses many genres beyond the narrative film, including documentary, animated, and avant-garde expression. The range and diversity of motion pictures suggest rich opportunities for appreciation and for study.

Twayne's Filmmakers Series examines the full panorama of motion picture history and art. Many studies are auteur-oriented and elucidate the work of individual directors whose ideas and cinematic styles make them the authors of their films. Other studies examine film movements and genres or analyze cinema from a national perspective. The series seeks to illuminate all the many aspects of film for the film student, the scholar, and the general reader.

Frank Beaver

PREFACE

Monster films have fascinated and disturbed movie audiences for decades, exerting an appeal that meets an evident psychological and emotional need. Despite the initial condescension and condemnation by critics and many others, such films have often endured the ravages of time far better than their superficially more respectable contemporaries.

At their best, monster films rarely convey clear-cut messages, but relate directly to humanity's inner nature, to the archetypal fears and fascinations shared by everyone: fear of the violence and irrationality that dwell beneath civilization's attempts at order, fear of what we ourselves may be capable of, fear of the distorted and deformed, fear of the unknown. These fears, which have hardly altered over time, make mundane existence magically, nightmarishly unpredictable.

The true character of monster films is less often articulated in their dialogue than embodied in situations. More important, it is inherent in images that create on screen not the world of tangible facts and concrete realities but that of the emotions, the instincts, and the imagination. This stress on images tends to attract filmmakers, for it permits—even requires—them to exercise their cinematic powers. It might be argued that the most successful of these filmmakers are the least self-conscious, because only they can draw frankly and thoroughly on their own instinctual, irrational dreads.

The filmmakers discussed in this volume are key members of this group. Three—James Whale, Terence Fisher, and Freddie Francis—are directors, and two—Willis O'Brien and Ray Harryhausen—are model animators who were thoroughly involved in many aspects of their films' creation. Each has a strong visual and/or technical background in such fields as set design, editing, photography, or special effects. Together, their careers cover much of film history, both American and British.

James Whale defined the horror film genre when he made the original *Frankenstein* in 1931. With *The Lost World* (1925) and *King Kong* (1933), Willis O'Brien similarly defined the fantasy-adventure film, which features dramatic encounters with gigantic creatures. Ray Harryhausen later refined O'Brien's approach, while extending it to include myth and legend, as in *The 7th Voyage of Sinbad* (1958) and *Jason and the Argonauts* (1963). Starting in the late 1950s, Terence Fisher revived and reinterpreted the traditional characters of Frankenstein and Dracula for a contemporary audience. More recently, Freddie Francis brought his expertise as an Academy Award–winning photographer to the genre and directed several moody, atmospheric classics.

These creators reveal a wide range of styles and tones as they seek to entertain and stir an audience. *The Men Who Made the Monsters* examines how they used their cinematic skills to tell dramatic stories and evoke powerful emotions. These individuals transcended the category of impersonal entertainers to become artists who shared their perspectives on existence. As a result, this volume takes as its thesis the fact that the films discussed reveal the personalities and outlooks of their creators. Sometimes this happened consciously, but more often it was an unconscious process that resulted from a commitment to their professions and from a compulsion to create meaningful works within a popular genre. Often, therefore, the films entertain while also conveying insights about human nature.

All five of these subjects were pragmatic people who needed to make a living, to earn money. At the same time, they found themselves engaged in an activity they loved, one they had to engage in to feel satisfied. Although they frequently worked on films with limited budgets, the depth and range of their talent and their commitment frequently triumphed. In a genre known for calculated exploitation, they convey sincerity of feeling and perspective with stylistic subtlety and even moral rigor.

I met and interviewed Ray Harryhausen, Terence Fisher, and Freddie Francis, as well as several people who worked closely with James Whale. I then filled out my understanding by consulting a wide range of published interviews and other records, including unpublished shooting scripts. Finally, after absorbing all of this, I found that my viewings (or, in most cases, re-viewings) of the films produced an unexpected effect. I had always liked the films, and I had come to like their makers. Now, I seemed also to understand their personalities: their strengths and limitations, their quirks and compulsions, their needs which were met and those which lay unsatisfied. As a result, I found myself admiring both the men and their films all the more.

In writing this volume, however, I tried to maintain a reasonable balance between enthusiasm and objectivity in treating the subjects' careers and their specific films. Similarly, I tried to deal—in varying proportions, as situations required—with background information, the filmmakers' thoughts about their work, the films' content, and their visual style. Such an approach seems to me the only enduring one, whether or not the volume in hand successfully illustrates it. At any rate, the reader should come away having encountered five sets of films that reveal the sensibilities of five individuals who are well worth knowing.

ACKNOWLEDGMENTS

This book probably would not exist but for the openness and generosity of Freddie Francis. In 1967, my attempt to contact a much-admired director had brought negative, disillusioning results. Still stinging from that experience, I decided to try again and sought an interview with Mr. Francis, the photographer-turned-director. To my relief, his response was both friendly and professional, both frank and diplomatic, and it has remained so ever since. His positive reaction also encouraged me to contact other creative figures, both active and retired. For those satisfying encounters, as well, I feel indebted to the support which Freddie Francis offered to a then-unknown correspondent.

In the preparation of this volume, the firsthand information and perspective offered by the following individuals proved invaluable: Terence Fisher, Robert Florey, Freddie Francis, Ray Harryhausen, Ted Kent, Elsa Lanchester, David Lewis, and R. C. Sherriff. Additional facts and insights were provided by Forrest J Ackerman, Ray Bradbury, Veronica Carlson, Peter Cushing, Pierre Fogel, Kevin Francis, Richard Gordon, Curtis Harrington, Carl Laemmle, Jr., Benn W. Levy, David Manners, Peter Saunders, Gloria Stuart, Milton Subotsky, and Hilda Walls. Far more than just cooperative and informative, these individuals received me with unforgettable graciousness.

Secondary research was made possible by the cooperation of SUNY-Oneonta's Milne Library, especially the interlibrary loan staff; New York City's Library of the Performing Arts at Lincoln Center; the Birmingham (England) Central Library; and, in London, the British Film Institute, the Westminster Central Reference Library, the Theatre Museum at Covent Garden, and the British Museum Newspaper Library at Colindale. Appreciation is also extended to SUNY-Oneonta for granting a sabbatical leave during the fall of 1994 and, for technical support, to the college's Intructional Resources Center, especially Hap Mancke and Charles Winters.

The photographs that appear in this volume do so courtesy of the following: Amicus Films, Cinerama, Columbia Pictures, First National Pictures, Fitzroy Films, Hammer Films, Museum of Modern Art/Film Stills Archive, National Film Archive, Paramount Pictures, RKO Radio Pictures, Tigon Films, 20th Century–Fox Pictures, Tyburn Films, United Artists Pictures, Universal Pictures, Warner Bros. Pictures, World Film Services.

The author wishes to thank the following individuals for their varied kinds of support and aid: David Anderson, Greg Boggia, Ronald V. Borst, Jack Brent, Jerrold Brown, Jim Danforth, William K. Everson, Mark Frank, Richard Koszarski, Jessie Lilley, Tim and Donna Lucas, Scott MacQueen, Leonard Maltin, Bryan Senn, Gary Svehla, and Richard Valley. I am indebted to Frank Beaver for his encouragement, to editor Mark Zadrozny for his commitment to this project, and to manuscript editor India Koopman for her acuity.

On a more personal level, I want to acknowledge the influence of the people who over the years have helped to prepare me for this project: Robert Allen, Donald Chattaway, Peter Christensen, George Gildersleeve, Arthur Loder, Vincent Quatroche, Fred Silva, Harry Staley, and Roger Watkins.

Special thanks are due to Richard Klemensen for generously making key research materials available; to Arthur Lennig for his close reading of the manuscript, perceptive suggestions, and general inspiration; and to Mark A. Miller for his continual encouragement, advice, and support.

This book is dedicated to my parents, who didn't understand why I like these films, and to Barbara Dobkowski, who does.

CHAPTER 1

James Whale

James Whale directed four of the most intelligent, witty, and visually striking horror films ever made: *Frankenstein* (1931), *The Old Dark House* (1932), *The Invisible Man* (1933), and *Bride of Frankenstein* (1935). With this quartet of classics he virtually created, and then dominated, the genre. Whale's monsters ranged widely, from Henry Frankenstein's brutish creation and a scientist seeking power through invisibility to the decadent perversity of Horace Femm (in *The Old Dark House*) and Dr. Pretorius (in *Bride of Frankenstein*). Unable to produce one-dimensional villains, Whale gave these characters individuality, depth, and complexity.

Probably the most versatile and sophisticated of all directors associated with horror films, the English-born Whale worked on 22 features during a Hollywood career just over a decade long. These include comedies, war stories, courtroom dramas, adventures, a musical, and a slice of contemporary British life. They are not all of equal quality, but many reveal sensitivity, eccentric humor, and a confident cinematic style. Whale's background as a painter, magazine cartoonist, and designer of stage sets and costumes polished his visual sense, while his experience directing and acting in plays heightened his feeling for drama, for character, and for good dialogue well delivered.

Although he worked in Hollywood's factory system, Whale often was the dominant creative force behind his pictures. His association with Universal—one of the smaller, less regimented studios—helped make this possible: Its "family" atmosphere fit Whale's temperament, as did the enlightened passivity of Carl Laemmle, Jr., the youthful vice president of production who hired talented people and let himself trust their judgment.

The best of Whale's films reveal his contradictory characteristics, which somehow seldom clash. Whale respected an author's intentions, while revealing his own distinctive personality; his films are both literate and highly visual, and they mix flamboyant theatricality with slice-of-life realism. Personally, Whale was soft-spoken and gentle but also forceful and decisive; elegant but gawky; sardonic yet vulnerable; introspective though engaging as a raconteur. Although he craved success and its trappings, he did so more on a social and artistic level than on a crassly material one.

During his years at Universal, Whale bypassed entrenched production methods, following through on his artistic decisions with unwavering determination. Uncomfortable among strangers, he frequently worked with people he knew but he rarely sought their advice or opinions. Despite his aloof and even imperious manner, Whale's charm and dedication usually won over his associates. Ted Kent, who edited many of his films, stated years later that Whale was "firm in his belief in his author-

The ever-artful James Whale in the real-life role he created for himself: the elegant and cultured film director.

ity—but as firm as he was, he was a very kind and considerate man." He added, "I can't remember any conversation over the years that didn't involve the picture that we were working on. Outside conversation never existed; it was just all the picture."[1]

Cinematically, Whale followed his instincts, creating films that have his stamp on every aspect. He generally collaborated with his scriptwriters, selected his performers and technicians, and guided department heads with sketches of sets, costumes, and makeup. Ted Kent recalled that the backs of Whale's script pages were full of drawings. "He was very talented," Kent explained, "in sketching sets for the art director, especially if it was a castle, or a ballroom, or places that had columns and arches and drapes. He would give them something to start with—you know, an impression of what he thought. Then the art director would come back with his detailed drawing." Elsa Lanchester, who acted in *Bride of Frankenstein,* agreed that Whale "conceived" his sets. In that movie, she added, the forest was built on a long but shallow sound stage, so Whale used forced perspective—he was a master at it—to create the impression that the set covered a large area.[2]

In addition, Whale designed the look of the Bride's hair, which stands stiffly away from her head, in contrast to the script's description of it as "curled close" and hanging "straight and dark on either side." Lanchester also described the director's meticulous concern about the dress she wore as Mary Shelley: He insisted that it be of "the finest possible white net, with iridescent, sequined butterflies and moons and stars on it," even though such details would not be obvious on the screen.

Whale's distinctive use of editing went against the accepted standards of the time. He often cut directly from a medium shot of a character to a slightly closer one of the same person, as opposed to the usual method of moving the camera nearer during a shot or cutting away to a different character before returning to the closer view. Ted Kent disliked Whale's editing style, calling it abrupt and "choppy." Working on a Whale film, he explained, was bad for his reputation among other editors, who would say, "It wasn't very well cut. It just jumped all over the place."[3]

Whale carefully prepared his shooting scripts to indicate these cuts and then added even more. Significantly, instead of filming an entire scene from various angles, as most directors did, he shot only those sections he intended to use. Gloria Stuart, who acted in three of his films, quickly realized that Whale on the set was "cutting the film the way *he* wanted it."[4] The result left an editor no choice but to construct the scene the way the director intended. To Ted Kent, this meant that Whale "was afraid the editor would botch it up. He probably was of the opinion that the director was the one that should edit the pictures and, if he had to have an editor do it, he'd . . . get everything nailed down: 'This is the way I want it and this is the way it's going to be.' That was the kind of guy he was."[5]

Whale's four horror films clearly illustrate this approach, as in the progressively closer shots with which he introduces the Frankenstein Monster and the Invisible Man. During conversation scenes, Whale also edits frequently, in ways that illustrate and emphasize the dialogue. A perfect example appears in *Bride of Frankenstein*'s prologue, where varied camera positions isolate sections of Lord Byron's speech, underlining them and expressing their meaning visually. What Whale had planned, in the shooting script, as a single medium-close shot becomes, in the film, the following four shots: [Medium shot of Byron] "I should like to think that an irate Jehovah was pointing those arrows of lightning directly at my head—[close-up of Byron's head]—the unbowed head of George Gordon, Lord Byron, England's greatest sinner. [Long shot of Byron and Shelley] But I cannot flatter myself to that extent. Possibly those thunders are for our dear Shelley—[medium shot of Shelley]—Heaven's applause for England's greatest poet." Audiences rarely notice Whale's unique editing, but it does have a psychological impact, as the viewer first senses the emphasis on Byron and then the shift away from him.

Because Whale made his basic decisions about editing in advance, he was free on the set to concentrate on the actors' performances. At this stage of production, he drew on a sensitivity to mood and character that developed during a theatrical career that included the first major English productions of Chekhov's *The Sea Gull* and *The Cherry Orchard,* as well as plays by Pirandello, Maugham, Shaw, and Molière. As a result, Whale spent much time rehearsing a film's cast, leading them to an understanding of the text. As Mae Clarke, who starred in three of his films, recalled, "Our objectives became: What did the *author* want? What did he not say, and assumed *we* would?"[6] Whale's method involved describing a scene's situation and the character's feelings in it. "He wouldn't say *how*" to play the scene, according to Clarke. Instead, "he would tell you *what* was happening." After, he would say, "Now let's see *what* you want to do."[7] Gloria Stuart elaborates: "He would say how he felt the scene, we'd play it, and then he'd start to work individually. Very politely, very thoroughly, very tactfully."[8]

Although the actors may have felt free to produce their own results, Whale actually guided them to his interpretation. "With James," said Stuart, "every single line, every single movement, your whole approach to the character was very meticulously discussed," and rehearsal continued "until James had everything exactly the way he wanted it."[9] At times, he even provided a demonstration. In *Frankenstein,* for example, all of the Monster's movements were Whale's. "I saw him do them," declared Mae Clarke, who explained that when Henry Frankenstein "first said, 'Sit *down,*' Whale mapped it all out. He said, 'Now you don't know what sit down means, but you know because his hands are going that way he means back. So you go. . . . You hit the chair, you go down.' "[10]

Generally, the actors gave Whale what he wanted, according to Gloria Stuart, but "if someone angered him or opposed him—said 'Yes,' and then did it their own way—he was very swift to notice and point it out, sometimes with an unkind word. There was never any yelling though."[11] Once, when Claude Rains tried to steal a scene from Ms. Stuart (in *The Invisible Man*), Whale told him, "Now, Claude—don't be naughty. We can take it over and over and over, because we'd like half of Gloria!"[12]

Even cooperative cast members sometimes found themselves frustrated or bewildered by Whale's attention to seemingly irrelevant details. Valerie Hobson, who appeared in *Bride of Frankenstein,* disliked the wedding dress she wore in her first scene—"it made me look like an elephant!"—and considered it "a lot of nonsense" when Whale told her, "You mustn't wear any underclothes."[13] Evidently the director didn't volunteer a reason for this, but when Gloria Stuart questioned why her character wore an evening gown in *The Old Dark House,* he explained that, when she runs through a corridor, "I want you to be like a flame, like a dancer." This is a revealing insight into Whale's poetic visual sense, but Stuart thought the idea "pretty ridiculous." Nevertheless, "that's what he wanted and that's what he got."[14]

Gloria Stuart's first impression of Whale was of someone "very austere, very cold, very English—very removed from the scene,"[15] but "once initial familiarities developed, the atmosphere became an easy, good one, although always very serious."[16] Mae Clarke also felt that everyone on the set developed a comfortable familiarity. "We all knew each other almost like a family excepting it wasn't a gooey family, it was a professional understanding of each other's motivations, etc. So we had a very pleasant association that way."[17] Because Whale had few close friends, this sort of professional "family" became his mainstay. He felt comfortable and in control when working, perhaps because he could be close to people without having to deal with them on a more intimate, personal level.

James Whale at work in his office bungalow on the Universal Studios lot. Like some of the sets for his films, Whale's real-life quarters were filled with flowers.

James Whale's personality—his private nature, his sensitivity, and his sometimes biting humor—derived from a basic insecurity that had its roots in childhood. Born on 22 July 1889 in the town of Dudley, he was part of a large, working-class family that struggled against poverty in the grim industrial Midlands of England. Although he soon revealed artistic ability and attended the Dudley School of Arts and Crafts, a more formal cultivation of his talent was out of the question. Whale seemed reluctantly destined for a life of physical labor, but at the same time this introspective, sensitive, and talented boy—who was also, according to actor Alan Napier, "skinny" and "slightly undersized"[18]—felt apart from his surroundings and was probably teased, and even ridiculed, by his more earthy peers.

Whale defended himself by taking the initiative and cultivating his differences. He adopted the manner of dress and precision of speech of a gentleman, not a factory worker, and he exaggerated his sensitive, artist's demeanor. Whale also cultivated a quiet self-confidence, which was usually justified but not always completely felt. At the same time, he positioned himself as an observer of his own existence, someone above and apart from events and people, commenting with ironic skepticism on others and, implicitly, on himself.

These tendencies would define Whale's adult personality, for even at the peak of his success he was—according to a close friend, author R. C. Sherriff—"a loner" whose defensiveness about his lack of education and social polish made him combative. Once, after Sherriff had introduced him to some upper-class acquaintances, Whale spoke on and on about how worthless those people were.[19] Having grown up in a rough-hewn family, he spent his adult life obsessed with refinement and class, and with the contradiction between his desire for good breeding and his actual origins. "Jimmy saw everything in terms of a step up the ladder," concluded Alan Napier. "He gloried in achieving success."[20] Whale truly enjoyed the work he did, but that was not enough, nor did he merely seek to live the good life. His need for achievement was also inspired by a resentment of those who had mocked him, a feeling that had lingered for so long that it became a part of his nature; success offered the satisfaction of being well-paid and respected for doing what those around him had for years disdained, thereby satisfying (but never totally venting) his need for revenge.

Such success, however, was still far off when in 1914, during World War I, Whale found himself a lieutenant in a Worcestershire regiment. He served his country, fighting in France and Belgium, until on 25 August 1917 his platoon was caught in a trap and captured by the Germans. As a prisoner of war, Whale passed the time doing charcoal sketches of other soldiers and helping to put on plays, for which he improvised sets as best he could. He also played a lot of bridge and won about £4,000 ($20,000 in those days). Returning to England at the war's end, Whale brought along the IOUs he had collected and cashed them all. Most of the money went to help his family.

In 1919 Whale, still an aspiring artist, had a few satirical cartoons published in the magazine the *Bystander,* but he soon relinquished art in favor of his new interest, the theater. He acted in the Birmingham Repertory Theatre's production of the seventeenth-century play *The Knight of the Burning Pestle,* by Beaumont and Fletcher; a program lists him in the catch-all category, "Soldiers, Gentlemen, Boys." The production ran for the standard two weeks, from 30 August to 12 September 1919. At the end of December, he played the role of Rugby in a Manchester production of Shakespeare's *The Merry Wives of Windsor.* Ernest Thesiger, who appeared as "Slender," later described the thirty-year-old Whale as "a frail ex-prisoner-of-war with a faun-like charm."[21]

During much of 1920, and into 1921, Whale served as stage manager and played various small parts in the Birmingham Rep's touring production of *Abraham Lincoln,* by John Drinkwater. Then, back in Birmingham, he designed the costumes for George Bernard Shaw's *Captain Brassbound's Conversion* and appeared as an extra in the production. Later in 1921, he joined the Liverpool Repertory Theatre, which had been taken over by the London-based Nigel Playfair. Whale's main job was as stage manager, but he also played small parts. In September 1922, Playfair brought his Liverpool production of Arnold Bennett's *Body and Soul* to London, where Whale served as associate stage manager during its run. He then stayed in London to stage-manage Playfair's *Polly,* an adaptation of John Gay's *The Beggar's Opera.*

At the Liverpool Rep, Whale had developed a close relationship with the company's set and costume designer, Doris Zinkeisen. Playfair also brought her to London, where she designed his 1923 production of Karel Capek's *The Insect Play.* "Miss Zinkeisen was very good-looking and wore exotic clothes," recalled John Gielgud (who acted in *The Insect Play,* along with Claude Rains and Elsa Lanchester). "She was at that time engaged to James Whale, a tall young man with side-whiskers and suede shoes." They "made a striking pair at the dances to which Playfair, with his charming hospitality, used to invite the company."[22] It was also during *Polly's* long run that Whale made his debut as a director with Geoffrey Whitworth's *Father Noah—A Mystery of the Ark,* for which Zinkeisen designed the sets and costumes. Performed on 12 June 1923, this curtain-raiser was part of a benefit for the Library Fund of the British Drama League.

Whale evidently enjoyed sharing this Bohemian period of art and outlandishness with a kindred spirit, but something happened around this time that caused him and Doris Zinkeisen to part company. Perhaps Whale simply recognized and accepted his homosexuality; this clearly had happened by the spring of 1925, when he invited Alan Napier to an all-male party.[23] However, the change may have been more deeply psychological than that. Elsa Lanchester, who knew him then, never fully understood the break-up with Zinkeisen, but, she said, "I think he believed that was to blame for his not having a 'normal' life."[24]

At any rate, Lanchester noted a shift in Whale's personality, a growing bitterness. "I don't think he liked humanity very much," she concluded, and this seemed particularly true of women.[25] However, Whale and Zinkeisen did remain friends: In 1936, she designed the costumes for his film *Show Boat* (1936) and also painted a large portrait of him; twenty years later, he remembered her in his will. This pivotal aspect of James Whale's life will probably forever remain vague, for he rarely spoke in personal terms about himself or his past. It seems clear, though, that he initially felt himself to be an outsider because of his social origins and artistic nature; his homosexuality then heightened that feeling.

Near the end of *Polly*'s run, Whale became involved with London's nonprofit theater organizations, which produced revivals or new plays on a showcase basis, usually on Sunday evenings. From September 1923 through September 1924, he was stage manager (or stage director) of six such offerings and also designed the sets for two of them, Shakespeare's *Measure for Measure* and *Much Ado about Nothing*. With this experience behind him, Whale was hired to aid J. B. Fagan, the director and designer for the Oxford Players, a repertory company in that university city that put on a new program each week of the academic year.

During the 1924-25 season, Whale served as assistant director, designed a majority of the sets, and played several supporting roles. The Oxford Players—who included John Gielgud and Alan Napier—performed a wide range of works, including Shaw's *Candida,* Synge's *Deirdre of the Sorrows,* Ibsen's *John Gabriel Borkman,* and Barrie's *The Admirable Crichton.* Two of these productions, which Whale designed and in which he acted, were so well received that Fagan later brought them to London: The first, Richard Hughes's *A Comedy of Good and Evil,* lasted for only fourteen performances, but the second, Chekhov's *The Cherry Orchard,* premiered on 25 May 1925 and didn't close until 19 September. The enthusiastic London critics, echoing their Oxford counterparts, noted that the production achieved the slice-of-life, human comedy style of the Moscow Art Theatre, with all of the characterizations kept in "almost perfect balance."[26]

As both designer and actor, Whale received special attention. *The Era* found his settings for *The Cherry Orchard* "particularly good and the second act, laid in the open fields, was exceedingly beautiful. The delightful background, the colours of the costumes, and the compositions of the figures made a picture of striking beauty."[27] At the same time, the influential James Agate singled out Whale's performance as the awkward Ephikhodof, who "cannot enter a room without tripping, hand a bouquet without dropping it, or play billiards without breaking his cue. . . . He is only a small character, yet he has his place, and when he speaks the world centers round him for the space of that utterance."[28]

One month after *The Cherry Orchard* closed, Gielgud and Whale returned in Chekhov's *The Sea-Gull,* with Whale again designing the sets. Then, during 1926–27, he rejoined Nigel Playfair for three consecutive productions. He was stage director for *Riverside Nights,* a revue that included a parody of Chekhov's plays, which Whale designed and in which he acted. Subsequently, Whale played "Baptiste" and stage-directed Molière's *The Would-Be Gentleman,* then designed George Farquhar's *The Beaux' Stratagem,* in which he portrayed Squire Sullen.

Nigel Playfair's son Giles later described the Whale of this period as "quiet, cynical, an entertaining conversationalist, but not quite the kind of man for whom I would have predicted great success [because] his manner was too precious and too docile to fit him well for the actual task of stage management. Stage hands like to be given their orders directly and in the roundest possible terms. James Whale would lead them aside and whisper confidentially, 'Don't you think it would be fun if we had a bit of green paint on that flat?' His methods of command did not win their respect."[29]

Nevertheless, through 1928 Whale found frequent employment as a stage manager or stage director, and also as a designer and actor. In the nearly four years after he returned to London from Oxford, Whale performed one or more of these functions in nine commercial productions and twenty nonprofit ventures. In addition, the non-profit world gave him three chances to direct: *Light o' Love* (7 December 1925), *Caged* (21 December 1927), and *The Young Visitors* (10 January 1928).

Finally, Whale directed his first commercial production, a double bill of *Fortunato* and *The Lady from Alfaqueque,* by Serafin and Joaquin Alvarez Quintero, which he also designed; it played from 22 October to 17 November 1928. Respectful reviews were undercut by the fact that Harley Granville-Barker—the theatrical legend who had, with his wife, written the English-language adaptations—periodically took charge of the production and even insisted that O. B. Clarence be hired to play Fortunato, a role that Whale had intended for himself. Not that this incident interfered with Whale's career, for from 7 to 20 November he acted in *High Treason,* while also directing and designing *The Dreamers,* a delicate tale about reincarnated lovers that had a two-week run starting on 12 November. Thus, for several days that month, Whale's efforts were represented on three London stages simultaneously.

Soon after, Whale directed and designed the Incorporated Stage Society's produc-tion of *Journey's End* (9 and 10 December 1928), a play by R. C. Sherriff about the pressures of trench warfare. Laurence Olivier starred as Captain Stanhope. The glow-ing reviews led to a commercial run, but Olivier had his eye on a different play, so Whale replaced him with a relative unknown, Colin Clive. Even as he conducted rehearsals to blend Clive with the rest of the cast, Whale re-created his role of Medve-denko in a one-week revival of *The Sea-Gull.* Then *Journey's End* premiered on 21 January 1929 and suddenly Whale, Sherriff, and Clive were famous.

After fulfilling commitments to design two other plays, Whale inevitably followed where his hit show led. He rehearsed a second company of *Journey's End,* offered six performances in London, then sailed to New York for a 22 March premiere. Next, Whale journeyed from New York to Hollywood, where he directed the dialogue scenes for Paramount's *The Love Doctor* (1929). By September, he was back in New York rehearsing the Chicago company of *Journey's End,* after which he returned to Hollywood to direct the dialogue scenes of *Hell's Angels* (1930), the World War I air epic that producer Howard Hughes had been shooting as a silent film since Novem-ber 1927. Then, in New York, Whale staged the Quinteros' *A Hundred Years Old;* after its premiere on 1 October 1929, he again headed to Hollywood, where he filmed *Journey's End,* with Colin Clive—on a leave of absence from the London produc-tion—as Stanhope. Finally, in April 1930, Whale returned to England, having been away for more than a year. While there, he directed R. C. Sherriff's next play, a small-scale comedy called *Badger's Green,* which premiered on 12 June 1930.

A chance to direct and design two one-act plays by Ferenc Molnar, *One, Two, Three* and *The Violet,* lured Whale back to New York; the program premiered on 29 Septem-ber 1930, but Whale's main interest now was films. When Universal's Carl Laemmle, Jr., asked him to direct *Waterloo Bridge,* based on Robert E. Sherwood's play about a

London prostitute's wartime affair with a soldier, Whale agreed and began a union with Laemmle and Universal that for six years provided nearly ideal working conditions. Although he would visit England often, Whale settled comfortably in Hollywood, where he established a long-term relationship with producer David Lewis, whom he had met in 1929. In 1936, however, Laemmle left Universal, taking with him Whale's power base and, ultimately, his confidence; this led to a lengthy retirement that began in 1941 and ended with Whale's suicide in 1957.

Through most of the 1930s, however, James Whale experienced both artistic and financial success, although he never lost his sense of personal insecurity. In 1936, he described Hollywood as a dreamland from which he hoped never to awaken. Having worked there since 1929, and currently at a professional peak, he nevertheless declared, "I always cash my check the minute I get it, to make sure it's real. That they should pay such fabulous salaries is beyond ordinary reasoning. Who's worth it! But why not take it." This view of his uncertain status reflected Whale's philosophy about the artificiality of existence. In the same interview, he declared: "And the architecture! And furnishings! I can have modernistic design one day, and an antiquated home over night! All the world is made of plaster of paris. I get to feel that maybe Buckingham Palace is, too!"[30]

Whale reassured himself about his own position through the people he knew and the fantasies he kept to himself. He was, said David Lewis, "very much interested in royalty, rich people, the beautiful people, the jet set of the time—he knew he couldn't make it, but he was going to *be* there, with them."[31] Thus, Whale enjoyed the company of Ernest Thesiger, who was reportedly related to royalty, and once kept a semifictional diary in which he imagined himself a lost prince. At times, Whale "borrowed" events from Lewis's life, incorporating them into his own anecdotes. Not that he couldn't distinguish reality from fantasy; such indulgences were more wish fulfillment than self-delusion.

Whale's elegance and artistry were quite real, but they also derived from a calculated performance in which he played the real-life role of "James Whale." The initial appeal of Hollywood may have been the chance to make a lot of money, but Whale quickly felt at home in this land of artifice, for he himself was a creature of illusion. Whale probably sensed that he could function better as an upper-class gentleman in America than in England, so he remained in California even after his film career ended. Physically, he cut an attractive figure, and to Americans he seemed the essence of a reserved but articulate English artist. In 1936, an interviewer declared that he "looks and sounds like Leslie Howard—but with more animation."[32] To a later eye, his strong but sensitive features evoke both Joseph Cotten and Peter O'Toole.

Just as Whale designed his own personality and stage-managed his life, he suffused his films with elegance and sophistication: The richly furnished settings through which his characters often move had much in common with Whale's own quarters; vases of flowers such as those seen on his sets also filled his home and office. In his work as in his life, Whale's appetite for style generally harnessed his personal bitterness, keeping it within the bounds of socially acceptable irony. In addition, his sensitive response to Chekhov-style realism resulted in scenes that possess an aura of naturalness. Horror stories, however, also presented Whale with the opportunity to develop heightened characters and situations into which he could channel his inner conflicts and defensiveness, resulting in a quartet of films unlike those of any other director.

Whale's theater work includes several precedents for his later direction of fantasy and horror films, including two 1928 plays in which he acted. The first, *A Man with Red Hair* (adapted by Benn W. Levy from Hugh Walpole's novel), starred Charles Laughton as the warped Mr. Crispin, who believes that pain is the most exquisite of all sensations. In his gloomy cliff house, Crispin indulges his love of torture, and the macabre production went all-out to evoke horror, prompting one critic to describe Crispin as "a thing so evil and malignant that it can paralyze one's power to combat it."[33] Whale played Crispin's son, a character described by reviewers as "strange,"[34] "masochistic,"[35] and "almost repulsive."[36]

A Revival of London's Grand Guignol consisted of five short plays, the longest being "After Death," by René Berton, "a gruesome and nerve-shaking piece of modern science, used to cause mere horror." In it, Whale played a condemned murderer who steadfastly claims his innocence. Guillotined, he becomes the subject of a scientific experiment to revive his dead brain. The process succeeds, and, when asked again about his guilt, the dead man still indicates "No," whereupon the prosecutor goes mad and "frantically endeavors to carry off the head, which he had demanded in the name of the law."[37]

To the horrific plots and atmosphere of these plays, we must add the ideas implied by two semi-allegorical fantasies in which Whale acted during 1925–26. In *A Comedy of Good and Evil,* an attractive young girl is really an emissary of the Devil (a duality later suggested in *Bride of Frankenstein*), and the theme of *Mr. Godly beside Himself* is "the inner tragedy of mankind," which involves "a longing for beauty, a yearning after something vast and almost undefinable; and when we try to . . . grasp this elusive something, we become inarticulate."[38]

When Whale, in 1928, directed *Fortunato,* he himself planned to play the good-hearted but unfortunate title character, "a creature of infinite pathos, [a man] bewildered all the time by the tossings of misfortune."[39] *Fortunato's* image of human helplessness—along with Mr. Godly's concept of elusive beauty—evidently stirred something in Whale's nature. Only three years later he directed Boris Karloff in a role that combined the essence of these characters, the Frankenstein Monster.

Although much work had already been done on the script of *Frankenstein* (1931) before Whale became involved, he turned what would have been a brutal, simplistic horror tale into a complex, sensitive, and surprisingly personal work. Not a direct adaptation of Mary Shelley's 1818 novel, the film owes its existence to Peggy Webling's 1927 play *Frankenstein: An Adventure in the Macabre,* which Hamilton Deane performed in repertory with his own version of Bram Stoker's *Dracula.* After touring England with both productions, Deane opened *Frankenstein* in London on 10 February 1930, where it played for two months.

Earlier, playwright John L. Balderston had adapted Deane's *Dracula* for the American producer Horace Liveright, who scored a success with it on Broadway and sold the rights to Universal Studios, which released its film version in February 1931. Seeking to repeat this process, Liveright had Balderston adapt Webling's *Frankenstein,* and this version (which included some significant changes) received a U.S. copyright on 11 March 1931. Less than a month later, on 8 April, Universal bought the film rights, before Balderston's play ever went to the stage.

Meanwhile, in March, writer/director Robert Florey met with Richard Schayer, the head of Universal's writing department, to discuss possible projects for Bela Lugosi, the star of *Dracula.* Florey, with Garrett Fort (who contributed the dialogue), prepared a screenplay of *Frankenstein* dated 15 May–20 June 1931, and on 16–17 June he directed two test scenes: Victor Moritz's conversation with Dr. Waldman and the coming to life of the Monster. Florey had envisioned Bela Lugosi as the scientist, but Universal decreed that because Lugosi had played a monster in *Dracula,* he had to remain a monster in *Frankenstein;* also in the scenes were two other *Dracula* alumni,

Edward van Sloan and Dwight Frye. According to Paul Ivano, who photographed the tests, Universal liked the results and screened them for all the directors on the lot.[40] Strangely, Universal's records do not mention the Florey-Fort screenplay, but do list separate scripts by Richard Schayer (18 May) and Garrett Fort (8 June).

During this time, James Whale shot *Waterloo Bridge* (1931), his first film under a five-year contract with Universal. Upon its completion near the end of June, Whale took an interest in *Frankenstein* because "it was the strongest meat and gave me a chance to dabble in the macabre." He added that it would be "amusing" to deal with a subject that "everybody knows to be a physical impossibility."[41] Having already made three consecutive films about World War I, Whale no doubt also wanted a change of pace. Carl Laemmle, Jr., readily deferred to his new star director, so Florey, with only a one-film contract, found himself writing and directing the lower-budgeted *Murders in the Rue Morgue* (1931) instead of *Frankenstein*. Lugosi, who disliked the nonspeaking role of the monster, joined Florey to play Dr. Mirakle, a character inspired by Florey's version of the scientist in *Frankenstein*.

Whale quickly began to modify *Frankenstein*'s screenplay, with John Russell providing some revised pages on 17 July and Francis Edwards Faragoh submitting a full script on 7 August. Faragoh and Garrett Fort received credit for the final screenplay, dated 12 August. Meanwhile, Whale—rejecting the studio's suggestion that Leslie Howard play Frankenstein—insisted that Colin Clive be brought from England for the role. Quite close to the start of shooting on 24 August, Whale also cast Mae Clarke (his lead in *Waterloo Bridge*) as Frankenstein's fiancée and Boris Karloff as the Monster.

Although Robert Florey claimed that he never consulted John Balderston's play, his initial script and the finished film both owe much to that work. All three, for example, take place in the town of Goldstadt and center on Henry (not Victor, as in the novel) Frankenstein; his fiancée; his boyhood friend, Victor Moritz (who loves Frankenstein's fiancée); and his former professor, Dr. Waldman. In addition, Florey retained the content and structure of the play's first half, while expanding on it by depicting events that the play's characters only report.

Balderston began with Waldman and Victor at Frankenstein's laboratory, where Henry, who has avoided everyone for weeks, is "nervous" and "at the point of hysteria." During a thunderstorm, he tells how he obtained corpses from a grave and the gallows and stole a brain from Waldman's dissecting room. Then, as his astonished visitors watch, he gives life to the new body he has fashioned. Florey adds the character of Fritz—a dwarf assistant with whom Frankenstein can talk while working—and actually shows them gathering body parts. He also adds a scene that introduces Victor and Frankenstein's fiancée (Amelia in the play, Elizabeth in Florey's script) and establishes their concern about Henry. Then, Victor visits Waldman and the two men go to the laboratory, where the action follows that of the play.

Florey, however, made the laboratory more isolated by placing it in a deserted windmill instead of Frankenstein's house. He also prolonged the actual creation and made it more dramatic. In the play, Frankenstein uses a large galvanic battery that "gives off queer lights" and "sends out sparks," explaining that he has captured "all the rays in the spectrum—the ultra-violet, beyond that—and the *great ray* beyond that—which in the beginning brought Life into the world." Variations on this dialogue appear in Florey's script and the final film. However, Balderston's Frankenstein also discusses alchemy and administers an "elixir of life" to help bring the body to life. Florey discarded the alchemy aspect and elaborated on the use of electricity by making the play's atmospheric thunderstorm functional, with Frankenstein using the lightning in his experiment instead of a battery. Balderston, Florey, and the film all end the creation scene with the Monster raising his arm; then, Balderston has Waldman declare, "You make yourself equal with God," which Florey changed into Frankenstein's line, "Now I know how it feels to be God!"

Both Balderston and Florey follow the creation with a scene set a few weeks later. In the play, Frankenstein has taught the Monster to talk, but he still views his creation as a soulless brute, chaining him in a dark cellar and, he explains, controlling him with a whip. The Monster now enters and, when Waldman opens a curtain, he "sees the sun, drags himself into the sunlight and kneels holding up his hands like a savage in prayer to the sun." When Frankenstein uses the word "fire," the Monster cringes, because earlier Frankenstein had burned him with a red-hot iron. During this scene, Victor and Baron Frankenstein enter and, later, Amelia arrives; the sight of her stirs the Monster's sexual awareness and he abruptly demands a woman for himself.

Florey obviously chose to prove Frankenstein right about his Monster by having Waldman identify the owner of the brain Fritz stole as "criminally moronic," a man who led "a life of brutality—of violence and murder!" Florey also omits the Monster's ability to talk and his encounter with sunlight. Instead, he shows Frankenstein whipping the chained Monster to make him stop howling. When the Monster picks up the whip, Frankenstein retrieves it by burning his creation with a red-hot iron. Florey also simplifies the character of Waldman, who in the play is a priest as well as a scientist. As such, when Frankenstein wants to kill his creation, Waldman resists, calling it murder. In Florey's version, Waldman is solely a scientist and it is he who declares that the Monster "should be destroyed!" As if to prove Waldman right, the Monster immediately kills Fritz, so Frankenstein and Waldman subdue him with a hypodermic injection.

The play's second act occurs some weeks later, at the Baron's house. As Frankenstein and Amelia prepare to marry, they learn of murders committed in the countryside. Then the Monster—having found the address on a letter in Henry's coat—enters and encounters Katrina, Frankenstein's gentle and innocent sister. Unafraid, Katrina offers her hand and the Monster touches it, pleased to have found someone who does not try to hurt him. Attracted to the "shin-ing wa-ter" of a nearby lake, he goes with her to examine it. Soon the bewildered Monster returns, carrying the drowned Katrina, and explains what happened: "Boat float—like leaves—like bird—shin-ing water. She beau-ty—I want her float—on shin-ing wa-ter—she not float . . . kill beauty—kill friend. Why did you not tell me the shining water could kill?"

Again the Monster demands a woman, explaining that in his travels he saw "woman—man—mate, bed." When Frankenstein refuses to create a companion for him, the Monster threatens to take Amelia and grabs her; in their struggle, he tears off her bridal veil and the top of her dress. Another six months pass as Frankenstein prepares a mate, but at the last moment he changes his mind and the angry Monster accidentally kills him. Agonized, the Monster follows Waldman's suggestion, prays for God's help, and is struck by lightning. He dies with a look of peace on his face, leaving Amelia comforted by Victor.

Florey, continuing his process of simplification, takes this part of the story in a different direction. He has Waldman prepare for "cranial dissection" of the Monster, who awakens and strangles the doctor. Then, Florey gives his Monster a more brutal form of sexual awareness by elaborating on Balderston's "mate, bed" line: Peering through a cottage window, the creature observes a young peasant couple as the woman undresses and they start to make love. Suddenly, with "eyes gleaming bestially," he bursts in, kills the man, and—it is strongly implied—rapes his wife. Then, after a short interlude establishing Frankenstein's wedding preparations, Florey offers his less innocent version of the "shin-ing wa-ter" scene. The childlike Katrina is now an actual child, Maria, who smiles at the Monster and holds out a flower. "Without changing the expression of his face, he starts to advance towards her. . . . The Monster's shadow falls across her face," and he reaches for her, as the scene ends.

News of Waldman's death interrupts the wedding preparations, then Maria's father carries the child's body to town. This leads to Florey's totally new ending, in which the townspeople hunt the Monster, who carries Frankenstein back to the old mill/laboratory. Initially, Florey had the Baron shoot the Monster, but in midscene he changed his mind and had Maria's father do it; then, the man fires again and hits Henry in the chest. The villagers set fire to the mill, the Monster hurls Frankenstein's body to the ground, and flames consume the mill and the Monster. In an epilogue, Victor consoles Elizabeth in the village church, as a new day dawns.

Balderston's play is limited to a few interior settings in which characters report significant events, but it also gives the Monster both a dangerous and a vulnerable side. Florey made his script more cinematic and dramatic by adding scenes that depict those events, but he brutally simplified the Monster and the emotions he provokes. Whale retained most of Florey's scenes, but he also reworked all of the major events and characterizations to increase their subtlety and significance. Frankenstein's ultimate success must, therefore, be credited to Whale, who elevated a shallow, if intense, melodrama by taking its subject seriously. Interviewed in 1931, Whale said, "I tried to make it seem as real as it was possible"[42] by applying a general rule he had stated even before filming *Journey's End:* "The simpler a big situation is presented . . . the harder it strikes."[43] *Frankenstein,* Whale told Colin Clive shortly before shooting started, contains "none of Dracula's maniacal cackles,"[44] so a reviewer's comment about the film that "beside it *Dracula* is tame"[45] must have pleased the director.

Henry Frankenstein, as depicted by Florey, possesses intelligence but lacks passionate idealism and nobility. Instead, he is fanatical and hysterical, an admitted paranoid who shifts between grimness and a "mad gaiety." Florey describes him, in the laboratory, as "disheveled and haggard, his surgeon's uniform stained with chemicals and looking as if he hasn't had it off for days—his eyes feverish, face glistening with sweat." After the death of Fritz, Frankenstein completely loses control, "reeling around the room, alternately laughing and crying, careening against whatever appears in his way."

Whale consciously avoided such a one-note, "mad scientist" approach. He saw Frankenstein as having a complex personality, one reminiscent of Captain Stanhope in *Journey's End,* who is nervous and high-strung from the strain of command and the tensions of trench warfare. In 1931, Whale explained that he chose Colin Clive for the part because he could project "tenacity" (as opposed to obsessiveness) and "levelheadedness," even "in his craziest moments."[46] Writing to Clive, he described Frankenstein as "normally and extremely intelligent, a sane and lovable person, never unsympathetic, even to the Monster."[47]

Whale's conception evolved in stages. In Florey's version, Frankenstein himself whips the Monster and burns him with the hot iron, but the shooting script shifts the blame to Fritz, who accidentally disturbs the Monster by striking a match. Finally, in the film, Whale has Fritz deliberately antagonize the Monster with a torch and Frankenstein tries to stop him. During the postcreation scene between Frankenstein and Waldman, the shooting script still has Frankenstein "nervously walking up and down" and speaking "in an excited, argumentative voice," as he had in Florey's version, but by the time he shot the scene Whale had clarified his vision, so in the actual film Frankenstein is seated, totally calm and thoroughly composed.

Whale wanted Frankenstein to be a "very strong, extremely dominant personality"[48] with the "kind of romantic quality which makes strong men leave civilization to shoot big game."[49] Thus, Whale gave the character a sensitivity missing from Florey's version. This quality is most directly seen in Frankenstein's speech to Waldman, which does not exist in Florey's screenplay or in the shooting script. "Have you never wanted to do anything that was dangerous? Where should we be if nobody tried to find out what lies beyond? Have you never wanted to look beyond the clouds and the stars or to know what causes the trees to bud and what changes darkness into light? But if you talk like that, people call you crazy. Well, if I could discover just one of these things—what eternity is, for example—I wouldn't care if they *did* think I was crazy!"

These lines, delivered with quietly powerful sincerity by Colin Clive, give the character depth and substance. No one can say who wrote the speech, but Whale surely inspired it, for its roots lie in *Journey's End,* when Stanhope contrasts a fellow officer's lack of curiosity with his own compulsive imagination. "I suppose if Trotter looks at that wall he just sees a brown surface. He doesn't see into the earth beyond—the worms wandering about round the stones and roots of trees. . . . Whenever I look at anything nowadays I see right through it. Looking at you now there's your uniform—your jersey—shirt—vest—then beyond that. . . . It's a habit that's grown on me lately—to look right through things, and on and on—till I get frightened and stop." Here, and throughout the film, Whale re-created Florey's Frankenstein in Stanhope's image.

Although Whale rendered Frankenstein sympathetic, he did not make him a totally positive figure. To present this aspect of the character, Whale had to change Dr. Waldman from a voice of moral authority, whose statements should be taken at face value, to someone who only seems knowledgeable. Early in the film, Waldman tells Victor and Elizabeth that Frankenstein is "interested only in human life—first to destroy it and then re-create it," but clearly Frankenstein never killed anyone to further his experiments. Later, even before he learns that Frankenstein used the abnormal brain, Waldman declares, "This creature of yours should be kept under guard! Mark my words, he will prove dangerous!" The news about the brain only confirms what Waldman already assumed. This scientist evidently feels no need to observe events before drawing conclusions; he starts out with a fully formed idea, and no events can shake him from that belief.

Initially, Frankenstein has an open mind about the Monster. "You must be patient," he tells Waldman. "Do you expect perfection at once? . . . I believe in this monster as you call it. . . . He's only a few days old, remember." Later events, however, shake his confidence until he starts sharing Waldman's assumption. In the cellar, Frankenstein protects the Monster from Fritz's cruelty by taking the whip from him and saying, "Come away, Fritz. Just leave it alone, leave it alone!" But Frankenstein does not enforce his order and instead turns away—literally and morally—leaving Fritz and the torch behind. Thus, the death of Fritz is due both to the dwarf's own provocation of the Monster and to Frankenstein's neglect, as he shirks his responsibility to both of those beings to whom he serves as a kind of guardian.

Eventually, Frankenstein accepts a degree of responsibility for the Monster when he tells Victor, "I made him with these hands and with these hands I will destroy him." That takes courage, yes, but it is easier to join a manhunt than to acknowledge that the manhunt would not have been needed if he had done his duty earlier. Frankenstein, to the very end, remains blind to his failure, oblivious of the fact that the Monster possessed the potential for a somewhat normal life and that he himself indirectly caused the deaths of Fritz, Maria, and Waldman—not because he gave life to a monster but because he ignored his responsibility to tend and teach the Monster.

Florey had deprived the Monster of even potential humanity; from the start, he is even more of a beast than his criminal brain warrants. In the first postcreation scene, Florey's monster wears "an expression of dumb animal hate and fear." Elsewhere, his eyes "gleam with animal cunning" and, when he recognizes Frankenstein near the end, his face shows "an imbecilic, terrible smile of triumph." Florey used the criminal brain as a blunt excuse for turning the Monster into a destructive brute.

The criminal brain device remains in the final film, but Whale consistently contradicts its implications. Throughout, his direction of Boris Karloff carefully creates sympathy for the Monster, returning to Mary Shelley's (and, to a lesser extent, Balderston's) concept of a newly born creature rendered violent by ignorance, chance, and the violent responses of others. As Karloff later recalled, "I don't think the main screenwriter, Bob Florey, really intended there to be much pathos inside the character. But Whale and I thought that there should be; we didn't want the kind of rampaging monstrosity that Universal seemed to think we should go in for. We had to have some pathos, otherwise our audiences just wouldn't think about the film after they'd left the theatre, and Whale very much wanted them to do that."[50]

Florey had dropped the Monster's encounter with sunlight, which appeared in Balderston's play, but Whale restored the scene and, in the process, gave the character dignity. The result is one of the film's finest moments. When Frankenstein opens a ceiling window, the Monster is drawn to the patch of brightness. He stands and stretches his hands upward, trying to grasp its intangible beauty. Afraid of agitating the creature, Frankenstein closes the window and, with the light abruptly removed, the Monster looks with bewilderment at his creator, who has bestowed a glimpse of unexpected radiance and then deprived him of it. Karloff's facial expression and empty-handed gesture eloquently convey the Monster's sense of loss and his confusion at the mysterious power that this "father" and "God" has over his life. If the addition of Frankenstein's speech about curiosity establishes Whale's mature conception of the scientist, this touching, almost allegorical scene does the same for the Monster.

Immediately after the light scene, Fritz enters with a torch and brings it close to the Monster, who backs defensively against a wall. As Fritz persists, what began as a delicate introduction to beauty becomes an ordeal. Whale, by juxtaposing the bright beauty and comforting warmth of sunlight with the pain and aggression of fire, has confronted the Monster with two opposing qualities of the same element. He has also dramatized, in a clear, schematic fashion, the positive and negative alternatives of human existence.

For the Monster, this scene represents the first and only fork in the road of his life, but one over which he has no power of choice, for Frankenstein and Waldman perceive him as out of control and overpower him. "Shoot it—it's a monster!" declares Waldman, in a typical misjudgment of events. As a result, Frankenstein loses confidence in his creation's potential, and ceases to protect and educate him. Therefore, this scene marks the beginning of the end for the Monster and turns the burning of the mill at the film's climax into the final triumph of flame over sunlight, of pain and destruction over beauty and sensitivity.

Appropriately, script alterations give the Monster motives for killing other than innate destructiveness. Fritz, himself a deformed outcast, vents his pent-up hatred on the confused Monster, taunting him into a frenzy with whip and torch. In both the Florey and Whale versions, the Monster kills Dr. Waldman out of self-preservation, but

Whale dropped the references in the Florey/Fort dialogue to his being "butchered" and "torn to pieces." Whale's attention to the Monster is also evident in a short scene of him leaving the laboratory after killing Waldman, which has no counterpart in either Florey's screenplay or the shooting script. In it, Whale's direction and Karloff's pantomime clearly convey the Monster's emotions (he recoils from the room where he was chained and tormented) and his childlike awkwardness (his arms dangle limply at his side as he stumbles down the stairs, and he reacts with surprise as a door swings open at his touch).

Whale also expanded the Monster's encounter with little Maria by returning to Balderston's concept. The Monster now accepts the flower from Maria, examines her tiny hand, and kneels down to make "boats" by tossing flowers onto the lake. Having rendered this part of the encounter innocent and gentle, Whale next showed the Monster throwing the girl into the water because he mistakenly thinks she will gain in beauty, as the flowers had. Whale followed this with shots of the Monster's bewilderment and concern, and Karloff's pantomime conveys with vivid pathos the full meaning of Balderston's line, "Why did you not tell me the shining water could kill?"

The death of Maria serves multiple purposes. Of course, it provides the main reason for the villagers to hunt down the Monster. It also reveals the Monster's childlike thought process, as we see him draw what seems to be a logical conclusion; but an actual child would be physically unable to put such thoughts into action, unlike the fully grown Monster. In this way, we can see the great injustice done by Frankenstein, who failed to protect his "child" from such mistakes. In addition, the distress felt by the Monster at the scene's end adds poignancy to his plight, for this moment of pleasure has, like the sunlight, been abruptly taken from him. According to Karloff, while shooting the scene he and the crew members "were all very hostile" about Maria's death and wanted her scene with the Monster to have a happy ending.[51] That response was doubtless the same one that Whale sought from the audience.

Universal ultimately shortened this scene so that it ended, like Florey's version, with the Monster reaching for Maria. But most of the added qualities remained and contradict any conclusion that the Monster molests the girl. Florey, however, may indeed have meant to suggest a sexual attack because, two scenes before, his Monster had observed the peasant couple making love and raped the woman. In recent years, Universal has almost completely restored the scene, although—based on the film's cutting continuity—it still lacks two close-ups of the Monster's puzzled expression and one of the water's surface after Maria sinks out of sight.

Surprisingly, Whale did not extract Florey's criminal brain device from the final script, despite its inconsistency with his concept of the Monster. In fact, he even stressed it by adding a normal brain, which Fritz drops, to serve as a contrast and alternative. This unfortunately resulted in the illogicality of Frankenstein not noticing the jar's label or the "degenerate characteristics" Waldman pointed out to his students. The shooting script weakly dismisses the whole problem, when Waldman reveals which brain had been stolen, by having Frankenstein look surprised, then offer the lame rationalization, "It's only a piece of dead tissue." However, Colin Clive's fine acting—his pause and glance over one shoulder before saying the line and his rising inflection at its end—makes this dialogue almost acceptable by suggesting that Frankenstein does not believe his own words. Unfortunately, this also implies that the Monster really is doomed to what Waldman called a life "of brutality, of violence and murder."

Considering the numerous changes that Whale made before and during filming, the fact that he retained the criminal brain can hardly be an oversight. Therefore, the obvious contradiction between Waldman's claim about the brain's influence and the observable facts of the Monster's actions and reactions may actually be part of Whale's point; seen in this light, the film dramatizes the difference between starting with an assumption, then interpreting events in a way that reinforces it, and starting with an open mind so that an observer (the viewer) will draw a different conclusion about the Monster than do Waldman and, eventually, Frankenstein.

In 1931, Whale mentioned drawing Boris Karloff's features and contributing to the makeup design.[52] True, he often did provide technicians with sketches to guide their work, but the Monster's basic appearance probably existed before Whale became involved; according to both Florey and Paul Ivano, Jack Pierce's makeup for Lugosi in the test was similar to that eventually used for Karloff, and one page of Florey's script contains a rough sketch of the Monster's familiar square-skulled head, with a notation that Pierce should add bolts to the neck. Whale, however, may have mellowed the Monster's appearance to increase audience sympathy, for a photo exists of Karloff in an unused version of the makeup, one with forehead clamps and a distortion of the lower lip that make him seem more vicious and fearsome than he does in the actual film.

Edward van Sloan's recollection that Bela Lugosi's Monster resembled Paul Wegener in the German film *The Golem* (1920) probably derives from the fact that Florey—who admired Wegener's performance—had directed Lugosi to walk stiffly, like the Golem. Whale, on the other hand, made Karloff's walk a loose-limbed one, thereby increasing the Monster's credibility as a person who does not yet have full control of his sewn-together body parts.

Besides altering Florey's tone and characterizations, Whale made many scenes more concise. The dialogue that establishes Victor's fondness for Frankenstein's fiancée is almost halved, conveying the information less bluntly, and Frankenstein's nervous collapse became shorter and less repetitious. A single interlude of Henry and Elizabeth on a patio replaces Florey's two scenes—of them walking by a lake and drifting in a canoe—which would have been more trouble to film than their significance justified. Whale also established the wedding celebration in a simple tracking shot of dancing and drinking townspeople, in contrast to Florey's plan for an elaborate camera movement past a puppet show, a dancing bear, a candy seller, a carousel, a shooting gallery, and the village inn. This might have accurately summarized European peasant entertainments, but it also would have placed undue emphasis on extraneous events.

In general, Florey's script tended to sprawl and needed tightening. This is well illustrated by an outline of his first scenes:

A. 1. Frankenstein and Fritz dig up a newly buried body.
   2. Frankenstein and Fritz obtain a body from the gallows.
B. Victor and Elizabeth discuss a letter from Waldman about Frankenstein. Victor leaves to talk with Waldman.
C. 1. Waldman lectures a class about the criminal brain.
   2. Victor talks with a secretary at Waldman's office.
   3. In a hallway outside the lecture hall, the secretary tells Waldman that Victor wants to see him.
   4. Fritz, in the empty lecture hall, steals the criminal brain.
   5. Victor talks with Waldman in the latter's office, and the two decide to visit Frankenstein.

The shooting script retained Florey's choppy structure and even added a new scene of the characters in a carriage, on their way to Frankenstein's laboratory. It also changed

The strangely sad Monster as he appeared in James Whale's *Frankenstein* (1931), as portrayed by Boris Karloff. Whale wanted to create a Monster that would inspire sympathy as well as terror in the viewer.

Boris Karloff made up as a more ominous version of Frankenstein's Monster; this version of the makeup was never used in Whale's film.

the letter received by Elizabeth to one from Henry, which makes the situation more personal for her while still prompting the visit to Waldman, and it has her accompany Victor to Waldman's office. After filming, however, Whale eliminated Waldman's secretary by dropping one scene and reducing another to a brief shot of Waldman and his students leaving the lecture hall. He also grouped all the body-stealing activities together by placing the lecture and Fritz's theft after the gallows scene. The result is much more succinct:

A. 1. Frankenstein and Fritz dig up a newly buried body.
    2. Frankenstein and Fritz obtain a body from the gallows.
    3. a. Waldman concludes his lecture on the criminal brain.
        b. The class and Waldman leave the lecture hall.
        c. Fritz steals the criminal brain.
B. Victor and Elizabeth discuss a letter from Frankenstein and decide to visit Waldman.
C. Victor and Elizabeth talk with Waldman in his office and decide to visit Frankenstein.

Next, we observe Frankenstein's laboratory activities, until the other characters arrive and he offers firsthand exposition. This intensely dramatic sequence climaxes with the Monster's creation, followed by an extreme change of pace as Baron Frankenstein grumbles to Elizabeth, Victor, and the Burgomaster. Then, while the Baron prepares to find his son, we return to the laboratory as the Monster encounters sunlight and, agitated by Fritz's torch, is overpowered. Next, the Monster kills Fritz, whereupon Victor, Elizabeth, and the Baron arrive to take Henry home. After the Monster kills Waldman and leaves the laboratory, scenes of Frankenstein at home and of the wedding preparations provide another breather, followed by the death of Maria. A return to the wedding preparations begins the unbroken climax, as the Monster invades the house and confronts Elizabeth, Maria's body is brought to town, and the Monster hunt leads to the deserted mill, where he is consumed by flames.

Thus, everything ties together neatly, without a wasted moment: Each intense climax is followed by a change-of-pace scene that also provides new information or introduces another character; later, the participants in these scenes enter a dramatic one. To achieve this efficiency, though, Whale had to modify the shooting script's structure, in which the Baron's first scene occurs after the subduing of the Monster and before the death of Fritz. Ultimately, Whale placed this scene earlier, where it separates the creation from the Monster's entrance; the relief it provides is more useful there, but the change does complicate the story's time sequence, for Victor, Elizabeth, and the Baron now take far too long to reach Frankenstein's laboratory. Also, Maria's scene originally followed the one between the Monster and Elizabeth, where it interrupted the momentum of the climax.

Most of Whale's structural changes help streamline the film, but one has the opposite effect. Robert Florey had placed Frankenstein's laboratory in an old mill, so at the climax the Monster carries Frankenstein there because it is the only refuge he knows. The shooting script and film, however, locate the laboratory in a watchtower, which renders the mill just an arbitrary setting for the finale. This change, though, was not complete, for at one point the film's dialogue still refers to Henry's laboratory as being in a mill.

Unfortunately, to maintain the pace and power of the film's final third, Whale permitted the inclusion of several contrived moments. Some are relatively minor, such as the failure to explain how Waldman's body was discovered in the isolated laboratory or why Maria's father is convinced that she was murdered; clearly, any attempt to explain these things would have clogged the narrative and interrupted the flow of events that builds to the Monster's inevitable destruction. More problematic, though, is the scene between the Monster and Elizabeth in her bedroom. Does he realize that this is his creator's home, and does he know this woman's identity? What, in fact, are his intentions as he approaches her? The scene appears designed to make viewers fear for Elizabeth's welfare, which it certainly did in 1931; "little gasps of terror burst across the house," reported one audience member.[53] However, the Monster does nothing but stand opposite Elizabeth and growl a response to her screams, in a weird parody of a conversation. Later, we see him depart as Elizabeth lies unconscious on the bed. The Monster may have attacked her—that is what Frankenstein seems to assume—but even if we believe otherwise, the film remains vague.

In Balderston's play, the Monster grabs and struggles with Frankenstein's fiancée in the context of his demand for a mate, but Florey dropped that aspect of the plot and never had his Monster confront Elizabeth. The shooting script reinstates the confrontation, but Whale, himself, was probably inspired less by Balderston than by *The Cabinet of Dr. Caligari,* which he screened in July "to get some ideas for *Franken-stein*"[54] and which also has a dark figure enter through a background window and approach the white-clad heroine in the foreground. Although the scene helps to motivate Frankenstein's pursuit of the Monster, Whale's writers did not justify its presence, so the result feels arbitrary. Even more awkwardly, to set the scene up Whale uncharacteristically allowed the blatant contrivance of having Frankenstein foolishly lock Elizabeth in her room.

Both Florey and Whale intended to end their films with Frankenstein's death, but Florey included a final scene of Victor comforting Elizabeth, while the shooting script concludes more starkly on the burning mill, without any superficial optimism. Shortly before releasing the film, however, Universal added a one-shot epilogue that establishes Frankenstein's survival; because Colin Clive had already left for England, the scene was staged with Frankenstein seen only in the distant background.

Aside from the peasant diversions, Florey's script offered no light touches. Whale, by casting the blustery Frederick Kerr as the Baron and having his dialogue rewritten, gave that character the added dimension of humor—although, in truth, he is not especially amusing. (Kerr had played a similar role in *Waterloo Bridge.*) More in line with the eccentric humor of later Whale films is the scene in which Fritz answers the knocking at the laboratory door; during shooting, the director added the hunchback's grumbling and his pause on the staircase to pull up a recalcitrant sock.

Whale also extended the creation scene's dramatic possibilities. In Florey's script, Victor and Waldman are the only observers; a synopsis in Universal's files has Elizabeth arrive with them, but Henry sends her away for her own safety; in the final film, she remains through the entire sequence and her presence adds a gentle facet to Frankenstein's treatment of the intruders, while providing characters with whom both sexes in the audience can identify. Whale felt that the creation scene must be convincing or the audience would not accept what followed, so he used the observers in the laboratory as surrogates for those in the movie theater.

He also turned Frankenstein into a kind of director who sets the stage to impress his visitors and, by extension, the audience. Whale noted that, in this scene, Frankenstein "becomes very conscious of the theatrical drama."[55] He "deliberately tells his plan of action" so that everyone "will settle down to see the show. Frankenstein puts the spectators in their positions, he gives final orders to Fritz, he turns the levers and sends the diabolic machines soaring upward. . . . He is now in a state of feverish excitement calculated to carry both the spectators in the windmill [*sic*] and the spectators in the theatre with him."[56] Some new dialogue—"Quite a good scene, isn't it? One man, crazy. Three very sane spectators!"—establishes this approach, as does a camera angle that places Henry in the foreground, facing the trio, who are grouped in the middle ground. During the experiment, the spectators sit on a raised platform a little apart from the scientist's "stage," and Whale periodically cuts to them for reactions.

Florey had planned to reveal the Monster's face in a close-up even before the experiment began. After that, the Monster would first be seen chained in the cellar. Whale kept Karloff's face covered and added a striking, gradual introduction to the Monster as he backs into the laboratory through a doorway, then pauses and turns around. Although Whale's editing is not as complex as it would become a few years later, his handling of the Monster's entrance anticipates that style: The shooting script calls for only a single medium shot, but Whale cuts from a long view to a medium shot (as the Monster turns), to a facial close-up, and finally to an extreme close-up (from forehead to chin). This extends the moment's impact, while allowing viewers a progressively better look at the creature.

Elsewhere, Whale imposed his visual style on Florey's ideas. In the original script, Florey planned to begin Victor and Elizabeth's first scene with a close-up of a photo of Frankenstein; then, the camera would track back to reveal Elizabeth with the letter and finally the whole room as the maid announces Victor's arrival. Instead of this camera movement, which would delay the action, Whale accelerates the pace by using four separate close-ups—the photo, the maid announcing Victor, Victor entering, and Elizabeth rising—before cutting to a long shot of the entire room. Florey had the initial audacity to open with the photo, but Whale's editing rendered the introduction more concise, dramatic, and involving. Not that Whale rejected the moving camera, but he used elaborate tracking shots sparingly.

Because most of the scenes created by Florey and Fort remain in the film in some form, Universal's failure to provide Florey with a writer's credit is a distressing "oversight" (which was rectified only on European prints and only after Florey complained). His initial script provided a useful skeleton, one that Whale and his writers fleshed out and infused with life, creating *Frankenstein*—a film that is spare yet complex, combining a forceful plot line with depth and perception. Still, despite the number of creative hands involved, this masterpiece is clearly dominated by Whale's skill and sensitivity.

Before its official release on 2 November 1931, *Frankenstein* was previewed in Santa Barbara. Far more brutal and macabre than *Dracula,* the picture must have been a shock to the unsuspecting audience. David Lewis attended the preview and recalled that from the first scene the audience was distraught. "They gulped and they started to run around the theater. You never saw such a performance!" The next day, according to Lewis, the theater manager telephoned "Junior" (as he was called) Laemmle and said, "I had about five calls last night from people at two and three o'clock in the morning, saying, 'I can't sleep and I'll be damned if you will.' " Laemmle, worried about the impact of this bombshell, asked others in the industry for advice. Opinions may have varied, but Edward Montagne's comment—as reported by David Lewis— was probably typical: "Tell him to leave it alone, he's got the hit of all time."[57]

Universal's advertising campaign made certain that spectators knew what to expect, with statements like "No thriller ever made can touch it" and "To have seen *Frankenstein* is to wear a badge of courage." Some ads even declared, "If you have a weak heart and cannot stand intense excitement or even shock, we advise you NOT to see this production. If, on the contrary, you like an unusual thrill, you will find it in *Franken-stein*." Others included misleading references to sex: "No man has ever seen his like—No woman's kiss has touched his lips!" announced one ad, and another juxtaposed a photo of Colin Clive and Mae Clarke with the line, "I gave him life, but he wanted love!" Also, the studio at the last moment added a prologue in which Edward van Sloan steps in front of a theater curtain and warns the spectators that the film "will thrill you, it may shock you, it might even—horrify you!" Such emphasis on sensationalism helped to prevent complaints, while attracting curious viewers.

From the start, *Frankenstein* was a tremendous success. At its Los Angeles premiere, lines formed for the 10 A.M. showing and remained until midnight; the theater dropped the usual shorts and newsreel to fit in more showings. In New York, *Franken-stein* drew crowds on a rainy opening night and became Broadway's biggest hit. Extra showings were scheduled, with the Mayfair Theatre selling tickets as late as 2 A.M. The film's first week set a new house record of $53,800 (a dramatic contrast to $19,000 for the previous week's film).

Frankenstein set similar records in both cities and small towns. At a time when tickets cost 25–50 cents and films seldom played longer than one week, *Frankenstein* often doubled the box-office take of the prior film and was held over. In Detroit, where children were barred and no one was admitted during the final reel, police had to control the waiting crowds, and the second week's income topped the first week's record. In Ottumwa, Iowa, "a midnight performance crowd broke the plate glass in front of the theatre in efforts to gain admission," while in Cedar Rapids "approximately 3,500 people attempted to enter and . . . it was necessary to call out the fire department to check the crowd after the police failed."[58]

The artistic and financial triumph of *Frankenstein* reinforced "Junior" Laemmle's confidence in Whale, but the director declined to imitate that work's straightforward intensity. Instead, he gave each of his three subsequent horror films a complex, idiosyncratic tone, one that combines dramatic impact with his often witty acknowledgment of a situation's theatricality. Thus, humor derives from danger, instead of alternating with it; the manner, actions, and personalities of the menacing characters are often both amusingly odd and potentially lethal. This blend is a delicate one, and Whale constantly risks slipping into simple parody, but for the most part he maintains his precarious balance.

The Old Dark House (1932) is Whale's most subtle and characteristic work in this vein. Universal no doubt envisioned only a follow-up to *Frankenstein* that would reunite Whale with Karloff, but this one-of-a-kind work creates an entirely different mood. Its basic plot—a group of people are stranded one stormy night in the isolated home of mysterious eccentrics—was already overused by 1932, but *The Old Dark House* is the final word on the subject, spoken by literate, sophisticated collaborators who shared an amused respect for the melodramatic formula.

To adapt J. B. Priestley's 1928 novel (titled *Benighted* in Great Britain and *The Old Dark House* in the United States), Whale turned to his friend, British playwright Benn W. Levy, who had written the stage version of *A Man with Red Hair* and the screenplay of *Waterloo Bridge*. Levy had also adapted Marcel Pagnol's *Topaze* for a 1930 London production that starred Raymond Massey, but he was best known as the author of several witty, ironic comedies, including *The Devil*, which premiered in London in 1930 with Ernest Thesiger as "an unsuccessful author who glories, or pretends to glory, in his decadency."[59] Thesiger repeated his role on Broadway, where the play—called *The Devil Passes*—opened in January 1932, ran for about two months, and

Stranded in *The Old Dark House* (1932) on a dark and stormy night, fellow travelers gather around the hearth with a bottle of gin provided by their host, Horace Femm (Ernest Thesiger, standing). From left to right are Lillian Bond, Melvyn Douglas, Gloria Stuart, Raymond Massey, and Charles Laughton.

closed not long before Whale began shooting *The Old Dark House*. Levy's experience with both sophisticated horror and drawing-room comedy made him an ideal choice to write the script for *The Old Dark House,* which smoothly combines those two styles.

After Universal purchased the novel's screen rights on 6 January 1932, F. Hugh Herbert wrote an incomplete script; then, Levy submitted a ten-page treatment on 29 January, followed by two script drafts (20 February and 8 March). Jack B. Clymer finished a screenplay on 17 March, and Levy handed in the final version eight days later. By the time shooting began in April, Levy had returned to England, so Whale's friend R. C. Sherriff—the author of *Journey's End*—visited the set and provided on-the-spot phrase polishing.

Because *The Old Dark House* is set in Wales, the director justifiably cast the film with actors he knew, and who knew each other, from the London stage. This resulted in the kind of ensemble acting usually found only in theatrical repertory companies. First to arrive at the old, dark house are Philip and Margaret Waverton (Raymond Massey and Gloria Stuart) and their friend Penderel (Melvyn Douglas), a cynical veteran of the war. Later, a self-made businessman, Sir William Porterhouse (Charles Laughton), and his chorus girl "companion," Gladys DuCane (Lillian Bond), join them. Massey, a Canadian, had for more than a decade directed and acted on the London stage; in 1925, he performed with Whale in *The Prisoners of War*. Laughton, of course, played Whale's father in *A Man with Red Hair* and was Elsa Lanchester's husband. At one point, Whale had contacted Colin Clive about playing Penderel; Melvyn Douglas's performance may lack Clive's distraught intensity, but he is one of the few American actors able to appear convincingly British. Studio ingenues Stuart and Bond effectively serve their mostly passive, reacting functions.

Whale hired Ernest Thesiger for the pivotal role of Horace Femm, the most prominent member of the film's unusual household. A familiar figure on the English stage, Thesiger began acting professionally in 1909 and played Captain Hook in *Peter Pan,* the Dauphin in *Saint Joan,* Mephistopheles in *Dr. Faustus,* and a social reformer in *Gentlemen Prefer Blondes.* Whale acted with Thesiger in 1919, and in 1927 he stage-managed two plays in which the actor appeared. Thesiger invested each of his roles with a distinctive, somewhat peculiar manner. Holding his tall, lean body straight, with tight control, he has the demeanor of a decayed nobleman or disdainful servant. To this, his brittle features add the look of a startled bird of prey; his nose—angling sharply upward and tapering to a pinpoint—turns his face into a living skull distressed by an unsavory odor. Speaking with amused, arrogant irony, Thesiger makes even ordinary lines sound droll. His looks and manner evoke both servitude and condescension, but always with a prissy hauteur that conveys a corrupted rationality, a sour dignity.

Eva Moore portrays Rebecca Femm, Horace's religiously obsessed, hard-of-hearing sister. In 1909, she was the romantic lead in *Old Heidelberg,* with Thesiger cast as a student. Her later stage roles included Miss van Gorder in Mary Roberts Rinehart's mystery *The Bat.* To play the aged and bedridden Sir Roderick Femm, Whale took the unusual step of hiring an actress, Elspeth Dudgen (billed as "John Dudgeon"), who inevitably gave her character an odd quality; in 1924, Whale had stage-directed a production of *Macbeth* in which she played one of the witches.

As Saul Femm, a pyromaniac, Brember Wills has only one scene, but his entrance has been so anticipated that much depends on the actor's ability. Wills's distinguished background includes a role in Karel Capek's robot play, *R. U. R.,* the main character in Elmer Rice's expressionist *The Adding Machine,* and Androcles in Shaw's *Androcles and the Lion.* In 1929, Whale designed the sets for two productions that featured Wills, whose diminutive stature and dramatic intensity are essential to the director's conception of the climax of *The Old Dark House.*

In adapting *The Old Dark House,* Levy remained remarkably faithful to his source. Most of the script's incidents, their overall structure, the characterizations, and even the dialogue derive from the novel. During the plot's single evening, the Wavertons and Penderel are admitted to the house by Morgan (Boris Karloff), a mute butler, and accept the reluctant hospitality of Horace and Rebecca. During dinner, Sir William and Gladys arrive. Later, after the drunk and brutish Morgan attacks Margaret Waverton, Philip knocks Morgan out; then, the Wavertons enter a room where the aged and helpless Sir Roderick lies bedridden. Meanwhile, Penderel and Gladys tell Sir William that they have fallen in love. Sir Roderick warns the Wavertons that Morgan will probably release the maniacal Saul, which he does. When Morgan and Saul descend the stairs, two of the men wrestle the butler into the kitchen and Rebecca locks the door, leaving Penderel to face Saul. The men struggle and Saul is killed. In the morning, the group leaves the fear, insanity, and darkness of the night and the house behind.

A good deal of the novel's philosophizing, in conversation and in the characters' thoughts, had to be eliminated in the interest of pacing and to keep the film from being talky. Yet a surprising amount of it remains, including a condensed version of the truth game, in which each character tells something private about himself or her-self. Even Penderel's cynical outlook is included, although adroitly changed from a lengthy monologue to a brief question and answer.

> Horace: I presume you are one of the gentlemen slightly, shall we say, battered by the war?
> Penderel: Correct, Mr. Femm—War generation, slightly soiled, a study in the bitter-sweet, the man with the twisted smile—and this, Mr. Femm, is exceedingly good gin.

These evocative lines were created for the film. Totally gone, though, is Priestley's symbolic use of the stormy, isolated setting to create a microcosm of helpless human-ity in the midst of "a gigantic hostile power." Instead, the storm is reduced to some rather less cosmic sound effects.

Otherwise, Whale and Levy re-created the novel in filmic terms. The dialogue is rendered more concise for dramatic effect. When Rebecca shouts, "No beds! They can't have beds!" Horace ironically declares, "As my sister hints, there are, I'm afraid, no beds." The tightness of this line lends itself better to Thesiger's sardonic intonation than the novel's clumsier version, "As my sister hints, there are no beds, I am afraid, at your disposal." Similarly, in the novel Horace discourses on his favorite drink: "It is not whiskey, which all you young men drink now, I believe. This is gin, which I prefer to all the other spirits, except, of course, the very old brandies. With some lemon, a little sugar perhaps, some hot water if you care for it, gin is excellent, and, remember, the purest of the spirits." This becomes the terse, and therefore amusing, "It's only gin, you know. Only gin. I like gin!"

In addition, Whale and Levy heighten aspects of the novel in a purely cinematic way. Priestley had treated the introduction of Horace and Rebecca Femm almost casually; they simply walk in together through a ground-floor doorway, followed immediately by Morgan. The film, however, keeps Morgan out of the way—he was already encountered at the front door—and provides the Femms with separate entrances. For example, Horace dramatically descends a staircase, which Whale stages in a single shot, with knowing skill: As Horace moves down the steps and into the foreground, the camera tracks forward and tilts up to provide a close, angled shot that emphasizes Thesiger's startled-skull features. This staging allows for a grad-ual revelation of Horace, while also exposing viewers to the staircase, which will be employed more fully in the climax. A little later, Rebecca receives her own intro-duction.

Whale did not just adapt and reconstruct Priestley's material in a faithful but cine-matic manner (although that in itself is no small accomplishment). He also made it his own by adding a more complex tone—a peculiar sense of humor that the novel con-sistently lacks. Whale never stretches for laughs, however; they arise naturally out of the characters, evoked by the director's cut to a certain shot or by the actors' vocal inflections.

During the opening scene in the Wavertons' storm-besieged car, when Philip com-ments sarcastically, "I love the trickle of ice-cold water pouring down my neck," Whale unexpectedly shows a tight close-up of his hat brim, as rain flows under his collar. Shortly after, Margaret examines their map and declares hopelessly, "It's all a stupid puddle!" Philip's reply, "It seems to represent this country very well!" is matched to a close-up of the limp and soggy map. These lines of dialogue are not par-ticularly funny in themselves, but they become so when juxtaposed with the close-ups mentioned. Thus, Whale achieves humor through the use of cinematic style. The novel merely mentions that Philip feels the rain go down his back, and the lines about the map, although lifted from the book almost verbatim, hardly evoke a smile there.

In keeping with his film's odd tone, Whale adds an entirely new bit of business for Horace Femm's first scene. After introducing himself, Horace picks up some cut flowers and a vase, and declares, "My sister was on the point of arranging these flowers." He then tosses the bouquet into a blazing fireplace. The unexpectedness of this action and Thesiger's matter-of-fact manner make the moment funny, but Horace's implied antagonism toward Rebecca makes it disturbing, as well.

Throughout, Whale develops Horace's personality through other additions to, or modifications of, the novel. While carrying the gin and glasses to his guests, he sniffs the top of the open bottle with muted pleasure, and when he says, "I like gin," Whale cuts to a close-up of Rebecca disdainfully wrinkling her nose. At the dinner table, as Horace mocks Rebecca's desire to say grace, he is shown in a close medium shot, his face framed by the carving utensils he holds—a fork and a wicked-looking knife. During the meal, Horace twice says, "Have a potato." This simple line, delivered with clipped precision by Thesiger, is simultaneously comic and threatening. Its only source in the novel is indirect and vague: Priestley simply mentions that Horace "somewhat fantastically proffered" some potatoes. In another change, the script turns Philip's speculation about the source of the house's electricity into a statement by Horace, who declares, again with matter-of-fact exactitude, "We make our own electric light here—and we are not very good at it."

Whale visually elaborates on the strangeness of the dinner. When Rebecca passes some bread stuck on the end of a fork, none of the guests feels like taking any, and Whale's camera follows the fork, in a close shot, as it journeys down the length of the table. The camera also tracks, in close-up, from plate to plate while Rebecca digs in and a visitor picks at a large black spot in a potato. Later, by moving the after-dinner conversation from the table to chairs by a fireplace, Whale avoids excessive exposure of one setting while creating a new mood by filming the speakers from across the top of the flames. Even a close shot is taken from this position, which gives the atmosphere and the image an otherworldly quality.

Various undercurrents, not present in the book, are suggested through Whale's staging. When Horace authoritatively directs Morgan to show the visitors where to put their car, the director cuts to Rebecca and Morgan: He looks toward her, she nods, and only then does he go. The image, not the dialogue, makes it clear who really is in charge. During dinner, Whale prepares the viewer for Morgan's later drunken attack on Margaret by showing him, while serving, pause and look her over each time he passes.

One of the high points of *The Old Dark House* occurs when Margaret Waverton enters Rebecca's room to change from her wet clothes. The old lady remains and starts talking about her sister, Rachel, who died in the same room. A fall from a horse had injured her spine and for months she lay in bed, screaming with pain. "She used to cry out to me—to kill her. But I'd tell her to turn to the Lord. She didn't. She was Godless to the last." At this point, Whale visualizes Rebecca's warped psyche by cutting during her dialogue from a direct shot to Rebecca's reflection in a mirror, then to her face distorted by a section of the mirror's glass, and finally—in what is really a jump-cut—to her face even more distorted. After that, he returns to a normal-looking shot of the two women. "[Normal image] They were all Godless here. They used to bring their *women* here. [Reflection] Brazen, lolling creatures in silks and satins, they filled the house with laughter and sin, laughter and sin. [Distortion] If I ever went down among them, my own father and brothers, they would tell me to go away

During an intense scene from *The Old Dark House* (1932), Rebecca Femm (Eva Moore, right) confronts her bewildered guest, Margaret Waverton (Gloria Stuart), with disturbing events from her family's past.

and pray. [Extreme distortion] They wouldn't tell Rachel to go away and pray! [Normal image] And I prayed, and left them with their lustful red and white women." Here, Whale's images and Eva Moore's edgily insane delivery combine to slip viewers out of the concrete world, providing a direct exposure to Rebecca's inner deformity and Margaret's perception of it.

Probably associating Margaret with the young and attractive Rachel, the old lady now turns on her guest. The two figures are in profile, in a medium long shot, when Rebecca starts to taunt Margaret, calling her, "Young and handsome, silly and wicked. You think of nothing but your long, straight legs and your white body—and how to please your man. You revel in the joys of fleshly love, don't you?" As Rebecca's speech becomes more intense, the camera tracks closer, finally pausing when she reaches for the other's dress and says, "That's fine stuff—but it'll rot!" Then Whale cuts to a side angle, shooting past Rebecca toward Margaret as the fanatic places an open palm against her victim's bare chest, declaring, "That's finer stuff, still—but it'll rot, too, in time!" Mrs. Waverton backs away and the camera moves forward slightly, putting Rebecca out of the frame and intensifying Margaret's repulsion.

In the novel, Priestley diluted the impact of this confrontation in two ways. First, the verbal attack is separated from the touch by a digression about Margaret's child (never mentioned in the film). Then, Rebecca says her final lines, only without the touch. Margaret has to ask, "What's finer stuff?" and Rebecca repeats, "That is," and touches her skin. It is to the film's advantage that Whale and Levy eliminated both Margaret's question and Rebecca's repetition.

After Margaret recoils from Rebecca's touch, the old woman finally leaves her alone. Having put the audience on edge, Whale here shifts the mood by having Rebecca pause near the door to check her hair in a mirror: The woman who has just called Margaret "wicked" and "vain" is oblivious of her own unjustified vanity. The deadpan inclusion of this incident, totally without precedent in the novel, is typical of the director's unpredictable flashes of humor.

With the tension reduced at Rebecca's departure, the camera moves with Margaret as she crosses the room and casually opens a window, as if to freshen the fetid air. Suddenly, all equilibrium is again lost as a burst of wind surprises Margaret and the viewer, throwing objects and curtains into confusion. (The fact that the wind's power and abruptness are funny in no way undercuts the distress caused by the event.) Her equanimity now totally shattered, Margaret sits in front of the dresser mirrors, which distort her young, attractive face. Her mind stops resisting, and the memory of her unsavory encounter floods in on her. The distorted shots of Rebecca are repeated, and the woman speaks a few phrases, followed by cackling laughter. Also edited into this scene are extreme close-ups of Morgan, who seems to be spying on Margaret, but perhaps only in her imagination. The result is a remarkable evocation of the woman's emotional condition.

Out of this entire sequence, only the dialogue relates closely to Priestley's original version. In the novel, while Rebecca talks, Margaret notices "a fungus cheek" on one side of the woman's face, which "looked like grey seamed fat, sagging into putrefaction." The distorted reflections in the film convey a similar impression, but with greater impact. Once Rebecca leaves, however, novel and film part. Margaret is described as sitting at "the little cracked mirror" as "the familiar reflection brought comfort to her." When she opens the window, wind and rain enter, but "the air was unbelievably fresh and sweet" and the darkness "friendly." Whale's version of the scene is much more disturbing and emotionally complex, and it is executed with visual ingenuity and impeccable pacing.

Later, these events are referred to in a short but startlingly imaginative vignette. It is, in fact, a practically perfect case of translating a novelist's account of his character's train of thought into visual imagery and thereby heightening the effect. Disturbed by Rebecca's touch and her own imaginings, Margaret, alone, observes a candle's flame.

Idly she held one hand above it and began twiddling her fingers, watching their play of light and shade. Then she saw the shadows they cast, a dance of uncouth crazy figures, savages leaping in the smoke of a ceremonial fire, and she brought her hand away. . . . Her mind swayed towards unreason. There came gibbering into it the fancy that she was the victim of a plot, that all the others had been deliberately spirited away by Miss Femm, who would lock them all up and then come creeping back to lay a toad-like witch's hand upon her. For one sickening moment she could feel that hand.

Because a filmed version of this would be impossible, Whale replaced it with a new, but related, incident. When Margaret begins making shadow figures on the wall with her hands, the camera moves forward, placing her body out of the frame and leaving only the shadow of her figure. Suddenly, Rebecca's distinctive shadow darts into view, faces Margaret's shadow, touches the shadow's chest, then darts away. Next, Whale cuts to the actual figure of Margaret who, startled, looks around but sees no one. There is never any verbal reference to this shadow fantasy, as if Whale trusted the viewer to draw the necessary conclusions. Such a subjective embodiment of a character's state of mind, while entirely appropriate, is also creatively daring, especially in 1932.

Even less like the novel is the film's climax, although the basic situation is the same in both versions: Morgan, drunk and out of control, has released Saul and the two descend to the top of the main staircase, with Morgan in full view but only Saul's hand showing around the corner, resting on the bannister. In the novel, Saul is big, heavy, and "unusually powerful"—a screaming maniac who attacks Penderel right away. Whale and Levy altered and expanded this situation to make it more dramatic and, in the process, characterize Saul more fully. The script has continually pointed toward Saul's entrance as the climactic event, with ominous references to him as the dangerous brother locked away upstairs; Horace is so frightened that he refuses even to go near the room. Whale realized that after all this fear and preparation, and with everyone's attention focused on the top of the stairs, no one who stepped into view could fulfill the viewer's indefinite expectations.

So, the filmmakers purposely disappoint their audience with a calculated reversal of expectations. Saul, when he emerges, is a small, weak-looking, shy man who pleads pathetically with Penderel. "Don't let them put me back. I'm not mad—I swear upon Heaven, I'm not mad. . . . They're frightened of me. I know something about them. Years ago, they killed their sister, Rachel—but I won't tell, I promised I'd never tell." Here, Saul acts and sounds reasonable, except perhaps that he eagerly blurts out his

Guests of *The Old Dark House* (1932) anticipate the appearance of the mysterious Saul Femm (played by Brember Wills), whose hand can be seen on the bannister behind the family servant, Morgan (Boris Karloff).

knowledge of the killing despite his promise not to tell. Penderel and the viewer begin to relax, whereupon Whale starts to build the tension again. At one point, when Penderel is not watching, we glimpse the real Saul as, in close-up, he raises one eyebrow and curls his upper lip. Coming from this seemingly gentle creature, the expression chills.

Seated at a table with Penderel, Saul declares that he has made a study of flame. As he talks, a single candle burns in the foreground. "Flames are really knives. They are cold, my friend, sharp and cold as snow. They burn like—ice." Brember Wills delivers these lines straightforwardly, but the ideas belie the rationality of his tone. Then Saul picks up a carving knife and gestures with it as he talks. "Did you know my name is Saul? Saul, my friend. And Saul loved David. . . . But Saul was afraid of David because the Lord was with him, and it came to pass on the morrow that an evil spirit came upon Saul, and he prophesied, and there was a javelin in Saul's hand, and Saul *cast* the javelin—." At this, Saul throws the knife at Penderel, just missing his head.

Although written for the film, this dialogue fits remarkably well with Priestley's plot. Horace's mockery of religion and Rebecca's religious fanaticism link neatly with Saul's Biblical parallel, while the javelin and flame references connect with Saul's attraction to knives and his reputation as a pyromaniac; earlier, Horace's statement that Saul wished to make the house "a burnt offering" had already tied his compulsion to religion. Thus, Whale and Levy provide what Priestley failed to attempt: a valid unification of Saul with the film's overall motifs.

Saul knocks Penderel out, grabs a torch, and climbs to the landing, where he ignites the curtains. Penderel regains consciousness, follows, and—in a situation evocative of *Frankenstein's* climax—man and "monster" fight on a high place, beside a railing, for possession of a smouldering torch. Saul is now fearsome, moving with imp-like agility. Suddenly, his head thrusts forward to bite Penderel's neck. In the novel, the struggle concludes with Penderel falling through the railing to the main floor and both men die, Penderel of a broken neck and Saul "perhaps from shock and a weak heart." One version of the script retained this ending, as indicated by a synopsis in the studio's files, but two changes were made before or during shooting. The final film explains Saul's death more specifically by having the two men fall together. Moreover, as had also happened with *Frankenstein,* the early plan to kill off the hero was dropped, so Penderel is permitted to survive.

Filled with unexpected subtleties of style and idiosyncrasies of tone, *The Old Dark House* is a brilliantly individual work. In fact, it was probably too individual for 1932. Although one trade reviewer mentioned the film's comedy content,[60] Universal advertised it as strictly a horror film. One ad read: "A Lifetime of Terror—Lived in One Mad Night! Ten Men and Women Storm-bound in a House Accursed—While Fear Played Havoc with their Bodies and Souls!" Newspaper reviewers generally praised the film, especially the performances, but were no more helpful than the ads in conveying its tone. Because of this, and because of the studio's emphasis on its new star, Karloff, *The Old Dark House* disappointed and perhaps confused audiences. It was not a financial failure, but during its first week in New York it did a little less than half the business of *Frankenstein.*

Before Whale shot his third fantasy film, *The Invisible Man,* in July 1933, it took almost two years to develop an acceptable script. Universal had acquired the rights to H. G. Wells's novel in September 1931, as a possible follow-up to *Frankenstein* and *Murders in the Rue Morgue,* and announced in October that Benn Levy would write the script and Whale direct. However, the studio soon assigned Whale to *Impatient Maiden*

(1932), and in December Robert Florey became writer-director of *The Invisible Man,* which would star Boris Karloff. In January 1932, Garrett Fort was listed as a writer, with Florey still directing, but a treatment by Whale dated 3 January indicates that Universal had more than one iron in the fire.

The next month Universal purchased *The Murderer Invisible,* a 1931 novel by Philip Wylie with a similar premise; the studio may have envisioned combining elements of both books, for Wylie's more menacing character was better suited to Boris Karloff than Wells's hero. Years later, however, R. C. Sherriff stated that he wrote the final script without referring to *The Murderer Invisible* and suggested that the studio bought the rights only to avoid any chance of a plagiarism suit.[61] (Despite some claims that Wylie himself worked on the screenplay, studio records do not list him among the many writers engaged.)

From April 1932 through June 1933, Universal accumulated at least nine treatments and eleven scripts, prepared by twelve different writers. Garrett Fort began the process with a screenplay submitted on 9 April. In May, John L. Balderston prepared a treatment, revised Fort's script, and prepared one of his own. Balderston's screenplay was in turn revised by Cyril Gardner. The studio next considered treatments by John Huston (July), Richard Schayer (September), James Whale (November), Governeur Morris (December), Whale and Morris (no date), and John Weld (January 1933).

While numerous typewriters rehashed Wells's plot, Whale and Sherriff concentrated on a sequel to Universal's highly successful *All Quiet on the Western Front* (1930). The studio had owned Remarque's continuation of the story, *The Road Back,* since 1929, and in 1931 Whale was chosen to direct, after finishing *Waterloo Bridge.* Universal postponed the picture because of its high budget, however, so Whale made *Frankenstein* and *Impatient Maiden.* Then, in February 1932, he had the studio ask R. C. Sherriff to adapt *The Road Back.* The playwright, who was studying history at Oxford University, accepted Universal's offer to work in Hollywood for several months during the spring and summer.

Upon his arrival, Sherriff received an office and secretary on the Universal lot, but he preferred writing at home, in the evening. At Whale's suggestion, he visited the office in the morning, gave the secretary his night's work to type, then observed activities at the studio, including the filming of *The Old Dark House.* At noon, he would leave, having officially put in his time. During this period, Whale suggested that Sherriff follow *The Road Back* with *The Invisible Man.* The idea of adapting Wells's novel attracted the writer. "I'd read the book as a boy," he recalled. "It had thrilled me, and I'd never forgotten it."[62] Sherriff was, however, anxious to return home, so the studio allowed him to write in England, with the stipulation that he return to Hollywood for conferences later. After discussing the project with Whale, Sherriff set to work at his country house near London. (In his autobiography, Sherriff states that he wrote *The Invisible Man* in Hollywood and adapted *The Road Back* in England, but news items in *Variety* at the time indicate otherwise and, during a 1971 interview, Sherriff confirmed the actual order of events.)

Whale sailed to England with Sherriff for a holiday and in September he returned, ready to start *The Road Back,* but the studio again delayed production and assigned him to *The Kiss before the Mirror,* filmed early in 1933. While Sherriff worked, other hands also tried to turn *The Invisible Man* into a horror film. Scripts were submitted by Preston Sturges in November 1932, Governeur Morris in December, and John Weld in February 1933. Sherriff finished his first version on 4 March 1933, two days before Laird Doyle completed his and two months before Preston Sturges submitted his second.

Meanwhile, Universal decided to make a sequel to *Frankenstein*. Whale opposed the idea and pinned his hope of avoiding it on Sherriff and *The Invisible Man*. Finally, on 12 June, Sherriff submitted a second draft, which more than satisfied Whale and the studio. *Variety* reported that Universal considered it "the perfect screen version of a novel."[63] Whale was especially pleased at the chance to sidestep *The Return of Frankenstein*.

In May 1933, Universal still expected to star Boris Karloff in *The Invisible Man*, but the studio refused to pay him the raise written into his contract, so Karloff walked out. This left Whale quite literally with an invisible man for his lead. Colin Clive turned the part down, although he admitted that the role appealed to him.[64] Whale then turned to Claude Rains, whom he had known in London, before the actor conquered Broadway in the late 1920s. Whale tested Rains and signed him shortly before the start of shooting. David Lewis recalled Whale's reasoning: "Rains has the greatest voice in the world and if he can't be seen, his voice has the needed presence."[65] But to get Rains, the studio had to give him star billing, an unusual situation for a filmic novice and one that caused the already-signed Chester Morris to leave the film. At close to the same time, Whale added Una O'Connor to the cast; she, too, had been evident on the London stage of the 1920s. As with *The Old Dark House,* the presence of these and other British actors helped give *The Invisible Man* an authentic atmosphere.

Shooting began at the end of June 1933 and didn't end until late August. This was a long period for the early 1930s, but a technicians' strike probably contributed to the undue length. First set for release on 24 August, the film didn't appear until November, owing to the meticulous laboratory work required for the shots in which the title character is seen partly clothed or disrobing. In 1934, photographer/technician John P. Fulton described the special effects he used for such scenes. First, the normal characters and their reactions were photographed and the negative developed in the usual fashion. Next, a special set was covered with black velvet and Rains costumed in black velvet tights, gloves, and headpiece. On top of this, the actor wore whatever clothes were required. Then, when the camera filmed him against the black background, the clothing seemed to move by itself in empty space.

For many shots, Rains's cloth head-covering could contain no openings, so he breathed through a tube that ran up his pants leg. The headpiece also muffled sound, so even a voice amplified by a megaphone could barely be heard. Because the actor's movements had to be carefully timed to match actors and a setting filmed separately, they required much rehearsal and many retakes. This material was later combined with the other footage to form a single shot.

One of the most difficult shots involved having the Invisible Man unwrap his head bandages while reflected in a mirror, which required the filming and combination of four separate pieces of film: the wall and the mirror, with the mirror's surface covered by black velvet; the character, seen from behind, performing the action; a front view of him, doing the same thing, to serve as his reflection; and the room's opposite wall, which would also be seen in the mirror. "All of these had to be perfectly coordinated—matched in viewpoint, perspective and action to a fraction of an inch," Fulton declared. "It was as difficult a shot as I have ever made."[66]

Thanks to Fulton, *The Invisible Man*'s illusions are smooth and convincing. Perhaps more important, though, Whale treats the special effects like any other element of a scene, using them in a dramatic and cinematic fashion; instead of being intimidated by the technical problems and presenting each effect in a single shot, he employs considerable editing during these scenes and thereby heightens their dramatic effect. The trick photography exists for the film, not the reverse, and the picture's ultimate success depends more on the script and the director's handling of it.

Universal had urged Sherriff to base his adaptation on the many prior attempts, few of which bore any relation to Wells's plot. For example, Richard Schayer's treatment has a scientist render his mutilated assistant invisible and later stand trial for a murder committed by the man. In a final courtroom scene, the invisible assistant's suicide solves the scientist's problem. Preston Sturges then added to this premise: After the doctor treats his "maniacal" assistant with the invisibility drug, the two journey to Russia to avenge the killing of the scientist's relatives during the Revolution.

Rejecting this grab-bag of "extravagant and fantastic and ridiculous" plots, Sherriff sought to return to the "charm and the humor and the fascination" of Wells's story.[67] But when he asked Universal for a copy of the novel he was told that the studio's was lost—and that everything worthwhile from it had gone into the scripts. Sherriff persisted and, after a futile search through Hollywood's bookstores, eventually located a secondhand copy. A rereading of the novel reinforced Sherriff's faith in Wells's approach. "His secret was a simple one. To give reality to a fantastic story, . . . it had to be told through the eyes of ordinary, plain-spoken people. If you tried to fasten extraordinary people to extraordinary events the whole thing fell to pieces."[68]

After analyzing the difference between a novel and a film script, Sherriff concluded that a scriptwriter must "prune away the side-shoots and keep to the main stem," so that "every line of dialogue was there to drive the story on." Because Wells had essentially done that in his book, Sherriff simply "dramatized it chapter by chapter, and it was mainly a matter of turning narrative into dialogue. I had to add ingredients here and there to tighten up the drama, and condense a lot . . . , but when it was finished I felt reasonably sure that this was the genuine, unadulterated story which Wells himself had conceived."[69]

Although not as close to the novel as Sherriff recalled, the film *is* an excellent adaptation that captures Wells's lightness combined with tension and that retains both his narrative structure and specific incidents. The film's opening section, in particular, recreates the novel with a purist's faithfulness. Each work opens with the bandaged stranger's arrival at an inn, develops his irritation at the locals' curiosity, and provides an initial climax when he strips off his clothes in front of them. After indulging in some impish and angry pranks in the village, the Invisible Man, Jack Griffin, contacts Dr. Kemp (William Harrigan) for help in creating a reign of terror. Sherriff has Kemp notify the police, but Griffin escapes and announces that he will execute Kemp as a lesson to all who would resist his power. Soon after accomplishing this, Griffin himself is killed and, at death, regains visibility.

In the middle of the novel, Wells's character has a long monologue in which he recounts his early experiments, his need for money, his robbery of his father, his problems in adjusting to invisibility, and his ways of stealing clothes from stores. No doubt to "keep to the main stem," Sherriff wisely dropped most of these details, for they would have required a prolonged recitation by Griffin, a major series of flashbacks, or an earlier beginning of the story. The first choice would have been dramatically static, the second would have interrupted the film's pace, and the third would have sacrificed the impact of opening with Griffin's mysterious arrival at the inn.

To counteract the reduction of Griffin's explanation to Kemp, and no doubt to provide the love interest demanded by American studios, Sherriff added two new characters: Dr. Cranley (Henry Travers), with whom Griffin had been working, and his daughter, Flora (Gloria Stuart), Griffin's fiancée. He also increased Kemp's importance by making him an associate of Griffin and a rival for Flora's affections, instead of just a slight acquaintance. These three people discuss Griffin's disappearance in scenes intercut with the main action and provide some of the exposition removed from the other scene.

The invisible man (Claude Rains), his face tightly bandaged, is first seen as he comes in from a severe snowstorm to an inn. James Whale introduces him in a series of long to medium to close shots, a technique he also used to introduce the Monster in *Frankenstein*. From *The Invisible Man* (1933).

Sherriff's changes help unify the action by providing characters who are involved in most of the film's major events. Further tightening the book, Sherriff eliminated the tramp who helps Griffin after the trouble at the inn and gave Kemp two of that character's functions: accompanying Griffin to the inn to recover his notebooks and seeking police protection when the Invisible Man threatens to kill him. In a major change, Griffin now carries out his threat, whereas in the book he is killed while chasing Kemp, who survives. The film therefore builds to a more dramatic climax.

The model for these added aspects was probably *Frankenstein,* for the two films share the situation of a passionate young scientist who has disappeared in order to experiment alone, leaving behind a worried fiancée, a fatherly associate (Dr. Cranley here combines Dr. Waldman and Baron Frankenstein), and a friend who is fond of the fiancée. Both films first introduce the menace situation, without explanation, followed by a scene in which those left behind provide exposition. Even the dialogue in the exposition scene evokes *Frankenstein,* as Flora speaks of receiving a cryptic note from Griffin. The plot then returns to the initial situation, which builds to a climax as the menace is "created." After another scene with the normal characters, the two groups of people converge.

These similarities could have resulted from Whale's contribution to story conferences with Sherriff, or perhaps from the writer studying Whale's prototype film. There is, however, an intriguing contrast in the way the two pictures use their similar elements. Whale had intended *Frankenstein* to end with the scientist's death, but the studio let Henry regain consciousness; something similar had occurred with Penderel at the end of *The Old Dark House.* It is tempting to think that the director, in preparing *The Invisible Man,* decided that this time he would kill off both the main character and the heroine's other suitor.

Of course, this ending's difference from that of *Frankenstein* develops logically from the changes made in Wells's plot. By increasing Kemp's importance, Sherriff and Whale provide Griffin with a specific antagonist, thereby creating a more precise conflict than exists in the novel—and adding an element that is not part of Henry Frankenstein's relationship with Victor Moritz. Such a conflict is dramatically necessary in *The Invisible Man,* because there is no overt struggle between the scientist and a monster, as there is in *Frankenstein.* Here, the scientist himself becomes the monster.

Because the conflict between Griffin and Kemp has gained in importance, it also must come to a definite resolution, and because viewers have been encouraged to relish the Invisible Man's power, they would feel shortchanged without this preliminary victory before his inevitable destruction. Thus, the film's fantasy of omnipotence is allowed a brief extension, but even modern audiences express surprise that Griffin is allowed to accomplish such a cold-blooded murder.

The movie prepares its audience for Kemp's death by emphasizing his cowardice, a trait that inhibits viewer identification and arouses some antipathy. The gentle, good-looking Victor Moritz hints at his affection for Elizabeth and then lets the matter drop, whereas Kemp has a sour personality and presses his case too hard. He is hardly an outright villain, but neither does he act like a gentleman in taking advantage of Griffin's absence, so we are shocked that he is killed, without being disturbed at his death.

Griffin's megalomania exists in both book and film, but Wells never lets him start his reign of terror, while in the film he causes one good-sized train wreck. But anything gained must be paid for, and the film pays for the train wreck by declaring that a drug used by Griffin has driven him insane. This reduces the character's moral accountability for his actions and allows the viewer to avoid the discomfort of vicari-

The Invisible Man (Claude Rains) enlists the aid of fellow scientist and romantic rival Dr. Kemp (William Harrigan). From *The Invisible Man* (1933).

ous guilt. The book's narrator considers the possibility that Griffin has gone insane, but rejects the idea, recalling instead the "extraordinary irascibility" of this "intensely egotistical and unfeeling man."

Sherriff gave Griffin two dynamic speeches about his plans for seizing power that have no counterparts in the book, and because of the vividness of these monologues, Griffin's megalomania gains in importance. The first such speech is delivered to Kemp. "The drugs I took seemed to light up my brain. Suddenly I realized the power I held—the power to rule, to make the world grovel at my feet. . . . We'll begin with a reign of terror. A few murders, here and there. Murders of great men, murders of little men, just to show we make no distinction. We might even wreck a train or two. Just these fingers, 'round a signalman's throat."

A pivotal figure in the development of horror films, Griffin is one of the first scientists to proclaim his superiority to the masses and revel in it, seeing no reason why he shouldn't rule the world. Of course, the attraction of power was implicit in most of the horror films that preceded *The Invisible Man*. Audiences relished the supernatural abilities of Dracula and Im-ho-tep, the ruthlessness of Dr. Mirakle, the brilliance of Henry Frankenstein and Henry Jekyll, and the physical force of the Frankenstein Monster and Mr. Hyde. They also were fascinated by these characters' independence and isolation, by their willingness to venture into the Forbidden and the Unknown. But all of these characters had limited goals, and few verbalized a desire for power. Griffin, however, embodies this Superman aspect completely.

This characteristic does exist in Wells's novel, but Sherriff's dialogue and Rains's dynamic performance heighten it considerably. In this regard, *The Murderer Invisible* may have influenced the script, for Wylie's novel does deal directly with its invisible character's megalomania, as when he declares, "Power has always been denied me. My compensation will come—and it will not be the power of Wealth—wholly—not power over a few thousand employees—it will be power over leaders—then power over a nation—and at the last power over the world."

Such a figure would naturally attract people who, boxed into a corner by the Depression, were intrigued by men who ignore the rules and take matters into their own hands, whether they be Jack Griffin, Little Caesar, or Franklin Delano Roosevelt. As a character in King Vidor's *Our Daily Bread* (1934) says, regarding the selection of a leader for a collective farm, "We got a big job here and we need a Big Boss!" This fascination faded in the late 1930s and early 1940s, as the Depression receded and reports from Germany revealed some of the realistic results of putting the Superman philosophy into practice.

Because Griffin is the film's central figure—the "hero"—viewers are led to identify with him; therefore, although each individual watching *The Invisible Man* would certainly not tolerate someone else having the total power that Griffin desires, he or she likely enjoys fantasizing about having it personally. Thus, Griffin's assertion of God-like omnipotence by killing Kemp is really the emotional climax of the film, with the Invisible Man's death merely a perfunctory requirement for returning the world to order. Even Whale seemed to lose interest at this point, for the discovery of Griffin sleeping in a barn occurs abruptly, and the actual trapping of the fugitive lacks the director's usual knack for pacing a scene to elicit its full quota of tension. Instead, the shots leading to this climax are too short and, when events happen, they happen too quickly. It is almost as if Whale, unable to show Griffin's reactions directly, stops treating him like someone with feelings. So, after the barn is set on fire, all we get is a shot of the straw moving when Griffin wakes up, then a shot of the barn doors opening as he leaves. After that, his footprints appear in the snow and he is killed. Very little dread is established in the police, and no emotion at all is created for Griffin. (The climax of *Frankenstein* makes a good contrast here, for in that film Whale evokes considerable terror and sympathy when the Monster is trapped in the burning mill.)

In general, though, *The Invisible Man* reveals the full flowering of Whale's visual style, especially in his editing among a large number of slightly varied setups. He knew when to cut and when not to—when a few extra shots can build tension, when a shift of angle will satisfy the viewer's eye during an expository speech, when a stationary medium shot will dramatize significant dialogue, when a close-up will heighten a revelation. Whale seldom returns to the exact shot from which he had cut away a few seconds before. Instead, he uses a new setup, perhaps one placed a little closer to the subject or one viewing it from a slightly different perspective.

The first scene between Kemp and Flora illustrates how Whale blends this fluid editing with dialogue. As the two discuss Griffin's disappearance, the shots shift directly from a medium long shot of the couple to a closer shot of them, followed by a tight close-up of just Flora as her comments become more intense and personal. Then, Kemp tries to undermine his missing rival in a medium shot of him and Flora, which leads to a close shot of them both.

Another scene that illustrates Whale's intelligent combination of editing and dialogue is a conversation between Griffin and Flora at Kemp's house. Again, the characters hardly move, yet the scene is far from static, for the image shifts among various medium shots of both and close-ups of each individual. The script had indicated only one shot for the speech, with which Griffin ends the scene, but during shooting Whale divided it into three: [Medium close shot of Griffin, who rises as he speaks and the camera tilts up at him] "Power, I said! Power to walk into the gold vaults of the nations, [close-up of Griffin] into the secrets of Kings, even the Holy of Holies. Power to make the multitudes run screaming in terror [medium shot of Griffin] at the touch of my little invisible finger. Even the moon's frightened of me. Frightened to death! The whole world's frightened to death!"

At other times, Whale chooses not to edit at all, as when Mrs. Hall first shows Griffin to his room at the inn. Aloof, he stands in the background, facing away from her and us. She putters around, too nosy to leave, hoping to learn something about the stranger. In a long shot, she stands on the right in the foreground, straightening something, then moves to the left to adjust a lamp, then back to the right as she brushes a chair, then again to the left after Griffin orders some food. Throughout, the camera pans back and forth with her, while always keeping Griffin in the frame, as the central point to which she is drawn. Here, the lack of cutting conveys the magnetic field of her curiosity, creating the scene's subtle humor.

There is, in fact, quite a lot of humor in *The Invisible Man*. Wells's novel, too, has a witty tone, so here—unlike in *The Old Dark House*—it is consistent with the source. But *The Invisible Man* veers closer to farce than did the earlier film, which is probably inevitable, because farce involves physical violence that deflates figures of respect and an invisible man can tweak noses with impunity. This unseen prankster swats a passerby with a broom, knocks over a baby carriage, tosses an old man's hat into a river, throws rocks through a store window, splatters ink on one policeman, and pulls the pants off another. In the midst of a chase, his shirt drops to the ground just as a cop swings his club—and hits another pursuer on the head. These events succeed as comedy by virtue of Griffin's impishness and a feeling that no one is ever really hurt.

Because such farce derives from Griffin's invisibility, Whale easily isolates it from the film's serious segments, in which Griffin can be seen, albeit wrapped in bandages. Occasionally, Whale mixes the two moods. At the end of the second invisible rampage, just after a policeman absurdly waves his club at nothing, Griffin chokes an official until he lies unconscious on the floor. Then he picks up a wooden stool and cracks the man's skull with it! In this impressive shifting of gears, Whale leaps from painless farce to brutal murder. An earlier shift in the other direction is less successful. After a tense confrontation between Griffin and Mr. Hall, the landlord is thrown down a flight of stairs. The tone of this scene is then disrupted by the screeching of Mrs. Hall (Una O'Connor). At this point, Whale departed from his shooting script by having the half-conscious man raise his head and in a weak voice tell his wife to shut up. Fortunately, this bit of contrived comedy is the film's only moment of overindulgence.

The film offers subtler humor in some of the dialogue and its delivery, such as policeman E. E. Clive's pompous statement of the obvious: "He's invisible, that's what's the matter with him!" It probably isn't a coincidence that as the Invisible Man removes his clothes to surprise the police he says, "This will give them a bit of a shock," just as he unzips his trousers. Griffin also reveals some of the arch, haughty manner associated with the coy madness of Ernest Thesiger's Horace Femm as he declares his intention to murder people of varied social classes, "just to show we make no distinction."

Most contemporary reviewers and audiences responded favorably to *The Invisible Man*'s humor, in contrast to their uncertainty about *The Old Dark House*. *Variety* noted that one audience laughed readily at the scenes involving moving objects or the

Invisible Man discarding his clothes.[70] However, Whale's mixture of moods still provoked some critical confusion, with *Variety* unsure whether all of the laughs had been intended. Richard Watts, Jr., in the *New York Herald-Tribune,* even described the scene of Griffin unwrapping his head as "properly frightening."[71] Such contrasting reactions were possible because the concept of the scene—and the film—contains both humor and horror, comedy and tragedy.

By 1933, Universal's horror films had already passed their peak of audience popularity. After *Frankenstein,* viewers had been disappointed in the overblown *Murders in the Rue Morgue* and the subtle *The Old Dark House* and *The Mummy.* Only a few fantasy/horror films caught the interest of a wide public: *King Kong* was a blockbuster in 1933, but *The Invisible Man* offered healthy competition. Also, at a time when reviewers had already revealed condescension toward horror films, *The Invisible Man* inspired a rare respect, owing both to its inherent quality and its literary origin. The *New York Times* called it "one of the best features of its kind. . . . in many ways a far better picture than was *Frankenstein.*"[72] Even H. G. Wells, at a luncheon given to publicize the film, praised Universal and Whale for "a triumph of production" and for the "almost complete suppression of romantic interest and the absence of a star."[73]

The Invisible Man's quality and success reinforced the reputations of Whale and Sherriff and established Claude Rains as a Hollywood presence. Seeing it remains a rewarding experience, given the film's knockabout farce, whimsical charm, adventure, fantasy, and brutal violence. It depicts human aspiration, human arrogance, human accomplishments, and human absurdities. It arouses emotions of omnipotence and helplessness, provoking both objective laughter and subjective sympathy. It inspires awe at technical ingenuity, while making us forget that what we are seeing is impossible. Most of all, amid the comedy and the spectacle, the fantasy and the illusion, it never forgets the tragic solitude of a man who has gone beyond the normal and is trapped there, isolated, unable to return—he has achieved his goal but lost everything in the process. Not surprisingly, as David Lewis recalled, this was the film of which Whale was by far the proudest.[74]

By making *The Invisible Man,* Whale had managed to avoid Universal's intended sequel to *Frankenstein;* the studio even announced that Kurt Neumann would make *The Return of Frankenstein.* Late in September 1933, Whale took over the direction of a comedy, *By Candlelight,* and also turned to another of the studio's ideas for a fantasy film, *A Trip to Mars.* Several writers had already labored over *Mars* during 1932. First, R. C. Sherriff wrote a screenplay, dated 3 March, but Universal may have been dissatisfied with it, for on 18 March the studio purchased an original story by Harry O. Hoyt. Ralph Parker submitted treatments on 19 and 24 March, and two months later Richard Schayer and Tom Reed offered another treatment (20 May) and a screenplay (13 June). After that, the project was set aside.

Universal's synopsis tells the far-fetched story of Professor von Saxmar, who launches an unmanned rocket to Mars, where it explodes. This angers the Martians, who retaliate with a rocket that destroys half of Europe. When an American reporter tells Saxmar that only a manned expedition can prevent more deaths, the scientist at first resists. "Then, an insane light appearing in his eye, he consents." So Saxmar, his daughter, and the reporter journey to Mars, where they encounter giant insects that possess almost-human intelligence; at one point, an army of large ants defends a Martian city from an attack by equally large spiders. In the glass palace of the Martians' Queen Meera, the reporter and the Queen fall in love, a process that renders her more human. When the ants rebel against their Martian masters, Saxmar and his daughter are killed and their Irish terrier, which had learned to talk on Mars, dies "with a cheerful wisecrack on his lips." The lovers, however, escape safely to Earth and a Niagara Falls honeymoon.

Considering the elaborate settings and Willis O'Brien–type special effects that *A Trip to Mars* would have required, it is not surprising that budget-conscious Universal shelved the project. However, in September 1933 Whale revived it as a vehicle for Karloff. R. C. Sherriff soon set to work on a new script, and in December Whale sailed to England for a combination holiday and conference. Two months later, he returned with the completed script, expecting to film it in March 1934.

Together, Whale and Sherriff completely rewrote the plot. Although publicity continued to use the title *A Trip to Mars,* both Sherriff and David Lewis insisted that the location was changed to the moon. The approach, too, shifted from fantastic adventure to realistic semidocumentary. A copy of this unproduced script has yet to appear, but in 1973 Lewis recalled the project quite vividly. "It was a brilliant script. . . . The blastoff, everything, was as it finally happened. It wasn't exactly as it happened, but it was damn close! And the moon was an absolutely desolate place. On Earth, they'd believed the moon was inhabited—they found no one there, it was darkness, they became lost, unable to breathe, and so forth."[75] According to Lewis, Whale wanted to make this picture—"It was his and Sherriff's 'baby' "—but even though the budget would have been smaller than that for the earlier version, Universal again backed off. So Whale turned instead to *One More River* (also from a Sherriff script), which he filmed in May 1934. Then, once again, he faced the specter of Frankenstein's creation.

In December 1931, shortly after the release of *Frankenstein,* Robert Florey had anticipated the possibility of a sequel and written a story entitled *The Monster Lives!* which drew a great deal from Mary Shelley's novel and was never used. Only in June 1933 did the writing department set to work. Tom Reed submitted a treatment on 10 June, then worked on three versions of a screenplay through the end of July. "They've had a script made for a sequel," Whale told Sherriff, "and it stinks to heaven. In any case I squeezed the idea dry on the original picture, and never want to work on it again."[76]

Late in 1933, Universal tried once more, with L. G. Blochman submitting a new treatment on 5 December and Philip MacDonald providing a 36-page story on the day after Christmas. No further writing was done until Spring 1934. Then, around the time Whale set aside his objections and agreed to direct, the studio hired horror veteran John L. Balderston (*Dracula, Frankenstein, The Mummy*), who submitted a screenplay on 9 June. After two more attempts, he completed his fourth and last version on 23 July. Balderston's script provoked some basic objections from the Hays Office, which enforced Hollywood's production code, whereupon Universal brought in William Hurlbut for rewrites during October and November. The final shooting script,[77] completed on 1 December, provoked a new set of concerns from the Hays Office. This time, Whale himself met with a code representative to discuss the problems, which ranged from religious irreverence and the large number of killings to the use of the word "entrails," which was called "offensive to mixed audiences"[78] (and was changed to "insides").

Production on what came to be called *Bride of Frankenstein* finally began in January 1935. About two months later, Joe Breen, of the Hays Office, screened the finished film and became "gravely concerned." The film, he declared, was "definitely" in violation of the code "because of its excessive brutality and gruesomeness." In addition, "the shots early in the picture, in which the breasts of the character of Mrs. Shelley are exposed and accentuated, constitute a code violation." But, he added, "careful and intelligent editing of the picture may remove the difficulties."[79] Universal made many of Breen's suggested cuts (along with others that tightened the film's pace) and reduced the movie's running time by about seventeen minutes.

Although Balderston did not receive a screenplay credit, elements from his adaptation of Webling's *Frankenstein: An Adventure in the Macabre* found their way into *Bride of Frankenstein*. These include the Monster's halting, monosyllabic speech, his demand for a mate, and his threat to kidnap Amelia/Elizabeth unless Frankenstein complies. Also inspired by the play and Robert Florey's script was a scene of the Monster observing a peasant couple as they make love, which arouses his sexual desire. Predictably, the Hays Office wanted Universal to turn that scene into "an unsuggestive, unobjectionable, and harmless picture of the pure and innocent affection felt between simple folk" by eliminating "Eric taking down Hilda's hair, and undressing . . . the kiss and the action of falling back on the bed." It also urged that the Monster not ask for a "mate," because it "suggests that he desires a sexual companion."[80] In response, Hurlbut completely omitted the peasant couple and had the Monster desire a "friend."

Whale did not want to make just an ordinary sequel, "to pick up the Monster and have him go like fury," according to David Lewis. "He said that if he had to make the sequel, he was going to make it different enough in conception and idea and treatment . . . that it would stand on its own."[81] Once Whale became involved, he conferred frequently with the writers and had them include the tiny creatures created by Dr. Pretorius and the prologue with Mary Shelley, Percy Shelley, and Lord Byron. As the script evolved, the totally new character of Dr. Pretorius became a pivotal figure who quite eclipsed Henry Frankenstein; Whale's decision to cast Ernest Thesiger in the role further determined the film's tone, making it a cross between the drama of *Frankenstein* and the arch humor of *The Old Dark House*. Through Pretorius, Whale includes and intertwines a coy fascination with death, an ambivalent attitude toward religion, a suspicion of women, and a disdain of human nature in general.

Referring to *Frankenstein,* Whale said in 1931, "I never intended this picture for children, but I would like to make a children's version."[82] Evidently, the director saw in the situation a mythical, almost fairy-tale quality. Although he certainly made *Bride of Frankenstein* for adults, in it he emphasized fantasy and humor over macabre realism. Faced with the basic implausibility of the Monster's survival, Whale deliberately selected artificiality as his style. The acting, incidents, and settings all exist on a level far above reality, and every emotion is pushed to its extreme. The Monster was a simple, tragic image of the human condition; now, he possesses a self-awareness that gives him a new majesty in defeat. At the same time, the Monster is almost comically human, as he talks, enjoys music, drinks wine, and smokes a cigar. He also cries at the blind hermit's kindness and at his bride's rejection.

In *Bride of Frankenstein,* Henry Frankenstein (again played by Colin Clive) is limited to various degrees of anguish, until scientific passion finally takes over in the creation scene. The enthusiastically perverse Pretorius dominates, as he entices the film into his bizarre world. Leaving the graceful arches and large, open rooms of the Frankenstein mansion, Henry and the viewers enter the cramped garret of Pretorius, with its angled walls and pointed shadows. There, Henry trades his relatively scientific methods for the vague procedures of his former teacher. The tiny figures that Pretorius claims to have grown "from seed" exist totally on the level of fantasy and justify Henry's comment, "This isn't science—it's more like black magic."

Because *Bride of Frankenstein* picks up events exactly where the original film ended, Whale refreshes the viewer's memory through a prologue in which Mary Shelley discusses her story. As Lord Byron offers a summary, we see shots from the earlier film (and one, of a murder, that is new). Then, Mary decides to tell the "rest" of her

Elsa Lanchester, who doubles as the Monster's mate and as writer Mary Shelley in *Bride of Frankenstein* (1935), appears here as Shelley flanked by poets Percy Bysshe Shelley (Douglas Walton, left) and Lord Byron (Gavin Gordon).

tale. Oddly, this prologue is set in the nineteenth century, whereas *Frankenstein* had been updated to the present, but the main portion of the new film circumvents this contradiction by existing in an uncertain time period that permits elaborate laboratory equipment while treating the telephone as a new invention.

The prologue also has a subtler purpose. Whale insisted that Elsa Lanchester play both Mary Shelley and the bride, thereby linking the two females. He stressed Mary's daintiness and poise, Lanchester explained, to imply that within the pretty and delicate woman existed "a nasty spirit, a real evil," that the two were "the same person."[83] Actually, the bride doesn't live long enough to reveal a nasty or evil side, but the basic idea of such duality remains valid and is, certainly, conveyed in the prologue. When Byron describes Mary as an "angel," she coyly asks, "You think so?" Later, he declares, "Astonishing creature. . . . Frightened of thunder, fearful of the dark, and yet you have written a tale that sent my blood into icy creeps. . . . Can you believe that bland and lovely brow conceived a Frankenstein—a monster created from cadavers out of rifled graves? Isn't it astonishing?" Mary responds, "I don't know why you should think so."

The film's main body begins as the villagers leave the charred remains of the mill. The parents of the drowned Maria remain behind, however, for the father must see the Monster's corpse with his own eyes. As a kind of punishment for his vengefulness, he falls through the floor into a pool of water and is killed by the Monster (Boris Karloff), who has survived there, burned and dangerous. Shortly after, the Monster

throws Maria's mother to her death. At each murder, Whale cuts to a sleepy owl looking passively on, a typically quaint touch that contrasts with the script's blunt description of a rat "quivering in a crevice between the stones." The Hays Office had
protested that showing a rat "has in the past proved offensive,"[84] so Whale improved
the scene by using the incongruous owl instead.

For the most part, Whale's humor in *Bride of Frankenstein* is witty and off-beat, but
because of his fondness for Una O'Connor, he encourages her to greater excess, even,
than she showed in *The Invisible Man*. She plays Minnie, a servant whose comments
and screams throw several scenes off-balance, irritating and distracting more than they
amuse. Just after the deaths of Maria's parents, the Monster stands quietly behind Minnie until she turns, screeches, and runs off howling. Later, the pompous Burgomaster
(E. E. Clive) tells Minnie to "shut up," a bit of business borrowed from *The Invisible
Man* and not part of *Bride of Frankenstein*'s script.

Soon, Frankenstein has recovered enough to converse with Elizabeth (now played
by Valerie Hobson). He tells her, "I dreamed of being the first to give to the world the
secret that God is so jealous of—the formula for life. . . . It may be that I'm *intended* to
know the secret of life. It may be part of the divine plan!" But Elizabeth calls his work
"blasphemous and wicked," adding, "It's the Devil that prompts you. It's death, not
life, that is in it all and at the end of it all." Having linked death with the Devil, Elizabeth unknowingly juxtaposes both with Pretorius. "When you rave of your insane
desire to create living men from the dust of the dead, a strange apparition has seemed

Dr. Pretorius (Ernest Thesiger, standing) and the reluctant Henry Frankenstein (Colin Clive)
toast "a new world of gods and monsters." From *Bride of Frankenstein* (1935).

to appear in the room. It comes, a figure like Death, and each time it comes more clearly, nearer. It seems to be reaching out for you, as if it would take you away from me. There it is—look—there!" This speech climaxes with a knocking at the door and a shot of the cloaked, death-like figure of Pretorius seeking admittance.

To Minnie, Pretorius declares that he has come "on a secret matter of grave importance," which the servant reports to her master as "on a secret grave matter." Aside from being an amusing pun, this phrase—coming when it does—further connects the intruder with death. We soon learn that Pretorius had been a doctor of philosophy at the university, but was booted out. "Booted, my dear Baron," he declares, relishing his own prissy superiority, "is the word—for knowing—too much." Inexplicably, Pretorius and Frankenstein talk as if the Monster is alive, without knowing it for certain or even acting concerned.

Pretorius takes Frankenstein to see the tiny figures he has created and keeps in jars: a King, a Queen, an Archbishop, a Devil, a Ballerina, and a Mermaid. (The shooting script called for a seventh figure, a baby, "already twice as big as the Queen, and looking as if it might develop into a Boris Karloff. It is pulling a flower to pieces." Wisely, Whale dropped both the baby and the script's self-conscious flippancy.) Pretorius is a manipulative God figure who gave these beings life, determined their identities, and controls their actions. He is also archly disdainful of them, which is revealing of Pretorius and probably of Whale, who conceived of them in the first place.

The King, a parody of the male sex drive, scrambles out of his glass "home" at every opportunity, trying to reach the Queen. Pretorius cavalierly picks him up with tweezers, drops him back in his bottle, and places a dish on top. "Even royal amours are a nuisance," he declares. (It is hardly coincidental that this figure resembles King Henry VIII, the womanizer portrayed in 1933 by Charles Laughton, who happened to be a homosexual, Elsa Lanchester's husband, and an actor in *The Old Dark House*.) Pretorius further reveals his purely academic interest in heterosexuality when he speaks of the mermaid, an experiment with seaweed. "Science, like Love, has her little surprises," he comments mockingly. In this context, one should note that the script's title page bears a quotation from William Blake's "The Garden of Love" (*Songs of Experience,* 1794): "So I turned to the Garden of Love / That so many sweet flowers bore; / And I saw it was filled with graves."

Whale satirizes religion by having the Archbishop discovered asleep; when awakened, he leaps up and gives blessings with an empty, mechanical gesture. The film's mockery even extends to high art, as Pretorius quips that his ballerina "won't dance to anything but Mendelssohn's 'Spring Song,' and it gets so monotonous." In fact, the only figure for whom Pretorius has any respect is the Devil, and the reason is clear. "There's a certain resemblance to me, don't you think? Or do I flatter myself?" He then adds, "Sometimes I have wondered—" and the script leaves the sentence unfinished, but in the film he completes his thought: "—whether life wouldn't be much more amusing if we were all Devils, and no nonsense about angels and being good." At the end of this scene, in a section edited out, Pretorius's assistant Karl (Dwight Frye) enters the room, catches a glimpse of the figures, and declares to another assistant, "He is the Devil, I tell you!"

Several times in his early scenes, Pretorius—the witty Devil-God—cynically blasphemes. Speaking of his pathetic human dolls, he says, "I also have created life, as they say, in God's own image." He urges Henry to follow the lead of nature, adding derisively, "or of God, if you like your Bible stories." (In the script, the line reads, "if you are fond of your fairy tales," but the Hays Office found this too "derogatory."[85] On the face of it, "Bible stories" is innocent enough, but Ernest Thesiger's voice could give any dialogue a haughty, condescending twist.) At one point, Pretorius drinks a toast "to a new world of Gods and Monsters," making a profane link between the two. Frankenstein, a comparatively reverent challenger of God's preeminence, is more repelled than attracted by what Pretorius represents. "I want no more of this Hell's spawn," he asserts.

Part of a conversation between Frankenstein and Pretorius illustrates how carefully Whale divided his dialogue scenes into shots. With both characters seated, there is virtually no action, but editing gives the footage variety and visual energy, while the changes from shot to shot control the emphasis placed on each part of Pretorius's speech:

> [Long shot of Pretorius] You think I'm mad. Perhaps I am. [Medium close-up of Pretorius] But listen, Henry Frankenstein. While you were digging in your graves, piecing together dead tissues, I, my dear pupil, went for my material to the source of life. [Medium close-up of Frankenstein] I grew my creatures—[Close-up of Pretorius]—like cultures. Grew them, as Nature does, from seed. [Extreme long shot of both men] But still, you did achieve results that I have missed. Now think, what a world-astounding collaboration we should be—[Medium close-up of Pretorius]—you and I, together.

This pattern of shots is far more imaginative than the standard setups called for by the script: a close-up of Pretorius and a medium shot of Pretorius and Frankenstein.

The carefully structured *Frankenstein* had alternated scenes of its different characters and then had their paths cross. *Bride of Frankenstein,* however, settles for a long segment devoted to the scientists, followed by an even longer one detailing the Monster's adventures. These two sets of characters and events remain separate for much of the film's length, creating a sense that each exists in an isolated world and leaving the viewer without a clear grasp of chronology and parallel action. Only as the picture nears its climax do the two lines of development merge and strike sparks off each other.

When we leave Frankenstein and Pretorius to rejoin the Monster, the mood shifts from decadence and perversity to more straightforward emotions. The Monster is discovered moving through a forest in the daylight, so he must have killed time for many hours after emerging from the mill. He pauses at a stream to drink and, repelled and angered by his reflection in the water, he splashes it away in a major step toward self-awareness. The Monster then makes friendly overtures toward a shepherdess, but she screams at the sight of him, loses her balance, and falls into the stream. Not yet totally alienated, the Monster rescues her, but she misinterprets his grasp. (Here, Whale sneaks through a blatant continuity error, intercutting a shot of the Monster holding his hand over the girl's mouth with close-ups in which her mouth is uncovered and she screams in panic.) The girl's cries attract two passing hunters who fire at the Monster, and he, wounded, flees into the woods. The hunters rouse the villagers, who set out after the hapless creature.

For the two forest scenes, Whale stylized his sets to reflect the action that occurs in each. The scene by the stream has a lush, pastoral quality created as much by the setting's foliage and underbrush as by the herd of sheep and the musical score. In contrast, the mob pursues the Monster across a barren landscape dominated by trees as tall, straight, and bare as telephone poles. Superbly visualized by Whale, this chase evokes the excitement and pathos of the first film as the Monster, a formidable adversary, crouches above his enemies and pushes over a boulder, crushing several men. The sequence ends with the Monster overpowered and tied to a post. Whale's staging of this suggests a crucifixion, as the Monster is raised upright and held for a few seconds before being dropped into a wagon. The editing emphasizes this moment by using six shots, in place of the single setup indicated in the script.

- Medium long shot of the Monster being raised into position.
- Closer shot of the Monster, upright.
- Extreme long shot of the Monster, the crowd, and the wagon.
- Long shot of the Monster's full figure, as he starts to fall.
- Extreme long shot, as the Monster falls into the wagon.
- Close shot of the Monster, pinned down by a pitchfork placed around his neck.

In this way, Whale forcefully conveys the script's description of the Monster "raised against the sky, a terrible but pathetic sight—friendless, persecuted and almost crucified."

Brought triumphantly to town, the Monster is placed in a cell and chained to a massive garroting chair. Again his pain is emphasized, as Whale cuts between the hammering of the chains into the stone floor and the Monster's face as he screams in angry agony. The scene's emotional force is great enough to obscure the fact that hammering the ends of the chains would surely not inflict such pain. The Monster then regains his composure, breaks loose, and wreaks havoc on the village. By now, the audience is rooting for him, so his escape has the desired effect, even though someone able to snap chains and rip a heavy door from its hinges would surely not have been held by the ropes that bound him to the post.

The impact of the Monster's imprisonment is also diminished by the presence of Minnie, who peers into the dungeon and calls out, "I'd hate to find him under my bed at night. He's a nightmare in the daylight, he is!" When the Monster reaches the street, the script had one man raise his gun to fire, then lose his nerve and start to run; the Monster catches him, "shakes him as a terrier a rat, and throws him to the pavement," trampling his body as he moves on. Whale, probably on the set, weakens this action with comedy by having Minnie thrust the man into the Monster's path, saying, "Why don't you shoot him?" and then running for safety herself. The rest of the Monster's rampage is depicted indirectly, in shots of the villagers discovering bodies— a choice which saves time and also softens the Monster's character. A dead girl, in her communion veil and white dress, is found outside a church, killed by our monstrous Christ. An elderly man and his wife lie dead inside their house (although groans were added to the sound track to suggest that they still live). Omitted from the final print are shots of the child's mother carrying the girl's body, of a female corpse lying in a mortuary, and of a dog howling over the body of its master, whose fishing pole lies beside him in the woods.

In one lengthy sequence that Universal deleted, the Burgomaster conducts an inquiry into the various deaths. After questioning several villagers, he determines that no one actually saw a murder committed. "Monster indeed!" declares the Burgomaster. "It's all nonsense and poppycock." Ordering the courtroom cleared, he adds, "Let me hear no more of this monster business!" As the Burgomaster mutters to himself about the people's foolishness, the Monster appears in a window and, reaching through, grabs the skeptic, drags him outside, and "cuffs him soundly, first from one side, then the other—and drops him, then turns away." Among those in flight are Uncle and Auntie Glutz (Gunnis Davis, Tempe Piggott), whose nephew, Karl (Dwight

Frye), has gotten an idea. After observing his uncle remove a bag of money hidden in his bed, Karl strangles the old man, takes some of the money, and leaves. Then Auntie Glutz discovers her husband's body and the sequence ends as Karl says to himself, "Very convenient to have a Monster around. This is quite a nice cottage—I shouldn't be surprised if he visited *Auntie,* too."

Whale may have cut the Burgomaster's investigation because of its similarity to Inspector Bird's inquiry in *The Invisible Man* and because the Monster's semicomic "punishment" of the Burgomaster would have weakened the mood. Also, the Hays Office had wanted the number of killings reduced, and specifically urged Universal to cut the subplot involving the Glutz family. But because these scenes distract from the Monster's adventures anyhow, they aren't missed.

With this footage gone, we follow the Monster without interruption as he—in an unscripted scene—encounters some gypsies camped in the forest. The Monster seems to ask for food, but the gypsies flee in terror. He reaches for a piece of meat still cooking over a fire and burns his hand, a new contact with flames that drives him back into the night. The scene effectively concludes the Monster's escape, but it leaves behind an inconsistency: Having gone out of his way to attack the people in town, the Monster here meekly "asks" for help.

Despite the cuts, the Monster has already attacked more people in this film than in the first film, yet Whale does not dwell on those deeds. Instead, he emphasizes the mistreatment of the Monster by others. No longer the uncontrolled embodiment of our nightmares, the Monster has become more victim than menace, an "outsider" persecuted by a society that refuses to understand and accept him. As a result, the Monster arouses greater audience sympathy.

Attracted to a hut by the light and the music of a violin coming from within, the Monster remains outside, wary. When the blind hermit who lives there senses his presence and goes to the door, the Monster still hesitates, expecting the usual fear and abuse. Instead, because of the gentle blind man's affliction, the Monster is for the first time treated like a human being. The hermit feeds and reassures him and gives him a place to sleep. This character has strong religious associations—he dresses like a monk, plays the "Ave Maria," and seems to have a crucifix on every wall—but unlike the tiny Archbishop, the hermit is presented without ridicule or irony. Beside the Monster's cot, he prays: "Our Father, I thank Thee that in Thy great mercy Thou hast taken pity on my great loneliness and now, out of the silence of the night, hast brought two of Thy lonely children together and sent me a friend, to be a light unto mine eyes and a comfort in time of trouble." The "Ave Maria" builds in intensity on the soundtrack and the Monster, having finally discovered warmth and security, sheds a tear.

All of this verges on the maudlin, but after the previous events the audience shares the Monster's feeling of relief, and Whale's careful handling keeps the scene in control. However, as the final shot fades out, a crucifix on the wall remains visible, glowing with a garish neon brightness. This touch, which pushes the scene's mood over the edge into bathos, was a last-minute idea of the editor, Ted Kent, who decided it would be consistent with Whale's aims; Kent had the laboratory print the fade so that the crucifix remained unaffected[86] and Whale probably did not even know about the effect until it was too late.

The amount of time that passes between this and the next scene is vague. The script states that a few months have passed. In the actual scene the hermit's line, "Remember our lesson?" implies that more than a day has gone by, yet the Monster's reactions to bread and wine are clearly those of a first encounter. After eating and drinking—and repeating the words "bread," "drink," and "friends"—the Monster tries a cigar. At first, he enjoys it, but on the set Whale modified this idyllic scene with a touch of comic realism, a close-up of the Monster starting to feel sick. Because the Monster reacts with alarm at the flare of a match and is reluctant to approach the blazing fireplace, the hermit explains that fire can be both good and bad; the Monster weighs the words, then reaches for the hermit's violin, saying, "Good!" He understands the concepts.

The Monster is seated at his friend's feet, puffing happily on a cigar and listening to the music, when two hunters blunder into this refuge and bring him suddenly down to earth. One of the hunters (John Carradine) declares, "This is the fiend who has murdered half the countryside," and the other adds, "He isn't human. . . . Frankenstein made him out of dead bodies," thereby adding another bit of information to the Monster's self-knowledge. Violence erupts, and the hunters pull the hermit from his home. During the struggle, fire spreads into the room and, changing from "good" to "bad," engulfs the Monster in a new inferno. When he finally reaches the door and safety, he is again alone, his brief exposure to pleasure ended. Standing quietly, he makes the familiar questioning gesture with his hands and calls out in vain for his only friend. It is an affecting moment.

The two scenes with the hermit are at least as important as any in *Bride of Franken-stein* and should not be minimized in favor of the more off-beat ones that follow. They establish the Monster's humanity, denying for all time that his "criminal brain" (never referred to in the film) had doomed him to villainy. The carefully depicted interaction of these two characters is both touching and amusing, and because the Monster has experienced this paradise, we understand why he helps Pretorius force Frankenstein to create a friend for him; later, having experienced kindness and companionship, he feels this new friend's rejection with a particularly sharp pain.

Abruptly deprived of a stability that came from understanding and acceptance, the Monster resumes the aimless journey of his existence. In the next scene, which heightens his feeling of bitter futility, the Monster emerges by a road just as some children pass; he pauses and, at the sight of him, they scream and flee. Unmentioned by the script, but prominent in the shot, is a roadside shrine with a crucifix that stands near him. Then, once more pursued by villagers, the Monster finds himself in a cemetery where, according to the script, he encounters "a huge Christus" and "sees it as a human figure tortured as he was in the wood. He dashes himself against the figure, grappling with it. The figure is over-turned. He tries to rescue the figure from the cross." As if in response to his sympathy, the fall of the statue reveals an underground crypt, which offers the Monster protection from the approaching mob.

After reading the script, the Hays Office evidently felt that the Monster's actions might be viewed as irreverent, so it urged the filmmakers to substitute "some other type of monument" for the statue of Christ. Whale complied and used the figure of a bishop instead, although the crucifix is clearly visible in the background. This change, of course, eliminates the possibility of making the intended point about the Monster's empathy and rescue attempt (which might, in any event, have been too subjective a motivation to depict clearly). As a result, in the reconceived scene the Monster appears to *attack* the statue, which replaces a positive urge with a negative one; in its hypersensitivity, the Hays Office had converted a moment that was pro-Christ into one that is starkly anti-Church. Also, it keeps the underground vault from being a reward and a place of protection, placing the emphasis instead on its nature as a chamber of death, where the Monster feels at home and declares, "I love dead! Hate living!"

In this cemetery scene, the Monster vents his rage and then declares sympathy with the dead around him: "I love dead. Hate living." From *Bride of Frankenstein* (1935).

Actually, such bitter resentment at hypocritical goodness is consistent with Whale's feelings, as revealed in the comments of Dr. Pretorius and the actions of his tiny Archbishop. In fact, the origin of the cemetery scene's final version can be found, three years before, in an unused treatment for *The Invisible Man* by Governeur Morris, a writer with whom Whale had collaborated. In it, a mutilated man is so physically repugnant to the woman he loves that she takes refuge in a convent. In an effort to overcome his appearance, he becomes invisible and instigates a reign of terror to make her return. "He is baffled by the spectacle of the holy cross round her neck as she approaches. In a demonic frenzy against all holy elements which seek to refute his own hellish impulses, he seeks to destroy a religious monument towering above them." Perhaps the version of the scene in *Bride of Frankenstein* that resulted from the interference of the Hays Office is closer to Whale's true feelings than the one in the shooting script.

Hidden in the death vault, the Monster observes the arrival of that other death figure, Dr. Pretorius, who has come for a skeleton to use in his new experiment (creating a "mate" for a creature he still has no reason to believe is alive). After completing his work Pretorius declares, "I rather like this place," and remains in its atmosphere of death and decay; next to a neat pile of female bones topped by a skull, he sets out his dinner, a chicken and a bottle of wine.

The Monster now steps into view and Pretorius, unruffled, says, "Oh—I thought I was alone." He offers the Monster a cigar, adding, "They're my only weakness." (He had earlier offered Frankenstein a drink of gin, saying, "It's my only weakness." Evidently, he has two "only" weaknesses, one of which jokingly refers back to *The Old Dark House*.) Pretorius tells the Monster that he will make a woman, a friend for him, and the Monster likes the idea. Evidently anticipating some resistance from Franken-stein, Pretorius decides that he can use the Monster to "add a little force to the argu-ment." Finally, the film's two plot threads have been knit together, and in a most appropriate fashion: The figure of Death meets a living corpse in the house of the dead, the God-like Devil and the Devilish Christ come face to face, and the two social outcasts join forces.

We then encounter Henry Frankenstein for the first time since early in the film. During the interim, he has married Elizabeth, and the couple are about to depart when Pretorius intrudes. After Elizabeth leaves the room, Pretorius confronts Frankenstein with the Monster and then secretly sends his new assistant to abduct Elizabeth. This forces Frankenstein to join Pretorius, and they set to work in a larger version of the first film's tower laboratory.

When a fresh, young heart is needed, Pretorius sends his assistant, Karl, out to mur-der for one. Frankenstein convinces himself that it comes from an accident victim, and Whale subtly improves on the shooting script to point up this self-deception. In the script, Frankenstein tells Karl to get the heart, adding, "There are always accidental deaths occurring." Karl replies, "I'll try," and leaves. The film's version of this is the same, except that Frankenstein says, "There are always accidental deaths occurring," *after* Karl departs, which makes the line more clearly a rationalization, and Pretorius then responds sardonically, "Always!"

A subsequent discussion of the new heart illustrates Whale's ability to depict the interaction of several characters, to imply more than is stated, and to do so in a highly cinematic way.

- [Close-up of Karl.] Karl: "It was a very fresh one."
- [Medium shot of Pretorius who, worried that Karl will give the truth away, drops something to distract him.]
- [Close-up of Karl, who turns, startled by the warning noise.]
- [Close-up of Henry, suspicious.] Henry: "Where did you get it?"
- [Close-up of Karl.] Karl: "I gave the gendarme fifty crowns."
- [Close-up of Henry.] Henry: "What gendarme?"
- [Close-up of Karl, who looks toward Pretorius.] Karl: "It was a—"
- [Close-up of Pretorius mouthing the word "police."]
- [Close-up of Karl, who finishes his sentence.] Karl: "—police case."

The scripted version merely noted that the dialogue would be delivered in a medium shot and made no reference to Pretorius.

The actual creation scene allows Whale to take full advantage of his larger budget and expand on the comparable sequence in *Frankenstein*. Impressive electrical instru-ments crackle with anticipation, each in its own shot, and the table containing the body soars majestically to the distant top of the tower laboratory, as the camera stresses the movement by simultaneously descending. When the scientists check gauges and give orders in intense close-ups, sidelighting molds their faces atmospherically and the camera tilts slightly. Through it all, the music maintains a pulse-like rhythm that builds tension, infusing the air with the life force that soon will enter the reclining form. At the experiment's peak, the Monster throws Karl from the high walls—a life is lost as one is gained. The table is lowered and the music, now gentle, anticipates what the sci-entists soon discover: They have succeeded.

The awe one feels in watching this cinematic choreography is only slightly diminished by the Monster's unmotivated appearance on the roof to attack Karl and by special effects, which, in combining live action with a model tower, render the struggling figures transparent. Nor does it really matter that the music turns a bit too gentle and changes moods a few seconds too soon. The awe is there, but despite the elaborate staging, we have seen it all before and the impact of the first time evades recapture.

A tongue-in-cheek quality soon enters the scene as Frankenstein and Pretorius, having unwrapped the woman and dressed her in a flowing white gown, present her to the camera. "The bride of Frankenstein," announces Pretorius, forgetting for the moment to whom the name belongs, and wedding bells peal forth on the soundtrack. However, Whale immediately regains his balance, elaborating on the script with a series of close-ups of the woman as she turns her head stiffly, surveying the world.

She is led to a seat and the Monster enters. There now remains only the playing out of the tragedy, for the outcast remains an outcast, even to his intended "friend." The Monster's painfully gained self-knowledge makes the hostility of his ironically labeled "bride" especially acute, to him and to the viewer. "I love dead! Hate living!" he had said, and now, realizing the futility of his existence, he declares, "We belong dead," and pulls the lever that destroys the tower, returning the two freaks of nature to their origins. His "we" also includes Pretorius, and appropriately so, in view of the many associations of that gaunt figure with death.

Elizabeth has somehow escaped her captivity and, in the shooting script, arrives at the tower in time to die with the others in the explosion. The climax was filmed this way, and in the scene's brief long shots Frankenstein can still be seen amid the avalanche of debris. However, footage was also shot of the Monster telling Frankenstein, "You—go. You—live," and of Frankenstein and Elizabeth reaching safety. Like *Frankenstein,* this sequel provides a token happy ending, even though the Monster has no reason to be generous to his creator. In any case, the final impression of the Monster is consistent with Whale's almost entirely sympathetic attitude. The script has him utter "an ugly cry," his eyes having "the gleam of a wild vengeance" as he pulls the lever, but in the film's final close-up the Monster's eyes gleam only with elegiac tears.

Whale's ambivalence about making *Bride of Frankenstein* shows in the final product: It both refuses to take itself seriously and contains some remarkably serious and moving scenes. "He knew it was never going to be *Frankenstein,*" recalled David Lewis. "He knew it was never going to be a picture to be proud of. So he tried to do all sorts of things that would make it memorable." The result is flawed, but it also is a success, with a wider, more flamboyant scope than *Frankenstein* and a more daring conception of the Monster. In a sense, it is less a sequel than an alternative to its predecessor. Although not as consistent a film as *Frankenstein,* it is equally memorable in its deliberate mixture of tones, and so it finally did become a picture of which Whale could be proud.

Bride of Frankenstein turned out to be the last film for which Whale gathered his extensive family of collaborators, though not his last good film. It also was his last horror picture. Universal did announce, in June 1935, that Whale would direct *Dracula's Daughter,* but although R. C. Sherriff worked on the script throughout the fall, Whale ultimately kept his distance, leaving Lambert Hillyer to carry out the assignment in 1936.

Whale's total output of films was wide-ranging; the horror films are only a small part of it—a part that, if taken in isolation, can be misleading about the nature of his talents and interests. However, these four films did permit Whale to be more personal than he was in most of his other films. Because horror had not yet been defined as a genre, there were few precedents to follow. Whale was able to create several new models, and in the process of developing them he placed much of himself—or, rather, his view of himself—in the central characters. Taken together, these figures compose a multifaceted self-portrait.

Whale changed both Frankenstein and the Monster into characters different from the ones he had inherited, turning them into people who interested and, presumably, satisfied him. For all their superficial differences, it is revealing that they have one major trait in common: Each functions as an outsider, someone generally set apart from and derided by humanity. Henry Frankenstein is set apart by intelligence, imagination, and sensitivity, but for him these qualities do not automatically result in isolation. A secure position in the social family awaits him, but pride and ambition prevent his accepting it. He refuses to compromise his nature—to deny his interests or temper his goals. Instead, he gives full vent to his distinctive abilities. In so doing, he consciously accepts the inability of society to understand or accept him ("I wouldn't care if they did think I was crazy"), and he deliberately isolates himself from the world ("I believe in this monster, as you call it, and if you don't—well, you must leave me alone"). Of what does Frankenstein's compulsive, solitary work consist? He seeks to bring into existence that which never existed before; to create something unfamiliar, something new.

Frankenstein shares this psychological and emotional position with Whale, who also willfully followed his own nature, who set himself apart from his mundane working-class background by accepting his homosexuality and engaging in artistic creation; ultimately, success permitted—and demanded—that he completely control every facet of his films. Seen in this light, Frankenstein's disappointment in the result of his creative effort echoes the inevitable response of all true artists: When the work takes on a concrete form, it somehow never matches the nebulous and profound ideal that existed in the creator's mind.

Frankenstein, the scientist-rebel, indirectly reflects Whale, the artist-rebel, and in *Bride of Frankenstein*'s prologue we find three artist-rebels who, in the shooting script, are clearly conceived as variations on Whale, himself: elegant figures disdainful of society and traditional morals. The demure Mary Shelley describes herself, Percy, and Lord Byron as "infidels, scoffers at all marriage ties, believing only in living fully and freely in whatever direction the heart dictates." As a result, "I am already ostracized as a free thinker," while Percy Shelley—"that pink and white innocence, gentle as a dove"—was "thrown out of Oxford University as a menace to morality . . . and reviled by society as a monster himself." The cheerful Lord Byron adds, "We're all for shocking 'em—eh, Shelley? 'The world is a bundle of hay; Mankind are the asses that pull.' " These three consciously place themselves above and apart from society and, in the process, court its antagonism. For all the inherent arrogance of their rebellion, however, these people do not seem like offensive monsters. They are, instead, intelligent, sophisticated, gentle, and—above all—creative. (Most of this material was probably shot, but cut before release.)

Frankenstein's Monster casts Whale's self-portrait in a different light. He too is an outsider, but not by choice. His physical characteristics—over which he has no control—inspire fear and hatred in the "normal" people he encounters, who instantly draw erroneous conclusions, who cannot see past the superficial facts of appearance and reputation to recognize the true self beyond. This, in turn, forces the Monster initially to defend himself and ultimately to develop a resentful aggressiveness, which then gives society further evidence to support its first reactions. The film's viewers should recognize in the Monster's reaction to sunlight a sensitive nature, an attraction to the beautiful and the delicate. But just as Henry Frankenstein tried to achieve an elusive goal, the Monster in his way is doomed to failure as he seeks to grasp that which can never be grasped, to possess and absorb that which will forever be outside himself.

The hermit scenes in *Bride of Frankenstein* are also interesting for what they reveal about Whale's identification with the Monster. This is the only gentle and honest relationship the Monster experiences in the film. Two lonely outcasts have found each other. "I will look after you," says the hermit, "and you shall comfort me." Together, they settle into a contented companionship; they have all they need, as long as the rest of the world remains shut out. But society will not leave them alone, and it disrupts their stability. The sincerity of this relationship contrasts with the pairing of the effete Pretorius with Henry Frankenstein, whom he lures away from his fiancée; these two form a much less wholesome couple, who serve as "parents" to an artificially created "child." The appealing combination of the Monster and the hermit also stands in sharp contrast to the grotesque incompatibility of the Monster and his female counterpart, as well as to Mary Shelley's "nasty spirit" and the tiny King's parodied virility. Only Henry and Elizabeth, the standard romantic couple, are free of such negative overtones, although Whale revealingly intended to kill them off at the film's end.

In *Frankenstein* (and, to a lesser extent, in *Bride*), the villagers—as in most traditional horror films—band together to rid society of a threat to its stability, an abnormal intrusion, and to reestablish a condition of balance and consistency. However, *Frankenstein* does not depict this process favorably. Yes, the Monster has become a nightmarish menace, but Whale treats the villagers like a lynch mob, engaged in what he in 1931 called "the pagan sport of a mountain man-hunt."[87] Lost in their anger and hatred, caught up in a mass compulsion to destroy, they become so unthinking that, when the Monster is trapped in the mill, they eagerly set it on fire and burn him alive; during this climax, Whale again and again cuts not to the triumphant villagers but to their frightened, helpless, and agonized victim. *Frankenstein*'s true monster is not Henry's creation but society itself; in *Bride,* the villagers only capture the Monster, but Whale maintains his outlook by turning the scene into a kind of crucifixion.

Both Frankenstein and the Monster embody the director's view of himself and his position in life and work, but Sir William Porterhouse (in *The Old Dark House*) and Jack Griffin (in *The Invisible Man*) reflect a slightly different aspect of Whale—a compulsion to rise above his humble origins and prove himself by gaining status and material success. Sir William, the earthy businessman from the industrial North of England, explains how he and his wife had been snubbed by the gentry. "That's what started me makin' money," he declares. "I swore I'd smash those fellows and their wives who wouldn't give my Lucy a kind word. Hah! And I have smashed 'em—at any rate, most of 'em." For Sir William, like Whale, financial achievement is less an end in itself than a means of punishing those who had been so disdainful.

Griffin, too, rebels against his economic status. "I wanted to do something tremendous," he tells his fiancée, "to gain wealth and fame and honor. . . . I was so pitifully poor. I had nothing to offer." Nothing, that is, except intelligence and ability and determination. Resenting how others had made him feel inferior, Griffin develops a heightened sense of superiority ("He's got the brain of a tapeworm, a maggot, beside mine") and a need for power that can grant him revenge on ordinary society ("to make the world grovel at my feet"). Whale, like these men, started life a poor and insignificant person, possessing only a keen mind and innate talent, and like them he felt the disdain of others; he shared their need to achieve something significant and, ultimately, to punish the world.

Neither character quite captures Whale's position, however, for the power he gained was not an ability to wreck trains, torment people physically, or crush them financially. Rather, it involved a calculated positioning of himself apart from and above others; then, from that privileged vantage point, he revealed to the world that he refused to take it seriously. This was conveyed less through the words he used than through his coy, overstated, not-quite-sarcastic manner of speech, a manner that blurred the distinction between honesty and irony; he could simultaneously mean what he said and sound as if he didn't mean it.

For example, after greeting Charles Laughton and Elsa Lanchester upon their arrival in Hollywood, Whale declared, "You don't know how wonderful it is, when you've had nothing, to be able to *pour* gold through your hair!"[88] In another instance, Whale recalled for Curtis Harrington how Boris Karloff had summoned him to see his makeup for *The Mummy* (1932). When Karloff's face was unveiled, Whale declared, "This is the most *marvelous* thing ever seen on the silver sheet!"[89] Whale's use of "silver sheet" instead of "silver screen" is typically arch, but neither statement is particularly witty; to understand their distinctive quality, one must imagine them being spoken with the vowels drawn out in a kind of ostentatiously insincere drawl.

Ultimately, Whale's manner reflected his disdain for life and his separation from it, but he usually stayed just short of sarcasm and condescension. Thus, Gloria Stuart, who socialized with Whale during the early 1930s, could say that he "had a very sharp sense of humor, and he could be very cutting, too. [But] he was charming and relaxed" and "a wonderful companion."[90] At times, though, he could be perceived as crossing the line if the listener felt strongly about the subject of a comment. When Whale said of Boris Karloff, "Oh, he was a *truck driver*," Elsa Lanchester—who liked Karloff—considered the statement "rather nasty" and "derogatory."[91]

This aspect of Whale emerges forcefully in *The Old Dark House* and *Bride of Frankenstein* through the wry irony of Ernest Thesiger's characters. According to Elsa Lanchester, Thesiger the man was exactly the same in the films as in life—"prissy and bitter and witty, too."[92] He was, she said on another occasion, "very acid-tongued—not a nasty person at all, just *acid!*"[93] Valerie Hobson found him not only "terribly funny" with "an amusing face, an amusing twinkle," but also "a terribly sweet man" with "a kind and gentle heart."[94] These English women perhaps understood Thesiger better than did Whale's American companion David Lewis, who disliked Thesiger: "He was just as nasty as he could be! He hated my guts when he first met me. He came to the house for dinner one night and treated me like . . . the butler or the secretary."[95]

Lewis felt that Whale's interest in Thesiger was mostly due to "the fact that he was related to royalty."[96] Ms. Lanchester, however, speculated that Whale enjoyed Thesiger's company because he empathized with his exaggerated manner, for Thesiger acted on the outside the way Whale felt under the surface.[97] In partial support of this theory, Gloria Stuart confirms that Whale spoke with some of the archness and irony that one hears, in a more extreme way, in Thesiger's voice.[98] Certainly, aside from their different economic and social origins, Whale and Thesiger had much in common. At school, Thesiger was "bullied by my contemporaries and disliked by my masters, both, probably, for the same reason, namely that I possessed a somewhat unbridled tongue combined with an uncomfortable knack of finding out people's weak spots. This does not make for popularity." Consequently, he spent his childhood "painting or wandering about with other physical outcasts, or, more frequently still, by myself. . . . To be unusual or unconventional was the one sin not forgiven by the British schoolboy."[99]

Later, during four years spent at an art school, he finally was happy. "For the first time in my life I was among people who were amused and not scandalized by any odd thing that I might take it into my head to do. Did I sit in the window threading bead-chains instead of painting, there were plenty of people to tell me that I was 'deliciously original.' Did I command the other students to tickle the palms of my hands with their paintbrushes during the 'rests,' I was considered rather attractively decadent and sybaritic."[100] Although he frequently performed in amateur or charity theatrical productions, Thesiger considered himself a professional painter until he concluded that he would "never make a fortune with my brush" and shifted to acting full-time.[101] By 1915, when he enlisted in His Majesty's Army, Thesiger had already established his lifelong style of viewing life as theater, with himself as a player who observed his own actions from a discreet distance. He readily adapted to his role of soldier: "I seemed entirely to have forgotten my real identity, but at the same time I never could quite forget that it was only a character part that I was playing."[102]

Whale carefully crafted the roles of Horace Femm and Dr. Pretorius for Thesiger, so when the former describes saying grace as one of "my sister's strange tribal habits" we can perhaps hear an echo of Whale's own style of speech, and when Pretorius states that life might "be much more amusing if we were all Devils, and no nonsense about angels and being good," we probably hear Whale's opinion of society's righteousness. One obituary of Thesiger summed him up by saying, "He never moved without grace or spoke without elegance, but implicit in his performances there was a quizzical mockery of those qualities."[103] This statement could also describe the style and essence that Whale sought for himself, and which to a considerable extent he attained.

A true psychological and emotional portrait of James Whale can only be achieved by combining elements drawn from all these characters: helpless persecution, intense commitment and ambition, powerful resentment, prim passivity, and cynical wit. The range of his personality was extensive, but all of these factors merge in the form of an outsider who hovers on the sidelines of life and society, shadowed by the prospect of doom and destruction.

These aspects maintained a balance within Whale during the 1930s, when he felt secure in the protective and reinforcing cocoon of "Junior" Laemmle's confidence, the familiarity of his collaborators, and the acceptance of his friends. When the Laemmles lost control of Universal in 1936, the studio passed into less sympathetic hands, and Whale never again received the combination of support and independence he required to work at his best. He made some films for other companies and some for the "new" Universal, but they only occasionally reveal his individual style and personality. In effect, he had accepted—or given in to—the standard directorial formula. In 1941, the struggle no longer seemed worth the limited gain, and Whale retired from films.

The motion picture medium fascinated Whale, to whom directing was, in David Lewis's words, "a sublime job which satisfied him inside and made it possible for him to function as a human being."[104] When he lost the power to control his working environment he also lost the ability to use his creative talent in the medium he loved. Whale's sense of futility increased, and he retreated, like Horace Femm, to his mansion—the only setting left for him to design.

At one point, when David O. Selznick offered him a job, Whale told Lewis, "I was quite embarrassed, because I'm not a beginner and I don't like to be treated like a beginner." In the mid-1950s, RKO considered making H. G. Wells's *The Food of the Gods,* a novel Whale had wanted to film, so the producer contacted him. "Jimmy, at that time, was disillusioned, unhappy . . . very lonely for films," explained David Lewis, but his professional confidence had disappeared and "he was frightened to death." After meeting with the producer, "Jimmy came home and said to me, 'I don't think I want to do it. I really don't think I want to do it.' "[105] Living well on his investments, Whale became a dilettante, directing only a few minor plays and a short film that was never released.

When Whale took up with a younger man, David Lewis moved out of their home, although the two remained friends. "Later on," said Lewis, "he filled his house full of, what I thought were sad young men, but I wouldn't judge him on it."[106] Whale painted in his studio and entertained. To an extent he did enjoy himself, as he put his past success behind him. At any rate, Curtis Harrington recalled, he did not want to be out there fighting for projects.[107] Instead, he led a life of aimless irony.

In 1956, Whale suffered several strokes and was twice hospitalized, for two weeks in September and for thirteen days the next month. When he returned home, Whale physically wasn't able to paint, so Lewis bought him a camera, hoping that would provide an artistic outlet, but he never used it. He seemed to have lost both the interest and the ability to create. From 19 January to 23 March 1957, Whale spent a total of four weeks at Las Encinas Sanitarium, which began a period of dependence on prescription drugs. Finally, on 29 May 1957, he wrote a message to "all I love," explaining that "for the last year I have been in agony day and night—except when I sleep with sleeping pills—and any peace I have by day is when I am drugged by pills. . . . The future is just old age and pain."[108] With that he obtained the peace he sought by drowning himself in his swimming pool.

At the peak of his Hollywood career, Whale exerted complete control over every facet of his films; "I don't believe he could have worked any other way," concluded Ted Kent.[109] Therefore, when he lost that power Whale simply ended his career. His personal life reveals the same kind of control, as he precisely defined both himself and his environment. Because Whale could not live any other way, when he felt even that ability start to slip away, he chose to make one last use of what power remained, ending his life as he had lived it, with an act of self-definition.

During his last fifteen years, Whale had set himself apart from his film career and he never lived to find his work truly appreciated. Although that career was regrettably short, during it he created many works of enduring merit. Not the least among them are his four horror films, which remain models of the genre and of sensitive moviemaking—and through which viewers can encounter the essence of this enigmatic and private individual.

Willis O'Brien's fabulous creation, King Kong.

CHAPTER 2

Willis O'Brien

Willis O'Brien inhabited two distinct, virtually incompatible worlds. As a technician, he mastered the intricacies of model construction, animation, and composite photography. Success for him depended on meticulous planning and the careful execution of those plans. He had to be as exact as a scientist, as precise as a watchmaker. At the same time, O'Brien felt the urges of a creative artist. Paper and canvas could not hold the contents of his active imagination; scale models in dioramas remained frozen. Only film could bring to life his images of fantastic adventure.

Overall, O'Brien's career boasts a dual triumph. First, although he often worked with a team of specialized artists and technicians, it was O'Brien himself who blended subject matter with technology to define and perfect a new type of motion picture. In this way, he established precedents for generations of future filmmakers. He was not, however, only a pioneer, for he also created three enduring films: *The Lost World* (1925) and *Mighty Joe Young* (1949) continue to amuse and fascinate viewers, while *King Kong* (1933) remains an unmatched work of adventure and imagination.

O'Brien was an innovator in the use of three-dimensional animation: the filming of a model one frame at a time, pausing after each exposure to move the model slightly. When this footage is projected at a rate of at least sixteen frames per second, the figure on screen seems to move independently and, if the animator has talent, naturally and with character. But this illusion of life remained insufficient, so O'Brien went further by constructing environments in which his fantastic creations appear at home, using both paintings and miniature sets. He then completed the illusion by combining these miniature worlds with living humans and full-sized sets through rear-screen or front-screen projection and stationary or traveling mattes. Finally, the fantastic and the real coexisted, forming a new, cinematic whole.

Despite O'Brien's achievements, a pall of frustration shrouds his career, though not the man himself. The American film industry of the 1930s and 1940s could not accommodate O'Brien, with most producers unable to share his vision and unwilling to finance his projects. As a result, he spent far too many years preparing ideas that never reached the screen. The limited aims and imaginations of Hollywood must bear the blame, but O'Brien did prolong his fallow periods. Because he refused to compromise the scale of his visions, only large budgets were acceptable, and he lacked the knack of self-promotion that would convince producers to invest in his fantasies. Also, his limitations as a writer led to the development of plots with more weaknesses than strengths. O'Brien needed a collaborator.

At the same time, O'Brien's personal life tended to be unstable. An ill-advised marriage led to the tragic deaths of his two sons in 1933. Only on his second marriage, to Darlyne, in 1934, did O'Brien at the age of forty-eight find a companion attuned to his personality. For many of their years together, however, the couple made do on a very limited income. Animator Ray Harryhausen, who knew O'Brien during this period, states that somehow, despite the "tragedy and disappointments in his life," O'Brien "was a very happy man and a very wonderful person. He had a great sense of humor."[1]

Born on 2 March 1886, Willis Harold O'Brien temporarily left his Oakland, California, home at the age of about eleven to work on cattle ranches. At thirteen he left again, working at a wide variety of unrelated jobs, including farmhand, factory worker, fur trapper, wilderness guide, and bartender. The young O'Brien's fondness for and understanding of animals, especially horses, and his inarticulateness around people soon developed into introspection, self-reliance, and a quiet, soft-spoken manner.

Although seemingly drawn to physical, working-class environments where he had to fend for himself, O'Brien also possessed a naive, trusting nature and a tendency to act on impulse; these qualities, combined with an obvious restlessness, prevented him from achieving success in any endeavor. For example, after a few years as a cowboy, he owned eight horses, but then lost them all in a single poker game. On another occasion, he gave a season's worth of fur pelts to some fellow woodsmen to take to town for him, and never heard from them again.

O'Brien's interaction with the local Indians, however, left an enduring, positive impression, and the time he spent guiding some scientists in search of prehistoric fossils began a continuing fascination with dinosaurs. Also influential was his experience working as a cowboy and competing in small rodeos: One of his unfilmed projects, *Gwangi,* involved cowboys who capture a prehistoric beast, and in *Mighty Joe Young* some rodeo riders try to lasso a giant gorilla. That film's hero, played by the very likeable rodeo veteran Ben Johnson, even shares the name Gregg with O'Brien's admired oldest brother.

A knack for drawing led O'Brien to some less physically demanding jobs, but the young man remained at loose ends, never following through when threatened with security and stability. His constant changes of occupation seem thoroughly random, revealing no clear progression, no attraction toward a goal, only a determination to get away from wherever and whatever he had been. O'Brien liked doing things, but evidently had little interest in accomplishments for their own sake. Starting out as an office boy for an architect, he quickly rose to the position of draftsman, but left to become a newspaper sports cartoonist. Then he entered professional boxing and won his first nine bouts, but gave that up after lasting only two rounds in his tenth encounter; the experience later contributed to the fighting style of his giant simians King Kong, Kong's son, and Joe Young. O'Brien also worked for the railroad as a brakeman and then a surveyor, assisted the head architect of the San Francisco World's Fair, and designed in clay the decorations for such stone structures as fireplaces.

While employed in the stonecutter's shop, O'Brien modeled a miniature boxer, but felt dissatisfied with the result. He wanted to see it move by itself. With the aid of a local newsreel cameraman, he used frame-by-frame animation to create a one-minute film using models of a dinosaur and a caveman. This led a San Francisco exhibitor named Herman Wobber to finance a five-minute short, *The Dinosaur and the Missing Link.* At the age of twenty-nine, O'Brien had stumbled on his life's work.

During this arbitrary, stream-of-consciousness existence, O'Brien seems to have lived in the experience of the moment, adapting to the present with little concern for

Willis O'Brien near the end of his filmmaking career in 1956.

the past or the future, a quality he retained throughout his life. Years later, when his second wife, Darlyne, asked him why he didn't get discouraged after having so many of his projects cancelled, "he said he was like a spider [and] whenever they tear down his web, he would build a new one." Along with this ability to accept outside influences and adapt to them, came youthful enthusiasm and unreliability. "He was a kid right up to the day he died" at age seventy-six, recalled Darlyne; "he was still a boy and a dreamer." O'Brien enjoyed attending horse races and "liked to go pub crawling to be around the different characters and talk to them." He also "loved his bourbon." He was "lovable" and "a lot of fun," but also "unpredictable" and "not very dependable,"[2] two parts of the same psychological package.

O'Brien was a good worker, but only on what he enjoyed, and he lacked assertiveness. He relied on others to set up projects because he "couldn't bring himself to go out and ask people for anything," Darlyne explained. "He didn't like to do that. He wanted to get away from it all and play and create something new. It was sheer luck that anything ever did come about."[3] According to Ernest B. Schoedsack, codirector of *King Kong,* O'Brien "worked hard and was always dependable except when we would be fighting for time," then he'd get worried and "head for the bar across the street."[4] Clearly, O'Brien did not learn to adapt to pressure or accept responsibility. His trustingly impulsive side also stayed with him, and his instincts did not always prove valid. Merian C. Cooper, *Kong's* other codirector, told researcher George E. Turner that he had "fired dozens of animators and effects men during production because so many of them were drinking buddies" hired by O'Brien.[5]

By the time the Edison Company purchased *The Dinosaur and the Missing Link* and hired O'Brien to make more such shorts, he had already completed *Morpheus Mike* and *The Birth of a Flivver.* Moving to New York, he set to work at Edison's studio, where his solitary labors resulted in *R.F.D. 10,000 B.C., Prehistoric Poultry,* and *Curious Pets of Our Ancestors.* All of these shorts were released as Conquest Pictures in 1917. (O'Brien reportedly also worked on *In the Villain's Power, The Puzzling Billboard,* and *Mickey's Naughty Nightmares,* but the exact nature of his contributions is not currently known.)

Most of O'Brien's shorts include no live-action footage; both humans and animals are animated models and, in their stress on caricature-like humor, the films resemble animated cartoons more than O'Brien's mature work. In *The Dinosaur and the Missing Link,* when a character is stunned by a tree limb, we even see stars appear around his head. The climax, however, includes a brief fight between an ape called "Wild Willie" (the missing link of the title) and a small brontosaurus. *Morpheus Mike* begins in the present, as a woman hangs her washing on a line. A goat devours the clothes, but Mike, a passing tramp, retrieves them from the animal's mouth and the woman rewards him with some food. Later, Mike imagines himself in a prehistoric restaurant, where he orders such treats as tiger stew and an ostrich egg, with each served by an elephant, using its trunk. The egg, however, cracks open and a baby ostrich emerges. When Mike orders "a trunk of soup," he gets sprayed in the face with it. At this, he wakes up, having had water poured on his head.

In *R. F. D. 10,000 B.C.,* Johnny Bearskin sends Winnie Warclub a love letter carved in stone, but a jealous mailman substitutes an insulting one. Winnie later cracks the innocent Johnny over the head with the missive. When Johnny and the mailman fight, a brontosaurus that pulls the mail wagon smacks the villain with its tail, knocking the top of his body off. The mailman's torso flies through the air until its arms catch hold of a tree limb; it hangs there until the body's lower half runs to the tree and rejoins the

A dream elephant and ostrich from one of Willis O'Brien's earliest films, a short titled *Morpheus Mike* (1917).

upper part. The mailman admits defeat, so Johnny wins both the girl and the mail delivery business.

O'Brien's affinity for animals prompted him to give the prehistoric creatures in these films such winsome personalities that they steal scenes from his animated humans. In *Prehistoric Poultry,* a chicken-like dinornis rolls its eyes cutely and a small brontosaurus licks its master's face. The brontosaurus in *Morpheus Mike* calmly observes the humans' actions, grazes quietly after the wagon tips over, and laughs at its former master's defeat. The three cavemen in *The Dinosaur and the Missing Link*—the Duke, Stonejaw Steve, and Theophilus Ivoryhead—vie for the hand of Araminta Rockface, and, perhaps revealingly, it is the less assertive Theophilus who wins the girl over his overtly aggressive rivals.

Otherwise, the films are interesting mainly as technical exercises. They look quite primitive: The human faces are expressionless, the elephant moves only its head and trunk, and the brontosaurus has a stiff-kneed walk. Some shots are fairly impressive, though, like one of Mike lighting his pipe and exhaling smoke. The films also offer such appealing, slice-of-life details as the mailman wiping his forehead after handling a heavy letter or Mike toying with a cane while waiting for his food.

O'Brien left Edison in 1917, when the studio abandoned its program of shorts, but soon Herbert M. Dawley, who had built and photographed dinosaur models himself, agreed to bankroll a new O'Brien film. Made in 1918, *The Ghost of Slumber Mountain* runs twelve minutes (projected at sound speed), but more than half of its footage consists of straightforward live action. Once again O'Brien depicted prehistoric life, but this time he omitted the cavemen and the broad humor. The animation itself easily surpasses O'Brien's previous experiments. It presents several different creatures, their movements are fairly smooth, and once or twice the camera even moves during a shot. However, cautious about involving his humans with the dinosaurs, O'Brien contrived a plot that places the creatures outside of the film's "reality."

Two boys ask their uncle, a writer, to tell them a story "about wild animals er sumpin." The film's main body consists of this story, in which the uncle and a friend explore the area around Slumber Mountain. After the men happen upon the grave and cabin of Mad Dick, a hermit, the friend tells of having once seen Dick leave the cabin and gaze through an unusual instrument. That night, the uncle is led from camp by Mad Dick's voice. At the cabin, a bearded ghost appears and directs the man to take the instrument to a mountaintop. He does so and, gazing through it, sees prehistoric animals feeding and fighting. Eventually, a tyrannosaurus chases the uncle and almost catches him. Then, at the last second, the man awakens, having dreamed about the ghost and the monsters while safe in camp. Finally, we return to the present, where the uncle has clearly made up the tale for his nephews' benefit.

In a simple form, *Slumber Mountain* reveals the basic elements found in many later, more ambitious features with animated monsters: explorers who enter some sort of wilderness, where they find beasts that battle among themselves and threaten the awed hero or heroes. It also reveals a definite, if rudimentary, sense of dramatic structure, with the animal vignettes becoming progressively more impressive. First, a brontosaurus and then a bird-like diatryma stand and graze, simply impressing us with their presence. Then, two triceratops start to fight, but one walks away, yielding the bout. After that, the tyrannosaurus enters and kills the remaining triceratops. Until this point, events have remained distantly objective to the watching uncle, and to the viewer, but in the climax the character himself is threatened. O'Brien suggests the chase by intercutting the man and the beast, not by combining the two in a single shot.

Back in Oakland, O'Brien had impulsively become engaged to Hazel Collette, a woman twelve years his junior. When the Edison job took him to New York, he hoped his absence would discourage Hazel, but instead she and an aunt followed him east and so, around 1918, they were married. Although the union was not stable or satisfying, it produced two sons: William, born in 1919, and Willis, Jr., in 1920.

O'Brien's films attracted the attention of Watterson R. Rothacker, who hired him to work on the advertising shorts made by his company. The two men soon developed larger ambitions and found themselves drawn to *The Lost World,* Sir Arthur Conan Doyle's 1912 novel about prehistoric animals on an isolated South American plateau. O'Brien began developing ideas, sketches, and camera tests, but work was delayed in 1922 when Herbert Dawley threatened a $100,000 lawsuit. O'Brien had never patented the articulated armatures he built for his models, so after *The Ghost of Slumber Mountain* Dawley obtained patents in his own name and O'Brien again found himself taken advantage of by a person he trusted. Eventually, he proved that he had used the method before working with Dawley.

In 1922, Conan Doyle exhibited some of O'Brien's footage as part of a speech he gave at a magician's convention. Referring to his well-known interest in spiritualism, Doyle hinted that the images might be genuine, obtained by some mediumistic means. Without taking a stand on their authenticity, a newspaper report described the scenes: "Dinosaurs of one tribe appeared on the screen and rubbed jowls in an affectionate manner. Then entered the tyrannosaurs [which] fought among themselves, interlocked their great jaws and wrestled. Finally one broke the back of the other and was about to devour it, when up dashed a triceratops, . . . who drove the tyrannosaur away."[6] The next day, Doyle explained his deception, admitting that the monsters were "constructed by pure cinema, but of the highest kind."[7]

Later that year, Rothacker officially purchased screen rights to *The Lost World.* When First National Pictures agreed to back the project, O'Brien received his first chance to use animation in a large-scale feature. Principal photography began in 1923, followed by more than a year devoted to animation and other technical work. *The Lost World* was so much more ambitious than *The Ghost of Slumber Mountain* that O'Brien sought out technical assistance.

Through First National he obtained the services of Ralph Hammeras, an effects specialist, and to construct the complex models he hired Marcel Delgado, a young, Mexican-born grocery clerk and aspiring artist he had met at the Otis Art Institute in Los Angeles. "Obie didn't know me from Adam," recalled the still-amazed and grateful Delgado years later. "He was just taking a chance."[8] This example of O'Brien's impulsive nature paid off, with Delgado contributing greatly to the appearance of the models in all O'Brien's major films. For *The Lost World,* he built nearly fifty prehistoric animals, covering O'Brien's metal armatures with sponge "muscles" topped by rubber "skins," using Charles R. Knight's well-known paintings of dinosaurs as his inspiration.

Because *The Lost World* placed its characters among the prehistoric creatures and even had one animal brought back to London, O'Brien for the first time combined live and animated action in the same shot. He usually accomplished this by first filming the actors on a set, but with part of the image (often the top or bottom half) blocked off and left unexposed. Then he rewound the film and, with the already-exposed section of the image blocked off, recorded the animated creatures and model landscape on the empty portion. Finally, the footage was processed and a composite picture obtained.

To create the impression of vast, exotic locations, O'Brien employed Hammeras's recently developed technique known as the glass shot. This involves painting a portion of the set in perspective on a piece of clear glass, which is then placed between the camera and the full-sized set on which the actors perform. The camera films both simultaneously, so that the area around the actors knits seamlessly with the painted, miniature portion.

Released early in 1925, *The Lost World* must have startled and awed moviegoers, many of whom had never seen model animation. The sense of fantastic reality created by this technique is attested to by contemporary critics, who generally were both convinced and thrilled. Although the film originally ran 104 minutes, for many years only a condensed version, running about one hour, has existed. This copy eliminates one major character, Gladys Hungerford, along with several complete scenes and shots from others, including some animation footage. (Recently, a print that may contain some of the missing footage reportedly turned up in Czechoslovakia.)

The scenario carefully follows the structure of Doyle's novel. In London, the characters are introduced and the expedition organized, then it follows the group's adventures in South America and concludes when they bring a prehistoric beast to London, where it escapes. In the book, Professor Challenger, a scientific maverick, had discovered an isolated plateau after studying the records of the explorer, Maple White, and Challenger had already sighted the creatures. His fellow scientists consider him a charlatan, so three skeptics accompany Challenger on his return: a rival scientist, Professor Summerlee; a big-game hunter, Lord John Roxton; and a newspaper reporter, Edward Malone.

The film's Challenger remains an arrogant rebel, but he has not yet seen the plateau, and the character of Paula White, the missing explorer's daughter, is added. Thus the expedition's motive becomes as much a search for Maple White as an attempt to document Challenger's assertion. Another change involves Edward Malone. In the novel, Challenger dominated the action, but Malone told the story; the film makes Malone the main character and reduces Challenger to a supporting role, although he remains the most interesting figure.

Both novel and film have Malone in love with Gladys Hungerford and driven to face danger by her demand that he prove himself. But Gladys is rarely around, so scenarist Marion Fairfax satisfies the assumed (and probably actual) audience demand for romance and a pretty face by having Paula White join the expedition. Ultimately, Malone is torn between Paula and Gladys, and a second triangle arises because Roxton also loves Paula. Much of this added material is overly familiar and tends to clog the story line, as does a sequence in a jungle trading post (cut from the condensed print).

Once his characters reach the plateau, Doyle divides his attention between the monsters and two native tribes. The primitive ape-men vie with a more civilized tribe for supremacy, and the Englishmen help the latter group to exterminate the ruthless brutes. The filmmakers eliminated both tribes, retaining only a solitary ape-man (played by a heavily made-up Bull Montana, but related to O'Brien's animated missing link character), who makes a few arbitrary appearances. To provide a visually impressive climax on the plateau, they added a smouldering volcano and a fire that panics the area's animals. In the scenario, Professor Summerlee's pipe starts the fire, but the condensed print omits this, leaving the vague implication that the volcano caused it.

The brontosaurus on the loose in London pauses at the British Museum in *The Lost World* (1925), the first feature to make extensive use of model animation.

The film's most useful change occurs in the story's final section. Doyle's Challenger brought a baby pterodactyl back to England and, in a lecture hall, unveils this trophy as his final proof. The creature escapes and, after circling over the audience, flies out through a window and is never encountered again. To give this segment greater scope, the film replaces the pterodactyl with a brontosaurus, which escapes when its cage breaks at the London docks. The confused creature makes its destructive way through the city, until the Tower Bridge collapses under it and the animal plummets into the Thames. The scenario includes a final shot of the brontosaurus passing an ocean liner on its way home, but in the shortened print it could—for all anyone knows—have found its way to Scotland and Loch Ness.

The animated action of the dinosaurs in *The Lost World* is generally smooth, and O'Brien gave his creatures bits of business that make them seem naturally alive. One beast pauses to examine its wound and another, in close-up, sneers at an opponent. O'Brien also elaborated on the action described in the scenario. Originally, an allosaurus was to fight and kill first a trachodon and then a triceratops. In the film, it kills the trachodon, then heads for the triceratops, which pushes its child to a safer position and successfully fends off the menace. In a separate sequence, not in the scenario, an allosaurus attacks a monoclonius and is killed by it. Another allosaurus then enters and kills the monoclonius. As it stands over its victim, the allosaurus spots a passing pterodactyl, plucks it out of the air, and kills it, too. With these additions, O'Brien increases the action, while developing the one creature's tendency to kill for the sake of killing and offering a contrast in the triceratops's protection of its young.

Still, the models lack the detail found in O'Brien's later work and sometimes move awkwardly. Another problem is the limited interaction between man and beast, owing to the primitive methods available for creating composite shots. Most of the time the characters, as in *The Ghost of Slumber Mountain,* simply observe animal activity from the sidelines. This severely reduces the chance for true drama and excitement, which require a direct threat to human beings. An exception is the allosaurus attack on the camp, during which Malone hurls a burning stick into the creature's mouth. This scene, like the animal fights, is a more ambitious and successful version of action first sketched out in *Slumber Mountain.*

Samuel Johnson once said that when a man is tired of London, he is tired of life, but perhaps that does not apply to prehistoric monsters. In *The Lost World,* the brontosaurus does a bit of smashing through the city streets and stops to toy with a street lamp, but in general it finds little to do in London. The most convincing effects here are in the shots that do not include live actors. When the two are combined, one can at times see right through the beast's body.

Most often, the beasts are viewed in long shots, with little cutting closer for impact or to show details, thus limiting the excitement. Similarly, the film does not introduce the menaces in a dramatic or atmospheric fashion, but instead cuts to them abruptly. This is true of both the animated beasts and the ape-man, and it typifies Harry Hoyt's straightforward, unimaginative direction, which faithfully follows the detailed scenario. (There is no way of knowing the extent to which Hoyt, or anyone else, influenced Ms. Fairfax's writing.) Perhaps the film's cinematic high point occurs in a now-missing scene of Gladys manipulating the smitten Malone. According to the scenario, his reaction to her beauty was to be intercut with shots of Gladys teasing a kitten with a catnip mouse, "its eyes shining with eagerness—its tail quivering with excitement." After Malone grabs and kisses Gladys, the kitten catches the mouse.

The Lost World was a financial success in 1925, and it endures as a moderately entertaining film, at least in the condensed version, which lacks most of the deadwood and broad comedy. It also stands as a major step forward for O'Brien, a work that moved him into the world of features and proved the validity of his interests and techniques. The next stage remained: to consolidate his gains and make a *great* film.

O'Brien's most immediate need, however, was to keep working. For a while, First National considered making a follow-up to *The Lost World,* and O'Brien spent several futile months preparing plot outlines and sketches for *Atlantis,* a film about a race of people who inhabit gigantic underwater caverns, fight sea monsters, and interact with a group that lives amid ice and snow. Available evidence suggests that, unlike *The Lost World,* this story was devoted entirely to creating a fictional world, one filled with spectacular, exotic sights but without central characters with whom viewers could identify—a kind of large-scale slice of fantastic life. O'Brien also started to plan a version of Mary Shelley's *Frankenstein* that would employ a giant animated Monster. Finally, he left First National.

In 1929, O'Brien and Harry Hoyt devised a new project, *Creation,* and in 1930 Hoyt convinced RKO Radio to produce the picture. By summer, O'Brien and his staff were hard at work preparing drawings, glass paintings, miniature settings, and dinosaur models. Meanwhile, O'Brien's home life had deteriorated. Throughout the 1920s, as tensions escalated, O'Brien turned more and more to work, bars, racetracks, and other women. Hazel's natural jealousy evolved into a paranoid resentment of everyone she perceived as luring her husband away, including his coworkers. This drove him still further from her, as cause and effect merged. Finally, in 1930—just as his professional life looked promising—O'Brien moved out of the house, although he frequently visited his sons and took them on outings.

Perhaps owing to Hoyt's influence, the plot of *Creation* draws more on *The Lost World* than did *Atlantis.* Its hero, Steve, loves the rich and fickle Elaine. To be near her, he takes a job on the family's yacht when it sails to South America. Also aboard is another suitor, Ned, so a romantic triangle develops. Instead of seeking an unexplored plateau, this group stumbles into its adventures. Warned of a typhoon, they take refuge in a Chilean submarine, and the storm causes an island to rise from the sea. The submarine surfaces, damaged, in a lake surrounded by jungle at the center of a volcano. On shore, they encounter prehistoric creatures, and an arsinoitherium kills most of the sailors.

Steve assumes leadership of the survivors, despite Ned's resistance, and they establish a camp. When the unreliable Ned shoots at a passing dinosaur, it destroys their hut, but Elaine drives it away with a burning stick (as Malone had in *The Lost World*). Later, Ned shoots a young triceratops and is himself killed by its parent. Exploring further, the survivors discover an ancient temple loaded with jewels. After Steve saves Elaine from being carried away by a pterodactyl, a stegosaurus chases them into the temple, where they encounter a tyrannosaurus. While the two creatures fight, the humans escape, only to be threatened by the volcano's eruption, a fire, and an animal stampede (as in *The Lost World*). Steve sends an SOS on a repaired radio and at the last moment seaplanes rescue the group, who have kept some of the temple jewels.

Although *Creation* has recognizable characters with which viewers can identify, its central element—the romantic triangle—is too thin to support the vast array of plot details. Like *Atlantis,* this story remains a sprawling, overstuffed series of events. The climax that starts at the temple reveals this most clearly, as one danger follows another in an arbitrary fashion. What *Creation* lacks is a character comparable to *Lost World*'s Professor Challenger, a forceful, dynamic figure whose scientific and personal quest adds narrative drive that transcends the film's romantic complications.

The humans in *Creation* are basically passive, avoiding confrontations and reacting to situations instead of initiating action; only Ned does that, and he's the villain of the piece. According to Ernest Schoedsack, O'Brien "didn't have a story sense,"[9] which may be true, but O'Brien's approach to stories probably derived from his own sense of life, which would explain his inability to imagine characters who do more than adapt to events that happen to and around them. *Creation,* if finished, might have become an impressive fantasy film, but probably not a truly exciting adventure.

The filming of effects footage began in November 1930 and included the typhoon and the emergence of the island, created in a tank with miniatures. The sole surviving test reel contains shots of Ned (Ralf Harolde) wandering through a primeval-looking forest, intercut with both real animals and an animated baby triceratops. Ned shoots the creature and its mother pursues him, but the reel stops before he is killed. The technical work here is O'Brien's most sophisticated to date, with extremely convincing models, very smooth animation, and an effective combination of the actor with back-projected miniatures. Work continued into 1931, but costs mounted as the production fell behind schedule.

In October 1931, David O. Selznick took over as RKO's head of production. With the studio feeling the pinch of the Depression, he halted work on all films, pending an inventory to determine which would be kept and which dropped as too expensive or troublesome; at this point, *Creation* nearly met the fate of *Atlantis.* O'Brien's financial status was equally troubled: On 20 October, *Variety* reported that he had gone to a bankruptcy referee, declaring assets of $5,866 against $1,752 in liabilities and a $5,516 uncollected judgment in a civil suit.

Luckily for O'Brien, and for film history, Selznick chose Merian C. Cooper to conduct the studio inventory. Then in his late thirties, Cooper had already had a varied and adventurous career as a flier, fighter, escaped prisoner of war, explorer, and filmmaker. In 1925, he, cinematographer Ernest Schoedsack, and journalist Marguerite Harrison had traveled to southern Persia, where they filmed the Bakhtiari tribesmen in their annual migration. The result, *Grass* (1925), was one of the first

Ernest B. Schoedsack (left) and Merian C. Cooper had long been filmmaking partners by the time they directed *King Kong* in 1933. Shown here as seen in their first joint work, the 1925 documentary *Grass.*

important documentary features. Schoedsack then joined a zoological expedition as photographer. Also aboard was Ruth Rose, whose father had been a playwright and theatrical producer; once an actress, she was now a research technician. On Schoedsack's return, he and Cooper took a filmmaking journey to the jungles of Siam, but their new picture, *Chang* (1927), was not planned as a strict documentary. Instead, the two men concocted a simple but exciting plot about a typical native family and then, filming entirely on location, staged the various spontaneous-seeming scenes.

After completing *Chang,* Schoedsack married Ruth Rose, who joined the team on their next trip. This was to Africa, where they shot backgrounds and battle scenes for *Four Feathers;* the stars were filmed later, in Hollywood, and the film reached theaters in 1929. Cooper then entered the aviation business, while Schoedsack and Rose went to the Dutch East Indies, where they made another feature, *Rango* (1931), about a native boy, his pet baby orangutan (Rango), and the animal's father.

Meanwhile, Cooper again felt the call of the wild. His friend, W. Douglas Burden—a scientist and explorer associated with the American Museum of Natural History—had in 1926 visited the island of Komodo and brought two giant lizards back to the Bronx Zoo, where they attracted crowds and were eventually "killed" by civilization. Cooper became intrigued, he wrote years later, "with the possibility of photographing and capturing a giant gorilla . . . in the hopes of getting one back alive to the United States." Cooper also imagined that a battle between his gorilla and one of Komodo's prehistoric throwbacks could be a dramatic part of his movie, and he decided that he would somehow make the animals appear unusually large.[10] "I wanted to go to Africa and film it in the real gorilla country," he said in 1933, "but I couldn't find anyone willing to put up the money."[11]

Cooper had written down some ideas for his proposed film and brought them with him to RKO. Fate was on his side, for he soon discovered Willis O'Brien's preparations for *Creation.* "When I saw all the prehistoric animals they had lying around this studio," he said in 1933, "I decided I'd make my gorilla picture anyway—and make it right here."[12] Cooper had always been more an adventurer and dramatist than a true ethnographer, and a jungle picture made entirely in Hollywood was the logical culmination of his previous projects: *Grass* was a standard documentary; *Chang* added a slight storyline and dramatic construction, while still being filmed on location; and *Four Feathers* was derived from a famous adventure novel, starred major actors, and was partly filmed in a studio. Cooper had traveled the world seeking the epitome of adventure that could, in fact, only be found in a jungle created from his own imagination.

With his inherent sense of drama, Cooper immediately spotted the weaknesses of *Creation,* but he felt that some of its elements might effectively combine with his own idea. "The present story construction and the use of the animals is entirely wrong," he wrote in a December 1931 report to Selznick. "My idea then is to not only use the prehistoric animals for their novelty value, but also to take them out of their present character of just big beasts running around, and make them into a ferocious menace. The most important thing, however, is that one animal should have a really big character part in the picture. I suggest a prehistoric Giant Gorilla."[13]

"I always believed in personalizing and focusing attention on *one* main character," Cooper recalled in 1964,[14] and this filled the dramatic gap in *Creation.* In addition, Cooper's choice of a gorilla added an important element that a brontosaurus or a tyrannosaurus could not have provided. "I got to thinking," he said, "about the possibility of there having been one beast, more powerful than all the others and more intelligent—one beast giving a hint, a suggestion, a prefiguration of the dawn of man."[15] A gorilla's kinship to human beings would inspire audience empathy in a way impossible for any other type of animal.

"Then the thought struck me," Cooper continued, "what would happen to this highest representative of prehistoric animal life in our materialistic, mechanistic civilization? Why not place him at the pinnacle of the tallest building, symbol in steel, stone and glass of modern man's achievement and aspiration, and pit him against modern man?"[16] Starting with this climactic image, Cooper considered how to capture this semihuman animal in the first place. "There is only one thing that may undo a brute," he decided, "provided the brute approximates man, and that is beauty! It is beauty that kindles the spark of something the brute never has sensed before. He is amazed, he is subdued by this strange thing of beauty."[17] So Cooper decided to draw on a latently human facet of the animal—the ability to feel emotion, to respond to abstractions—as the element that raises him above the other beasts and also renders him vulnerable.

These decisions led Cooper to a plot that differs from *The Lost World* and O'Brien's unfinished projects in a very significant way: An animal would serve as the emotional and narrative center of the film, and would be as much its "star" as any of the human actors. In addition, the importance of "beauty" to the storyline would make the inevitable female lead an integral part of the plot, not just an arbitrary addition.

RKO had recently hired the British mystery novelist and playwright Edgar Wallace, so Cooper assigned him to develop a script based on his ape ideas. Not long after, Wallace wrote to his wife that "it is much more his story than mine," adding, "the story has got to be more or less written to provide certain spectacular effects"[18] described by Cooper. At the same time, O'Brien was already filming some effects footage. A full week before Cooper wrote his report to Selznick, Wallace watched him work on a process shot. "The camera shoots against a blue background lit up by about fifty orange arc lamps. It was two men making an attack upon a prehistoric beast. The beast, of course, was not there; he is put in afterwards, and every movement of the men is controlled by a man who is seeing the beast through a movieola, that is to say the film of the beast, and signals by means of a bell every movement that the men make."[19]

Thirteen days later, on 25 December, Wallace noted that Cooper had received preliminary approval for the film from RKO's New York executives. On 30 December, he visited the animation room and "watched the preparation of the giant monkey which appears in this play. Its skeleton and framework are complete. . . . There are two miniature sets with real miniature trees, on which the prehistoric animals are made to gambol."[20] Clearly, Cooper had been so confident of approval that he gave his production a head start, and a script was needed only to provide a context for action scenes that O'Brien was already filming in the guise of tests. The script of what eventually would be titled *King Kong* continued to evolve during shooting, and, thanks to his status at the studio, Cooper the perfectionist could permit as many rewrites, tests, and retakes as needed to give form to his vision. "I wanted to produce something that I could view with pride and say, 'There is the ultimate in adventure.' "[21]

O'Brien's feelings at this point must have been mixed. On the one hand, he finally had full studio backing for an animation project and could indulge to the full, in a sympathetic environment, his loving passion for minute detail. He also surely recognized Cooper's inherent sense of dramatic structure. At the same time, his project was no longer his. It now was Cooper's, although O'Brien certainly remained a major collaborator. "Frankly," said Cooper in 1933, "I didn't know the details of how we were going to produce these strange prehistoric animals and mingle them with real persons in modern settings,"[22] and in later life he stated that *King Kong* "is as much his [O'Brien's] picture as it is mine."[23] It was both Cooper and O'Brien who met with Edgar Wallace on 5 January 1932 to discuss his almost-complete script page by page. Nevertheless, final decisions were made by someone other than O'Brien. Without Cooper, O'Brien would probably still be known as *the* master animator, but with Cooper he became *a* creator of the finest adventure movie ever made and an enduring modern myth.

The Lost World, via O'Brien and *Creation,* had a considerable impact on *King Kong.* The earlier film, and Doyle's novel, provided the plot's basic framework: An expedition explores an isolated location and transports a beast back to civilization, where it escapes. However, the addition of the gorilla and his attraction to the heroine provided a new dramatic core, one that extends the full length of the film and motivates both the humans and the animal.

The Lost World also influenced *King Kong* in more specific ways. Its brontosaurus had knocked loose a fallen tree trunk that bridged a chasm, thereby trapping the characters on the plateau, and this became the giant log that Kong shakes to drop his pursuers into a ravine below. In both films, a normal-sized monkey is fond of the heroine, but in *Lost World* this fact is used only as a means of getting a ladder to the stranded explorers, whereas in *Kong* it has a thematic function. Later in the 1925 film, as Malone descends on the rope ladder, an ape-man pulls the ladder up; this situation evolved into Kong pulling up the vine by which Jack Driscoll and Ann Darrow try to escape from his cliff domain. In London, the brontosaurus had stuck its head through a window and disrupted a chess game, and a scene filmed for *Kong,* but discarded, had the ape do the same to a New York poker game. Both creatures arrive at a major urban landmark, but the brontosaurus simply happened upon Tower Bridge, whereas Kong heads for the area's highest spot, the Empire State Building, because he had lived in a cave on Skull Island's highest cliff.

In January 1932, Ernest Schoedsack returned from India, after shooting exteriors for Paramount's *The Lives of a Bengal Lancer.* When the studio then delayed production on that film, Cooper brought his friend to RKO. Eventually, Schoedsack directed most of the non–effects scenes of *King Kong,* but first, in May and June, he codirected (with actor Irving Pichel) the adventure-horror film *The Most Dangerous Game* (1932). Simultaneously, Cooper used *Game's* elaborate jungle set in a test reel of *Kong* that he was preparing for the studio's executives. He initially planned to use in *Kong* three cast members from *The Most Dangerous Game*—Fay Wray, Robert Armstrong, and Joel McCrea—but McCrea dropped out and Bruce Cabot replaced him.

For the test reel, Cooper filmed a lengthy action sequence that probably began with the sailors fleeing from a brontosaurus. It continued as an arsinoitherium chases the men onto the fallen tree trunk and Kong drops them into the ravine as Driscoll takes refuge in a cave. When a tyrannosaurus approaches Ann, Kong battles with the intruder, then carries the woman off, with Driscoll in pursuit. This footage impressed RKO's officials, as well it might, and they gave final approval to the production. Selznick, in turn, fully backed *Kong.* "One of the biggest gambles I took at RKO," he later commented, "was to squeeze money out of the budgets of other pictures for this venture."[24]

In Edgar Wallace's version of the screenplay, most of the animal action scenes resemble those in the final film, probably because they were Cooper's (and O'Brien's) contributions. The fact that the Carl Denham character is a circus man seeking wild animals to exhibit also derives from Cooper's notes. Wallace, however, didn't so much develop what Cooper provided as alternate it with a new plot thread involving exconvicts who, with a woman and another man, have survived a shipwreck and find themselves on the island. One of the convicts is about to rape the woman when Kong arrives and carries her off. Wallace then mixes the action scenes with some coy interplay between Kong and his captive: He fixes a nest for her, imitates her washing her face in a pool of water, and brings a pterodactyl egg as a gift. Cooper disliked the way Wallace split the plot line and felt that the convicts were too violent and the ape too gentle.

After Edgar Wallace's premature death on 10 February 1932, other writers worked on the script, including Dudley Nichols, Bartlett Cormack, and Horace McCoy. Finally, James Creelman and then Ruth Rose (Mrs. Schoedsack) took over. It is not clear what changes the interim writers may have made, but Creelman (with input from Cooper and Schoedsack) appears responsible for the final order of events, although his version still introduced Kong during the attempted rape of the heroine. When Cooper suggested having the natives sacrifice her to the giant ape instead, Creelman's imagination dried up, so Cooper turned to Rose and she added that aspect, while playing up the beauty-and-the-beast parallel and rewriting the dialogue.

A key contribution to the film's future success was the decision to base the three main characters on Cooper, Schoedsack, and Rose. In the final script, Carl Denham is a documentary filmmaker and explorer who has teamed with Jack Driscoll, the ship's first mate, on several expeditions. Denham readily fits Fay Wray's description of Cooper as a "voluble visionary,"[25] and the solid, almost stocky Robert Armstrong evokes Cooper's appearance, complete with his ever-present pipe. Driscoll (Bruce Cabot), taller and more overtly virile, fits Wray's description of Schoedsack—the self-styled "strong, silent one"[26]—equally well. Ann Darrow, the actress-turned-adventurer who falls in love with Driscoll, corresponds to Ruth Rose, although Marguerite Harrison, who had accompanied Cooper and Schoedsack on the *Grass* expedition, may have been another model.

Driscoll, however, is a sailor and not a filmmaker, so Denham also reveals some of elements of Schoedsack. In real life, Schoedsack was generally the cameraman and Cooper the dramatist, but Denham is both, and some of his dialogue derives from the recent filming of *Rango*. For example, Schoedsack's trouble with a photographer so afraid of the jungle that he drank himself into uselessness turned into Denham's explanation of why he operates his own camera: Once, in Africa, "I'd have got a swell picture of a charging rhino, but the cameraman got scared."

When Denham is chided for taking a woman into danger, he responds sarcastically, "I suppose there's no danger in New York!" This line originated with Schoedsack who, when asked in 1931 about the dangers of jungle filming, replied, "As dangerous as your poison liquor and your automobiles here in New York, I suppose." On the same occasion, Schoedsack complained, "Everyone seems to think that stories, to be vital, must contain a love interest. A picture can't be good unless it's built around a throbbing scene between a male and a female. That's a mistake, as Cooper and I tried to show with *Grass* and *Chang.*"[27] The team's alter ego, Denham, voices the same opinion in *Kong*. He doesn't want to bring a woman along, but "the public—bless 'em!—*must* have a pretty face to look at. . . . Isn't there any romance or adventure in the world without having a flapper in it? . . . I go out and sweat blood to make a swell picture and then the critics and exhibitors all say, 'If this picture had love interest, it would gross twice as much. All right! The public wants a girl and this time I'm gonna give 'em what they want!' " This drawing upon the experiences and personalities of real people gives the film's characters an inner integrity that helps support the fantastic situations they encounter.

King Kong also reflects the basic theme of its makers' prior films, which Schoedsack summarized in 1931 as "the elemental clashes . . . between man and nature."[28] *Chang's* titles even list the jungle as a character, describing it as a "timeless" and "unconquered" force against which Man, the intruder, must struggle for survival. This image of the jungle as "a great green threatening mass of vegetation" was carried over into the fantasy world of Skull Island.

In *Chang,* the natives also fear certain beasts: They build high walls to protect their animals from tigers, but even more intimidating is the "giant Chang" or elephant. When a family captures a baby Chang that had trampled their crops, the creature's mother comes to rescue it, destroying their house in the process. The animal chases them to the village and soon a herd of elephants knocks over the buildings, causing general panic. All of this evolved into the Skull Island natives' fear of Kong, a jungle creature that Denham describes as "monstrous, all-powerful—still living, still holding that island in the grip of deadly fear."

The main thematic difference between the two films lies in Kong's nearness to humanity. The elephants in *Chang* may be strong, but "stronger still is Man's Mind," and so "brawn surrenders to brain" when the beasts are captured and domesticated. To an extent, this is also true of Kong's capture, but, unlike the elephants, he is never tamed. Kong's destruction results not from a lack of intelligence but from his attraction to beauty, which makes *King Kong* not only a human-versus-nature story but also a parable about humanity's emotional vulnerability.

The parallels to Cooper and Schoedsack and their careers are interesting in themselves, but they also give the film a remarkable resonance. Real filmmakers who want to make a picture that is "the ultimate in adventure" end up making a picture about a filmmaker who wants to make "the greatest picture in the world," and when Denham describes "the idea of my picture," he describes the very film in which he is a character. In a similar boxes-within-boxes situation, actress Fay Wray, playing in an adventure film opposite a giant ape, portrays Ann Darrow, an actress hired to play in an adventure film opposite a giant ape. These characters then find themselves in a "real" adventure that resembles Denham's fictional plot. In effect, Darrow acts out in "real" life what her director expected her to act out on the screen. Appropriately, a key scene in this "real" adventure takes place on a theater stage, in front of an audience that has come expecting to see a movie, and, as this "real" audience in a theater watches a girl and an ape, it echoes the real audience watching a movie about a girl and an ape, and watching the "real" audience watching. Kong then leaps from the secure distance of the theater stage into his audience's midst, even while remaining safely on the movie theater's screen.

This inward spiral of illusion and reality probably interested Cooper and Schoedsack and Rose, but it began as an eminently practical solution to the problem of creating a plot. Thus, by having Denham feel the need for a female lead, they have automatically introduced their own female lead, and Driscoll's love for Darrow becomes his very necessary filmic motivation for chasing through the jungle after her.

Some intriguingly uncomfortable implications arise from this subject matter. The movie's audience is intended to sympathize at least partially with Kong, shackled helplessly as an exhibit to be gawked at by a jaded paying public, and yet this is very close to what Cooper and Schoedsack have done with their own created Kong (and with the natives and animals appearing in their previous features). The implied criticism of Denham and his audience thereby becomes an implied criticism of Cooper and Schoedsack themselves, and of the film's audience. Cooper, who may or may not have been aware of this, would probably reply that, unlike Denham, he had left his natives and animals safely in their own environment without transporting them to a world where they, like Kong or the Komodo dragon lizards, would have to die.

This valid argument, together with the film's (and, ultimately, Denham's) sympathy for Kong, does mute what would otherwise be a disturbingly negative overtone. Certainly, during the long period spent making *Kong,* the two directors became so closely involved with their creation that Cooper declared, ambiguously, "We should kill the sonofabitch ourselves."[29] So the two aviators seen machine-gunning Kong in the film's climax are in fact those two real-life aviators, Cooper and Schoedsack; the men who unloosed this creature on an unwary populace have, unlike Carl Denham, fully faced their own unpleasant responsibility and destroyed it.

As directors, Cooper and Schoedsack were far from subtle stylists, but they did understand dramatic structure and pace. In their bid to make the definitive adventure film, they rightly kept dialogue and character development to a minimum, while including many exciting encounters between people and animals. Unlike many makers of action films, they also realized that a continual series of such encounters satiates and wearies an audience, reducing instead of increasing the excitement. In an early interview, Schoedsack declared that a film should be constructed like a musical composition. It "should build up to climaxes, then allow some rest, then build again. I believe in pace. If necessary I use a stopwatch on the actors."[30] Both *The Most Dangerous Game* and *King Kong* evidence the speed and excitement generated by this approach.

King Kong begins with a series of scenes that lead to and depict the journey to Skull Island. Here, the directors establish all the necessary information, so that the rest of the film can be an uninterrupted series of encounters, chases, climaxes, and pauses. However, they keep these early scenes as short and interesting as possible, with the exposition conveyed in ways that simultaneously move the story forward.

First we meet a theatrical agent who joins Denham, Driscoll, and the Captain on the ship. The arrival of this outsider provokes dialogue that conveys the basic situation, as he reports that no actress could be found to join the mysterious expedition, which in turn motivates Denham to find someone himself and leads directly to the next scene. With its rapid pace, the film sometimes enters conversations after they have started. For instance, Denham spots Ann Darrow trying to steal some fruit from a vendor and decides to take her to a restaurant, but when we join them there, she has already finished eating, so the scene includes the important dialogue while omitting much unneeded action. Such efficient use of screen time continues throughout *Kong.*

Several scenes conclude with dramatic "curtain lines" that imply more than they state. After finally explaining about Skull Island and its unknown beast, Denham is asked what would happen if it didn't like having its picture taken. He replies, "Well, now you know why I brought those cases of gas bombs," followed by a fade out. Soon after, Denham films an on-deck screen test with Ann, asking her to look upward higher and higher and then to scream for her life. After the shock of her screams, the film cuts to Driscoll asking the Captain, "What's he think she's really going to see?" and the scene ends. The point has been made, without overstatement.

The developing romance is concisely conveyed in three short scenes. As the ship sets sail, Driscoll calls Ann a nuisance and barely manages to apologize for an accidental sock in the jaw. Later, he says that she's "swell," but adds that "women can't help being a bother." Finally, after the natives have expressed an interest in sacrificing Ann to Kong, Driscoll admits, "I'm scared for you! I'm sort of—I'm scared *of* you, too. Ann, I—I guess I love you." They kiss. When Ann is kidnapped by the natives immediately afterward, Driscoll is ready to risk death to get her back.

Behind the scenes on Skull Island in *King Kong* (1933).

Visually, these early scenes are efficient and informative, with the directors using film technique to place subtle stress on the more dramatic moments. Denham's explanation about the island to Driscoll and the Captain is shown mainly in group shots. Then, during a pause, Denham takes a few steps and we cut to a shot of him alone, as he says, "Did you ever hear of—Kong?" This isolation of Denham heightens the impact of his line, the first mention of the film's true star.

The staging and structure of the action sequences are ideal. We follow the natives as they tie Ann to an altar and close the giant gate on her. The script says only that Kong "steps from jungle opening," but Cooper and O'Brien give his entrance a more dramatic buildup. As Ann squirms and the natives wait, the sound of growls and music that evokes a walking rhythm create anticipation. Some trees move, but we cannot discern the shape behind them until more trees are knocked aside and the ape's imposing figure emerges.

Only after Kong absconds with Ann does the ship's crew reappear, and our first real exposure to the jungle comes through them. This section is wisely constructed so that the incidents escalate in danger, intensity, and excitement. First, the crew passes one of Kong's footprints. Then, they spot a stegosaurus grazing placidly. It sights them and charges, but is quickly knocked out with a gas bomb before doing any harm. Starting with a spectacular scene would have made subsequent events anticlimactic, and because this is the crew's (and the viewer's) first contact with the local fauna, what we see is impressive enough. Even so, viewers receive a bonus when the beast, thought unconscious, stirs and is shot. Then it rises, collapses again, and is finished off with another shot.

Next, the men reach a lake, so they stop to build a raft. Maintaining a rapid pace, the film dissolves immediately to the task's completion, efficiently eliding this unexciting activity. As the men pole their craft across the lake, a brontosaurus surfaces beneath it and sends them swimming to shore. But the land offers no safety, for the lumbering animal pursues them there. One seaman seeks refuge in a tree (as a native had when chased by a tiger in *Chang*), but is plucked from his perch by the long-necked dinosaur. The survivors run onto the fallen log, but Kong, at the opposite end, twists it, dropping them to their deaths. Having eliminated the anonymous sailors, Kong turns his attention to Driscoll, who has entered a cave in the ravine wall. When Kong reaches down, Driscoll slashes at the giant hand with his only remaining weapon, a knife. Kong pulls his hand out and viewers are tempted to relax, but suddenly a lizard-like creature climbs up from below. At the last second, Driscoll notices this and cuts the vine, which sends the animal plummeting.

When Ann, who had been placed in a tree by Kong, screams at the approach of a tyrannosaurus, Kong rushes to her aid. As the two giant creatures struggle, Cooper and O'Brien pull out all the stops, providing spectacular fight choreography and fairly rapid editing. Naturally, ex-boxer O'Brien has the ape throw a few punches at his taller opponent. Kong also tries to topple the dinosaur by grasping its leg, and the two do a somersault together. After Kong falls and knocks over the tree containing Ann, he jumps onto the tyrannosaurus's back and sets about cracking its jaw. The entire fight, lasting nearly three minutes, contains thirty-one cuts between several camera setups, all of which keep Ann in view so the audience never forgets the danger the huge figures pose to her. (One must remember that separate camera angles require far more effort in an animation film than in live action.) After this impressive climax, toward which the film has carefully built, the audience finally has a chance to rest while the two survivors, Driscoll on one side of the ravine and Denham on the other, decide what to do.

As originally planned, the film up to this point contained even more animal action. Escaping from the brontosaurus, the crew watches a fight between Kong and several triceratops in an asphalt pit. The shooting script describes the scene: "In the centre is a dry mound to which Kong springs. . . . Kong picks up boulders and hurls them down on the beasts as they try to reach him through the asphalt mire. He kills two. The third retreats." This last triceratops then pursues the men. (It is not certain that this scene was ever filmed.) When one of the sailors hides behind a tree, the triceratops knocks it over, pins him to the ground, and "gores him to death."

The rest of the crew, running onto the log, spot Kong on the other side and hesitate, but an arsinoitherium blocks their retreat, and Kong drops them into the ravine, where horrible creatures dwell. The shooting script describes the sailors' fate in nine shots.

> [Long shot] The men at the bottom of the ravine are attacked by giant insects who come out of caves and fissures to eat them.
> [Close-up] The surprised face of a sailor lying in the mud as he sees this.
> [Close-up] Face of another sailor staring up in horror from the mud.
> [Close-up] Face of a third sailor in the mud, horrified as he sees—
> [Medium shot] An insect with octopus arms takes a man.
> [Semi-close-up] Its arms wind about the struggling man.
> [Semi-close-up] Two men on their backs staring up at a spider who attacks them.
> [Close-up] The face of a fourth sailor, fallen in mud, staring in horror as he sees—
> [Full shot] A giant lizard takes a man.

While animating the ravine sequence, O'Brien evidently elaborated on this action and varied the nature of the creatures. As his camera operator recalled, "Obie wanted *real snakes* for the closeups" and after he got them "we filmed stuntmen screaming as the snakes wrapped around their bodies."[31]

Cooper rightly discarded both the asphalt pit scene, which didn't directly involve the characters, and the ravine footage, which deflected attention from the dangers faced by Ann and Driscoll. The result focused the action on the key characters and tightened the film's pace. Because he completely removed the insects, Cooper also took the trouble to have the spider that had climbed the vine toward Driscoll's cave replaced with the lizard-like creature. According to Cooper, when he removed the ravine sequence "O'Brien was heartbroken; he thought it was the best work he'd done, and it was, but it worked against the picture, so out it came."[32] Such editorial ruthlessness, exercised for the good of the total film, made Cooper an invaluable collaborator for O'Brien and helps *Kong* surpass every similar feature made before or since.

Having already provided more excitement than is found in most adventure films, *Kong* again starts building tension as Driscoll pursues Kong and Ann, while Denham returns to the gate. When Kong reaches his cliffside lair, another series of scenes leads to a smaller climax. First, the ape fights a serpent-like creature, and in every shot care is taken to include either Ann, huddled in fear, or Driscoll, hiding behind a rock. These shots are made even more complex, technically and visually, by the inclusion of a pool of real water, another pool of bubbling lava, and wisps of rising steam—all of which had to be photographed separately and then combined.

Next, Kong examines Ann, pulling off some of her clothes. Although Schoedsack stated that this scene was O'Brien's idea and "done by Obie himself on his own,"[33] a version of it appeared in Edgar Wallace's early script. Not even the shooting script, however, mentions that Kong tickles Ann several times and sniffs her scent on his finger, so those details were added during production. The combination, in a single shot, of Fay Wray in a full-sized hand with the animated model of Kong's body and his other hand is totally convincing.

When the ape investigates a sound made by Driscoll, a pterodactyl starts to fly off with Ann, so Kong again bounds to the rescue. By this time, the menace has, in his defense of Ann, also become a kind of hero. During the fight with the flying reptile, Driscoll and Ann try to escape by climbing down a vine. Kong, victorious over the pterodactyl, pulls the vine up, "reeling" them in. With no other alternative, the couple drop to the river below. (In the shooting script there is no vine, and the two simply

Preliminary sketch by Byron Crabbe of a scene in *King Kong* (1933) in which Kong exhibits both the heroic and fierce sides of his nature, here rescuing the character Ann Darrow from a pterodactyl.

jump into the water.) Some shots of Driscoll and Ann swimming and of Kong in pursuit were ultimately cut, briskly condensing the fugitives' return to the wall.

After this minor climax, another slight pause occurs when Driscoll and Ann are welcomed by Denham and the others. Suddenly, the action picks up again as Kong appears and breaks down the barred gate. His rampage through the native village (evoking that of the elephant herd in *Chang*) brings the film to a new level of excitement. Here, Kong's threat is dramatized as he chomps natives between his teeth and stomps others into the mud. This third climax ends as Denham tosses gas bombs at Kong and the giant ape collapses on the beach.

Following the lead of *The Lost World* (the novel, but not the scenario), *King Kong* skips the practical details of hauling the captive back to civilization, dissolving directly to the first night of his public exhibition. After another brief pause, tension again builds until Kong, mistaking the photographers' flash bulbs for an attack on Ann, breaks loose. The film now provides more thrills, but without just repeating the kind experienced on Skull Island: This time, Kong is the outsider who encounters a strange world.

Kong bites a man plucked from an automobile, then climbs a building in search of Ann. In a horrifying scene, he reaches into an apartment and takes a young woman from the security of her bed, holding her upside-down, many stories above the street. Her scent is not Ann's, so he casually drops her to her death. After locating Ann in another room and carrying her off, Kong demolishes an elevated subway train, no doubt thinking it a kind of serpent. This incident, conceived by Cooper after filming had been completed, filled a key gap in the pacing of the New York sequence by providing a needed subclimax.

In the film's final pause for breath, Driscoll and Denham listen to radio reports of Kong's approach to the Empire State Building and decide to attack him with war planes. From here on, the picture moves rapidly to its tragic-heroic conclusion, as the giant ape is shot by these mechanical pterodactyls and falls to his death. Because of the empathy created for Kong, this one-sided battle becomes the film's most emotionally involving scene, and the film thereby avoids the danger that its ending might not surpass some of the earlier sequences.

After Ann's abduction from the ship, *King Kong* is almost nonstop action, superbly orchestrated for maximum excitement and imbued with a rare emotional resonance. Thanks to Cooper's insistence that Kong be shown doing brutal things, and not just defending himself or Ann, our feelings about him are subtly mixed. He is not just a sympathetic victim, although he is that, too.

Nor is the film just a beauty-and-the-beast fantasy, for dialogue extends that concept into the normal, human world. When Denham sees Ann with the ship's pet monkey, he comments, "Beauty and the Beast, eh?" Driscoll jokingly misinterprets this, saying, "Well now, I never thought I was good lookin'." The sturdy first mate then voices concern about Ann's safety. "I never knew it to fail," retorts Denham. "Some big hard-boiled egg gets a look at a pretty face and—bang!—he cracks up and goes sappy. . . . You're a pretty tough guy, but if beauty gets you—" he warns, then explains: "It's the idea of my picture. The Beast was a tough guy, too. He could lick the world. But when he saw Beauty, she got him. He went soft, he forgot his wisdom, and the little fellows licked him." Here, the film broadens its premise to apply to all male-female relations, and the valid idea about vulnerability takes on a tinge of misogyny that (probably unconsciously) adds another edge to viewer response.

Although not a horror film, *King Kong* has much in common with films in the genre. *The Murders in the Rue Morgue* (1932), for instance, has an ape kidnap the heroine and carry her over the city's rooftops. *Variety*'s description of "the gigantic gorilla and the frail, defenseless girl" in its review of that film (16 February 1932) sums up the horror-monster's embodiment of primitive passions, of the sexual drive, of the id unleashed and out of control. That, too, is one of the qualities that makes Kong so appealingly dangerous, but it is tempered by his bewilderment and gentleness when faced with glowing blonde beauty, just as *Frankenstein* (1931) balanced the Monster's physical menace with a sensitivity revealed by his attraction to sunlight.

Carl Denham, too, has a double edge due to characteristics shared with horror films. Though not a scientist who creates a monster, he does discover one and, in the process, reveals a blend of admirable ambition and arrogant excess similar to that in Henry Frankenstein, as portrayed by Colin Clive in 1931. Denham's goal is to do "something that nobody's ever seen or heard of," and he is willing to bend the rules to achieve it, by sneaking out of the harbor with a load of ammunition and gas bombs. This and his "reputation for recklessness" lead even Driscoll to ask, "Think he's crazy, Skipper?" to which the Captain replies, "Just enthusiastic."

Denham is so obsessive that he loses human perspective. Upon seeing the natives' ceremony he exclaims, "What a show!" and, when told that a native will be the "bride of Kong," he responds, "Great!" Denham's detachment is most apparent when he considers using Ann as bait to lure the ape from his mountain ("We've got something he wants"), but his ruthlessness isn't put to the test because Kong takes the initiative. It is to Cooper's credit that he allowed, even encouraged, this complexity in his surrogate figure.

The full extent of O'Brien's contribution to this collaborative enterprise is hard to assess. Certainly some of the incidents originated with him, and his skill and sensitivity brought Kong to subtly characterized life. Archie Marshek, Cooper's production assistant, called O'Brien "a husky, hard-drinking Irishman" and stated that "as we watched a certain personality develop in the ape we could see something of Obie showing through."[34] Darlyne O'Brien agreed: "I could see him in every one of its gestures and movements."[35] At the same time, his characterization of Kong is eminently realistic, without any caricature-like excesses. Even the more extreme moments—when Kong wiggles the cracked jaw of the dead tyrannosaurus, when his nostrils and the ridge above his eyes move as he sniffs Ann's scent, and when he plucks a villager's spear from his behind, tosses it aside, and strides away—avoid the taint of exaggeration.

The script describes Kong as killing the serpentine creature in his cave by squeezing it to death, but O'Brien has him grab one end and slap the body against the ground like a whip, a much more visually dramatic action, but still a natural one. Kong's reaction to the gas bomb is full of gestures, unmentioned in the script, which prolong his collapse without overstating it: He wipes his eyes, clasps his throat, rubs his eyes with the other hand, slumps onto one elbow, then crawls on all fours until he loses consciousness. Similarly, his end atop the Empire State Building elaborates subtly on the script's limited description ("He staggers, turns slowly, and topples off roof"). Injured by an airplane's bullets, he touches his chest wound and inspects the blood on his fingers; it is while he pets the reclining figure of Ann that more bullets hit him; he looks up and sneers weakly at a plane; drained, he tilts backwards but grasps the building's tip, then he leans back again, his grip loosens, and he falls. These actions present Kong's death simply and straightforwardly, without milking it for sentimentality, building up its brutality, or turning it into an operatic aria.

O'Brien's attention to detail made the settings into a convincing primeval world. To create depth and dimension, he used four or five layers of glass paintings depicting trees, mountains, and sky. In between, he placed animation tables containing portions of model sets with real and artificial foliage and creatures to animate. To this, he often added separately filmed bits of actual landscape. The explorers' plunge into the jungle of Skull Island had to feel like a descent into the imagination's deepest, most unconscious fears. The plot's events provide the needed sense of unbridled animal energy, but at least as important are O'Brien's dense, engulfing jungle and his craggy, barren cliffs and caverns.

King Kong was a triumph for all those involved with it, and especially for O'Brien, who had fought to establish the validity of his techniques and to use them in a fantastic adventure. Humans and models are extensively combined in the same shot, but not by the primitive double-exposure method of *The Lost World*. O'Brien often rear-projected live-action footage onto tiny screens placed within the miniature sets, then rephotographed it frame by frame as he animated the models. Having designed this procedure and devised the necessary equipment, he no doubt recalled Herbert Dawley's actions of years before and this time he patented his idea. He also used the Williams and Dunning matte processes and the recently developed optical printer, which combined separately filmed images onto a new negative.

But superb technical work alone would not have been enough. O'Brien's feeling for physical form and texture, his ability to create bigger-than-life creatures out of tiny models, and the many-faceted plot combine to make *King Kong* the "escapist entertainment pure and simple"[36] that Cooper had sought. It also became such a basic, evocative fable that later viewers could, with some validity, see it as an allegory about ecology, colonialism, or slavery. Such a masterful combination of insights and talents—and such a lavish investment of production time on detail, on trial and error—would never again occur in the field of stop-motion animation.

When *King Kong* premiered on 2 March 1933 in two of New York's largest theaters, the Radio City Music Hall and the RKO Roxy, it did such impressive business, despite President Roosevelt's "bank holiday," that the studio bragged in a *Motion Picture Herald* ad, "*With no money* last week *King Kong* played to 189,402 paid admissions."[37] Such receipts immediately inspired a sequel, which began shooting in April, but one with a small budget, short shooting schedule, and elements discarded from *Kong* and *Creation:* some violent and rebellious crewmen, an ancient temple and treasure, and an earthquake that destroys Skull Island. Cooper, who had recently replaced Selznick as RKO's head of production, now had less time to devote to a single film, so Schoedsack directed alone.

Knowing they could never equal *Kong,* the filmmakers wisely took a different approach with *Son of Kong* (1933). More than half of this short film is spent getting the characters to Skull Island, and the "little" Kong they encounter acts more like a mascot than a menace. In the words of Ruth Rose, "It was a case of 'if you can't make it bigger you'd better make it funnier.' "[38] Unlike its intense predecessor, *Son of Kong* provides relaxing diversion. Even so, its plot is surprisingly realistic, even grim.

The story joins Carl Denham (Robert Armstrong) a month after the death of Kong. Once the epitome of confidence, he now hides from process servers, dodges lawsuits, and voices regret at the ape's fate. Penniless, Denham flees the city with Captain Englehorn, hoping to survive by hauling cargo among the islands they know so well. Meeting with little success, the former showman pauses on Dakang to attend a tiny circus. Its owner, Petersen, has a drinking problem that cost him a job with a big circus, so he and his daughter find themselves trapped by poverty on the furthest fringe of show business. Their pathetic acts include some costumed musical monkeys and the untalented Hilda Petersen (Helen Mack) singing the aptly titled "Runaway Blues," as the natives in the audience stare uncomprehendingly.

Petersen's drinking buddy, Helstrom, is also a runaway, hiding from the law after losing his ship in an insurance fraud. During a drunken argument, Helstrom hits Petersen with a bottle, and an upset lamp starts a fire. Waking, Hilda frees the monkeys and drags her father from the flames, but he dies and the monkeys flee. Meanwhile, in a coincidence that is the plot's biggest weakness, Denham recognizes Helstrom as the man who originally gave him the map of Skull Island. Hoping to escape from Dakang, Helstrom concocts a story about treasure on the island and Denham swallows the bait. After they set sail, Hilda is discovered on board. Like the others, she "just didn't have anywhere to go," so she joins this ship of failures.

By the time they reach Skull Island, Helstrom has stirred up a mutiny, and, in the film's biggest surprise, the villainous crewmen suddenly spout communist propaganda. "You don't give us a living wage," they tell Englehorn, as they set the Captain, Denham, Hilda, and the cook adrift. Although Helstrom expects to take command, he is told, "We're through with captains on this ship" and the revolutionaries toss him overboard "with the rest of the bosses."

This unnecessary political overtone must be a case of the filmmakers venting their own negative opinion of Marxism. Cooper had, years before, fought for Poland against the Bolsheviks, and Schoedsack's greatest anger while making *Kong* had been directed at by-the-book union men. "The rest of us were working all night trying to finish up animation scenes, because if you left those little sets standing too long between frames the tiny plants shrink and ruin the effect," he recalled. One particular employee would "walk off and leave them and it caused us to have some pretty crude scenes. I tried to congratulate him once—'that's good, you got fifteen feet finished today'—and he snarled and muttered something like, 'yeah, tomorrow you'll probably want me to do twenty feet!' "[39] The snarling and muttering mutineers in *Son of Kong* represent Schoedsack's revenge.

On the island, Denham and Hilda discover a young, twelve-foot gorilla caught in quicksand. The two help him escape, and from then on the grateful Little Kong serves as their guardian angel: He defends them from a cave bear and a dragon-like creature, shakes a tree to provide coconuts, and helps them enter an ancient temple where there really is a treasure. Another dragon conveniently kills Helstrom, then an unexpected earthquake causes the island to sink. Little Kong saves Denham from drowning, and the survivors are rescued by a passing ship. By helping Kong's son—and having the son like him—Denham has shed the burden of guilt he had carried. At the end, he still has some of the temple jewels, he wins the girl, and the two are presumably freed from lives of aimless futility.

The Dakang scenes contain a realistic sense of human desperation, but on Skull Island one never feels the presence of real danger. Still, the earthquake provides impressive spectacle, and Little Kong's fights are lively, especially the bout with the bear, which is full of tumbling, rolling, and punching. Elsewhere, Little Kong reveals the kind of cuteness avoided in *King Kong*. After one battle he salutes his friends, then clasps his hands in a boxer's victory gesture. When Denham and Hilda walk away, the gorilla looks directly into the camera, scratches his head, and shrugs his shoulders. Denham befriended Little Kong because "I felt I owed his family something," but despite this he—like the film itself—shows little respect for the youthful simian, calling him a "half-wit" and a "big dummy."

In the climax, as the island sinks, Little Kong stands on a mountain top with Denham in his hand; the animal's foot is caught, but he continues holding Denham above water, even after his own head submerges. When the rowboat pulls near, Little Kong's hand releases Denham, then disappears underwater. This ending has tragic overtones only if a pet's self-sacrifice for its master can be called tragic. It is quite touching, however, and not as sentimental as it sounds. At least the filmmakers didn't have the hand wave a final goodbye before sinking!

One of *King Kong*'s few weaknesses was the use of a full-size mechanical head for most of the ape's close-ups. This head, with a different physical structure than the model's and hardly any expressiveness, always broke the illusion created by the animated figure. In the sequel, all of Little Kong's close-ups use animation, so the overall effect is much more consistent. *Son of Kong*'s blending of live action and miniatures in the same frame is also more thoroughly convincing than in the first film.

One cannot tell who, besides Schoedsack, determined the different tone of *Son of Kong* and its title character. The film lists Ruth Rose as author of the story, but includes no screenplay credit at all. According to Archie Marshek, Cooper "was ill during much of the shooting,"[40] and researcher Don Shay states that O'Brien "washed his hands of the entire project, refusing to contribute anything substantial in the way of personal creativity."[41] Reportedly, he left much of the animation to Buzz Gibson, a former grip whom O'Brien had trained. But why would O'Brien react this way? Perhaps he resisted the jokey quality and felt it demeaned the initial accomplishment, yet his early shorts had a broad sense of humor, as did O'Brien himself; Orville

Goldner, who worked on *King Kong,* has even claimed that O'Brien was "always trying to corn things up" and that Cooper and Schoedsack "had to sit on him about it."[42] If O'Brien did have that tendency, surely he would have enjoyed working on *Son of Kong.*

Darlyne O'Brien believed that her husband "felt it was too soon to follow *King Kong* with a picture of the same type" and took offense at his employers, who "felt that they didn't even have to *consult*" him on technical and creative matters any more.[43] Another possibility must also be considered. Schoedsack's comment that O'Brien disappeared into the nearest bar when faced with deadlines could easily apply to this film, for unlike *Kong,* the sequel was made under extreme time pressure. O'Brien's mood may also have been affected by a news item published by *Variety* while *Son* was still in production. The trade paper stated that, despite *King Kong*'s profitability, RKO's New York executives had "rung the finish gong on horror pix" for the studio. The reported reason was the executives' sensitivity to "the kidding *Kong* has received inside the industry. Kidding was based on the ultra fantastic angles in the beauty-and-the-beast tale."[44]

Nor was O'Brien's personal life pressure-free. In the years since he had left his wife, she became a victim of tuberculosis and cancer. His older son, William, also contracted tuberculosis and the disease left him blind. These events and the drugs Hazel took for her illnesses probably affected her already precarious mental state. Matters reached a breaking point in early October, just as *Son of Kong* was being readied for release, when Hazel shot and killed both William (aged fourteen) and Willis, Jr. (aged thirteen), then turned the gun on herself. "My husband is not to blame in any way," she was quoted as saying. "I just couldn't sleep and there was no one to leave the kids with."[45] Hazel survived her suicide attempt, but was considered too ill to stand trial; she died in November 1934. As if this were not enough, a woman O'Brien was dating near the end of 1933 was diagnosed with breast cancer and killed herself.

With all of these elements linked together in his mind, it is not surprising that, even fifteen years later, O'Brien was reluctant to discuss *Son of Kong.*[46] At one point in the film, after Denham has bandaged Little Kong's injured finger, the curious monkey inspects the result with his wrapped middle finger extended. It is tempting to imagine O'Brien, overwhelmed by circumstances and three sheets to the wind, dropping in at the studio and leaving behind this gesture as his comment on life in general.

Ironically, *Son of Kong*'s Skull Island sequence contains a rapid-fire series of arbitrary but exciting events that recalls O'Brien's plots for *Atlantis* and *Creation,* and however much or little he contributed to the film, it probably reflects his inclinations more than is generally realized. Overall, *Son of Kong* may not be as "serious" as its parent, but it does capture a young boy's sense of adventure and is, like the title character, quite likeable. It also illustrates how lucky was the conjunction of personalities and circumstances that produced *King Kong.*

Life for Willis O'Brien took a turn for the better in 1934, as he courted Darlyne Prenett, whom he married on November 17, shortly after Hazel's death. Darlyne evidently matched his personality well, and the two embarked on a stable, enduring relationship. Far less stable, though, was O'Brien's relationship with the film industry. When Merian Cooper produced *She* (1935), he changed the setting of H. Rider Haggard's story from Africa to the Arctic and considered including some O'Brien-animated mammoths, but budget reductions cancelled that plan. O'Brien did work on Cooper's *The Last Days of Pompeii* (1935), using miniatures and glass paintings to extend partial sets of buildings and to depict the volcanic eruption that destroys the city. For Cooper's Technicolor feature *Dancing Pirate* (1936), a tedious musical about a nineteenth-century dancing teacher mistaken for a pirate, O'Brien provided a shot that combined live action with glass paintings to depict a distant ship at anchor.

Finally, in 1938, O'Brien and Cooper began work on a new animation project, this time with MGM's backing. Entitled *War Eagles,* this grandiose story had much in common with *The Lost World* and O'Brien's unmade features, but with an emphasis on flying that surely appealed to airman Cooper. A young pilot and a Challenger-type professor with an eccentric theory venture into an unknown section of the Arctic (as the heroes of *She* had done). There, they discover a race of Viking throwbacks who ride giant prehistoric eagles and live above a lush valley inhabited by dinosaurs. The pilot engages in some O'Brien-style cowboy action when he ropes and rides a wild eagle. He also romances a Viking woman, after saving her from a tyrannosaurus when a bomb buries the creature in a landslide. At one point, the evolving screenplay also had the Vikings capture an allosaurus and transport it in a large wagon.

When the explorers learn that America is at war, they and the Vikings ride their eagles to New York, where, in a midair battle, they defeat the enemy's airplanes. At the end, they perch in triumph on the Statue of Liberty, yielding a patriotic collage of American symbols that probably reveals the response of Cooper, the anti-fascist fighting man, to the growing threat of war in Europe.

Much time, effort, and money were spent making drawings, paintings, and miniature settings, and Marcel Delgado built several models of people and eagles. O'Brien even shot a short test of animated spearmen on their eagles attacking a tyrannosaurus. At about this time, the teenaged Ray Harryhausen contacted O'Brien and described his own experiments with animation, which had been inspired by *King Kong.* O'Brien invited Harryhausen to the studio, looked at some of his work, and offered much-needed encouragement. Gradually, O'Brien became a mentor to the aspiring animator, who had been born in the same year as one of the sons he had lost.

Some time later, O'Brien told Harryhausen he had, from the start, felt "an antagonism by the staff at MGM—against somebody coming in from outside and trying to do a picture there."[47] After the outbreak of a real war in Europe prompted Cooper to reenlist in the Army Air Corps, MGM quickly dropped the film. O'Brien then took whatever work he could find, which included joining the team that animated George Pal's Puppetoon shorts, a team that also included Ray Harryhausen.

At the same time, O'Brien developed new ideas for features, and in the summer of 1941 he and producer John Speaks (who had worked on *Pompeii* and *Dancing Pirate*) started effects work at RKO, which had agreed to finance *Gwangi.* This plot revived several aspects of *War Eagles,* but on a less elaborate scale. In it, a group of Wild West show cowboys discover a valley in the Grand Canyon that contains prehistoric monsters (but no lost civilization). They try in vain to rope Gwangi, an allosaurus, but only when it is trapped in a landslide can they cart it back as an exhibit. The creature breaks loose, fights some of the show's lions, and wreaks havoc in the town until a truck forces it over a cliff to its death.

While Delgado constructed an allosaurus model, O'Brien drew detailed storyboards to illustrate the planned action scenes. Ray Harryhausen also recalls seeing "a series of Dioramas in three-dimensional cardboard cutouts for each set-up."[48] After several months of work, but no actual filming, *Gwangi*—like *War Eagles* before it—was shelved and by February 1942 Speaks and O'Brien had left the studio. O'Brien then spent about a year in Chicago, doing effects work for military documentaries. Returning to Hollywood, he created glass paintings for such traditional films as *Going My Way* (1944) and *The Bells of St. Mary's* (1945). Even that sort of work was in short supply.

By 1947, O'Brien had celebrated his sixtieth birthday, and, as he struggled to make a living, Merian Cooper—along with Schoedsack and Rose—reentered his life. Together, they began work on O'Brien's last major feature. A script was completed by September 1947, with revisions added throughout the fall. Then, after more than a year spent on animation and live-action filming, RKO released *Mighty Joe Young* in the summer of 1949.

As with *King Kong,* Cooper built this story around an animal. He even borrowed *Kong*'s premise: A callous showman brings a giant ape to civilization, with destructive results. However, for *King Kong*'s 1938 re-release the Hollywood Production Code had compelled RKO to remove Kong's more violent actions and the scene of him undressing the heroine. As if in response, Cooper turned *Mighty Joe Young* into a film without emotional complexity, a sentimental fairy tale with no deaths or even injuries, and with a happy ending for the ape.

From *Rango,* in which a young boy raised an orangutan in the jungle, came the device of having a child, Jill Young, adopt and raise a baby gorilla, whom she names Joe. Years later, this animal has become more than a pet; "Joe's the only friend I have," says the now-orphaned girl. (The fact that Joe somehow grew to abnormal height goes unexplained.) Unlike Kong, Joe is a consistently sympathetic figure, although as an animal and because of his size he is still potentially dangerous.

The pivotal character of showman Max O'Hara plans to open the Golden Safari, an elaborate nightclub with an African motif. "Nobody's ever seen anything like what

Jill (Terry Moore) and Joe suffer indignities on the stage of the Golden Safari in *Mighty Joe Young* (1949).

I'm gonna give 'em," he announces. Borrowing an idea from O'Brien's unfilmed *Gwangi,* Max brings some rodeo cowboys to Africa, to capture animals for use as decor. When the giant gorilla shows up, they try to rope him, too, but without success. Eventually realizing that Joe is tame, Max convinces Jill to perform with her friend as the nightclub's star attraction.

Like Carl Denham, Max O'Hara derives from Cooper himself. His refrain, "It isn't *big* enough," even echoes a comment made by Cooper during the filming of *King Kong.* Max, however, reflects Cooper (and Denham) in a distorting mirror. Denham had taken his films and expeditions seriously, and the dangers he faced were real, but Max (played, as was Denham, by Robert Armstrong) makes up his adventures from the relative comfort of a camp chair. His goal is publicity, not adventure. This urban type is a fish out of water in Africa, and broad satire turns to farce as Max struggles to saddle a resisting horse. Although Max is a comic figure, the film mocks him affectionately. He may be a self-centered, fast-talking manipulator, but he is also honest, appealingly enthusiastic, and ultimately sincere in his effort to help Jill and Joe.

Max has built his nightclub in Hollywood, and Cooper's treatment of the film capital is far less gentle than his handling of Max. Ruth Rose's screenplay refers to the Golden Safari's architecture as "very garish and in the worst possible taste," a description that also fits its grotesquely excessive decor, with lions pacing in glass cages behind the bar, a clutter of fake trees and vines, and the orchestra perched in an elaborate "tree house." Over the years, however, some viewers have mistaken this satiric tackiness for the real thing.

The nightclub's customers—the inhabitants of Tinseltown—also receive harsh treatment in the script, which describes them as "over-dressed" and "underbred." The fans who besiege Jill outside the theater are equally pushy and rude ("Gimme your autograph!"). Originally, the film also contained a long scene in which Max introduces Jill to Taylor Z. Bascombe, "the biggest shot in town," who embodies the worst aspects of Hollywood producers as he and his friends make condescendingly crude jokes about "the farmer's daughter" and reveal their arrogant ignorance of Africa. After clumsily spraying the distraught Jill with champagne, Bascombe embraces her "with mock solicitude." However, after a preview of *Mighty Joe Young,* Cooper eliminated this scene (and a few other, shorter segments), which tightened the film's pace but also weakened its criticism of Hollywood's denizens. Nevertheless, the shallow, obnoxious customers and fans remain in the film. With Cooper drawing on his own nearly two decades of exposure to Hollywood, the glamor and bright lights with which Max tempts Jill are shown to be much overrated.

The film treats the full-grown Joe's first appearance in Africa matter-of-factly, by abruptly cutting to a full shot of him, but Joe's entrance onstage at the Golden Safari is much more impressive and ingenious. As Jill sits at a piano playing his favorite song, "Beautiful Dreamer" ("Old Black Joe" in the screenplay), the nightclub's audience starts to feel cheated. Then Jill's platform rises and Joe emerges into view standing on an elevator stage, holding the platform above his head. While the stage below him slowly rotates, Joe poses like a Las Vegas showgirl and the amazed patrons gasp, then burst into applause.

This introduction is quickly followed by a tug-of-war between Joe and several wrestlers. Although relatively innocuous, this act subtly shifts the performance's mood as the customers' response changes from awe to laughter. The show is a hit and seventeen weeks pass, but spending his off-hours in a cage depresses Joe, and their new act disturbs Jill: Joe is dressed like an organ grinder's monkey, and the customers throw fake coins at the stage and at Joe. (This sad, demeaning treatment of an animal recalls the costumed musical monkeys seen in *Son of Kong.*)

Just when Jill (Terry Moore) and cowboy Gregg Johnson (Ben Johnson) find themselves in love and decide to take Joe back to Africa, three drunken customers shatter their hopes by sneaking backstage and plying Joe with liquor, then burning his hand. Joe loses control, breaks free, and destroys the nightclub. No one is injured, and Jill guides Joe back to his cage, but a judge nonetheless orders Joe shot. Max finally realizes that Joe and Jill "don't belong here" and arranges to smuggle them and Gregg back home. On their way to a waiting freighter, they pass a burning orphanage and stop as Joe helps the couple rescue some trapped children. After this good deed, Joe is officially forgiven and allowed to return to Africa.

Mighty Joe Young's exaggeration and simplicity keep it from equaling the achievement of *King Kong,* but the changes do give the new film a distinctive, independent identity. With his slouch and low-hanging arms, Joe looks more like a real gorilla than Kong did, and numerous animated close-ups allow him to register curiosity, concern, and anger, while his bright eyes and expressive mouth further define a winning personality. True, Joe's cuteness sometimes goes too far, as when he sits in the back of a truck drumming his fingers on his knees, but, more important, the film evokes the desired emotions. Even reluctant viewers will find themselves rooting for Joe's survival and possibly shedding a tear or two at the climax.

Realizing that he needed an assistant, O'Brien typically followed his nature by hiring Ray Harryhausen, the young man who had first met his mentor nearly ten years before. "Most of Obie's time was, by necessity, consumed in planning and devising ways of doing the many complicated shots," Harryhausen recalls. "He only had time to actually animate four or five scenes. He animated several shots of the nightclub and two or three of the roping scenes."[49] Ultimately, Harryhausen did 80–85 percent of *Mighty Joe Young*'s animation.

One of the film's grips, Pete Peterson, also expressed an interest in animation, so O'Brien gave him a chance, and Peterson, who suffered from multiple sclerosis, revealed patience and skill. "Obie was *so* sympathetic to anyone who had an illness like Pete's," recalled Darlyne O'Brien. "Even if he hadn't been a good animator, I'm sure that Obie would have put him on the film. As it turned out, he was a *wonderful* animator."[50] Peterson's work can be seen in the piano act and Joe's escape in the truck, plus occasional shots elsewhere. Peterson married after completion of *Joe,* but his wife died three months later; O'Brien was bound to identify with Peterson's troubles, and, after Harryhausen left to make his own films, O'Brien and his new surrogate son continued to work as a team during the 1950s.

Part of O'Brien's time during preproduction was spent in debate with Merian Cooper. Don Shay records that O'Brien "wanted to have another ferocious gorilla escape from its attendants in the cellar [of the nightclub] and come up on stage where Jill Young is performing. Her screams were to have reached Joe, who was then to have broken out of his cage and engaged in a destructive battle with the other gorilla."[51] Cooper overruled O'Brien on this point, and rightly so, for this action—like many aspects of O'Brien's unproduced plots—lacks originality: It is too much like *Kong*'s theater scene, whereas Cooper's version omits the visual redundancy of a second gorilla, lets Joe's drunken stagger add to his personality, and ultimately arouses more sympathy for the animal.

For the film's climax, according to Harryhausen, O'Brien argued to have Joe and a second gorilla "let loose in San Francisco on top of a cable car, beating the heck out of one another as the cable car broke loose going down the hill!"[52] Cooper also rejected this visually striking but far-fetched idea and replaced it with the more emotionally involving orphanage sequence, even though it meant that the film lacked an all-out fight between giant creatures, something which O'Brien clearly desired.

Technically, *Mighty Joe Young* functions on a high level of accomplishment, with totally natural animated movements and the flawless knitting together of live and animated action in a single shot. The roping sequence is a fine example, as horsemen gallop across the screen in front of and behind Joe, tossing ropes over his head and being plucked off their mounts as they pass. Rapid editing among various camera positions further increases the excitement. Other highlights are Joe's destruction of the nightclub, which includes considerable interaction with people and lions, and the rescue at the orphanage, which faces the major challenge of combining fire with animation.

These spectacular scenes are supplemented with quiet but affecting moments, as in the epilogue of Max watching a filmed greeting from Africa. At first Joe just stares into the camera. Then he sees Jill and Gregg waving and, after awkwardly trying it himself, finally catches the rhythm and waves a friendly goodbye to Max and the film's viewers. *Mighty Joe Young* also manages to avoid *King Kong*'s few flaws, such as the dummies that fall limply into the ravine and the mechanical head and foot used for close-ups, but unfortunately the miniature humans and vehicles used in several shots are unconvincing.

O'Brien and his staff filled *Mighty Joe Young* with bits of action, many of which were added during the animation. In Joe's first scene, the script has him push over a lion's cage, which breaks, freeing the occupant. The film, instead, has him smash the cage open with his fists, trip on it as he pursues the lion, and throw a rock at the escaping feline. In another addition, during the roping sequence Joe tackles a horse and picks the rider up by his foot. The orphanage climax is extended beyond what the screenplay includes by having Joe save the last child a second time, when the building's wall starts to fall. The shooting script was already full of events, but these and other additions further contribute to the film's richness of detail and to the gorilla's personality.

For this film, O'Brien again used large glass paintings to fill out the settings and miniature projection to combine live action with animation, but less extensively than in *King Kong,* for *Mighty Joe Young* is narrower in scope—there are no prehistoric beasts or dense jungle settings. However, production costs in general had risen since 1933 and the film cost far more than its predecessor. In addition, as Harryhausen explains, "all the overhead of the studio got dumped on our picture," which made it appear to be even more expensive.[53]

As a result, *Mighty Joe Young* did not make much of a profit, so discussions about a possible sequel (*Joe Meets Tarzan*) did not progress far. But O'Brien won an Academy Award for the film's special effects and he managed to interest producer Jesse Lasky and Paramount Pictures in another of his stories, known variously as *Emilio and Guloso, El Toro Estrella,* and *Valley of the Mist.* This is the first of O'Brien's original stories to include a human interest element, one resembling that in *Mighty Joe Young,* only with the sex and nationality changed: A Mexican boy raises a pet bull, but unlike Joe Young, this animal is normal sized. In need of money, Emilio's father sells the bull, Guloso, to a producer of bullfights. Knowing that this means death for his friend, the boy is distraught.

Onto this situation, O'Brien rather awkwardly grafted the remnants of *Gwangi.* Emilio investigates tales told by the local Indians, discovers the inevitable valley of dinosaurs, and—with the Indians' help—captures an allosaurus, which he intends to trade for the life of his pet. When plans go awry, the dinosaur escapes and enters the ring, where Guloso kills it after a furious fight. In one version of the story the bull then dies of its wounds, but in another it gets to live.

Because O'Brien reportedly wrote this story in 1944, it very likely influenced *Mighty Joe Young*. By the same token, O'Brien himself had probably been influenced by "My Friend Bonito," a similar tale about a boy and his bull—but no dinosaurs—written by Robert Flaherty; in 1941, while O'Brien was preparing *Gwangi* at RKO, "Bonito" had been set for inclusion in Orson Welles's never-finished RKO film, *It's All True*. At any rate, O'Brien spent six months preparing *Emilio and Guloso*, with Harryhausen again assisting, but money problems arose and Lasky terminated the project.

O'Brien later sold his story to producers Edward and William Nassour, whose all-animated short feature, *Emilio and His Magical Bull*, did not appear until 1975, and then only briefly. Incidentally, another story about a boy and his bull, also without dinosaurs, was filmed as *The Brave One* (1956) and won an Academy Award, which caused turmoil in Hollywood when its credited author, Robert Rich, turned out to be the then-blacklisted Dalton Trumbo. It remains unclear whether Trumbo conceived his plot independently or derived it from either O'Brien's or Flaherty's.

Around 1952, Ray Harryhausen told O'Brien that he had a chance to work on a low-budget project, *The Beast from 20,000 Fathoms*. Darlyne O'Brien recalled that the older man responded, "I would prefer to make better pictures. I don't want to make the smaller, cheaper pictures."[54] But O'Brien was still unwilling or unable to promote himself and, according to Darlyne, "he just sat back and waited, thinking that someone would come along with a story that they would want him to do. But nothing happened."[55] Cooper did contact O'Brien about filming H. G. Wells's *The Food of the Gods* and also considered using the new Cinerama process for a picture about events that occurred during the transfer of Kong from Skull Island to New York. Neither of these ideas moved much beyond the talking stage.

O'Brien was not financially secure and needed to work, so he eventually had to deal with the independent, low-budget producers who were making imitations of Harryhausen's *The Beast from 20,000 Fathoms*, but his luck was bad even in that realm. To the Nassour brothers, he sold another story spin-off from *Gwangi*, in which a rancher, accused of killing cattle and murdering a business rival, claims that a giant animal is actually responsible. When the deputy sheriff and an Indian companion investigate, they find and capture the creature, but on the way to town it escapes and terrorizes the citizens until the deputy kills it with an improvised spear. O'Brien, expecting that he would later be hired to do the animation, also sold his Gwangi model to the Nassours, whereupon they "promptly dismembered" the creature,[56] studied its construction, and supervised the animation themselves! Then, in publicity for *The Beast of Hollow Mountain* (1956), they rubbed salt in the wound by bragging about the originality of their "Regiscope" process.

The final screenplay eliminates the murder, adds a romantic rivalry, and spends so much time developing the characters' rather familiar problems that the dinosaur doesn't even appear until the last quarter of the film, at which point it conveniently resolves those problems. It also has the rancher do his own investigating and limits the scope of the climax by having the monster threaten only a few people in a cabin. Its new finale, however, is well-conceived, as the hero (Guy Madison) swings out over some quicksand to lure the creature to its death. Despite these changes, the juxtaposition of cowboys with an allosaurus remains pure O'Brien, and *The Beast of Hollow Mountain* may also reveal his influence in its Mexican setting, its references to native legends, and the supporting character of a poor Mexican boy.

Even working on a low budget, O'Brien would surely have created a far more convincing beast than the one the Nassours provided, which runs awkwardly and holds its floppy forearms like a begging dog's paws. In close shots, the creature repeatedly bares its teeth and waggles its unbelievably long tongue, but otherwise the model reveals little flexibility. Most of the time, animated shots are intercut with separate shots of the live action; when the two are combined, the background figures sometimes appear out of focus.

O'Brien had more success with producer Irwin Allen, who employed him to supervise the prehistoric sequences of his documentary *The Animal World* (1956), with Ray Harryhausen doing the animation. Of course, humans did not coexist with dinosaurs, but Allen wanted to include a little menace, so after the narrator states that man had not yet been created, he adds, "but if he had been—" and we see a brontosaurus pick up an animated cave man and walk out of the shot with him in its mouth, screaming. The film includes a confrontation between a brontosaurus and an allosaurus, but no fight. A brontosaurus egg hatches. A ceratosaurus kills a stegosaurus, then another ceratosaurus leaps into the shot, and as the two fight over the carcass they fall over a cliff (in live-action model footage). When a triceratops and a tyrannosaurus are about to fight, a volcano erupts, the ground shifts, and the tyrannosaurus falls into a newly opened crevasse—a cataclysm the film uses to represent the end of the dinosaur era.

"Irwin Allen said take all the stops out and make it bloodthirsty," recalls Harryhausen, "because he had a lot of shots in the picture of lions and tigers tearing animals to pieces . . . so I went completely wild, having a ceratosaurus rip off a big slab of a stegosaurus's flesh, dripping blood."[57] After a preview, however, Allen backed down and removed the gory shots, both animated and live action. Nevertheless, O'Brien and Harryhausen made this nine-minute slice of dinosaur life the most memorable portion of *The Animal World*.

In a frustrating twist of fate, O'Brien, who disdained the kind of low-budget film that Ray Harryhausen had begun making, next found himself working for the same producer, Jack Dietz, and director, Eugene Lourie, with whom Harryhausen had made *The Beast from 20,000 Fathoms*. According to Paul Mandel, Dietz initially hired Lourie to direct *The Black Scorpion* (1957), and Lourie contacted O'Brien and Pete Peterson to do the effects. The two were then "working out of Peterson's garage,"[58] so O'Brien was reduced to the improvised conditions that Harryhausen himself had recently escaped.

After some preliminary work, Lourie left the project and Edward Ludwig took over as director, but O'Brien and Peterson stayed, despite the short time (about three months) budgeted for the animation. The pair spent part of their working time in Mexico City. "We lived in a hotel rather than having an apartment," said Darlyne, "and we didn't come home with any money at all. But it was fun, it was worth going."[59] O'Brien, now in his seventies, supervised the effects for *Scorpion*, with Peterson doing the animation sitting down because of the pain caused by his illness.

Them, the popular 1954 movie about giant ants, provided the model for *The Black Scorpion*'s screenplay, but although O'Brien made no acknowledged contribution to the writing of *Scorpion*, aspects of the new film suggest that he had some input. Whereas the menaces in *Them* are mutations caused by atomic radiation, the giant scorpions are prehistoric creatures freed by an erupting volcano from their cavern far below the earth's surface. Other elements by now associated with O'Brien are the Mexican setting, the natives' superstitious belief in a "demon bull," and the climactic confrontation in a bullring. In both *Scorpion* and *The Beast of Hollow Mountain*, mysterious disappearances (of people in one case, cattle in the other) frighten the natives, and fearful cowboys desert their ranch. Each film also features an orphaned boy played by Mario Navarro; in addition, two other Mexican actors have roles in both pictures, which at least reveals that the producers were familiar with *Hollow Mountain*.

Although *The Black Scorpion*'s humans have little personality, the script's major weakness is the way characters often announce important revelations to each other. A local doctor tells the hero (Richard Denning) about a wound in the back of a victim's neck, the venom in his system, strange bacteria found in soil samples, and a large, clawed footprint. Later, the second male lead (Carlos Rivas) shows him a scorpion embedded in a piece of obsidian, a doctor from Mexico City offers more information, a military man reveals that some scorpions may have escaped from the sealed cavern, and a news broadcast announces that the largest beast has killed all the others and is headed for Mexico City. The film's failure to include scenes that dramatize these discoveries may be due partly to its low budget, but it also reveals the writers' limited imaginations.

But if the human actions lack vitality, the scenes with animation—the parts over which O'Brien and Peterson exerted control—look impressive and stir the imagination. In the scorpions' first appearance, as they kill three telephone linemen, we discover the threat posed by their massive size, their rapid movements, and the lethal sting in their raised tails. They also demonstrate the agility and strength of their front claws, plucking a man from his pole and hurling a truck into the distance. In one especially intimidating shot, a scorpion runs toward and over the camera. This builds into an attack on the ranch, then on the nearby town.

During the film's centerpiece sequence, the geologists played by Denning and Rivas (along with the boy, a stowaway) explore the cavern, eluding numerous scorpions and other, even more exotic, denizens of the shadowy depths. One scorpion kills an equally large worm-like creature, then an even bigger scorpion kills the first and devours the worm. Later, a trapdoor spider chases the boy, until killed by the men's gunfire. This thirteen-minute adventure in an alien world offers viewers an exciting range of horrifying encounters and bizarre images.

Before the film's climax, O'Brien and Peterson provide another striking scene as a railroad train crashes into a scorpion that straddles the tracks. Even though this event derives from one in *King Kong,* the turmoil that ensues has its own grotesque power: Scorpions swarm over the wrecked cars, grasping people in their claws and fighting among themselves. Finally, the remaining creature is lured into the stadium, where it uses its powerful claws to destroy several helicopters and tanks before being electrocuted.

Despite the film's low budget and the less-than-ideal working conditions, O'Brien and Peterson provided first-rate animation, but other factors sometimes undermine their efforts. The cavern sequence contains far too little interaction between the humans and the models, with the men reduced to watching events from the sidelines and taking pictures. Elsewhere, interaction usually occurs only in long shots that can include animated models of people. One shot of scorpions moving past the camera is used several times in the cavern to suggest a large mass of creatures, and the same shot turns up again during the train scene. Simple cost-cutting is probably to blame for these lapses.

In other scenes, the action feels incomplete or unresolved. The scorpions' attack on the town, for example, just fades out during the panic, and we never learn how the creatures were repelled. During the cavern sequence, whenever the men are threatened, the danger passes abruptly, and the attack on the train doesn't build to its climax, forcing the newscaster to fill in the gaps. In some shots that combine a scorpion with live action, the creature is seen as a giant silhouette, which suggests that the process work that would have matted the model into that space was never completed. These weaknesses give credence to a report that the film's producers ran out of funds and left the effects unfinished. Another weakness is the frequent use of a mechanical, constantly drooling, and totally unconvincing scorpion face.

O'Brien worked again with Eugene Lourie on a low-budget British film released in 1959, *Behemoth the Sea Monster* (U.S.: *The Giant Behemoth*). Producer David Diamond assigned the effects to a company headed by Jack Rabin and Louis DeWitt, who had contributed to *The Brave One* and *The Beast of Hollow Mountain*. They, in turn, subcontracted the animation to O'Brien and Peterson, who this time had even less money to work with and only about six weeks to do the animation.

Lourie modeled his screenplay for *Behemoth* on *The Beast from 20,000 Fathoms*. In both, a dinosaur emerges from the sea and terrorizes a major city; explosives cannot be used on the creatures for fear of contaminating the city (with germs in *Beast* and radioactivity here). Because the behemoth is already dying from its radioactive charge, scientists suggest hastening the process with a dose of radium. In the climax, a specially prepared torpedo is fired into the menace from a submarine, a situation taken from another of Ray Harryhausen's films, *It Came from Beneath the Sea* (1955). Also from *The Beast from 20,000 Fathoms* comes an eccentric, enthusiastic paleontologist (with lean Jack MacGowran replacing the avuncular Cecil Kellaway). Discarded, however, is the earlier film's attempt to explain the origin of its creature, which here simply exists.

Making *Behemoth* in England seems to have released Lourie's creativity as both director and screenwriter, for his noncreature scenes reveal a satisfying use of British-style documentary realism, with much on-location filming. At the same time, his visual style makes consistent use of tightly framed compositions and expressive camera angles, such as a high-angle shot with a woman in the foreground on the left, her fisherman father on the shore below in the center, and, on the right, his boat and a rock that counterbalances the woman's form.

The film takes the time to show its hero, Steve Karnes (Gene Evans), using a photographic process to test some specimens of fish for radioactive contamination. This activity is interesting to watch and provides the kind of dramatized discovery of information that *The Black Scorpion* had avoided. Also noteworthy is the concise depiction of a ferry's departure, which cuts together a series of well-chosen details that summarize the action and identify the passengers. This sequence could stand alone as an effective documentary, but here it takes on a poignant overtone because the viewer assumes—rightly—that the behemoth will soon disrupt this familiar, orderly activity.

Lourie gives his characters personality, while avoiding exaggeration. For example, he contrasts the American scientist's impulsive impatience with the discreet diplomacy and quiet seriousness of his British counterpart (Andre Morell), but does so without making them opposites or putting them in conflict. As written and acted, the film's humans are often distinctive and always natural. In keeping with this approach, Lourie avoids involving his main characters in a romance.

One rather original plot point is the fact that this creature carries a charge of electricity, which projects its radioactivity outward, burning anyone nearby. This characteristic allows the behemoth to kill people without making physical contact with them, which in turn permits Lourie to involve the beast throughout the story—despite the very limited effects budget—by focusing solely on the victims' reactions. Of course, it would be more interesting and dramatic if the creature were shown at these times, but the compromise serves its desired purpose and is preferable to avoiding such scenes entirely.

Later, when we do see the animated creature roaming London, its radioactive aura remains the main danger, so Lourie can intercut animated shots with live action and avoid the added expense of shots that involve both. The radiation is not projected continuously, however, and on one occasion the animal's neck pushes against the top of a building, followed by a live-action shot of a wall landing on some people. Only once does the behemoth attack anyone directly, but because it picks up an occupied automobile in its mouth, then tosses it into the river, a model vehicle is used in a totally animated long shot. The few images that combine the creature with live action are unimpressive, with the creature placed in the background, behind a building.

Overall, the alternation between dramatic angles of frightened citizens and close shots of the beast's head or side give the sequence energy and create a limited sense of involvement. The animal model itself appears to have less flexibility than it should, or else O'Brien and Peterson lacked the time to provide fluid movement. Nevertheless, the animation is always at least competent and makes the best of the limited activity granted the creature, which mostly just strides and roars.

While guiding the giant behemoth around London, and especially when the creature's weight shatters a bridge and plunges it into the Thames, O'Brien must have recalled *The Lost World* and the very similar climax he had animated more than thirty years before. Once the originator, O'Brien was now—in his seventies—reduced to cutting corners on a deliberate copy of a film made by his own protegé. Under the circumstances, he surely felt elated when producer-director Irwin Allen revealed his plans for a major remake of *The Lost World* and hired O'Brien as technical adviser. The two had previously collaborated on *The Animal World,* so Allen knew the virtues of animation and understood what was involved. At last, after a decade in the wilderness of low-budget productions, O'Brien could envision his career coming full circle with one last elaborate feature. Perhaps his patience would finally be rewarded.

Allen's production was backed by 20th Century–Fox, which in 1959 released the popular *Journey to the Center of the Earth*. The studio's executives no doubt saw their new film as a follow-up to that success, and they wanted to have it in theaters the following summer. That meant that Allen had to work fast, faster than O'Brien's time-consuming techniques would allow. *Journey to the Center of the Earth* had used live lizards instead of animated models, and that hadn't hurt its box-office reception, so why not—for the sake of efficiency—adopt that method? At some point, Allen became convinced and would not be dissuaded, although O'Brien prepared drawings and paintings in an attempt to convince the producer of his error. Shortly after the film's release, O'Brien told an interviewer, in his typically reserved way, "They claim that the live technique looks smoother, that animation is jerky. I don't think so."[60]

Ultimately, O'Brien had no influence on the film's special effects, the absurdity of which is heightened by the fact that lizards with appendages attached are explicitly identified as dinosaurs. In addition, the characters are unconvincing and the film itself condescends to its subject. Allen, probably hoping to make a sequel, even omits the original's climax, ending the film before Professor Challenger (Claude Rains) returns to London with a baby tyrannosaurus. "The story is completely changed," O'Brien told an interviewer. "You wouldn't recognize it."[61] All in all, the fact that O'Brien's name appeared in the credits of *The Lost World* (1960) simply aggravated his by-now substantial wounds.

But instead of nursing those wounds, Willis O'Brien—as he had so many times before—set to work and wrote a new story that he could animate, one that incorporated some of his rejected ideas for *Mighty Joe Young: King Kong vs. Frankenstein.* This contrived plot has two sets of showmen separately discover Kong and the fifty-foot

Frankenstein Monster and bring them to San Francisco, where the creatures break loose and fight on top of a cable car. Producer John Beck purchased the story, then drifted out of contact.

Meanwhile, Linwood Dunn, who had contributed to the optical effects of *King Kong*, hired O'Brien to work on *It's a Mad, Mad, Mad, Mad World* (1963). For this long and rather ponderous comedy, director Stanley Kramer planned to use animation during an elaborate climax in which the characters dangle from a loose fire escape. At about this time, O'Brien learned that *King Kong vs. Frankenstein* had found its way to Japan and been filmed as *King Kong vs. Godzilla*, with the monsters played by men in clumsy, unconvincing suits. An English-dubbed version, with numerous scenes added by John Beck, was released in 1963.

These two events marked the end of O'Brien's life and career. On 8 November 1962, he suffered a heart attack and died. In familiar fashion, he had placed his confidence in someone who had let him down. In equally familiar fashion, he was depending on that person to put together a production that would give him work and a creative outlet. He was still the dependent independent, the vulnerable youth who decades before had lost his horses and his furs to some acquaintances. At the same time, at the age of seventy-six, he was still adapting, still optimistic, still nurturing his imagination. He never retired and was just starting to work on *It's a Mad, Mad, Mad, Mad World* when the end came.

Reporters rarely interviewed the taciturn Willis O'Brien. However, during the 1950s he sketched out numerous ideas for films, ranging from mere fragments to more fully developed plots, and in some of those which have been published[62] he unconsciously reveals himself far more clearly than any interview would have done. First, though, one must pare away the borrowings from films made and unmade: the entrepreneurs who hunt for animals to exhibit and the cowboys who rope elephants in Burma, the Yeti who saves a human friend by holding him above water, the bearlike creature that shakes a cable car until its occupants fall to their deaths, and the captured dinosaur that is pulled in a portable trap on wheels. These situations reveal O'Brien casting about for a new success by placing modified fragments of his cinematic past in fresh contexts.

At times, however, O'Brien breaks away from the formula that he helped define, and when that happens the inner man shines through. Children appear several times as key figures in the imaginings of this man in his seventies, and here O'Brien forgets about dinosaurs, concentrating instead on the boys themselves. Nothing about these sketches suggests that O'Brien was dwelling on his own lost sons; rather, he seems to be casting back to his own youth, while embodying in these figures an idealized image of his adult nature.

In "Bounty," two paragraphs of semiautobiographical musings, a lonely, independent twelve-year-old who had been a farmhand finds himself on the San Francisco waterfront. He "thought that he might like to work on one of the ships and travel to far-off lands, but his stomach told him he was hungry." In this one line, O'Brien concisely reveals his life-long attraction to the adventurous fantasies that real life withheld, and the continually conflicting pull of mundane needs.

Another such character, a Mexican boy obviously inspired by the one in *Emilio and Guloso*, possesses a "persistent optimism" much like O'Brien's own. Despite poverty and numerous tribulations, Pepe's "heart was pure," and therefore things always seemed "to work out miraculously" for him, if not for the man who created him. A different story contains one of the more distinctive figures that O'Brien had hoped to animate: the gentle, childlike Umbah, a fifteen-foot giant with a "simple heart." Also surprisingly childlike is the Yeti encountered in still another tale. This quality of simplicity and purity extends to O'Brien's more sympathetic adult males and their relationships with animals. One man keeps a giant eagle as a pet and another has his face licked by a brontosaurus (as the farce of O'Brien's early short films evolves into a kind of sentimentality). These docile creatures offer no threat to their sensitive friends.

People, however, are a different matter. Interaction with humans works out well in the idealized life of little Pepe, but O'Brien's adult males—like the boy on the waterfront—seek escape from the real world, from responsibility and other people. They look for refuge in their own imaginations, in the secure affection of animals, and in nature and solitude. "It seemed like a man ought to be able to do about what he wanted, away off in the country," thinks a character named Andy, "but he guessed people made everybody's business their own in this day and age." So he mounts his giant eagle and flies on its back to the mountains. "This was a new experience for Andy, and he enjoyed every minute of it," writes O'Brien, enviously.

Such adventurousness, however, represents only one aspect of O'Brien, an aspect that resided more in his mind than in his deeds. The man's internal conflict emerges clearly in the contrasting main characters of "Matilda." Elmos is "shy" and a "dreamer," a man who "didn't want his dreaming disturbed by conversation" and has a "penchant for making pets of animals." The essentially passive Elmos is paired with his friend Horace, a promoter who has "a flair for fantastic ideas," but whenever Elmos tries one of Horace's plans, it fails. During their main adventure, the two find themselves stranded on an island and Horace, "ever the optimist," looks forward to the unknown, while Elmos misses "his quiet life at home."

In reality, O'Brien endured the vicissitudes of life and work with patience and humor, immediately rebuilding his web each time it was destroyed, adapting and accepting rather than setting forth aggressively. Yet he was neither impossibly virtuous nor naively blind. Frustration was not foreign to him, and he clearly felt the ironies and inequities of his career. At times, he even let it show, as when a model–maker asked him if the miniature cranes he had built for *Behemoth* were good enough and O'Brien replied, "They're too goddamned good."[63]

Responding to publicity gimmicks, such as the "Regiscope" animation process used by the Nassours on *The Beast of Hollow Mountain,* O'Brien wrote in a foreword to his Yeti story, "If my third-dimension animation requires a name, it could be 'Origimation,' since I was the first in this field." In this story, O'Brien states that "greed continues to be a constant companion" of the explorers, and the showmen who embody that quality are suitably punished. An even more explicit revelation of anger and wish-fulfillment appears in "The Last of the Oso Si-Papu," in which the villain is a producer of low-budget monster movies who wants to film a real creature to save the cost of special effects. This man hijacks the animal from the scientists who captured it and in the climax is killed, as it were, by his own cost-cutting greed.

Willis O'Brien couldn't help but see himself as a lonely dreamer buffeted by the selfish materialism of Hollywood's film industry, but bitterness never controlled him. The fact that O'Brien's career had peaked in 1933 was not for him the tragedy it might have been for many others, because he lived life in his own way and seems to have placed limited demands on existence. If good things and bad things are equally arbitrary, one simply takes what comes and carries on, without overreacting to either the good or the bad. If this means not savoring the heights of elation, it also means not suffering the depths of depression. What O'Brien had, instead, was satisfaction in the moment. His glass, more often than not, was half full, not half empty. "He was," recalled his widow twenty years after his death, "very young for his age, and childlike, enjoyed playing and having fun, and I did, too. I can't find anyone else like him."[64]

He may not have amassed a fortune, but Willis O'Brien left much behind at his passing. He created one motion picture destined to endure as an unmatched master-piece, and others that still offer distinctive rewards. In the process, he originated and perfected a new type of adventure film, one that continues to fill viewers with excitement and awe. He also left an indelible imprint on the memories of those who knew him, including Ray Harryhausen, who carried on O'Brien's legacy: his techniques, his vision of fantasy, and his personal good humor.

Special effects master Ray Harryhausen with a tyrannosaurus from *The Animal World*, the 1956 film he worked on with pathbreaking animator Willis O'Brien.

CHAPTER 3

Ray Harryhausen

Ray Harryhausen occupies a unique position in motion picture history. Although neither a director nor a scriptwriter, he has exerted far more control over his films than most of the directors and writers with whom he worked. Without this "Creator of Special Visual Effects," there would have been no *20 Million Miles to Earth* (1957), no *7th Voyage of Sinbad* (1958), no *Jason and the Argonauts* (1963)—and the world of fantasy film would be the lesser for it. After Harryhausen's retirement in 1987, at the age of sixty-seven, we have the complete career of a man whose willpower and individuality brought to life an impressive body of work.

Like Willis O'Brien, his inspiration and mentor, Harryhausen brought the illusion of life to three-dimensional models through animation, then caused those figures to interact with living humans. But Harryhausen achieved the extensive career that had eluded O'Brien; ultimately, he managed the almost impossible task of fusing the worlds of technician and artist. Recognizing that large budgets would not be forthcoming, he developed procedures that could, for the most part, be accomplished cheaply, quickly, and by one person alone. He also joined with a compatible businessman, Charles H. Schneer. For a quarter of a century, these two initiated projects and produced them independently, often with the financial backing of Columbia Pictures.

Driven by a need to give form to his mental images of exotic fantasy and wishing only to create the kinds of films that he himself wanted to see, Harryhausen accepted the need for compromise and, therefore, substantially achieved his goal. By satisfying his own needs, he admitted viewers into his private world of sights and experiences, which in turn stimulate the viewer's imagination. Harryhausen embodies the technician as generous visionary; author Ray Bradbury, Harryhausen's friend since boyhood, has aptly praised "the delicious monsters that moved in his head and out of his fingers and into our eternal dreams."[1] In addition, as Harryhausen's career developed, the entertainer evolved into an artist who expressed his complex personality and outlook.

Unlike most filmmakers, who must collaborate with their actors, Harryhausen is a God-like creator who constructs his "stars" and their performances. But despite such total power, he is no brooding eccentric confronting the mysteries of the universe in a mountaintop tower. Instead, he is modest and practical, yet the ambitious goals and the solitary creative struggle do exist, in a very modern blend of the ethereal and the mundane, of passion and patience. However, even the pragmatic technician withholds many details of his methods. "You'll no longer be interested in the magician if he gives away all of his secrets," he asserts.[2]

The artist within Harryhausen, the inner, intuitive man, is only fleetingly glimpsed behind the careful planner and is perhaps vague even to himself. In a rare moment of introspection, Harryhausen once said, "I've been spending my life trying to duplicate a life-like action. Maybe I've got a Frankenstein complex. Maybe I'm an alchemist who wants to make the perfect Homunculus. I don't know. But I wouldn't attempt to analyze this desire. I find that if you analyze things too much, you analyze yourself out of existence. You can analyze *anything* out of existence!"[3] Paradoxically, Harryhausen's work involves the very essence of analysis—analysis of movement, of muscle flexing, of expressiveness. He can, in fact, analyze anything into existence! But for Harryhausen, analysis is a method of creation, a means to an end, whereas he wants viewers to respond with a spontaneous and emotional "appreciation of the 'wondrous.' "[4]

What we know about Harryhausen's early years helps clarify his attraction to solitary work, his blending of art and technology, and his compulsion to control the worlds in his films and the world of the filmmaker. An only child, born in Los Angeles on 29 June 1920, Harryhausen spent much of his youth either alone or with his parents. They encouraged his interest in dinosaurs and lost civilizations by taking him to the LaBrea Tar Pits and the Museum of Natural History, and they bought him a book illustrated with Charles R. Knight's dramatic paintings of prehistoric life. Somewhat shy and introspective, the young Harryhausen must have enjoyed the secure excitement of these ancient, imagined worlds. An ability to sketch was redirected by a school assignment to build models of old Spanish missions, which produced "a yen for three-dimensional objects rather than flat ones"[5] and a satisfaction in construction that links him to his father, a machinist.

Harryhausen combined his varied interests by building prehistoric dioramas. Then, in 1933, he saw *King Kong*. "I came out of the theater stunned and haunted,"[6] he recalls, and "haven't been the same since."[7] Somehow, his models and settings had come to life. *Kong* inspired an interest in film technique, but less as a way of expressing thought and feeling than as a means of giving life to his dioramas, of showing the unshowable.

After learning about single-frame animation, Harryhausen borrowed a 16mm camera and, with an improvised cave bear model, shot his first footage. His father helped build the articulated skeleton, an old coat of his mother's provided the fur, and the family garage became a studio. "It was a thrill to see the object move by itself," says Harryhausen,[8] and that thrill—that feeling of power—would be conveyed, years later, by the magicians in his Sinbad films. When Sokurah, in *The 7th Voyage of Sinbad,* uses the force of his will to invest a skeleton with life-like movement, he probably evokes Harryhausen's own feelings of control and of achievement. But Harryhausen went further. In one early experiment, the young filmmaker himself interacted with the giant bear. Later, the adult Harryhausen appeared in test footage for the unmade *The Elementals* and for *It Came from Beneath the Sea* (1955). Convenience was no doubt his motive, but the self-sufficient boy and man must also have enjoyed inhabiting his own created world.

In 1939, Harryhausen met Willis O'Brien, whose "interest and encouragement," he recalls, saw him "through many a difficult period."[9] The serious-minded young man was already obsessed with animation: "If I wasn't doing something, learning something, reading something useful, I felt that I was wasting time."[10] He therefore took college courses in acting, in art and anatomy, and in film editing and art direction. While "doing puppet shows and stringing puppets for a doll company,"[11] he built models with his father and filmed them in the family garage. Finally, he got a full-time job doing animation for several of George Pal's Puppetoon shorts, including *Hoola*

Boola, Jasper and the Watermelons, and *Tulips Shall Grow.* Meanwhile, he began his own film, *Evolution,* but left it unfinished when he saw the "Rite of Spring" segment of Disney's *Fantasia* (1940), which covered similar territory.

According to a friend from Pal's crew, Harryhausen never grew up: "He's just a kid at heart."[12] At the same time, though, he never had a "normal" childhood or adolescence. Ray Bradbury recalls, "We used to talk for hours on the phone, and we'd never talk about girls—we'd talk about dinosaurs!"[13] Even at the age of twenty-seven, Harryhausen's social life was "negligible. My main interest was my job."[14] To director Eugene Lourie, the thirty-two-year-old Harryhausen was "a very old, young man."[15] Not surprisingly, he remained a bachelor until he was forty-two. This is not to say that Harryhausen was antisocial. "He was not gregarious," explains a different member of Pal's crew, "but he was fun to be around and laughed easily."[16] His interest, however, was not in reality or the exploration of human nature through art and literature but in creating a private world and controlling an illusion of life.

While working for Pal, Harryhausen's "real desire was to be involved with a serious feature fantasy film,"[17] but the difficulty of achieving that goal was dramatized in 1942, when Willis O'Brien joined the Puppetoon crew. Harryhausen's pleasure at working with his idol must have been muted by the fact that the only full-time professional in his chosen field had settled for the same job as a novice.

During World War II, Harryhausen spent about three years in the army, making training films until his discharge in 1945. Back in Los Angeles, he bought some outdated 16mm film and animated four nursery rhymes: "Little Miss Muffet," "Old Mother Hubbard," "The Queen of Hearts," and "Humpty Dumpty." To these he added a brief introduction, in which Mother Goose makes a movie projector appear and uses it to present the scenes, a situation that—by blending film, magic, and storytelling—suggests Harryhausen's view of his activity. A nontheatrical distributor then bought the eleven-minute *Mother Goose Stories* (1946) for sale to schools and libraries.

In 1947, Willis O'Brien hired Harryhausen as his assistant on *Mighty Joe Young* (1949). Under O'Brien's supervision, he did 80–85 percent of the film's animation. It was "a long-awaited dream come true"[18]—with one disturbing aspect. According to a friend from that period, "I'd never heard him complain about anything before, but he'd have tears in his eyes. 'I can't work,' he'd say. 'It's just impossible!' He couldn't do anything because of the unions! He couldn't light a scene—he'd have to have an electrician and two gaffers. . . . He couldn't paint a puppet, because that was a union job, too. He was terribly upset."[19] Not only did this assembly-line approach hinder creativity, but it made the end-product far too expensive.

After completing *Mighty Joe Young,* Harryhausen received a taste of the frustration O'Brien had long endured. He assisted in O'Brien's futile preparations for *Valley of the Mist,* while his sketches and test reel for a production of H. G. Wells's *The War of the Worlds* aroused no studio interest. So he continued to hone his skills by making more shorts, this time with narration written by his former drama teacher, Charlott Knight. In *Little Red Riding Hood* (1949), Harryhausen gives the wolf a muscular, slinky stride that anticipates his saber-toothed tiger in *Sinbad and the Eye of the Tiger.* The film also reveals a wariness of violence: the wolf doesn't eat Grandma, and he dies off-screen. An amusingly gawky bird in *Hansel and Gretel* (1951) predates the phororhacos of *Mysterious Island* by ten years, and the image of Hansel locked in a cage returns in *The 7th Voyage of Sinbad.* In *Rapunzel* (1951), Harryhausen varies his usual long and medium shots with a few close-ups, a subjective shot, and a dramatic moment when a character strides so close to the camera that an image of her hand holding a pair of scissors fills the screen.

Then chance, or fate, introduced Harryhausen to Jack Dietz and Hal Chester, independent producers who had a script for a low-budget picture about a sea monster called *The Monster from Beneath the Sea*. In June 1951, a story by Ray Bradbury had appeared in the *Saturday Evening Post*. "The Beast from 20,000 Fathoms" (later retitled "The Fog Horn") told of a lonely sea creature's attraction to an isolated lighthouse, which, in confusion and frustration, it destroys. Months later, Dietz and Chester asked Bradbury to revise *The Monster from Beneath the Sea;* he declined the job, but noted a similarity between the script and his story. As a result, the producers bought the film rights to the story, which they integrated into the finished film. Dietz and Chester also adopted Bradbury's title. In addition, the film's rhedosaurus closely resembled the *Post's* illustration by James R. Bingham, except that Harryhausen made the head and forearms larger.

The Beast from 20,000 Fathoms (1953) also owes a debt to *The Thing* (1951), because both films begin at an Arctic military post. *The Thing,* however, featured an alien from outer space that remained in the Arctic, while *The Beast* borrowed from *King Kong* (successfully re-released in 1952) by making its creature prehistoric and bringing it to Manhattan. *The Arctic Giant* (1942) may also have provided inspiration. In this Superman cartoon, scientists discover a frozen prehistoric creature; after thawing out in Metropolis, the beast breaks through a building, steps on cars, and causes the collapse of a bridge.

Before employing Harryhausen, Dietz and Chester hired set designer Eugene Lourie to direct. Lourie supervised a week of location filming in New York City, then shot the rest of the live action in California, after which Harryhausen spent about six months doing the special effects. The small budget limited what he could accomplish, but Harryhausen "found it a fortunate experience because it taught me to design and achieve certain effects without going into very costly processes."[20] To save time and money, he animated the model creature in front of rear-projected, live-action shots, which eliminated the need for much postproduction laboratory work.

The Beast from 20,000 Fathoms delays introducing its characters and basic situation by adopting a semidocumentary style, with a narrator intoning about "Operation Experiment" over shots of airplanes and servicemen. Not in the shooting script, this opening emphasizes the experiment—the test dropping of an atomic bomb—so the introduction of the film's true subject will surprise viewers. It also establishes a realistic context for the fantastic events to come and lets the producers pad the film with cheap stock footage. More narration was added to identify Professor Tom Nesbitt (Paul Christian) and Colonel Evans (Kenneth Tobey), a task the script had overlooked. The documentary style disappears when Nesbitt and another man investigate the explosion's effects. After they glimpse the dinosaur, its movements start an avalanche, which knocks Nesbitt unconscious and kills the other man. Rescued, Nesbitt is shipped to a New York hospital. So far, the characters are just bundled-up, anonymous figures seen in static long shots, but the brief views of the monster have impact. Usually, it appears behind a curtain of snow, then strides quickly out of sight.

In the film's main section, Nesbitt tries to prove the truth of his story. Of course, the viewers have also seen the creature, so we *know* that he's right, but the characters keep us interested. As Nesbitt, Paul Christian has a straightforward and pleasantly honest manner. That alone would not be enough, but he is supported by Cecil Kellaway's charm as Dr. Elson, a paleontologist; by Kenneth Tobey's firmness as Colonel Evans; and by Donald Woods's vitality as a Coast Guard officer. In the role of Lee Hunter, Dr. Elson's assistant, Paula Raymond conveys a sincerity that helps transcend stereotype. The dialogue also gives the characters dimension, as when Lee Hunter says, "I make coffee strong enough to enter the Olympics," and Colonel Evans, wary of being thought crazy, jokes that "eagles on a straitjacket are not regulation uniforms." The comments of two lighthouse keepers neatly reverse our expectations: The old man mentions hearing a new song he liked, and the youth waxes nostalgic about old ballads "that warm ya even when the fog is a foot thick."

In one satisfying scene, Nesbitt and Lee examine drawings of dinosaurs to identify the one he saw. Nesbitt notes that he is an atomic scientist and she a paleontologist. "Between us," he says, "we span the ages. You deal with the past, I with the future." When she responds, "Look how uncomplicated the past was," he adds, "And how bright the future can be." The comment about their professions has shifted gracefully into a hint at mutual attraction, and the actors support this implication with their delivery and the pause that follows. "Well," Lee finally says, "let's get back to the present," and they look at more drawings. At the scene's end, Lee says, "Phone me if anything exciting happens." Nesbitt replies, "I'll phone you even if nothing happens." This line sounds like the kind of flirtation he might indulge in with any attractive woman, but it could also be the comment of someone truly interested in knowing her better. Thanks to such moments, their romance seems less like a plot requirement and more like the interaction of recognizably real people.

The rhedosaurus appears only three times during this central section. In a scene of it attacking a ship, the script describes only two shots of the beast: one of its head, seen through the pilot house window, and a final one of it overturning the vessel. Harryhausen provides more, including an impressive entrance as its head rises in the foreground and two views of the ship's destruction. During the lighthouse sequence, Harryhausen develops a poetic quality by placing the animal in silhouette. The creature's third appearance occurs after Dr. Elson descends in a diving bell to find it. This sequence develops an emotional pull, as we enjoy Elson's pleasure at seeing alive what he previously knew only in fossil form, while we also anxiously anticipate his expected loss. Unfortunately, although Elson says he can see only the monster's leg and shoulder, we view the entire creature in diorama-like long shots that prevent us from sharing Elson's sense of claustrophobia. Other shots (not in the script) do present Elson's perspective by showing the creature's head as it moves toward the camera. Here, Harryhausen again gave the producers more than the script demanded, but the extra shots do not always fit the scene's dramatic needs.

When Elson dies, the filmmakers wisely trade spectacle for feeling: Instead of seeing the bell destroyed, we stay on shipboard as communication stops, which leads to a scene in the museum as Lee reacts to Elson's absence. Here, she cries in Nesbitt's arms and he comforts her. This—plus a quick kiss before Nesbitt leaves to kill the monster and an embrace afterward—is as far as the romance develops. Such restraint adds to the relationship's believability.

The loss of Elson, the film's most likeable character, signals a general loss of contact with the characters as people. From here on, spectacle dominates as the film jumps rapidly from place to place and person to person. When the monster climbs ashore in lower Manhattan, anonymous figures flee or are killed. After a news broadcast becomes narration over impersonal stock footage, Colonel Evans learns that the creature's blood carries a "virulent disease," so shooting and explosions must be avoided. Then, Nesbitt reemerges to suggest firing a radioactive isotope into the beast's open wound.

As the rhedosaurus tromps through the city streets it shakes a car here, eats a policeman there, and knocks over a building or two. Harryhausen's animation of this is smooth and detailed, with effective visual touches. One striking shot, not called for by the script, shows the monster from a low angle turning away and swishing its tail close to the camera. At night, a spotlight moves restlessly across the creature, and there are dramatic flashes when the animal touches some high-voltage wires. Harryhausen also provides more complex images than the script demands. In one case, we see the monster's jaws grasp a policeman and pick him up, whereas the script has that part of the action occur off-screen. Two incidents in the screenplay, however, do not appear in the film. In one, a young woman—"partially dressed, evidently having just taken a shower"—is shocked when the beast's head appears at her window; in the other, the monster tears the Brooklyn Bridge apart.

Only when one recalls Kong's New York quest for Ann Darrow does this film's weakness become clear: The rhedosaurus has no purpose or goal as it wanders about, and when it stands amid the curlicues of a roller coaster, it has nothing to do but chew the scenery. In the script's version of this climax, the beast dramatically, and pathetically, becomes tangled in the coaster's collapsing girders. When Nesbitt and a sharpshooter set out with the isotope, the sharpshooter is crushed by falling debris, so Nesbitt does the fatal deed himself. Meanwhile, a fire starts, and Colonel Evans rushes to Nesbitt's rescue. Owing to Harryhausen's suggestions, the film offers a more elaborate finale in which the girders do not collapse around the monster. Seeking a clear shot, Nesbitt and the sharpshooter (Lee Van Cleef) ride the roller coaster to a high position, then get out to take aim. The isotope hits its target, and, as the beast's writhings jar the structure, the coaster breaks free and races wildly along the track, crashing and starting the fire. The two men climb down, avoiding both the fire and the monster.

This sequence has some impact, but it never creates a strong sense of confrontation or even substantial risk, because events rarely feel connected to each other. From the moment the men run to the roller coaster until they stop and load the rifle, we have fourteen shots of them and the people watching but none of the beast; with the menace thus omitted, the segment feels prolonged. When Van Cleef aims and fires, he does so quickly, with no suspenseful obstacles to overcome. The film then intercuts between the empty coaster rushing along the track and the men walking the opposite way, but the car does not endanger the men and the monster receives only one shot of the thirteen used, so the editing creates little suspense. After the car merely falls off a broken end of the track, Lourie intercuts between the beast reacting to the isotope and the men climbing down, but the monster has no impact on the men and their need to avoid the fire lacks urgency.

This climax doesn't build consistent excitement, but the sights we see do hold considerable interest, thanks to their novelty. At the end, the film is turned over to Harryhausen's beast, which finally has something meaningful to do. It circles, falls onto its elbows, rears up for a final scream, then collapses and is still. The rhedosaurus had never been a sympathetic monster, but it is sad to see an animal in pain. Appropriately, the final shot is of the creature, not the human survivors.

Dietz and Chester grabbed a quick profit by selling *The Beast from 20,000 Fathoms* to Warner Bros. which, after adding a new musical score and one shot of a ballet performance, made a much bigger profit. Meanwhile, Harryhausen returned to his fairy tales. *King Midas* (1953)—which includes a malevolent-looking, bald-headed magician who anticipates Sokurah in *7th Voyage of Sinbad*—demonstrates Harryhausen's increasing visual skill. One dynamic sequence, of Midas testing his golden touch, builds from long shots to close-ups of his hand entering the frame to change a series of objects into gold.

Harryhausen was working on another fairy tale when Charles Schneer contacted him. The producer, Harryhausen recalls, "was interested in making something new and different from the normal type of adventure films."[21] Schneer's idea of "new and different" was to have a monster from the sea attack a city! Specifically, he wanted a giant octopus to pull down San Francisco's Golden Gate Bridge, an event similar to the Brooklyn Bridge sequence omitted from *The Beast.* The live-action octopus/shark fight seen in *The Beast* may have inspired the use of an octopus, an idea reinforced by the giant squid in Disney's *20,000 Leagues under the Sea* (1954). The new film even used the same working title as *The Beast,* but its final title—*It Came from Beneath the Sea*—derives from the science-fiction film *It Came from Outer Space* (1953). Working with an even lower budget than he had on *The Beast,* Harryhausen saved animation time by giving the octopus fewer than its natural eight tentacles. As he explains, "Time is money and the more time one can save the better."[22] Money was also saved by including more stock footage than *The Beast* had, which gives the film a cut-rate, padded look.

Like its predecessor, *It Came from Beneath the Sea* (1955) starts in documentary style, with a narrator discussing atom-powered submarines, which again misdirects viewers before the first encounter with the creature. Unfortunately, this script never discards the crutch of using narration to provide information. "What was the nature of that nameless substance found caught in the damaged diving plane?" asks the anonymous voice. "A substance so strange, so inexplicable and alarming, that the best minds in the nation had to be called upon to solve the problem. Behind the guarded door . . . three people met." The presence of this device makes the writers so lazy that they sometimes avoid dramatizing events even when narration isn't used. We first learn about a newly devised torpedo, for example, *while* it is being loaded onto the submarine. As a result, the film becomes a fragmented series of highlights and not an evolving story.

At least, the opening scenes do improve on those of *The Beast.* Pete Mathews (Kenneth Tobey), who commands the submarine, is clearly established as the main character, and, when something unknown grasps his craft, the viewer remains within the ship and sees no more than the characters do. Later, as Mathews and two scientists examine the rubbery material that was caught on the sub, they wear protective suits and helmets. Here, unlike in *The Beast,* our inability to "see" these people has a purpose: We are meant to be surprised when her voice reveals that one of the scientists is a woman, Professor Lesley Joyce (Faith Domergue).

The three main characters lack the kind of personal involvement in the situation that Nesbitt had in *The Beast,* so the writers fill the gap by elaborating on a romance between Mathews and Joyce. Happily, they approach this familiar task in a fairly fresh way. Mathews is more than just flirtatious; he is a sexual predator, pushy and aggressive, cornering Joyce at every opportunity. (*The Thing* had cast Kenneth Tobey in a similar role.) This overconfident chauvinist assumes, once they've kissed, that she will immediately drop her plans for a research trip and stay with him—but she doesn't. In *The Beast,* Lee Hunter had only been the professor's assistant, but this heroine is the professor—the "head of Marine Biology at the Southeastern Institute of Oceanography"—and, as such, figures prominently in the plot. She determines that the rubbery mass is part of a giant octopus, she explains that it left the deep ocean because of hydrogen bomb tests, she designs the torpedo that will remain fixed in its target's flesh, and she talks back to the skeptical higher-ups. Her male teammate, Dr. Carter (Donald Curtis), is just along for the ride.

The conflict between Mathews and Joyce reaches its peak after they first sight the monster. Mathews insists that Joyce be sent to safety, speaking to Carter as if she were not even present. Carter suggests asking her opinion. "What's the difference what she says?" replies Mathews. Carter explains, "There's a whole new breed [of women] who feel they're just as smart, just as courageous as men. And they are! They don't like to be overprotected. They don't want to have their initiative taken away from them." Carter's speech, however, is forgotten when the submarine sets out to fire Professor Joyce's torpedo at the creature and no one even suggests that she go along. The film's final scene, though, returns to the original concept: Joyce won't marry Mathews because she's too busy, but she suggests that they collaborate on a book. The two kiss, and Mathews admits to Carter, "You were right about this new breed of woman." A relationship has been established, but an untraditional one that blends work, romance, and independence in a way that has always been rare in American films.

This unexpected anticipation of feminism grants the film a limited distinctiveness, but the blunt characterizations dilute its impact, with Mathews so irritating that no one could find him desirable. When Joyce gives in to romance during a beach embrace, Faith Domergue abruptly adopts a pouty sensuousness, and the extreme contrast with her earlier manner is jarring. Equally disruptive is director Robert Gordon's handling of Domergue in an earlier scene. After Mathews asks if she is romantically involved with Carter, Joyce stands next to Carter and stares at him. When he asks her a question, she gets flustered and keeps staring. The idea of having her decide if she might really be interested is a good one, but the exaggerated execution doesn't fit this self-possessed woman's personality. Carter presents a different problem. The writers seem to have included him to create a romantic triangle, but after planting the seed, they let it die. The director never finds anything else for poor Carter to do, but still includes him in shots of Mathews and Joyce, so the character becomes a boring appendage.

Visually and dramatically, the film's energy increases when the monster arrives in San Francisco. Unlike in *The Beast,* the main characters participate in the action and confront the creature directly. The Golden Gate Bridge is electrified to keep the beast out of the harbor, but (unexpectedly and without explanation) electricity attracts it, so Carter drives out to shut off the power. This scene offers impressive spectacle and a sense of Carter's vulnerability, as tentacles rise in the background, break through the bridge's surface, and crush his car. Mathews drives to Carter's rescue, but at this point the filmmakers' control falters. Carter gets in the car and it speeds off in reverse. After a long shot of the octopus grasping the bridge, we see the car moving forward (without ever having turned around). Another long view shows the octopus starting to pull down a portion of the bridge, followed by four shots of the car driving off the bridge and reaching safety. Finally, in still another long shot, the creature continues to pull at the bridge. As happened in the climax of *The Beast,* the people at this point have no connection with the creature, but this is the only time such is the case in *It Came from Beneath the Sea.*

The octopus next surfaces at the city docks (just as the rhedosaurus had). Clearly, a sea creature can threaten only a limited amount of harm on land, but Harryhausen justifies public panic by having its tentacles snake their way through the adjacent streets. Like a whip cracking in slow motion, one giant appendage rolls down on a group of fleeing figures and, in a brilliantly gruesome touch, drags back, presumably spreading their bodies along the road like strawberry jam on bread. Another tentacle moves through a window and its tip waves about inside, as if looking for someone (evoking an unused incident in *The Beast*'s script). A third knocks a helicopter out of the sky. The octopus must be driven back into the water, so soldiers with flame throwers send the tentacles into retreat.

Because the creature's destruction has to be "complete and instantaneous," the scientists aim their torpedo at its only vulnerable spot, the brain. Thus, we have the same

Ray Harryhausen's giant octopus comes from beneath the sea to terrorize San Francisco residents at the city docks. From *It Came from Beneath the Sea* (1955).

basic challenge as in *The Beast*, but in a revised and improved version. The torpedo hits its mark, but before it can be detonated the tentacles grasp and hold the submarine. The plot has come full circle, with a situation like the one in the first scene, and a character appropriately declares, "This is where we came in!"

Detonation would mean self-destruction, so Mathews swims into action. He fires a spear into a tentacle, only to be knocked unconscious. Carter then tries the same thing, though he is hardly qualified for the job. True, Mathews had rescued him on the bridge, but a reciprocal gesture would be dramatically necessary only if the script had developed their relationship. This weakness, though, matters less than having the main characters directly involved with the creature. In an impressive shot of Carter poised in front of the creature's giant eye, he fires point-blank. (Unfortunately, a poor technical effect makes Carter's figure translucent.) The sub is released, Carter swims away with Mathews, and the torpedo is detonated. *The Beast* had ended on a shot of the monster, but *It Came from Beneath the Sea* simply blows its creature to bits, and we end with an epilogue that ties up the romantic loose ends.

After finishing *It Came from Beneath the Sea*, Harryhausen joined Willis O'Brien to animate the prehistoric segment of the documentary *The Animal World* (1956). Reminded once more that O'Brien's insistence on large budgets had limited his output, how could Harryhausen resist the lure of Charles Schneer? A finished work—even a low-budget one—is far more satisfying than unproduced plans. One cannot wait for backing. One must take control and make one's own fate! By teaming with Schneer, Harryhausen surely made the right decision. Twelve films exist to prove it.

Convinced that the only way to make such movies cheaply was to work alone, Harryhausen developed a one-man assembly-line technique. Believing that "it is most important to start off with essentially a strong visual impression,"[23] he first made about a dozen large drawings of possible creatures and encounters. He and a writer then created a screenplay based on these images. "The picture is built around the fantasy sequences," he explained in 1974. "It has to be!" Harryhausen also planned the basic set design and sometimes sketched every shot in a sequence, especially those involving special effects. "It's important to get what we want on paper first," he has said, "because it's terribly costly to try to invent on the set" or "to shoot more than we intend to use."[24] This detailed planning would occur before a director was even hired.

During live-action filming, the director handled the scenes without animated figures, but with Harryhausen usually on the set. If the schedule was tight, he might direct one scene while the director worked on another. As for the effects sequences, either Harryhausen directed them or, he said, "I let the director know what I need and he directs it."[25] Much later, Harryhausen animated his models and combined them with the previously shot footage. "I usually edit those sequences myself, then talk it over with Charles [Schneer]. If we see that we can improve it, he gets his two cents in. Then the director looks at it."[26] It is not clear how many cents worth of input the director got.

By dominating this process, Harryhausen made his pictures in an efficient, economical way, while shielding himself from conflict by hiring people who knew from the start that they would be working for him, not with him. Unsurprisingly, his

A rare photo of Ray Harryhausen at his solitary work. Here he animates the death of the dragon for *The 7th Voyage of Sinbad* (1958).

favorite part of the procedure was the planning, because "that's where most of the imagination comes in." Later, "there's also a great deal of enjoyment in the animation."[27] The middle stage, which involved the most work with other people, satisfied him least.

Harryhausen's determination to create the effects alone derived from both practical and personal motivations. Because animation requires monitoring many small stages of movement, attention has to be completely focused on the work; "sheer will power" kept Harryhausen going.[28] Concentration also allowed him to establish a personal connection with his models. "This illusion depends on an inward feeling for movement," he says, which is "locked inside the animator until it is freed by the use of stop-motion photography."[29] Solitude freed his imagination to add the spontaneous character details that give a creature individuality and create a performance. The young Harryhausen's flirtation with acting here found its perfect, indirect form. "I suppose," he admits, "that I act through my models,"[30] and these actors "never talk back or criticize what I'm doing."[31]

Before animating a dueling skeleton for *The 7th Voyage of Sinbad*, Harryhausen took fencing lessons. "It's very difficult to explain," he says, "but . . . you have to almost put yourself in the figure, and I felt it was very important that I got the feel of it."[32] While working on *Mighty Joe Young*, Harryhausen felt comfortable with just one of the four gorilla models. "It was the only figure . . . which I could successfully manipulate into the many complicated poses I visualized in my mind. It's really quite fascinating how one can become attached to a mass of metal and rubber." As if self-conscious about this admission, he adds, "It may be that it was all in my own mind."[33] The technician is forever ill-at-ease with the artist who drives him on.

Harryhausen's working method, which "requires you to have the mentality of a monk sometimes,"[34] grew naturally from the personality of the boy who filmed in his parents' garage. He did not move out into the world and find a job. Instead, the man who, in director Nathan Juran's words, is "complete unto himself"[35] designed a career that fit his private needs, providing the security of complete control. "I managed to find my little niche," he says, "and stayed there out of everybody's sight."[36] In effect, he turned the vast, intimidating film industry into the neighborhood garage.

At the same time, Harryhausen took on so many creative tasks that no individual could possibly excel in them all. Harryhausen explains that he bases his decisions on technical demands and budgetary limitations, and it is hard to argue with this, yet such argument would have to occur for a Harryhausen film to rise to the level of *King Kong*. He worked hard to make good, imaginative pictures, but he never worked with a person who could take him further than he might go alone, as Merian C. Cooper did for Willis O'Brien.

This limitation could already be seen in 1955. *The Beast from 20,000 Fathoms* had been an original work, the first film in which humans confront a creature revived (or antagonized or mutated) by atomic energy. As such, it created a formula that other films copied. *It Came from Beneath the Sea* was merely one of those other films. Significantly, Eugene Lourie had dominated *The Beast*, but Harryhausen dominated *Beneath the Sea*. He devised a visually striking creature and he refined the action climax, but he lost what believability *The Beast*'s human characters had possessed. The next two Harryhausen-Schneer projects—*Earth vs. the Flying Saucers* and *20 Million Miles to Earth*—also feature attacks on major cities—further variations on the formula.

In the 1950s, "flying saucers were a big news item," recalls Harryhausen, "and Charles wanted to make a science-fiction film about them."[37] They were an item not only in tabloid newspapers but also in Hollywood production offices, as witness *The*

Thing (1951), *It Came from Outer Space* (1953), and *The War of the Worlds* (1953). So the two men joined the bandwagon, concocting (with horror veteran Curt Siodmak) a story in which beings from a disintegrating solar system attack Washington. Although "suggested by" Major Donald E. Keyhoe's 1953 book *Flying Saucers from Outer Space,* the final script of *Earth vs. the Flying Saucers* (1956) takes only a few details from that nonfiction work. Unlike the film's authors, Keyhoe emphasizes the saucers' *lack* of aggressiveness and states that the Air Force ordered its pilots *not* to fire on them.

Typically, Harryhausen approached the film as a technical and imaginative—but not a dramatic—challenge. He was attracted to "seeing just how interesting one could make an inanimate object such as a rounded metal spaceship."[38] He even made his task more difficult by designing saucers that constantly whirl and that create around themselves a transparent, shimmering shield. As a result of this emphasis on technical execution, the film is the most simplistic of all Harryhausen's features. Little distracts from the basic subject: an alien encounter of the hostile kind. Even the now-expected opening narration declines to mislead viewers, instead presenting the "facts" of some saucer sightings and quoting a fictional Air Force order "to fire on sight at any flying objects not identifiable." From the start, we expect impressive scenes of battle and destruction.

The filmmakers do not even try to give their characters personalities. Romance is avoided by making the male and female leads newlyweds, and their relationship hardly matters to the plot. They also face no major decisions or conflicts. For example, the aliens contact Dr. Russell Marvin (Hugh Marlowe) because he heads a satellite launch program, and from then on all he does is react to them. Marvin's wife (Joan Taylor) suffers a worse fate. Unlike the heroine of *It Came from Beneath the Sea,* she has no identity of her own, existing only as a scientist's wife and secretary and as a general's daughter. Instead of people and feelings, *Earth vs. the Flying Saucers* stresses factual details. The "foo lights" that sometimes float about are remote-controlled spy devices, an "Infinitely Indexed Memory Bank" extracts a person's knowledge and stores it, and the aliens operate in a dimension in which time moves much faster than in ours.

The screenwriters included many useful suggestions for building energy and character throughout the film, all of which the filmmakers ignored. Harryhausen himself may be to blame in the scene of the Marvins sighting their first saucer. In the script, it appears behind their car, then in front. Marvin tells his wife, who is driving, "Go after it!" She "steps on the gas and drives ahead at full speed. The saucer easily outspeeds them. . . . Then with startling suddenness, it reverses direction and comes back at the car with incredible speed. . . . It looks as though it is about to crash into the car." Carol swerves "off the road and across the adjoining empty field. The speeding car rocks and bounces dangerously over the uneven ground, threatening to flip." In the film, after the saucer appears in front of the car, Carol merely pulls over and Marvin gets out and looks up, as the object quickly departs.

In other scenes, director Fred F. Sears omits the script's ideas and finds no alternatives. When a messenger interrupts the Marvins' dinner with important news, the script has him arrive in a medium shot that pans as his jeep "skids through a tight turn and stops close to the barbecue party." Sears settles for a stationary long shot of the jeep pulling up, so the effect is calm instead of tense. In a later scene, Carol is loaded with supplies and "nearly bumps into" her father. As they talk, he "helps her recover a falling package." Then, he "holds the lab door open for her." The film omits these reasonable, if not especially novel, interactions; the two just meet, talk, and part. When Marvin tries to contact a saucer, he "wipes the sweat off his brow and looks anxiously around for a place to dispose of his cigarette which is burning his fingers. Finding no ashtray, he drops it on the floor." Such details, which heighten the intensity of events, cannot be found in the film, which the director's failure of imagination dooms to flat-ness.

The writers' ingenuity, however, was limited to such touches, and in the basic plot they resort to arbitrary manipulation. As soon as the military decides not to use atomic weapons on the invaders, Marvin gets an idea for a new kind of weapon. When his prototype isn't satisfactory, an otherwise unnoticed scientist recalls a sugges-tion made between scenes by a doctor from New Delhi. "Of course!" exclaims Mar-vin, and the solution has been found. To keep the final battle limited to Washington, the film assumes—without explanation—that all the saucers have converged on that city from around the globe.

The script's biggest weakness, though, is its vagueness about the aliens' purpose, which may reflect a conflict between the optimism of Major Keyhoe's book and the filmmakers' desire for a saucer attack. At first, the aliens seem like victims of our shoot-first mentality: When a saucer lands and three figures emerge, soldiers immedi-ately open fire. The aliens respond by killing people and blowing up buildings. Later, a tape recording reveals that they thought they had set up a meeting, and Marvin learns that they feared our satellites might be weapons directed against them.

The aliens seem sympathetic, if overreactive, until they demonstrate their power by destroying a battleship and declare that they could easily conquer us. The result, though, would be a wrecked planet and a hostile population, so why not avoid fight-ing and reach an agreement? They give Earth fifty-six days to arrange a meeting of world leaders for this purpose. Instead, Marvin and the military devise a weapon and test it on a saucer that lands nearby. One alien dies and the saucer fires back, killing people and blowing up a vehicle, a bomber, and a building. It then drops the bodies of two brain-drained prisoners and leaves. When the time limit runs out, the aliens cause an explosion on the sun, which leads to eight days of "meteorological convulsions" (and many stock shots) that cripple the earth and lead to the final battle—Earth's counterattack.

The film implies that the aliens want us to capitulate without resisting, but was that their intention from the start or did it result from our firing on them? Would they have settled for some kind of immigration and resident-alien status? The exposition of this issue is so confused that the film cannot quite be the simple them-against-us action picture that it evidently wants to be.

Such limitations aside, *Earth vs. the Flying Saucers* is a film of action, and that action is fairly spectacular. Marvin's weapon nullifies the magnetic force that powers the saucers, causing them to crash impressively: One hits the Capitol dome and another topples the Washington Monument. "The collapse of the buildings," recalls Harry-hausen, "had to be animated frame by frame. That meant that each brick was sus-pended with invisible wires and had to change position with every frame of film. Dust and debris were added later. It was something I would never do again."[39]

This climax is noteworthy, but a few brief moments remain at least as long in the memory. These fragments use photography not just to show events but to dramatize them. A close-up of the captured general is taken from an extremely low angle, with the aliens' ominous brain machine visible above him. After the attack on the launch center, when the Marvins realize they are trapped in their underground command post, we see them in an extreme long shot, as the walls and a staircase press toward their tiny figures.

Such shots may be the work of the director and/or photographer, but others include Harryhausen's effects. The final destructive binge ends with the Marvins standing in front of the gaping Capitol dome, with a crashed saucer on the building's steps, and the graphic power of this image transcends the facts of what it shows. An even more resonant moment occurs when Marvin meets the aliens on a beach. A shot of him walking into tight close-up is followed by an extreme long shot from above as he stands by the previously unseen saucer. Marvin's unexpected nearness to the camera and the abrupt shift of angle and distance create, for a few fragile seconds, an almost primal sense of mystery: A man alone, by the vast ocean, in darkness, steps toward the massive unknown. Who needs a big budget when a creative sense of cinema is available? What counts is not the special effect but how it is used. These moments were not described in the shooting script. Did some alchemical blend of talents suddenly produce art here?

Discussing *Earth vs. the Flying Saucers,* Harryhausen reveals a limited grasp of its elements. At one point, he justifies the pale human characters: "When you're trying to tell a tale such as we do in the saucer picture, you either spend the time trying to develop characterization, or you spend the time developing the destruction, which is what these pictures are all about." Two sentences later, he declares, "That picture, I thought, had good, rounded characterizations in it."[40] Trying to have it both ways, he develops a defensiveness that can blind him to the reality of his own work. A complete filmmaker dare not view action and characterization as mutually exclusive, nor can he confuse competent acting with rounded characterizations.

Just after completing *The Beast from 20,000 Fathoms,* Harryhausen had felt "a longing to go to Europe."[41] Without the funds for a vacation, he outlined two films that would require European locations. In *The Elementals,* large, winged creatures invade Paris, and *The Giant Ymir* placed an animal from Venus in modern Rome. One of *The Beast's* producers had bought *The Elementals,* but nothing resulted. After *Earth vs. the Flying Saucers,* Charles Schneer evidently ran out of ideas for films, so Harryhausen offered *The Giant Ymir.* The outline "had most of the key situations in it,"[42] he recalls, but "its many faults stood out like the boot of Italy on a map."[43] He turned for help to Charlott Knight, who "rounded out the live characters and put a great deal more substance in the story."[44] A script was written, and Harryhausen got his trip abroad.

Retitled *20 Million Miles to Earth* (1957), this film solidified Harryhausen's creative position: He wrote the original story, supervised the screenplay's development, and shot the on-location footage. His fondness for *King Kong* clearly influenced the plot's structure. An early version had first recounted events on Venus, with that planet substituting for Skull Island as an isolated spot where monsters are found. The final story omits Venus, but the parallel remains, with the monster discovered and overpowered on an island (Sicily), then brought to a major city (Rome). There, held in place by metal belts, it is exhibited to reporters. Like Kong, the Ymir breaks loose and stalks the city's streets, wreaking havoc and lowering real estate values. Finally, it falls from the city's most famous building.

Unlike Kong, this creature has no clear goal except survival—although survival can be a strong and valid goal on its own, and viewers readily empathize with the Ymir as a lonely victim defending itself in a strange, unpredictable world. Still, this limited goal weakens the plot's development. Kong broke his bonds because of what he perceived as danger to Ann Darrow, but the Ymir escapes because an accident short-circuits the electrical system that keeps it unconscious. This accident is not even explained; it occurs for the filmmakers' convenience. Equally arbitrary is the setting of the climax at the Colosseum. "I rather fancied having the Ymir in the final reel leave a mass of new ruins among the old," is Harryhausen's reason for choosing that location.[45] By contrast, Kong headed for the tallest building because he had lived on Skull Island's highest mountain.

In one significant respect, Harryhausen here surpasses both *King Kong* and his previous films. He designed the rhedosaurus to look like a dinosaur, and his octopus was, like Kong, derived from reality, but the Ymir is totally imaginary. Like a tyrannosaurus, it stands upright on two muscular legs and has a heavy tail for balance. Unlike a tyrannosaurus, it has long, muscular arms that end in three large talons. Its face, less fierce than a dinosaur's, is sensitive and even vulnerable, with an almost feline quality owing to its whisker-like folds. A truly impressive conception, the Ymir combines stature and ferocity with mobility and expressiveness. It also offers variety. The other beasts had entered their films full-sized and ready for action, but the Ymir arrives on Earth unborn, in a small canister. Because our atmosphere upsets its metabolic rate, the creature rapidly grows to the size of a man, and then even larger. This allows the film to introduce the alien early and to save the giant menace for later.

The script provides no information about the Ymir's intelligence, but Harryhausen's animation of the creature's movements—its "performance"—adds details that suggest a subtle nature. When quite small, the Ymir is startled by the sudden switching on of a light. It turns away, shielding its eyes, then rubbing them. It also brushes its snout ingenuously and looks, by turns, curious, confused, and quizzical. At other times, of course, it snarls menacingly. This wide range of expression creates a distinct identity, making the Ymir as striking an entity as anything devised by Willis O'Brien.

Thanks to careful writing, the film's human characters move into and out of the action with unobtrusive ease. Two fishermen and Pepe (Bart Bradley), a young boy, rescue Colonel Calder (William Hopper) and another man from a spaceship that crashed in the sea. With the local doctor away, a villager recalls the presence of Dr. Leonardo (Frank Puglia) because Pepe had sold specimens to him. Leonardo is only a zoologist, but his granddaughter, Marisa (Joan Taylor), attends medical school, so she cares for the injured men. Meanwhile, Pepe discovers the canister and sells its contents to Leonardo. Thus, the characters' paths cross in a logical, efficient manner that continues throughout the film, and this occurs without a reliance on narration.

The supporting characters are quickly, but vividly, sketched. Although the aggressive salesmanship of Pepe grows somewhat overbearing, his scene with Dr. Leonardo has a relaxed humanity as Leonardo teasingly humors the boy, while clearly feeling affection for him. In the role of General MacIntosh, Thomas B. Henry is an acceptable military figure (as he was in *Earth vs. the Flying Saucers*), but his harsh voice makes the statement "It's tragic the others died in the moment of their glory" sound like an insincere afterthought. In *Flying Saucers,* John Zaremba played a scientist who steps out of the background to offer important information, then disappears. This awkwardness is avoided in *20 Million Miles* by combining several minor figures into one continuing character, Dr. Uhl, also played by Zaremba.

The hero and heroine are better matched than any pair in Harryhausen's earlier films. Marisa is independent and assertive, but not overpowering, and the crisp arrogance of Colonel Calder is justified by the pressure of circumstances. In four effective scenes, their initial antagonism develops not into romance but into a more convincing affectionate respect.

They first meet in the village hospital, where Marisa tries to stop Calder from disturbing the other survivor with questions. Worried and impatient, he snaps at her to leave him alone. Because he assumes she's a nurse, Marisa retorts that she's a doctor, then adds, "Or, almost a doctor." Calder continues talking to the dying man, so she injects him with a sedative. Throughout, we understand both characters' perspectives:

Calder must obtain information before the other astronaut expires, while Marisa is insecure as a "doctor" but determined to do the right thing. The scene contains edgy tension and real anger.

When they meet again, on the road to Rome, Calder greets Marisa with, "Well, hello, Almost-a-doctor," which (to William Hopper's credit) sounds slightly more nasty than teasing. Later, when the two are more relaxed, Marisa admits to having been "inconsiderate and self-centered," and Calder responds, "All you've done is try to help. All I've done is snarl at you." He offers to make it up to her "over a table for two in a dark café." "With a candle burning on the table?" she asks, knowing the routine but interested nonetheless.

During their next encounter, at the Rome zoo, the two flirt in a friendly fashion. "You caught me unprepared," she says. "I've been cooking over a hot creature all day." He responds with, "You're getting lovelier every time I see you—or is it the lights in this room?" "Well," she replies, glancing toward the Ymir, "next to that, I look dandy." This banter enlivens the characters in an appealingly unexpected way. Then Marisa takes the initiative, reminding Calder about the dinner offer and warning that the candle is "burning lower and lower and lower." This is as involved as the two ever get, so the film does not have to push them too far, too fast. The result—characters who strike an appropriate balance between being distinctive individuals and filling the needs of the plot—was not achieved easily, for the apology scene is not in the shooting script and the zoo dialogue was changed considerably.

Director Nathan Juran responds well to these characterizations. During the hospital scene, he reinforces the conflict by having the actors speak at the same time, which happens there but nowhere else (and isn't indicated in the script). The mutual apologies are exchanged while Marisa changes a bandage on Calder's arm. When someone calls him, he starts to leave but is pulled back by the bandage roll, which Marisa still holds. As she cuts him loose they exchange looks, having noticed that this bit of business reflects a new link between them.

Often, Juran devotes extra visual attention to Marisa. At the end of the hospital scene, she moves to a window and closes the shutters; then, as she turns around, the camera tracks in for a close-up of her. After a shot of Calder from her point of view, we return to the close-up as she says, in an angry tone and mostly to herself, "Pleasant dreams." Here, Juran conveys both Marisa's professional dedication and her personal resentment. In another scene, she and Leonardo discover that the Ymir has grown larger overnight. When the man leaves, instead of following the script's direction that Marisa watch him, "fondly amused," Juran has her stare with interest at the off-screen cage, then move closer to it. These few seconds support her later ability to draw conclusions about the Ymir, such as, "I guess I frightened it as much as it frightened me" (a line not in the shooting script). Joan Taylor's characterization gains much from such thoughtful, essentially cinematic, opportunities.

Overall, Juran uses images more creatively than Harryhausen's previous directors, and his background as an art director probably influenced the scene of two fishermen searching the spaceship for survivors. The interior shots are claustrophobic and threatening, with vague foreground shapes, deep shadows, and pervasive steam mingling in tight compositions. Modest and unpretentious, Juran has described himself as "just a technician who could transfer the script from the page to the stage and could get it shot on schedule and on budget."[46] He admired Harryhausen's specialized skills, saying, "I learned real fast from him."[47]

In return, Harryhausen enjoyed working with Juran, but only because he "understood the problems" of making a special-effects picture.[48] Dwelling on the compromises imposed by his small budgets, Harryhausen never seems aware of what directors actually do, aside from working with actors. He once even declared that "the quality of each picture a director works on depends largely on how much money is in the budget."[49] Generally, he employed only directors who fit his image of them as crafts-men and who accepted his plans without asserting themselves. By "learning" from Harryhausen and viewing himself as a hireling, Juran evidently struck the right chord, while unobtrusively improving the film with his own contributions. Not surprisingly, Juran and Harryhausen made two more films together, whereas only one other direc-tor (Don Chaffey) returned for even a second stint.

Harryhausen's special-effects scenes in this film represent his most cinematically effective work thus far. A confrontation with the Ymir in a barn provides a good example. As Calder prods the creature from its hayloft perch and toward a waiting wagon, long shots of the whole area are intercut with shots of just Calder. Only when the Ymir becomes angry and hits at the pole do we also have close views of the crea-ture. When a farmer panics and attacks the animal, a series of varied shots keeps the viewer involved in the action: Calder stops a man from firing his rifle; the farmer picks up a pitchfork; he advances on the Ymir in a long shot of them both, followed by close shots of the farmer thrusting and of the Ymir's back with the pitchfork stuck in it. Further close-ups of the farmer and of the Ymir in pain build the moment's intensity. Finally, as the men back out through the doorway, we have a close, intimi-dating view of the Ymir advancing toward the camera.

The Venusian Ymir from *20 Million Miles to Earth* (1957), a monster created entirely from Ray Harryhausen's imagination, takes on an elephant in the streets of Rome, Italy.

The film's monster-in-the-city climax resembles, but improves on, the endings of *The Beast* and *Beneath the Sea*. The escaped Ymir's fight with an elephant starts in the zoo, then progresses to a street. When the victorious Ymir moves on, Calder follows. He knocks the creature down with his car and pursues on foot, until it takes refuge in the Tiber. Here Harryhausen borrows some action from *Beneath the Sea:* The monster rises behind the men, disappears again, then erupts through the bridge surface. But even as he recycles these events, Harryhausen improves on their staging. This time, the beast appears in the foreground of the shot and its bulk fills the screen, blocking our view of the people. By placing the creature so near the camera and varying what we see, Harryhausen heightens the impact.

The hunt for the Ymir in the Colosseum contains striking compositions taken from high or low angles and with extreme contrasts in depth. Also notable is a shot that tracks along a row of corridors, following Calder's wary movement in the background; the series of empty spaces extending into the distance adds to our uncertainty about where the monster might next appear. All of these shots can be credited to Harryhausen, who had supervised the location filming in Rome.

"I always find it rather upsetting to have to kill off the 'villain,' " admits Harryhausen, adding that he prefers to do so "with a touch of pathos."[50] The death of the rhedosaurus had some emotional force, but his octopus and saucers remained sterile Enemies. In *20 Million Miles,* Harryhausen creates his first semitragic death scene. The creature stands atop the Colosseum in futile defiance. Wounded, it clasps its side and struggles to stay upright, then loses its footing and hangs onto the building's edge with one arm. The soldiers fire at the structure, the stones give way, and the Ymir falls with them to its death. The pathos here develops not from the fact that it dies, as happened with the rhedosaurus, but from the effort the Ymir makes in its struggle against death. The sight of this creature clinging desperately but heroically to life is followed by a shot of only the barrel of a tank's cannon as it fires the final barrage—an image that is both dramatic punctuation and an almost abstract summation of the act of killing.

A balance of relief and regret at the Ymir's demise is evoked by a high-angle shot of the plaza far below, as Calder's tiny figure moves from the cluster of soldiers to Marisa standing on the sidelines, a point of view that puts humankind in its insignificant place. This mood is unfortunately broken by a blunt medium shot of Dr. Uhl and General MacIntosh, as Uhl utters the pretentious and unnecessary statement, "Why is it always, always so costly for Man to move from the present to the future?"

With *20 Million Miles to Earth,* Harryhausen came as close as he ever would to matching *King Kong*. Its creature is truly central to the film, and the hero and heroine arguably have more personality than Jack Driscoll and Ann Darrow in *Kong*. Yet those qualities which make *Kong* great continued to elude Harryhausen. None of the characters has an emotional relationship to the creature's predicament, and even that predicament remains vague. We see the Ymir on its own in just one extended sequence, as it explores a farm, and then its actions are ambiguous. Why, for instance, does it stare at the sheep or move toward the sound of the barking dog? Is it hungry? Does it want to communicate with these animals? Is it afraid, or only curious? The viewer's imagination can provide answers, but few clues are given to help it along.

Ultimately, the film lacks the nuances found in *King Kong*: the beauty-and-the-beast motif that relates Ann to both Jack and the gorilla, the filmmaking context that comments on the very film we are watching, the overtones of colonialism that derive from the white man–native relationship, and the forceful leader's overreaching quest. Probably another achievement of that sort and on that level is impossible. It is part of Harryhausen's heroism that he sought to match the unmatchable, to do as if for the first time what had already been done. It is part of his achievement that he came as close to success as he did.

Having made four horror-adventure films in which a monster threatens the familiar, civilized world, Harryhausen may have felt a need to diversify. Perhaps he also realized that *20 Million Miles to Earth* was an accomplishment in that vein that he might never top. At any rate, the search for his next story again led him to an earlier idea, a fantasy-adventure that sends his characters to an unknown, exotic land. In a sense, he turned for inspiration not to the final, Manhattan portion of *King Kong* but to the earlier, Skull Island section. He also replaced the modern world with the "much more colorful" mythic past.

Around 1954, Harryhausen had prepared some drawings and a ten-page outline describing the adventures of Sinbad the Sailor. Similar Arabian Nights material had appeared in two versions of *The Thief of Bagdad* (1924 and 1940), but later films replaced the fantasy elements with broad comedy and tame female flesh. Harryhausen wanted to shift the emphasis back to magic and adventure, but when RKO's *Son of Sinbad* (1955) proved a box office disappointment, producers rejected Harryhausen's idea. In 1957, though, Charles Schneer accepted the challenge, so writer Kenneth Kolb, in Harryhausen's words, "tied the drawings together with a story line."[51]

The result, *The 7th Voyage of Sinbad* (1958), reveals how completely Harryhausen reacted against *Son of Sinbad*. His hero is not a reckless, picaresque thief but a sturdy ship's captain who avoids unnecessary risks. Instead of rebelling against the Caliph, Sinbad is treated like a prince. Uninterested in seducing every female around, he is a one-woman man engaged to a princess. Also dropped is *Son of Sinbad*'s comic tone. Nor does Harryhausen's hero resemble the Sinbad of the *Arabian Nights,* however, for that seaman is not a ship's captain or even a crew member but a merchant who sets off on trading expeditions only to be stranded in unfamiliar locales. Harrowing experiences make him regret his ambition, but he always survives and returns home rich. Harryhausen's Sinbad owes more to Douglas Fairbanks and Errol Flynn than to the *Arabian Nights.*

In visualizing Sinbad's adventures, Harryhausen took only two concepts from the seven voyages in the *Arabian Nights:* the giant, flying roc whose newly hatched chick is killed for food and the man-like giants who roast their captives on a spit. Harryhausen embellished these creatures by giving the roc two heads and making the giants one-eyed, like the cyclopes in *The Odyssey.* From elsewhere in the *Arabian Nights* came a genie in a lamp and an evil sorcerer, while *The Odyssey* provided its sirens, now called "demons." To all of this, Harryhausen added a fire-breathing dragon and a dueling skeleton. "*The 7th Voyage of Sinbad* was unique," Harryhausen rightly asserts. "Nothing quite like its contents had been seen on the screen before."[52] It is a fast-moving adventure filled with real magic, a feature that broke new ground for Harryhausen and for fantasy films in general.

The 7th Voyage of Sinbad immediately plunges viewers into a tense situation, with Sinbad's ship lost on a foggy sea at night. In the morning the fog lifts, revealing the island of Colossa, so Sinbad (Kerwin Mathews) and his men row ashore in search of fresh water. When Sokurah (Torin Thatcher) rushes out of a cave pursued by a cyclops, the sailors try to help, while the magician summons a genie from the lamp he carries. The genie constructs an invisible barrier to protect the men, but Sokurah drops the lamp and the cyclops strides off with it. Onboard ship, Sokurah offers "the treasure of a hundred years" if Sinbad will help him regain the lamp. Sinbad refuses because his bride-to-be, Princess Parisa (Kathryn Grant), is on the ship and her safety takes precedence. This opening grabs the viewer's interest with its dramatic, unex-

A cyclops from *The 7th Voyage of Sinbad* (1958).

pected events, while introducing the main characters and setting up the plot's premise. Because the film is not a horror fantasy, nothing is lost by revealing a major menace like the cyclops so soon, and much is gained by offering a sample of the wonders to come.

In Bagdad, the Caliph refuses Sokurah's request for a ship and crew, so the magician shrinks Parisa to only a few inches in height. When the Sultan of Chandra blames the Caliph for his daughter's condition and threatens war, Sinbad asks Sokurah for help. The magician knows of a potion that can restore Parisa to normal size, but it requires a piece of a roc's eggshell from Colossa. Sinbad agrees to set sail, and because the potion can be used only in Sokurah's castle, the tiny Princess goes along.

From here on, the film moves quickly from one spectacular action scene to another. The crew mutinies, but wailing demons drive the men mad and Sinbad, using earplugs, regains control. On the island, some sailors find the cyclopes' treasure but are caged by one of the giants; Sinbad blinds the cyclops with a torch and lures it over a cliff to its death. The hungry sailors discover a roc's egg, killing and eating the baby roc that emerges. In a calm interlude, Parisa enters the lamp, where the young genie (Richard Eyer) reveals his desire to be a real boy and explains how to summon him. The roc carries Sinbad to her nest, and Sokurah kidnaps Parisa.

After Sinbad evades a fire-breathing dragon and forces the magician to restore the Princess to normal size, Sokurah brings a skeleton to life and orders it to kill Sinbad. The two duel until the skeleton falls from a staircase and shatters. Sokurah destroys a stone bridge, but the genie provides a rope, so Sinbad and Parisa swing across the chasm. The dragon snaps its chain, and as it fights a cyclops, Sinbad and the Princess sneak out. Then Sokurah leads the dragon out of the cave, but the sailors stop it with an arrow fired from a giant crossbow. The dragon falls on the magician, crushing him, then staggers to the shore, where it dies.

Harryhausen's tendency to start with ideas for dramatic sequences had earlier challenged his writers to justify those scenes and link them together smoothly. *The 7th Voyage of Sinbad* reduces those burdens. Because the adventure format usually involves a quest that takes the hero through a series of dangerous encounters, it is almost by definition episodic, and in a mythic world exotic creatures simply exist and are accepted.

The script manipulates its characters and their actions less than the *Arabian Nights* tales do, but more than is desired in a modern plot. Often, events happen solely because they are convenient or dramatic. Because Sokurah has extensive magical powers, his desire for the lamp, which drives the plot, seems overstated. Also, the magician has announced that "there is nothing I would not do" to regain the lamp, and the Caliph knows he is manipulative, yet when the Princess shrinks, Sokurah's blatant scheme goes undetected. After the roc carries Sinbad to its nest it just flies away, and Sinbad descends without difficulty. The dragon breathes fire except when forced to stand near the wall, so Sinbad can walk past. Later, it snaps its chain because the writer wants it to fight the cyclops. Sokurah's castle contains a spiral staircase that leads nowhere because the skeleton needs a place from which to fall and because one of Harryhausen's drawings had included it. Nonetheless, these contrivances do not seriously damage the film. The events themselves are so striking and occur at such a rapid pace that the viewer is successfully distracted.

Characterizations of the hero and heroine also had presented a problem in Harryhausen's films. *Earth vs. the Flying Saucers* avoided the issue by making the couple newlyweds, and *The 7th Voyage of Sinbad* does something similar: Sinbad and the Princess are due to be married, but an obstacle must first be overcome. The people in this film enter fully formed and do not change, and their choices are clear-cut and simple, but the actors flesh out the characters in a satisfactory way. As Sinbad, Kerwin Mathews is sturdy and reliable without being stiff or excessively nice. Kathryn Grant's Princess Parisa is giddily cheerful, but that appears to be a deliberate decision. In the role of Sokurah, Torin Thatcher creates, without self-consciousness or camp, a larger-than-life figure of considerable intensity. His ironic voice, penetrating eyes, stern jaw, and shaven skull make for a character almost more intriguing than the monsters.

Beneath the magic and *Arabian Nights* paraphernalia of the film, the bones of *King Kong* may still be detected, providing solid support: A strong-willed obsessive (Sokurah/Carl Denham) leads the stalwart hero (Sinbad/Jack Driscoll) and his loved one (Parisa/Ann Darrow) to an uncharted island inhabited by giant animals. The foggy approach to both islands reinforces the parallel. This time, however, the obsessive is an out-and-out villain who lives there and controls some of the creatures.

The creatures themselves also have precedents in *Kong*. The upright cyclops evokes a tail-less and semihuman tyrannosaurus, the dragon echoes the long-necked brontosaurus, and the roc suggests a pterodactyl. Only the skeleton is a totally new menace. But these similarities do not mean that Harryhausen's designs lack freshness and individuality. The cyclops is an especially vivid concept, with its block-like head, horn, single eye, and flat nose blending with a hairy, satyr-like lower body to form a harmonious whole. Still, the similarities reveal how thoroughly *King Kong* embodies the essence of fantastic adventure and how hard it is to break free of its influence.

Harryhausen's casting of a child as the genie—and the character's desire to be a real boy, which is unrelated to the main plot—suggests that he and Schneer were seeking a preadolescent audience. Happily, the film as a whole does not condescend to its viewers the way works geared for children often do. However, the filmmakers are wary of making their dangers too extreme or intense. For every evocatively gruesome incident, such as a cyclops crushing sailors with an uprooted tree, several others are deliberately undercut. For example, a cyclops ties one victim to a spit that rotates over a fire, but instead of developing the man's plight, the film cuts to other events, ignoring him until help arrives. An adventure film should create real fear for its characters' welfare, but Harryhausen worried about going too far: "We would have lost a great number of children from our audience."[53]

The 7th Voyage of Sinbad minimizes other emotions, too. We do find a hint of sadness when Sinbad discovers his first mate's body and gently touches his face, but the moment passes quickly. Also, Sinbad's voice holds a note of true concern when he calls out for the Princess after Sokurah has taken her away. But the filmmakers seem uncomfortable with such strong feelings and rarely even suggest them.

Director Nathan Juran's command of the camera is evident in the lively action scenes. During the mutiny, for instance, Sinbad is attacked in the background of a shot, then slams onto a table in the close foreground; the camera frequently pans with the characters' movements; and there are several tight close-ups, such as one of Sinbad's fist hitting a villain's bare stomach. However, these efforts are damaged by the fact that many blows don't land forcefully, and a few don't land at all. The demon sequence put Juran's skills to the test. Unexpectedly forced to film with the ship docked, he improvised the illusion of a rough sea by synchronizing a rocking camera with the actors' staggering movements, while an airplane propeller acted as a wind machine and the Barcelona fire department sprayed water all over the deck. Because Juran had to keep these shots brief and close to the action, the scene gains in impact.

Elsewhere, Juran's visual sense heightens a scene's effect in small but significant ways. Shadows move across Sokurah's face when he tries to convince Sinbad to return for the lamp, which adds to the actor's menacing intensity. Later, when Sinbad approaches Sokurah in his castle, an extreme long shot of the two men includes chains and a skeleton's legs hanging in the foreground; this adds depth to the action, while establishing the skeleton's presence for later use.

The need for editing is just as great in a special effects sequence as in other action scenes, but one cannot just shift the camera's position and film additional shots the way one can with living actors. The animator must therefore keep reminding himself that a distant view can establish the general layout, but other shots are needed to develop the drama. Also, having models move toward or away from the camera while interacting with live actors requires the time-consuming calculation of perspective and relative proportions. The cyclopes scenes reveal Harryhausen struggling with these issues.

The first cyclops emerges from the cave in an extreme long shot and moves from left to right, remaining at a constant distance from the camera. This viewpoint keeps the audience outside the action and Harryhausen, realizing this, immediately cuts to a powerful close shot facing the cyclops and taken from a low angle. As the scene progresses, the film cuts between the long shot and closer views of Sinbad slashing at one of the cyclops's legs, a sailor attacking the other leg, and Sokurah calling on the genie for help. In contrast, the scene of the cyclops lifting the intruders out of its treasure cave and putting them in a cage includes only the minimum shots necessary. Most of the action occurs in a single static long shot of the cage, the cyclops, and the rocks containing the cave. The only other shots are of the men in the cave and of the cyclops's face peering down through a hole in the roof. The scene is impressive

One of Ray Harryhausen's preliminary sketches for the sequence in which Sinbad fences with a skeleton in *The 7th Voyage of Sinbad* (1958).

because of what we see happening, but its animated-diorama look severely limits its power.

Sinbad's duel with the skeleton, beyond being a technical tour de force, is also an exciting bit of filmmaking, owing to the way the action was planned and shot. With a fencer standing in for the skeleton, Juran filmed the entire sequence in live action. Then, each shot was recorded again, this time with Sinbad fighting alone. Much later, Harryhausen animated his skeleton model and combined it with the figure of Sinbad. Because the scene was choreographed like a traditional, live-action duel, the shots seem chosen with the action, not the animation, in mind. As the fight moves from the magician's lair to an outer area and up the spiral staircase, we see the combatants sometimes together and sometimes separately, as well as shots of the magician and Parisa watching. From the moment the skeleton takes its sword until it lies shattered on the ground, the film cuts thirty times. This sequence takes the special effects for granted and was directed without evident regard for the needs of the technician; as such, it appears to be a true collaboration between Harryhausen and Juran.

In 1958, *The 7th Voyage of Sinbad* was an eye-filling, imagination-stirring spectacle (one that still holds up quite well). It was also Harryhausen's biggest financial success to date. In England, though, children under the age of sixteen could see it only if accompanied by an adult. "I was incensed and outraged," recalls Schneer.[54] He later had the film reclassified by removing the skeleton duel and part of the dragon-cyclops fight. The United States offered no such difficulties, so Schneer and Harryhausen shifted their base of operations to London, where they could confer in advance with the censors. Another major lure was the availability there of a new sodium backing process for combining separate images into one shot.

The 7th Voyage of Sinbad marked the end of Harryhausen's artistic apprenticeship and led directly to a quartet of equally ambitious and confident films. Unlike the previous features, these four adapted preexisting stories, yet they also reveal—sometimes consciously and sometimes not—the evolution of concepts, images, and attitudes that mark them as Harryhausen's first truly personal creations.

Jack Sher and Arthur Ross had already written an adaptation of Jonathan Swift's Gulliver's Travels when Charles Schneer took on the project. Harryhausen then had their script revised "to incorporate our techniques,"[55] and Sher stayed with the project to direct The 3 Worlds of Gulliver (1960). In Swift's 1726 novel, Dr. Lemuel Gulliver visits four countries, but the film retains only the first two: In Lilliput the people are six inches tall, so to them Gulliver seems a giant, but in Brobdingnag the situation is reversed, with the inhabitants ten times larger than Gulliver. (The third "world" of the title refers to Gulliver's home, England.) Swift's satire of eighteenth-century English life is, of course, dated, but his exposure of human nature's absurdity remains relevant. The book has a complex tone, with some of Gulliver's comments meant to be taken at face value, while elsewhere Gulliver is mocked.

Written in the style of contemporary travel accounts, Gulliver's Travels lacks a conventional dramatic structure, so the filmmakers added incidents to give the action an orderly progression. In addition, over the centuries the book had been "cleaned up" and treated as a children's story. Harryhausen and Schneer continued this tradition, while keeping some of the satire. "We *could* have told a straight adventure story," Harryhausen explains, but "we retained the message phases that were intrinsic to the plot."[56] The result may tilt more toward cuteness than irony, but Harryhausen deserves credit for trying something different. Taken on its own terms, the film has virtues.

It first introduces the life Gulliver (Kerwin Mathews) leads in England, where, owing to the poverty of his patients and his own generosity, his medical practice is floundering. Elizabeth (June Thorburn), Gulliver's optimistic fiancée, wants him to buy a rundown cottage for their home. "Can't you be content with what we have?" she asks. "But we don't have anything," he replies, adding "I want to help the sick without being sick inside myself with worry and debts." One incident epitomizes their world: When Elizabeth trips and drops some money, the greedy landlord picks up the coins, while Gulliver helps Elizabeth to her feet. Concluding that "you have to be rich and important to be anything in this world," the disillusioned idealist sets sail for the East Indies in the hope of making a fortune. This opening sequence has lively, entertaining dialogue and is very efficient—too much so, perhaps, for it lasts just six minutes and feels rushed.

Swift paid little attention to Gulliver's private life, so the film's version is mostly new material, with the romantic couple (like Sinbad and Parisa) facing an obstacle to their marriage. The writers also created a more precise motivation for Gulliver's journey, one that allows him to learn the emptiness of ambition and self-importance. When Gulliver returns home he is, we are meant to believe, happy to settle for the rundown cottage. Thus the film teaches a neat and conservative moral that tames the book's expression of anger at humanity.

Elizabeth stows away on Gulliver's ship, which fits her assertive nature to an extent but is still largely a manipulation that keeps her involved in the plot. During a storm, Gulliver is lost overboard and washed ashore at Lilliput. The events in this part of the film follow the novel closely: Gulliver is tied down with numerous tiny ropes attached to stakes driven into the ground; he is granted freedom after swearing a loyalty oath; he steals the fleet of Lilliput's enemy, Blefuscu; and he puts out a fire in the Royal Palace, which ironically inspires the Empress's resentment. Swift's Gulliver extinguished the fire by urinating on it, but in the film he spits a keg-full of wine on the flames, which is more tasteful, while still allowing the Empress to be angry at this "uncouth, vile, filthy, evil, dirty, spitting, and spewing animal." Gulliver also antagonizes the Emperor by refusing to annihilate Blefuscu. Accused of treason, and unwilling to use his strength to oppress either Lilliput or Blefuscu, Gulliver flees from the island.

The Lilliput segment retains much of Swift's ironic commentary on human nature and social institutions. The candidates for prime minister must prove their ability by walking a tightrope and juggling. "A man in high political office," explains the Emperor, "must always maintain his balance in a crisis" and be able to juggle problems so that they seem to disappear. The Emperor admits he doesn't need a prime minister to fight a war, "but I need one to blame in case we lose it." He also says, "I trust and have abiding faith in the integrity and reliability of any man that I can kill." Later, the Empress tells her husband that she knows Gulliver is in danger because "criers are going through the square now, proclaiming your kindness, and that means that some-body's going to be executed soon." This witty dialogue does not derive directly from Swift, but it is consistent with his outlook.

Unfortunately, most of the dialogue is delivered so that instead of sounding reasonable until we realize its absurdity, it immediately sounds unreasonable. The only exception occurs when the Minister of Defense criticizes Gulliver's capture of the fleet. "Who ever heard of a war without anyone getting killed? Where's the sacrifice, above and beyond the call of duty? Where's the heroism?" He says this as if he believes it, and for a few seconds the film's style almost matches the book's. Also, Swift's Lilliputians are skilled in mathematics and mechanics; their Emperor is a "patron of learning," his movements are "graceful," and he courageously stands his ground when confronted by Gulliver. The film turns these people into clowns. Fearful of Gulliver, they stumble clumsily down a flight of steps and could never be a valid threat to any-one. In Lilliput, farce overwhelms satire.

When the film visits Brobdingnag, all that remains from the novel is the fact that a young girl, Glumdalclitch, affectionately cares for Gulliver, which allows Harryhausen to give children in the audience an identification figure. In the book, Gulliver at first fears the giants, assuming that anyone that large must be savage and cruel. The Brob-dingnagians, in turn, assume that anyone as small as Gulliver couldn't be rational or dignified. Once they realize that he is like themselves, they treat him well.

Although Gulliver comes to like the Brobdingnagians in the novel, he can't help but be nauseated by the sight of them eating, by their body odor, and by the giant spots and pimples on the fashionable ladies' skin. He is astute enough, though, to real-ize that he probably looked to the Lilliputians the way these people look to him, and that his countrymen would seem the same if viewed closely. In short, he recognizes the gross nature of the human animal, despite its pose of civilization. Similarly, for all the kindness and respect they show him, the Brobdingnagians can't help but treat Gulliver with condescension. Ultimately, he is just their pet, forced by his size to be humble. With his self-esteem undermined at every turn, he feels demeaned and humiliated. In short, he recognizes the insignificance of the human animal, despite its delusions of stature.

The film omits all of this and radically alters Swift's tone. Initially the film's Gulliver is afraid, but because he acts like a fool by hiding his face and not his body, we are urged to laugh at him instead of fearing with him. From here on, the Brobdingnagians are consistently benevolent, with no overtones of condescension. Only near the end, after he defeats the King at chess, does Gulliver feel a loss of dignity when he must, in effect, apologize for winning. Unfortunately, this occurs at the expense of the King's character, for he suddenly becomes a childishly poor loser. Until that point, Brobdingnag is a paradise for Gulliver. He is even joined by Elizabeth, who had earlier been washed up on shore.

Swift failed to offer the scriptwriters a dramatic climax, for his Gulliver departs from Brobdingnag abruptly and accidentally. To solve this structural problem, Harryhausen adds a new character, Makovan, the court's alchemist. Seeing Gulliver as a threat to his position, Makovan accuses him of being a witch, but Gulliver uses his knowledge of chemistry to defeat the alchemist in a test. Despite this scientific one-upmanship, Gulliver is put on trial before the King. Elizabeth urges that he save himself by saying what they want to hear, so he concedes that science does not exist and that only a witch could beat the King at chess. Such self-abasement does Gulliver no good, for he is sentenced to death as a witch anyhow.

This situation may seem to go against Harryhausen's fondness for magic, but we can gain insight into his thinking from the unused narration that was written to begin *The 7th Voyage of Sinbad:* "To a man out of the distant past we live in a world of unbelievable magic. At a touch of our fingers we produce light, heat, or sound. Men travel swiftly through the air and beneath the sea. We speak with friends thousands of miles away through a tiny wire. Familiar things, yet fantastic." Science and magic are linked here, as they are in the activities of Makovan and Gulliver.

Until this point, Harryhausen had included only one use of animation, when a squirrel takes Gulliver to its nest. This occurs after he and Elizabeth, having been married by the King, foolishly sneak out of the palace for a honeymoon. The entire sequence, irrelevant to the main action, could easily have been omitted. Now, the King—who has a collection of (to him) miniature animals—decides to use his crocodile as Gulliver's executioner, a rather sadistic plan that is inconsistent with the King's character. It does, however, provide an impressive and exciting confrontation. The Queen tosses the helpless Gulliver a round pin, which he uses as a weapon, whacking the beast on the snout with it until the crocodile bites one edge and, after a short tug of war, tosses the object aside. Gulliver then grabs a latch pin from a jewel box and with it dispatches the monster. During this action we have several dramatic shots of the crocodile from Gulliver's point of view, and the physical interaction as both hold onto the pin is amazingly precise. The illusion is so convincing that one wishes the scene were a more natural part of the film as a whole.

Glumdalclitch then flees with Gulliver and Elizabeth, as a lynch mob pursues. Finally, the couple float to sea in a basket. Later, they find themselves on an English shore, with no basket in sight. The dialogue suggests that, as in *The Wizard of Oz* (1939), their adventures might all have been a dream. At any rate, Gulliver has learned the folly of ambition. This is an odd moral for Harryhausen to advocate, for his own career illustrates that an individual can achieve major goals through ability and determination, but it is less contradictory to what Harryhausen stands for than Swift's conclusion, in which Gulliver has come to see himself as merely unimpressive.

Technically, *Gulliver* is almost seamless. Nearly the entire picture depends on visual effects (if not on animation), and they are so smoothly integrated that the viewer takes them for granted, responding as if it were a "realistic" work. Although one might wish for greater complexity, the film is reasonably intelligent and offers more food for thought than most movies designed for children.

Like *Gulliver,* Harryhausen's next film had a finished screenplay before he and Schneer became involved—an adaptation of Jules Verne's 1875 novel *The Mysterious Island,* which takes place during the American Civil War. In it, some Northern soldiers escape from a Confederate prison camp in a hot-air balloon, only to be stranded on an unknown Pacific island. No doubt the involvement of Captain Nemo and his disabled submarine, the *Nautilus,* hooked Harryhausen's imagination. The book, however, completely avoids fantasy, dealing in a practical fashion with the castaways' survival. "We had to take great liberties" with the story, Harryhausen admits,[57] to include giant creatures that the characters could fight and he could animate. At one point during revisions, the island was populated by dinosaurs (as in *King Kong*); at another stage, it had an Egyptian origin.

Eventually, the writers let Captain Nemo solve the problem. Like the novel, the film *Mysterious Island* (1962) includes several strange events that are ultimately explained as the benevolent, anonymous actions of Nemo (Herbert Lom): Captain Cyrus Harding (Michael Craig) is discovered safe on shore after being lost at sea, a bullet is found in some meat, a chest floats ashore with items the castaways need but can't make, and an attacking pirate ship unexpectedly explodes. To these incidents, the film adds the discovery of large oysters, a giant crab, and massive bees as another facet of the same mystery. Nemo, it turns out, has created them to provide the world with an inexhaustible food supply. Thus, the animation scenes feel like a natural part of the plot. Harryhausen did, however, retain from the earlier concepts a prehistoric phororhacos (which viewers naturally assume is some kind of chicken), a giant nautiloid cephalopod, and the underwater remains of an ancient city that combine Greek buildings with Egyptian statues.

The addition of Nemo's experiments is consistent with Verne's confidence in science and his rejection of fantasy. Just as Harryhausen's *Gulliver* explains the alchemist's "magic" as a form of chemistry, his *Island* provides a pseudoscientific explanation of what seems to be fantastic. After he finds a large oyster, one character in the film remarks, "It's almost supernatural, isn't it?" Verne offers a precedent for this, when a man is so impressed with the way his companion creates fire that he thinks, "If Cyrus Harding was not a magician, he was certainly no ordinary man."

At the same time, the plot change does have a result that Verne would not have condoned. All of the seeming magic now originates with Nemo, the sorcerer-like outsider who has his own secret methods. Verne's faith had been embodied not in Nemo but in Captain Harding, who is "a compound of every science, a possessor of all human knowledge." Under Harding's guidance, the castaways do more than survive. They recreate modern industrial society, complete to the manufacture of steel, and do so with available contemporary knowledge. The film's castaways accomplish much less.

The novel also emphasizes the group's cooperation in a common effort, with Harding's knowledge and ingenuity making him the natural leader. He is far more an engineer than a soldier. The film's writers, recognizing that such a situation lacks conflict, alter the relationships. Pencroft (Percy Herbert), a Northern sailor in the book, becomes a Southern soldier who resents working under a Northerner. Gideon Spilett (Gary Merrill), a war correspondent, now has an edge of sarcasm that antagonizes Harding. The new Captain Harding takes command because he is the ranking officer, and as such he assigns duties, gives orders, and inspires resistance. He has become more soldier than engineer. In another change, Herbert Brown, a fifteen-year-old orphan in the novel, has aged a few years and functions as the obligatory teenage heartthrob (Michael Callan). He also has more personality than in the novel because of his cowardice, which he overcomes during the attack of the phororhacos.

To explain Nemo's experiments, the film tempers his anger. Verne's Nemo is (like Jonathan Swift) a disillusioned idealist disgusted by humanity; Harryhausen's Nemo is disturbed not by people but by the concept of war. As a result, he seeks to eliminate famine and economic competition, the presumed causes of war. He hopes to achieve a paradise similar to the one Harryhausen's Gulliver imagined he could create on Lilliput, what Gulliver called a country where "none of you will ever be hungry again, no man will ever steal or be jealous of what another has." This turns Nemo into a man with whom the sincerely wholesome Harryhausen can feel comfortable. Even though Verne might have disliked these alterations, his characters are too idealized and similar to each other, so the changes help create a more solid, satisfying film.

A more arbitrary addition involves Lady Mary Fairchild (Joan Greenwood) and her niece, Elena (Beth Rogan), who are washed ashore after an unseen shipwreck. But if one accepts this contrived arrival, the women's presence is far from disturbing. Their English cultivation contrasts nicely with the Americans' practicality, and the script neatly avoids the usual complications. Instead of being arrogant, Lady Mary realistically adapts to the need for work; Elena does not adjust as easily, but neither does she become a problem. There are no romantic triangles, and the inevitable romance between Elena and Herbert is understated. (A plan to have the couple married by Nemo near the film's end was wisely discarded.)

The film's climax contains the largest amount of new material. In the book, the island's volcano erupts after Nemo dies; the movie retains the eruption, but Nemo plans to escape by patching and raising the sunken pirate ship. Work begins, but when the eruption starts sooner than expected, Nemo gives up and Harding suggests placing the balloon inside the ship and inflating it, an idea that neatly links the film's end with its beginning. But the filmmakers, not content with this race against the volcano, also include a confrontation with the giant nautiloid cephalopod. "The tentacles required almost microscopic movements in order to give the illusion of a slow undersea effect," recalls Harryhausen,[58] but that very slowness limits the scene's excitement. After this digression—which interrupts the suspense, instead of adding to it—the plan works, although Nemo dies in the process. As the survivors sail off, they vow to work "for a peaceful and bountiful world."

Harryhausen carefully introduces all of *Mysterious Island*'s creatures. Searching the beach for food, the men do not realize they are standing on the back of a massive crab until it rises under them. The phororhacos initially appears only as a shadow that falls on Spilett while he is fishing; we do not see the beast itself until it bounds into the camp. When Herbert and Elena discover a honeycomb, the sound of buzzing is heard well before an inhabitant returns. The nautiloid cephalopod has perhaps the most dramatic introduction: The camera starts on some men working underwater, then moves into darkness until it comes upon a giant eye that fills the screen.

In staging these encounters, Harryhausen rarely finds much for his creatures to do, but one hardly notices because they are just opponents for the humans to defeat (and, often, to eat). For example, the excellent crab conflict makes the men the focal point of the action as they dart about trying to master the monster, and the editing gives a feeling of activity despite the humans' useless lunges at the stoical creature. The story is the people's, and the creatures are just part of their environment. We do not feel that the film exists for the sake of showing the animals, which was the case in Harryhausen's films prior to *The 3 Worlds of Gulliver*.

The success of *Mysterious Island* derives not from the convincing special effects, which can be taken for granted in a Harryhausen film, but from the fact that the "normal" scenes are also worth watching. Because the novel contains no giant ani-

Castaways in *Mysterious Island* (1961) battle a giant crab.

mals, the basic plot is interesting in itself, and director Cy Endfield supports it with tight pacing and active visuals that grip viewers from the start. After a vigorous, economical impression of Civil War battle, we cut to the inside of a cell as the prisoners prepare to escape. Here, and in the balloon gondola scenes that follow, Endfield achieves visual variety in a constricted setting through multiple camera setups and continual shifts of actor and camera position. These scenes involve viewers in the characters' plight, so we needn't endure patiently until a monster arrives.

The film never returns to this level of energy, but Endfield doesn't completely relax his grip, either. He also has the discipline to underplay moments that someone else might have overstated. For example, he stages an early exchange of looks between Herbert and Elena by placing them near the camera, but on opposite sides of the screen, while two others interact in the background. Such discretion avoids cliché and makes the characters more believable.

Although *Mysterious Island* derives from the basic fantasy-adventure formula (uncharted island, stranded humans, giant beasts), it possesses enough integrity and originality in all departments to stand solidly on its own. It may not contain Harryhausen's most spectacular effects, and viewers are as likely to recall the story and the relationships as they are the monsters, but the film is one of his best.

Harryhausen next returned to his own pet project, *Jason and the Argonauts* (1963). In filming Jason's quest for the Golden Fleece, he wanted to include the interaction of humans and the gods, an element which previous films on related subjects had ignored. After Harryhausen made his drawings, Jan Read wrote a script, which Beverley Cross revised. "Ray was very positive about which special effects he wanted to do," recalls Cross. "It was just a question of how we would string them all together in the neatest, most lucid way."[59] Harryhausen had first been attracted to Greek mythology when, as a child, he learned about the Colossus of Rhodes, a gigantic statue of Apollo that stood at the entrance to that island's harbor. "If I could only *build* a statue that big!" he had thought, and the wish "stayed with me through the years."[60]

Existing for centuries only in oral form, the Greek myths accumulated multiple layers of often contradictory details, until they became a complex fabric of sudden digressions, inexplicable assumptions, and seemingly arbitrary actions. As a result, the screenwriters faced a daunting mass of elements to choose from and modify or replace. That they achieved a coherent plot is in itself a major accomplishment. No adaptation could ever be truly faithful to the source—there is no definitive source—but *Jason and the Argonauts* does capture the Greek view of existence. At the same time, the film repeats and clarifies some of the concepts and images already encountered in *The 7th Voyage of Sinbad, The 3 Worlds of Gulliver,* and *Mysterious Island,* turning it into an unexpectedly personal work. Of all his movies, says Harryhausen, *Jason* "pleases me the most."[61]

In the legend, Jason is rather easily convinced to seek the Golden Fleece, so the screenwriters had to clarify his motivation. First, they introduce Pelias (Douglas Wilmer), who wrests the throne of Thessaly from King Aristo. Warned that he will eventually lose the kingdom to one of Aristo's children, Pelias tries to kill all of his rival's offspring, but Aristo's son Jason is taken to safety. Twenty years later, the goddess Hera (Honor Blackman) arranges a "chance" meeting between the two men: She startles Pelias's horse, which throws him into a river so Jason (Todd Armstrong) can rescue him.

Afterward, not realizing the King's identity, Jason complains that during Pelias's rule Thessaly has changed "from the pride of Greece to a savage, evil land" whose people "need more than a leader—they must believe the gods have not deserted them." To achieve this, he plans to seize the throne and obtain the Fleece, which "has the power to heal, bring peace, and rid the land of plague and famine." Pretending support, Pelias advises Jason to get the Fleece first, hoping that he will be killed in the process. This adaptation clarifies matters by establishing a clear need for the Fleece. One might wish that the current state of the kingdom had been shown, not just described, but much time has already been devoted to exposition and the filmmakers understandably elected to be concise.

The god Hermes brings Jason to Mount Olympus, where Hera explains that she can help him, but only five times. Then Jason gathers his crew and the ship *Argo* is readied for a journey that parallels the one in *The 7th Voyage,* with the distant Colchis replacing Colossa. When the Argonauts grow weak, Hera directs Jason to the Isle of Bronze, but warns him to take only food and water. Once ashore, though, Hercules and Hylas discover a hoard of treasure within the pedestal of a huge metal statue. Because Hercules takes a giant brooch pin, the statue—of the warrior Talos—comes to life and attacks the Argonauts. This situation matches that of Sinbad's crew in the cyclops's cave, except this time Harryhausen establishes a more precise cause-and-effect relationship between the discovery of treasure and the giant creature's attack.

The initial movements of Talos inspire awe and dread: Its head turns to gaze on the thieves, then it slowly descends from the pedestal, steadies itself, and advances. After that, as the figure trudges along the beach and the men run about, the sight's novelty fades and the scene loses its intensity. True, Talos reaches through a stone arch and drags its hand back through the sand, but that action was performed more menacingly by a tentacle in *It Came from Beneath the Sea*. Excitement returns when Talos, standing astride a channel, picks up the ship and shakes it so that the crewmen fall to the water below (as Kong had once done with a fallen log). Finally, Hera tells Jason, "Look to his ankles." He does so and finds a pin, which he unscrews, while Talos patiently waits. With its life-fluid draining out, the figure clasps its throat, cracks, and crashes to the ground.

Very little of this derives from the myth. In fact, the original figure was not even a giant, but Harryhausen used Talos to satisfy his desire to re-create the Colossus of Rhodes. His impressive animation fully captures the statue's creaking stiffness, and he carefully tailored its movements for something of such size. The result looks stunning and feels as if it *might* be an actual mythic encounter.

The *Argo* is repaired, and Hera tells Jason to sail to Phrygia, where Phineas (Patrick Troughton) will give him further information. Blinded for misusing his gift of prophecy, Phineas has fallen victim to the bird-like harpies, who steal his food and otherwise torment him. Phineas cries out to Zeus, "I was a sinner—I've never tried to deny it—but I didn't sin every day. Why then do you punish me every day?" Rebelling against Zeus, Phineas refuses to provide information until Jason frees him from the harpies, so the men enclose a ruined temple with nets and trap the creatures within. The Argonauts then enter the improvised cage and wave their swords at the creatures. This causes a lull in the action, for despite a lot of running around, nothing happens. Finally, Phineas and the Argonauts emerge and the net is dropped directly onto the harpies, which could have been done right away. Phineas now reveals that the way to Colchis is between the Clashing Rocks.

In Harryhausen's version of the Clashing Rocks, ships entering a narrow channel are threatened with an avalanche of boulders. This is demonstrated by the destruction of a vessel from Colchis, which works neatly into the plot because Jason rescues Medea from the wreck. Jason's method for passing between the rocks is visually striking, but also inexplicable. Hera supposedly can no longer aid Jason, yet we see her move the figure of Triton, a giant merman, on the Olympian gameboard. Phineas had given Jason a pendant of a similar-looking figure, and now Jason, angry at the gods' cruelty, rips this pendant from his neck and throws it into the water. Thereupon, the giant figure of Triton emerges and braces both sides of the channel, as the *Argo* passes under one arm.

The reason for Triton's emergence is far from clear. We don't know the nature of the pendant, and because Jason rejects the gods, why would his throwing of it cause a god to help him? If Hera's movement of the Triton gamepiece summons him, how can she break the rules and help when Jason is supposedly on his own? This kind of "illogic" can and does appear in myth, but probably should not in art.

Jason's meeting with King Aeetes of Colchis presents some fascinating thematic points. Medea has said that the Fleece brought "peace and prosperity" to her city, and Aeetes insists that its loss will cause "plague and famine and the destruction of our country." (This important part of the film's plot does not derive from the myth.) Aeetes then has Jason and his men arrested and condemns them to death. Like Gulliver, Jason has so far done only a good deed—rescuing Medea—yet he is treated like a traitor. Unlike Gulliver, he really does intend to undermine the country's welfare, so we cannot help but consider Aeetes's position valid. The irony is pointed and even profound: In order to bring peace and prosperity to his own land, Jason must undermine a country that has done him no harm.

Meanwhile, Medea has fallen in love with Jason and wishes to help him, but as a Priestess of Hecate and a loyal citizen, doing so would make her a traitor. The film plays down this predicament: In the myth, Medea was also Aeetes's daughter, so the film's omission of that detail makes her choice less difficult. Also, from *The 7th Voyage* on, Harryhausen's films avoided love and romance as much as possible. The shooting script did confront this subject, for in it Jason flirtatiously comments on Medea's beauty, she realizes that he had undressed her after the rescue, and she thinks aloud about "the way he held me" and "the feel of his skin under my fingers." The film, however, omits this preparation for Medea's actions. As a result, we see her set him free, but must assume her motive. Still, Medea's dilemma remains in the film—albeit weakly—and helps give it substance.

In the script, Medea leads Jason to Hades, where they pass the two-headed guardian dog Cerberus and Charon ferries them across a lake, as floating figures grasp at their boat. Then Jason enters the Pool of Hecate, the waters of which will protect him from injury. Harryhausen never filmed this lengthy and rather passive sequence, so Jason continues to function as a traditionally vulnerable hero.

Before gaining the Fleece, Jason must defeat a hydra. This creature (borrowed from Hercules's adventures) is a triumph of choreographic animation, with its seven heads and necks all moving at the same time. In a powerfully dramatic introduction, the heads seem to burst into view and toward the camera. During the fight, editing creates a good illusion of activity as Jason waves his sword and dodges, while the hydra's heads bob and weave. The only physical contact occurs when the beast picks Jason up with its tail, then puts him down again. Finally, Jason plunges his sword into the

Dueling skeletons attack Jason in one of the most spectacular special effects scenes of Ray Harryhausen's career. From *Jason and the Argonauts* (1963).

hydra's chest and the waiting is over. The mythic hydra had presented a greater challenge for Hercules, because whenever a head was severed, two grew back in its place. Harryhausen wanted to have Jason slice off a few heads, too, with at least one new one growing back each time, but fear of the British censor restrained him. Unfortunately, he had nothing with which to replace that action.

After the Argonauts flee with the Fleece, Aeetes gathers the hydra's teeth. Confronting Jason, he spreads the teeth on the ground and armed skeletons emerge. Using the myth as a starting point, Harryhausen here borrows from himself: The skeleton duel had dominated *The 7th Voyage of Sinbad,* and he probably assumed that multiplying the numbers would increase the impact. He was right, for although the viewer's attention is spread out and one doesn't know or care who is fighting alongside Jason, the almost constant physical interaction between the humans and the models makes this one of the most amazing effects scenes in Harryhausen's career. No doubt it contains more action than the Talos, harpy, and hydra segments because, as in *The 7th Voyage,* Harryhausen first staged the duel with stuntmen standing in for the skeletons.

Significantly, Aeetes's situation is very different from that of Sokurah, so we understand and half support his actions. This time, the cry "Kill, kill, kill them all!" comes from an outraged victim, not an obsessed villain. We still root for Jason, because skeletons do not evoke empathy, especially when they outnumber the humans, but the scene conveys a subtle, morally ambiguous overtone.

In revealing and not always conscious ways, certain aspects of Harryhausen's three previous films here flower on a thematic level. Sinbad's desire to prevent an unnecessary war between two similar sides had functioned only as a superficial plot device and was soon forgotten; other than peace, we have no idea what success offers. *The 3 Worlds of Gulliver* takes this further, with its emphasis on the Lilliput-Blefuscu war and Gulliver's description of a paradise that the Lilliputians' desire for power and revenge denies them. In Brobdingnag, Gulliver finds himself in just such a paradise, but it is lost through the King's childish whim and Gulliver's need for self-respect. Similar situations in *Mysterious Island* involve Nemo's attempt to end war, which would produce some vague sort of paradise, and the attempt of the castaways to establish a civilized society despite their personal conflicts.

Finally, in *Jason and the Argonauts,* we discover a rather mature vision of war's causes and ironies: Both Colchis and Thessaly need the Fleece to make them feel the gods have not deserted them, and both seem justified in their determination to have it. Stability and happiness are fragile conditions, and those who seek them are neither purely good nor maliciously evil. Such concepts would not exist in this form in *Jason and the Argonauts* if the previous films had not already handled them in more limited ways.

Another concept that evolves through these films, and one possessing even wider implications, begins with Sinbad's physical relationship to the tiny Princess, which is a detail included only for its novelty and plot function. Differences are more important to *The 3 Worlds of Gulliver,* which relates size to dominance and subservience. The giants are concerned about the tiny ones' welfare, but cannot escape feeling a sense of their own power and some degree of condescension, while the tiny ones struggle to assert their strength, such as it is, and establish their self-worth. *Mysterious Island* contains no large humans, but Nemo is a mental and technological giant who manipulates the lives of the relatively "tiny" castaways in a benevolent way, but always with the implication that his influence could as easily be destructive. In a sense, Nemo is a subtler, more complex variation on the blunt villainy of the equally manipulative Sokurah in *The 7th Voyage of Sinbad.*

The stress on the gods' relationship to humanity in *Jason and the Argonauts* links Nemo's god-like involvement in the other characters' struggle to survive with the explicit size contrast found in *Gulliver*. In *Jason,* a view of existence embedded in the previous films, but left unrecognized and undeveloped, finally becomes clear and conscious. These gods' control of human life is summed up in two images: the tiny Jason held in the palm of Hermes' hand, and Jason standing on the gods' table-top map, where they move models of people and ships like pieces in a game to produce real effects below. Earlier, Gulliver's standing on the Brobdingnagians' chessboard was only a plot detail, but the comparable image in *Jason* has the resonance of a metaphor.

A key point is that although the gods aid and hinder humans, they also leave those earthly mortals a degree of independence and responsibility. "Zeus has given you a kingdom," Pelias is told. "The rest will be up to you." And Pelias, in his human weakness, is not satisfied and seeks to avoid losing the kingdom later. When he learns that he has killed one of his rival's children needlessly, he asks why Zeus drove him to it. "Zeus," he is told, "cannot drive men to do what you have done. Men drive themselves to do such things." Similarly, Hercules goes against the gods' command by taking Talos's brooch pin, after finding the chamber door temptingly ajar; he rationalizes that if the gods left the treasure unguarded, they obviously do not want it.

Just as humans have the freedom to go against the gods' will, they also must contribute to the help the gods offer. Zeus assures Pelias that he will defeat the King of Thessaly, but Pelias must nevertheless fight the battle himself, and when Jason asks how to defeat Talos, Hera says, "Fight Talos with your wits. Look to his ankles. There is nothing else I can tell you." Later, instead of explaining how to get to Colchis, Hera sends Jason to ask Phineas. The gods' help goes only so far, and humans have to work for success and survival. This concept could already be seen when the genie in *The 7th Voyage* does not rescue Sinbad and when the Queen of Brobdingnag does not rescue Gulliver. Instead, they provide tools and/or information, which the heroes must make use of themselves. Nemo does the same kind of thing for the castaways.

Harryhausen probably empathizes with the independent Jason, who uses his strength and will to achieve a goal despite obstacles and resistance, but he also has much in common with the gods themselves. The scripts of his films had frequently indulged in god-like manipulation of characters and events, and in Jason the gods' involvement in the characters' lives offered Harryhausen the perfect subject, with behind-the-scenes manipulation becoming part of the film's subject. Instead of the scriptwriters giving Jason an unexpected means of defeating Talos, Hera does it, and it is the gods who inflict fantastic creatures on the characters, in a sense actually bringing them to life. The gods also reveal an interested, but distant, response to the characters. Harryhausen, the emotionally austere manipulator, has given himself a place in this film.

The overall tone of *Jason and the Argonauts* also reflects its creator's personality. Harryhausen is a man who in one breath says "I don't like depressing pictures"[62] and in another states that he likes "subjects that are overshadowed by doom."[63] This seeming contradiction embodies his basic nature. When a future Argonaut defeats Hercules in a contest, Zeus says, "Let Hylas have his moment of triumph—while he may." This statement illustrates the way the film (and the Greek worldview) undercuts human pride and delusions of achievement, yet does so not in a cynical or defeatist way. Individuals may be helpless pawns in the hands of powerful, mysterious forces, but those same individuals have the freedom to make their own success through strength, determination, and skill. "I think you can make your own destiny," Harryhausen once declared, "but only up to a point."[64] Only after understanding *Jason and the Argonauts* can one realize that the film *Gulliver* avoids the bitterness of Jonathan Swift not just for commercial reasons but also because it is foreign to Harryhausen's outlook.

In 1963, both critics and audiences dismissed *Jason,* which Harryhausen attributed to people confusing his film with Italian "spear and sandal" epics. The public's resistance, however, was more likely due to the film itself. Its moral complexity and the characters' lack of control over their actions dilute the heroic adventure that audiences were led to expect, and the gods' involvement keeps pulling viewers away from the action, so that the plot feels more abstract than immediate. The ending of the film exemplifies this tendency. As the *Argo* sails away, we see it not directly but from the gods' point of view. Zeus states, "For the moment let them enjoy a calm sea, a fresh breeze, and each other. . . . I have not yet finished with Jason. Let us continue the game another day." With that, he waves his hand and the image of Jason and Medea fades from sight. We are left in the mists of Mount Olympus, unable to share the characters' moment of triumph. By concluding in this way, the film almost willfully refuses to satisfy the very audience it seeks to entertain.

Harryhausen could not have expected this material to be quite as personal as it became, for—like most artists—he bases his most interesting choices at least partly on instinct. Even thirty years later, commenting on a scene from the film, he stated, "I always had an intense interest in relationships between big people and little people," adding, "I don't know what it is about it—it just fascinates me."[65] Harryhausen need not articulate such matters. In *Jason,* the images and situations explain for him, but such a fortuitous combination of elements would never occur again.

After completing *Jason and the Argonauts,* Schneer and Harryhausen turned to H. G. Wells's *The First Men in the Moon.* As Harryhausen's last adaptation of a literary work, it appropriately resembles the first, for both Swift in *Gulliver's Travels* and Wells in *First Men in the Moon* use an imagined society to criticize their own worlds. Wells, however, offers *two* main characters: Cavor, a narrowly focused inventor, and Bedford, a narrowly focused businessman.

Harryhausen wished to retain the novel's turn-of-the-century setting, but Columbia Pictures wanted it updated, so scriptwriter Nigel Kneale added a modern prologue in which UN astronauts land on the Moon, only to discover a note dated 1899 claiming the satellite for Queen Victoria. Investigators then locate Bedford in a nursing home, where he recounts his tale and the film moves into the past, returning to the present only for a brief finale. This compromise satisfied both parties, but the studio also considered Kneale's adaptation too serious-minded. "The front office complained that women would not be able to identify with this picture, that it needed charm," states Harryhausen,[66] consciously echoing Carl Denham's lament in *King Kong.* So another writer helped add both a woman and a sense of humor.

First Men in the Moon (1964), like the book, begins with Bedford (Edward Judd) eluding creditors after a business failure. He rents a country cottage, where he plans to make money and avoid real work by writing a successful play. Readily distracted, he listens as a neighbor, Cavor (Lionel Jeffries), explains his attempt to develop Cavorite, an antigravity substance. Cavor seeks knowledge for its own sake, while the pragmatic Bedford remains unimpressed until he sees a chance for wealth and power. When Cavor reveals his own intended use for Cavorite, a trip to the Moon, Bedford resists until he learns that gold exists there. Having discovered a practical purpose for the journey, Bedford insists on going along.

Using *The 3 Worlds of Gulliver* as a model, the filmmakers added the character of Kate Callender (Martha Hyer), Bedford's supposed fiancée. Kate, like Gulliver's fiancée, tours the cottage and speaks of marriage, but Bedford, like Gulliver, wants to "sail away" to make a fortune. Gulliver, however, is a generous man frustrated by poverty, whereas Bedford is a self-indulgent manipulator. Here, the scriptwriters develop Bedford's deceitfulness further than Wells had. It is not certain that he ever planned to marry Kate, and he improvises a series of lies to her, claiming that he owns the cottage, that he has made progress on the play, and that a producer anxiously awaits it. He even illegally signs the cottage over to her and has her sell it to Cavor, so he can invest the money in Cavorite.

Such duplicity makes the film's Bedford more unpleasant than the merely self-deceiving, ambitious businessman of the novel. Consequently, because there was a need to present him as an acceptable romantic companion for Kate (and something like a traditional hero for the viewer), the filmmakers tried to soften the character in the actor's performance. As guided by director Nathan Juran, Edward Judd avoids the necessary balance between charm and callous calculation, with charm winning out; despite a hint of swaggering foolishness, the man and his actions do not quite blend. Juran also uses farce to distract viewers from Bedford's less positive qualities. At one point, when Bedford sits on a chair coated with Cavorite and rises to the room's ceiling, Juran has Cavor bustle about, shout for help, and struggle with a ladder while Bedford delivers dialogue that the script had placed later. As a result, his passionate words—"It'll revolutionize shipping, locomotion, building. . . . We're onto the chance of a thousand years! . . . Cavorite could rule the world!"—disappear into the background.

Like Elizabeth in *Gulliver,* Kate goes on the journey, although not as a stowaway. Having been served a summons by the cottage's real owner, she angrily strides to the sphere and is pulled in just before it takes off. Once on the Moon, Bedford stakes his claim and the two men explore. The film omits the giant plants that grow up around the sphere, but the men's adventures in the caverns below do follow Wells's plot. When the novel's characters return to the surface, they cannot find their sphere amid the thick vegetation. Here the film's writers, having omitted the plants, borrow a plot twist from Wells's *The Time Machine:* The Selenites have dragged the sphere under-ground.

The subsequent search for the vehicle and Kate occupies time that could have been devoted to the lunar civilization and the men's responses to it. Even so, the film includes a few pointed facts about the aliens, such as their putting unneeded workers to sleep in cocoons. "A unique way of dealing with unemployment," admires Cavor, who adds, with a revealing touch of uncertainty, "Entirely reasonable—I suppose." The more realistic Kate then identifies a disadvantage of this reasonable procedure: "They'll treat us the same way if they find they have no further use for us."

The film contrasts the two men's views of the aliens. Cavor seeks to communicate and share knowledge; he is curious about a society "different from ours," one with "different standards." It doesn't at first occur to him that those very differences might place him in danger, but when it does, he's willing to take the risk. Meanwhile, the skeptical and defensive Bedford attacks the Selenites as soon as they press in on him. "You've certainly given them a taste of human violence," chides Cavor. Bedford later declares, "I haven't your boundless confidence in those insects," and Cavor responds, "You don't try to understand."

Without quite advocating Bedford's aggressiveness, the film does suggest that Cavor's scientific rationality is not the ideal perspective. During Cavor's interview with the Grand Lunar, the ruler's questions and Cavor's replies reveal the absurdity of Earth's society. The Lunar concludes, rightly enough, that if humans detest war but still engage in it, they must be "defective." This puts Cavor in the rather unscientific position of defending imperfection. The Lunar, knowing that violence will result if more earthlings arrive and that only Cavor can make Cavorite, decides to keep him on the Moon. As Bedford accurately warns, "This is not an audience. You're on trial!" Bedford's suspicion of "those insects" appears to be borne out, and Cavor's confidence just impractical naivete; at the same time, Bedford's violence had inspired the Lunar's decision, so in a sense he himself created the situation that seems to validate his initial violence. Like *Earth vs. the Flying Saucers,* this film presents an alien race that is both victimized by and dangerous to humanity, but here the combination feels less like confusion than sincere ambivalence.

Despite an opportunity to escape, Cavor chooses to stay behind when Bedford and Kate leave in the sphere. We then return to the present, as the modern astronauts discover the deserted and crumbling lunar city. What happened? "Poor Cavor," mutters old Bedford, "he did have such a terrible cold." The implication that germs from Earth destroyed the Selenites is a letdown for several reasons: It is a blatant steal from Wells's *The War of the Worlds,* Cavor had clearly not had a terrible cold (he coughs slightly once), and Edward Judd's delivery of the line evokes no particular feeling, so that the event is neither a tragedy nor a sick joke.

Like *Gulliver's Travels,* Wells's novel contained little opportunity for animation, so Harryhausen spent most of his time creating the outer space sequences and the Selenites' world. In general, he dislikes science fiction because it seems "terribly cold and you're always dealing with gadgets."[67] The bland, semidocumentary realism of the UN Moon landing in *First Men in the Moon* both illustrates his point and reveals his lack of interest in the genre. Thanks to the turn-of-the-century setting, however, Harryhausen can relate to the main story as a fantasy, with the Moon serving as the equivalent of some remote, unexplored island.

Because Charles Schneer insisted on filming in Panavision—an anamorphic widescreen process—Harryhausen couldn't use his standard method of front- or rear-screen projection to combine elements into a single shot. Instead, he filmed miniature settings and used a traveling matte to add the live actors. By this means, he created vast caverns and a gigantic staircase, a massive horizontal world punctuated by the vertical lines of towering crystalline forms. In designing the Selenites, Harryhausen followed Wells's description of them as upright, humanoid ants. Although opposing the use of people in suits, he avoided "an eternity in animating the creatures en mass"[68] by placing children in costumes for long shots and fights. He did animate the taller, "intellectual" Selenites who interact as individuals with the humans. The two approaches do not blend smoothly, but the animated figures, at least, have a strikingly alien quality.

Aside from Bedford's fight scenes, the film's action highlight involves a massive Moon creature with an elongated, caterpillar-like body appropriate to the rectangular shape of the screen. The book's characters merely watch some "Mooncalves" grazing, but Harryhausen has one of his monsters chase Bedford and Cavor around a cavern, until the Selenites kill it and cut it up for food. The sequence doesn't feel out of place, but it is less a necessary part of the story than a token gesture for Harryhausen's fans.

Consistently interesting and at times spectacular, *First Men in the Moon* is sustained by the acting of Lionel Jeffries as Cavor, who keeps the film's energy level high, while somehow finding a human center in his wildly flamboyant performance. The addition of Kate and a sense of humor inevitably led to a muting of Wells's stress on the flaws in Bedford and Cavor, and in what they represent, but the shift in tone also bears the imprint of Harryhausen's personality: The film's acknowledgment of those flaws is tempered with understanding, even sympathy, for both men.

After *Jason and the Argonauts* and *First Men in the Moon* failed to perform well at the box office, Schneer and Harryhausen must have begun to question their choice of subject matter. Meanwhile, England's Hammer Films decided to remake *One Million B.C.* (1940) and purchased the rights from its producer-director, Hal Roach. Electing to use animated dinosaurs and not the magnified lizards of the first version, the studio hired Harryhausen to provide the special effects. *One Million Years B.C.* (1966) thus became his first effort without Charles Schneer in a decade. Although, he said, "the Hammer executives and I worked pretty closely together"[69] and he had previously collaborated with director Don Chaffey and photographer Wilkie Cooper, it is safe to say that Harryhausen had less than his usual degree of control in this project. The film was not "built around" his sequences, and the publicity stressed not special effects but the poster-girl sexuality of its star, Raquel Welch.

The intelligently conceived plot depicts, in almost allegorical fashion, a stage of humanity's evolution. First, we meet the dark and brutish Rock people, whose relationships are based on physical power. During a fight with his father, the chief, Tumak (John Richardson), falls from a cliff. Wandering alone in unfamiliar territory, he is befriended by the blonde and moderately more refined Shell people, through whom he discovers tools (a spear), art (a necklace and cave paintings), sensitivity (tears), ideals (mercy shown to a helpless opponent), rituals of respect (burial), and innocent amusement (swimming). This process permits the logical integration of a romance, as Tumak develops an affection for Loana (Raquel Welch), a voluptuous Shell. (The slightly longer British version of the film includes several shots that establish the burial and cave paintings more fully than the American print does.) In turn, the Shell people learn physical prowess and courage from Tumak: When an allosaurus invades the village, he confronts and defeats it after everyone else takes cover. Throughout, the characters use only—to us—unintelligible words and grunts, and director Chaffey generally meets the challenge of making events and relationships clear visually.

Location filming on the volcanic Canary Islands created a believably bleak, inhospitable prehistoric world, but one that is probably too barren to justify the presence of large animals. Science, of course, insists that humans never coexisted with dinosaurs, but viewers generally accept such artistic license for the chance to see the confrontations that result. More disturbing is the fact that, although most of the creatures were based on museum restorations, the first two seen in the film are not even dinosaurs, just an enlarged lizard and spider. "I have never favored" this approach, says Harryhausen, but he adds that "we felt it might add to the realism if the first creature we saw was a living specimen."[70] It didn't, and this unconvincing rationalization denies the merit of Harryhausen's technique. He did, however, save animation time.

Harryhausen's creature encounters and the climactic eruption of a volcano derive from previous films, but all are impressively executed and most improve on their sources. For example, the pterodactyl here and the roc in *The 7th Voyage of Sinbad* both carry main characters to their nests. The roc, however, simply left Sinbad there to find his way back. In *One Million Years B.C.*, Harryhausen reconceives the sequence for greater impact and plot relevance: The pterodactyl carries Loana to its nest, where some hungry babies wait, and in midair it fights with a similar creature for possession of the shapely morsel. During the struggle, she falls to the surf below. After this, events do not simply go on as before. Tumak believes she has been devoured, and Loana brings the Shell people to help Tumak against his brother and rival.

Despite their evidencing the filmmakers' technical skill, most of the action scenes inspire limited audience involvement because of the characters' helplessness and relative passivity. Chance saves Loana from the pterodactyls, she and Tumak cower behind rocks as a triceratops struggles with a ceratosaurus, and Tumak barely escapes from the lumbering lizard. This, and the abrupt way the creatures enter their scenes, may create an accurate picture of humanity's precarious vulnerability in an unpredictable, primitive world, but it does so at the expense of a viewer's respect for the characters.

In this context, Tumak's battle with the allosaurus stands out as an instance of humanity both in the grip of a larger force *and* in the process of taking independent, meaningful action. Tumak does not just rush out to face the menace. Shortly before, he had helped a child gather fruit by lifting her into a tree, so now, when the allosaurus approaches the girl, he reveals a new protectiveness by coming to her aid. Then, as he pokes and prods at the towering threat, the Shell men are emboldened to help him. Finally, the encounter turns into a one-on-one struggle, a classic scene of action and courage that builds to a stunningly theatrical moment (and a technical tour de force) as Tumak falls on his back and impales the charging beast on the pole he is holding. It hovers, balanced above him, for a second or two, then topples over as Tumak scurries out of the way.

A brontosaurus, glimpsed in passing early on, was originally to have attacked the Rock people just before the volcanic eruption. The sequence was dropped and the script rewritten during live-action filming because, according to Harryhausen, "there were more than enough animated creatures throughout the rest of the film and to keep it in would add another two to three months to the already excessive animation schedule."[71] Translated, this means that the film was overbudget and something had to go. To replace it, Chaffey filmed the Shell people invading the Rock tribe's cave, the motivation of which is not fully clear. The event also places an emphasis on aggressiveness that does not fit the supposedly peaceful Shells.

During the eruption and earthquake that follow, people fall into crevasses and are crushed by boulders or buried under debris. Sensing that this cataclysm, despite its impressive spectacle, is too arbitrary and impersonal, the filmmakers blend this large-scale action with the themes and conflicts that had already evolved by including a final confrontation between Tumak and his brutal brother. Thus, Tumak kills the embodiment of his old existence during the eruption, and the two events climax simultaneously to mark the end of a way of life. Afterward, Tumak, Loana, and the other survivors emerge and move tentatively off into their future.

Working for Hammer Films on *One Million Years B.C.* allowed Harryhausen to step aside from major career decisions, but only temporarily. A new project had to be developed. One day, he happened upon a copy of the 1941–42 screenplay for Willis O'Brien's unproduced *Gwangi,* which he and Schneer agreed "still had great production values for an action film."[72] When Columbia Pictures deemed their budget too large, Warner Bros. stepped in to back the production. The result is an homage to Harryhausen's mentor and a technical triumph in its own right, but Harryhausen, by turning to a twenty-five-year-old project, was also marking time instead of advancing.

The Valley of Gwangi (1969) retains O'Brien's basic plot, in which Wild West show cowboys follow a tiny prehistoric horse to an isolated canyon where they encounter prehistoric creatures and capture Gwangi, an allosaurus. The showmen place their creature on exhibit, but it breaks loose, endangers the town, and is destroyed. This outline obviously owes much to *King Kong,* and also reveals elements—cowboys roping the beast from horseback and the tiny horse responding to a music box tune—which O'Brien had transferred from the discarded *Gwangi* to *Mighty Joe Young.*

Harryhausen wisely set this tale at the turn of the century, to avoid the "problems in disposing of Gwangi with present-day weapons."[73] In the process, he replaced O'Brien's climax (a truck herds Gwangi off a cliff) with a more atmospheric and

emotional one, which has the monster consumed by fire in the town's cathedral. Harryhausen also substituted a "Forbidden Valley" in Mexico for the Grand Canyon and
has Gwangi battle an elephant once he escapes, as the Ymir did in *20 Million Miles to
Earth*. "I had wanted to animate just the fight and use a real animal in the remaining
scenes," says Harryhausen, but the only elephant available was too small, so he also
animated shots of the animal performing tricks in the show.[74]

To flesh out the characters, Harryhausen also turned to *20 Million Miles to Earth*.
Again we have a male lead's antagonistic romance with an independent woman (T. J.,
who owns the Wild West show), a business-minded native boy (Lope), and a scientist
who is one of the boy's "clients" (Professor Bromley). This time, though, the romantic
antagonism is more serious, for Tuck (James Franciscus) had earlier walked out on the
now-bitter T. J. (Gila Golan). Harryhausen himself had married during the production
of *Jason and the Argonauts,* and intriguingly the next two films over which he exerted
script control stress a male's reluctance to commit to a woman. In *First Men in the
Moon,* Bedford had never explained himself, but here Tuck reveals that after living "on
my own so long" and having to "pitch [and] hustle my way into whatever I am now"
in the entertainment business, he couldn't face settling down.

Surprisingly, Tuck becomes quite unpleasant in his selfish manipulation of others.
Edward Judd had minimized Bedford's negative side, but James Franciscus lacks the
skill or charisma to make Tuck comprehensible and sympathetic. That Tuck takes an
instant liking to Lope when the boy mentions that his father is dead suggests that he
sees himself in the young hustler, but his reaction—and his selfless rescue of the boy
from a bull—is too abruptly inserted to fit with the rest of the characterization.

Even more surprisingly, the other male characters reveal similar negative qualities.
Champ (Richard Carlson), a friend of T. J.'s father, hates Tuck for deserting T. J., but
the force of his feeling suggests that he really suffers from jealousy. Carlos (Gustavo
Rojo), who works for T. J., also reveals jealousy and has an angry, petulant manner,
while the professor (Laurence Naismith) starts lusting after scientific fame and a
knighthood. Even Lope (Curtis Arden) goes too far, selling drinks of water in the
wilderness. The script might have included these qualities to give the characters substance, but because the actors never get past the obvious surface, they form an irritating, unlikable group. Only T. J. elicits empathy when she refuses to sell the show's star,
her "Wonder Horse," because that would put her companions out of jobs. The others,
however, don't seem worth her concern.

It appears that somewhere along the line the script intended to have physical action
embody psychological situations that the characters do not verbalize, as happens when
Tuck rescues Lope from the bull. Similarly, just when Tuck agrees to settle down with
T. J., a man (Prof. Bromley) is caught in a trap that Tuck himself set. Often, though, the
event fails to accomplish what seems to have been its original purpose. Tuck first
appears during T. J.'s act, as she is about to leap on horseback from a tower into a pool
of water below. When she sees Tuck she hesitates for long seconds, then "takes the
plunge," an action which would reflect her response to his return—uncertain about
again becoming involved, she decides to take a chance—except that the event occurs
at the wrong time, for she immediately rejects Tuck and doesn't reenter a relationship
until later.

In somewhat the same way, the script seems designed to resolve the conflicts
among the men during the Forbidden Valley sequence. When a fight nearly breaks out
in their camp, T. J. interrupts, asking, "Where do you think you are, civilization? We
have all got to stick together." Ironically, in this forgotten, primitive world the men
will at last work as members of a team. No single rope can hold the allosaurus, so

there is no single hero. Whenever one man drops his rope or falls from his horse another rides in to take his place, and when one is endangered by a creature, another risks his own life by luring the animal away. Instead of providing excitement for its own sake, this action sequence reveals the characters' flaws giving way to skill, courage, and interdependence. Once back in "civilization," though, only Tuck has been improved by the experience; in fact, the professor is now overtly unpleasant and T. J. has herself become ambitious, now that she "owns" Gwangi.

When Gwangi escapes and stalks T. J. and Lope, the film again almost succeeds at using action to reflect and create psychological change, as the ordeal or ceremony in the cathedral reestablishes the relationship between Tuck and T. J. At the end, they stand with Lope, looking like a newly minted family. Unfortunately, a few shots had explicitly shown T. J. and Tuck reunited *before* this climax, so the ending's potential power is defused, as if the filmmakers had not trusted their ability to convey the situation indirectly.

Although someone tried to create a film that uses its action meaningfully, the finished product does not follow through on that intention. It is not clear whose idea it was, or what went wrong, but Harryhausen himself had sometimes revealed an instinctive, not fully developed tendency to use action in this way. At any rate, Harryhausen responded to this film's approach, because his remaining features continue the attempt, with varying degrees of success.

Despite this fascinating but frustrating incompleteness, *Gwangi* offers two sequences that stand among Harryhausen's best: the events in the Forbidden Valley and the cathedral finale. In the former, the animation is superlative and its combination with the live action almost always convincing, as when a pterodactyl plucks Lope off his galloping horse. Even more impressive is the roping scene, which closely follows O'Brien's original storyboards. To give the horsemen something to rope, Harryhausen used a jeep with a long pole attached. Later, while animating the sequence, he positioned the allosaurus model in front of the back-projected jeep and blended the real ropes with those on the animated creature, creating the illusion of actual contact. From Gwangi's first appearance, through the roping and Gwangi's fight with a styracosaurus, until a landslide knocks the creature unconscious, this entire section is excellent, fast-paced adventure.

Gwangi is a much larger model than the allosaurus used in *One Million Years B.C.,* because he "had to be able to snarl, bleed, blink, and do many more things in front of the cameras."[75] The only thing he lacks is a sympathetic personality, and yet Harryhausen keeps Gwangi from becoming an outright villain. We view his actions as self-defense and animal aggressiveness, not cruelty or maliciousness. We even sporadically root for him, without exactly rooting against the humans. The film's climax carries this double-edged tone still further. Of course, Gwangi must be prevented from razing the town and killing its citizens, but he is also a creature forced from his native habitat and confused by his new surroundings. We can worry about the characters while still sympathizing with this lost animal, whose fate we assume to be sealed.

Tuck risks his life distracting Gwangi from the trapped woman and child. Then, positioned on a balcony, he encounters the allosaurus at eye level and the struggle becomes a one-to-one confrontation. When Tuck grabs a spear from the cathedral wall and prods the creature with it, Gwangi's teeth clamp down on the point, initiating a brief tug-of-war between man and monster. This direct manifestation of conflict is so apt that the viewer almost forgets to admire the precision with which Harryhausen has created a physical link between the actor and the model.

When Gwangi relaxes his grip, Tuck falls backward against the organ and a chord reverberates, startling and distracting the animal. Tuck seizes this moment to hurl the spear, which drives deeply into the side of Gwangi's head. While the creature painfully attempts to knock the spear loose, the humans run for the door, the organ's howl blending with the screams of the wounded animal. At the door, Tuck flings a brazier toward the creature. Trying to avoid the flames, Gwangi knocks over another brazier and the fire spreads, trapping him like the Frankenstein Monster in James Whale's 1931 film.

Outside, the hero, heroine, and boy stand with the townspeople. There is no cheering, no rejoicing. Silent and solemn, they watch the cathedral go up in flames and imagine the agonized terror within. It is a moment of glorious tragedy and Harryhausen, in an uncharacteristically grim mood, refuses to let the viewer off the emotional hook, repeatedly cutting to inside the church as Gwangi falls onto his back, is engulfed by flames, and writhes helplessly under the collapsing roof. The scene is not brutal, but it is painful to watch. For the first and only time, Harryhausen achieves the liberating effects of fear and pity, and he does so without the benefit of a humanoid creature. Then Harryhausen, reluctant to leave his audience too distressed, follows "The End" with each actor's name superimposed over a shot of his character; Gwangi is the last figure shown, which lets the viewer carry away an image of him alive and active.

The Valley of Gwangi did not reach much of an audience. Released during a change in management at Warners, it was "dumped on the market" with very limited publicity, explains Harryhausen.[76] He also blames the changes in film content that dominated the late 1960s. His resistance to "the permissive film"[77] and "the rise of the antihero"[78] developed into a wider concern about the self-indulgent state of American society in general. Harryhausen's comments have validity, but another factor may also be involved. Owing to the mixed emotions of the climax and the rather unpleasant human characters. *The Valley of Gwangi* leaves the viewer uncomfortable. In a way, Harryhausen had created his own antiheroes, and the public did not want them.

Now in considerable need of a hit, Harryhausen and Schneer retreated to their biggest success, *The 7th Voyage of Sinbad*. Harryhausen came up with two premises for a sequel: the gathering of three interlocking pieces of a medallion and the rescue of a human who has been changed into a baboon. "I was trying to incorporate the two ideas, but they wouldn't fit. . . . So I shelved the idea of the monkey and used it later."[79] To the medallion device and the inevitable magician-villain, Harryhausen added elements discarded from previous films (a Fountain of Destiny, which like *Jason*'s Pool of Hecate endows invulnerability, and a tribe of Green Men who derive from a green-skinned character in the script for *Mysterious Island*). He also included a Greek oracle, an Indian goddess, Babylonian carvings, and a Stonehenge-like structure. From this melange of details, he and writer Brian Clemens fashioned one of Harryhausen's most personal plots.

Jason had sought to bring peace and healing to a corrupted country, and *The Golden Voyage of Sinbad* (1974) contains a similar situation, with Sinbad (John Phillip Law) helping a Vizier (Douglas Wilmer) whose land "is being choked alive" by the evil magician Koura (Tom Baker). If Koura gains complete power, "freedom and happiness would be lost to Marabia forever." (As in *Jason and the Argonauts*, the country's condition is stated, but not illustrated.) Sinbad has chanced upon one piece of a medallion and the Vizier has another; discovering that the pieces form a nautical chart, Sinbad sets sail with the Vizier to the mysterious island of Lemuria. Koura—

who knows that placing the medallion in the Fountain of Destiny will bring its owner youth, invisibility, and "a crown of untold riches"—follows Sinbad's ship. Using a tiny, flying homunculus as a spy (a variation on the "foo lights" in *Earth vs. the Flying Saucers*), Koura learns Sinbad's plan and the pursuit becomes a race.

Because Sinbad just stumbles into this conflict, Harryhausen tries to create a substitute for personal involvement by stressing the concept of destiny. After the medallion piece drops from the sky to his ship, Sinbad has a vision of a woman with an eye tattooed on one palm; in a dream she returns, and the dream leads into a sudden storm, which throws the ship off course, then abruptly ceases. Arriving at Marabia, Sinbad concludes, "We've been brought here by some mysterious force." The Vizier voices the same thought: "Only Destiny could have brought you here." Returning to his ship, Sinbad is lured into a shop and its owner asks him to take his lazy son, Haroun, as a crewman. Sinbad resists until he sees a slave, Margiana (Caroline Munro), who has an eye tattooed on her palm. Convinced that she is part of some plan, he takes both her and Haroun with him. Much later, because of the tattoo, the Green Men try to sacrifice Margiana to a giant one-eyed centaur that lives near the Fountain of Destiny.

Thus, Sinbad's involvement is justified because it was preordained. *The Golden Voyage of Sinbad,* explains Harryhausen, "was based on the Middle Eastern point of view of Destiny: that everything is the will of Allah. You're not your own free-will agent; there's some sort of pattern. The whole of life is plotted out ahead of time."[80] *Golden Voyage* does establish such a pattern, but because the force that determined it (whether gods or god-surrogates) is not introduced, the function of destiny is both more obvious and less well integrated than in *Jason.*

This time, destiny is the sole cause of events—a substitute for character motivation—not an explanation involving interaction between control and independent human action. At the same time, the film also includes references to exactly that kind of interaction, which Sinbad sums up in the aphorism, "Trust in Allah—but tie up your camel." Trapped in the Temple of the Oracle, Sinbad declares that "a man's Destiny lies in his own hands" and figures out a way to escape. Even the Oracle states that as good and evil struggle, it is the "deeds of weak and mortal men that may tip the scales one way or the other." In *Golden Voyage,* the emphasis on destiny does not mesh smoothly with the possibility of human choice.

A much more interesting aspect of the film involves Koura, a magician who works with a finite pool of power. Because Koura grows older and weaker with every use of his magic, the very process of seeking the medallion increases his need for the youth it promises, making Koura a more complete character than most of those in Harryhausen's films, a man who sacrifices—at least, temporarily—and takes risks for his goal. Also significant is the fact that nearly all of this film's creatures are literal extensions of Koura's eyes, ears, and hands. He creates them or brings them to life, and they do his bidding, just as an animator controls his models.

Fifteen years and seven films earlier, Sokurah reflected Harryhausen's confidence in his own power to infuse the inanimate with life; in *Golden Voyage,* Koura reveals the mood of Harryhausen in his fifties. The exertion of willpower, the strain and struggle of intense concentration, now leave the magician drained. "You will *die* if you go on this way," cautions a concerned aide, to which Koura replies, "To summon the demons of darkness there is a price and each time I call upon them, it consumes part of me." This is then visualized when Koura uses his own blood to bring a homunculus to life. The shooting script describes the effect of this process with sympathetic understanding: It causes "extreme physical distress," leaving Koura both "exhausted" and "frustrated by his own weakness." By the time he reaches the Fountain of Destiny,

Koura is reduced to crawling. Finally, he places one part of the medallion in the water and declares with triumph, "The energy of youth is mine again!" Koura is a remarkably revealing surrogate for Harryhausen, who reportedly had considered retiring after the failure of *Gwangi*.[81]

The Golden Voyage also touches on the issue of age through Haroun, an Arabian "hippie" who reflects Harryhausen's impatience with contemporary permissiveness. Haroun is broadly ridiculed in the guise of comic relief, but, more meaningfully, he takes his youth for granted, misuses his energy, and disdains any age slightly greater than his own. When told he might be at sea for three years, he whines, "I'll be an old man before then! I'll be ancient!" Haroun's laziness also irritates the hard-working Harryhausen, who converts him (not very gradually) into a reliable and courageous crewman. This evolution recalls that of Herbert in *Mysterious Island,* except that Haroun's flaws are not as sympathetically presented.

Most of the creatures animated by Koura lack an independent ability to feel pain or think, and although the ship's figurehead and the statue of Kali look human, the wood and metal of which they are made inhibit characterization. They are also nearly invulnerable, which reduces the chance for exciting battles. The figurehead performs its simple task—bringing Sinbad's chart to Koura—without meeting much resistance, and in the duel with the six-armed Kali, the sailors merely defend themselves until it is pushed from a parapet and shatters (revealing the medallion's third part within). In contrast, the tiny homunculi, which resemble Ymirs with wings, offer personality as well as spectacle. When one eavesdrops on the Vizier's conversation with Sinbad, its flexible body reacts to what it sees and hears. Lurking by a window, it leans forward attentively, then pulls back at a particularly important comment.

Only in the film's climax does Harryhausen turn to his more traditional creatures. The cyclopean centaur and griffin are both amalgams of different animals: The centaur combines the head, arms, and chest of a man with a horse's body, and the griffin blends a lion's body with the head, beak, and wings of an eagle. Each must have been difficult to design and animate so that the parts appear harmonious. The centaur, in particular, could easily have looked off-balance, but Harryhausen meets the challenge with deceptive ease.

Thematically and in terms of plot, the final battle between Good (the griffin) and Evil (the centaur) is more confusing than powerful. Challenged by Sinbad, Koura summons the centaur to fight in his stead, but his control of it is questionable because he had not previously known it existed. Even more awkwardly, the griffin's origin is never explained. In the script, its abrupt entrance and link with Good were quickly justified when Margiana prays, "In Allah's name—save him [Sinbad]. . . . in the name of goodness and *love."* Although footage of this was shot, Harryhausen explains noncommittally, it "failed to work out" and couldn't be used.[82]

When the griffin appears to be winning, Koura slashes its leg with his sword, tipping the scales enough for Evil to triumph. Then Sinbad tips the scales in the other direction by leaping onto the centaur's back and, with repeated stabs, killing the beast. Finally, the conflict reverts to a human level, but Koura has an advantage. Having thrown the medallion's second part in the fountain, he grows progressively more invisible as he and Sinbad duel. Then, when totally invisible, he foolishly steps into the fountain's geyser; the water reveals his form, and Sinbad stabs him. Although depicted in a satisfactory fashion, this duel cannot help but be anticlimactic, coming as it does after the giant creatures' struggle.

Could the two fights have occurred in the reverse order? "We thought about that," admits Schneer, "and structurally we really couldn't change it because the dramatics of the piece require that the conclusion be a final confrontation between Koura and Sinbad."[83] The problem, of course, lay in the way the script had been developed. Having conceived the special-effects scenes before writing the story, Harryhausen was so committed to those scenes that he couldn't imagine an alternative.

Although Tom Baker had played Rasputin in *Nicholas and Alexandra* (1971), his performance as Koura lacks stature and intensity. Still, by capturing the character's subtler, more vulnerable side, Baker does serve as this film's backbone. Sinbad cannot be as interesting a figure as Koura, but he could have been more than the cardboard character provided by John Phillip Law. The script describes Sinbad as irrepressible, filled with "exhilaration" and a "devil-may-care optimism," but the best Law offers is a shallow confidence. As Margiana, Caroline Munro has an exotic beauty that makes her a pleasing adornment, but only her eye tattoo contributes to the plot. Director Gordon Hessler—despite overuse of a hand-held camera—does a workman-like job of staging the action, but overall the film has a slow, even ponderous, pace.

Nevertheless, *The Golden Voyage of Sinbad* captures the pulse of mythological adventure and dispenses several unforgettable events, including the rapidly edited duel with Kali, the crack and splinter of wood as the figurehead pulls loose from the ship's prow, and everything involving the homunculi. It is also, thanks to the conception of Koura, one of Harryhausen's most complex and subtly confessional films.

Columbia's publicity department backed the film to the hilt, and, despite its oppressive mood, it was a financial success. Encouraged, the studio re-released *The 7th Voyage of Sinbad* to good results. Naturally, Columbia agreed to back a new Sinbad adventure, so Harryhausen elaborated on his idea about the baboon, and Beverley Cross turned the result into a screenplay. But despite new settings, creatures, and other details, the basic plot of *Sinbad and the Eye of the Tiger* (1977) resembles that of *The Golden Voyage*. Again a magician—this time a woman, Zenobia—schemes to seize power from a good ruler and Sinbad must counter her spells. Ultimately, he sails to Hyperborea, a green land near the North Pole, seeking the power contained in its Shrine of the Four Elements. Zenobia, like Koura, sails after Sinbad and uses her magic to spy on him, hoping to learn his destination.

This time, though, Harryhausen replaces the previous film's emphasis on destiny and the emotionless search for the medallion with a character-based situation inspired by *The 7th Voyage*. In that story, Sokurah had altered the Princess's form to get his way, and Sinbad brings her to Colossa to return her to normal; in *Eye of the Tiger*, Zenobia prevents the coronation of Prince Kassim by changing him into a baboon, and Sinbad takes him to Hyperborea to change him back to human form. Such characters as Cavor (in *First Men*) and Bromley (in *Gwangi*) probably inspired Melanthius, an elderly scientist-alchemist who is ahead of his time professionally, sloppy in his housekeeping, often garrulous, sometimes grumpy, always charming, and eccentric in a very English way.

Despite its debts to other films, *Sinbad and the Eye of the Tiger* stands solidly on its own, for Harryhausen had recognized the problems of *The Golden Voyage* and solved them here. This film also contains only one brief, but revealing, mention of age: Melanthius asserts that he is too old to join the expedition, but then develops a commitment to the task that belies his claim. In much the same way, the fast-paced *Eye of the Tiger* reveals in Harryhausen a revived energy and fresh enthusiasm.

In one key change, Harryhausen limits the number of creatures the magician controls. This leaves room in the plot for other kinds of animated beings, two of which remain involved throughout most of the film: the baboon, who accompanies and interacts with the humans, and the Minaton, a bronze figure created by Zenobia to do

The battle between Trog and a giant saber-toothed tiger is one of the most fully developed fight scenes ever staged by Ray Harryhausen. From *Sinbad and the Eye of the Tiger* (1977).

her heavy work. (The human-bodied and bull-headed Minaton is based on the actual Talos of Greek myth.) In Hyperborea, Harryhausen introduces a giant prehistoric human, a Troglodyte, which is also integrated into the action.

Moreover, Harryhausen makes two of his animated characters totally sympathetic, a step he had never taken before. The fact that the baboon is really Prince Kassim justifies giving it human qualities, and Harryhausen's subtle animation develops a personality that rivals that of *Mighty Joe Young* (without Joe's comic eye-rolling). In one of the film's highlights, the skeptical Melanthius hands "Kassim" a mirror, but the animal does not attack his own reflection, as a true baboon supposedly would. Instead, his simian countenance reveals completely human emotion as he gazes at the form in which he is trapped. Finally, he turns away and weeps silently. Melanthius, of course, is convinced. It is a moving scene for both the characters and the viewers, one that finally offers Harryhausen the opportunity to "act" through his model. He is also able to vary his animated characterization, because the longer Kassim remains in baboon form, the more his humanity disappears.

When the Troglodyte first enters, everyone (including the audience) assumes him to be a menace, so the film provides a neat twist when he converses with the baboon and helps Sinbad find the Shrine of the Four Elements. Although Trog doesn't have as much personality as the baboon, he is human enough and has sufficient screen time to develop sympathy.

The film's final battle pits Trog against a giant saber-toothed tiger. Trog has already participated in the action, so his involvement here is natural and the viewer immediately roots for him. The tiger had not been previously introduced, but because Zenobia projects herself into its ice-encrusted body, it is less a new creature than Zenobia in a new form. The fight—with many long, medium, and close shots of the action—is one of Harryhausen's most fully developed and violent confrontations. After Trog is killed, Sinbad himself faces the tiger, which (in an effective reprise of the allosaurus scene in *One Million Years B.C.*) leaps toward Sinbad, who impales it on the Minaton's

In *Sinbad and the Eye of the Tiger* (1977), Princess Farah (Jane Seymour) plays chess with her brother after he has been changed into a baboon. Such scenes allowed Ray Harryhausen to create a wide range of emotions through animation.

pike and pivots its body over his head. This sequence resolves the structural awkwardness in the climax of *Golden Voyage* by combining the animal fight with the human fight by the simple but ingenious method of having one of the animals actually be the magician. The new version works perfectly.

The careful structure of *Eye of the Tiger* stands out as another virtue. Especially effective is the way it apportions expository information while continuing to advance the plot. The first scene depicts Prince Kassim's coronation, which involves the audience through close-ups that reveal the various characters' relationships. As the crown is lowered toward Kassim's head, Zenobia (Margaret Whiting) casts a spell and smoke obscures the Prince. Exactly what has happened remains unknown, whetting the viewer's appetite.

Some time after, when Sinbad (Patrick Wayne) arrives at the city, a local merchant lures him to his tent. After dialogue informs us about Sinbad's friendship with the Prince and his sister, Farah, the merchant attempts to poison Sinbad and his men. This provokes a fight, during which Zenobia enters and conjures three ghouls—flesh-covered skeletons with large, insect-like eyes—which attack Sinbad. Harryhausen had regretted that the skeleton fight in *Jason and the Argonauts* "did not take place at night. Its effect would have been doubled,"[84] so in *Eye of the Tiger* he proves his point by having the duel with the ghouls move out of the tent and into the darkness. The action ends when Sinbad cuts the ropes holding a pile of logs, which tumble on top of the ghouls. Princess Farah (Jane Seymour) then appears, and Sinbad escapes with her to his ship.

The couple's conversation onboard the ship provides the first extended exposition, and by now the viewer is sufficiently curious to listen with interest. However, we learn only that something serious happened to Kassim and that unless he is crowned "in seven moons" he will lose his right to be Caliph. The romance between Sinbad and the Princess is established here, too. A year before, Sinbad—like Tuck in *Gwangi*—had left her because he was unwilling to give up his independence. Now that he has changed his mind and returned, the wedding must be delayed until an obstacle has been overcome (as happened to Sinbad in *The 7th Voyage*).

The next morning, Sinbad prepares to seek help from Melanthius, on the island of Casgar, and Zenobia makes her official entrance; she is Farah's stepmother, a sorceress plotting to put her own son, Raffi, on the throne. When sailors bring a covered cage onboard ship, they stumble, revealing a large baboon inside. Quickly, he is taken below. The viewer can now deduce what happened to Kassim, but it still has not been stated outright. Later, as the baboon plays chess with Farah in Sinbad's cabin, a sailor glances in and panics. Only now does Sinbad explain, to the sailor and to us, that the baboon is Kassim. Soon Sinbad reaches Casgar, where Melanthius (Patrick Troughton) tells about Hyperborea, which initiates the journey's second stage.

Aside from Zenobia's Minaton, which is more workman than menace, the film has presented no animated danger since the ghouls, but the efficient script has kept viewers intrigued by starting Sinbad on his journey and setting up Zenobia's pursuit, while still parcelling out information. Interest continues as a new plot element develops. Although Sinbad's romance with Farah is taken for granted, the film finds time to let Melanthius's daughter, Dione (Taryn Power), develop an affection for the baboon.

On the way to Hyperborea, Zenobia spies on Sinbad by changing herself into a gull, flying to his ship, and entering the cabin as herself in miniature form. After she is captured and placed in a bottle, Melanthius questions her and reveals what she wants to know in the process. Finding her vial of magic fluid, he makes another mistake by testing the liquid on a hornet, which increases in size and attacks. Sinbad enters and fends off the hornet, as Zenobia escapes from the jar, drinks the fluid, changes back to a gull, and flies off. This engrossing scene works because of the strong personalities of Melanthius and Zenobia, uncertainty about how it will develop, and imaginative direction that includes distorted shots through the jar's glass. Although Melanthius's actions don't support his reputation for intelligence, at least the script has him apologize for his misjudgments. In another good decision, Zenobia is not all-powerful. She cries in agony during the first transformation and, lacking enough fluid for a complete return to human form, spends the rest of the film limping with one webbed foot.

The masts of Sinbad's ship prevent it from using the tunnel entrance to Hyperborea, so the expedition takes a land route, but Zenobia's Minaton-powered vessel can pass through the tunnel, so she arrives first at the pyramid. To create an opening she has the Minaton remove a huge stone block, which crushes the Minaton, leading to the script's sole lapse in logic: Zenobia dismisses the loss of the Minaton, saying that he has done his job, evidently forgetting that she would have to get home again somehow. From here on, the story moves quickly to its climax, and Kassim is finally crowned Caliph while the end credits roll.

The film's human characters are well conceived and, for the most part, well acted. Noteworthy is the presence of three strong, intelligent women. Margaret Whiting makes Zenobia both believable and larger than life in her ironic and angry determination; the actress even redubbed her dialogue to add an exotic accent. Farah and Dione transcend the attractive adornment category, for both have a personal connection with Kassim and the actresses effectively convey distress, sympathy, or irritation as required. Patrick Troughton's Melanthius successfully embodies the garrulous eccentricity that had eluded Laurence Naismith as Professor Bromley in *Gwangi*. Only Patrick Wayne fails to measure up. He looks the part of Sinbad, but is diminished by a flat and strained delivery of dialogue. Director Sam Wanamaker, better known as an actor, probably helped elicit these mostly convincing performances, and his use of camera movement and close shots provides the visual vitality missing from *Golden Voyage*.

Eye of the Tiger contains some technical flaws—for example, Harryhausen filmed stand-ins on location in Petra and later matted in closer shots of the actors, with some inconsistency—but they rarely relate to the animation or its combination with live action. The film's fantasy characters mark a kind of breakthrough for Harryhausen. Not since *Mighty Joe Young* had he created animated, feeling companions for the humans, a challenge he meets with great skill. Although it may lack the personal implications of its predecessor, *Sinbad and the Eye of the Tiger* succeeds admirably as entertainment.

Ever since *Jason and the Argonauts*, Harryhausen had wanted to make another film based on Greek myth. He was especially intrigued by the confrontation between Perseus and Medusa, the gorgon with snakes instead of hair and a face that turns all who gaze on it to stone, but he couldn't fit a plotline around this encounter. Beverley Cross, however, suggested a solution, so at the completion of *Eye of the Tiger* he worked with Harryhausen on a script for *Clash of the Titans* (1981). Columbia considered the project too expensive, but Metro-Goldwyn-Mayer, seeking to reestablish itself as a production company, was looking for films. In fact, MGM wanted a big and important feature, so the studio encouraged Harryhausen to make *Clash of the Titans* elaborate and even hired such mainstream performers as Laurence Olivier, Maggie Smith, and Burgess Meredith. Finally, Harryhausen had a chance to become "respectable."

In the myth, Perseus has already killed the gorgon when he discovers Princess Andromeda chained to a cliff as a sacrifice to a sea monster. Falling immediately in love, he destroys the monster and marries Andromeda. The film changes the order of events, so that Perseus meets Andromeda first, then obtains the gorgon's head to use in rescuing her. Thus, as in *The 7th Voyage* and *Eye of the Tiger*, the union of hero and heroine is delayed until an obstacle can be overcome.

To provide Perseus with an ongoing antagonist, Cross created a totally new character, Calibos, who schemes against Andromeda and her country. The script also establishes the hero's origins and adds an earlier challenge that Perseus must meet to win Andromeda. This results in two almost completely separate adventures, with the film's entire first half becoming exposition that sets up the main situation. Although this awkward structure disrupts audience involvement, the added material helps make *Titans* a richly textured work.

Like *Jason* before it, *Clash of the Titans* dramatizes the gods' control over humanity. Especially apt is the use of the theater as an image for that manipulation: The gods place terra-cotta figurines of the characters in a model amphitheater whenever they, as "authors," influence the people's lives. Taking this concept further, Cross sets part of the earthly action in a real amphitheater and includes a playwright as a major character. Like any good author, Ammon (Burgess Meredith) is always ready to move the plot along by giving Perseus (Harry Hamlin) some useful information or suggestion.

Desmond Davis had perhaps the ideal combination of talents to direct *Clash of the Titans*. His years as a camera operator gave him the necessary technical expertise, and he also had experience as a scriptwriter. His first films as a director—notably *The Uncle* (1964) and *I Was Happy Here* (1965; U.S.: *Time Lost and Time Remembered*)—emphasize small, sensitive moments conveyed in an understatedly cinematic style. In *Clash of the Titans*, Davis often captures a scene's essence in a close-up detail, such as hands separating when Perseus parts from Andromeda (Judi Bowker) or the dust of a crushed figurine blowing from Zeus's palm.

Likewise, Davis's editing lets us share the perspective of Perseus as he first encounters the sights of Joppa or glances at an executed man, then at Queen Cassiopeia, and finally at the tower that contains her daughter, Andromeda. In the opening scene, the filmmakers are not content to let the camera merely observe the setting's impressive cliffs, waves, and mist. Instead, carefully chosen angles and close shots build the impact. Harryhausen, in his effects scenes, also uses film technique creatively and not just as a means of recording events: When Perseus and the gorgon stalk each other among a temple's columns, the flickering firelight and extensive editing build considerable tension.

In *The Golden Voyage,* an evil force was causing a nation's decline, a situation that reflected Harryhausen's concern about America's "permissive society." That film, though, had only stated the country's condition in dialogue, whereas *Clash of the Titans* makes its similar situation both thoroughly visual and more extreme. Harryhausen's final film is permeated with cruelty and ruthlessness on the part of both the gods and humanity, and its physical world is often ugly and decaying. Only the innocence of Perseus and Andromeda, and a few scenes of peaceful beauty or calm, relieve this surprisingly grim tone.

In essence, the film reveals Harryhausen's personal struggle to assert a positive outlook in the face of his growing disillusionment. Certainly Perseus resembles Harryhausen's familiar hero fated for individual achievement: Zeus tells him to "Find and fulfill your Destiny"; after falling in love with Andromeda and realizing her danger, Perseus declares, "I have found my Destiny"; then, after defeating the gorgon, he recalls Zeus's original words. Yet this heroic theme does not fit naturally into the film. The references to Destiny were, in fact, added at the last minute. They do not exist in the shooting script, which instead has Perseus chased from the gorgon's lair by her "poisonous" blood, which "spreads across the vast stone floor—lapping against the petrified dead, filling the ritual pool—slowly covering the abandoned fields." Through these changes, Harryhausen seems to want to reclaim heroism from what had become a bleak and even cynical vision.

Before introducing the adult Perseus, the film thoroughly establishes the context. In a prologue, King Acrisius of Argos orders his daughter, Danae, and her newborn son, Perseus, placed in a coffin-like chest and has it thrown into the stormy sea. This, he claims, will punish her "sin" and restore his honor. At the same time, he believes, "Their blood is not on my hands," because he did not actually kill them. Observing events from Olympus, Zeus (Laurence Olivier) angrily punishes Acrisius for his "cruel and ruthless crime" by releasing the Kraken, a sea monster, which creates a tidal wave that destroys Argos and drowns its citizens. Zeus also crushes the figurine of Acrisius, killing the King. This punishment is hardly less ruthless or vengeful than Acrisius's original deed, nor is Zeus an objective judge, for he had caused Danae's "sin" by fathering Perseus.

Zeus is, at least, a benevolent father who brings the castaways to a safe shore and watches over Perseus's growth to manhood on an idyllic, isolated island. At this point, the goddess Thetis (Maggie Smith) speaks to Zeus about her earthly son, Calibos, who is about to marry Princess Andromeda of Joppa. Calibos had been given a beautiful area to rule, but, complains Zeus, he "hunted and destroyed every living creature" and "trapped and killed my sacred herd of flying horses," leaving only Pegasus. "His crimes are unforgivable," says Zeus, and he must be punished. Thetis pleads for mercy, but Zeus is adamant and alters Calibos's appearance, making him "abhorrent to human sight" so that he must "live as an outcast in the swamps and marshes." Thus are the weaknesses of humans dealt with on Olympus.

The resentful Thetis then arranges that no one else will ever marry Andromeda, and, just to make trouble, she lifts the sleeping Perseus from his peaceful island. "Time you saw something of the world, Perseus," she says. "Time you came face to face with fear. Time to know the terrors of the dark and look on Death. Time your eyes were opened to grim reality!" Thetis's giant hand places Perseus in an amphitheater in Joppa. When Zeus discovers this "deliberate and malicious act," he forces three other goddesses to provide his son with help: a sword, a helmet, and a shield.

The reality to which the bewildered Perseus awakens is, indeed, grim. Aside from Ammon, the place is deserted. Why has the theater been neglected, Perseus asks. "It's a sign of the times," replies Ammon. "This kingdom is under a curse and the city is in despair and everyone goes around muttering, 'Call no man happy who is not dead!' " Conditions are so bad that he urges the youth to return to his island, but when Perseus discovers the three gifts, Zeus's image appears in the shield and delivers his "fulfill your Destiny" line. Perseus then rushes off to Joppa, forgetting his sword.

Entering the city, Perseus absorbs the exotic sights of its crowded streets, which seem to be filled with sideshow performers, climaxed by the charred remains of a man burned at the stake. "These are complicated times," says a soldier, who explains that the man, the latest suitor of Princess Andromeda, had failed to answer the required riddle and met the consequences. This, evidently, is part of Thetis's revenge. The soldier points out the tower where Andromeda lives, "above this smoke and stench."

Intrigued, Perseus sneaks into Andromeda's chamber and there falls spellbound at the sight of her sleeping form. Then, he watches in confusion as a giant vulture brings a cage and carries away Andromeda's spirit, which has emerged from her body. Determined to follow the vulture on its next visit, Perseus, at Ammon's suggestion, ropes and tames the winged horse Pegasus, on which he pursues the vulture to the marshland home of Calibos. Part human and part satyr, this deformed creature still seeks Andromeda's love. "Remember me how I was," he pleads, and caresses her shoulder with his claw-like hand. Andromeda feels pity, but that is all. She pleads with Calibos to be merciful and cause no more human bonfires. Pathetic, but dangerous in his resentment, he refuses and makes up a new riddle (written out by an assistant, the Huntsman, using the bloody end of a bird's leg).

After Andromeda leaves, Calibos and Perseus struggle in the swamp. Later, in Joppa, Cassiopeia asks if there is a new suitor for her daughter. Perseus enters and gives the riddle's answer: the ring of Calibos, which he exhibits still on the creature's severed hand. He had, however, pitied Calibos and spared his life, on the condition that he remove his "curse" from Joppa. "There will be no more bonfires, no more nightmares," declares Perseus. "Light has conquered darkness." The film appears set for an early happy ending, except that Calibos complicates matters by praying to Thetis. "In wounding me," he argues, Perseus "has insulted you. Then, surely, he must be punished." Thetis replies that with Zeus protecting Perseus, she can do nothing. "Then punish those Perseus loves: the Queen, Andromeda, the people of Joppa. . . . I demand justice!" Thetis sees through this, asking, "Justice—or revenge?" But she is, after all, on her son's side.

At the wedding ceremony, Cassiopeia in her enthusiasm describes Andromeda as "more lovely than the Goddess Thetis herself." This angers Thetis—or, rather, it lets her justify the punishment-revenge sought by Calibos. Cassiopeia asks for forgiveness, but Thetis refuses: In thirty days Andromeda must be sacrificed to the Kraken or the beast will destroy Joppa and its inhabitants. The mercy that Perseus granted Calibos has now brought even greater danger to Andromeda.

No one knows how to defeat the Kraken, but Ammon suggests asking the three blind Stygian Witches, who "have a craving for human flesh." So Perseus sets out with some soldiers, and the assertive Andromeda accompanies them part of the way. Meanwhile, Zeus orders Athena to replace Perseus's lost helmet with Bubo, her "all-knowing, all-seeing" owl. Unwilling to part with Bubo, Athena has a mechanical replica made, which is all-knowing, all-seeing, and all-cute. From the air, this pseudo-Bubo points the way to the witches' temple. There, in their filthy abode, the cackling hags stir the contents of a cauldron. At one point, a human hand rises to the surface and the fingers squirm, but a witch shoves it back below the surface. They have similar plans for Perseus, who is, one says, "not plump, but well made." Bubo helps by grabbing the crystal orb that serves as their shared eye, which Perseus threatens to destroy unless they help him. When they suggest that Medusa's head could destroy the Kraken, Perseus tosses the eye onto the rat-infested floor and, as the witches crawl about in search of it, leaves.

Ammon explains that Medusa had once been beautiful, but the god Poseidon seduced her in Aphrodite's temple and, as punishment, the jealous goddess turned her into "an apparition so horrible" that she petrifies anyone who looks at her. Ferried across the River Styx by the skeletal Charon, Perseus and the soldiers reach Medusa's temple, where Dioskilos, a two-headed guard dog, attacks. After defeating it, Perseus and the two surviving soldiers cautiously enter. One of Medusa's arrows kills the first soldier and the other is turned to stone, but Perseus swings his sword from behind a column and beheads her.

Dramatically, the film should move directly from the death of the gorgon to the rescue of Andromeda, but Calibos has not yet been dealt with, so Harryhausen includes three more events, which crowd the climax and interrupt its momentum. While Perseus sleeps, Calibos pierces the gorgon's head and her blood flows to the ground, turning into scorpions which grow to giant size. Upon defeating these foes, Perseus is attacked by Calibos. This time, he kills the vengeful mutation. Exhausted, Perseus has Bubo fetch Pegasus from the lair of Calibos, which it does after driving out the Huntsman and giant vulture. Finally, on the coast, Andromeda is chained to a rock, and, as the tentacled Kraken approaches, Perseus flies to the rescue. When he reveals the gorgon's head, the Kraken freezes, then shatters. Perseus and Andromeda marry, and Zeus grants them a happy future.

Life in *Clash of the Titans* consists of vengeful punishments and little mercy. The world it depicts is cruel and ugly—though not as repulsive as the one Beverley Cross describes in the script. There, we discover the "cracked and filthy" floor of the amphitheater; in Calibos's lair, a "greenish, sluggish vapour" rises "from the seething, bubbling marsh sludge"; the witches' temple is "streaked with soot and grease" and littered with "yellow, rotting bones"; the soldier shot by Medusa turns into "a smoking, shapeless blotch"; the scorpions are preceded by "a writhing, squirming pool of blood-bloated maggots, swollen worms and all forms of venomous insect"; and Bubo's talons "leave the face of the Huntsman a raw bloody pulp." Even though the film tempers Cross's descriptions, this remains the most unpleasant of all the worlds created by Harryhausen.

In the script, Zeus offers the bleak view that time is "a *human* tragedy" because "poor earthly man is in the grip of Age from the instant he is born. And in the end, he passes to the deep land of the dead and is forgotten." Although this statement was omitted from the film, at times Ammon expresses the older Harryhausen's impatience with youth and current artistic creation. After Perseus rushes off to Joppa, Ammon says to himself, "Impetuous. Foolish. The young—why do they never listen? When will they ever learn?" Ammon calls himself an optimist—"the last optimist," in a line dropped from the film—because he believes "in the ability of man to overcome most obstacles." As such, he writes comedies. "I was partial to tragedy in my youth," he reveals, "before experience taught me that life is quite tragic enough without my having to write about it." (Harryhausen has often voiced similar opinions, such as: "For me the cinema is essentially for entertainment, not for sending depressing messages."[85])

But a person who describes life as "tragic" is surely not an optimist. Instead, Ammon is so disillusioned that he turns away from life and, through art, creates alternatives to reality. This has also been Harryhausen's admitted aim, yet the Harryhausen of this film differs from Ammon because—like Perseus—he has emerged from the security of his private island to face (and create) the "grim reality" of the world at large. And in doing so, he has granted the mercy of understanding to his chief villains. Both Calibos and Medusa are themselves victims of the gods' anger, enduring excessive and endless punishment for past weaknesses. Perhaps the film's true villains are the gods, who combine a human kind of ruthlessness with an Olympian power over humanity.

The film clearly tries to end on an optimistic note, but cannot quite achieve it. Even as Zeus grants a happy future to Perseus and Andromeda, Hera asks, "What if one day there were other heroes like him? What if courage and imagination were to become everyday mortal qualities?" Zeus replies, "We would no longer be needed. But, for the moment, there is sufficient cowardice, sloth, and mendacity down there on Earth to last forever!" Courageous and imaginative individuals will always be in short supply, and they, like Harryhausen himself, are bound to feel besieged by the corruption around them.

For most of its length, *Clash of the Titans*—following *Eye of the Tiger*'s lead—integrates its animated figures with the ongoing plot; they are not monsters that enter only to be confronted and defeated. Often, as when Bubo snatches the witches' eye or the vulture carries Andromeda to Calibos, the animated action is an accepted part of the film's world. Harryhausen initially intended that Calibos, like the baboon in *Eye of the Tiger,* would be totally animated, but the final script gave the character dialogue, so Harryhausen used an effectively made-up actor (Neil McCarthy) for the close shots and a smoothly animated model for more distant views. Together, the two form the ultimate synthetic figure. Medusa and the Kraken may have only one major scene each, but their existence has been established earlier, so their presence hovers over the preceding action.

Only the two-headed dog and the scorpions are traditional walk-on creatures, and the fights against them reveal the familiar lack of activity. In both cases, Harryhausen tries to enliven the scenes by leaving Perseus for a time without a sword. The mechanical Bubo represents a special case: Resemblances to R2D2 of *Star Wars* aside, his broadly comic spinning head, twirling eyes, and pratfalls continually disrupt the film's otherwise subtle mood. Such misjudgments, however, are minor compared with the evocatively developed atmosphere in scenes that have nothing to do with action-adventure. For example, Perseus first sees Pegasus in a setting of pastoral beauty that fits the horse's shining purity, and the crossing of the River Styx possesses an almost Germanic misty mysticism.

Although *Clash of the Titans* reveals a high level of personal accomplishment, in one respect the film must have disappointed Harryhausen. To finish on schedule, he for the first time hired others to work on the animation. The choice of assignments is not surprising. Harryhausen, with little interest in comic characters, relinquished Bubo to Steven Archer; years before he had dropped a flying horse sequence from *Jason,* and now he let Jim Danforth animate the shots of Pegasus in the air. Danforth also worked on the Dioskilos sequence. Harryhausen had planned to have Perseus cut off one of the dog's heads, but decided that would be too gruesome. Danforth, though, liked the basic idea, "so I had Perseus appear to cut a nerve or something. Since the background hadn't been shot with that in mind, there was really no timing in Peseus's action to allow for that, but I managed to squeeze in just enough frames so that you can see one of the heads go limp and drop, and then the other head keeps on snapping and barking."[86]

MGM's promotional campaign for *Clash of the Titans* positioned the film as an event, scheduled a display of Harryhausen's drawings and models at New York's Museum of Modern Art, and sent Harryhausen himself on a tour of universities and museums. This film, asserts Schneer, "was our biggest financial success ever."[87] But that was not enough. In the words of actor Burgess Meredith, Harryhausen "had great hopes for *Clash of the Titans* to be accepted as a work of merit."[88] The critics, however, saw it differently. Most settled for the usual condescension, but *Variety*'s review was calculatedly cruel, calling the film "an unbearable bore" with "flat, outdated special effects."[89]

"Ray was hurt by [the film's] critical reception," says Meredith.[90] In a line dropped from the movie, Ammon (no doubt speaking for Harryhausen) mutters, "I never did like critics," but this time Harryhausen couldn't take refuge in his usual reverse-condescension toward what he considers overly intellectual critics. The reaction was too strong (at least in a few quarters), and perhaps he had invested too much of himself in this work or was too tired to fight back.

Despite the negative critical response to *Clash of the Titans,* Harryhausen did start to plan new films. Some writing was done for *Sinbad Goes to Mars* and *Sinbad and the 7 Wonders of the World,* and Beverley Cross completed a script based on Virgil's *Aeneid.* Harryhausen also prepared drawings for *People of the Mist,* a script brought to him by director Michael Winner. But, as *Clash of the Titans* revealed, Harryhausen's method of working had become impractical; it took too much time, and therefore cost too much. He had always enjoyed solitary labor. It made him comfortable and it allowed him to "put my mark on the work," resulting in "a personal attachment to my films. Now that that is no longer possible, I have lost interest in continuing. I don't want to just be part of a committee, with other people also putting their identification on the end result."[91]

Simultaneously, the length of time he would have to spend on a new project began to intimidate Harryhausen. In 1981, he admitted that "I find it more and more difficult to keep up my enthusiasm and strength throughout a whole year of work."[92] As he entered his sixties, he decided that the process was too all-consuming. "I never got to see my family," he explains. "It's not the right way to live, particularly when you're over a certain age. . . . I don't feel I can confine myself to a dark room for a year anymore."[93]

The industry itself was also draining his energy. "When you make a movie today, you face defiance from *every* direction. I marvel that anybody can actually finish a film, and get it released, because of all the obstacles." Audiences, too, presented a problem: They are "bombarded with entertainment everywhere. They take it for granted. . . . I don't know if the audience even cares any more about having a story."

Filmmaking was no longer fun, and, he concluded, "There's no point in knocking my head against the wall."[94]

The vacation that Harryhausen planned after finishing *Clash of the Titans* grew progressively longer. Tributes and festival appearances kept him busy, and he satisfied the urge for solitary creation by sculpting bronze versions of his creatures. Finally, in 1987 at the age of sixty-seven, he announced his official retirement. Did Harryhausen finally concede defeat in his personal struggle to achieve a goal despite obstacles? In a narrow perspective, yes, but not in a larger sense. Looking back, "I had a vision in my mind and I wanted to do it more than anything else in the world."[95] He did it—he obtained his goal by creating a career and an extensive body of work—and so he could retire from the conflict gracefully, with his dignity and stature intact.

That body of work stands as an evolving thing, offering a process of discovery for viewers, just as it must have been that for Harryhausen. In it, we can see him starting out as an entertainer, aiming for nothing more (or less) than stirring the feelings of an audience. Then, as he explored the ideas of Swift, Verne, Wells, and the Greek myths, he gradually defined his own view of existence. Finally, he found himself expressing that view as it applied to life around him, but did so indirectly, in the language he spoke fluently, in the context of fantasy. Inevitably, Harryhausen's most personal films contain inconsistencies and uncertainties of tone or thought, for he worked on a level that mixed conscious intent with unconscious compulsion. Consequently, the results are perhaps all the more rewarding.

It is appropriate that Harryhausen should ultimately follow the advice implicit in his final film: Like Perseus, he left his isolated workshop-island and entered the world. That there will be no more Harryhausen films means a loss for the viewing public, of course, but also a private gain for the man himself. And viewers can always turn to the existing films for consolation, immersing themselves once more in impossible worlds, accepting the flow of miraculous images as wonders to be savored, while exploring with the Master Magician some of the implications of those images. They can also consider the total achievement of the person behind the films, who serves as a prime example of, in Ray Bradbury's words, "the creative powers of single individuals in the world."[96] Through the films, we can continue to encounter Ray Harryhausen, the self-made cinematic conjurer, the modern Pygmalion who used technology to breathe life into improbable Galateas.

Known for his modesty and amiability as well as his calmness on the set, Terence Fisher here directs actor Edward de Souza, who plays the romantic lead, Harry Hunter, in Fisher's interpretation of *The Phantom of the Opera* (1962).

CHAPTER 4

Terence Fisher

At the age of fifty-four, Terence Fisher unexpectedly found himself a horror film specialist after directing *The Curse of Frankenstein* (1957) and *Dracula* (1958; U.S.: *Horror of Dracula*). These two pictures revived interest in the classic subjects that had faded from the screen in the 1940s. They also identified Britain's Hammer Films as a reliable source of such pictures, linked actors Peter Cushing and Christopher Lee with the genre, and established Fisher as its central creative figure, which he remained for a decade. During that time, he—and the tightly knit Hammer team—provided contemporary versions of a gallery of familiar characters: Baron Frankenstein, Count Dracula, the Mummy, the Werewolf, the Phantom of the Opera, and Dr. Jekyll and Mr. Hyde. In the process, Fisher put his distinctive imprint on material already made memorable by others. In some cases, the new films surpassed their predecessors. More significantly, they were independent works, with themes freshly interpreted and a consistent, rigorous visual style.

The results, however, made Fisher a controversial director, for his films were described as indulging in gore and violence for the sake of audience titillation. C. A. Lejeune, in the *Observer,* wrote of *Dracula*'s "sickening bad taste" and Nina Hibbins, in the *Daily Worker,* said that the film "disgusts the mind and repels the senses."[1] Such extreme responses temporarily obscured Fisher's real accomplishment: He was, in fact, more interested in sensation than sensationalism. But the films were popular and profitable, and time has vindicated the instincts of both the director and his audiences.

A down-to-earth Englishman, Fisher felt little kinship with the abstractions of German expressionism. To him, "the only reason for making films" is to play on viewers' "emotions for an hour and a half. . . . and perhaps make them believe that the unreal is true" for that period. Even when his subjects were supernaturally fantastic or scientifically improbable, Fisher stressed the human element, grounding his plots in the characters' emotional reality. "I want to work always towards the people who are involved in a situation," he said. "Of course, the surrounding situation is important, but somehow you've got to get your audience not only to be interested in the situation, you've got to get them feeling with the people."[2]

Fisher was equally intent on establishing the physical reality of the characters' world. Many of his films are set in a concretely realized Victorian milieu created by Hammer's masterful production designer, Bernard Robinson. Fisher described that period as a time "when superstitions still had all their power. The fantastic was an everyday affair,"[3] and so it existed as a facet of physical reality. In this light, Fisher's determination to show, as explicitly as possible, the staking of a vampire or Baron Frankenstein's surgical procedures becomes understandable. At the same time, Fisher made entertainment and did not want to veer too close to the contemporary world. "I would rather go into the past, into superstition, into legend, into anything, than to delve into actual events which people are seeing and experiencing in a lot of cases in their ordinary life."[4] By keeping to superstition and to the allegory implied in it, he could deal with fundamental issues and treat them realistically, without alienating viewers.

Unfortunately, because of the circumstances of low-budget filmmaking, Fisher was seldom involved in a project from its inception. More often than not, a script had already been completed and Fisher then determined to be faithful to it. "The written word is the basis of everything. Most important, the idea, and after that, the dialogue."[5] Yet Hammer scripts tended to be superficially conceived and Fisher often had to hunt for something that interested him. "You find within a script that which should perhaps be more accentuated, but isn't," he once said.[6] A director, he explained, can take a script and "*pick* at it, go *underneath* it, and *underline* certain things."[7]

Generally, what interested Fisher in his scripts was the implied struggle between the powers of good and of evil. "You've got to say something about good and evil in every film you make, I think,"[8] he stated near the end of his career. In a separate interview, he said: "I have endeavored, in the actor's performances and in the interpretation of the material scene by scene, to underline, wherever possible, that conflict."[9] On another occasion, he declared, "If my films reflect my own personal view of the world in any way, it is in their showing of the ultimate victory of good over evil, in which I do believe."[10] This goes beyond being a facile justification for happy endings. It is a distinct moral stance that pervades even Fisher's response to other people's films, such as *Witchfinder General* (1968; U.S.: *The Conqueror Worm*), in which the character who embodies good also possess the seed of evil, which grows and makes him evil as well. "I found it—in a strange way—not satisfying, but upsetting . . . and worrying," commented Fisher.[11]

Although a rejection of good as a valid possibility has dominated films since the late 1960s, many of Fisher's works still retain their power, because they are not emotionally simplistic. In them, the force and appeal of evil are depicted vividly and with insight. While making *Dracula,* Fisher decided that "one of the greatest things that the Power of Evil has is [the ability] to make its temptation tremendously attractive." Thus, his villains are often handsome, magnetic aristocrats who draw their victims to them through sexual desire and satisfaction. This is especially true of Fisher's vampires. To the director, "vampirism" is synonymous with "the power of evil," of sexual temptation, and of control. The male vampire's female victim, Fisher declares, "is really saying, 'Don't do it to me, but, please God, come and do it to me!' "[12] This relationship is decadent, even depraved, and totally unrestrained.

Fisher regularly links the supernatural force of evil to earthy decadence. Uninterested in the vampire's inhuman facets, he is fascinated by the creature's ability to exert control "sexually, emotionally" and by "the power of his mind."[13] The result is a master-slave relationship that exists on a solidly physical and emotional plane. Similarly, some of Fisher's most involving scenes depict powerful aristocrats tormenting some helpless beggar or servant girl, and the prostitutes who sometimes tempt his characters have a kinship to Dracula's promiscuous female victims, who are the id unleashed, embracing and attacking both male and female with an indiscriminate, sexually evangelical fervor.

The contrasting worlds of the Victorian era naturally lend themselves to this situation, for its primly controlled, deceptively civilized society masks the sensuousness and irrationality boiling below. "The era was damn good," declared Fisher, "because it was so full of hypocrisy,"[14] and in his films the linked forces of sexuality, decadence, vampirism, and animality break in on orderliness, sometimes in quite literal ways. One of Baron Frankenstein's creations, deformed and cannibalistic, disrupts a countess's musical evening (*The Revenge of Frankenstein*, 1958); a body bursts through a stained-glass window, shattering the seeming calm (*The Hound of the Baskervilles*, 1959); a degraded woman falls through a skylight, crashing to her death amid dancing couples (*The Two Faces of Dr. Jekyll*, 1960; U.S.: *House of Fright*); demons attack in the placid home of an ideal family (*The Devil Rides Out*, 1968; U.S.: *The Devil's Bride*); and death disturbs the refinement of an opera house (*The Phantom of the Opera*, 1962). In Fisher's three vampire films, the figure of evil invades progressively more cloistered quarters: the home of those fighting him, a strictly supervised girls' school, and a monastery.

Many times, a character's attractive appearance cloaks an evil nature, as with Fisher's elegant vampires and his procession of scientists and aristocrats, whose sophistication barely masks an inner ruthlessness. Such duality is linked to Fisher's fascination with the ambiguities and contradictions of identity. In each of his five Frankenstein films, one individual's personality is placed in the body of another, usually through a brain transplant. No conflict results in the creature of *Curse of Frankenstein*, because his brain does not retain the prior owner's characteristics. In the second film, *Revenge of Frankenstein*, a conflict is imposed from outside when an accident injures the subject's brain, arousing cannibalistic urges. *Frankenstein Created Woman* (1967) has a young man's "soul" placed in his girlfriend's reanimated body, but this film concentrates on his revenge, so the "emotionalism" favored by Fisher is lost. It "dodged the issue a little bit," acknowledged the director.[15]

Frankenstein Must Be Destroyed (1969) is another matter. Here, Fisher was fascinated by "the whole concept of who we are and . . . how do we know who we are. Are we this bit of physical body and is this lump of crap which Frankenstein takes from one person and puts into another, is that the person?" Fisher liked the fact that this brain "went from one normal physical human being into another normal physical being" and that, afterward, the original owner's feelings and memories remain. "A brain transplant is coming bloody quickly, isn't it?" Fisher speculated in 1974. "It is a terrifying thought, in actuality," he added. It is one thing to have someone else's kidney or heart, but "it's a very different thing if you look like somebody else completely and you have all your past experiences and emotions."[16]

Frankenstein and the Monster from Hell (1972) also faces this issue. "Underneath the story progression and Hammer's idea of what is entertainment," concluded Fisher, "there are moments when it gives you food for thought, I think." This time, what Fisher "found fascinating" was the subject of organ rejection: "Does the liver reject its new body, or does the body reject its new liver?" In *Monster from Hell*, "the brain didn't reject the body. . . . but the body started to reject the brain and kept its previous impulses of homicide, murder, and so forth."[17] Though scientifically dubious, this idea does have metaphorical and emotional validity, with the conflict between the brain and the body evoking a struggle between humanity's higher nature and its more physical, animalistic, and uncontrolled side.

Christopher Lee based his first two performances for Fisher on this kind of internal conflict. As the creature in *Curse of Frankenstein*, the actor explained, "Everything I did was almost as if it was forced out of me as if I was rather unwilling to do it, controlled by somebody else's brain not my own." Lee also viewed Dracula as a person dominated "by a force that is beyond his own powers of control," by a "demon that is within him" and "clawing to get to the surface."[18]

An especially graphic embodiment of identity conflict occurs at the end of *The Two Faces of Dr. Jekyll,* when Edward Hyde speaks in Jekyll's voice. This device reappears in *Frankenstein Created Woman,* with a male voice dubbed in for actress Susan Denberg. Generally, though, the identity pairs within Fisher's characters do not appear simultaneously: The bland Dr. Jekyll alternates in dominance with the urbane and ruthless Hyde, a youth periodically releases his animal nature in wolf form, a naive composer becomes the menacing Phantom of the Opera, and Dracula's female victims cast aside their prior inhibitions.

Despite the consistency of his horror film career, Fisher is not a self-consciously personal creator. He is a journeyman, a craftsman, a director for hire buffeted and controlled by economic factors. "I've had to earn my living, by the sweat of my bloody brow! I didn't mind anything they offered me, because I found I could do them reasonably well." Fisher's self-appraisal is clear and balanced: unembarrassedly aware of his works' limitations and quietly sure of their strengths. Both pretension and false modesty are foreign to his personality. "If you don't forget—without being pompous—your ideals, you can drag something out of anything you're presented with."[19]

Because Fisher readily admitted his reliance on the written contributions of others, it is fair to say that he did not originate the themes and situations expressed in his films. Rather, he received a script and searched through it for something of interest. "My themes remained what I was given to translate from the written word into a visual form. You see, I'm only a working director. I'm not a director who can pick what he wants to do."[20] In this context, he discovered an affinity for the concepts he found in the scripts of others, which he then stressed through his direction, thereby making them his own.

In addition, one must consider the close relationships among members of the Hammer team, which Fisher joined in 1952. With these collaborators, he directed eleven features before making *Curse of Frankenstein;* afterward, they made seventeen more. Such constant contact over a period of twenty years led to each individual knowing the interests and strengths of the others, which permitted much give-and-take and could easily have resulted in Fisher, directly or indirectly, influencing Hammer's scripts.

This seems even more likely when one considers who wrote most of Hammer's horror scripts. Jimmy Sangster, Fisher's assistant director or production manager on at least nine earlier films, wrote or cowrote seven of his horror pictures; Peter Bryan, the camera operator on two of Fisher's 1952 films, contributed to scripts in 1958–59; and producer Anthony Hinds, with whom Fisher had a close relationship since 1952 ("Tony Hinds and I understood each other and we worked well together"[21]), wrote five films under the pen name John Elder. When a writer has a continuity of experience with a director and knows what situations he responds to and handles well, that writer will probably—with or without the director's knowledge—gear his work to those strengths.

Fisher declared in 1974, "I can't write. I don't pretend to write. But I can dissect writing and analyze writing . . . in emotional terms."[22] Here, in his self-deprecating way, Fisher ignored the fact that in 1953 he was a credited coauthor of *Mantrap* (U.S.: known as *Woman in Hiding* or *Man in Hiding*) and *Four-Sided Triangle* (U.S.: *The Monster and the Woman*), two of his most interesting pre–*Curse of Frankenstein* productions for Hammer. Clearly, Fisher was both willing and able to write films, yet he never again received a script credit and is known to have participated in the writing of only one other picture, *Frankenstein Must Be Destroyed*. "I came in early on and there was a threesome of discussion," he explained. "I think Bert Batt and Tony Keys [the credited authors] will agree on that, because they used to come here and we used to kick it around" (for "hours and hours and hours, day after day," added his wife, Morag).[23]

Not only was Fisher capable of effective screenwriting, but during the early 1950s he teamed productively with writer Richard Landau, who wrote or cowrote *Stolen Face* (1952), *Spaceways* (1953), *Murder by Proxy* (1954; U.S.: *Blackout*), and *Mask of Dust* (1954; U.S.: *Race for Life*). Fisher also mentioned "participating closely" with writers on "last-minute changes."[24] Nor did he feel so respectful of the scripts he received that he wouldn't revise them during production. "On every day of shooting, I've sometimes [prepared] a complete overhaul" of the story's development, he acknowledged.[25] Sometimes, Fisher's revisions were extensive, as one of *Dracula*'s key scenes—Jonathan Harker's first meeting with Dracula—reveals.

Much of Jimmy Sangster's dialogue was rewritten to make it more concise. In the script, just before Dracula appears, the Vampire Woman tells Harker the same thing four consecutive times: "You can help me escape. He never lets me go out. I am confined to this house. He's keeping me prisoner." The film condenses this repetitive dialogue. Later, Sangster gave Harker the unwieldy speech, "As I told you sir in my letter, it will be a pleasure for me to be able to stay here where it is quiet and peaceful. The work I shall do on your behalf is small payment for the seclusion that your house offers." In the film, this becomes the much more direct, "I like quiet and seclusion. This house, I think, offers that." Elsewhere in the scene, Fisher eliminated dialogue and replaced it with something visual. For example, he cut two of the script's verbal references to the food that was left for Harker, keeping only the most general one ("I trust that you have found everything you needed"), which is followed by a shot of Harker and Dracula, with the table and its contents prominent in the foreground. Fisher also added a line in which Dracula explains the absence of a housekeeper and moved his comment about having to leave from the scene's middle to its end.

Such changes retain the essence of Sangster's script, while making it more compact, dramatic, and natural. But Fisher went further by rejecting the writer's conception of Dracula. According to Sangster's stage directions, "When he speaks we may notice that his two canine teeth are slightly longer than normal, and definitely more pointed. One gets the impression that unless he makes a conscious effort to the contrary, these teeth would lay along his lower lip." Sangster also wrote, "We have perhaps noticed that this suitcase is obviously heavy by the manner in which Jonathan has carried it heretonow. . . . But Dracula takes it up as though it weighed nothing, swinging it in front of him as he moves up the stairs." Finally, when Dracula shows Harker to his room, he walks so rapidly that when the guest enters the passage, Dracula stands waiting for him. Sangster obviously planned to reveal Dracula's abnormal aspects—his teeth, strength, and stride—from the start, but Fisher chose to establish Dracula as a normal, if austere, presence and to save his otherworldly qualities for later.

Because Fisher's modifications of this scene are so extensive, it is clear that his translation of a script into visual form could constitute a form of rewriting. One might similarly question Fisher's overly modest statement about his influence on the casting of his films. On only two occasions, he said, did he have control: "One was Freddie Jones in *Frankenstein Must Be Destroyed* and the other was Charles Gray as Mocata" in *The Devil Rides Out*.[26]

While it is true that Hammer cast both leading and supporting roles from a standard roster of performers, this explanation does not fit the fact that Thorley Walters ("great friend of mine, love him," said Fisher[27]) appears prominently in six of the director's films, including two made for other studios. It also is hardly coincidental that people who had acted for Fisher in earlier, non-Hammer features turn up again, later. These include Arnold Marle, Carol Marsh, Andre Morell, Guy Rolfe, Freda Jackson, and Felix Aylmer. In addition, Aylmer and Martita Hunt had crossed Fisher's path in films he edited before becoming a director.

Fisher's refusal to overstate his creative impact, which sometimes led to understatement, illustrates some of his personal characteristics. Actor Charles Gray spoke for almost everyone ever directed by Fisher when he described him as "easy to get along with."[28] Madeline Smith added, "He was one of the kindest . . . directors I've ever worked with,"[29] and Richard Pasco considered him "a director whom I could trust very much indeed [and] a deeply compassionate man."[30] According to Barbara Shelley, Fisher was so "understanding" and "gave out such a warmth" that he inspired his casts "with tremendous confidence."[31]

One reason for this confidence was the fact that he was, said Yvonne Monlaur, "always very calm, whatever the circumstances or problems,"[32] so the performers never felt rushed or pressured. As Hazel Court recalled, "with Terence Fisher you had all the time you wanted."[33] Fisher's crew felt the same way. "I never saw him lose his temper," recalled production manager Hugh Harlow.[34] "He was well aware of tight schedules," added camera operator Len Harris, "but was always able to cope with them in a calm way."[35] Photographer Jack Asher concluded that Fisher "was well liked, even possibly loved," by his colleagues,[36] and editor Bill Lenny called him "a very sweet man, well loved by the unit."[37]

The man who inspired such devotion was, however, in the words of his wife, Morag, "fundamentally shy, a loner."[38] Fisher's colleagues also noted this aspect of his personality. "He was a quiet sort of chap," said Len Harris, "but he could inspire me [and others] by his enthusiasm."[39] To producer Michael Carreras, he was "self-effacing,"[40] Jack Asher used the word "unobtrusive,"[41] and Bill Lenny called him "slightly introverted."[42] Perhaps actress Veronica Carlson expressed this best when she said that Fisher "would never throw his arms around me and say, 'How are you, Veronica?' or anything like that. . . . He was not as outgoing as Freddie [Francis]."[43]

Such reticence did not prevent him from establishing a relationship with his coworkers and eliciting their commitment to the film. Instead, they responded to the clearly sincere feeling that lay just below the surface. In every respect—personally and professionally—Fisher "was the most honest person that I've ever known," declared Morag.[44] Yet, despite his close involvement with others on the set, Fisher viewed film direction as "one of the most lonely jobs in the world," because "you're surrounded by people and they are all looking out of the corners of their eyes at you and saying, 'What are you going to do with my talent?' " He would "take everybody's ideas," but "there's only one person who decides [and] you have to be diplomatic in rejecting ideas."[45]

Fisher's desire for control and the security it brought is revealed by the fact that he didn't just tolerate the shooting of scenes out of sequence—he preferred it, because it meant carrying the continuity around in his head and being the only one with a complete grasp of how a given shot would fit the overall pattern. "In cinema, there is a fascination about working out of sequence," he said. "It all has to be crystal clear in your mind, and that makes for perfection."[46] By the same token, Fisher preferred working on sets to filming on location because, he explained, "in a studio, you can control things in a way you can't outside."[47]

Fisher was "such a gentle person," said Morag, that he "didn't want trouble. Never trouble of any kind."[48] This led to his calm and diplomatic manner on the set, which was personally necessary and artistically productive. It also led him to control his feelings to maintain the atmosphere he required. Sometimes, reported Morag, during "the last week or so" of his shooting schedule, a studio "would suddenly cut back on the number of days he had left. . . . When something like this was presented to him, he would get very quiet,"[49] instead of arguing or indulging in emotional outbursts. Fisher accepted things. "If he had a failing," noted Anthony Hinds, "it was being too kind. Kind people tend to get trodden under in the rat race."[50]

In his personal life, Fisher also revealed a need for control and stability. "He liked coming home and relaxing," recalled his wife. "We didn't mix in the film crowd very much. . . . but we always had people coming here. . . . He was happiest being a homebody."[51] However, visitors are not the same as friends—close friends—and in that respect Fisher remained a loner. According to Morag, "He had one really good friend, Marcel Baclet," with whom he could "really talk." When Baclet died, "Terry missed him very, very much because he didn't have what I thought were close friends. If you read the letters, everybody was his friend, but it was only business."[52] Perhaps, though, Fisher didn't want close involvement. From all indications, he was satisfied with friendly acquaintances and the comradeship of his working environment. Beyond that, the privacy and security of home and wife were enough.

Fisher's emotional self-discipline led him to view as wrong anything he perceived to be self-indulgence. "One must never be self-indulgent in making a film," he told one interviewer,[53] and Morag stated, "That's what made him angry with all the new directors—self-indulgence."[54] Fisher did not apply this concern only to his profession. Once, when discussing the merits of horror films set in contemporary times, he expressed a fear that they might "encourage indulgence" in susceptible viewers.[55]

Because Fisher was a loner, it is not surprising that his most interesting characters are also cut off from emotional involvement with others. Whether heroes or villains, such men lead independent, often solitary lives. Sherlock Holmes epitomizes the positive version of this figure, while Baron Frankenstein embodies the negative form. Holmes has a single friend and confidant, Dr. Watson, and Frankenstein has only "business associates," doctors who provide assistance but are not, as people, necessary to him. Was it just by chance that Thorley Walters—whose companionship Fisher enjoyed—played Holmes's companion in *Sherlock Holmes and the Deadly Necklace* (1962) and Frankenstein's associate in *Frankenstein Created Woman*?

In some of Fisher's horror films, the loner falls in love with a woman and is torn between his need for independence and his desire to have her with him. In almost every case, the nature of the man makes such a union impossible. The title character of *The Man Who Could Cheat Death* (1959) has stayed youthful for more than a century through periodic operations, so he cannot have a long-term relationship with someone who will age without him. When he finally decides to commit himself to a woman, he plans to perform the same operation on her, a decision that leads to his destruction. Other frustrated love affairs appear in *The Mummy* (1959), *The Phantom of the Opera,* and *The Gorgon* (1964). Only in *The Curse of the Werewolf* (1961) is the male offered a real possibility of happiness with a woman, whose presence helps him curb the animal instinct that at times makes him lose control of himself. Fate, however, separates them, and so this loner, too, is doomed.

When Fisher responded to the conflict between good and evil that he found in his horror scripts, and as he developed his ideas about the attraction of evil, he naturally interpreted those concepts from his own perspective, based on his own assumptions.

Because he sought to live a calm, secure life by controlling his emotions and because the loss of such control felt threatening, Fisher equated the characters who embody rationality, intelligence, and self-discipline with good. Conversely, those who indulge their emotions embodied a dangerous decadence synonymous with evil. Thus, Holmes and Dr. van Helsing are solitary, self-controlled heroes, while Fisher's vampires give in to unrestrained instinct, to passionate self-indulgence.

This opposition is not as simplistic as it might at first seem. Baron Frankenstein, for instance, takes the qualities associated with good to such an extreme that he has no empathy for others, which makes him selfish and egocentric. He thus reveals a different, but equally ruthless, form of self-indulgence, one that makes him not a productive creator but someone who tramples people's feelings and, often, their lives. In contrast, van Helsing's intense objectivity and emotional reserve are tempered by sympathy for others, which motivates his fight against vampires. Frankenstein has so sublimated his feelings that, for all practical purposes, they no longer exist, but feelings play an important part in van Helsing's life, although he keeps them under control.

Fisher's films present both kinds of characters with such honest force that the director must have understood each of them quite deeply. In a sense, Baron Frankenstein can be seen as what Fisher unconsciously feared he might have become without the "moral strength" Morag mentioned[56] and without the love and support of Morag herself. On the other hand, van Helsing can be seen as the Fisher who disciplined his impulses but also concerned himself with the feelings of his characters, his coworkers, and his viewers. Fisher trusted his instincts and those of his actors, while maintaining the objectivity required to produce an effective film.

Fisher's concern for stressing the emotional content of a scene and for making the characterizations as real as possible shaped his approach to his work. "I'm not an intellectual director—I've said this many times—I'm an emotional director. I work by intuition and emotion. . . . Of course, I've got to know my bloody script and everything, but I'm *not* an intellectual director to the point where I say this is exactly what I'm *going* to do." Instead, he let a scene find its form when he rehearsed it just before taking shots. For him, working with actors involved "an interchange of emotion" between "director and artists." Although Fisher started out with "certain things that you have in back of your mind," the reactions of the performers to him, to one another, and to the settings helped build a scene's dramatic identity. "It comes out of the emotion, the action, at the moment of rehearsal," he explained, and "movements arise out of it and ideas arise out of it." Through that chemistry, "the whole thing— evolves."[57]

By drawing on the ideas and feelings of his cast, Fisher made them an important part of the creative process. "Most of the time, I only give them a general outline. I believe it is indispensable to leave a little freedom to the actors. . . . It seems to me that there ought to be a large amount of improvisation. Besides, it is much more fun to work that way."[58] In addition, he knew that he might get a good idea about how to improve a scene from an actor. This, of course, pleased and flattered his performers. "He always listened to everything you had to say," recalled Hazel Court.[59] Madeline Smith concurred: "He would always ask you what *you* wanted, how *you* felt about something, and that's rare in a director."[60]

During the filming of *Dracula*'s climax, Peter Cushing (who played van Helsing) felt he needed an alternative to pulling one more crucifix out of his pocket. Recalling a scene from the movie *Berkeley Square* (1933), he suggested that his character grab a candlestick with each hand and with them improvise a cross. Fisher agreed, and the prop department came up with the necessary items.[61] Christopher Lee probably suggested one change that Fisher made in *Dracula*'s screenplay. Sangster had Dracula get Harker's attention by calling his name from off-screen, but Lee wrote in his copy of the script, "Is it not more effective to have presence bring J. round—no voice." Fisher modified this idea, and in the film the vampire woman's departure prompts Harker to wonder what caused it, so he turns to look behind him. This keeps viewers uncertain for a bit longer and saves the sound of Dracula's voice for a more dramatic moment.

A particularly delicate example of Fisher at work occurred during the filming of *The Brides of Dracula* (1960). The elderly actress, Martita Hunt, was too vain to be seen wearing fangs, so she told Fisher, "I really don't need those. I'll just cover my mouth with my shawl!"[62] To an unaware observer, this might be an instance of an actress dominating her director, but Fisher took this idea and emphasized it, so that the character seems so humiliated at having been made a vampire by her son that she must hide the evidence of it, which becomes one of the film's emotional highlights.

Fisher's openness led some actors to believe that he did not really direct them. Andree Melly, for one, thought that Fisher was more "interested in lighting and cutting" than in his actors,[63] and Oscar Quitak, who called Fisher "not one of the great inspirational directors," spoke about inventing his limping walk for Karl in *Revenge of Frankenstein*.[64] (Separately, Fisher cited that walk as one of the details that pleased him most in that film.[65]) Christopher Lee reacted similarly, stating with regard to *Dracula,* "I don't think anyone on the film had a clear idea of where to go, including dear Terence Fisher." The way Dracula "was played and interpreted—this came from me."[66]

These actors evidently felt that Fisher didn't know what he wanted and concluded that they achieved their performances on their own. To an extent, that is true, because he viewed his actors as professionals who, if they understood their characters and the situation, could take it from there themselves. Once he knew they understood a scene, he would not tell them *how* to perform. If he noticed that they were taking it in a direction other than the one he sought, he would make a comment to move them closer to his intention, but he was sufficiently self-effacing that he did not have to *seem* to be in charge, even though he was.

Many of the actors who worked with Fisher understood his method. Barbara Shelley explained that he put a lot of psychological thought into the characters, "and the marvelous thing about it was that you never catch him at it. He doesn't go into a lot of talk and chatter about the conclusions he has reached, but it is obvious after you've discussed a scene for a while that you know exactly what he wants and of course he's always right."[67] Yvonne Monlaur agreed, stating that "he had the gift of being subtle: he directed us precisely without our being aware of it."[68] Andrew Keir described Fisher's technique in greater detail. "Terry knew what he wanted, and he could get rid of your excesses and then bring it back to what he wanted. . . . Terry had a way of pulling people back into the scene, and it was always *gently* done. Never a wrong word or done with any cruelty, just a nudge here and a nudge there, to get what he wanted. Sign of a great director."[69]

Richard Pasco offered an additional insight. Fisher, he said, "was the kind of director who would come up to you just before you went for the take and give you what we actors call a 'golden umbrella.' He'd give you pure gold in one short sentence or maybe just a few words. He'd say something and suddenly you'd be all clear about what you were after in that particular shot."[70] A good example of this involves Melissa Stribling, who played Mina Holmwood in *Dracula*. When Mina returns after her first encounter with Dracula, she pauses for a moment in the doorway. Fisher recalled that he told the actress, " 'I'm going to go very close at this moment . . . and I want a reaction from you, please.' She said, 'What reaction do you mean, Terry?' " Stribling, reasonably enough, couldn't imagine how a woman who had been attacked by a vampire would feel, so Fisher offered her a "golden umbrella" that solved her problem, while guiding her in the direction he wanted. "I said, 'For God's sake, you've had the most wonderful sexual night you've ever had in your world.' And this is true, this was the important thing at that moment—she had become part of Dracula. . . . And she *played* it, too! . . . She conveys every bit of it!"[71]

In addition to helping actors understand their characters, Fisher was alert to visual details that might add to a scene. In 1964, he cited two examples from *Revenge of Frankenstein*. "There's a man in a hospital bed, with no legs because the Baron has cut them off to put them on his Creature. So the man sits with his arms coiled round just where his legs were, as if he would have liked to rest his elbow on his knee but couldn't any more. We only 'saw' this on the floor. And did you notice the scene where Frankenstein lights the bunsen burner in front of the eyeballs in the tank? The reflection of the flame in the glass seems to be touching the hand. And you feel the helpless fear of these dismembered parts. This sort of thing can hardly be visualised at the script stage."[72]

Only after he finished developing a scene would Fisher decide how to divide its action into shots and where to place his camera. Only then, he said, did he "break the scene into dramatic set-ups and start punching and punctuating" where he wanted.[73] In this area, he felt free to deviate from any descriptions of camera position and editing included in the screenplay, which he considered intrusions into the director's domains—"that is your own personal interpretation" of how "to turn the written word into visual form."[74]

A major element of Fisher's visual style is deep focus, which uses the foreground, middleground, and background depths so that everything important to a scene is present in a single shot. "I love to *see everything* in focus," he declared. "You can always get the narrow depth of view when you need emphasis." He also tended to keep the early part of a scene in one long take, which lulls the viewer into a calm state, so that when he does cut to medium or close shots, the change has considerable dramatic force. Often accused of using static setups, Fisher actually does move his camera quite a bit. "But I don't want the audience to be conscious of the movement," he said, "until such moment as it's got to hit them emotionally and dramatically! . . . Otherwise, they're buzzing about, being dragged along after a camera the whole time." When a technique is used too often, he declared, it "ceases to have any emotional impact on the audience."[75]

A good example of his style appears in *Dracula,* during a conversation between van Helsing and Arthur Holmwood. With the latter seated in a chair, van Helsing walks around and does most of the talking. Throughout this scene, the camera pivots slightly to adjust as van Helsing moves to the right and the left of Holmwood and between the background and foreground. Without elaborate tracking and without editing, the scene is visually varied, thanks to Fisher's control of the viewer's attention. He knows that a character who is standing, who is close to the camera, and whose face is visible attracts the eye and gains emphasis, so he keeps shifting van Helsing's position to stress important lines and minimize others. Thus, this one shot creates an understated dramatic rhythm, and, as Fisher pointed out, "You're getting your cutting, really, by the movement of the characters, of the people within the scene."[76] Then, after the general statements about vampirism have been made and the men start to talk about their situation, Fisher shifts gears, cutting between more intimate medium shots of each character. Most directors would have used such shots from the start, but Fisher's restraint grants them the power to involve the viewer.

Fisher also uses this style during scenes of action. In *Curse of Frankenstein*, Franken-stein ascends a flight of stairs with an elderly professor whose brain he covets. When they pause to examine a painting, the professor steps back for a better view and Frankenstein pushes him against the railing. All of this occurs in a single take, as the camera moves with the characters. Then, having lulled the audience, Fisher shocks them with a sudden cut to a disorienting shot looking directly down, as the railing gives way and the professor falls to the floor below.

Near the opening of *Dracula,* Jonathan Harker talks with a seductive and frightened woman. They stand, in medium shot, near a large, free-standing globe—"the most wonderful prop in the world, that globe," recalled Fisher[77]—and, as the woman pleads for help, she walks behind it to the other side, then across the front of the object until she is again near Harker. Fisher's camera pans with her, moving to the left until Harker leaves the frame, then back to the right until he is again visible. The shot is a quiet one, but it subtly offers visual variety by contrasting the two-shots with the view of the woman alone and by differentiating between her position when partially blocked by the globe and her closeness as she comes around it. This, Fisher pointed out, was a case of the "intuition and emotionalism of a director . . . who suddenly sees a prop" and decides to use it. The resulting blend of actor and camera movement "was a physical thing which expressed something—without cutting, thank God!"[78]

When Harker comforts this woman and she moves to bite his neck, Fisher sud-denly cuts to a long shot as Harker pushes her from him, while, in the background, Dracula is glimpsed in the doorway. An extreme close-up of Dracula's blood-smeared face follows, then we return to the long shot as Dracula leaps forward over a table and hurls the woman aside. Here, Fisher uses three kinds of visual shock—the sudden cut to a new position, the extreme contrast between a long shot and a close-up, and the movement within the frame—combined with the aural shock of musical chords and Dracula's loud hiss. These work together in a few seconds to create a dramatic explo-sion.

One scene that never uses cutting, but still employs the impact of changing from a long view to a close one, occurs in *Revenge of Frankenstein*. After Karl, Frankenstein's escaped subject, has turned cannibal, a young girl heads home down a flight of steps, along a landing, and down some more steps. In a long shot we see her descend the first steps toward the camera; when she walks to the right on the landing, the camera moves with her, then tilts downward to center on the back of Karl's head, as he hides below. Suddenly, the head turns and we get a close-up of his distorted features. We next move with him to the right as he confronts the girl at the bottom of the second set of steps. The camera pulls back into a long shot as Karl drags her into some bushes and holds on the bushes while we hear her scream. This uninterrupted shot makes a remarkably varied and emotionally powerful use of distant and close views.

Low-budget filmmaking always limits money, time, and opportunity to participate in preproduction activities, but Fisher seemed to thrive under such conditions. He successfully placed his stamp on these films, both visually and thematically, and unlike many large-budget directors he rarely had his films altered by their producers. "I do most of my editing in the camera," he explained. "Not entirely, but I'm a most eco-nomical shooter. This doesn't mean that every shot falls together like a bloody jigsaw puzzle, but I shoot to the extent of having no extraneous cover at all, except for moments of intercutting . . . closer shots" and for instances in which "you have to gauge the length of time that you will hold anything before you [snaps fingers] do that! [cut to startle the viewer] So I cover myself there."[79] This approach made Fisher an ideal director of films with short shooting schedules, but it also meant that editors (and producers) could not veer far from his intent. Happily for the viewer, Fisher's instincts often proved worthy.

Terence Fisher's instincts, his solitary nature, and his need for a stable, controlled life can be traced to his youth. Born on 23 February 1904 in Maida Vale, London, he had what he called "a funny upbringing."[80] An only child, he lost his father when he was about four years old, and his mother appears not to have been a major presence in his childhood. "My grandparents looked after me," Fisher revealed, "until I went to the Bluecoat school where I stayed until I was sixteen."[81] On another occasion, he said, "I had an Irish grandmother. She brought me up—very badly—but I loved her deeply."[82] The unusual nature of his childhood, Fisher believed, led to the fact that "I never really decided what I wanted to do" in life.[83]

When Fisher was about sixteen, his mother decided that a period at sea would be "good discipline"[84] and "give some direction to my life; in fact, of course, it put me in the way of a great many temptations."[85] After three years of apprenticeship on a merchant navy training ship, the young man "got a second mate's ticket, joined the P&O [line] as a junior officer,"[86] and spent a total of five or six years on his own. "You can write my sea experience down to my sexual education," he once said.[87] In a separate interview, he added, "I loved going to sea. I learned a lot. It wasn't so much a question of seeing places as meeting people I'd never met before in my life. That was exciting."[88]

Despite the excitement, Fisher "decided that a lifetime at sea was not for me,"[89] but there was nothing else he wanted to do. After leaving the merchant marine, he took a job at a department store or, as he later put it, entered "the rag trade."[90] "The only reason I can remember for working there was that we happened to live near the shop at the time."[91] Fisher arranged the store's windows and, eventually, became assistant display manager; "five to seven year[s] I think I was there."[92] During that time, he became a moviegoer and found himself drawn to the industry. "Love at first sight came rather late," he recalled. "I don't think I had the chance to visit movie theatres regularly before the age of twenty-seven or twenty-eight. But since then, I never lost my passion for everything about films."[93]

In 1933, Fisher—nearly thirty years old—began his third career and once again started at the bottom, as "the oldest clapper boy in the business."[94] Within a year, he had become an assistant editor. Two years later, he was a full-fledged editor and spent the next decade editing a wide range of films. In the process, he consciously studied film technique. "Most of what I learned filmwise was in the cutting rooms. That gives you a great sense of the pattern of a film, the overall rhythm."[95] This was an excellent opportunity to analyze both editing and the staging of action within shots. During World War II, Fisher expected to be summoned for military service, but "film editors were classified as a reserves occupation, which meant you weren't called up."[96] After the war, in 1947 (when Fisher was 43), the J. Arthur Rank company initiated a training program for potential directors. "I thought I'd like to direct," recalled Fisher, "so I applied for the course and was accepted."[97] Morag Fisher recalled his description of the interview for this position: "It was like going to see God with this huge desk, and a long way from the door up to it. And Terry was like a little boy. And this man was much younger than Terry was!"[98]

Each trainee received three short features to direct, and Fisher's trio offered the novice considerable variety: *Colonel Bogey* (1948) was a pleasant ghost comedy, *A Song for Tomorrow* (1948) a romance with music, and *To the Public Danger* (1948) a tale dramatizing the danger of drunk driving. Fisher followed these films with *Portrait from*

Life (1948; U.S.: *The Girl in the Painting*), which depicted the plight of displaced persons after World War II and placed him fairly high in the ranks of serious directors. After making *Marry Me!* (1949), a comedy-drama about the clients of a marriage bureau, Fisher solidified his position by replacing the veteran Anthony Asquith as director of *The Astonished Heart* (1950), a romantic drama by Noel Coward and starring Michael Redgrave, Celia Johnson, and Margaret Leighton. When Coward grew dissatisfied with Redgrave's performance, he took on the role himself. Next, Fisher directed *So Long at the Fair* (1950), a suspenseful thriller in which Victoria Barton (Jean Simmons) investigates the disappearance of her brother during the 1889 Paris Exposition.

With his career going so well, it seems surprising that in 1950 Fisher left Rank's Gainsborough Studios, where he had worked with major stars and rewarding material, to align himself with low-budget companies. From 1951 through the end of 1954, he directed fifteen features, eleven of them for Hammer Films. Fisher later explained that Rank had become "a little doubtful as to what they were going to do with me."[99] He also said that "Rank began to be very wary about their investment in films and the whole industry in Britain began to go through a very bad time—apart from Hammer, who were applying themselves very seriously to improving their product. And so I joined Hammer."[100]

Although small, Hammer produced a steady output of films and could offer the security-minded director regular employment. In addition, the close Hammer organization filled a need in Fisher. "Being in a small studio one got to know everyone connected with it," he explained. "The crews didn't change from picture to picture."[101] Shooting schedules were short, at most about thirty days, but apart from that, he had "complete freedom."[102] Fisher summed up Hammer's appeal when he said, "They had a certain amount of confidence in me and they did leave me alone to get on with the job."[103]

Another motivation may have been the fact that Antony Darnborough, the producer of *Portrait from Life,* served as Fisher's codirector on *The Astonished Heart* and *So Long at the Fair.* The topic of Darnborough's involvement and their division of labor went unexplored by Fisher's interviewers, but one can speculate that the situation made him uncomfortable. As Morag remarked, "he didn't really like visitors on the set,"[104] and a codirector would be the ultimate visitor, someone looking over his shoulder and interfering with the chemistry of direction. From this perspective, Fisher probably preferred to be an independent fish in a small pond, with Hammer giving him the chance to make films his way.

Fisher's earliest pictures for the studio suggest that this gamble was paying off. Two of his first three Hammer features boast superior, if small-scale, scripts. *The Last Page* (1952; U.S.: *Man Bait*), a tightly knit story of realistic characters involved in a blackmail scheme, was written by Frederick Knott, author of the 1952 Broadway hit, *Dial "M" for Murder.* Even better was *Stolen Face* (1952), about a plastic surgeon who tries to change the life of a bitter criminal by repairing her scarred visage. Only *Wings of Danger* (1952; U.S.: *Dead on Course*) was a standard mystery melodrama, but even it contained fairly complex characters.

Fisher then took a step forward by collaborating on the above-average scripts of *Mantrap* (1953) and *Four-Sided Triangle* (1953). These were, however, the last films for which he would be credited as a writer and his next Hammer productions were mostly just effective second features. Then, in the mid-1950s, the demand for Hammer's product declined, and in 1956 the studio produced more shorts than features. Thus, during 1955–56, Fisher worked elsewhere and even formed a production company, in partnership with producer-director Francis Searle, which turned out to offer no security. "We dissolved the association by mutual consent," he said, "because of the difficulties involved in film promotion at that time."[105]

Many of Fisher's prehorror films are minor mysteries that imitate the American film noir style of the 1940s, with plots in which a man suspected of murder has to solve the crime himself. *Murder by Proxy* (1954) at least has a sense of humor about its roots, as when someone suggests that the hero try detecting and he says, "I can do that—I've seen enough movies." *Face the Music* (1954) includes some acceptable Raymond Chandler-type narration—"I felt like yesterday's corpse when I finally got away that night"—but in *Blood Orange* (1953; U.S.: *Three Stops to Murder*) Tom Conway wanders around a fashion house making tedious attempts at investigating.

One should not, however, dismiss—as Fisher himself did—these early films as "a training ground for learning something about film craft."[106] When he began directing at the age of forty-three, Fisher's personality and his use of film technique were already fully mature. Granted, *Curse of Frankenstein* and *Dracula* offered fertile material, but his previous films reveal an assured visual style and a sensitivity to the kinds of characters and situations that would reappear in the horror films.

Starting at least with *To the Public Danger,* Fisher used his camera in a concise manner that creates impact and conveys information with a minimum of cinematic means. Such an approach, which avoids attracting attention to itself, inevitably depends on the quality of the subject matter for its success. Fortunately, several of these scripts are strong enough to justify Fisher's honest, direct observation. The first shot of *Portrait from Life* illustrates this style. The camera films from inside a pub's telephone booth, with the bar visible in the background. When a man decides to place a call, he moves from the bar to the foreground telephone; at one point, he exchanges waves with someone in the background, who is leaving. Here, Fisher provides everything the viewer needs in one compact image. He also does this in *Stolen Face,* when the main character discovers that the woman he loves has departed. Here, Fisher uses one clear, but understated shot, looking past the man through a doorway at an unmade bed and an open, empty wardrobe. In *Murder by Proxy,* Fisher employs deep focus to create suspense when a man wanted for murder checks out of his hotel in the shot's foreground, while in the background a police inspector telephones his description to headquarters.

It is not unusual to find, in these films, visual approaches that reappear in the horror pictures. When, in *The Last Page,* a secretary enters her employer's office to report his wife's death, Fisher uses a medium shot of the two, with the man's desk and a photo of his wife prominent in the foreground. He follows the same principle in *Dracula,* placing a food-laden table in front of Harker and Dracula. Also in *The Last Page,* Fisher holds an ordinary shot of a man and woman talking for more than a minute. Then, when the man abruptly turns and puts a hand over her mouth, Fisher matches the action with an equally abrupt cut to a closer shot. Here, the director lulls his viewers into a calm mood in order to jolt them with the sudden movement and change of shots. He again does this in *Brides of Dracula.* While van Helsing, having been bitten by a vampire, heats a piece of iron and wraps a rope around his free arm for support, Fisher's camera slowly tracks closer. Then, when van Helsing presses the iron against his neck, Fisher cuts to a close-up just as the man's body writhes in agony. The suddenness of this cut and of the movement within the frame vividly conveys the hot iron's impact.

Other details from these films also anticipate Fisher's horror pictures. Leaves blow in the wind at unhappy or threatening moments in *Portrait from Life,* much as they do in *Curse of Frankenstein, Dracula,* and *The Gorgon.* Also in that film, an underground bunker, with its staircase leading to a doorway where a figure lurks, evokes the crypt seen near the beginning of *Dracula.* The blackmailer in *The Last Page* (Peter Reynolds) has a kinship to Baron Meinster (David Peel) in *Brides of Dracula:* Both are handsome and urbane, in a slippery sort of way, as they manipulate susceptible young women into doing their bidding. A murder in *Blood Orange* occurs when a fashion model falls to her supposedly accidental death through the railing of a staircase landing, a plot device that Jimmy Sangster, the film's assistant director, reused in his script for *Curse of Frankenstein.*

Some of these early plots evoke both Fisher's personality and the horror films to come. The most interesting ones center on independent men committed to their work, men without close emotional involvements. At times, these honest, even idealistic, loners lose their perspective when tempted to indulge their emotions or when confronted by the self-indulgence of others. This frequently involves a relationship with a woman, which tends to result in a story not of love but of loss. The ambiguity of identity is a recurring motif, and the need to identify or define a personality is often presented in artistic terms, through the creation of a painting or a statue; even a plastic surgeon acts like an artist in this way.

Two of Fisher's first three films include elements that would reappear over the years. *Colonel Bogey,* although a fantasy, is a romantic comedy and therefore quite different from his more typical works. However, based on a plot summary,[107] *A Song for Tomorrow* incorporates several significant story details. A surgeon (Ralph Michael) successfully operates on the wounded Shawn Noble (Derek Wardell), but when the patient recovers, he has amnesia. The voice of opera singer Helen Maxwell (Evelyn McCabe) is Noble's only link with the past, and the two fall in love. Later, after the surgeon stages a fake operation, Noble regains his memory and realizes he actually loves a woman to whom he originally had been engaged. This linkage of surgery, identity, and frustrated romance anticipates Fisher's future works.

To the Public Danger is less an anti-alcohol tract than a drama that contrasts two very different personalities. Fred (Barry Letts) is a moral man, but weak, a bit dull, and vulnerable—the victim of his fondness for the self-centered Nan (Susan Shaw). Captain Cole (Dermot Walsh) is immoral, ruthless, and manipulative, but charming when he chooses and, to Nan, attractive in his strength, control, and confidence. Cole indulges his impulses, and, like the vampires and other arrogant noblemen in Fisher's later films, he uses others in cruel, impulsive ways.

Having worn out their welcome at one pub, the group drives on and their car hits what they think is a man on a bicycle. Cole doesn't stop and, later, argues against returning, while Fred speaks up for common decency. After Cole beats him in a fight, Fred flees and hides. Now on his own, and better off for it, he calls the police, but at the site there is no sign of an accident. Having built an extremely uncomfortable situation for Fred, the film finally offers him relief: A poacher admits that a car had hit his bicycle, which was parked with a sack of potatoes on it. Although this vindicates Fred, he feels foolish for being so concerned about a minor incident. Meanwhile, Cole's control of events and people turns into an out-of-control situation, as he gives his impulses free reign. Epitomizing dangerous self-indulgence, he imagines himself so powerful that he can drive with no hands. The film ends with Fred, unaware that the Cole and Nan have died in a car crash, doubting the merit of his own positive qualities.

Portrait from Life, Fisher's fourth film, summarizes his future interests even better than *To the Public Danger.* Its plot is set in motion when two lonely men meet while gazing at a painting of a young woman. Major Lawrence (Guy Rolfe) has just commented, in his narration, "You can feel lonelier in a crowd than anywhere else on earth"; Professor Menzel (Arnold Marle), a war refugee, hasn't seen his daughter in nine years, but recognizes her in the portrait. Lawrence, intrigued by the woman's face and the man's plight, helps him find the dying, alcoholic artist (Robert Beatty) who declares, as if speaking for the filmmaker, "You saw my picture, didn't you? . . . It's all in there—all the little lonely souls, lost, looking for one another." (Later, in a flashback, the painter also evokes Fisher, who didn't like visitors on the set, when he says, "I can't stand people watching me. It puts me off.")

Touring the displaced-person camps in Europe, Lawrence searches for the painting's subject. When he finds her, he learns that she had loved the painter but he had not let himself accept her love or his love of her. Lawrence also tries to reclaim the woman's forgotten childhood, to determine if she is Menzel's daughter or the daughter of the man whom she believes to be her father (Herbert Lom). Eventually, she recalls her past and Lom's character is exposed as a Nazi war criminal.

Lawrence is the earliest example of the ideal Fisher hero, the type of person exemplified by van Helsing in *Dracula* and *Brides*. He is a solitary man, emotionally distant in his dealings with people. This serves him in good stead, for it permits him to be organized and efficient, able to get a job done and done well amid the overwhelming misery of the camps. But Lawrence is also sympathetic and caring, a man guided by his feelings for others. At no time do these emotions control him in selfish ways, however. He never seeks to please or satisfy himself, and there is no indication that he is attracted to the woman in the painting. If he does harbor such feelings, he has too much self-control to indulge them and does not suffer the inner turmoil revealed by the artist. Because of this, it is unfortunate that the studio had the film's ending reshot to hint at a future romantic link between Lawrence and the woman.[108] (At least the new ending only *hints* at this.)

Fisher's early Hammer films also include relevant characterizations, such as *The Last Page*'s central figure (George Brent), who is, like Fred, a quiet, rather nice man, but one too tolerant for his own good. Revealingly, his medical report states that he is "liable to lose control in emotional situations." The most meaningful of these films, however, are the six written in various combinations by Paul Tabori, Richard Landau, and Fisher himself: *Stolen Face, Mantrap, Four-Sided Triangle, Spaceways, Murder by Proxy,* and *Mask of Dust.*

Stolen Face, written by Richard Landau and Martin Berkeley, centers on Dr. Philip Ritter (Paul Henreid), an idealistic plastic surgeon unconcerned about a poor family's inability to pay and critical of an egocentric rich woman's request for a face-lift. "Learn to live with yourself as you are," he tells her. Ritter believes that "a physical deformity might cause someone to become unbalanced enough to commit a crime," and he has tested his theory by operating on convicted criminals. "I thought you were stark, raving mad," says the prison doctor, but he admits that only one of the prisoners Ritter treated has been arrested again since the surgery. Ritter assures his latest subject, the badly scarred Lily (Mary Mackenzie), that he will make her "as attractive as [she] always wished to be." He is, at this stage, sincerely unselfish, but so involved in his work that he has no other life and never relaxes. When he finally takes a vacation, he meets and falls in love with Alice (Lizabeth Scott), but she flees from him and from her emotions because of a commitment to David (Andre Morell), a dignified and gentle older man.

Later, Alice telephones Ritter and tells him, "I want so much to be honest with you." He replies, "Are you honest with yourself?" The point is well taken, but, without his realizing it, the disappointed Ritter has become selfish and self-indulgent: He turns Lily into a facial double of Alice and, shortly after, marries her. When Ritter declares, "If I don't believe in my work, what can I believe in?" his associate replies, "You're gambling with your future, just to prove a theory." Overconfident of his ability to control and define Lily, Ritter asserts, "I know what I'm doing." In fact, he has lost his objectivity. He is no longer interested in his theory for its own sake; an act previously performed for the other person's benefit has become one done for himself.

"I'll be everything you want me to be," says the grateful Lily (played, after the operation, by Lizabeth Scott), and Ritter guides her selection of hairstyle and clothes. If he cannot have the real thing, he will have a duplicate. At first, Lily tries to satisfy Ritter, but she's bored at the opera and he's bored at a jazz nightclub. She grows to resent his domination and, in rebellion, starts to shoplift and mingle with petty criminals. "Why don't you stop trying to make me something I'm not?" she asks. Ritter, in his self-deception, has discovered the limits of scientific planning. His experiment has become his life, but, having omitted the human element from the equation, he lost track of the nature and needs of his subject. "You left love out of your calculations," he is told.

Mantrap, cowritten by Fisher and Paul Tabori, also involves a woman with a dual identity, although a less blatant one than in *Stolen Face.* Thelma (Lois Maxwell), the beauty editor of a magazine and the wife of an engineer, had earlier been married to Mervyn Speight (Kieron Moore), an artist convicted of murder. "I was a front page face," she explains, and to escape from that notoriety, she says, "I gave up all but one or two of my friends. I changed my name. I hoped I would have a little peace." Her scenes with her new husband (Bill Travers) evoke those between Alice and David in *Stolen Face* because, like David, he is patient and sincere. "I want to do the right thing, darling," are his first words in the film, to which he adds, "I feel I may lose you any moment, even though you *have* taken my name. You see, that's all you've let me give you." She responds, "You've given me the hope of a new life, Victor—love, devotion, and security."

Meanwhile, Speight escapes from prison, and a lawyer, Hugo Bishop (Paul Henreid), is asked to help him. Bishop's fiancée warns that his involvement could cost him his practice and put the couple's future in jeopardy. But Bishop says he was asked by a friend for help, and that's enough. Besides, Bishop has a semiscientific approach to his work. "I like to help because I'm curious, because I'm human, and above all because I'm interested in people under stress," he tells Thelma. When she replies, "Like animals under a microscope?" he declares, "Most certainly not! Any human being is a wonderful creation one should do everything to preserve from destruction. . . . That isn't a laboratory procedure, believe me." Before they part, he (like Dr. Ritter) insists on his honesty. "You must promise to trust me," he says.

Speight had suffered from amnesia, but while imprisoned he regained his memory and started drawing a man with a "face all twisted with passion, fear, and hate." He's determined to explain this recollection. "I'm not mad," he tells Thelma. "I'm not going to be on the run for the rest of my life. I'll be out of this mantrap, for good." At present, though, he doesn't trust anyone. "Do you trust yourself?" Thelma asks. He replies, "I know I'm not my own enemy . . . , but everyone else is my enemy. You, too. But I wish—I wish you weren't my enemy. If there was only one, just one!" But he is completely alone, at least until Bishop enters his life and helps resolve matters.

Stolen Face and its two versions of one woman clearly intrigued Fisher, for he cowrote (with Paul Tabori) *Four-Sided Triangle,* which has a very similar premise. In later years, he dismissed this film as "science-fiction," but, when pressed, he acknowledged that it "touched and scratched" at the worthwhile subject of confused identity.[109] In actuality, *Four-Sided Triangle* does much more than that, and only at the end does the script lose its grip on the intriguing plot.

The story, told in flashbacks by a doctor who had known the main characters since childhood, deals with two friends, Bill (Stephen Murray) and Robin (John van Eyssen), who invent a machine that can duplicate anything. After their success, the "solid and dependable and conscientious" Robin marries Lena (Barbara Payton), another childhood friend. During their honeymoon, Bill works alone in the laboratory. Although he speaks of "detached scientific curiosity," he is far more emotionally involved in his work than he admits. He also loves Lena, but is "too sensitive" to tell her. Driven, in the doctor's words, "by a force he couldn't control," Bill hopes to create another Lena. When the idea is suggested to her, the doctor tells Lena, "Be quite sure of yourself." As she considers what to do, Fisher's camera tracks closer to her reflection in a mirror. She agrees to the experiment and it succeeds, but the new woman—called Helen (also played by Barbara Payton)—attempts suicide. Everyone, it seems, has overlooked the fact that she would be an emotional as well as physical duplicate of Lena. Therefore, she retains her now-futile love for Robin, who remains married to Lena.

"In all my life," Bill says, "I've only wanted two things—knowledge and, I suppose, love. I used the first to try and gain the second." Now, even if he accepts his own loneliness, that won't lessen Helen's. So Bill decides to "erase" her memory. Like Phillip

Early in his career as a director, Terence Fisher relaxes with actress Barbara Payton during the filming of *Four-Sided Triangle* (1953). Fisher also coauthored the screenplay of this feature.

Ritter and Hugo Bishop before him, Bill tells Helen before the experiment begins, "You trust me, don't you?" She does, but the machinery begins smoking and then explodes, destroying the building and the couple, leaving only Lena and her husband to survive.

The key virtue of *Four-Sided Triangle,* despite the far-fetched "science," is its sense of reality. Rarely have the dangers and attractions of playing God been presented in as natural a manner. After all, Bill's attempt does seem the logical thing to do, and yet there is also something inhuman about it. The plot only fails to satisfy at the end, when the ultimate implications are avoided in favor of an arbitrary conflagration. One wonders, for example, whether Bill would still love Helen after she received a new personality. At its heart, *Four-Sided Triangle* is not really a film about science; like all good science fiction (or fantasy), it deals with the emotional and personal results of a hypothetical situation. The final impression left by the film, which links with Fisher's attitude toward temptation and emotion, is summed up in the doctor's statement, "There's often less danger in the things we fear than the things we desire."

Fisher's other science-fiction film from this period, *Spaceways* (written by Paul Tabori and Richard Landau), is not as successful, but it still has much to offer. Appropriately, it places greater emphasis on the tensions between the characters than on technology. Like *Four-Sided Triangle,* it involves a "creative" effort, but this time the experiment and the human aspects are less thoroughly blended. When Vanessa (Cecile Chevreau), the dissatisfied and unfaithful wife of scientist Steve Mitchell (Howard Duff), disappears with another scientist, Philip Crenshaw (Andrew Osborn), Steve is suspected of killing the two and hiding their bodies on a now-launched rocket. The need to prove his innocence provides the motive for a manned flight to retrieve the rocket. Surprisingly, Steve is allowed to pilot the spacecraft himself. Also surprisingly, the mathematician with whom he has fallen in love, Lisa Frank (Eva Bartok), disguises herself as a man and joins him. Preparations for the launch are intercut with the discovery of the fugitives—Crenshaw is a foreign spy fleeing with both Vanessa and scientific secrets—but because the mystery is solved before the launch occurs, the space flight becomes unnecessary and anticlimactic.

Although Howard Duff is unconvincing as a rocket scientist, his character is Fisher's familiar work-obsessed, self-controlled loner. This time, he is married, but mismatched with the self-centered Vanessa. "She could see herself moving in high circles, leading a very glamorous life," Steve says. "It's an old story. A guy with a one-track mind, nothing but rockets in his head, meets a beautiful woman with—something entirely different in hers." The film does not present Vanessa sympathetically, but she is comprehensible. To her, the scientific facility with its military security was "a prison" from which she had to escape.

Unlike Vanessa, Steve reveals an appreciation of human limitations. Early in the film, before Vanessa's disappearance, Lisa asks Steve if he is happy. "Happy?" he replies. "It's a very inexact word for a higher mathematician, Lisa." She then wonders whether "the achievement of the mind, the creative effort," is "the only thing that counts." Steve responds, "All I do know is that we can do almost anything with matter or energy, we've streamlined science, but as for the human being, we're still muddling around in the stone age as far as our emotions are concerned." By the film's end, these two scientists have formed an emotional link. "We can work it out together," she says. "Prove them wrong!" Only such a combination of rational science and "inexact" emotions—not merely romantic feeling—permits success.

This aspect of *Spaceways* is further developed through the character of Smith (Alan Wheatley), a biologist working for military intelligence, who investigates the disappearances. A bit of an eccentric, he has a crisp, preoccupied, almost arrogant manner that anticipates Peter Cushing's future performances. He also combines rationality and intuition in a way that typifies Terence Fisher and his work. "I'm a great believer in atmosphere," says Smith. "Hunches may not be scientific, but sometimes they pay off." On one occasion, he declares, "Somehow, I smell death in this room—my grandmother was Irish, you know." So was Fisher's, and the director also shares Smith's blend of the uninvolved and the intuitive. As if to cement this link, Smith sports a pair of heavy-framed, Fisher-like glasses.

Although its human element provides some substance, *Spaceways* remains an unbalanced mixture of genres that jumbles together spaceships, infidelity, possible murder, a detective, and spies. More important, while the characters' nature as scientists is well mixed with their human aspects, the experiments do not link directly with the characters' emotions and relationships (at least, not until the end). As a result, the early footage devoted to a rocket launch seems arbitrarily inserted; it alternates with the people's lives, instead of merging with them. In *Four-Sided Triangle* (and Fisher's Frankenstein films), the experiments are performed on the characters, and that makes all the difference.

After *Spaceways,* Fisher's early films are driven more by their standard mystery plots than by the characters' personalities. Some—like *Face the Music* and *The Stranger Came Home* (1954; U.S.: *The Unholy Four*)—are well made and hold a viewer's interest, but they are less personal and probably were less satisfying for the director. (Admittedly, several of these features remain unseen and may offer surprises.) A partial exception is *Murder by Proxy* (written by Richard Landau), in which Casey Morrow (Dane Clark) becomes involved with the deceitful Phyllis Brunner (Belinda Lee). Casey has been on his own for years, drifting through life in a vague form of escape from his origins in a Chicago slum. Phyllis, too, is running away, from her fiancée and from her family's wealth and control. Casey is drunk and broke when, in the film's first scene, Phyllis offers to pay him to marry her. The next morning he has no memory of what happened: He may or may not have married her and he may or may not have killed her father.

Selfish and emotionally manipulative women are no strangers to Fisher's early films, but usually they—like Lily in *Stolen Face* and Vanessa in *Spaceways*—are understandable and even sympathetic. *Four-Sided Triangle,* however, offered Fisher's first ideal female character, someone the narrator describes as "the most wonderful thing in the world, a woman who is also a companion and a comrade." Lisa, in *Spaceways,* also illustrates this ideal, as does Maggie Doone (Eleanor Summerfield) in *Murder by Proxy.* An attractive artist who helps Casey, Maggie has an ironic sense of humor and is independent but vulnerable. By the film's end, Phyllis has been so consistently untrustworthy and Maggie such a good-humored "buddy" that it is hard to accept the script's arbitrary conclusion, which exonerates Phyllis and lets Maggie drop from sight.

Early in *Murder by Proxy,* Casey says, "I've always been 'away,' even when I was a kid." Here the film implies that an isolated, unsatisfactory childhood led to his drifting alone through life. Later, in a ten-minute sequence, Casey and Phyllis visit his mother, whom he has not seen or contacted in eight years, and his stepfather, with whom he has an initially strained encounter. When Casey's mother asks why he didn't return sooner, he replies, "I don't know. You wait and try to become somebody and the years pass. Then, you're ashamed to come back." Shortly after, Phyllis tells Casey, "You can't run away from yourself, you know," to which he responds, "No one can say I didn't try." Finally, Casey declares, "No more running. We stay and we clear up this mess once and for all," which refers not only to the murder mystery but also to his personal life. This sequence stands out because it has little relation to the main plot and because, in an otherwise artificial (if entertaining) melodrama, it is emotionally sensitive in a reserved and natural way.

It also evokes what little we know about Fisher's childhood and probably stirred an empathy in the director that prompted the shift in tone. In the process, Fisher may also have revealed his current feeling of professional frustration, a sense that as he neared the age of fifty he still had not "become somebody." A year earlier, in *Four-Sided Triangle,* the script he cowrote had the narrator describe Lena as "a self-confessed failure. She had tried many things—art, music, writing—but without success." Lena says, "There are many scapegoats for our sins and failures. . . . [but] I shan't blame anyone but myself."

This element of professional frustration becomes a central issue in *Mask of Dust,* which was released in the same year as *Murder by Proxy* and was also written by Richard Landau. In it, a race-car driver past his prime (Richard Conte) refuses to quit. "Driving's my life, my career," he explains. "It's what I was meant to do. I've got no choice!" Morag Fisher spoke in similar terms about her husband: "He made pictures because he loved making pictures, and he made pictures to live."[110] The parallel continues when the character declares, "I can't walk away and leave a string of failures behind me. I've gotta prove I can still win. . . . A man's gotta be able to live with himself. If he can't do that, he's no good for *any* woman." Later, an employer says, "While you're under contract you'll do what Bellario and I tell you!" Fisher may have felt similarly frustrated and helpless in his profession.

Mask of Dust may be a familiar and, unusual for Fisher, sentimentalized story about a stubborn sportsman, but it also seems to reflect the mood of a director who in 1950 almost achieved his goal of creative freedom and stability, but then saw it slip away. Significantly, Fisher had four films ready for release in 1952, four in 1953, and six in 1954—but only two in 1955 and one in 1956. His career was, in truth, stagnating when in the fall of 1956 Hammer proposed that he direct their new version of Mary Shelley's *Frankenstein.* The rest, as they say, is history.

Until this point, Fisher observed, "my career had been attempting to find a line of direction which I was good at. *The Curse of Frankenstein . . .* put my career into perspective."[111] Having had no particular attraction to horror or fantasy before, Fisher said, *Curse of Frankenstein* "revealed to me an entire aspect of myself of which I was totally unaware. . . . If I had not worked with Hammer, I undoubtedly would not have chosen this film on my own."[112] From 1957 through 1974, Fisher directed eighteen more films for Hammer and five for other companies. Virtually all were horror films.

In 1956, the popularity of Hammer's *The Quatermass Xperiment* (1955; U.S.: *The Creeping Unknown*) started the company looking for a suitable follow-up. "We suddenly realised," recalled James Carreras, the studio's head, "that nobody had made a classic horror film—by which I mean the Frankensteins and the Draculas—for many, many years."[113] Hammer, satisfied with the screenplay that Jimmy Sangster wrote for *X—The Unknown* (1956), assigned him to adapt *Frankenstein.* According to Peter Cushing, Sangster's script needed "a little attending to,"[114] so producer Anthony Hinds offered creative advice. "I worked as a co-writer without credit," Hinds explained, but Sangster "did all, or most, of the actual writing."[115]

"I was owed a film by Hammer," Fisher later said, "and the next one happened to be the *Frankenstein.*"[116] However, Michael Carreras, the film's executive producer, recalled that Fisher had "expressed to Tony [Hinds] his desire to handle more gutsy subject matter."[117] Hinds also questioned Fisher's version of events. "I know that he kept saying till the end that he was only engaged to direct the first one because Hammer owed him a picture, but it just is not true; Terry and I had been friends for many years before that and I knew he had just that right combination of discretion and lets-give-'em-something-to-make-'em-sit-up that the shows needed."[118]

Hammer had decided to make the film, in Fisher's words, "for a lark" and planned to shoot it in black and white on a three-week schedule. The idea of remaking a classic on such a short schedule "staggered" Fisher, and, after reading the script, he said, "I need money, but not fifteen days, please!"[119] Ultimately, Hammer lengthened the schedule and shot the film in color. Fisher chose not to screen James Whale's 1931 *Frankenstein* before making his version. "There was a long period of time between theirs and ours. The whole way of living had changed so it would have been pointless to try and copy them."[120] Instead, he "tried to forget the idea that I was continuing the central horror tradition in the cinema. I wanted the film to grow out of personal contact with the actors and out of the influence of the very special sets."[121]

The most important of the actors was Peter Cushing, cast as Baron Victor Frankenstein. An experienced and versatile performer, Cushing had begun his career in English repertory theater but made his screen debut in America as a bit player in *The Man in the Iron Mask* (1939); this was directed by, of all people, James Whale, and Cushing also appeared in Whale's last feature, *They Dare Not Love* (1941). He then returned to England and acted in the theater, in films, and on television. Cushing's sharp features and dignified bearing were ideal for the character, conveying a quality of polite, ironic ruthlessness, of gaunt intensity. Hammer also employed a good supporting cast and a team behind the camera that would remain together for numerous films. These included Fisher, Sangster, photographer Jack Asher, composer James Bernard, editor James Needs, and production designer Bernard Robinson.

"The great temptation was for the actors to try and send it up, to overdo things," Fisher remembered. "That's always the danger with these films."[122] But he knew that the tone had to be completely serious. "The first thing Peter Cushing and I said together" was that "we will play this fundamentally with integrity." Their agreement set the mood for the entire production, but it was still just another assignment for Fisher. "The moment I really got interested was about a third of the way" into filming, because then "I knew we had something . . . through the association of the people who were acting in it."[123]

Aspects of Jimmy Sangster's script derive from *Four-Sided Triangle*, on which Sangster did not work but which Fisher cowrote and Sangster certainly knew about. In both films, an older man teaches a young boy all he knows, then becomes his assistant for a reckless experiment. Also, both scripts employ a flashback structure and narration (this time, by the central character instead of the older one). "I became his teacher," we are told in *Four-Sided Triangle*, "but only for a little while, for he soon outpaced me as a hawk would a sparrow." In *Curse of Frankenstein*, Frankenstein says, "In two years, I'd learned all he had to teach, but we went on together, probing into the unknown, investigating, recording, searching. . . ."

Curse of Frankenstein begins with Victor Frankenstein imprisoned and about to be executed. When a priest enters his cell, Frankenstein tells him, "Keep your spiritual comfort for those who think they need it. I sent for you because I could think of nobody else." These lines—the character's first—establish Frankenstein's sardonic self-sufficiency. But, at the same time, Frankenstein *did* send for the priest and *is* trying to stay alive by convincing the authorities that not he but his creation is the murderer. (It is a logical flaw that, in the long flashback representing his account of events, Franken-stein admits to killing Professor Bernstein.) By the end of the film, after finishing his story, Frankenstein begs his former teacher, Paul Krempe (Robert Urquhart), for help. It is as if Hammer, having made the scientist far more ruthless than viewers expected, decided to cushion the impact with these framing scenes. Frankenstein's confidence, his superiority over mundane emotions, and his ruthlessness are what make him inter-esting. By undermining this quality, Hammer reassures the audience's moral sense at the expense of the character's distinctiveness.

After this opening, we meet Frankenstein at the age of fifteen (Melvyn Hayes). He is totally on his own: His father has been dead "since I was five years old"—a reminder of Fisher's youth—and relatives have just paid their respects after his mother's death. Victor now possesses the family fortune and the title of Baron. Although haughty and willful, young Victor seems to be a responsible person, espe-cially compared with his unctuous aunt, who worries about her allowance and tries to set Victor up with her prenubile daughter, Elizabeth. Polite and efficient, Victor assures the woman that the payments will continue but remains uninvolved. (Fisher probably filmed other scenes of the young Victor, because publicity material identifies actors who play a schoolmaster and a mother.)

After Victor hires Paul Krempe as his tutor, the film rapidly summarizes their years of study. We rejoin them, with Victor an adult, performing an experiment that has lit-tle impact because we are not told what is happening. Finally, water is drained from a tank and a puppy removed. Victor, in extreme close-up, listens for a heartbeat. There is little dialogue here, with emphasis placed on Cushing's gaze and the subtle changes at the corners of his mouth, until he says, "Paul, it's alive." Such understatement will dominate all of Fisher's horror films.

Having restored the animal to life, Frankenstein intends to build an ideal human being, "a man with perfect physique, with the hands of an artist and with the matured brain of a genius." Paul, his tutor-turned-assistant, resists, calling the idea "a revolt against nature," but Frankenstein convinces him to help. The first stage of Victor's plan involves body-snatching. As he tells Paul, "I'm harming nobody. Just robbing a few graves, and what doctor or scientist doesn't? How else are we to learn the complexi-ties of the human animal?" This historically accurate way of obtaining bodies gives *Curse of Frankenstein* a realistic context lacking in the updated Universal films. It also helped Cushing understand his character. "There had to be a reason behind his actions," he explained, "so I more or less based him upon Dr. Robert Knox, the famous anatomist who . . . shut his one eye as to how Burke and Hare got him bod-ies—he didn't care where they got them from." So, Cushing envisioned Frankenstein as "a man who is, fundamentally, trying to do something for the good of mankind."[124]

Frankenstein's methods, however, are thoroughly pragmatic. "There is nothing—do you hear me?—nothing more important to me than the success of this experiment," he tells Paul. To Fisher, Frankenstein was "a complete idealist," a man consecrated to a noble goal and, "like most consecrated people, he is single-minded and completely ruthless in what he does. But he is governed by an idealism, he is not inhuman. He is not doing it to achieve evil in any shape or form, or to achieve riches for himself."[125] Paul Krempe points this out to Frankenstein's cousin and fiancée, Elizabeth (Hazel Court), saying that he is "neither wicked nor insane. He's just so dedicated to his work that he can't see the terrible consequences that could result." At first, Frankenstein merely bends the laws of his hypocritical era, but soon he places himself totally out-side the consideration of good and evil by believing that his end justifies any means. He has, in Fisher's words, "metaphorically sold his soul to the Devil."

James Whale's film had skimmed over Frankenstein's gathering of body parts and omitted his piecing them together into a complete figure. It dwelt, instead, on the method of infusing it with life and on the results: the nature and actions of the Monster, the conflict between creator and created. Fisher's film does the reverse, emphasizing Frankenstein's preliminary activities. This difference in emphasis can be seen in the way two similar events are handled. In Whale's version, Henry Frankenstein has his assistant cut a hanged body from a gallows, while in Fisher's, Victor Frankenstein does that dirty work himself. Henry immediately declares that because the neck is broken the body is useless, and at that point the segment ends. Fisher and Sangster, however, have the body brought to Frankenstein's laboratory, where the scientists note that birds have pecked out the eyes and "half the head's eaten away." So, Frankenstein coolly cuts the head off, wraps it in burlap, and eases it into a vat of acid.

This sequence typifies Fisher's decision to stress concrete detail and factual realism, but in a straightforward, unsensational way. The director started by insisting that a stuntman play the corpse when it is cut from the gallows. According to camera operator Len Harris, Fisher stated "that a dummy wouldn't fool them like a body would."[126] Later, the gruesome actions are not shown directly. The severing of the head occurs below the frame's edge, and, as Frankenstein handles it, his arms partially block the action. Elsewhere, though, *Curse of Frankenstein* offers good views of detached eyes and severed hands. (At one time, the film probably did show Frankenstein placing the head in the acid, but current prints offer a shot of Paul in the next room instead.)

Frankenstein is out collecting the hands of a recently deceased sculptor when Elizabeth arrives and mistakes Paul for the fiancée she hasn't seen for years. Soon Victor returns, gives Elizabeth a quick "hello," and whisks Paul off to see his trophies. Paul again resigns, which Frankenstein takes in his stride. "If you really mean you're not going to help me," he says, "I'll be glad if you'll leave me alone. I've work to do." That evening, Elizabeth ignores Paul's urgings that she leave, and Paul learns of the wedding plans. The transition from this scene to the next is dramatically effective, delivering a typical jolt to our preconceptions: After Elizabeth declares that marriage to Victor "has always been my dearest wish—his, too," Fisher cuts to Victor kissing the maid, Justine (Valerie Gaunt). Our discovery of his affair is a surprise, but Fisher has prepared us for it by having the maid show her awareness of Frankenstein by straightening her dress or glancing his way. The affair itself is quite consistent with Frankenstein's character; he is no Lothario of the laboratory, but he is a man and Justine satisfies his physical needs with fewer complications than someone from his own class. He uses her, but no more than she tries to use him. A social climber, she has her calculating eye on marriage. Justine is not even discouraged when Frankenstein, true to form, follows the kiss by reminding her to call him "Baron," not "Victor."

After Frankenstein obtains a pair of eyes at the Municipal Charnel House, Fisher wittily (but atypically) cuts to a close-up of Victor examining his delicacy with a magnifying glass that isolates his own functioning eye. Later, Frankenstein shows the completed body to the still-reluctant Paul. "Look, I admit he isn't a particularly good-looking specimen at present," he says, but "one's facial character is built up of what lies behind it, in the brain. A benevolent mind, and the face assumes the patterns of benevolence. An evil mind, and an evil face. For this, the brain of a genius will be used and when that brain starts to function . . . the facial features will assume wisdom and understanding."

Paul asks where Frankenstein will get the brilliant brain he needs, but Victor merely says, "I'll get it." Fisher then cuts to Frankenstein entertaining Professor Bernstein

(Paul Hardtmuth), and the Baron's intention is immediately clear. From the second floor, he pushes the professor to an "accidental" death, but before this happens the elderly man serves as a voice of maturity and wisdom, reminding Frankenstein that "one can spend too much of one's life locked in stuffy rooms seeking out obscure truths, searching, researching, until one is too old to enjoy life." Bernstein also raises an issue that surfaced in *Four-Sided Triangle* and *Spaceways:* the misuse of scientific discoveries. "There's a great difference between knowing that a thing is so," he says, "and knowing how to use that knowledge for the good of mankind." During Bernstein's speech, Fisher contrasts the two men by intercutting a close shot of the professor with one of Frankenstein, who is clearly not really listening to him.

After Frankenstein obtains Bernstein's brain, he is interrupted by Paul, and in the scuffle between them the jar holding the brain shatters. Frankenstein picks fragments of glass out of the precious organ and, between scenes, places it in the creature's skull. He then sets his machinery in motion, and from here on *The Curse of Frankenstein* is surprisingly unimpressive. Frankenstein, unable to operate the apparatus alone, leaves to fetch Paul. While he is absent—and more than halfway into the film—the creature comes to life. When Frankenstein returns to the lab, his creation (Christopher Lee) immediately tries to strangle him. To save Frankenstein, Paul hits the creature on the head with a chair. Soon after, Frankenstein reminds Paul of the broken glass and blames him for everything. He plans to repair the damaged brain the next day, but instead finds the creature gone. The escape is not shown.

In a nearby forest, a small boy leads his blind grandfather to a clearing, then goes to the side of a lake. The creature emerges, but recoils when the man reaches out to touch him. Worried, the blind man pokes at him with his stick. When the creature grabs the stick and snaps it, the man runs, falls to the ground, and cowers. The creature walks slowly to him and kills him. From the staging and the creature's limited expressions, it is hard to know how to react to this scene. Fisher has said that the creature "didn't want to kill" the blind man. "He was pleased with him, quite friendly. Then the silly old man got frightened and poked at him with his stick. Suddenly the Monster's mind went wrong and he killed the old fellow."[127] However, although the creature is not immediately antagonistic, he never seems friendly and too much time passes after the incident with the stick for that to be the direct cause. The creature almost seems to realize that the man is helpless. If so, the killing must be due to the damaged brain, but the creature acts too wary for that to be the case. The script's inclusion of a damaged brain probably put Fisher and Christopher Lee in a situation similar to that of James Whale and Boris Karloff in 1931: They have to make the creature both monstrous and semisympathetic. The result here is confusion and uncertainty.

By placing the boy next to a lake, like little Maria in Whale's *Frankenstein,* Fisher and Sangster prompt viewers who remember that film to assume, mistakenly, that the boy will be a victim. Then, when the boy checks on his grandfather, Fisher holds on a shot of him moving out of sight behind some bushes. A viewer expects to hear screams as the boy discovers his relative's body or is himself killed, but nothing happens and the scene ends. The blind man and the boy are not referred to again, which suggests that further action may have been shot but omitted during the final editing.

Paul shoots the creature in the eye, and, as the figure falls, for the first and only time a slight wind stirs the leaves that carpet the forest floor. With the creature dead, Paul is relieved, but Frankenstein secretly restores him to life (again, off-screen). Later, on the night before his wedding, Frankenstein shows Paul the revived creature and demonstrates that he has taught him to obey simple commands. When Paul rushes out to contact the authorities, Frankenstein follows. With both men out of the house, the creature pulls his chain from the wall and wanders onto the roof. Elizabeth, curious, enters the laboratory and makes her way to the roof. Frankenstein and Paul spot the creature and head for the roof, too. When the creature grasps Elizabeth, Frankenstein shoots, hitting her in the shoulder. As the creature advances, Frankenstein throws a lantern and the creature catches fire, staggers, and falls through a skylight into the vat of acid. The body is destroyed and Frankenstein ends up in prison, where he finishes his story. Paul, visiting, denies the tale and departs with Elizabeth, as Frankenstein is marched off to the guillotine.

Once Frankenstein's creature is created, the plot feels rushed, as if the filmmakers had become unexpectedly interested in the Baron's activities and then found they had to hurry through the rest of the story. To compound the problem, the film skips several potentially dramatic scenes, and the script includes two redundant confrontations with the creature instead of building to a single, gradually developed one.

Peter Cushing exudes energy and intensity as Frankenstein and even during the film's later scenes his character has moments that keep him human. At one point, after dishing out some food for the creature, Frankenstein tastes it, then adds a lot of seasoning. Also during this section, Frankenstein reaches his peak of ruthlessness: When the pregnant Justine tries to blackmail him into marriage, he locks her in a room with the creature and listens as she screams. Fisher follows this with a transition to Frankenstein, at breakfast with Elizabeth, calmly asking her to "pass the marmalade." Once, when Elizabeth asks, "Can I come and watch you working in your laboratory," Frankenstein replies, "No, my dear, not yet—but one day, very soon," hinting, as he had previously, that he will introduce Elizabeth to his work in some disturbing manner.

Unfortunately, Christopher Lee is only adequate as the creature, but that is not really his fault. Fisher saw the character as someone who "can't control himself,"[128] and Lee agreed, calling him "an ill-coordinated, childish creature who had no control over his emotions."[129] The actor gave considerable thought about how to convey this. "I had a damaged brain so therefore I walked slightly lop-sided,"[130] he recalled. He also decided that the creature's "hands must have an independent life" and that its "movements must be spastic and unbalanced."[131] Lee shambles around and wears a coat with sleeves that emphasize his dangling hands, but effective movements don't disguise the fact that the creature has very little to do, and, because the brain evidently retains no memory, he is without identity or purpose. Unlike Boris Karloff, Lee is simply a creature.

Another problem is Lee's pasty makeup, which looks like hastily applied lumps of putty. According to Phil Leakey, the makeup man, Hammer had no idea what it wanted. "We really needed months—or at least weeks—to experiment with different materials and try different approaches. But we just didn't have that amount of time."[132] Instead, he was "due to start shooting in twenty hours time and nothing settled. . . . The idea evolved that we would just try sticking lumps of flesh on a skeleton or skull and stitch it all up."[133] The final result was, said Leakey, "the most dreadful thing I'd ever seen in my life. I was utterly ashamed of it."[134]

But *The Curse of Frankenstein* was, after all, only a first step. The follow-up film, *Dracula*, retains the first work's emphasis on realism and characterization, while eliminating its weaknesses. This time, Sangster's script is tightly constructed, with a conflict between two strong figures, Dracula (Christopher Lee) and van Helsing (Peter Cushing), that provides a solid dramatic core. "One of the best films I've made," said Fisher of *Dracula*, quite correctly. "*Everything* worked well."[135]

Like Baron Frankenstein, Dracula is attractive in appearance and manner but ruthless in his exploitation of others. Although polite but reserved in his first scene, from then on he is ferociously physical and unrestrained. Lee makes a powerful impression in the role, supporting the script with his imposing stature (he stands well over six feet tall) and a haughty maturity that suggests strength and experience. Dracula is not on screen much more than Frankenstein's creation had been, but his presence hovers throughout, determining the other characters' actions.

Peter Cushing's van Helsing resembles Baron Frankenstein in that he is the embodiment of reason, an idealist who controls his emotions to do his work—work that also involves bodies and blood. However, van Helsing is a force for good, a mixture of doctor and priest who "operates" on a vampire's physical form to release its spirit. Fisher himself called van Helsing "the rationalist, the moralist who is trying to break an unholy pleasure."[136] Neither van Helsing nor Dracula has the complexity of Baron Frankenstein—and appropriately so, for what had been merged in the previous film's central character is here separated into two distinct figures, with each possessing traits the other lacks. The resulting conflict between the forces of good and evil gives *Dracula* a dynamic dramatic tension.

As he had with *Curse,* Fisher stresses emotional and physical reality. Because he "tried to make the vampires a bit more human than they usually are,"[137] Fisher was pleased that Sangster's script denied Dracula the ability to change into a bat or a wolf or a mist. Once a vampire is shown doing those things, Fisher felt, "credibility stops." This freed him to isolate and dwell on the link between vampirism and the power of evil, which to him meant Dracula's sexual appeal. "I think my greatest contribution to the Dracula myth," he later said, "was to bring out the underlying sexual element in the story."[138] The sexual connotations of the vampire's bite have always existed, of course, but in the 1931 *Dracula,* women simply waited passively as he leaned toward them. Later, they felt humiliated. In Fisher's film, the women want Dracula to visit them. They carefully prepare for his arrival and relish the moment. This was inherent in the script, but Fisher developed it clearly and subtly, imbuing even the air that rustles among some drifting leaves with unsettling sensuality.

Equally sensual, in its way, is the other physical aspect stressed by Fisher. Never one to be coy about emotionally provocative material facts, he starkly confronts the staking of vampires, which, he noted, "was never destruction. It was, of course, release and liberation." He added, in a comment that could be his overall credo, "It's important that you should see what's happening."[139] Why is it important? For one thing, because of the release involved. True, that could be indicated merely by showing the figure's peaceful expression after the deed is done, but that would make the change seem too abstract and too easily achieved. The activity is in fact far from easy, both for van Helsing and for his "victim." It is a harsh and difficult task, physically, ethically, and emotionally. Fisher doesn't just want his audience to know what has occurred; he wants each viewer to *feel* the impact of the hellish ritual that must be endured before release is granted, so he refuses to ignore its uncomfortable aspects.

Three stakings occur in *Dracula.* Early in the film, Jonathan Harker (John van Eyssen) dispatches the Vampire Woman (Valerie Gaunt); a bit later, van Helsing does the same for Harker. Neither event is shown graphically: Fisher cuts to shadows on the wall in the first case and, in the second, the scene ends before van Helsing begins. Only the staking of Lucy Holmwood (Carol Marsh), much later in the film, contains close-ups of the point entering the body, as blood wells forth to discolor her white negligee. The decision to emphasize Lucy's staking in this way is dramatically astute. The Vampire Woman's staking had considerable impact, owing to her screams and the crack of hammer on stake and the woman's shrivelled appearance afterward, yet it also left something for use in the later, more emotionally charged scene. (The editing of the earlier scene does suggest that, at one time, there may have been a shot of the stake entering the Vampire Woman's body, but it might not have been in the film's release print.)

The circumstances of the two stakings differ greatly. We have seen very little of the Vampire Woman in the film, and nothing at all of her in a normal, human state, so we have little empathy for her, personally. Because of this, the sight of her blood and pain would just be callous spectacle. Besides, something else occurs in the scene simultaneously: As the stake is driven into the woman, Fisher cuts to a close-up of Dracula in a nearby coffin, and his eyes pop open, seemingly in response to her screams. He looks to one side and we cut to a window, with the sun setting beyond. Dracula smiles to himself. Only then do we return to Harker, who, unaware of this, leaves the body of the woman and moves to Dracula's coffin, which is now empty. Looking up, he sees Dracula step into view and close the crypt's only door. Harker is trapped.

So this scene deals less with the woman's spiritual release than our realization that Dracula has awakened. The aftermath of the staking, for the audience, is not relief but further tension. In contrast, the staking of Lucy is the sole emotional line of that scene. We have encountered the living Lucy, have liked her, have hoped for her recovery, and have shared the concern of van Helsing, her brother Arthur (Michael Gough), and her sister-in-law Mina (Melissa Stribling). We have watched her fade, then die, only to be reborn as an "undead." She is not an unknown quantity, so we are

Dracula (Christopher Lee) appears just after Lucy (Carol Marsh), in anticipation of his visit, has carefully arranged herself in bed. From *Dracula* (1958).

emotionally involved and we know that the participants in the staking are even more involved. Because the event is meaningful in this way, Fisher shows it in detail.

Fisher had to change the script to build this emotional impact. Sangster had Lucy's brother do the deed. "It is my responsibility," Arthur argues, "and it is my fault that it happened." This is logical and appropriate, but Fisher improves on the situation. In the film, van Helsing drives in the stake, and as he does so Fisher not only shows the penetration but also cuts to shots of Lucy screaming and Arthur writhing in sympathetic agony against a wall. This gives Fisher a character for the viewer to identify with, a vehicle to carry the emotion. If Arthur had wielded the hammer, his emotional response—and the viewer's—would have been limited.

By the same token, Fisher does not dish out the gore on occasions when a less-conscientious director would jump at the chance. Only once is Dracula shown with blood on his face, and that's when it has the greatest impact—when we and Harker first see him not as an aristocrat but as a ferocious animal. From then on, we know what he is capable of, so further emphasis would only have a diminishing effect. Nor does Fisher dwell on the actual neck-biting. To him, the victims' anticipation is more important, because it reveals their responses to Dracula and all he embodies, including his control over them. Thus, we observe as Lucy, alone in her bedroom, goes through her ritualistic preparations. She locks the door, opens the French windows, removes a crucifix from around her neck, then arranges herself on the bed. When Dracula appears and bends over her recumbent form, the cape hanging from his arm blocks our view. The next time he visits her, the scene ends before he even arrives. Later, when Dracula bites Mina, we see more, but even then the emphasis is on his foreplay: a claw-like hand placed roughly against the side of her face as his mouth grazes her cheeks and forehead and then makes the final lunge to her neck.

Although Fisher always gave due credit to Sangster's well-conceived screenplay, he also pointed out that "both female characters in *Dracula* were so loosely written that it didn't mean a thing. . . . I had to emphasize that these two women who were involved with Dracula were under a special influence. His attraction, sexually, to both of them was a different sort of attraction."[140] Through the way he isolates and stresses material in the script, Fisher conveyed quite clearly the women's different responses to this sexual force. Lucy is the young virgin just discovering sensual experience, so her scenes are romanticized. From the way she prepares the room and herself, we sense that this night has been constantly on her mind since her "lover" last visited, and now she lies and waits with tingling anticipation. When Dracula arrives he does not step into view but quietly appears between shots, and his movements are graceful, even gentle.

With Mina, the married and more mature woman, things are subtly different. We do not see her prepare for Dracula, and she goes to him instead of waiting for his arrival. Dracula's movements here are forceful and his treatment of her distinctly physical. Later, Mina glows with the knowledge of her illicit pleasure, smiling inwardly with controlled satisfaction. In one shot, as her husband and van Helsing in the foreground wonder how to locate Dracula, she sits in the background, fulfilled but alert, forgotten by the men but not by Fisher's camera.

A particularly important moment for the director is Dracula's first entrance, when he greets Harker in the castle. Fisher anticipated that viewers would be "ready to laugh their bloody heads off," thinking "they were going to see fangs and everything."[141] So he decided to surprise them and, at the same time, heighten the character's credibility. "I said, 'Play it in silhouette, please, until the last moment,' " and then, when Dracula is seen, "he isn't like that at all—he has all the seduction, the charm of

Evil."[142] In a long shot, Dracula stands in shadow at the top of a flight of stairs. After a moment, he steps forward and descends toward the camera and into the light, stopping only when his face is in close-up. The revelation of Dracula's appearance is gradual and dramatic, even though only one camera position is used. The script, however, had him stand in a ground-floor doorway and made no mention of shadows. (In *Stolen Face,* six years before, Fisher offered a version of this scene when he revealed Lily's badly scarred face by first placing her in the background, facing away as she looks out a window. Then, in a medium shot, she turns and moves into the light.)

Thanks to the tightness of its storyline, *Dracula* feels dramatic and fast-moving. As in Bram Stoker's novel and Universal's 1931 film, Jonathan Harker arrives at Dracula's castle, followed by a transition to "civilization" and the Holmwoods. Otherwise, most of the details are new. Instead of being a real estate agent acquainting Dracula with his purchased property, this Harker is to index the Count's books (a rather unlikely situation). Soon, we learn that Harker's real mission is to destroy the vampire and that he is in league with van Helsing. This allows van Helsing to search for Harker at the castle and to stake his now-vampiric friend, and it gives him a reason for meeting the Holmwoods, when he reports Harker's death to them. Quincey Morris and the insane Renfield have been dropped, the asylum eliminated, and its director, Dr. Seward, changed into the family physician. As a result, the plot follows a small group of characters—Arthur, Mina, and Lucy—as they interact with van Helsing and Dracula, which narrows the dramatic focus. Also, the real estate aspect is replaced with a new, more personal reason for Dracula's travels: Because Harker has staked his female companion, the vampire intends to replace her, first with Lucy, then with Mina.

Throughout the film, scenes are juxtaposed to create transitions of maximum efficiency and impact. As van Helsing pauses, about to stake Harker, the scene changes to sometime later, when he finishes telling the Holmwoods of Harker's death. A direct connection between events results, with unnecessary scenes and dialogue omitted. Later, after Lucy prepares for Dracula's visit, a scene of van Helsing using a primitive Dictaphone gives us information about vampires and adroitly delays the previous scene's climax. Then, when van Helsing states that Dracula must be found and destroyed, we cut abruptly to a close shot of the Count in Lucy's bedroom. Similarly, Lucy's second wait for Dracula ends before he arrives, because the dramatic impact comes from the transition—to the girl lifeless in her bed.

In the final chase, Arthur and van Helsing pursue Dracula, who has abducted Mina. The two men arrive at the castle just as Dracula places Mina in a grave and starts to bury her. Interrupted, he flees into the building. This attempted burial makes little sense, and the middle of a chase is no time to confuse audiences. Even the director did not find Dracula's action here convincing. He candidly declared, "It was there in the script" and "I excused it by saying that he had no more use for her," that he was himself unconsciously attracted to the permanent death of the grave. Looking back, Fisher would have added a close-up of Dracula to imply, "Pray God, that should be I."[143] (The script contains an earlier scene in which van Helsing speculates that Dracula would try to bury himself and Mina to keep her with him, but this explanation was not included in the finished film.)

Some important on-set changes occurred while filming the climax. In the script, van Helsing interrupts Dracula as he tries to escape through a trapdoor. The vampire pauses, "his blood red eyes flooded with anger, unable to do anything for a moment. Then even while he is standing there a ray of sunlight creeps across his face. He claps his hand to his face and screams, then he turns," but Van Helsing uses a crucifix "to force Dracula back into the pool of light." This conclusion was too rapid and easy, so

Fisher added a short struggle that almost defeats van Helsing. Then, he notices sunlight just beyond the curtains of a large window and runs along a table top to leap onto the curtains, pulling them down as he falls. The beam of light hits Dracula, trapping him. When he tries to move out of its range, van Helsing uses two candlesticks to form a cross and forces Dracula back into the light. The result is an exciting finale that builds creatively on what the script provided.

Dracula had considerable impact at the time of its release, and it remains effective, despite the greater explicitness of later films, because its realism is linked with characterization and emotion. This film fully reveals Fisher's virtues as a director. "I found that, emotionally, it had achieved more than I had expected," he said.[144] According to his wife, "Terry had nightmares when he was making" *Dracula,*[145] which suggests that this director had indeed tapped into something personally relevant. Financially, the film confirmed *The Curse of Frankenstein*'s success and ensured that the next few years would be remarkably productive, with Hammer releasing another Fisher film in 1958, four in 1959, and three in 1960. Several of these stand among the director's best.

Hard on the heels of *Dracula* came Fisher's first Frankenstein sequel, *The Revenge of Frankenstein,* which carefully avoided the flaws of its predecessor. Ignoring Frankenstein's cringing and pleading at the end of the earlier film, it consistently depicts him as an aloof, superior outsider. In addition, Frankenstein's new creation is a memorable character in his own right, one with clearly established and fully conveyed feelings. Jimmy Sangster also wrote this screenplay, but Hurford Janes provided "additional dialogue." According to producer Anthony Hinds, "Peter Cushing did not think much of Jimmy Sangster as a writer and was always complaining about his dialogue, so I used to sometimes get in someone to 'give it a polish' just in order to keep Peter happy."[146]

For the most part, Sangster's horror scripts lack humor, but in *Revenge* Frankenstein has a cool wit only hinted at in *Curse of Frankenstein.* For example, when Hans Kleve (Francis Matthews) tries to force Frankenstein to make him an assistant, Frankenstein casually says, "Surely this is blackmail—an ugly trait in a doctor." Then, wondering aloud if he can trust Kleve, he says, as he polishes a large carving knife, "Uncertainty is part of life's fascination, isn't it?" Shortly after, Kleve stumbles while descending a flight of steps and Frankenstein comments, "It would be a pity to lose you—so soon." It may well be this aspect of the dialogue that was contributed by Hurford Janes.

The Baron had escaped execution by convincing Karl (Oscar Quitak), a prison employee, to substitute the priest as the guillotine's victim. In return, Frankenstein promised to give the crippled hunchback a new body. Three years later, calling himself "Dr. Stein," he has a thriving practice as a society physician, while also volunteering at a hospital for the poor, where he shops for body parts to use in his secret experiments. Dr. Ritter in *Stolen Face* (on which Sangster was assistant director) also had a distinguished practice and helped the poor, but Ritter disdained catering to rich and vain patients. Frankenstein, however, tolerates Countess Barscynska's attempt to interest him in her daughter and reveals no empathy for his unwashed patients. He is at his crisply independent best when confronted by a delegation from the city's Medical Council, which he has refused to join. "I have built up a highly successful practice, alone and unaided," he tells them. "Having grown accustomed to working alone, I find I prefer it." But he doesn't continue working alone, for Kleve guesses Dr. Stein's identity and becomes his aide.

Frankenstein has already pieced together a body in his laboratory, so the film avoids duplicating *Curse*'s emphasis on gathering parts and devotes more attention to the experiment's results. Also, Frankenstein has concluded that he must use a living brain.

"Unlike the limbs," he says, its "life cannot be restored, once life is gone." This leads to a realistic stress on surgical procedure rather than life-giving machinery, and it permits Frankenstein's creation to retain the memories and feelings of the brain's first owner. The filmmakers also avoid the need for a monstrous makeup by having the creation be thoroughly human looking. In another change, the fact that Karl is a volunteer makes Frankenstein less unpleasantly ruthless than before. Indeed, after the operation he even seems pleased for Karl's sake.

Fisher does not show the operation's details, which must wait for a more permissive cinematic era, but we get a good look at the brain before it is placed in the body. At the end of the process, the new Karl (now played by Michael Gwynn) is placed in a locked attic room and strapped down to keep him quiet until fully healed. When Karl does get up, he tests his walk, responds to finding his side no longer paralyzed, and surveys his new form in a mirror. Here, his human, vulnerable nature is conveyed in a quiet, understated way. In *Curse,* the creature began life in an abnormal state, but Karl has a chance to live happily ever after. Thus, when things go wrong, the loss of what he has gained brings an emotional depth to the horrific results.

Whereas the creature's brain in *Curse* had been injured by a single chance action, *Revenge* constructs a better-motivated series of events that lead inexorably to disaster for Karl. At the same time, the irony of good intentions leading to bad ends is thoroughly developed. A patient (Richard Wordsworth), who helps with the chores, spies on the doctors as they take Karl to the attic room. Hearing a scream, he assumes that they are torturing him. Meanwhile, Margaret (Eunice Gayson), a society do-gooder, has used her father's influence so she can help in Frankenstein's clinic. With beamingly naive sympathy, she wanders the ward offering soap, writing paper, and tobacco—only one of which interests the patients. When the spy tells Margaret of the mysterious patient, she enters the room and, trying to be helpful, loosens the straps that bind him to the bed.

Earlier, Kleve had unthinkingly told Karl that people "will come from all over the world" to see him alongside his old body. He had been stared at enough in his crippled state, so Karl leaves the room before fully recovering and, in the laboratory, burns his former body. Hearing noises, a janitor (George Woodbridge) discovers the intruder and strikes him with a chair. When Karl begs, "Don't hit me," the man gives him a brutal beating. This would be bad enough, but a side-effect noted in a prior experiment complicates matters: An agitated monkey had injured its new brain, which turned him into a cannibal. The janitor's blows have a similar effect, so Karl becomes a "monster" through a chain of misunderstandings and attempts to do good.

Because Karl knows about the monkey's condition, he recognizes the symptoms in himself. Racked by understood and undesired urges, he is simultaneously pathetic and fearsome. Later, Karl's anguish increases when his paralysis returns. After killing a village girl, he breaks in on Countess Barscynska's musical evening. The Baron is present, and Karl staggers toward him, pleading, "Frankenstein—help me," before he collapses, dead. When the Medical Council investigates, Frankenstein admits his real name but denies that he is the infamous scientist. The patients in the poor ward, however, have long suspected him of unnecessary mutilations; believing their suspicions to be confirmed, they corner him and beat him mercilessly. With Frankenstein near death, Kleve secretly transfers his brain to a new body. The film ends in London, where "Dr. Franck" sets up medical practice. As Frankenstein had told Kleve earlier, "They will never be rid of me."

Fisher followed the tight, tense, and emotionally involving *Revenge of Frankenstein* with *The Hound of the Baskervilles.* In this, Peter Cushing's fourth consecutive Fisher film, the actor creates his third memorable portrait of utter rationality. As Sherlock Holmes, Cushing combines Frankenstein's curt dismissal of his mental inferiors with van Helsing's commitment to fighting evil and his disciplined empathy for its victims. Cushing's vivid characterization is especially impressive because he creates it in only two scenes (totaling about twelve minutes). Holmes then disappears from the film for nearly half an hour, but Cushing has made such a forceful impression that it easily carries the viewer through until he reappears. In addition, the scenes without Holmes are supported by Andre Morell, who gives Watson the sturdy intelligence and quiet reliability he brought to his characters in *Stolen Face* and *So Long at the Fair*.

Peter Bryan's adaptation of Sir Arthur Conan Doyle's novel heightens the book's horror overtones by including a prologue depicting the misdeeds of Sir Hugo Baskerville—"a wild, profane, and Godless man; an evil man, in truth"—who pleases himself and entertains his friends by tormenting a servant. He hurls the man through a closed window, then holds him near the flames of a fireplace. "This may teach you to criticize my pleasures," says Sir Hugo. When the servant protests that the pleasures in question involve his unwilling daughter, Sir Hugo is incensed at the man's resistance, saying, "You should be proud that a Baskerville should so much as look at your miserable child!" Deciding to share the girl with his companions, Sir Hugo finds that she has fled, which further inflames his anger. With a pack of hunting dogs, he rides across the moors in pursuit. The Hound's howl intimidates the dogs, but not Sir Hugo, who intercepts the girl in a ruined abbey, where he stabs her to death and is himself killed by the unseen Hound.

Sir Hugo indulges his power and virility with a controlled ruthlessness that makes his actions especially offensive. Not only is he the center of his own world—to him no other world exists. "What does she think I am, that she does this to me?" he seethes when he finds that the girl has escaped. His ego does not permit such a slight, and no moral sense restrains his reaction. Fisher, in his staging of this sequence, fully captures Sir Hugo's menace, while resisting any temptation to overstate it. He is greatly supported by David Oxley's performance. Whether marching briskly down a corridor or delivering his "miserable child" line in full-face close-up, Oxley treads a fine line by depicting an excessive character without becoming excessive in his acting.

After Sir Hugo's death, the prologue is revealed to be part of the Baskerville legend, which has been read to Holmes and Watson by a potential client, Dr. Mortimer (Francis de Wolff). The scene that develops sets the film's present-tense plot in motion, while using Mortimer as a foil to establish Holmes's personality and, to a lesser extent, Watson's. When Mortimer starts reading from a newspaper report about the recent death of Sir Charles Baskerville, Holmes interrupts, saying with almost angry force, "I want just the plain facts in your own words!" A little later, when he asks, "Where was the body?" Holmes anticipates a useless answer, so he adds, with a condescending smile, "Somewhere on Dartmoor, I know, but exactly where? It's a very big place."

At one point, Mortimer states, "There were no footprints," and Holmes smugly declares, "That cannot be quite true, can it? There were the servant Barrymore's, for instance; your own; and Sir Charles's." Then, with the careful enunciation of a schoolmaster lecturing a slow pupil, Holmes states his credo: "Facts are only of value when they're clear, concise, and correct." Finally, when Mortimer says he will not be "ungenerous in the matter of fees," Holmes snaps back, "My professional charges are upon a fixed scale. I do not vary them, except when I remit them altogether." This statement reveals both Holmes's irritation at the thought that money could influence him and an implied sympathy for the poor, which differentiates him from Dr. Victor Stein and establishes a kinship with the idealistic Dr. Ritter in

Stolen Face. (Unfortunately, the script undermines this point, because at the end Holmes accepts a "very generous" check from Sir Henry Baskerville.)

Although this scene involves considerable dialogue delivered by three men in a single setting, Fisher's varied camera positions prevent it from feeling like a filmed play. However, the director lets the important dialogue and skilled acting carry the main burden, as when Holmes impresses Dr. Mortimer with a long list of deductions about him. Fisher stages this in a long shot that includes all three characters; he avoids stressing Holmes and what he says through the use of close-ups or even medium shots, because Cushing's rapid-fire delivery and the impressiveness of his statements are so strong that further emphasis, visually, would be overwhelming. Fisher does, though, cut to the silent Watson, who conveys, through subtle glances, an amused awareness of Mortimer's pomposity.

In the next scene, Holmes and Watson arrive at the hotel room of the man they are to protect from the "curse" that may have killed Sir Charles. The new master of Baskerville Hall is Sir Henry (Christopher Lee), who immediately assumes his visitors to be the hotel employees he'd sent for to complain about a missing boot. Sir Henry realizes his error, apologizes, and relaxes a bit, but he never loses his aristocratic manner. To a degree, Sir Henry parallels Holmes himself, but the former's impatience reveals an arrogance based on social position, whereas Holmes's derives from intellect, ability, and accomplishment.

Creating yet another convincing portrait of rationality for Terence Fisher, Peter Cushing (far left), here playing Sherlock Holmes, greets the self-consciously aristocratic Sir Henry Baskerville, played by Christopher Lee (far right). Next to Lee is Andre Morell in the role of Dr. Watson; to Morell's right is Francis de Wolff as Dr. Mortimer. From *The Hound of the Baskervilles* (1959).

Cushing is delightful in his interplay with Lee during this scene, as he stands very close to the taller actor and stares intently up at him. After he asks if Sir Henry intends to live in Baskerville Hall, a questioning expression freezes on his face; he then purses his lips in exaggerated concern when Sir Henry replies that nothing will stop him. Clearly, Holmes is unintimidated by either Sir Henry's physical height or his status. Nor is he impressed when Sir Henry says, "I can look after myself." The foolishness of such unjustified confidence is immediately illustrated when Holmes rescues Sir Henry from a tarantula that crawls out of his remaining boot and onto his shoulder.

The Hound of the Baskervilles may not deal with a supernatural force of evil, but Holmes's similarity to van Helsing is established when, upon first meeting Sir Henry, he warns, "The powers of evil can take many forms." Later, on the moors, he declares, "There is more evil around us here than I have ever encountered before." And he tells Bishop Frankland (Miles Malleson), "I am fighting evil, fighting it as surely as you do." As it turns out, the main form that evil takes in this film, as in *Dracula*, is seductive and sensual: The wild and beautiful Cecile Stapleton (Marla Landi) had lured Sir Charles to his death and tries to do the same for Sir Henry.

Her deeds, however, are made possible by the inherent nature of the Baskerville men. As Cecile points out, Sir Hugo had died because of a girl and Sir Charles died "because he wanted me, like you." In the prologue, we saw Sir Hugo engaged in his "pleasures," and, while we never meet Sir Charles, Bishop Frankland sums him up in a deceptively amusing scene. Sir Charles, he says, "knew his creature comforts, alright. I've seen him with some very attractive creatures, at times. Yes, he knew a woman when he saw one, did Sir Charles." Sir Henry may not share his predecessors' self-indulgence, but this solitary man—the last of his line—possesses the Baskervilles' hereditary heart ailment. "They all seem to suffer from the same weakness," explains Dr. Mortimer, thinking he refers only to a medical issue, but in fact pointing out a susceptibility to women that, in Fisher's terms, means a vulnerability to emotional temptation. It is not surprising, therefore, that Sir Henry suffers his first heart pains not long after being kissed by Cecile.

What places Holmes above other mortals is his stress on facts, not feelings. "We must make certain," he says after the tarantula incident, "never to be caught off our guard again." His channeling of emotion into practical action is exemplified when he and Watson believe that Sir Henry has died: Watson dwells on his feeling of guilt, but Holmes insists, "We are to avenge his death, not mourn over it." Also, just as van Helsing revealed sympathy for others when he comforted the child, Tania, in *Dracula*, Holmes is surprisingly gentle with Mrs. Barrymore, the servant who secretly aided her brother, an escaped convict.

The Hound of the Baskervilles is not a perfect film. Holmes's throwing a dagger at Dr. Mortimer is too melodramatic a gesture, the pace flags during the exploration of an abandoned mine, and the climactic encounter with the Hound lacks some of the power it demands. But the film's plot and characters are intriguing and draw from Fisher the utmost empathy. The same is true of his next film, the often-overlooked *The Man Who Could Cheat Death*, which features a central character whose self-inflicted solitude and commitment to work has caused him to lose his sense of moral balance. It is a story about age and time, about idealism and ego, about love and companionship and loss.

Decades before the film's start, Georges Bonner (Anton Diffring), a doctor and sculptor, discovered a way of retaining his youth. Now, at the age of 104, he still looks only thirty-five. At the unveiling of his new statue, a guest describes him as "charming and elegant," a man with "wonderful taste." To Dr. Pierre Gerard (Christopher Lee), Bonner states that "the patients I get require a great deal of individual attention. . . . I think their money gives them an overblown sense of their own importance." This reveals him as a society doctor catering to the indulgent rich, but he himself has developed a similar sense of self-importance. Like Frankenstein, he has placed himself and his work above all else. For Bonner, the two are synonymous, with his life literally depending on his experiment. Bonner ends the party by saying that an emergency has arisen. "My main duty," he explains, "is the care of my patients. Their needs must come before everything else." But the film never shows Bonner with his patients because he is, in fact, his own main patient and his statement actually refers to his own needs.

For Bonner to remain young, every ten years his now-elderly associate, Dr. Ludwig Weisz (Arnold Marle), must operate to replace a certain gland with a new one. When we meet Bonner, Weisz is already three weeks late and Bonner stays alive by drinking a special liquid. Anticipating Weisz's arrival, Bonner had obtained a fresh gland, but it went bad. This happened four times. Then, when he "couldn't get access to any more cadavers," he killed someone for a new gland. At this point, the "undead" Bonner becomes more than just egocentric. Like Count Dracula, he sustains his own life at the expense of others.

In another complication, Weisz has suffered a stroke and cannot perform the operation. Weisz convinces Dr. Gerard to do it instead, under his guidance, but then he learns that Bonner committed murder. Serving, like Professor Bernstein in *Curse of Frankenstein,* as a voice of morality and wisdom, Weisz demands, "Have you become God all of a sudden, to judge that you are more important than the other man?" Bonner replies, "Of course, I'm more important. He was nothing. Nothing at all. A nonentity." Bonner then explains why he lost his original idealism. "It's being alone, so utterly alone. Again and again, every few years, having to sever all contacts, cut all traces. Having to disappear and start a new life." He adds, "I often think that I can't bear it any longer," and breaks down in sobs.

"No man can live alone all his life," says Weisz. "It's not natural. It rebels against human nature. But as long as you continue, you *must* remain alone." When Weisz realizes that Bonner intends to perform the operation on a woman so she can join him, he rebels. "You are truly alone now," he declares, refusing to help with the operation and smashing the glass that holds the life-maintaining liquid. At this, Bonner strangles his "oldest and dearest friend"—his *only* friend, the one whose support sustains his life—and he starts to put his plan into action.

A parallel plot thread involves Bonner's work as a sculptor and his relations with women, who are attracted to this sophisticated, talented man. He has satisfied his need for love and companionship with a series of models, but each relationship lasts only until the sculpture is finished; that point coincides with his need for a new operation, so he breaks off with the woman, disappears, and begins a new life. Art, therefore, is for him equated with companionship and love, and the sculpture, when completed, becomes a substitute for the actual woman. "Sculpting is something I do for my own pleasure," he tells a man seeking to buy his latest statue. "I find it quite impossible to give up the completed work." Instead, he keeps it where he can "look at it and be reminded of my beautiful young model." Bonner is clearly what Fisher sought never to be, the ultimate self-indulgent artist.

At the film's start, the completed statue of Margo (Delphi Lawrence) is unveiled. Unwilling to be set aside, but unaware of Bonner's true nature, Margo interrupts him as he prepares to drink the liquid. "You know I love you," she declares. "You make me tell it to you time and time again! You make me humiliate myself!" She is shocked at the sight of him when he starts to age and, as he grabs her, she collapses. After drinking and returning to normal, he gazes at her body and says, with regret, "I tried to make you go. I tried very hard." This scene reveals Bonner's need for love, his attempt to save his victims, and his ultimate indifference to the women he has grown accustomed to using. Later, we learn from a police inspector that Margo has been reported missing and that something similar had happened in different cities every ten years. Thus, the models' romantic desire resulted in their deaths. The women's vulnerability is sad, but the film also evokes the tragedy of Bonner who, torn between human feeling for others and the desire for self-survival, is his own monster, a man who knows that his life has been reduced to mere existence.

The departure of Margo coincides with the return of Janine (Hazel Court), a woman Bonner had met in Italy. He admits to falling in love with her—"I've tried not to, I've tried very hard"—and "the impossibility of the situation" made him flee. As she looks at his unfinished statue of her, she says that it is lovely. "It's you who are lovely," he replies. "I only copied." Fisher stages this key moment with a subtle combination of actor and camera movement, which expresses both Bonner's use of the statue as an alternative to the real thing and his strongly felt need for the real thing. Fisher starts by positioning Bonner between the sculpture and Janine, but facing the statue. As he speaks, Bonner reaches out almost despite himself and grabs Janine's arm. Only after that does he turn from the statue to face her and, as he does so, the camera moves closer, shifting the statue out of the picture.

Having accepted the love he fears, Bonner asks, "Would you like to pose for me again?" "When?" she asks. "Now," he replies. This simple exchange, coming when it does, makes clear the equation between posing and a romantic liaison. Still, Bonner knows that this cannot last and, later, tells her that he must leave and never return. Her question, "Is it necessary for you to go alone?" then makes him think that he could take her with him, and he gives in to the ultimate commitment, a decision that proves his undoing.

After killing Dr. Weisz, Bonner learns that Gerard refuses to operate without Weisz's assistance. Unable to find another surgeon, he locks Janine in a warehouse among his statues and, knowing Gerard's fondness for her, forces him to help. Gerard makes the incision, but does not replace the gland. Then, thinking himself rejuvenated, Bonner slips away, reneging on his promise to release Janine and intending to perform the operation on her himself. Gerard notifies the police and locates the warehouse. Meanwhile, Bonner explains the situation to Janine, who resists. Suddenly, Bonner starts to age and realizes the truth. As he dies, Gerard and the police arrive and rescue Janine.

The Man Who Could Cheat Death contains a great deal of dialogue, but it is rewarding dialogue, delivered with such involvement and restraint that the characters stir our feelings, at least if we meet the film on its own terms. Overtly horrific action is limited and, in some cases, seems added solely for the sake of the genre audience. In the warehouse, for instance, Janine discovers the mad and mute Margo imprisoned in a cell with her statue. Margo's unexplained reappearance is awkward (she seemed dead when last we saw her), it confuses our understanding of Bonner, and it is unnecessary to the plot. Nonetheless, her laughter, heard as we watch Bonner decay, adds force to the scene and, by throwing a lamp that sets fire to him and the building, she stages a fittingly overwhelming finale, as flames engulf the row of statues that embody Bonner's needs and his limitations.

Another unnecessary element is the fact that the liquid Bonner drinks reportedly has "an unpredictable effect" on his mental balance, so that he temporarily becomes "without reason at all." This undermines the change in Bonner's personality by excusing his more extreme actions. The casting of Christopher Lee as Dr. Gerard also affects that character and his contrast to Bonner. When Gerard resists agreeing to the operation, Weisz says, "You lack the spirit of the pioneer." Gerard replies, "Being a surgeon is a practical business, Professor. It is necessary to make a living. It doesn't leave very much time for—pioneering." He also considers the moral issue involved. Because Lee is stern and stiff in his manner, Gerard evokes less viewer empathy than he should. The quiet strength and intelligent sincerity of the younger Andre Morell, who played Ritter's romantic rival in *Stolen Face,* would have made Gerard more of an acceptable contrast to Bonner.

Starting with *The Hound of the Baskervilles,* several of Fisher's Hammer films feature a horror initiated by events from the past and leading to a story that extends across a period of years. This posed no difficulty in *The Hound of the Baskervilles,* for its prologue establishes the past events, after which the plot stays in one time period. *The Man Who Could Cheat Death* solves the problem by using a single time frame and a tightly constructed script, which provides all the information we need through dialogue. Past events are not shown, because they are less important than the characters' present situation. Jimmy Sangster's script for *The Mummy,* however, fails to solve a similar plot problem. It is burdened by a choppy structure that (in less than ninety minutes) covers the events of three years in chronological order, while also including two major flashbacks.

The film begins as three archeologists—Stephen Banning (Felix Aylmer), Joseph Whemple (Raymond Huntley), and John Banning (Peter Cushing)—uncover the tomb of Princess Ananka. Stephen and Joseph enter it, despite the warning of Mehemet (George Pastell), an Egyptian priest. Left alone inside, Stephen examines the Scroll of Life. A secret door swings open, and soon Stephen is found insane and babbling. The next segment occurs six months after he has been placed in an English nursing home, as the others seal the tomb. Elsewhere, Mehemet vows to avenge their desecration. *The Mummy* then shifts to England, three years later, when Stephen is killed by a reanimated mummy (Christopher Lee). At this point, John tells Joseph the history of Ananka, which is illustrated in a lengthy flashback to ancient Egypt. A priest, Kharis (Lee), had loved Ananka and attempts, at her death, to return her to life. Interrupted, he is buried alive as the guardian of her burial place. Back in the present, the mummy kills Joseph and is seen by John, who tells a police inspector what had happened to Stephen in the tomb. Then, in another flashback, we see Kharis's mummy come to life while Stephen reads the scroll. The film then progresses to the mummy's attack on John and its destruction.

This episodic construction prevents a steady development of tension and leaves little time for characterization. In addition, the flashbacks are placed arbitrarily. It is hard to believe that Joseph, a member of the expedition, would be unaware of the story of Kharis and Ananka until John tells it to him, and the only reason to withhold the mummy's return to life would be to increase suspense by maintaining uncertainty about its existence, but Stephen already spoke about it and the creature is seen in action long before the flashback occurs. In addition, this flashback shows Mehemet enter, order Kharis back to his secret compartment, take the scroll, and leave—events that neither Stephen nor John knew about. A more practical solution might have been to follow the model of *The Hound of the Baskervilles* and start with a scene set in ancient Egypt, then reveal everything else as it occurs; the presence of Mehemet in the tomb footage even suggests that it might not originally have been intended as a flashback.

With so much to depict and so little time to do it, the film frequently resorts to plot manipulation. Mehemet could have saved time if he had Kharis kill Stephen in the tomb and taken the mummy out with him. Instead, he spends years digging through the rubble caused by the explosion that seals the tomb. A full hour into the film, John for the first time notices that his wife, Isobel (Yvonne Furneaux), resembles a drawing of Ananka; this happens only minutes before the resemblance is needed in the plot to distract Kharis when he attacks John. The resemblance is not explained and no mention is made of reincarnation, although that would have been an interesting aspect to develop.

Later, John is surprised to learn that an Egyptian has rented a house near the nursing home, although the rest of the town seems to know about it. The final confrontation between Kharis and John is far too similar to the earlier one, with Isobel again distracting the mummy as he strangles her husband. The main difference is that Mehemet, who had always sent Kharis off alone, this time accompanies him (and brings the scroll) so that he (and it) can be destroyed. For no clear reason, Mehemet orders Kharis to kill Isobel. Then, when the mummy hesitates, Mehemet moves to do it himself and Kharis kills him, picks up the scroll, and—although he didn't do so before—carries her off. In a final contrivance, Kharis takes Isobel not to Mehemet's house but to the swamp from which he had emerged, after the box containing him was accidentally dumped there.

The Mummy attempts to establish its characters' personalities and relationships, but lack of time limits this. The opening scenes suggest that Stephen and his son, John, are committed to their work above all other considerations. When Mehemet warns against desecrating "the graves of Egypt," Stephen tells him to "mind your own business," oblivious of the fact that his own job involves minding someone else's business. John, meanwhile, has a broken leg but chooses to stay, knowing that the injury will not heal properly as a result. Inside the tomb, Joseph says that he will report their find to John, but Stephen is too intent on "his" business to notice. Months later, Joseph asks after Isobel, but John, her husband, only half-listens. Another effective, if isolated, reference is John's comment that his father, although otherwise methodical, could not deal with such business matters as the paying of bills.

These are revealing details, but too much emphasis is placed on the fact that Stephen allows his son to decide whether to stay or not. Although Joseph states that Stephen should have ordered John to go, that is an unreasonable way to deal with an adult son, and it hardly qualifies as evidence of emotional disinterest. Thus, while John's limp throughout the rest of the film seems intended as a reminder of his father's human limitation, it really represents only John's decision to stay. Otherwise, John's personality is vague. "The best part of my life's been spent amongst the dead," he says early on, but this has not clearly affected his involvement with the living. He does have a wife, after all, which says something about emotional commitment, and the fact that their relationship is barely established hardly means that he shares his father's limitations.

Another difficulty involves *The Mummy*'s uncertain attitude toward the situation it depicts. Prior to sealing the tomb, John declares, "I've never worked in a place that had such an aura of menace. There's something evil in there, Uncle Joe. I've felt it." The film never questions this judgment, and it sides with John as he defends himself and protects Isobel, yet Mehemet's argument against the desecration of burial sites does sound reasonable. The result is a divided tone that results more from a lack of focus than from subtlety.

Christopher Lee's performance as the mummy conveys some pathos and helplessness, but he is not involved in the scene that most fully evokes Fisher's strengths. Near the film's end, John visits Mehemet, seeking to determine his possible involvement. Fisher places the two opposite each other and intercuts medium shots with a controlled austerity that matches the polite reserve of their articulate duel. At first, Mehemet questions the ethics of "opening the tombs of beings who are sacred," to which John replies, "If we didn't, the history of your country . . . would still be unknown." Nevertheless, Mehemet counters, "You are an intruder. You force your way in. You remove the remains of the long-dead kings and send them to places like the British Museum, where thousands of people can stare at them. Does this not trouble you at times?" John, still feeling out his opponent, responds, "No. It's my job. But it troubles you?" To this, Mehemet says, with caution and carefully weighed irony, "I'm a civilized man, Mr. Banning. To me the dead are the dead. Clay."

During a lull in the conversation, as Mehemet offers John a drink and a cigar, Fisher includes both men in a single shot. John then adopts a tactic used by Sherlock Holmes in *The Hound of the Baskervilles* when he deliberately antagonized Sir Henry by referring to his "peasant friends." Here, as John calls Karnak "a third-rate god" with "nothing to commend him to anyone with the slightest degree of intelligence," Fisher again intercuts medium shots and, as the confrontation builds, closer ones. Finally, Mehemet reveals his true attitude: "You pry and meddle with unclean hands and eyes. Profanity, blasphemy, religious desecration—all these you are guilty of, but the powers with which you have meddled do not rest easy." Finally, he retreats to politeness and explains, "We like to think that our European dress, our liberal education, have buried the past, but occasionally one is forced to realize that all this is only a veneer."

This scene exemplifies what *The Mummy* might have been, had the script given more attention to Mehemet and the two men's contrasting viewpoints. For example, the discussion of desecration might have been placed earlier and events could have built to a later encounter in which John provokes Mehemet. Overall, *The Mummy* feels the lack of such a clearly defined pair of antagonists, but in this one scene George Pastell achieves a subtle force that matches Cushing's.

The Stranglers of Bombay (1959) also deals with a clash of cultures. In *The Mummy*, Mehemet came to Britain seeking revenge, but in *Stranglers,* the British are the foreigners and George Pastell plays the High Priest of a secret religious group whose members worship the goddess Kali. In a precredits sequence, he explains the sect's history to three initiates, describing an ancient time when "a monster walked this land. He ate the young, the strong, the old. The blood of our ancestors poured from the monster's mouth, it poured like the water in the great river. No one dared battle with him—no one, but Kali!" When Kali defeated the monster, each drop of its blood produced a new monster, and when she killed them, their blood produced even more monsters. So, by devising a way to kill without shedding blood, she eliminated the monsters. Now, her followers continue to use the "sacred cloth," with which they strangle people for the glory of Kali.

This tale appears to imply an equation between the multiple monsters slain by Kali and the British presence in India, but the Kali cult does not fight against imperialism. Its members kill indiscriminately, and their actions have no political context. Only Patel Shari (Marne Maitland), who has become ruler "in name only" and is the cult's leader, has something to gain from undermining the British influence, but his motivation is more personal than political, racial, or national. The Kali worshipers themselves strangle and steal solely for their goddess. Thoroughly idealistic and cruelly passionate in their religious commitment, they punish members who commit robberies on their own. "You set out to steal," one pair is told, "not for sacrifice to our great mother, but to fill your own filthy stomachs."

Significantly, the Englishmen in this story do not represent the British government. They are planters and soldiers who work for the East India Company and seek "order and stability" for the sake of business. They are, therefore, no more interested in the welfare of the natives than are the Kali worshipers. The film contrasts both groups with one man, Captain Lewis (Guy Rolfe), who shares the virtues of Major Lawrence in *Portrait from Life* (also played by Rolfe). When the planters complain that caravans of goods have disappeared, Lewis interjects, "and people. . . . Thousands a year, every year." Unlike his peers, Lewis relates on a human level to the locals and cares what happens to them. He has, on his own, patiently investigated the situation, but only when the company faces a loss of profits does his superior agree to appoint someone to look into the issue.

Assuming that he will be that man, Lewis tells his wife, "I realize that our financial position isn't as good as it might be if I were engaged in private commerce, and I know I'm not getting any younger, and I know if ever I'm going to make a move now is the time to make it—but, Mary, this is something I've been thinking about and working on for years. It's terribly important to me." Describing the missing people's "sad-eyed relatives," who have approached him for help, he asks, "Do you think I could take another job, just for the additional money? . . . I'm better equipped than anyone for this task. Do you want me to evade my responsibility?"

The soft-spoken, responsible Lewis is, like Fisher, moral and patient and selfless, perhaps to a fault. When the position is given to the arrogant and shallow Captain Connaught-Smith (Allan Cuthbertson), Lewis offers him the information he has gathered in "two years of hard work" and wishes him luck, but Connaught-Smith drops the papers in a drawer, dismissing both Lewis and his theory. Lewis expresses his disappointment only indirectly, to a servant who thinks he has spotted his missing brother and asks permission to find him. After offering support, Lewis warns, "Don't build your hopes too high. I've done that a few times and it isn't too pleasant." Even the Kali worshipers use Lewis's kindness against him. One of them trips a beggar, and when Lewis stops to help the man, they grab Lewis, beat him, and take the only piece of evidence he has, one of the sacred strangling cloths.

When Lewis's servant is captured by the sect and his severed hand sent as a warning, Lewis presses his case with his superior and, told that he is "insolent and disrespectful," resigns. "What a time to act on impulse," says his wife. "The right time and the only time," he replies, "when someone you care for has been hurt." As he investigates independently, Lewis finds that he is even more alone than he thought. His peers refuse even to consider the existence of such a sect. At the same time, although Lewis, unlike Connaught-Smith, mingles with the natives and is sympathetic rather than intimidating, no one will tell him anything. "Are you not interested in what happens to your own kind?" he asks one man, who replies, "I am a merchant, Sahib, and he is a servant." Another says, "He is not our kind. I am a Muslim and he is a Hindu." Such internecine conflicts among the Indians are summed up by the fact that the servant's lost brother, a member of the Kali sect, is the one who kills him.

The Stranglers of Bombay is a catalogue of physical atrocities performed by this corrupt and inhuman cult: The arms of initiates are slit and the wound seared with a heated iron; men are blinded, their tongues are cut out, and they are kept in a cage until they act like ravenous animals; Lewis is staked out on the ground, his arm slit, and a cobra set loose; many strangulations occur, and the corpses' stomachs are slit so they will not swell and disclose their shallow graves; other corpses are placed on a funeral pyre to provide Kali with "the greatest gift of all—human flesh." Few of these horrors are shown in detail, but they are presented with Fisher's usual directness. Their cumulative impact would be overwhelming, except for the presence of Lewis, a strong but quiet man who is a tower of moral strength. Eventually, despite skepticism and physical hardship, Lewis destroys the High Priest, exposes Patel Shari, and convinces the authorities that the sect exists. However, the cult's members remain at large, so the task of eradicating it has only begun as the film ends.

Fisher's next picture, *The Brides of Dracula,* marks a return to Gothic fantasy, but it also employs the concept of evil found in *The Stranglers of Bombay,* which first appeared in *Dracula,* where vampirism was referred to as an "unholy cult." *Brides,* a follow-up to *Dracula,* follows the lead of Hammer's Frankenstein sequel by choosing not to revive its original monster. As the opening narration states, Dracula "is dead, but his disciples live on—to spread the cult and corrupt the world." So, in *Brides,* Dr. van Helsing must vanquish an entirely new vampire. The present horror of this story, like that of *The Mummy* and *The Hound of the Baskervilles,* derives from some profane activity in the past. However, *Brides* exists firmly in the present, and the script lets the characters' dialogue suggest the background. Thanks to this compactness, the film surges forward from the first scene with constant dramatic energy. It also contains some of the finest performances in any Fisher film and expertly combines theme, excitement, and pathos.

Marianne (Yvonne Monlaur), a young woman on her way to a teaching post, stops at an inn, where she meets the elderly Baroness (Martita Hunt), who invites her to stay overnight at Castle Meinster. That evening, the handsome Baron Meinster (David Peel), chained in his room, talks Marianne into stealing a key and freeing him. He then vengefully attacks his mother, after which their hysterical servant, Greta (Freda Jackson), shows Marianne the Baroness's corpse and the bewildered guest flees blindly into the woods.

Marianne may be just a traditional innocent heroine, but the film deftly and subtly defines its other characters. The Baroness is regal, but tired and lonely, starved for normal companionship, drained by years of suffering and guilt. Greta, the Baron's former nurse, has alone remained faithful to her mistress and to the child she raised, though the death of the Baroness pushes her sanity past the breaking point. Through looks and gestures, Fisher's actresses convey the unspoken bond between these two women, a bond forged from untold evils endured together. As the Baron, David Peel, with his blond hair, pretty face, and aristocratic bearing, shifts effortlessly from ingratiating prisoner to stern villain, making the line "Mother—come here!" chillingly memorable. Fisher liked Peel's performance "tremendously," but "never made real contact with him as a person. I never knew him. I knew him as a performer, we understood each other, but he had an inner independence."[147] Peel retired from acting after this film, at the age of forty, and later ran a London art and antiques dealership.

The film's tension relaxes when van Helsing (Peter Cushing) happens upon Marianne. Gentle and benevolent, he offers comfort, then escorts her to the school. After he subtly deflates the pompous headmaster, van Helsing proceeds to the inn and talks to the local priest, who had sent for him. Wisely, the script saves its exposition about vampires for this scene, after viewers have become involved in the story. Rapidly, the tension again builds and is sustained in a striking series of potent scenes. Van Helsing goes to a cemetery, where a village girl, the vampire's victim, has been buried. We watch with him as Greta lies on the ground and talks to the corpse below, laughing and urging her on in her effort to reach the surface. "No, I can't help you. You've got to be strong. . . . Yes, I know it's dark, but you've got to push. . . . There's my little beauty! Ah, the clever one!" The earth pulsates, a hand emerges, and the undead figure rises into view.

The revived girl escapes to Castle Meinster, with van Helsing in pursuit. He enters, walking quietly through the deserted rooms. Fisher precisely controls the mood here: There is no background music and no sound but footsteps and the regular, pulse-like ticking of a clock. Using long shots and lengthy takes, Fisher saves his arsenal of effects—sharp musical chords, close-ups, rapid cutting—for van Helsing's discovery that the Baron's coffin is gone and for his encounter with Baron Meinster. In a flurry of movement and editing, Meinster attacks and van Helsing drives him off with a cross. In contrast, the next scene, between van Helsing and the now-vampiric Baroness, is remarkably compassionate. "There's no release," says the frail victim, "from this life—which isn't life—or death. And I know I shall have to do whatever hideous thing he asks me to." There is one release, van Helsing assures her, and the scene ends on a close-up of her face, with its look of relief.

At the school, Meinster arrives and announces his engagement to the naive Marianne. Later, he attacks her friend, Gina (Andree Melly), another student-teacher. After van Helsing stakes the Baroness, he returns to the inn, where a bumbling doctor (Miles Malleson) reveals that someone has died at the school, so van Helsing accompanies him there and examines Gina's corpse. When Marianne is left alone to guard the coffin, her friend rises and tries to take her to the Baron. Van Helsing's entrance scares Gina off, but Marianne tells him that Meinster is at an old mill. Once there, van Helsing encounters the village girl and Gina, both vampires; to render him helpless, Greta grabs van Helsing's cross, after which she falls to her death. Choked by Meinster, van Helsing loses consciousness and is bitten. Upon waking, he cauterizes the bites on his neck by searing them with a heated iron bar and splashes holy water on the wound. This method (adapted from *The Stranglers of Bombay*) is new to the vampire legend—Jonathan Harker should have known about it!—but it is consistent with the film's parallel of vampirism with corruption and disease.

Meinster then enters with Marianne. "She's going to join us, Doctor," he says, sounding like the High Priest in *Stranglers,* "and you are going to watch her initiation." Van Helsing stops the vampire by throwing holy water on him. As the liquid eats at his face like acid, Meinster kicks over the brazier of glowing coals and, roaring like a wounded animal, flees outside. To escape the spreading flames, van Helsing runs upstairs, where he leaps onto one of the mill's vanes. His weight causes them to rotate, until the moonlight creates a giant cross-shaped shadow that pins Meinster to the ground until he is destroyed. (The mill itself casts no shadow, only the vanes do, but in the excitement this manipulation of reality tends to go unnoticed.)

An early version of the script for *The Brides of Dracula,* credited to Jimmy Sangster and Peter Bryan, contained a different version of this climax, as does the novelization of the film by "Dean Owen" (but with the copyright in Sangster's name). In both, van Helsing uses black magic, summoning the powers of evil to punish Meinster. "You have taken the blood of your mother," he declares in the novel. "You have taken the blood of this girl. And you have permitted her to live in order to satisfy your carnal desires. This is forbidden amongst the undead, even by your own code. I demand the penalty!" In response, a swarm of bats appears and drives the Baron from the mill, whereupon van Helsing finishes him off with the shadow. The replacement of the bats with fire in the film may have been due to the expense of the special effects, but producer Anthony Hinds also had the script revised because Peter Cushing "insisted on it."[148] That was perhaps due to Cushing's reported belief that van Helsing would not have allied himself with the forces of evil.[149] At any rate, the change was a wise one, for it keeps the confrontation on a human, realistic plane. (In 1963, the bats appeared, more appropriately, in Hammer's *Kiss of the Vampire*.)

The Brides of Dracula does contain some inconsistencies, such as Marianne's acceptance of the Baron when he arrives at the school and her surprise when he says that his mother is dead. (This part, too, is quite different in the novelization.) It also contradicts a "fact" established in *Dracula* by allowing Meinster to change into a bat, which should have made the chain attached to his leg useless. Nevertheless, the film works powerfully in dramatic and thematic terms. Especially interesting is the way the script links vampirism with sexual degeneracy. Past decadence, of a vague but very human sort, has resulted in a metaphorical decadence, a warped kind of love.

The nurse's monologue to the Baroness's corpse helps establish this. "You spoiled him, oh yes. He was always self-willed and cruel, and you encouraged him—aye, and the bad company he kept, too. You used to sit and drink with 'em, didn't you? Yes, and you laughed at their wicked games. 'Til in the end one of them took him, made him what he is. You've done what you could for him since then, God help you—keeping him here a prisoner, bringing these young girls for him, keeping him alive with their blood. But the powers of darkness are too strong. They've beaten you!" Later, the vampiric Baroness admits as much to van Helsing. "It was all my own fault. I loved his wildness, I encouraged it, and when this monstrous thing took possession of him I didn't send for a priest or a doctor. I hid him and helped him to live."

Most of the relationships in *Brides of Dracula* are distortions of normal affections, of acceptable loves. The mother-son tie develops implications of incest, with the Baron taking his mother's blood. The faithful attentions of a nurse are perverted into a struggle to keep her vampiric charge safe. The natural friendship of two women becomes a variety of lesbianism, with the risen Gina calling Marianne "my darling" and saying, "Put your arms around me, please. I want to kiss you, Marianne. Please be kind to me." Traditional marriage, too, is warped into a ménage à trois, as Gina tells Marianne, "We can both love him." Among the main characters, only van Helsing remains outside this epidemic of corruption.

In *The Two Faces of Dr. Jekyll*, Edward Hyde serves as a one-man epidemic of moral corruption. Written by a Hammer outsider, Wolf Mankowitz, the script for *Dr. Jekyll* reverses the traditional approach to Robert Louis Stevenson's classic story. This time, Dr. Henry Jekyll is bearded and bland, while the youthful, handsome Edward Hyde is insidious rather than grotesque, with a sleek, clean-shaven magnetism. Although the basic idea to have Hyde embody the elegant, aristocratic attraction of evil came from Mankowitz, it was entirely consistent with Fisher's outlook. "That's why I liked it," the director acknowledged.[150] Also consistent with prior Fisher films are the characterization of Jekyll and the general emphasis on ambiguous identity.

Jekyll (Paul Massie) typifies the negative version of Fisher's main characters. Solitary and cold, he pours all his energy into his work. "I can't think about anything else," he admits. Jekyll has only two friends. One, Paul Allen (Christopher Lee), is a libertine who takes advantage of Jekyll's kindness by "borrowing" money to pay his gambling debts. The other is Litauer (David Kossoff), a fellow doctor who—like Bernstein and Weisz in earlier films—offers sympathetic criticism, to which Jekyll pays no heed. Jekyll has isolated himself from his peers because of their ridicule. "Who in the profession has been fair to me?" he asks Litauer. "Who, apart from yourself, has even given me a hearing?" Jekyll and his wife, Kitty (Dawn Addams), live in what she calls a house "unused to visitors," a house he seldom leaves. When Kitty wants to attend a dinner party, he disdains mingling with "a lot of braying asses full of cant and hypocrisy." Kitty protests that "these are my friends. . . . You may not need friends, but I do."

Jekyll feels cut off from his wife because he believes they have nothing in common. "In six years of marriage," he says, "Kitty has never thought about my work." It doesn't occur to him that he never considered his wife's interests during that time. Litauer tries to help by telling Kitty, "You are married to a man of very great talent. . . . Such men are always difficult to live with," but it is too late. Jekyll's coldness has driven her to take his "friend," Paul Allen, as her lover. Kitty serves as a natural parallel to the artificially induced duality of Jekyll and Hyde: Just as Jekyll's two selves inhabit the same body, Kitty, in Paul's words, shifts "from perfect wife to perfect mistress and back again to perfect wife, and always in a few hours."

In his work, Jekyll seeks to understand the one thing that he, as a human being, understands least. "Man has always known," he tells Litauer, "that his personality is an uneasy and unsatisfactory combination of conflicting elements." In his smug confidence, Jekyll thinks he can control "every resource of the human personality by science." He injects himself with a drug he developed and becomes a person "beyond good and evil. . . . free of all the restrictions society imposes upon us, subject only to his own will." As Edward Hyde, he indulges his impulses by visiting a nightclub-bordello, where he encounters Kitty and Paul. He also becomes violent, beating an unconscious man (Oliver Reed) until Paul stops him.

On returning home, Jekyll goes to his wife's bedroom. Disturbed by what he has discovered about himself and about her, he says, "I need you, Kitty. I need you desperately," but she rejects him. He then asks, "What are you *really* like, Kitty?" When she replies, "I'm your wife, that's all I am," he continues: "But the woman inside you, is that woman my wife? . . . Will we ever know who we really are? Who are you, Kitty? . . . Who am I?" As Jekyll continues his explorations, Hyde seduces Maria (Norma Marla), a dancer and high-priced prostitute, who succumbs because he "simply takes" instead of buying or begging. That, however, was too easy, so Hyde decides it would be "amusing" to seduce Jekyll's "nice, cold wife." He visits Kitty and, thinking they both seek "the pursuit of pleasure, the fulfillment of desire," he can't fathom her resistance. Why, he asks, would she be faithful to the "weak, unscrupulous, and utterly unreliable" Paul? "I merely happen to love him," she answers.

Distressed at what, in his journal, he calls a "life of frustrated isolation and loveless misery," Jekyll decides "to discover all that Hyde can reveal." With Paul Allen as guide, he tours London's dens of iniquity, but that still is not enough. Realizing that "no degeneracy is low enough to satisfy" Hyde, Jekyll destroys his formula and drugs. "I must exorcise him," he writes, but Hyde returns by his own will and enters a new level of ruthlessness. He kills Paul, then rapes Kitty in the bed of the prostitute, "the bed you deserve." He completes the pattern by having sex with Maria in Kitty's bed; afterward, he strangles her. Meanwhile, Kitty awakens in the prostitute's bed, sees her "real" self reflected in the mirror of the bed's canopy, and discovers Paul's body. Dazed, she loses her balance and crashes through the nightclub's skylight windows to the dance floor below.

Soon after, Hyde tells Jekyll that he is determined to remain free, saying, "everything I do is directed toward that end." With callous precision, he has ensured his survival by implicating Jekyll in the murders and forcing him to stay hidden. He then shoots a workman, places the body at Jekyll's desk, and douses the room with gasoline. When the police arrive, the place is aflame and Hyde rushes out to safety. The authorities assume Jekyll killed himself, but as Hyde leaves the inquest Jekyll forces his way to the surface and is arrested. "Only I could destroy him," says Jekyll, with muted triumph, "and I have!"

In a sense, Hyde exerts the same power over others that Dracula does, only in a nonsupernatural context. Women are attracted to his confidence, his physical directness, and his aura of perverse sensuality. Fisher even stages his first appearance as he did Dracula's: Hyde stands in the middle distance, then turns to face the camera and walks into a close-up and bright light as we realize that his appearance is the opposite of what we expected. Also like Dracula, Hyde indulges his impulses without restraint and lacks human emotion. At one point, he admits to Maria, "I can't love, I know nothing about love," and when Jekyll asks if he hates him, Hyde replies, "I have no feelings towards you whatsoever. I do only what is logically necessary." Hyde is a villain because he is ruled by indulgence and rationality, whereas Jekyll becomes heroic because he gains feeling and, combining it with self-discipline, sacrifices himself by mastering Hyde.

Hyde "couldn't have been more decadent or degenerate or evil," Fisher stated in 1974 and yet "he never became an obvious physical bastard." This is partly due to underemphasis by actor, director, and makeup man. It is also due to the fact that Hyde is honest and direct, in contrast to the other characters' hypocrisy. As Fisher explained, Hyde "brought evil in his train to people who allowed him to do so, who consented." However, unlike Dracula, Hyde destroys people who already are immoral, only not as immoral as Hyde. "They were basically a shoddy lot, weren't they?" Fisher noted on another occasion.[151] In this way, the film deviates from a premise voiced by Fisher in 1964: "The monsters must outrage innocents or semi-innocents, because it wouldn't mean so much if they wronged hardboiled people."[152]

The fact that Hyde is surrounded by hardboiled hypocrites is part of this film's originality, but it also limits viewers' emotional involvement, leaving them the fascinated observers of a nest of writhing adders. Those adders, however, eventually reveal a quality which sets them apart from Hyde and which redeems them. Kitty truly loves the disreputable Paul, and Paul is shocked into morality when Hyde tells him to "obtain" Kitty for him. Even Maria feels for Hyde a selfless, unquestioning love.

This film is full of intriguing concepts, but it often presents them verbally rather than visually. This is particularly true of the opening, in which Jekyll tells Litauer his theories, then Kitty tells him that she heard Henry shouting "in a strange voice." As an impressive contrast, the film embodies its meaning in the action when, near the end, Hyde asserts the similarity of Kitty and Maria by switching their identities. Also satisfying is the way both Jekyll and Hyde inhabit one body at the same time, with actor Paul Massie shifting back and forth between voices and identities as the two struggle. This culminates in the striking image of Jekyll looking in a mirror and seeing Hyde's face.

The Two Faces of Dr. Jekyll marked the last collaboration between Fisher and photographer Jack Asher. They first worked together on *Portrait from Life* and *The Astonished Heart;* then, starting with *The Curse of Frankenstein,* Asher shot eight more Fisher films. *Curse* allowed Asher to test his ideas about shooting in color. Previously, with Technicolor, photographers had to follow the company's strict rules for using its process. "The lighting," Asher explained, "had to be flat, with no recourse to shadow content. This was completely opposed to what I already had in mind" for *Curse.* Because Hammer used Eastmancolor, Asher could experiment. "Even my photo colleagues were skeptical about my plans to shoot what amounted to be an overall majority of low key scenes, but with very vivid and vibrant colors always present among the highlights."[153] Fisher enjoyed Asher's approach to color, which also drew on the talents of Hammer's production designer, Bernard Robinson. "We understand each other very well," Fisher said of Robinson in 1964, adding, "I attribute enormous importance to the questions of set decoration and color."[154]

Examples from *Curse* include the red or blue decorations on Elizabeth's dresses and the laboratory's container of red liquid, which stand out in the otherwise muted settings. After Frankenstein's machinery starts to function, Fisher shows the creature's bandaged body start to breathe in a close shot that lasts for nearly half a minute. Then, he cuts from this *white* shot to one completely filled with *red*—the back of Paul's dressing gown. Because the creature's coming to life is not physically dramatic, the director created a visual-psychological shock with this sudden cut from white to red. Similar color effects can be seen in such films as *The Hound of the Baskervilles,* where Sir Hugo discovers the girl's escape in a shot filmed through a canopied bed, with its red curtains forming a three-sided frame around the angry, red-coated man.

Asher also, in Fisher's words, created "a completely unreal mood" in a "very stylized" way.[155] According to Len Harris, the camera operator, Asher "tended to paint the set in light and color,"[156] using "a lot of little lamps" with colored gels to place pinpoint highlights around the set. *Dracula* reveals a confident use of this style. In one shot of Jonathan Harker and Dracula, Harker is lit normally, but Dracula's face has a cold, blue-green tint. Asher and Fisher also use blue or green tints to create a horrific or emotionally barren mood in their other collaborations, notably *The Man Who Could Cheat Death* and *The Mummy.*

Although pleased with Asher's work, Hammer felt that he took too long and replaced him with the speedier Arthur Grant, who photographed five of Fisher's eight remaining Hammer films. Len Harris recalled that Grant did not use Asher's pinpoint color highlighting. "Arthur's was more of a general kind of lighting. But when I say general, I don't mean he just sort of turned the lights on, because he didn't. He took a lot of trouble."[157] From Fisher's point of view, Asher and Grant had "nearly opposite" ideas about color. Grant, he said, "is very sensible" and "a realist. Asher is a true romantic. . . . The tone of the photography is very different and that undoubtedly affects the entire style of the film. I am obliged to modify my approach to the subject, as a result."[158]

In a brief interlude, Fisher next directed *Sword of Sherwood Forest* (1960), which starred Richard Greene. This was a reunion of sorts, for Fisher had directed some episodes of Greene's television series, *The Adventures of Robin Hood,* a few years before. Then he returned to horror with Hammer's *The Curse of the Werewolf,* a film placed into production prematurely. Based on Guy Endore's 1933 novel, *The Werewolf of Paris,* it had been scheduled to follow *The Rape of Sabena,* a story about the Spanish Inquisition. Sets had already been built when the studio learned that the Catholic Church intended to condemn the picture, so it dropped *Sabena* and moved the werewolf film into its place. As a result, *Werewolf* inherited *Sabena's* sets, shifting its location from France to Spain. The change did not please Fisher. "I fought against this stupid idea," he said in 1963, but the producers were determined.[159]

Hammer's script for *Werewolf* was the first one credited to producer Anthony Hinds, who used the pen name John Elder (which he borrowed from the studio's former art director, J. Elder Wills). According to Hinds, an earlier script was "totally unfilmable" at a low budget, so he wrote a new one himself, because there was no money to pay another writer.[160] Hinds stripped away the historical and metaphorical trappings of *The Werewolf of Paris,* but retained several plot elements: a man imprisoned until he turns into an animal, a rape (by a priest, not the animal-man), the werewolf's birth on Christmas Day, the boy's blood-lust awaked during a hunting incident, and a woman who temporarily cures him through love. In the process, he ran into more problems of structure and content than he could solve.

The Curse of the Werewolf begins when the Marques Siniestro (Anthony Dawson), during his wedding celebration, entertains himself and his guests by tormenting a slow-witted beggar (Richard Wordsworth), getting him drunk, having him dance, and making him beg, "like a good dog," for food. Like the prologue in *The Hound of the Baskervilles,* this sequence is prime Fisher. The ruthless, unpredictable Marques is horrifically human, an aristocrat who indulges his whims and enjoys the distress of others, especially when he is inflicting it. At the same time, the beggar is sympathetic without being sentimentalized. We feel sorry for him as he awkwardly tries to dance, and yet he starts to enjoy it, unaware of his own humiliation or the danger he faces. Finally, when the Marques starts to leave with his bride, the grateful beggar leeringly wishes him "a good night." Offended, the Marques has the man locked in a dungeon.

Years later, when the jailer's daughter (Yvonne Romain) resists the advances of the elderly, syphilitic Marques, he has her locked in a cell with the beggar, who has reached the level of a shaggy animal. The beggar immediately rapes the girl, even though she had pitied and fed him. The girl's punishment over, the Marques tries again. This time, she kills him and flees. A kindly artist, Don Alfredo Carido (Clifford Evans), finds the pregnant girl and brings her to his home, where he and a servant, Teresa (Hira Talfrey), tend her. The girl dies during childbirth, but her baby lives. At the age of six, young Leon (Justin Walters) first turns into a wolf and kills some animals, but through loving care Alfredo and Teresa control the affliction.

The bestial tendency returns after the nineteen-year-old Leon (Oliver Reed) leaves home and takes a job at a vineyard. He visits a bordello with a coworker, and there, under the influence of alcohol and lust, he changes into a wolf and kills three people. Leon also falls in love with Cristina (Catherine Feller), the daughter of the vineyard's manager. Cristina is his salvation, for when she is with him, Leon does not succumb to his curse. The situation appears to be under control, but just when they are about to leave together he is arrested for murder. After a period of psychological agony, Leon changes once more, escapes from jail, and is killed when Alfredo shoots him with a silver bullet.

This story, spread across what the script identifies as sixty years, is presented in little more than ninety minutes. Like *The Hound,* it first shows the actions of an arrogant nobleman that affect the rest of the plot, but this time the film does not jump forward into the "present." Instead, it lurches along, periodically introducing new characters and situations, yet lacking the time to develop them. Two key events, the death of the beggar after the rape and that of the mother after childbirth, occur simply because the writer needs to be rid of those characters. A larger weakness stems from the fact that the truth about Leon's affliction is kept from him until late in the story, which limits the tragedy of self-awareness to the film's last section. Even then, Leon is helpless in the grip of a force over which he has no control, except through Cristina. As a result, the film lacks the drama of a struggle against an inner being who seeks to emerge, a struggle forcefully conveyed in *Dr. Jekyll.* Leon remains a passive victim who succumbs to sobs of fear and frustration.

Curse of the Werewolf also reveals confusion about the cause of Leon's affliction. Initially, the script had the beggar imprisoned in a kennel, where he took on an animal's characteristics. To an extent, this would have explained his son's nature. However, the British censor reviewed the script and, according to Fisher, "said that we must not combine sex and horror, and he made us remove all references to the beggar being a werewolf."[161] So the kennel became a dungeon and, when Richard Wordsworth arrived to be fitted with fangs for the scene, he was told, "The censor says no fangs. You can either have fangs or relations with the girl but not both."[162]

Judging from indications of revisions in the shooting script, Hinds made up for this lost explanation by elaborating on a religious aspect drawn from Endore's novel. Leon is born on Christmas and, says Teresa, "For an unwanted child to be born then is an insult to heaven." Later, a priest tells Alfredo that "elemental spirits" of beasts seek to invade the human body. Sometimes, one succeeds, "usually at the moment of birth," and "the soul and the spirit war with each other" to control the body. Then, continues the priest, "Whatever weakens the human soul—vice, greed, hatred, solitude—" gives power to the spirit of the beast and "whatever weakens the spirit of the beast—warmth, fellowship, love—raises the human soul. Now, little Leon has no real father or mother and yet he needs their love and care far more than any normal child." The script notes that this dialogue had been revised "on advice from Catholic Film Institute," so Hinds clearly struggled to explain Leon's problem under the watchful eyes of both the censor and the Church.

The script also reveals uncertainty about what solutions are possible. According to the priest, "only love" is a cure, but not a permanent one, which is evident in the success that Alfredo and Teresa, and later Cristina, have with Leon. However, the priest elsewhere urges that Leon "enter a monastery under special supervision," although it is not clear how the monks would keep him from changing or, afterward, keep him from breaking loose. As for permanent destruction, Leon and the priest agree that burning alive is "the only way," but Leon also tells Alfredo to use a silver bullet fashioned by a villager who had called that "the only way."

Despite its flaws, *Curse of the Werewolf* offers sincere acting, careful direction, and high production values (including a good werewolf makeup). It is, however, seldom moving or exciting. Even the climax fails, because it is too passive. Alfredo and Cristina stand on the sidelines and watch as Leon, in wolf form, leaps from building to building, going nowhere and doing nothing, while a crowd tags along below. Eventually, Alfredo climbs to the church's belfry and confronts Leon, who swings forward on the bell. Alfredo reluctantly shoots and a tear wells up in the dead creature's eye. These events evoke some emotion, but they miss their potential because they occur inside the building, where Cristina cannot see them and so we cannot feel them through her reactions.

By submitting its scripts to the censor in advance, Hammer rarely encountered problems once a film was shot, but *Werewolf* is an exception. The censor "took a little bit out" of the rape scene, recalled Fisher, because "it went too far for him," but "it never went far beyond what you saw" in the released version.[163] More disappointing to the director was the loss of a bit of the aged Marques's characterization. "On the set," he said on another occasion, "the actor was fiddling about, just getting into the part, and I saw him scratch a flake of skin off his nose, and I said, 'That's it—do that when we shoot.' " However, "this one detail was not allowed to stand."[164] Today, though, viewers of the film on laser disc can see Anthony Dawson flick some skin from under his eye. What they cannot see is the full scene in which Leon kills a prostitute, which has obviously lost some footage; whether or not that is the state of the original materials is uncertain.

Many of Fisher's previous films contained attitudes that match those of the director and situations that evoke his position in life. *Curse of the Werewolf* takes this parallel further, following the life of a boy raised by surrogate parents in an atmosphere that, although loving, left him isolated and emotionally vulnerable. The naive young man then leaves home "to make his own way" in a world filled with unfamiliar temptations, especially sexual ones. He finds that he can survive only by developing a self-discipline that involves restraining such emotions as anger. A simple, earthy man, he wants only to live a steady, quiet life, but his urges are strong and the struggle difficult.

Eventually, this loner finds that the loving support of one person, a woman, is all he needs to achieve his goal. "You've saved me," he says. "We'll be together every minute of the day and night." At this point, of course, the parallel ends, for Leon is separated from Cristina and loses control one last time, while Morag remained Fisher's lovingly supportive companion. It is unclear how the film's almost-autobiographical aspect came about, but considering all the changes made in the script prior to production, it may be that Anthony Hinds, the novice writer, conferred with his intended director as he worked. In any case, Fisher had been Hinds's friend and colleague for nearly ten years and the two reportedly understood each other well.

Fisher may not have been fully aware of the ways *Werewolf* reflected himself, but he consciously responded to at least one aspect of it. "If you're talking of love stories," he told an interviewer, "then the one you want is *Curse of the Werewolf.* It was a love story."[165] Actually, it is only partly a love story, but that is the aspect that appealed to him. In 1963, less than three years after making *Werewolf,* he spoke of wanting to direct "a genuine love story, simple and sentimental." It would, he said, be "in the style of those of [Frank] Borzage, whom I regard as the greatest director in the world."[166] Borzage's most typical films, revealingly, depict a financially struggling couple who find solace in each other amid an indifferent, sometimes intrusive, world.

Fisher never made that film, and pictures like *The Mummy* didn't capture what he sought, for they involved love lost or never attained. *Werewolf* comes closer, dealing with love found as well as lost, but that facet of the plot receives little screen time. *The Man Who Could Cheat Death* is probably Fisher's purest love story. Not only does it tell of love found, then lost, but it thoroughly integrates the ill-fated romance with the plot's other elements. Fisher's next film, *The Phantom of the Opera,* however, marked another incomplete attempt. "I emphasized the tragedy of the film which was the important thing to me: this man who had his music stolen, his association with the girl."[167]

In *Phantom of the Opera,* the relationship between the title character and the singer he kidnaps and coaches traditionally contains a strong element of doomed love. However, Anthony Hinds's script for this version loses track of that aspect. Its Phantom (Herbert Lom) has never met, or even seen, Christine (Heather Sears) before she is hired to star in the opera he wrote. As Fisher admitted two years later, "What he loves is her voice, [but] that is not exactly my idea of true love." In fact, the Phantom is more concerned with improving Christine's voice and her performance, for the benefit of his opera. For him, Fisher continued, the girl is "more a means, than an end in itself."[168]

The film's true romantic lead is Harry Hunter (Edward de Souza), the opera's director, who protects Christine from the advances of Lord Ambrose d'Arcy (Michael Gough), the supposed composer. Too conveniently, Christine's landlady turns out also to have been Professor Petrie's, and because he left some sheet music at their lodging, Hunter discovers that Petrie composed the opera, not d'Arcy. Investigation also reveals that Petrie broke into the building where his stolen music was being printed and, when a fire started, tried to put it out using nitric acid. After some of the acid splashed on his face, he ran out, fell in the river, and presumably drowned. (This explanation of the Phantom's origin derives from Universal's 1943 film, not the 1925 Lon Chaney version or the Gaston Leroux novel.)

The Phantom's background may be clear, but his intentions and motivations are inconsistent. During the film's first part, he sabotages the opera's production by causing the star to quit. Then, after Christine is hired, the hidden Phantom tells her, "You sang well, but you will sing better. I shall teach you. When you sing, it will be only for me." The script increases the Phantom's aura of menace when Hunter says, "I think there's something evil in this theatre, Christine—something or someone trying to

Christine (Heather Sears) with Lord Ambrose d'Arcy (Michael Gough), the true villain of *The Phantom of the Opera* (1962).

stop the opera from ever being performed." Shortly after, the Phantom's voice warns Hunter not to meddle. "My threat is not an idle one," he says. "There are forces of evil at large in the Opera tonight." Soon, he unsuccessfully tries to bring Christine to his lair. All of this indicates that the Phantom is destructive and that while his interest in Christine may not be romantic, it is personal and private.

Later, he brings Christine to the catacombs beneath the opera house and tells her, "I am going to give you a new voice, a voice so wonderful that theatres all over the world will be filled with your admirers. You will be the greatest star the opera has ever known. . . . And when you sing, Christine, you will be singing only for me." Here, the implication has changed. The "for me" is less literal than before, with the Phantom expecting that Christine will eventually leave, but remain in his debt. Finally, after Hunter tracks them down, the Phantom pleads to be allowed to finish teaching her, saying, "She will sing for me as she has never sung before and I will hear my work performed." Then, he adds, "You may never see me again, but you will never forget." Hunter and Christine evidently agree, because the film jumps ahead to the premiere, with Christine performing while the Phantom watches and nods approval. By now, the Phantom has become a supporter, not a saboteur.

Evidently, Hinds started out imagining the Phantom as angry and vengeful, then changed his mind, but did not remove from his script the confusion that resulted. Ultimately, he made the character a sympathetic victim and not a "monster" at all. He even changed the famous falling chandelier from the Phantom's ruthless attack on the audience to an accident during which he sacrifices himself to save Christine from being crushed on stage. Compared to Lon Chaney's Phantom, this one seems almost saintly—and too good to be true.

Because the writer nevertheless did want to include horror elements, he took up the dramatic slack by providing this passive and pleading Phantom with an ugly, mute assistant (Ian Wilson), a dwarf who looks after him and commits the requisite murders. The Phantom has no idea who this person is or where he came from, nor does the viewer. The dwarf has no personality, and his actions are ambiguous. He brutally stabs a harmless rat-catcher in the eye (possibly on the Phantom's orders, but this is not clear). Later, he shows sorrow after accidentally causing the Phantom's death. An additional attempt to counteract the Phantom's weakness is the emphasis placed on Lord Ambrose d'Arcy, the repulsively suave lecher and music thief.

Another problem lies in the film's structure. The 1943 *Phantom* had presented the background of its title character first, then progressed to after he had established his presence in the Opera House. That didn't work, because it delayed the interesting situation for too long. In contrast, this *Phantom* starts with the interesting situation, then presents the background in a seven-minute flashback. This doesn't work, either, because the flashback occurs just before the film's climax and interferes with the plot's forward motion. Even more seriously, the flashback redundantly illustrates facts already learned during the hero's investigation of the Opera House's mysterious inhabitant. Fisher's use of tilted camera angles during this sequence—the kind of visual indulgence he usually avoided—suggests that he felt it needed artificial respiration. "There is a great deal of padding," admitted Fisher not long after making this film.[169]

One more weakness is the fact that when the Phantom confronts his nemesis, d'Arcy pulls off his mask, then runs out, and this is the last we see of d'Arcy. Although he is the villain of the piece, his fate is left unresolved. The Phantom's uninteresting mask is also a problem. According to makeup artist Roy Ashton, the studio executives could not make up their minds about what to use, so three weeks after shooting started, when it was necessary for the Phantom to be seen, Ashton quickly "turned out a job with camera tape rag and string and rubber in about five minutes."[170] The result looks like a rush job, as does the Phantom's scarred face, which is seen only for a second when he unnecessarily rips off his mask before leaping to save Christine.

An explanation for some, but only some, of the film's characteristics lies in its inception. As Anthony Hinds explained, "Cary Grant came to us and said he wanted to make a horror film." (This was at about the time that Bette Davis and Joan Crawford were filming the horrific *Whatever Happened to Baby Jane?* [1962] in Hollywood.) "The only thing we could think of was *Phantom of the Opera*. I knew he'd never make it, but he was insistent, so I wrote the thing for him. . . . I knew that once he got back to the States his agent would tell him he couldn't make it. And that's what happened."[171] This explains the script's whitewashing of the Phantom, and perhaps there wasn't time to rewrite it before production began.

Although *Phantom* tries to be a respectable, mainstream drama instead of a horror melodrama, the central romantic couple are attractive but nondescript and the Phantom is bland rather than interesting or pathetic. The inclusion of the opera, while necessary to the plot, gives the film a feeling of pretentiousness, even though composer Edwin Astley valiantly tried to make it relevant by having its subject, Joan of Arc, sing about the voices that inspired her, just as the Phantom's initially disembodied voice inspired Christine's performance. The film is aided, though, by its Dickensian supporting characters, including the excessive but vivid d'Arcy, the opera's cackling cleaning women, and the rat-catcher, who advises that the squealing contents of his sack would "make a lovely pie, y' know."

While acknowledging the film's weakness, Fisher said, "nevertheless, I understand 'my' Phantom rather well. I have a sort of sympathy for him, because he is a character who has been deceived and bruised."[172] This sympathy probably ran deep, for the Phantom is an artist who must abase himself by accepting less money than his work is worth and even apologize for resisting, only to find that another claims credit for what his talent produced. Although Fisher never said so, he must also have identified with Harry Hunter, the opera's director, who is gently reassuring with his artists. He also is at the mercy of his employer, d'Arcy, whom he calls a man of "little musical taste."

More than usually, the character of d'Arcy (described by the Phantom as "a vile and vicious man") embodies everything that Fisher disliked. Not only does he try to use his position to seduce the innocent Christine, but he is so egocentric that, after a stagehand dies and his star has been frightened away, he says only that the situation is "acutely embarrassing for me." When d'Arcy learns that Hunter has held auditions for a new singer, he fumes, "I shall decide what is best and what is not best for my opera. How dare he!" Not only is d'Arcy arrogant, but that arrogance is based on a lie, for the work is not even his. After d'Arcy's attempted seduction fails, he fires Christine from even the chorus. "Fairness," says Hunter, "isn't one of his virtues." Hunter is also fired and, when the conductor talks back, he too is fired and the entire orchestra walks out. "How could they do this to me," asks the self-absorbed d'Arcy. Fisher later described the Phantom (the artist) as "a victim of circumstances" and d'Arcy (the employer) as "the evil force of the film."[173]

After dismissing Hunter, d'Arcy takes over as director, but he is a harsh one, browbeating his new singer. "No, no, no," he says, "not like that. Now start again." D'Arcy offers his performer no reassurance, no advice, and no golden umbrella. But the Phantom is also hard on Christine, slapping her and throwing water in her face when she collapses. "You think you can become a great singer without suffering? Do you think that I have not suffered?" Could these actions, by a character Fisher understood and sympathized with, embody the director's own frustrations? Actor Edward de Souza has said that Fisher "wasn't very well" while making *Phantom*,[174] so perhaps he felt unusually put-upon and vulnerable at the time.

The aspect of *The Curse of the Werewolf* that had interested Fisher most was its tragic love story; in that film, Leon was both romantic lead and monster, which offered a potential conflict. Unfortunately, all the Phantom shares with Leon is his nature as a helpless victim who feels sorry for himself and sheds a tear at the end. Fisher always achieved better results with strong, forceful characters, and *Phantom* was not financially successful. "I cannot understand it being a box-office loss even to this day," Fisher said a decade later. "I thought it was very good."[175]

Hammer had given *Phantom* a larger than usual budget, so its failure had a significant impact on Fisher's career: He made no more Hammer films for nearly two years. During that period, he took whatever jobs were offered, which meant traveling to Germany, where (with Frank Winterstein as codirector) he made *Sherlock Holmes and the Deadly Necklace* (1962). The experience was unfortunate, despite the reassuring presence of Christopher Lee (as Holmes) and Thorley Walters (as Watson). The international cast spoke English, French, and German in their scenes together, so it was hard for anyone to gauge a response to dialogue delivered in a foreign language. Walters referred to "trouble with the management,"[176] and Morag Fisher, who visited the production for a week, offered a stronger, but no more specific, recollection, saying, "They were so insulting. It was horrid. It really was horrid."[177]

Deadly Necklace is both mediocre and without energy. Lee looks reasonably secure in the part and gets to wear two disguises, but his voice and that of Walters were dubbed into English by other actors. The script pits Holmes against Professor Moriarty (Hans Sohnker) for possession of an Egyptian necklace, but it also replaces Holmes's deductions with a feeble running joke about the merits of the London *Times*. "Everything I could possibly require to know," says Holmes, "is in the *Times*. It is the best-informed and most reliable newspaper in the world." Visually, the only aspect of *Deadly Necklace* that reminds one of Fisher's other films is the use of tilted angles in a flashback sequence.

After a period without work, Fisher found himself in the ironic position of making two films for Robert Lippert, the American who had distributed many of Fisher's films in the early 1950s. The first of these was a spoof of the genre, *The Horror of It All* (1964), itself an imitation of Hammer's 1963 comic remake of James Whale's *The Old Dark House* (1932). The script, by Ray Russell, contains several references to that classic: Both films involve a house of menacing eccentrics, with one fond of gin, one old and bedridden, and one bearded and mute. In this case, Jack Robinson (Pat Boone) arrives, seeking to marry Cynthia Marley (Erica Rogers), only to find himself involved in a series of murders and farcical chases.

The script's humor is illustrated in a scene in which one inhabitant comments of the previous night, "There was evil about. I could feel it. I could *smell* it," whereupon another announces breakfast: "Haddock, kippers, kidneys." The eccentric Marleys possess some whimsical charm, thanks to Dennis Price (as an actor "between engagements"), Jack Bligh (as a scientist who "discovers" electricity), and Valentine Dyall (who had played a Jack the Ripper character in Hammer's 1950 film *Room to Let*). The standout, however, is the wildly exotic Natalia, who drinks Bloody Marys and says things like "Blood is thicker than water." Andree Melly, who makes this role a comic variation on her vampire in *Brides of Dracula,* recalled that Fisher created "a very easygoing, happy atmosphere" in which the cast provided "odd touches of improvisation."[178] The director, however, felt uncomfortable. Shortly after finishing the film, he called it "a kind of experiment," adding, "It is perhaps a compromise."[179] Several years later, he said, "I don't talk about it much. . . . I don't believe I will be ever very good at sending up horror."[180]

Equally unsuitable, in theory, was Lippert's science-fiction film, *The Earth Dies Screaming* (1964), because a director interested in "the charm of evil" would hardly respond favorably to an invasion by robots from outer space. Right after making the film, Fisher said that it "is not very important. It is a science-fiction film." However, he did like the fact that "everything happens very discreetly."[181] This comment probably refers to the lack of spaceships and war machines. Instead, humanity is decimated quietly, by means of a gas, and the robots (which appear only occasionally and no more than two at a time) are just faceless figures in spacesuits. The script supplements their menace by having dead Earthlings revived as "sightless and mindless slaves." The robots and the zombies, however, do not look very threatening. Unlike Fisher's vigorous vampires, they shuffle along quite slowly.

The lack of spectacle in *The Earth Dies Screaming* was probably due to its extremely low budget, but this played into Fisher's hands, making it necessary to put emphasis on the human survivors, including a mechanically minded test pilot who figures out how to destroy the robots, an untrustworthy criminal, an alcoholic weakling, and a surly young man with his pregnant wife. Despite being a familiar cross section, these characters reveal several qualities with which Fisher could identify. "I think," the director once said in a different context, "what one achieves is an emotional relationship to all the characters within the story,"[182] and that seems to be true of *The Earth Dies Screaming.*

The pilot, Jeff Nolan (Willard Parker), is knowledgeable and disciplined, a natural leader who uses his self-reliance for the benefit of all. A pragmatic optimist, he automatically carries on, "as long as there's a chance." Asked if he had ever felt that no chance existed, he replies, "No and I don't think I ever will." Although Nolan may be sure of himself, he has an inner uncertainty that he keeps under control; when someone tells him, "I wish I had your confidence," he responds, "I do, too." Nolan's caution and reserve ensure the group's survival, except for one person who rushes out at the first sight of the robots, thinking them soldiers. Her impulsiveness causes her death.

In opposition to Nolan, Quinn Taggart (Dennis Price) is wary, private, and independent in the selfish sense. From the start, he has no interest in staying with the group. "None of us," he declares, "know who our friends are," and after the aliens take over it will be "every man for himself." When the young couple arrive, Taggart's first reaction is, "That's all we need—a cheeky kid and a pregnant girl," but the far-sighted Nolan responds, "They're probably the most important people on Earth right now." Only Taggart doesn't admit the truth about himself, although he reveals it indirectly: He easily breaks into a locked building, can handle a pistol, and compulsively retrieves money thrown into a fire. Significantly, Taggart dies when he goes off on his own. Then, as an undead corpse, he becomes what he always had been, the "enemy."

Except for Taggart, there is something of Fisher in each of the film's male characters. Despite having achieved a degree of success, the director—as he reached the age of sixty—had again experienced the instability inherent to his profession. Fisher had always been sensitive to the need to earn a living and the economic struggle that implied. "I'll do anything for anybody,"[183] he once said. In addition, according to his friend Thorley Walters, Fisher "enjoyed his drink, but never did it affect his work or his endearing behavior toward his fellow beings."[184] A few years after Fisher directed *The Earth Dies Screaming,* however, Hammer would "put him up in a hotel next door [to the studio] to watch over him because he was a drinker."[185]

Prior to the alien attack, Jeff Nolan had faced a personal problem involving age and employment. "I passed the age for flying," he explains, "and the company wanted to give me a desk job." Typically, Nolan doesn't have the expected emotional response to this. "I just reached one of those turning points," he says, "where I thought I might take some inventory of myself." The young husband (David Spenser) is frustrated by his dependence on earning money, and at one point he enters with a case full of cash taken from a bank. "Three days ago," he says, "I'd have done *anything* for that much money!" Edgar Otis (Thorley Walters) takes refuge from his ineffectuality and fear in alcohol. Otis's indulgence threatens the welfare of everyone else by making him a useless watchman, so Nolan tells him, "You're *needed,* now." In the climax, Otis awakens from his drunken sleep in time to rescue the others from the undead Taggart.

Nolan's concluding comment, "All of a sudden, people mean something again," could express Fisher's relief at this reasonably human encounter with science fiction. It might also be his reaction on returning to Hammer horror. Shortly after making *The Gorgon* (1964), Fisher was enthusiastic. "There are many of my films which I do not like," he said, "but I admit without any modesty to being very proud of *The Gorgon.*"[186] He liked it because it revolved "more around the poetry of the fantastic than around horror," because its characters were "more complex than usual," and because it contained a mystery, whereas in fantasy films "very often only the spectacle counts, to the detriment of psychological motivations."[187]However, John Gilling, the script's author, later complained that "John Elder [Anthony Hinds] . . . re-wrote the opening, changed much of the dialogue and generally, I suspect, murdered what might have been a very good movie."[188]

Despite the accuracy of Fisher's comments, *The Gorgon*'s shooting script has several weaknesses. It offers hardly any explanation of the gorgon's presence in Vandorf or its link with Castle Borski. A character states that one of the three gorgons, Megaera, "fled to these parts" after the death of her sisters in ancient Greece. It is later revealed that Megaera's spirit survived her death and, for five years (starting in 1905), has possessed Carla Hoffman (Barbara Shelley), but only during the full moon. The film does not reveal why Megaera's spirit selected Carla or why the moon is involved. These are the story's premises, yet they are only arbitrary facts that must be accepted as a given. Nor does it mention Megaera's status during the intervening centuries or say if she ever possessed anyone before Carla. An ambiguous printed statement, which opens the film, doesn't clarify matters: "Overshadowing the village of Vandorf stands the Castle Borski. From the turn of the century a monster from an ancient age came to live here. No living thing survived and the spectre of death hovered in waiting for her next victim."

Also, the script is awkwardly structured as a series of three nearly isolated segments, with new characters regularly entering (and leaving) the plot. First, after artist Bruno Heitz and his model/lover argue, she sees something in the forest and dies. Soon after, Bruno hangs himself. This leads to the entrance of Professor Heitz (Michael Goodliffe), Bruno's father, who suspects that Dr. Namaroff (Peter Cushing) and the police have lied about events. Viewers know he is right, for we have seen that the girl's body had turned to stone. Professor Heitz then sees a figure and turns to stone himself. Finally, near the film's midpoint, Bruno's brother, Paul (Richard Pasco), arrives and begins the investigation that solves the mystery, but even more time passes before the film's last main character, Professor Meister (Christopher Lee), becomes involved.

This plot leaves little time for developing the characters' relationships, including Dr. Namaroff's jealous protectiveness of Carla, and what Fisher saw as the core of the film, Paul and Carla's "frustrated love story."[189] The script has Paul and Carla fall in love automatically, but Fisher, Richard Pasco, and Barbara Shelley make this aspect believable. As Pasco has said, "Terence did try very hard in this one to make it certainly much more a romantic story between Paul and Carla."[190] When the two first meet, Fisher uncharacteristically intercuts close-ups of the two, in which their facial expressions transcend the script by revealing an emotional response to each other. Fisher also altered the script's tone by revising a line at the scene's end. After Paul says, "I'm not really very concerned about what happens to me," Carla replies, "I am concerned." The script then had him say, "I don't know why, I'm sure. But as I say, I'm grateful to you." This curt dismissal became, in the film, the simple and sincere, "Thank you. I'm very grateful to you," and the dialogue is accompanied by lingering gazes. Several scenes later, Fisher adds and underlines a detail not found in the script. When Carla escorts Paul to Namaroff's office, he briefly (in close-up) touches her hand before she departs, which reveals their developing relationship both to the viewer and to Namaroff.

Carla's past dependence on Namaroff and his repressed love for her are pivotal to the film, but the script limits our contact with these elements of the story by introducing the characters as their relationship disintegrates. Similarly, Namaroff's power over Inspector Kanof (Patrick Troughton), who seems to represent authority in the "police state" of Vandorf, is insufficiently explained by their shared desire to cover up the seven murders that occurred during the past five years. As for Vandorf's citizens, they remain a nebulous presence. Although spoken about, they are seen only once, when a mob tries to drive Professor Heitz out of town.

Fisher's attempt to maintain a mystery about who is possessed by Megaera fails, for the only other suspect is an insane woman in Namaroff's sanitarium. She has no function in the plot except as an alternative to Carla, so an alert viewer will dismiss this ruse and guess the truth well before Professor Meister does. The director succeeds better with "the poetry of fantasy," taking a conversation that the script set indoors and staging it outside, with the sunset casting a warm, orange-brown glow on Meister but leaving Paul in cool, gray shadow. Fisher also makes extensive use of wind and swirling leaves. Even though the shooting script specifies the presence of the wind (but not the leaves), this is thoroughly consistent with Fisher's inclination in previous films.

The Gorgon is basically a transposition of Leon's relationship with Cristina in *Curse of the Werewolf,* with the sexes reversed. Like Leon, the helpless Carla is possessed during the full moon by a destructive force and later has no memory of what happened. Also like Leon, she seeks to leave with the person she loves, but whereas Leon knows that Cristina's presence will prevent the change from occurring, Carla only vaguely assumes it and viewers cannot be certain she is right. In another contrast to Leon, Carla is never told of her condition. To fill this gap, Fisher and actress Barbara Shelley work hard to suggest, through her manner, that Carla suspects more of the truth than the dialogue indicates.

There is also a link between *The Gorgon* and *The Man Who Could Cheat Death* (and, to a lesser extent, *Stolen Face*) in the way the characters' loved ones are replaced with statues. Here, the woman who models for, and loves, Bruno Heitz and who vents her feelings to him becomes a kind of sculpture. Later, Paul is partially turned to stone when he gazes at Megaera's (Carla's) reflection. Because this happens shortly after he first meets Carla, the fact that Fisher changed the earlier scene into one in which Paul feels attracted to her creates the implication that the process of falling in love, and thereby losing objectivity, weakens him. Paul is not completely destroyed, however, until his feelings lead him to discard all rationality and to ignore the evidence against Carla.

In a more general way, this turning-to-stone metaphor also applies to Namaroff, whose cool, stony manner masks his vulnerable inner self, his unrequited feeling for Carla. Namaroff, too, has given in to his emotions, but secretly—by protecting Carla from the truth about herself and by keeping her near him, as he selfishly ignores both her needs and the lives of Megaera's seven victims. Only at the end does Namaroff transcend his weakness when he tries to kill the gorgon and dies in the attempt. Peter Cushing has described this character as "a reserved thinking man, shy, retiring, rather sad and without very much to say,"[191] which is intriguingly similar to the actor's description of Fisher as "very shy and a little inarticulate."[192]

In contrast, the gruff and blunt efficiency of Professor Meister does not hide anything, including his affection for Paul. Rather, it is employed on his friend's behalf by this open, assertive man, even when it means going against Paul's impulsive desires. At one point, Paul is about to rush off to Carla, so Meister hits him—with great force and equally great reluctance—saying, "I can't let you destroy yourself." Earlier, when Meister reveals that he suspects Carla of being possessed by Megaera and Paul asks if he really believes that, the script had Meister reply, "Why shouldn't I? Because you're in love with her?" The film changes this to "Why shouldn't I? I'm not in love with her." The new line makes clear why Meister is able to kill the gorgon and survive, while Paul remains vulnerable and is killed by Megaera's gaze. Giving in to emotion means losing rationality, which causes destruction, whereas Meister is selfless and sympathetic, but not swayed by his feelings. *The Gorgon*'s climax evokes the staking of Lucy in *Dracula,* with Meister, after dispatching Megaera, saying, "She's free now, Paul. She's free," and we see the gentle face of Carla replace the gorgon's grim features. This time, however, the film offers no relief for the viewer or the characters. It is as though Mina, not Lucy, had been staked and the man who loves her dies immediately afterward, unable to survive the loss.

More than a year passed before Fisher shot *Dracula—Prince of Darkness* (1966), his third vampire feature, the second to feature Christopher Lee as Dracula, and his last installment in the series (Lee acted in five more, for other directors). It contains some powerful scenes, and Lee still has great presence, but the picture is damaged by the studio's decision to discard van Helsing and deal again with Dracula, which meant devoting a great deal of time to reviving the vampire and introducing a new set of characters, including a different vampire fighter. This automatically reduces the opportunity to stress the basic conflict between Dracula and his adversary.

The film's screenplay is credited to "John Sansom," the pseudonym of Jimmy Sangster, "from an idea by John Elder [Anthony Hinds]." Sangster, however, hardly recalls working on the film.[193] Possibly, his contribution originated in an unfilmed script, dating from before the filming of *The Brides of Dracula,* which Hinds revised into *Dracula—Prince of Darkness.* Hinds, meanwhile, stated that "Sangster wrote it exactly to my outline. We had worked this way before. He did not want to use his own name as it was a combined effort."[194] Another contradiction relates to Dracula's lack of dialogue in the film. Hinds said that he wrote it that way and that Christopher Lee " didn't realize it until he had already signed to do the picture. He paged through the script, looking for his lines—and there weren't any! So he never really forgave me."[195] Lee, on the other hand, claimed, "There was a great deal of dialogue originally, but it was so bad, that I refused to deliver it."[196]

. Although the details of its development remain unclear, at no point in the script's evolution did anyone solve the problem of structure and dramatic focus such a sequel poses. As a result, the story divides into two distinct parts, which never mesh into a satisfying whole, a situation symbolized by the use of different typefaces for each of the two sections in the shooting script. In the first part, four travelers arrive at Dracula's castle, where one man is killed, the vampire is revived with his blood, and his wife is turned into a vampire. Then, the surviving couple takes refuge in a monastery headed by Father Sandor (Andrew Keir), where the vampires pursue them. After the woman is staked, the others venture forth and destroy Dracula at his castle.

The film does not really have a plot. Instead, most of the first section is a long prologue that initiates an extended chase climax. The construction is so rough that a pivotal character, Ludwig (Thorley Walters), appears for the first time in the film's last third. Wisely, however, Father Sandor does cross paths with the other characters at the beginning. When the two couples stop at an inn, they meet the robust Sandor, a cleric who takes his pleasures seriously: He drinks mulled claret and warms his backside at the fireplace. "These are," he says, "earthly pleasures to be enjoyed while one is able," adding, "I enjoy shocking people's susceptibilities." With his rumbling voice and blunt comments, Sandor is the most interesting character, but he then disappears for almost an hour.

The other characters are quickly defined during this scene. Charles (Francis Matthews) and his wife, Diana (Suzan Farmer), are open and spontaneous, while Charles's brother, Alan (Charles Tingwell), and his wife, Helen (Barbara Shelley), are dignified and reserved. The main contrast is between Charles and Helen, with the optimistic, fun-loving man blatantly opposed to the primly disapproving woman, the kind of person who resists a change in plans because it disrupts their schedule. At this point, the audience knows that it should favor the likeable Charles, not the repressed and foolish Helen. Fisher, though, might have felt otherwise, for Charles says, "What I do, I do for my own satisfaction, nobody else's," and such self-centeredness does not fit with Fisher's personality ideal.

When the group finds itself at Castle Dracula, Charles is the first to enter, while Helen hesitates. As a result, Charles indirectly causes his brother's death, while Helen's fear ("Everything about this place is evil") turns out to be justified. The result is more a confusion in the film's attitude toward Helen than a subtle shift in its presentation of her. Despite the correctness of her judgment this time, she continues to seem a prude. The problem, perhaps, lies in the fact that both characters are too broadly conceived to combine reserved rationality with emotional sensitivity.

Dracula's servant, the lean, grim-faced, frock-coated Klove (Philip Latham), greets the visitors, feeds them, and shows them to their rooms. That night, when Alan awakens and wanders through the corridors, Klove stabs him and drags the corpse to the cellar. There, he ties a rope to its feet and raises the body until it hangs upside-down above a large sarcophagus, in which he places Dracula's ashes. Klove then rotates the corpse to face him and slashes Alan's throat. Blood drips into the sarcophagus, mixing with the ashes. A mist forms, in which the vampire's body starts to materialize. Finally, in a close shot, a hand emerges and grasps the coffin's edge with fingers that move like a spider's legs. Klove then lures Helen to the cellar, where Dracula attacks her. At the time of the film's release, Klove's actions seemed very brutal (although the shooting script went further by having Klove behead Alan). The procedure still has impact, even though the victim is already dead and the corpse faces away from the camera when Klove slits its throat. During filming, Fisher told Philip Latham, "Play it like a religious ritual,"[197] so the actor uses slow, precise movements—despite the fact that the script says he "works quickly and feverishly." Such dignified orderliness makes the events insidiously disturbing.

The next morning, Charles and Diana find themselves in the position of Vicky Barton in *So Long at the Fair:* There is no evidence that their companions had ever been at the castle. As Charles investigates, he finds Alan's body in a trunk (the script calls for a shot of it, with the severed head placed on top, but the film shows only Charles's reaction). Meanwhile, Helen approaches Diana, saying, "Come, sister. . . . You don't need Charles." Now that she is a vampire, the inhibited Helen has literally and emotionally let her hair down, becoming a sensual seductress. "Terry pointed out," Barbara Shelley recalled, "that when one becomes a vampire, one's sexual proclivities are no longer heterosexual so my character was then fancying the character that Suzan Farmer was playing." By viewing her vampire "as the epitome of evil, and decadence,"[198] Shelley fully embodies Fisher's concept of evil as a loss of self-discipline, a giving in to passion and instinct.

When Charles and Diana confront Helen and Dracula, Fisher handles the action with typical directness and impact, but the scene is less intense than the script's version. At one point, Charles takes a sword from a wall display and attacks Dracula, who (in the screenplay) grasps the blade and, ignoring the blood that "leaks out from between the fingers," pulls the weapon away and snaps it in two. In the film, Dracula merely grabs Charles's wrist. Then, in the script, Diana tells Charles to "make a cross" with the broken sword. This was shot, according to Francis Mathews,[199] but the footage was dropped during final editing, so that Charles seems to have the idea himself, which undercuts Diana and turns him into a traditional, ingenious hero.

Charles and Diana flee the castle and, by the time they are rescued by Sandor, most of the film's highlights have passed, with only the staking of Helen and Dracula's destruction offering thrills later on. At the monastery, we meet Ludwig, a deceptively mild-mannered eater of flies inspired by Renfield in Bram Stoker's *Dracula*. Thorley

Walters, who plays Ludwig, does not fit the script's description of the character as "cadaverous," so one wonders if Fisher's identification with his actor friend prompted him to cast Walters as "a brilliant craftsman" and "a harmless enough soul, but he has been known to erupt." It is Ludwig who, under Dracula's influence, undermines the monastery's security by inviting the vampire inside.

The script reveals its spliced-together quality when an important event—and potentially exciting scene—is merely reported. Speaking of the vampiric Helen, a monk tells Sandor, "We have caught the woman. She was hiding in the stables." The script then manipulates events by having Sandor order Helen brought to Ludwig's room. There is no internal reason for this, but it requires Ludwig to be moved, which allows him to escape and bring Diana to Dracula. The destruction of Helen avoids repeating similar scenes from *Dracula* because it involves an active, resisting vampire, not one in passive repose. In *Dracula* and *The Brides of Dracula,* the idealistic purity of van Helsing's purpose balances the harsh violence of his method. Here, however, that balance is not achieved, as monks overpower the struggling woman and, holding her arms and legs, pin her to a table so that Sandor, in a distinctly rape-like manner, can approach and attack her. Although the script does not call for showing the stake being hammered into Helen, Fisher includes a close-up of it, as he had in *Dracula*. The result is an emotionally impressive, but disturbing, scene.

The encounter between Diana and Dracula also contains a new element. After the vampire forces his victim to remove a crucifix from around her neck, he compels her to drink *his* blood from a cut he makes in his chest with a fingernail. Unfortunately, the hypnotic control over human will that Dracula possesses here was nowhere in evidence earlier, in the castle, when it would have been useful to him. Things happen in *Dracula—Prince of Darkness* not out of an inner logic but only because the filmmakers want them to happen. The film's climax depends on such manipulation. When Klove arrives at the castle driving a carriage containing coffins occupied by Dracula and Diana, a too-convenient wheel accident stops his progress and causes the carriage to tilt. This sends Dracula's coffin—only his—sliding down an adjacent embankment and onto the frozen moat. Such reliance on chance turns the characters into helpless pawns. Only Diana shows some initiative. While Charles engages in a futile fight with Dracula, she takes Sandor's rifle and shoots, hitting and cracking the ice. This unexpected result gives Sandor an idea and he takes over, firing more bullets until the running water traps Dracula, who sinks to his destruction in it.

Dracula—Prince of Darkness holds a viewer's interest from scene to scene, but its weaknesses overpower some gripping moments and underutilized characters. Even less successful is *Island of Terror* (1966), a monster film with a science-fiction basis that Fisher made for Protelco-Planet. What bothered Fisher about such films is the fact that their characters spend too much time discovering what is happening, why it is happening, and how to make it stop happening. This emphasis on the situation leaves little room for the people involved in it. The director found little of interest in this story about slugs that feed on bone, turning people's bodies into shapeless masses.

Despite its limited characterizations, occasional padding, and unconvincing creatures, *Island of Terror* is a competent work with a few limited virtues. The plot involves many of the island's residents and, although this aspect is not stressed, the film creates a sense of a community composed of mutually dependent individuals. Fisher is aided in this by his supporting cast of solid, earthy types, including Sam Kydd (who had appeared in Fisher's first four films), Niall MacGinnis, and Eddie Byrne. Although the script limits their characters' personalities, the actors' distinctiveness gives each some substance.

The main characters, however, are outsiders: Dr. Stanley (Peter Cushing), a patholo-gist; Dr. West (Edward Judd), a bone specialist; and Toni Merrill (Carole Gray), West's most recent sexual conquest. The script makes a token attempt to establish West as a ladies' man and Merrill as an indulgent rich girl, and then to have them change as they fall in love while facing danger, but their relationship remains stereotypical. Dr. Stanley, though, has a few small, human moments. Only he reveals a sense of humor, as when he approaches a large house and says, "Good Lord, it looks like Wuthering Heights," or when someone declares, "Let's not take any unnecessary risks," and he responds, "No, especially with me!" Such lines are atypical of the film as a whole, so one suspects Cushing and Fisher of supplementing the script.

An example of how the Cushing-Fisher team can add interest to a superficial script is seen when Stanley says, "I'm not very keen on going down in that cellar again," just before he descends. The obvious approach would be for him to make this statement, pause, then move cautiously ahead. Instead, Cushing says the line while striding pur-posefully to the stairs. The contradiction between his words and his manner reveals a man determined to do what must be done, without giving in to his fear. This brief insight helps to validate Stanley's later warning to the villagers, "Fear and panic will defeat us just as surely as the silicates."

The final mass attack of the silicates creates some tension, but the film's most intense moment involves just two people and one creature. A silicate's tentacle has caught Stanley's wrist and, unable to free himself, he extends his arm and West chops off the hand with an axe. This incident blends the physical reality of danger and pain with the powerful emotions of Stanley's insistence and West's reluctance. Here, as two men discipline themselves to do a difficult but essential deed, the film draws on Fisher's greatest strength; his close-ups of facial expressions and of the hand being sev-ered strike dramatic sparks. Nothing else in *Island of Terror* equals this brief, but mem-orable, scene.

Next, Fisher directed Hammer's fourth Frankenstein film (and his third). A key aspect of *Frankenstein Created Woman* bears a revealing relationship to the identity con-flict of Lily in *Stolen Face*, which is hardly surprising, for the script was written by Anthony Hinds, the producer of *Face*. The film also evokes such other split female personalities as Lena/Helen in *Four-Sided Triangle* and Carla/Megaera in *The Gorgon;* another precursor is *The Two Faces of Dr. Jekyll*.

In *Frankenstein Created Woman,* Fisher directs his camera and dramatizes the charac-ters' relationships with clarity and precision, but the individual scenes are far more interesting than the overall plot. The script's biggest problem is its premise, which shifts Frankenstein's experiments from medicine to mysticism: He fools around in some vague way with keeping a soul alive after the body's death. This is difficult to understand or accept, although Frankenstein manipulates his machinery with confi-dence and Peter Cushing convinces us that the character, at least, knows what he is doing.

Hans (Robert Morris), a young man who assists Frankenstein, loves the scarred and crippled Christina Kleve (Susan Denberg, a former *Playboy* centerfold). When three young, arrogantly insolent "gentlemen" taunt Christina, the hot-tempered Hans defends her. Later, the three kill the woman's father, and Hans is convicted of the crime. His execution drives Christina to suicide, so Frankenstein places Hans's soul in her body, which he then revives (although the script fails to mention how). In the process, Frankenstein eliminates her disability and improves her appearance. (The script ignores the fact that, had he done so earlier, the couple would still be alive—and the film without a plot.) Christina/Hans then kills the three murderers (without having a way of knowing that they are guilty) in a series of scenes that replaces suspense with grim inevitability. Afterward, Christina/Hans drowns herself/himself. This story, for the most part, evolves without Frankenstein's involvement or even his knowledge; he only serves as a catalyst and then a bystander.

As usual, Fisher responds not to abstractions such as transplanted souls but to the confusion of identity within Christina, but this aspect of the film is not fully satisfying. Although disfigured, the original Christina is too good-looking to justify the dialogue's accusations of ugliness, a weakness underlined by having Susan Denberg play both the original Christina and the beautiful "new" Christina. Hammer probably should have cast two different actresses in the roles, as it did in *Stolen Face*. The new Christina's desire "to know what I'm like" is touching, but because she recalls nothing of her former self, the situation offers less dramatic potential than an awareness of the change would have. (This contrasts with Karl's self-knowledge in *Revenge of Frankenstein*.)

Matters become more complex when the "soul" of Hans periodically occupies the new Christina's body. At times, he even talks to her in his male voice. Thus, the separated lovers have achieved the ultimate unity by becoming one person, but the new Christina's lack of memory means that she cannot know who Hans is, so the situation fails to resonate fully. Also, when the new Christina kills the three youths, she is apparently not possessed by Hans but is only carrying out his orders, yet she never acts

On the set of *Frankenstein Created Woman* (1967). Susan Denberg (who plays Christina Kleve, the woman Frankenstein re-creates) plies a cleaver to her birthday cake rather than to a man, as she does in the film. Next to her from left to right are costar Peter Cushing (Frankenstein), director Terence Fisher, costar Thorley Walters (Dr. Hertz), and producer Anthony Nelson Keys.

confused about this. Again, the emotional relevance of these events to Christina is lost. During the film's last part, the new Christina shifts between what the script calls "the scrubbed country girl" eager to please her medical mentors and an independent, dangerous seductress, but her seeming obliviousness to this alternation further limits the character's impact.

Although the plot places Christina at the film's center, she never becomes its heart or its soul. This failing has its roots in the script, but Fisher might have evoked something more emotionally coherent if Miss Denberg had been a more experienced actress. As it is, Christina is more interesting as a concept than as a character. When her scenes work, it is due less to her own inner turmoil than to the characteristics of the men she encounters. The sincere affection of Hans is complicated by his inability to control his temper—the temptation of emotional impulsiveness—and the three murderers seal their doom by giving in to the new Christina's sexual lure.

The most consistently rewarding aspect of the film involves not Christina but Frankenstein's aide, Dr. Hertz (Thorley Walters), a character almost irrelevant to the main plot. At first, the unimaginative Hertz appears to exist only for comedy relief, with Walters's charm keeping the chuckles good-natured. "Haven't you grasped anything of what I've been doing for these last six months?" demands Frankenstein. "I confess—very little," replies the bewildered Hertz. In one scene, after Hertz and Frankenstein do something with a machine, Frankenstein declares "Good!" and walks away. Hertz pauses, stares at the machine, and mutters to himself, "Good?" Later, after an experiment, Frankenstein states, "We have succeeded," and Hertz responds, in an accepting but uncomprehending tone, "We have?" After Frankenstein explains, Hertz asks, with polite curiosity, "Baron, one question, please: What is it for?"

Thanks to Thorley Walters's carefully balanced performance, the gentle innocence of Hertz gives the film life and warmth. From the start, he is much more than a self-described "broken-down, drunken old muddle-head." In a revealing contrast to Frankenstein, Hertz is both impractical and sensitive, a person concerned about the feelings and welfare of others. He is, in fact, a truly nice man. In his first scene, after reviving the frozen Frankenstein, Hertz suggests that they celebrate. Frankenstein, whose emotions remain unthawed, assumes it is because the experiment succeeded, but Hertz corrects him: "I want to celebrate your safe return." When Frankenstein decides to capture Hans's soul after his execution, it is Hertz who asks, "Is it right?" The oblivious Frankenstein replies, "What has 'right' to do with it?"

This contrast is clearly seen in the men's dealings with Christina. After her facial bandages are removed, Frankenstein abruptly orders, "Keep still!" while Hertz, sensitive to the girl's fears, reassures her, saying, "It's alright, my dear. It's alright." When Christina asks who she is, Frankenstein replies, "Your name is Christina and you're a very healthy young girl. That's all you need to know for the time being." Hertz, responding to the same question, says, "You're a very, very lovely girl, my dear." Christina also asks to see her face, which Frankenstein dismisses with the question, "What on earth for?" Later, Hertz brings her a mirror. Soon after, Frankenstein plans an experiment to stir Hans's memory in Christina, which prompts Hertz to ask, "Will it be safe?" Frankenstein replies, "I've no idea. . . . This test will be interesting and possibly informative. That's enough reason for me to carry it out." Thus, the bumbler has become thoroughly sympathetic and his empathy for Christina puts Frankenstein's scientific objectivity in stark perspective.

It is tempting to view Hertz, as embodied by Fisher's friend Thorley Walters, as an extension of the director, for he reveals the comforting humanity often cited in descriptions of Fisher at work. However, Hertz's function in the film—his juxtaposition to Frankenstein—is more subtle than that. Frankenstein may be unfeeling and even rude, he may epitomize amoral rationality, but he is not immoral or evil. He injures no one and, at the end, tries to stop the new Christina from killing the third youth and herself. In another significant detail, this is the first film in which Frankenstein truly needs someone's assistance. He has, before the film's start, injured his own hands somehow and therefore depends on Hertz to do much of the physical work during his experiments and surgery.

These facts join with the men's contrasting personalities to create a truly resonant pairing of mind with hand, thought with action, knowledge with feeling, and austerity with empathy. Each man, alone, is incomplete. Together, they combine to form a single, whole being. Instead of a simple conflict of opposites, we find the two necessary aspects of an identity achieving an unsteady balance: Each in his own way tolerates the other's limitations, Frankenstein impatiently and Hertz with understanding. "The hands were mine," says Hertz to Christina, about his surgery on her, "but the skill was his. He directed my every move." The implication here, and throughout the film, is that warm sympathy requires a foundation of cool rationality, while cool rationality must be tempered with warm sympathy. Each is an essential part of a successfully functioning personality.

In *Frankenstein Created Woman,* Fisher found thoroughly compatible material that encouraged a full flowering of the visual style that typifies his best work: clear, concise, and understated, yet carefully designed to express the human drama of a scene. This can be illustrated by Frankenstein's appearance as a witness at Hans's trial. As the Chief of Police questions Frankenstein, Fisher intercuts two reverse-angle medium shots of both men. In one, the three youths who are really guilty can be seen in the background, between the protagonists; in the other, the jury occupies that position. When one of the youths heckles Frankenstein, Fisher uses the first angle, and when a statement by Frankenstein draws laughter from the jury, he uses the second shot. In this way, the director keeps both principal characters prominently and continually in visual opposition, while depicting their interaction with others without cutting between individuals or groups.

Then, as the dialogue becomes more intense, Fisher shifts to slightly closer two-shots of Frankenstein and the Chief, from angles that place the men nearer each other in the frame and eliminate the other people. Later, when Frankenstein admits it is "not impossible" that Hans could have killed someone, Fisher finally uses a close-up of the speaker. Rarely do medium shots and close-ups carry such dramatic impact, because rarely do directors so carefully save them for key moments. As with much of Fisher's work, this scene stands as a textbook example of classical editing and composition, of style that brings out the qualities of a scene without drawing attention to itself.

Fisher next returned to Planet Films for another science-fiction picture, *Night of the Big Heat* (1967), which has also been called *Island of the Burning Doomed* and *Island of the Burning Damned.* During an unnaturally hot spell in the middle of winter, people hear a strange whirring sound, then stare in horror as a bright glare engulfs them. Eventually, the characters learn that aliens "composed of high-frequency impulses in heat form" have invaded. When finally seen, they look like glowing rocks that slide forward to incinerate their victims. Unlike *Island of Terror,* however, this script devotes considerable time to the people involved. Even without the presence of danger from outer space, their relationships would form an interesting plot.

The central conflict involves novelist Jeff Callum (Patrick Allen), who runs an inn on the island; his wife, Frankie (Sarah Lawson); and Angela Roberts (Jane Merrow), who arrives to serve as his secretary. Jeff, we soon learn, has fled to the isolated island after an extramarital affair with the compulsively seductive Angela. Frankie, unaware of the facts but sensitive to Jeff's nature, warns Angela off by telling her that a previous secretary had been infatuated with her husband. "That made her a complication," she says, "and Jeff doesn't like complications." Like the leading characters in some of Fisher's 1950s melodramas, such as *Murder by Proxy*, Jeff has avoided such "complications" by running away from them, not by mastering himself.

But Jeff cannot escape, for Angela has pursued him. "I'm not going through your special brand of madness again," he tells her. "For three months I wrote nothing. I nearly wrecked my marriage. I'm not going through it again!" In fact, this "brand of madness" has as much to do with Jeff's vulnerability to temptation as with Angela's efforts. The satisfying stability of work and marriage have been threatened by his inability to control passionate impulses. "I *wanted* her! I wanted her *body!*" he later tells Frankie, with an intensity that reveals the grip that irrationality still has on him. Jeff may not love Angela, but neither is he in control of himself, as suggested by his outbursts of anger at her ("I'll break your little neck!") and others.

Angela, too, is recklessly self-indulgent. On impulse, she tells Frankie the truth, then declares she lied. Why did she lie, Frankie asks. "I was angry," Angela replies. "It's an automatic reflex when I'm being warned off." Much later, she demands to see the local doctor. "I'm ill!" she yells. "I need him! Where the hell is he?!" The now-resentful Frankie blurts out a truth about Angela when she replies, "He can't come, you selfish bitch—he's dead!" During the film's climax, when Angela and Ken Stanley (William Lucas) are besieged by the aliens, she takes his gun to kill herself. Understanding her more than she understands herself, Ken tells her to shoot him first, saying, "For once in your damn life do something for someone else."

Throughout the film, Angela's background and motives remain vague, so she is more an embodiment of Jeff's weakness than a person in her own right. She seems to provoke him mainly because she knows she can and enjoys the power it gives her. At one point, she holds a cigarette, asks Jeff for a light, and—in a good directorial touch—stays where she is until he crosses the room to her. In the only clue about why she relishes her manipulations, Angela tells Frankie, "Men are all the same. There's nothing to choose between any of them." Evidently, something once disillusioned her in males and now she punishes them for a weakness she knows they all have. But distinctions should still be made, as she learns when a village man loses control completely and attempts to rape her; she also may realize this from the honest concern of Ken Stanley.

The film links these personal matters with the alien menace in two ways. We first hear the aliens' whirring sound when the newly arrived Angela stops to check her appearance before presenting herself at the inn. This connection between Angela and danger is maintained when the sound is again heard just before she kisses Jeff. It is also heard after she places his hand on her breast and says, "You know you want me. Why try to deny it?" A different form of this connection occurs in a later scene. A man at the inn sees Angela and says, "No wonder the temperature's way up!" whereupon the heat makes the bottles behind the bar explode. Shortly after, the heat and Angela cause human pressure to explode when the same man attacks her. Thematically, the possibility that heat is "bound to lead to irrational behavior" becomes an objective expression of the danger posed by sensual impulses.

The alien–menace part of the plot is also relevant to its human aspects through the presence of a scientist named Hanson (Christopher Lee), who has secretly been searching for proof of the invasion. Although Hanson is stern and abrupt, his manner derives from true concern, which has been channeled into a commitment to his work. Hanson's determination to be rational, even under the most trying circumstances, makes him a vivid contrast to the emotional indulgences of the others, especially Jeff. "I base my conclusions on observations of fact," he tells Jeff. When the two discover the remains of a victim, Hanson is distracted by an important clue and Jeff angrily declares, "This doesn't affect you at all, does it?" Keeping his emotions in check, Hanson says, "I appreciate how you feel. I know he was a friend of yours. But that won't do any good, now." Later, he warns, "Getting emotional isn't going to help."

It is Hanson who offers explanations and who plans what to do. When he suggests going to the local meteorological station to warn the mainland, the local doctor (Peter Cushing) volunteers and is killed. Then Jeff volunteers, but Hanson insists that he should go instead. "I'm not being heroic about this, I can assure you," he explains. "I think I'm better equipped to deal with a situation of this kind." He is right and, unlike Jeff, is being logical instead of emotional (although one wonders why he let the doctor go earlier). After Hanson is killed in the final confrontation, his function as a positive figure is picked up by Ken Stanley. When the hysterical Angela says, "Leave me alone," Ken tells her, "At least we have a chance by sticking together," and "I'm just as scared as you are, but we mustn't give up."

The film ends abruptly, without including some necessary final moments of characterization, but viewers can at least understand its incompletely achieved intention. While the seemingly indestructible aliens advance, both Angela and Jeff appear to achieve a measure of personal control. Angela has some sort of private breakthrough with Ken, while Jeff and Frankie embrace nearby. As if in response, rain starts to fall and destroys the creatures, extinguishing the heat that was wrecking lives and relationships.

Night of the Big Heat has several weaknesses. Rewriting could have filled in some pivotal gaps in characterization, while the horror aspect succeeds less well than the character presentation, developing limited dread. Also, too many scenes take place in the inn, with people interacting as if in a play, although this does contribute to a sense of claustrophobic frustration, as emotions flare. Visually, the film is direct without being especially vivid. Overall, however, the final impression is positive, because Fisher and his cast worked to create meaningful human drama camouflaged as a horror film. As Jane Merrow, who played Angela, recalled, "Terence and I decided that rather than hating her we had to have some sort of center, and it had to be pity."[200] At the same time, Fisher "was the ultimate professional. With him, it was let's get on with the job, use what we have in hand, and don't let us cry about spilt milk if they [the effects] aren't absolutely right."[201] Thus, Fisher on the set embodied—as always—the self-disciplined and realistic, yet emotionally sympathetic, ideal often depicted in his films.

Most of the main characters in this script are more thoroughly victimized by their passions than is usual in a Fisher film. Therefore, despite the familiarity of its implications, *Night of the Big Heat* doesn't feel typical of the director. Fisher's next film, however, is both one of his most typical and one of his best. *The Devil Rides Out* is, like *Dracula,* a fast-paced, exciting adventure in which the forces of good and evil clash through two powerful adversaries. Here, the Duc de Richleau (Christopher Lee) sets out to rescue his friend Simon Aron (Patrick Mower) from the seductive clutches of Mocata (Charles Gray), a practitioner of black magic.

The script, by Richard Matheson, faithfully follows Dennis Wheatley's 1934 novel, while condensing the wide-ranging narrative and pointing up its similarity to a vampire story. Thus, de Richleau corresponds to van Helsing and Mocata to Dracula, with the Duc drawing on the powers of good—light, a crucifix, and holy water—to fight an evil force that threatens the characters' souls. Like a vampire's victim, this film's heroine has been contaminated by evil and suffers an inner struggle between attraction and resistance. Ultimately, daybreak brings the destruction of Mocata and the recovery of the heroine's soul.

A story about black magic might seem inconsistent with Fisher's realistic orientation, but, as with the Dracula films, the director avoids stressing mysticism and the nebulous. Evil and Satan are given tangible form, and they pose concrete threats. "The power of Darkness," declares de Richleau, "is more than just a superstition. It is a living force which can be tapped at any given moment of the night." Mocata even asserts that magic is "merely a science," and he reveals a kinship to Baron Frankenstein and Mr. Hyde by noting, rationally, that it contains "neither good nor evil." Mocata becomes even more the ideal Fisher villain when he relates black magic to the mind. "The power of the will," he says, "is something people do not understand, attributing to it mysterious qualities which it does not possess, being merely the power of mind over matter or . . . the power of mind over mind."

The main difference between this film and its source is in the characterization of Mocata. Wheatley, who evidently used the real-life magician Aleister Crowley as a model, has de Richleau describe Mocata as "a pot-bellied, bald-headed person of about sixty, with large, protuberant, fishy eyes, limp hands, and a most unattractive lisp. He reminded me of a large white slug." The script does not contain a description of

Terence Fisher discusses a scene with actor Christopher Lee on the set of *The Devil Rides Out* (1968). In a change of pace, Lee portrays this film's hero, the Duc de Richleau.

Mocata, but Fisher insisted on casting Charles Gray in the role. This choice and Fisher's direction make the character just the opposite of Wheatley's version. With his gloves, cane, and red carnation, Gray is polished and urbane enough to mix with the highest levels of society. "He had all the charm and wickedness of evil," said the director.[202]

But *The Devil Rides Out* is much more than a simple conflict between the Duc and Mocata, between supernatural good and evil. Equally important is an underlying conflict between private self-indulgence and supportive friendship. To save Simon, the Duc enlists the aid of their mutual friends Rex Van Ryn (Leon Greene) and, later, Richard and Marie Eaton (Paul Eddington and Sarah Lawson). In the process, Rex falls in love with Tanith (Nike Arrighi), another potential initiate. The film establishes that Simon and Tanith are voluntarily giving themselves to evil, but only the novel reveals that they do so to gain personal power over others. Although this part of the explanation should have been included to clarify the self-indulgent nature of their temptation, the film does illustrate the licentious indulgence of the Satanists' ceremonies. It also establishes the position in which this places the Duc, who must save Simon not only from Mocata but from his own willingness to indulge in a "desperately dangerous adventure." Like Professor Meister in *The Gorgon* (also played by Lee), the Duc knows what is best for his younger friend and acts in his interests by knocking him out and kidnapping him from his own house.

The Duc succeeds through knowledge, strength, and self-discipline, but also through the friendship of Rex and the Eatons. The protective power of good, it seems, lies as much in mutual, unconditional support as it does in religious paraphernalia. As de Richleau tells Simon, after extricating him from the coven, "Your mind is troubled, but you are with your friends now and there is nothing more to worry about." Later, the group takes refuge with the Eatons who, with their daughter, Peggy, epitomize what Wheatley called a "sane and happy household." At one point, after Mocata gains mental control over Marie, it is the innocent Peggy who disrupts his hypnotic spell. The Eatons' healthy affection becomes a major factor when they, Simon, and the Duc take refuge in a pentagram during a long night of struggle against demons summoned by Mocata. In a later confrontation, the men are helpless and victory is achieved only by the two loving women and the pure child, when Tanith's spirit possesses Marie and has Peggy recite the words of the Sussamma Ritual, which destroys Mocata and returns Tanith to life.

Mocata may summon a giant spider and the Angel of Death on horseback, but these figures cannot reach those within the pentagram, so he turns their struggle into an internal one. When Mocata tries to use Richard's skepticism to lure him out of the circle, de Richleau reminds him of their years of friendship and begs him not to move "for the sake of that friendship." Mocata also tempts them with the voice of Rex, heard pleading to be admitted, and a vision of Peggy menaced by the spider. Here, he plays on the characters' feelings by sowing divisiveness in the girl's parents, as they are torn between an urge to help her and their confidence in de Richleau. Ultimately, the issue is less one of physical conflict than, in Fisher's words, "emotional tensions."[203]

Matheson's screenplay does not dwell on these psychological and emotional elements but lets them emerge naturally out of the action, while maintaining a breathless—but never rushed—pace. The first scene plunges viewers immediately into the plot, as Rex arrives, de Richleau briefs him on the situation, and they head straight for Simon's house, where Mocata's coven has gathered. Often, the script eliminates the usual transitions between scenes. After the Duc tells his chauffeur to drive to Simon's house, in the next shot he and Rex are already standing at the door. Elsewhere, although the script includes arrivals or departures, they were omitted from the final film.

Further tightening the pace is a revision that eliminated several scenes, representing more than nine pages. In the script, Rex arrives at a hotel, converses with the Countess D'Urfey, and takes Tanith for a drive. He brings her to the Eatons' home and, during a picnic, Tanith receives mental orders from Mocata. When they arrive back at the house, Tanith commandeers a car and flees, with Rex in pursuit. The film cuts most of this, moving directly from a shot of Rex about to leave to one of him and Tanith already in the car, and it is here that Tanith receives her orders from Mocata. Then, when they arrive at the Eatons', Tanith immediately drives off. Although the conversations in the cut scenes would give greater substance to the romance between Rex and Tanith, little else is lost and the film's compactness gains as a result.

Richard Matheson was, however, unhappy about changes made to his version of the pentagram attack. Actually, most of the sequence in the film does follow the novel, except for the presence of the giant spider. "They always go for the god-damned spider!" Matheson declared. "That wasn't in my script."[204] Wheatley had the Eatons' "daughter" menaced by a blobby thing with "whitish pimply skin, leprous and unclean, like some huge silver slug." Matheson probably retained that concept for, although the shooting script identifies the demon as a spider, it usually refers to it as the "Thing" and even mentions that it "begins to laugh, a distorted parody of Mocata's laughter." Perhaps understandably, the studio opted for a more easily filmed menace. Another change involves a demon seen earlier. What the script describes vaguely as "a greyish face . . . about seven feet above the ground" and "a hideously malignant creature" becomes, in the film, just a tall black man standing in the room. Compared with the elaborate special effects in current features, Hammer's choices look relatively unimpressive, but the essence of those scenes lies in the characters' responses, so it is hard to fault the film on this level.

A confrontation between Mocata and Marie Eaton reveals Fisher at perhaps his most typical and, visually, it evokes the scene in *The Mummy* between Mehemet and John Banning. Fisher starts with a long shot of the two seated at opposite sides of the frame with a great deal of space between them. As the conversation begins, he intercuts shots that include both people. Then, when Mocata's presence becomes more forceful, we have a medium shot of him intercut with a long shot of her. A very slow movement toward her evokes his growing power, until his full control is established through intercut close-ups. Finally, when he asks about Simon's location, Mocata leans forward into that rarity in a Fisher film, an extreme close-up. When Marie replies that Simon and Tanith are both "upstairs," Fisher cuts to a startling overhead shot of Mocata, as he looks upward. This leads to a movement in on his face and shots of his mental impact on the two people he seeks. The struggle between Mocata and Marie is thoroughly embodied in Fisher's counterpoint editing, with his choices of shots matching the stages of their interaction.

Aside from the special effects, the film's one possible weakness is its ending, which is too abstract to be comprehended fully on first viewing, and perhaps not even later. After Tanith has died, the reciting of the Sussamma Ritual defeats Mocata, whereupon the characters suddenly find themselves in another location, with Tanith alive but Mocata still dead. As de Richleau hastily explains, the ritual has somehow reversed time so that while the events after a certain moment really happened, they now have been undone, except for Mocata's death. Such a concept can be conveyed in a novel, which has the space to devote to explanations, but it is almost impossible to grasp in the few seconds it is allotted in the film. However, this is as much a challenge as it is a weakness.

His reading of Dennis Wheatley's novel probably helped focus Fisher's concept of the struggle between good and evil, as he expressed it in later interviews. Wheatley wrote of "an utter faith in the ultimate triumph of good" and, in 1974, Fisher said that "ultimately and inevitably good must be triumphant—not in every particular case in our experience of life, but ultimately and inevitably it is going to be."[205]

Shortly after directing *The Devil Rides Out* in 1967, Fisher was hit by a car while crossing the street and suffered a broken leg. As a result, he couldn't make *Dracula Has Risen from the Grave* (1968) and didn't direct again until more than a year later. *Frankenstein Must Be Destroyed* (1969), which Fisher also helped write, blends plot and character with a vitality not seen in the series since *Revenge of Frankenstein*. The experiments of the Baron (still Peter Cushing) are once again at the center of a tightly constructed script, and the character, although capable of great charm, has regained the ruthless methods and cold self-confidence of *The Curse of Frankenstein*. What extends the bleak outlook of this film, however, is the fact that his assistants and his patients are involved unwillingly. Frankenstein blackmails Dr. Karl Holst (Simon Ward) and his fiancée, Anna (Veronica Carlson), into helping him, but they are hardly innocent victims. For a year, Karl has stolen drugs from the asylum where he works and sold them, although only to subsidize the medical care of Anna's mother.

Frankenstein's goal is to cure the insanity and restore the memory of the hospital-ized Dr. Brandt, but his motives mix idealism with selfishness in typical fashion. He and Brandt had, separately, experimented with removing human brains at the moment of death, preserving them by freezing, and then transplanting them into new bodies. Frankenstein knows how to do the surgery, but only Brandt has the secret of preservation. So, while Frankenstein's long-range aim is to help humanity, on the immediate, personal level his motives are inhuman. He is less interested in helping Brandt the man than in obtaining Brandt's knowledge, and his actions are motivated not by feeling but by the needs of his work, which take precedence over all other considerations.

To save the lives of unknown future patients, Frankenstein leaves a trail of human wreckage—of dead bodies, shattered relationships, and compromised principles. Karl's murder of a watchman while helping Frankenstein steal equipment places him more firmly in Frankenstein's grip and, by heightening his sense of guilt, alienates him further from Anna. Ironically, the operations work perfectly, and Brandt's brain functions normally in the body of the murdered Dr. Richter. Yet this success immediately breeds failure, for Brandt reacts against what has been done to him and his wife recoils from this unfamiliar figure. In the film's grim climax, only Mrs. Brandt survives contact with Frankenstein's idealism.

The Baron easily dominates all of his scenes, whether lecturing some complacent fellow lodgers ("I'm afraid that stupidity always brings out the worst in me"), declar-ing that he won't let Anna leave ("I need her to make coffee"), responding to Karl's skepticism ("Your medical education is soon to be vastly improved"), or concluding a backyard burial ("I shall be down for breakfast at 6:30 . . . I should like two lightly boiled eggs"). Even when Frankenstein's personality is not central to the action, emo-tional involvement remains. A police search of Anna's house, where the operations are conducted, arouses suspense, as does the rupture of a water main in the garden, where a body is buried. The latter scene contains the vividly grotesque image of the corpse's arm held erect by a fountain of water and seeming to gesture. When Frankenstein and Karl kidnap Dr. Brandt from the asylum, a fellow patient starts to scream, and her cries echo through the corridors, building tension and giving voice to the doctors' violation of propriety. The presence of this woman and her reason for screaming—she believes that spiders are crawling over her—have been carefully established during an earlier scene, one that also introduced Karl, Dr. Brandt, and Dr. Richter. Such compact writing indicates the care taken with this film, in contrast to the more arbitrary inclusion of the mad women in *The Gorgon* and in the climax of *The Man Who Could Cheat Death*.

The earlier Frankenstein films, as if unsure about how far to carry their realism, had omitted all scenes of surgery. In *Frankenstein Must Be Destroyed,* however, Fisher spends a good deal of time on the operations. Such scenes, however, are neither vulgar nor extravagant, for the director avoids shocking with the gratuitously gruesome. Little is actually shown on-screen, as we watch the surgeons instead of the patient, but the film's calm precision, our knowledge of what is happening just below frame level, and the grinding sound of a metal drill scraping on bone produce considerable discomfort. Fisher is justified in lingering on such events, because this is what Frankenstein *does,* this is his *work,* so he and Fisher both take it for granted, just as would a surgeon or a doctor performing an autopsy. Fisher's restrained observation keeps such scenes under control, and only people unfamiliar with such activities, like the viewers and Frankenstein's assistant, recoil at them. Fisher knows he must show the man at his work in order for us to understand Frankenstein and in order to create the desired emotional response in the audience.

Despite the centrality of Frankenstein to all that occurs, the other characters add considerably to the film's substance. As he had in *Frankenstein Created Woman,* Fisher cast Thorley Walters in a major supporting role. Here, in his last performance for his friend, Walters plays Inspector Frisch. Accompanied by a doctor (Geoffrey Bayldon), Frisch follows Frankenstein's trail but never crosses paths with his quarry. Frisch and the doctor serve as an interesting reversal of the Frankenstein-Hertz pair in Fisher's previous Frankenstein film. If Hertz, the bumbler, revealed more feeling for others than did the efficient Frankenstein, this time the blustery, pompous, and distracted Frisch truly is a bumbler, and he shows as little sympathy as Frankenstein ever did. Tactless and blunt, he informs Ella Brandt that her husband has been kidnapped and then interrupts her to say, "Kindly listen to me and answer my questions!" Later, he calls her "stupid" for visiting Anna's house. Fisher makes a point of keeping the reserved but reasonable doctor in view, so that he can reveal distress at Frisch's manner. Ironically, the impatience and sarcasm of Frisch, the film's one representative of good, derive from shallow overconfidence, whereas Frankenstein's arrogance is justified by his intelligence and rationality.

More relevant to the main plot of the film are its two male-female pairs. Karl Holst and Anna are at first likeably affectionate, then sadly helpless as Frankenstein undermines their relationship. An even more subtly revealing couple is Brandt and his wife, Ella (Maxine Audley). Brandt, the asylum patient, epitomizes emotional passivity as he sits, unmoving, in his room. He has, it is explained, been sedated because he occasionally flies into "violent and murderous rages." Such a contrast of elements in one person immediately evokes characters from Fisher's other films. A new element, however, is the cause of his condition. "The pressure of his work," we are told, "had broken him." At this point, Brandt has no memory of his past life and, therefore, has lost his identity. To his wife, however, he still has an identity as her husband, and so she faithfully continues to visit him, even though he does not recognize or respond to her.

After Frankenstein places Brandt's brain in Richter's body and cures his illness, the character is in a marvelously evocative situation. It is here that, Fisher felt, the film "became emotionally dynamic."[206] The sadness of Brandt's plight is much less melo-

After he receives another man's brain in *Frankenstein Must Be Destroyed* (1969), Professor Richter (Freddie Jones) becomes the most human and tragic of Frankenstein's creations.

dramatic than that of the comparable character in *Revenge of Frankenstein,* and also more rewarding for Fisher. During these final scenes, Freddie Jones gives a touching and sorrowful performance as Brandt-Richter, achieving exactly the complex human dimension that had eluded the character of Christina in *Frankenstein Created Woman.*

Brandt has regained his memory and, therefore, his inner sense of self, but he has lost the external marks of identity, a discontinuity that inevitably disturbs him. When he attempts to communicate with his wife, who of course would not recognize him, he first hides behind a screen and only later reveals himself. Now that Brandt once more recognizes Ella and treats her in a sensitive, caring fashion, his hitherto supportive companion cringes at the sight of him. Brandt may have found himself, but to her he has become a stranger. This situation echoes, with the sexual roles reversed, the scene in *Dr. Jekyll* in which Kitty identified herself as "your wife" and Jekyll responded, "The woman inside you, is that woman my wife?" The challenge of self-definition is exceeded only by the challenge of understanding another, even the other that one knows best.

Unfortunately, Hammer's need for an efficient, dramatic resolution limited Fisher's chance to explore this situation. Because Brandt has been stabbed by the frightened Anna, he arrives at his home already dying. Frankenstein, angered by events, stabs Anna and pursues Brandt. When Karl finds Anna's body, he sets out after Frankenstein. Brandt, meanwhile, arranges for Frankenstein's destruction and, when Karl interrupts his revenge, Brandt shoots him and carries Frankenstein into the burning house. As was the case as far back as *Four-Sided Triangle,* the filmmakers have used a conflagration so that neither they nor the characters must face the final results of the experiment. This climax does convey a tragic futility, even as it feels a bit too arbitrary. Nevertheless, the dignified pathos of Brandt's final contact with his wife is what remains in the viewer's memory.

Near the end of filming, the head of Hammer, James Carreras, appeared on the set and announced that the film didn't contain enough sex. Someone then wrote a scene in which Frankenstein rapes Anna, which was added so hastily that, of the forty-five pages of revisions in the shooting script, it is the only one undated. The crassness of the scene's motivation is revealed by its written version, which concludes by saying, "The struggle continues—with appropriate cries and noises. FRANKENSTEIN eventually succeeding (as far as the censor will allow)—having torn ANNA's nightdress off her shoulders at least." This arbitrary afterthought disturbed everyone, especially Fisher, who had contributed to the writing of the film. As Veronica Carlson recalls, "Terry argued at length to keep it out, but was overruled, so we had to shoot the scene. Peter and I hated doing it . . . when my gown was ripped on camera, Terry yelled, 'Cut! I can't take anymore!' and turned his back and walked away. It was the only time I had seen him walk off the set."[207] For the accepting, professional director, this was a rare sign of rage. Five years later, Fisher still felt incensed. "It was dragged in," he said of the scene, " . . . to follow the trend." He then declared, with unexpected passion, "I'm not going to talk about this, because I thought it was diabolical."[208]

Not that Fisher was inherently opposed to a rape scene. He would, for example, have considered having Brandt, in his new body, rape his own wife. That, he said in retrospect, "would have been tremendous," because he saw it as "a justifiable thing within a situation, a human situation."[209] The intellectual and emotional overtones of such a scene would have been consistent with Fisher's interest in confusions of identity. In fact, he had already filmed a version of that scene in *Dr. Jekyll,* when Edward Hyde rapes Jekyll's wife.

Veronica Carlson was especially distressed because all of her later scenes with Cushing had already been shot, "and I hadn't interacted with him as though he had raped me."[210] Naturally, she felt that her performance had been undermined, although viewers probably add the new interpretation themselves every time she cringes at something in subsequent scenes. The problem is less that the addition damaged the acting than that it is a spur-of-the-moment action that occurs to Frankenstein only when he passes Anna's open bedroom door. Nowhere else does sex seem to enter Frankenstein's range of awareness; he already has as much control of Anna and Karl as he needs, and his methods have typically been more austere. The rape is inconsistent with the character's personality as established and developed elsewhere in the film.

Although *Frankenstein Must Be Destroyed* is a tight, intense, suspenseful drama, from Fisher's point of view it might be considered a film about wasted lives and lost abilities, about people who have run out of time and hope. As Karl says, "there's no cure" for Anna's mother, "just temporary relief." Dr. Brandt, too, "can never be cured" of his illness, and Dr. Richter comments, "What a terrible waste." Frankenstein, himself, is most appealingly idealistic when he describes the work in which he and Brandt had been engaged. "We were seeking to preserve for all time the great talents and geniuses of the world. When they die, their brains are at the height of their creative power and we bury them under the ground to rot, because the bodies that housed them have worn out. We want to remove those brains at the instant of death and freeze them, thus preserving for posterity all they contain." Does this reveal a consciousness in Fisher of his own advancing age and physical fragility? That seems likely, given that

Frisch recommends hiring "younger men" as watchmen. And of the murder victim, he says, "That old chap was seventy if he was a day." In the script, the age cited is sixty, but during filming of *Frankenstein Must Be Destroyed,* Fisher was approaching his own sixty-fifth birthday.

After completing *Frankenstein Must Be Destroyed* early in 1969, Fisher was to direct *Lust for a Vampire* (1970), but only a few days before shooting started he again broke a leg—being hit by a car in the same manner as before. Fisher's next and final film, *Frankenstein and the Monster from Hell,* was not shot until 1972. Almost as powerful as its predecessor, it is even more negative as it catalogues a variety of lost abilities. This time, Baron Frankenstein (Cushing) is an asylum inmate who also serves as the institution's physician and unofficial head, a position he achieved by blackmailing the venal director. As he had in the poor ward of *The Revenge of Frankenstein,* the Baron uses the patients as raw material for his experiments. Because his hands, like the man himself, have "lost all sensitivity," he requires the aid of others, first a female patient called Angel (Madeline Smith) and, later, Simon Helder (Shane Briant), a young doctor incarcerated for trying to duplicate Frankenstein's experiments.

Monster from Hell is full of intriguing implications and associations. The claustrophobic asylum feels like a metaphorical microcosm of the world, in which authority is pompous, corrupt, and crazier than the inmates, while an insensitive rationalist functions behind the scenes with the imperious omnipotence of a ruthless god. Frankenstein also exemplifies superior intellect, unable to disassociate itself entirely from the rabble because it must rely on average individuals to implement its ideas.

Frankenstein's subjects embody several of humanity's contrasting facets. Professor Durendel composes music, plays the violin, and understands pure mathematics ("more beautiful even than music," he says). Another, Tarmut, was a delicate craftsman who once carved small, exquisite figures. These two contrast with the "superior" Frankenstein, who admits to being tone deaf and cannot control his own hands. A third man, Schneider, has a powerful, primitive body and a mind with homicidal tendencies. "More animal than human," comments Frankenstein. "He was fascinated by broken glass. He liked stabbing people in the face with it." When he grafts the brain of the first man and the hands of the second to the body of the third, Frankenstein produces only a grotesque caricature of the impossible "ideal man." In this figure (Dave Prowse), we see humanity's separate natures warring with each other, as the animal instincts of the body seek to dominate the inner creative urge. Ultimately and inevitably, this "monster" of bits and pieces is torn apart by the unreasoning crowd.

Monster from Hell contains Fisher's most explicit operation scenes. We watch Helder sew an eye into the creature's head ("Pop it in," directs Frankenstein) and, as the hands are reattached, Frankenstein helps by holding an artery between his teeth, a bit of business cut for the film's American release. We also see the top of Durendel's skull lifted off and the brain removed. Later, when Frankenstein discards Schneider's old brain, he plops it into a dish on the floor, which he then accidentally kicks over. During these activities, Frankenstein pauses, unconcerned, for lunch. "Ah, kidneys!" he sighs.

Some elements of this film are familiar from earlier ones. For example, the ambiguity of identity is revealed in a semicomic scene as the asylum's director mistakes Helder for an outsider and treats him with respect. Then, when he realizes that Helder is a newly arrived inmate, deference becomes disdain and fear. On another occasion, Frankenstein interrupts the director's seduction of a female patient. "You may find it

Baron Frankenstein (Peter Cushing), no longer able to operate himself, assists Dr. Helder (Shane Briant) in attaching the Monster's hand by holding a blood vessel between his teeth. This action was cut from the film's American release. From *Frankenstein and the Monster from Hell* (1974).

impossible to restrain yourself," he says, "but you will not behave like an animal towards my patients!" Although Frankenstein has taken restraint to unnatural extremes, he does defend the inmates and reflects Fisher's antagonism to emotional and physical indulgence. Professor Durendel reverses this contrast, for although his gentleness and artistry represent the essence of goodness, he is quite capable of losing control. "When roused," explains Frankenstein, "that 'harmless little man' is as savage as a wild cat."

Fisher directs *Monster from Hell* with concise, reserved visual strength. This and the film's narrow focus—its confinement to a single major setting and only a few prominent characters—result in a leanness that produces an almost allegorical feeling of compression. Especially striking are several compact, expressive compositions that contain all the necessary information in a single shot but that also resonate with emotional overtones. Near the beginning, we see the title page of *The Collected Works of Baron Frankenstein;* there is a blood stain near an illustration of the author, on which Helder tosses a scalpel. Later, after Durendel hangs himself with his violin strings, a single shot shows the professor's feet, a kicked-over stool, and the violin on a table. We also get a close-up of the stringless instrument, an image that, while nondescript and purely factual on the surface, sets off a remarkably poetic series of associations about creativity and destruction, beauty and desperation, achievement and loss. This shot demonstrates, as well as any, a refined intensity of expression that surpasses Fisher's earlier films.

Many of the film's characters inspire similar associations. As usual in Fisher's films, their personalities are divided between self-control and indulgence, but this time one finds an almost obsessive concentration on creativity and futility. The sensitivity with which these figures are presented can derive only from Fisher's sense of his advancing age and physical infirmity. His identification with Frankenstein here reaches a point where the character, for all his ruthlessness, becomes sadly sympathetic in a way unprecedented in the series. He has become vulnerable, and therefore human.

It is this vulnerability that reveals the perspective of the nearly seventy-year-old Fisher at the end of his career. Like the director, Frankenstein at this stage in his life must struggle harder than ever just to continue and must make do with limited opportunities, but he is determined to carry on. "I knew you couldn't give up your work completely," Helder tells Frankenstein, who replies, "No, I haven't given up. I never shall!" However, he suffers from diminished physical abilities. Helder says that he thought Frankenstein was a "brilliant surgeon," yet the results he has seen belie that. "I was," responds Frankenstein, quietly. "I still am, in here," he adds, pointing at his head, and then explains about his burned, useless hands.

"You really are looking very tired," the asylum director tells Frankenstein early in the film. "Overwork, that's what that is." Much later, when Frankenstein decides that the creature's body is rejecting its new brain, he appears weary and drained, crushed by apparent failure. The brain, he says, will "deteriorate, decay, and finally rot to nothing." The creature, finally, will "become a cabbage and then he will die." Frankenstein here could be describing all of humanity, as age has its inevitable way with mind and body. Although the character's enthusiasm returns, the film never loses its aura of futility and desperation.

Other characters refine this sensitivity to lost creativity. Durendel, when he learns that his condition is incurable, gives up completely and kills himself. He, at least, could still produce art, but Tarmut is the embodiment of creativity lost. He had been a sensitive craftsman, until his brain atrophied. Now, all he can do is stare silently into space with an expression of lament and longing on his face. The sight of this man who has lost his ability to create is one of several such moving moments in the film.

Frankenstein's infirmity resulted from his work and Tarmut's has a biological explanation, but other characters have passivity imposed on them. Frankenstein insists that Durendel take medication, even though the patient doesn't want to "relax." Before the film's start, Frankenstein had done something similar to Schneider. After sedating him, he "removed a section of the sensory area of his brain. That made him unaware of his agony—or lessened it, at any rate." Schneider's pain was physical, but sedation is also available to lessen psychological pain.

Once Schneider's body contains Durendel's brain, this creature of contradictions suffers a psychological pain that resembles that of both Tarmut and Frankenstein. After examining his clumsy, misshapen body, he pleads, "Help me," and cries. As Frankenstein and Helder congratulate each other on their success, they (unlike Fisher) ignore their subject, who asks, "Why? Why?" Later, the creature that isn't quite Durendel can hardly pick up his violin, which he crushes in frustration. Fisher's handling of these characters' predicaments has a purity and a sensitivity that reveal his empathy with the plight of someone once able to produce creatively and now facing a loss or diminution of that ability.

Hammer producer Michael Carreras, years later, expressed regret that "the only picture I was able to give him [Fisher] in his later years was *Frankenstein and the Monster from Hell,*" a film with "the smallest budget and the tightest schedule he had had in a long time."[211] Fisher, however, remained true to his professionalism and, indeed, transcended it. Like Baron Frankenstein in the asylum, Fisher did the best he could with the materials available, in the end creating a film that, while it may be rough-hewn, has an inner intelligence and feeling.

The plot of *Frankenstein and the Monster from Hell* is direct and intense, and its many subsidiary overtones add to the film's power and stature. With this picture, Fisher bid farewell to the character of Frankenstein and, in effect, to his career. At the end, when dispersing the crowd of inmates, Frankenstein speaks as much for the filmmaker as for himself when he says, "There's nothing more for you to see. It's all over, now. All over." Shortly after, though, he speaks with renewed optimism of starting fresh, of continuing his work. There's "plenty of time," Frankenstein declares, but the scene's ironic, empty mood undercuts his words.

According to his wife, Fisher "enjoyed making" *Frankenstein and the Monster from Hell.* But, she added, "He was very sad because he always said that he was too old when he first went into the business. He said there were things he wanted to do, if he hadn't been so unwell. . . . But he could not do it, and he was very sad."[212] Although Fisher later spoke of possibly directing a film of Dennis Wheatley's *The Haunting of Toby Jugg,* there would, for him, be no more opportunities to continue his work. He died in 1980.

Fisher's last films reveal a refinement of style and feeling that, while appearing effortless, results from decades of polish and purification. He surely could have done more work, and spending the final years of his life in forced idleness could not have been pleasant. But he at least had the benefit, before he died at the age of seventy-six, of receiving the praise and attention of filmgoers who took his work as seriously as he did, sometimes more seriously.

Fisher noted that before he made *The Curse of Frankenstein* his career "had been attempting to find a line of direction."[213] With that film, everything coalesced. Stylistically and thematically, he had found his rightful milieu, one in which he discovered situations that interested him and, simultaneously, an unrecognized side of himself. But, he insisted, "a situation is worth nothing unless you are interested in the people who are involved,"[214] and Fisher's concern for the characters in his films helps make his work distinctive. "I came too late, in a way," Fisher said in 1974,[215] but he also came at just the right time, for his personal and professional maturity allowed him to put on the screen characters who changed the nature of horror films, while reflecting their director's outlook.

Terence Fisher preferred security and stability to status and, having found what he liked to do, he simply wanted to continue doing it. "The real task of the fantasy film director," he said, "is to bring integrity of intention to his film-making."[216] Because he achieved that, Fisher created strong, dramatic images of people confronted by what van Helsing called "a sickness partly physical, partly spiritual"—the insidious charm of timeless evil. To Fisher, the personification of that evil was also the personification of emotional temptation, of egocentricity. One must resist such temptation, his films imply, through self-discipline or else be destroyed by giving in to it. But cool objectivity can be equally destructive, so one must also nurture a basic feeling for humanity and act on it in a controlled, productive manner. Fisher clearly understood this aspect of the human condition and, because of his convincing depiction of how it falters, he must also have understood the alternative. Stability, he knew, is deceptive, and destructive passion can break through its surface at any time.

An instinctive and modest filmmaker, Fisher once referred to himself as "a simple old sod," then added insightfully that others, "who are far more talented than I am," have tried to make his kind of films "and they haven't made them as well. Really, I mean that. You have to be simple—but not inner simple, which is a different thing altogether."[217] Terence Fisher was a shy and private man, a loner who was also a loving husband and father, a compassionate man, a tower of moral strength. He understood human weakness and exemplified human virtues. He represented the best and contemplated the worst of human nature. Far from being "inner simple," he had an innate comprehension of the human personality's complexity. "Will we ever know who we really are?" asked Henry Jekyll. That was also the question posed by Terence Fisher many times, in many ways. It may be, though, that directing horror films helped Fisher to find an answer and contributed to his much-desired stability, for this gentle man's affinity for the genre surely reveals a need to vent, in a vicarious way, those strong emotions that he himself kept well controlled.

CHAPTER 5

Freddie Francis

At first glance, the directorial career of Freddie Francis closely resembles that of his fellow Englishman, Terence Fisher. Both men started directing fairly late in life and found themselves specializing in horror films almost by chance. Both worked for Hammer Films and often directed actors Peter Cushing and Christopher Lee. Francis even made sequels to Fisher's Dracula and Frankenstein films. Together, they dominated the British horror boom of the 1960s. However, their kinship exists only on the surface. In terms of professional background, visual style, plots, and themes—Freddie Francis stands apart as a distinctly individual artist. His most impressive films—such as *Paranoiac* (1963), *The Skull* (1965), *The Psychopath* (1966), *Torture Garden* (1968), *Mumsy, Nanny, Sonny, and Girly* (1970), *Tales That Witness Madness* (1973), and *The Doctor and the Devils* (1985)—could have been made by no one else.

Horror films had rescued Terence Fisher from the relative obscurity of impersonal programmers. Discovering within himself an affinity for the genre, he settled into a relationship with Hammer Films that brought him prominence and professional satisfaction. In contrast, Francis had already achieved wide acceptance as a subtle artist years before turning to direction. As a cinematographer—and, before that, as a camera operator—he had worked with major directors on big-budget, prestige pictures, some of which brought new styles and subjects into the British cinema. Critics often praised Francis's photography, and for *Sons and Lovers* (1960) he won an Academy Award. When Francis took over the director's chair in 1962, he surely hoped to make films as varied and substantial as those he had photographed. Instead, he became typed as a horror-film specialist. After making several good horror films on low budgets, he was offered nothing but more of the same. This thrust Francis into a world of filmmaking separate from the one he had known, and he found no lines of communication between it and the mainstream. "The sort of people I've been mixed up with as a cameraman," he explained around 1975, "that sort of circle of my friends, they obviously never see horror films. I don't even discuss my films with them, we don't talk about it."[1]

Such a circumstance must have felt like a retrogression, for low budgets and short schedules had not been an issue on a John Huston or Jack Clayton film. "It's jolly difficult to get the results I was used to getting as a cameraman on these sorts of budgets and schedules," Francis admits. However, as an artist and a dedicated craftsman, he refused simply to churn out a mediocre product. He also felt responsible for completing each picture on time and on budget. "I always say, because I think I have certain

Freddie Francis on the set of *The Skull* (1965). Equipped with roller skates, a hand-held camera, and a mock-up of the skull, Francis was rolled around the set so he could shoot from the skull's point of view.

standards, I try to make an eight or nine week picture in six weeks."[2] Although some-times defeated by the poverty level of a script, a budget, or a producer's sensibility, Francis did succeed with surprising frequency and many of his films reveal a visual subtlety rare on any level of filmmaking. In his best works, this stylishness blends with the content to create a truly cinematic whole.

At the same time, frustration inspired in Francis a tense ambivalence toward his suddenly circumscribed career. Although he generally enjoyed making his films, he often voiced antagonism toward the genre. "I would give anything not to be involved in this so-called horror realm," he declared in 1967. "I just seem to have gotten caught up in it. In this country, at least, it is rather difficult to break out of this rut."[3] Seven years later, he summed up the situation concisely: "Horror films have liked me more than I have liked horror films."[4]

Francis is particularly dissatisfied with traditional monster tales. "I simply cannot believe in monster films at all," he once declared.[5] Eight years later, he felt the same way, saying, "The thought of trying to *scare* somebody with a monster . . . just doesn't thrill me at all."[6] As a result, his contributions to Hammer's monster mythology—*The Evil of Frankenstein* (1964) and *Dracula Has Risen from the Grave* (1968)—reveal little empathy for their subjects. Francis lacks Terence Fisher's fascination with physical sensation and the stern morality of good confronting evil. His forte lies elsewhere, with stories of mood and suggestion, with atmospheric films that evoke the unseen terrors of someone victimized by his obsessions or those of others. On a practical level, this affinity for sug-gestion derives from Francis's natural fondness for using the camera to tell his story. From this perspective, an actor in monster makeup is a blunt and unconvincing pres-ence. Whatever can be seen can also be accepted and perhaps mocked, but intangible threats compel viewers to draw on their own dread of the nameless unknown.

To some people, and possibly to himself, Francis might seem an impersonal, unin-volved professional. He is not driven to make a "Major Statement" or to exorcise inner demons through the creative act, and his gentle good nature comes out when he comments, "If I thought the people were going to see this blood and think it was real and it was going to frighten them, I wouldn't want to make these sort of stories."[7] Francis considers his films to be games he plays with willing viewers. "I like to pull the audience's leg," he said in 1967,[8] and his best films work because he can manipu-late that audience through his command of movie technique. In fact, Francis is more aware and articulate about *how* he works than about any broad implications found in his films. Such a lack of self-consciousness is natural and necessary, but it should not be mistaken for the full person. There is more to Francis than a nice man playing harmless games. His films frequently contain intriguing resonances—implied links between evil and innocence, with subtly disturbing mixtures of tone—that cannot be dismissed so easily.

Like many people who have spent their lives in the movie business, rising gradually from the ranks, Francis views what he does as a highly satisfying occupation, little else. "I'm rather old-fashioned as far as films are concerned," he explains, "and I think the great days of films were when they were make-believe. I really have no other ambi-tion than to make films that will amuse or please the audience. There is very little more I want to get over to an audience." In fact, he declares longingly, "the only sort of film I should make is comedies," particularly sophisticated romantic comedies.[9] Over the years, Francis has nurtured several such projects, but financing could never be arranged.

Although Francis feels this pull toward comedy, he found "very few opportunities to introduce comedy into horror films," which he believes require a sincere approach.[10] "You can't do it tongue-in-cheek," he says, because audience laughter, except when it relieves tension, is "absolute death" for such a picture.[11] He does, however, respond when a chance appears. In the vampire segment of *Dr. Terror's House of Horrors* (1965), a doctor (Donald Sutherland) is convinced by the town's other physician (Max Adrian) that his wife is a vampire. After driving a stake through her heart, Sutherland is taken away by the police and Adrian denies all knowledge of the situation. Then, left alone, Adrian turns to the camera and declares, "This town isn't big enough for two doctors—or two vampires!" "I still think that the line is extremely funny," asserted Francis several years later, "and that any actor would give his right arm to say such a line."[12] He may be right, but a horror purist would probably view this story's flippant twist as an arbitrary and frustrating anticlimax.

A sequence in *The Evil of Frankenstein* is comic in a different way, because its humor derives less from dialogue than from Francis's staging. Baron Frankenstein (Peter Cushing), having returned to his hometown, learns that the Burgomaster has taken over his possessions. In anger, he rushes about the room identifying items stolen from him ("My chairs—my desk—my carpet—"), then looks into the bedroom and adds, "even my bed!" The statement is not in itself amusing, but Francis's composition juxtaposes Frankenstein's face with the bed containing the Burgomaster's young wife, and this prompts a viewer to notice how oblivious Frankenstein is to the voluptuous woman, which provokes at least a chuckle. Then, when the police arrive, Frankenstein locks himself in the bedroom. At this point, Francis cuts to the woman sitting up in bed, smiling with alert expectation. Here, her unexpected response—and its implications about her life with the Burgomaster—provokes understated humor, as the director uses editing to create a joke where none would otherwise exist. Frankenstein quickly makes a rope of some blankets, ties one end to the bed, and tosses the other over a balcony. After he says a polite "Goodnight" to the still-attentive woman, his weight pulls the bed across the room, and the Burgomaster's wife appears to enjoy the ride.

Taken on its own terms, this sequence maintains an effective balance between serious events and a humorous tone. However, its humor does disrupt the mood expected of a Hammer horror film, and its action requires a major shift in the character of Frankenstein, forcing this otherwise self-controlled individual to throw caution to the winds.

On a few occasions, Francis has even ventured into farce, usually in movies that feature his friend, entertainer Roy Castle. But such broad comedy ignores Francis's strengths, for it relies on the action itself and not on the manner of its presentation. Francis admits that the heavy-handed misadventures of Castle's character in the short feature *The Intrepid Mr. Twigg* (1969) "wasn't the sort of comedy I would like to do" and that he only directed the film "as a favor" to Castle.[13] That performer's self-conscious humor in *Dr. Terror's House of Horrors* and *Legend of the Werewolf* (1975) falls into the same category, as do the clumsy cavortings of almost everyone in *The Vampire Happening* (1971).

Francis's own, more idiosyncratic form of humor must be found elsewhere, often in isolated moments of perverse visual wit. In *The Skull's* prologue, for example, Francis cuts from the whiteness of a steam-filled room, as acid eats away at a severed head, to a plate of marshmallows on which a lounging woman nibbles. This quaintly sick visual pun, however, is surpassed by one in *The Psychopath*. While stalking a police inspector, a man falls to the floor and giant links of heavy chain pour down upon him, breaking his back. The sequence ends with a shot of his head protruding from this tangled pile, followed immediately by an equally tangled plate of spaghetti being eaten in a restaurant. In both of these cases, Francis views unpleasant facts through a half-amused eye as he places two carefully chosen images in unlikely juxtaposition, contrasting their subjects while finding a visual connection.

Francis makes extensive use of his subtle, personal humor in two productions that he originated, *Mumsy, Nanny, Sonny, and Girly* and *Tales That Witness Madness,* in which a stylistic twist thrusts grim events into an eccentric light. This tone develops logically out of the director's conception of horror films. "My approach to these films is that no one is really going to believe that these sort of things happen," he has said. "Though people may find it horrid for a while, they find it horrid in a *giggly* sort of way. Whether this is true or not I don't know. I may be fooling myself."[14] It may or may not be true, in general, but Francis finds the films horrid in this way and that outlook determines his approach to them, an approach that at its most successful creates a mood that is neither serious nor comic but an intriguingly individual fusion of the two.

All of this ambivalence provoked a good deal of psychological distress for Francis and led him into a fluctuating directorial career. His lack of affection for the genre sometimes allowed him to accept scripts from which nothing of merit could be fashioned, such as *Trog* (1970). At the same time, his resistance to the traditional monster tale channeled him into other, more appropriate paths. Given the opportunity, Francis can combine crisply efficient storytelling with a subtly oppressive mood, all executed in an admirably, even gracefully visual manner. Beyond this, he has used his quite British sense of morbid, understated humor to create scenes laced with a sadism made palatable by controlled style and dry irony. The resulting droll undertone turns the potentially repulsive into a distinctive form of wit that provokes a half smile instead of a grin or a laugh. Although Francis might have wished for a more stable and balanced career, his very special accomplishments more than outweigh the lapses. In fact, some of his best films draw on the inner tension between his skill at making horror films and his resistance to them.

Francis was born on 22 December 1917, in the Islington section of London. His early education was geared toward a career in engineering, but on leaving school in 1934, at the age of sixteen, he was apprenticed to a stills photographer at a nearby film studio. After two years he became a clapper boy and camera loader, and then moved up to the position of focus puller. "I was hovering somewhere between being a camera assistant and a camera operator" at the outbreak of World War II. In 1939, he joined the army, where he spent the next seven years. "Most of the time I was with various film units within the service, so I got quite a bit of experience in all sorts of jobs, including being a cameraman and editing and generally being a jack of all trades."[15]

On his return to civilian life, Francis rejoined the film industry. Except for work on *The Macomber Affair* (1946) as a second-unit photographer on East African locations, he "reverted back to being a camera operator" for ten years.[16] During this period, Francis operated on four major films written and directed by the team of Michael Powell and Emeric Pressburger: *The Small Back Room* (1948), *The Elusive Pimpernel* (1950), *Gone to Earth* (1950), and *The Tales of Hoffman* (1951). All of these were photographed by Christopher Challis, and Francis worked with Challis on three other films in 1952–53. He also made six films with cinematographer Oswald Morris, the best known of which were directed by John Huston: *Moulin Rouge* (1953), *Beat the Devil* (1953), and *Moby Dick* (1956).

By teaming regularly with the same photographers and directors, Francis no doubt became more of a creative collaborator than would someone hired for just a single project. This is especially relevant because a British cinematographer (or "lighting cameraman") concerns himself mainly with the lighting of a shot, while the operator handles those aspects directly related to the camera. Some cinematographers rarely even look through the viewfinder, so an operator's considerable responsibilities make him far more than an assistant.

Both Michael Powell and John Huston had an impact on Francis's approach to film production. From Powell, he "learned the adventure side of movies"[17] and "how to enjoy making films."[18] Powell himself described movie making as a journey of discovery on which he embarked "with people whom I like and admire."[19] For Powell, the key to this process was spontaneity, so he improvised his shots on the set, which turned work into exciting fun. Francis, too, thrives under such circumstances; he also shares Powell's belief that in films "images are everything," with dialogue and sound effects "used like music to distil emotion,"[20] creating an organic whole that blends "music, emotion, image and voices"[21] in a manner impossible in other art forms. *The Tales of Hoffmann* stands as Powell's ideal work, "the perfect composed film,"[22] and in *The Skull* Francis achieved something similar.

Francis also admires John Huston, declaring that several of the "most valuable lessons I've learned have been learned from him." Especially influential was Huston's desire "to tell as much of the story within any single frame as possible." Working with Huston, Francis realized that "whenever one lines up a shot one should say, 'What is the intent of this shot?' then look through the camera and if your intention doesn't at once strike you, then you've got the wrong shot!"[23] Although Francis in his films, leans more toward complex camera movements than Huston did, his compositions certainly reveal the influence of these lessons. In addition, Huston's *Beat the Devil* may have stirred Francis's sense of humor, for it was such a wry, unsmiling takeoff on tough mystery films that few contemporary viewers and critics found it amusing. Years later, two of Francis's most personal films would meet a similar fate.

Francis worked in several capacities on Huston's *Moby Dick*. Initially, he was the second-unit cameraman in charge of location shooting. "I photographed some live whaling out in Madeira. They still did whaling there with the old methods. We were chasing whales in an open boat."[24] Then, back in the studio, Francis headed a unit filming the model whales. During this time, he found himself in a situation "which nearly killed me. John and Greg Peck could only stay in the country a certain number of days. I was doing the special effects in the tank on the back lot. I was also operating on the main unit because Arthur Ibbetson was ill. To save time they had another second unit on the stage and John insisted that I operate on that unit, as well. So I was operating on two units and running my own at the same time! . . . It was a mad situation!"[25]

Huston was so pleased with Francis's efforts that "he just wanted me to stay operating for him for the rest of my life,"[26] but after *Moby Dick* Francis broke away to become a full-fledged cinematographer. His first film in that position was *A Hill in Korea* (1956), but the first truly important film he photographed was *Room at the Top* (1959), directed by Jack Clayton. "I'd known him for a long time, even before he started directing," explains Francis. "There was always an understanding between us that if he directed a film, I would photograph it."[27] *Room at the Top* follows a working-class youth (Laurence Harvey) in his ruthless rise to a higher social level. Clayton's sensitive direction and Francis's evocative photography of the gritty locations helped move the British cinema out of its traditional concern with polished urbanity and into an "Angry Young Man" period of social observation.

Francis also photographed the equally realistic *Saturday Night and Sunday Morning* (1960), which starred Albert Finney as a factory worker who counters his stifling job and environment with weekends devoted to seductions, beer, and back alley brawls.

This was the first feature directed by Karel Reisz, and the producers hired Francis "as a kind of insurance," as someone who is "there to be leaned on." He suspects that this occurred against the director's wishes. "Karel—with his background making documentaries—thought that because I was a features man I would therefore make everything look like a Hollywood musical, all glossy. But we became very firm friends, once Karel realized that I could be trusted to make the sort of film *he* wanted."[28]

Sons and Lovers (1960) continued Francis's association with working-class subjects. This adaptation of D. H. Lawrence's semiautobiographical novel dealt with the rebellion of a sensitive young man (Dean Stockwell) against the life represented by his coal miner father (Trevor Howard). *Saturday Night* had required calculatedly simple, lean photography, but this time Francis contrasted the sooty mining town with richer, more luxuriant images of the surrounding fields and forests, in keeping with Lawrence's almost Romantic response to nature.

Francis's last film as a photographer before turning to direction was *The Innocents* (1961), which reunited him with Jack Clayton. A considerable contrast to *Room at the Top,* this was an adaptation of Henry James's psychological ghost story, *The Turn of the Screw.* Deborah Kerr portrays Miss Giddens, a governess caring for two children on a large, isolated estate. Gradually she comes to believe that the spirits of Peter Quint, the perverse gardener, and Miss Jessel, her predecessor and Quint's lover, have taken control of the children. James's novella maintains a carefully ambiguous tone, refusing to establish for certain if the governess is correct about the ghosts' corrupting influence or if she is the victim of her own sexual frustration.

The film, too, maintains a note of subtle ambiguity, particularly in the performances of the children, Pamela Franklin and Martin Stephens. Film, however, is by its photographic nature a much more concrete medium than the written word, so although Francis's shots of the ghosts convey a hazy sense of subjective reality, the fact that they are seen at all gives the governess's conclusions a kind of validity. On the other hand, we are only perceiving things as the woman herself does. But no matter how a viewer reacts to this issue, *The Innocents* stands as a visually evocative, emotionally involving, and morally provocative ghost story—perhaps the cinema's finest.

Because Francis had already collaborated with Clayton on *Room at the Top* and because *The Innocents* depended on a mood created by its visuals, Francis worked closely with the director, exerting more influence on this film's style than he had on any other's. "I credit a lot of the film's success to Freddie," Jack Clayton has declared,[29] and in 1991 Francis admitted, "in that one, I achieved everything that I tried to achieve."[30] *The Innocents* is filled with images that provoke shivers without resorting to the blatantly grotesque. Some are realistic sights given disturbing overtones by their context and the heroine's point of view. In one case, the young girl cheerfully watches as a spider kills a trapped butterfly. At another time, Miss Giddens, alone in the garden, notices a broken piece of statuary in which one figure clasps two now-disembodied hands, holding tightly to an unseen figure. Then, in close-up, a large beetle crawls out of the figure's mouth, as if embodying the evil that dwells within the human form.

Generally, when we see the ghosts of Quint or Miss Jessel, some photographic quality keeps their figures from looking quite real. Miss Jessel, standing at the opposite side of a small lake, seems to be part of a cluster of reeds, while a shimmering veil of rain renders the image insubstantial. Similarly, when Quint is shown at the top of a tower, the sky's intense glare softens the figure's outline. Later, when the governess sees Quint peering through a window at her, the man's face emerges from pitch blackness and then disappears into it, which severs this vision from any surrounding realistic element.

When agreeing to produce *The Innocents,* 20th Century-Fox insisted that the film be shot in CinemaScope. "Neither Jack nor I," recalls Francis, "considered that this was a CinemaScope subject. We thought it was much too intimate for that." So Francis devised some camera filters that isolated a portion of the wide screen. "Instead of just centering our action and letting the rest of the frame go black, we graduated it off into dark areas of semi-exposure from which it seemed that something or somebody might pop out at any moment."[31] By this means, Francis turned a disadvantage into another way of suggesting the woman's perception of her surroundings, particularly when, with candle in hand, she hesitantly explores the corridors and rooms of the large house that she feels is possessed by evil spirits.

While working on *The Innocents,* Francis received an Academy Award for *Sons and Lovers,* an event that gave him, at the age of forty-three, a chance to start directing. "I had always been interested in making films, in any capacity, and one of the troubles with being a cameraman is purely and simply that so often one has to work with directors who are not very exciting. . . . And one always wants to get ahead, so I decided that I would direct my own films and make my own decisions. If the pictures were dull, it would at least be my fault."[32]

Francis directed six films and part of a seventh in about three years. "I wanted to do a lot of pictures very quickly," he recalls, to "make people think of me as a director rather than as a cameraman" and also "because I was enjoying myself so much . . . I could rarely refuse to do a picture." As a result, he "woke up one morning and found out that . . . I was classified as a horror film director."[33] From then until 1980, Francis's sole significant break from such low-budget genre films involved a temporary return to photography, on Karel Reisz's second film, the much underrated *Night Must Fall* (1964).

"I suspect it's a form of demotion," said Francis at the time, "but I respect Karel too much to refuse him this once."[34] *Night Must Fall* contrasts dramatically with Reisz's *Saturday Night and Sunday Morning,* and the differences suggest that Francis had considerable influence on its style. While making the earlier film, the two men had become friends and even joked about Reisz's static camera setups (which can also be seen in that director's subsequent films). But *Night Must Fall* features the kind of carefully choreographed moving camera shots that had already become a hallmark of Francis's horror films. "I guess, possibly because of his confidence in me as a cameraman and because I had become a director in my own right, Karel was able to let himself go more on *Night Must Fall.*"[35] While *Saturday Night* had a hard-edged, semidocumentary look, *Night Must Fall*—about a psychopathic murderer—possesses a brooding, sinuous, introspective quality.

Francis discounts any suggestion that *The Innocents* or *Night Must Fall* had struck in him a sympathetic chord that led to his directing psychological horror films. Still, the visual style of Francis the director does lend itself to such pictures. In other respects, as well, Francis felt comfortable making low-budget films. For one thing, he likes improvising on the set, which those films not only allowed but required. Actually, Francis explains, "the story of virtually every film I've been involved on has been told completely off the cuff, with a tremendous amount of improvisation. Most of these scripts have been no more than a pencilled working idea and, in fact, I have gone onto the floor with this pencilled idea and have told the story directly in my own way. With low-budget films, there are so many things one doesn't know until the last moment, such as what sort of actors and sets you are going to use, that it's almost necessary to improvise. Fortunately, I enjoy doing it this way."[36]

Although Francis rarely had much say in the selection of stories, he did have considerable independence in making most other artistic decisions. In the casting of actors, "I've had almost 100% choice except with a slightly higher budget film like *Torture Garden* (1968), for which we did have two artists—Jack Palance and Burgess Meredith—imposed on us. Fortunately, both were an absolute joy to work with and apart from them I had complete control of the casting, even of that picture."[37] One result of this has been the frequent re-use of certain performers. A director's familiarity with an actor—his knowledge of what to expect from him or her—proves invaluable when a film has a short shooting schedule. This applies not only to people like Peter Cushing, who starred in eight of Francis's features, but also to supporting players like Frank Forsyth and Geoffrey [Hedger] Wallace, who appeared in ten and eight films, respectively. No fewer than thirteen individuals have acted in at least three of Francis's movies. The same is true of the production crews: Francis worked with editor Oswald Hafenrichter and photographer Norman Warwick seven times each, and with photographer John Wilcox nine times.

"I've had complete control of the visual appearance of all my films," states Francis, and this is borne out by his approach to preparing a production. Initial readings of the script familiarize him with the film's content, but then he does not return to the actual script for some time. It is during the casting stage that the film's general concept begins to take concrete form. "Unless the writer is very good indeed," says Francis, "there are no characters at all in these scripts—just cardboard figures performing certain actions."[38] With the hiring of particular performers, these figures start to gain identifiable personalities.

Next, Francis selects locations, which adds more substance to the plot outline. Throughout this period, the need to answer questions about the characters, the story, and the settings prompts Francis to discover further facts about his film. Finally, a few weeks before shooting starts and while the sets are being constructed, he returns to the script, changing dialogue and making other specific adjustments. "I do plan out shots ahead of time, but that's usually just to have something I can deviate from on the set."[39] Thus, the film when shot has been completely visualized by the director, not simply transcribed from a script.

Francis enjoys working with actors, "but I'm terribly conscious that while they're working with me their careers, their reputations are in my hands and therefore I'm terribly sympathetic towards actors. . . . One has to work very hard to get their confidence."[40] A case in point is Veronica Carlson, whose inexperience on *Dracula Has Risen from the Grave* made her insecure, but she found Francis to be a "kind, gentle, lovable man, infinitely patient, as he needed to be with me."[41] Carlson was, she explains, "terribly naive," and Francis "controlled that naivety and . . . channeled it. He got exactly what he wanted."[42] In contrast, when working with the more experienced Peter Cushing, Francis would "just discuss the part at the beginning with him."[43] Cushing agreed, saying, "By the time I arrive to shoot, all the talking's finished."[44] On the set, Francis said, "I let Peter go ahead until I think it's time to change something."[45] Other actors, like Frank Finlay or Patrick Wymark, require still another approach. "This type of actor wants to have a reason for everything he does, and it's up to the director to give him a reason."[46]

Rarely has Francis had a preproduction period for rehearsal. Generally, his budgets permitted only a run–through before taking a shot. However, although the long takes and intricate camera movements that Francis favors require considerable time to set up, they are ultimately more efficient than filming a scene a number of times from different camera positions. Once such a shot has been planned out, there is little difficulty in running through it more than once for retakes, and several pages of the script can be filmed at once. This, of course, helps the actors, because they can perform without interruption, while making it difficult for producers to alter the film by reed-iting it later.

Much of Francis's work with his camera crew occurs before shooting starts. "It's important to get the right people working for you so that you have to spend as little time as possible with them when you're actually shooting. . . . One has to devote a lot of time in advance to working out the photographic style of the picture, try to get this across to the people doing it for you, and then not have to worry too much about it during the actual shooting."[47] Despite the complexity of his visual style, Francis main-tains efficiency because he can talk to the camera crew in their own language.

How would Francis's procedures have differed, had he been granted larger budgets? "I don't think one would like to have too much more time or money," he speculated in 1974.[48] He would want "a little more time" to work on the script and would "spend more on the actors playing the smaller parts and . . . on a little more coverage, which would in itself give us more time to characterize the people." As for the set-tings, "If I'm not capable of creating an atmosphere I don't think more expensive sets are going to help that." Even under low-budget conditions, he adds, "the quality of the lighting in these pictures would compare with any in films today." So, for this kind of picture, he would have liked an extra "week rehearsing the artists and possibly another week for shooting."[49]

Francis's first film as a director was *Two and Two Make Six* (1962), a flimsy romantic comedy with slightly serious overtones. Caught AWOL by a superior officer, an American soldier stationed in England (George Chakiris) shoves the man and, believ-ing he has killed him, flees on a motorcycle. He meets a girl, Irene (Janette Scott), who insists that he take her with him. Later, as they leave a diner, he and Tom (Alfred Lynch), another cyclist, accidentally switch girls. Most of the film depicts the romances that develop between these new pairs. Producer-scriptwriter Monja Danis-chewsky offered Francis this assignment "because I had photographed a film for him in the past [*The Battle of the Sexes* (1959)] and we had got on well together."[50] Look-ing back, Francis calls it a film "I should never have made. I didn't believe in the script but I got caught up with it and there was nothing I could do about it."[51]

The result is a not-unpleasant but minor work that draws its comedy less from the main characters than from such peripheral figures as a broken-down actor who clears a room of Americans by reciting Shakespeare. *Two and Two,* which offered Francis few chances to exercise his visual imagination, is at its most entertaining and stylish when Tom and Irene visit his eccentric Aunt Phoebe (Athene Seyler). Francis introduces this scene by moving his camera across a tapestry depicting graceful figures, down to an old-fashioned figurine on a mantelpiece, on to a phonograph, and then—in stark contrast—stopping on a chubby little girl dancing to the music. Here, the director uses a technique that would soon become typical of his style: He presents the viewer with a series of details, but does so gradually and gracefully in a single shot.

Dissatisfied with his first film, Francis agreed to help rescue *The Day of the Triffids* (1963), directed by Steve Sekely, in which a shower of meteorites renders most of the world blind and creates large plants that threaten to destroy humanity. "When they finished the film," recalls Francis, "they didn't think it stood up. I believe the distribu-tor would not accept it. I think that what went wrong with the film was that they thought this was a special effects film, so they'd just crash off the live action, get rid of the live action, and stress the special effects—but they hadn't done their homework on the special effects."[52] The film's uncredited producer, Bernard Glasser, acknowl-edges that he had difficulty "getting the Triffids to perform action called for in the script." Then, after he dropped "the special effects sequences that did not play," the picture's running time was too short[53] and the Triffids had become peripheral figures. In addition, the human characters are quite passive in their remaining Triffid encounters, and the survivors never devise a way to defeat the threat. Thus, the film lacked both energy and a climactic resolution.

To supplement this footage, Francis directed—without screen credit—a new subplot, set in an isolated lighthouse inhabited by a married couple. Tom (Kieron Moore) has lost interest in life, for reasons that remain unclear, whereas Karen (Janette Scott, who starred in *Two and Two*) still cares "what happens to us." Their struggle against the Triffids gives Tom a new reason to live, and the two work together to find a way to kill the plants. Ultimately, Tom discovers that sea water will dissolve them. "You hunt and you search and all the while the answer's right in front of you," he says at the end, referring to the discovery, but also to his newfound bond with Karen. The six lighthouse scenes offer what the film had previously missed: These characters are active, the threat of the Triffids is relevant to their personal situation, the limited setting creates a unity of focus, and the discovery of a solution provides an emotional and dramatic resolution.

Sekely's sequences for *Triffids* are competently crafted, but Francis's look far better in terms of lighting and camerawork, and they easily become the picture's highlights. Partly, this is because Francis recognized the absurdity inherent in the sight of ambulatory giant plants, so in his characters' first conflict with a Triffid he intercuts close shots of the creature with equally close shots of Moore lunging with a harpoon, which makes for an exciting fight and almost hides the plant's silly appearance. To his credit, the producer did not skimp on these scenes and allowed Francis a full five weeks for filming. *Day of the Triffids* as a whole is still only adequate, but Francis's nearly twenty-five minutes of footage could, if excerpted, stand as an independent and satisfying little story. Francis, however, feels that the lighthouse sequences are notable "not because they're particularly good, but because the other stuff is particularly bad."[54]

Although Francis's strengths had not clearly emerged in his first film, they were evident in *Day of the Triffids,* and he fully exercised them in his next film, *Vengeance* (1963; U.S.: *The Brain*). This loose adaptation of Curt Siodmak's 1942 novel *Donovan's Brain* was a West German–British coproduction filmed in England.

When the rich and ruthless businessman Max Holt dies in an airplane crash, Dr. Corrie (Peter Van Eyck) secretly removes his still-living brain and preserves it. Before long, the strong-willed Holt takes control of the doctor's thoughts and actions, causing him to suspect that the crash had not been an accident. Corrie, sometimes on his own and sometimes as "Holt," compulsively questions the relatives and associates of the deceased, discovering that no one regrets his death. Holt's daughter, Anna (Anne Heywood), and his lawyer (Cecil Parker) figure prominently, but Corrie also encounters Holt's wastrel son, his mistress, his chauffeur, and Immerman, a business partner and rival. After tunneling through a number of complications, Corrie learns (in the film's English-language version) that the daughter had arranged for the crash to prevent her father from keeping a newly discovered wonder drug off the market. At the end, although the brain has been destroyed, Corrie remains under Holt's influence.

Vengeance turned out to be a satisfying blend of science fiction (the doctor's experiments), horror (his possession by an outside force), and murder mystery (his investigation into the crash), and Francis staged the action with considerable imagination. Unfortunately, the production became the first of several unpleasant professional experiences for the director. A day or two before shooting began, he met with the film's English and German coproducers "to have a pleasant little get-together, but the outcome was that the German producer stated categorically that he wanted one of the German artists he was supplying to be the murderer. Raymond Stross, the English producer, was equally adamant that his wife, Anne Heywood, should be the murderess."[55] When neither man relented, the best solution would have been to shoot separate versions of the whole film for release in the two countries. But that would have lengthened the shooting schedule, which the producers refused to permit. Only the final confrontation could have dual versions, which meant that other scenes had to be written and acted with enough ambiguity that both endings would make sense.

"Every evening during shooting," recalls Francis ruefully, "I would have a talk with Pamela Davies, my continuity girl—who fortunately was a fabulous continuity girl—and we'd discuss what loopholes were left open. We'd say, 'The scene we shot today is alright for the version where Anne's going to be the murderer, but it won't work for the other one.' So I'd have to go home and rewrite the scene to plug up the hole the next day. But the whole thing was stupid, because we'd have scenes with the two people who were going to be the murderers at the end reacting completely wrongly for any situation." This problem was compounded by the fact that Peter Van Eyck took a strong dislike to Anne Heywood. By the time Francis shot the denouement scene, "Peter didn't want to do *any* scenes with Anne, so they had to be shot separately. Plus, we could only get Cecil Parker, who was in the same scene, on certain days, so he had to be done separately, too." The whole experience, declares Francis, "was absolute Hell—I'd never go through it again!"[56]

The scene in question does have two shots containing both Van Eyck and Heywood, but otherwise Van Eyck is isolated in large close-ups. At first, these are intercut with shots of Heywood and Parker together; then, as the scene builds, the director alternates between separate close-ups of Van Eyck and Heywood. It says much for Francis's talent and ingenuity that, having had this style imposed on him, he made it appear to grow naturally out of the scene, with Dr. Corrie visually isolated from and opposed to the others, who resist his questions. (The comparable scene in the German version unveiled Immerman as the guilty party.)

Francis rarely chooses to handle dialogue by intercutting static shots. Instead, he prefers long takes in which he varies the scene's stresses by shifting his characters between the background and the foreground and by moving his camera to follow one person or another. For example, an early scene begins with a stationary close-up of a television screen, on which a newscaster announces Holt's death. After someone enters the frame and switches off the set, the camera tilts up slightly, revealing the faces of Corrie and his female assistant; it then moves with them as they walk forward, talking. When they pass Corrie's other assistant (Bernard Lee), the camera stops on a close shot of him as he speaks, while the others continue into the background. Although Francis has, in effect, divided this scene into separate "shots" (the television set, Corrie and the woman, Lee), he has avoided the abruptness of cuts, opting instead for the fluid grace of actor and camera choreography.

Francis's direction frequently enlivens potentially ordinary scenes, such as the death of Holt's chauffeur. While Corrie questions him, a western is playing on a television set in the background. We leave the room with Corrie to take a telephone call, whereupon Francis cuts abruptly to an extreme close-up of a pistol on the television screen, which fires directly at the camera and momentarily shocks the viewer. Finding no one on the line, Corrie hangs up and returns to the room, where he discovers the man's dead body still sitting in front of the television set. Corrie flees and takes refuge in a dance hall. Hoping to lose himself among the couples, he grabs a partner but finds that a spotlight keeps seeking him out. When Corrie and his partner win the dance contest, the girl is urged to step forward. Francis stages this with deceptive simplicity: The girl walks toward the camera, away from the other dancers, and the women behind her suddenly scream. Bewildered, she turns around to face them and we see the cause—Corrie's bloody handprints on her back.

The basic situation of *Vengeance*—an invisible force asserting its will over the main character—brings out the best in Francis's style by allowing him to suggest this control visually, through such devices as the light bulb and graph attached to the brain or Corrie's thumb tapping, a habit associated with Holt. It also encourages the use of subtle lighting and camerawork to suggest a strong, unseen presence. One of Francis's many careful and appropriate compositions appears as Corrie talks with Immerman. When the doctor starts to take on Holt's personality, he is standing by a window, his back to the other man. Francis films this through the window, so that a vertical strip of wood separates the two opponents. Also, Immerman, seated in the background, is lit normally, but foreground shadows obscure Corrie's identity.

Francis is especially in his element when Corrie, just beginning to feel Holt's control, enters a room that replicates the Romanian kitchen where the tycoon was born. The scene begins with a parrot greeting Corrie with cries of "Hello, Max." A shot of Corrie looking around is followed by one of Holt's rocking chair swaying gently back and forth, as if still occupied by the man's indomitable personality. After another shot of Corrie, Francis uses a subjective tracking shot that moves around the room, examining objects. Suddenly, the camera starts tilting up and down; we aren't sure why, at first, but soon realize that we (Corrie) have taken over Holt's rocking chair. Cutting to an objective view of this, Francis wisely shows Corrie from behind, as the doctor experiences Holt's memories of the crash. By avoiding Corrie's face here, Francis seduces us into sharing the sensation of slipping into Holt's identity.

Because *Two and Two* and *Vengeance* received limited distribution and Francis was not credited on the more widely seen *Triffids,* it was his next four pictures—all directed for Hammer Films—that established him as a skilled and efficient director. They were *Paranoiac* (1963), *The Evil of Frankenstein* (1964), *Nightmare* (1964), and *Hysteria* (1965). Even the *New York Times* deviated from its usual condescension toward horror films, reviewing *Paranoiac* as an "economical little chiller" and praising Francis, who "detailed the incidents like a sharp-eyed hawk."[57] Although Francis did not realize it at the time, the quality and financial success of these films undermined his career plans, for they began the process of trapping him in the horror genre.

Paranoiac, Nightmare, and *Hysteria* form a trio of thrillers—inspired by Alfred Hitchcock's *Psycho* (1960)—that center on mentally unstable individuals. These films, all written by Jimmy Sangster, are concerned more with menacing moods and unexpected plot twists than with meaningful characterizations. "One occasionally had to make changes" in the scripts, Francis recalls, "because obviously there were great holes in them, but the trick was to keep them moving so that you didn't have time to see the holes."[58] *Paranoiac* has the tightest plot of the three, progressing rapidly through an impressive series of revelations. Eleanor (Janette Scott), a young woman living on a large estate, feels herself near madness when she "imagines" seeing the adult figure of her brother Tony, who had supposedly drowned himself as a child, an event from which Eleanor never fully recovered. Soon we discover that her other brother, the self-indulgent Simon (Oliver Reed), is plotting with a phoney nurse to hasten her complete collapse. The estate's executor has limited the funds Simon receives, but Simon in turn controls the executor's son with his knowledge of the young man's embezzlement.

When "Tony" (Alexander Davion) makes himself known, the question is whether or not he really *is* Tony. After he seems to satisfy the family—and the audience—that he knows everything Tony would know, we learn that the executor's son had hired him to fool the others and receive the inheritance. But "Tony" has fallen in love with Eleanor and reveals this to his coconspirator. Now, the emphasis shifts to attacks on "Tony," one of which involves a robed and masked figure wielding a longshoreman's hook. Meanwhile, Eleanor feels attracted to the man she believes is her brother. Crying, "I'm insane, I'm dirty," she attempts suicide, but "Tony" saves her and explains the truth. Ultimately, Simon is revealed as the insane one: As a child, he had murdered his brother and bricked the boy's body into the wall of an old chapel on the estate. Aunt Harriet, the current head of the household, has comforted and protected Simon, even to the extent of joining in a bizarre ritual by pretending to be young Tony, still alive.

Francis recounts this involved plot in a mere eighty minutes, so the viewer is kept in an almost-constant state of uncertainty. As a result, little opportunity exists for characterization, but the cast's solid ensemble acting helps cloak this fact, as do the characters' relatively believable actions. The work of Oliver Reed stands out, if only because the dissolute, sardonic, and hot-tempered Simon is the film's most dynamic figure.

The plot of *Paranoiac* separates neatly into halves—"Tony" as intruder, then "Tony" as potential victim—but the events are so tightly knit that the seam is barely noticed. *Nightmare,* however, breaks more obviously into two parts, and therein lies its main weakness. In this story, another young girl, Janet (Jennie Linden), has suffered a childhood trauma: On her birthday, she discovered her mother standing, knife in hand, over her father's dead body. Subsequently raised in a boarding school, she remains haunted by this memory. Near the film's start, Janet returns to her home, an isolated mansion. There, her fear that she has inherited her mother's madness grows, as a female specter lures her through the building's nighttime corridors to a room where she finds the specter's dead body and a birthday cake. Eventually, dream and reality blend for Janet when, at another birthday party, her sympathetic relative, Henry (David Knight), introduces his wife, who resembles the menacing specter. Janet, in a panic, grabs the cake knife, kills the woman, and ends up in an asylum.

The film's attention now shifts to Henry, who, with his lover, had planned the simultaneous elimination of Janet (his rival for an inheritance) and his wife. Together, they staged the girl's recent "visions," with the lover wearing a rubber mask modeled on the wife's features. These conspirators, however, soon start bickering, and the woman begins to suspect that Henry plans to eliminate *her.* In a sense taking Janet's place, she stabs Henry. Any viewer who pauses for a moment's thought during this part of the film would realize the truth—that the criminals' own tactics are being used on them—but events move so rapidly and the viewer is so intrigued by revelations about the first half that the climax tends to be a surprise.

For *Hysteria,* Sangster made his central character a man instead of a vulnerable young woman, and he eliminated the inheritance angle, but in general the formula remained the same. After an auto accident, Chris Smith (Robert Webber) suffers from amnesia, on top of which some inexplicable events prompt him to question his sanity: An unknown person has paid his hospital bills, then provided him with an apartment; he hears angry voices from the empty rooms next door, where a bloodstained knife turns up, then disappears; he has fleeting visions of a woman who had supposedly been stabbed to death in the building months before.

Finally, the same woman, Denise (Lelia Goldoni), introduces herself as his benefactor and the widow of the man who drove the car at the time of the accident. But she claims to have only just returned to London, and the voices continue. The script then admits us into Smith's memory of the events that led to the accident, and although the writer inserts these scenes abruptly, Francis provides a gradual transition through a shot that moves from detail to detail, slowly revealing information. First, we note that the room is unfamiliar; the sight of male and female feet at the end of a brass bed adds another piece to the puzzle; we follow a woman's hand as it brings a cigarette to her lips and lights it (we don't recognize her), then she passes it to her partner (it is Smith). We now understand the nature of the new scene and are ready for the dialogue that explains its context.

Ultimately, it turns out that Denise and Smith's psychiatrist have conspired to frame him for the murder of the doctor's wife, which explains the preceding inexplicable events. Like *Paranoiac* and *Nightmare,* this film has a major break partway through, but it is only the shift to the flashback. Unlike the other films, *Hysteria* has only one major plot twist, the final explanation. Denise's arrival does not quite qualify as a twist and Smith's statement at the end that he really had his memory all along may prompt us to re-view the film, but it doesn't change our interpretation of events. *Hysteria* is interesting, but it has a slow pace, with too little plot and too few characters for feature length. In all three films, however, Francis's camera prowls darkened corridors with the main character, making us share that person's feeling that the very air is laden with irrational menace. Such scenes are reminiscent of *The Innocents,* and, at times, Francis even uses the special filters he developed for the earlier film.

Paranoiac's script is the most complex and convincing of the three, and Francis rises to the opportunity. In the opening sequence, he introduces the main characters and conveys Simon's personality with remarkable economy. First, outside a country church we see the tombstone of "Antony Ashley," which informs us that he died in 1953 at the age of fifteen; his parents' inscription establishes their deaths as occurring in 1950. Inside the church, as the vicar speaks about the situation, the camera moves from him to the listeners, pausing on the faces of first Aunt Harriet and then Eleanor just as those individuals are mentioned. When the vicar adds that Simon plays the church organ, Francis cuts to some sheet music propped against the behind-the-scenes instrument. A puff of forbidden smoke enters the frame, followed by a hand holding a cigarette; it adjusts the music and the camera follows it to a close shot of Simon's face. As the vicar speaks about Simon's "sorrow," we see the contradiction of his sarcastic smile. In just a few shots, Francis has identified the background events and most of the main characters, while establishing their relationships and conveying Simon's nature. The director has also provided some purely aesthetic satisfaction, through his gracefully moving camera, his careful apportionment of subjects within the frame, and his creative juxtaposition of sound and image.

For harsher scenes, Francis trades tracking and panning for rapid editing. In *Nightmare,* he uses this technique for the flashback in which Janet discovers her parents. After a tracking shot of the girl arriving home, greeting the housekeeper, and running upstairs, Francis cuts abruptly to a close-up of the child screaming, followed by a point–of–view shot of the birthday cake, the father's body, and a hand holding a bloodstained knife. He next reveals the murderer's identity with a close shot of the mother holding the knife, followed by an ironic close-up of the cake. Only then does he provide a long shot that includes the girl with the father's body and the mother. In this way, Francis builds the scene's impact by parceling out the tableau's details.

At the same time, this scene's distant shots reveal carefully balanced compositions. For example, the final shot places the body along the bottom of the image, with the mother on the right side, counterbalanced by the bed's headboard on the left. The remaining space in the center reveals Janet screaming in the background doorway. The

A carefully composed shot of George A. Cooper, Moira Redmond, Irene Richmond, and Brenda Bruce in *Nightmare* (1960) illustrates Freddie Francis's use of the wide screen.

large shapes that fill the screen's sides make Janet appear surrounded and helpless, and although she is the smallest figure in the shot, her central position attracts the viewer's eye and gives her prominence. In this brief shot, Francis follows one of the "rules" he learned from John Huston: His composition instantly conveys what is most important, and it does so in a visually satisfying manner.

Francis directed only two other Hammer films, both of them sequels to films made by Terence Fisher. *The Evil of Frankenstein,* the studio's third feature in its series, was released on a double bill with *Nightmare;* four years later, Hammer brought Francis back for *Dracula Has Risen from the Grave* (1968). Both pictures reveal his lack of response to traditional Gothic material, and his visual handling rarely improves on the derivative, episodic scripts by John Elder (producer Anthony Hinds).

The plot of *The Evil of Frankenstein* consists of four almost-independent segments that never cohere into a unified whole. During the first ten minutes, Frankenstein (Peter Cushing) obtains a body and returns its heart to life, then is interrupted by a priest who smashes the equipment. Later, in his deserted "chateau," Frankenstein tells his assistant, Hans (Sandor Eles), why he had been banished from the village. In a ten-minute flashback, we see the creation and short life of his first monster (Kiwi Kingston). Next, the film spends ten more minutes on Frankenstein's adventures in the village, where he crosses paths with Zoltan (Peter Woodthorpe), a "mesmerist" who is himself ordered out of town for lack of a performance permit. After Frankenstein attempts to reclaim his belongings from the Burgomaster, a deaf and mute girl (Katy Wild) gives him and Hans refuge in a mountain cave. Now, at its middle point, the film's meandering plot gains focus. In the cave, Frankenstein finds his first creation frozen in ice. He revives it, but the brain remains dormant, so he has Zoltan hypnotize the monster. Then, Zoltan uses the monster to punish those who banished him. In the climax, the mesmerist dies, Hans escapes with the girl, and an explosion destroys Frankenstein and his creation.

Because Universal-International financed and released this movie, its storyline integrates Hammer's conception of Frankenstein with undigested elements from earlier Universal films: The laboratory draws electricity from lighting, as in *Frankenstein* (1931); the fair and its menacing mesmerist derive from *The Cabinet of Dr. Caligari* (Germany, 1920), by way of its Universal clone, *The Murders in the Rue Morgue* (1932); Zoltan's use of the monster for revenge originated in *Son of Frankenstein* (1939); the discovery of the monster in ice comes from *House of Frankenstein* (1944); and a defective heroine appeared in *House of Dracula* (1945).

Francis felt "fairly worried" about *The Evil of Frankenstein.* "I did think the original Karloff *Frankenstein* was really a great film," he said, and he feared that his small budget would limit his film's quality in contrast to James Whale's production. Deciding that one of the most important ingredients was "a good-looking, interesting, and exciting" laboratory set, he convinced the studio to spend a large share of the budget on elaborate electrical machinery. An equally important element, he felt, was the depiction of the monster as "a gentle giant."[59]

In the main laboratory sequence, Francis devotes more than nine minutes to totally visual storytelling. Unfortunately, although the equipment glows and flashes as Frankenstein throws assorted switches, this action occurs early in the film and during a flashback, so it has little dramatic impact. As for the monster, Francis's attempt to present him as a sympathetic victim fails. The monster's makeup, created by the usually reliable Roy Ashton, looks like a cross between Boris Karloff's square skull and the blobs of putty applied to Christopher Lee for *The Curse of Frankenstein* (1957). As a result, Kiwi Kingston's head is an exaggerated box, and his face looks like a white mud pie. In addition, this monster's reactions to fire and food reveal the difference between a wrestler hired for his build and an actor. On top of everything else, the sequence completely contradicts Hammer's account of events in *Curse.*

In another break from Hammer tradition, this Baron Frankenstein (played, as before, by Peter Cushing) is not the person found in Terence Fisher's films. In the flashback, no one is killed and only Frankenstein and the monster are injured; during the main body of the film, Frankenstein is a thorough victim who does little damage himself, especially in contrast to the righteously destructive priest, the blustery and irrational Zoltan, and the pompous, corrupt officials of Karlstaad. Frankenstein's arrogance has become a kind of self-mocking wit, as when Hans says, "You were right, as always," and the Baron replies, "Not always, Hans. Frequently—not always." Frankenstein even makes a joke, as he and Hans head to town for dinner. The worried assistant asks, "Do you think it's safe?" and Frankenstein, with a smile, responds, "What—the food?" He also reveals an almost gentle solicitude when he asks, "Why do you stay with me, Hans? . . . You get nothing but misery with me." Equally unprecedented is the way Frankenstein loses his composure when confronting the Burgomaster.

Francis may have chosen to elaborate on the flashback's events and on Frankenstein's semicomic encounter with the Burgomaster, while confining the contrived main plot to the film's second half. Revealingly, his best, most atmospheric work appears before the script's limitations intrude. The film's first shot uses a moving camera for dramatic impact and to provide a variety of images. From a distant view of trees, the camera tilts down past a lake to a cabin; an elderly couple leave and the camera pans to follow them. The calm mood is suddenly disrupted when a man's hand enters the frame in the extreme foreground and grasps a tree limb, then the man's body rises into a medium shot as he watches the now off-screen couple. Finally, he turns and moves into a close-up. Inside the hut, Francis shifts between objective and point-of-view shots to control the information we receive. First, he shows a corpse laid out on a rough-hewn table. When a confused and frightened girl looks into the room, a breeze blows out the candles that illuminate it. The film proceeds with the following:

- Medium close shot of the girl, startled.
- Close-up (from the girl's perspective) of the corpse's feet, which start to move as the body slides slowly to the right. The camera pans, keeping the feet in view.
- Medium close shot of the girl. She screams and starts to run.
- Medium long shot of the girl reaching a door and trying to open it, her back to the camera.
- The camera still follows the feet until it reaches a window at the end of the table. Through it, we see the man observed earlier as he hefts the corpse onto his shoulder.
- Medium long shot of the girl at the door. She turns and looks past the camera.
- Medium shot of the window and table, with both corpse and man gone.
- Medium long shot of the girl at the door, which opens, and she runs out.

In these shots, Francis conveys the child's perception of events, compelling us to share her sense of the irrational. Then, at just the right moment, he reveals what the girl has failed to notice and lets us in on the rational explanation. By solely cinematic means, the director has involved the viewer in a scene that, as the story progresses, remains the film's psychological and emotional highlight.[60]

During these years, Francis's only nonhorror film was *Traitor's Gate* (1964), an Edgar Wallace crime drama about an attempt to steal the Crown Jewels from the Tower of London. "I didn't think it was a very good picture," the director admits.[61] As with his earlier Anglo-German coproduction, the international politics weighed heavily on this picture. As a result, its generally tight construction is disrupted by the periodic intrusions—insisted on by the German producer—of a comic German tourist (Eddi Arent).

After making all of these films, Francis spent four years in close association with Amicus Productions, which—like Hammer—specialized in low-budget horror films. Milton Subotsky, the studio's creative head, had a fondness for the genre and for visual filmmaking that resulted in several imaginative and expensive-looking features. Francis's first Amicus film was the multi-episode *Dr. Terror's House of Horrors* (1965). Subotsky, who admired the 1945 episode picture *Dead of Night,* decided that "the time was ripe for another film like it."[62] The success of *Dr. Terror* led to more short-story compendia from Amicus, including Francis's own *Torture Garden* (1968) and *Tales from the Crypt* (1972). Explaining his attraction to such films, Subotsky said, "It's very hard to sustain a single story over ninety to 100 minutes. . . . With a multi-story film, we can tell four or five stories, with no fear of boring the audience."[63] For Francis, these pictures presented a "creative challenge because each story has to have a style of its own."[64] In addition, he said, one of the episodes might be a story "that you would like to make a feature of, so it's like enjoying yourself on a film you like, in a film that maybe you don't enjoy as much."[65]

Of course, the virtue of variety is countered by the episodes' brevity. Most of the stories are so full of events that they offer little room for characterization. Such concise narrative can result in a satisfying economy of means, but it just as often creates a feeling that everyone is going through the motions, making the plot points that must be made to reach the end. This problem is compounded by the fact that viewers

Passengers on a train with Dr. Terror (Peter Cushing, second from left), who in telling their futures provides the framing story for *Dr. Terror's House of Horrors* (1965). (From left to right are Christopher Lee, Cushing, Alan Freeman, Neil McCallum, Roy Castle, and Donald Sutherland.)

familiar with the usual type of framing story know from the start that each main character will probably meet an unpleasant end.

At times, the presence of the framing story itself causes logical problems. In *Dr. Terror,* the mysterious Dr. Schreck (Peter Cushing) tells the future of five other railroad passengers. The episodes illustrate his predictions; after each story concludes, a card from his Tarot deck presents death as an alternative to that future, yet at the film's end the men learn that the train has crashed and that they are already dead. Similarly, *Tales from the Crypt* has a cluster of people tour a crypt, where a robed figure informs them of their future experiences. At the end, they too realize they are already dead, so there is no time when those future events could occur. This leads to another contradiction: Although all of *Crypt's* characters are supposedly dead at the end of the framing story, not all of them die in their episodes. In fact, one story ends with a man brought back from the dead and granted eternal life. Of Francis's three Amicus anthologies, only *Torture Garden* avoids such inconsistencies.

Dr. Terror has the best of the framing stories because it is interesting in itself. This is partly due to Peter Cushing, whose performance as Schreck shades from gentle charm to grim intensity, and partly to the quietly chilling climax. The script reportedly had the train simply enter a tunnel, with a newspaper headline then announcing the characters' deaths in a crash. Francis elaborated on this by having the train emerge from the tunnel, only now Dr. Schreck is gone. The train stops at a station, and the men disembark onto a dark, deserted platform. A newspaper blows into view; examining it, they read of the train accident and their deaths. Looking up, they see Schreck standing with his back to them. The figure turns, revealing a skull instead of a face, then walks off into the shadows and the men resignedly follow.

The main body of *Dr. Terror* consists of five "original" stories by Milton Subotsky, who included every "classic" (or clichéd) plot device: a werewolf, a vampire, a creeping vine, a crawling hand, and a voodoo curse. These stories are stale, but the excellent production values and Francis's lavish dispensing of atmosphere and detail help cloak their weaknesses. Only the "disembodied hand" episode comes close to total success because it centers on a single dramatic situation, which eliminates the need to rush through several complications and explanations. This, in turn, allows time to develop the situation and its thrills. With only two main characters, one of whom dies partway through, the segment has a powerful, pared-down simplicity.

Both characterizations are swiftly, deftly etched in the first scene, as a smug art critic, Franklyn Marsh (Christopher Lee), publicly ridicules the work of soft-spoken Eric Landor (Michael Gough). Lee, with his imposing voice and demeanor, immediately convinces us of Marsh's ruthless arrogance, and Gough succeeds equally well at what may be the harder task, arousing our sympathy without appearing pathetic. Gough also tends to hold his hands at chest level, in a natural-looking gesture that subtly draws our attention to his character's artistic tools. After mocking Landor's paintings, Marsh overconfidently praises an unknown artist's canvas. He then is introduced to the artist—a chimpanzee! Humiliated, Marsh later runs Landor down with his car, and one wheel crushes the artist's right hand. Landor lives, but the hand is amputated.

Next, in a well-executed series of shots, Francis combines efficiency and emotional insight. Starting with a close-up of a painting displayed in an art gallery's window, the camera pans away, past a close-up of Landor's name on the exhibition's poster, and pauses on a close-up of his reflection in the glass (which creates a visual link between the man and his work). The camera then moves to a close-up of Landor himself, an expression of tormented sorrow on his haggard face. As Landor looks down, the camera descends to a close-up of his bandaged stump. Having established the man's condition in a single moving-camera shot, Francis changes settings by dissolving to a close-up of the stump as the other hand pulls open a drawer that contains a pistol. After a medium shot of Landor's head and shoulders, the hand in close-up grasps the pistol; the camera rises with the hand, then centers on a medium view of Landor's reflection in a mirror as he starts to point the pistol at himself. In an extreme close-up, the gun barrel turns to point directly at the camera. It fires and drops, and the hand descends, claw-like, out of the frame. Then, a new scene begins with a close-up of Landor's severed hand crawling slowly into view on the back of an automobile seat, approaching Marsh.

This brief sequence reveals Landor's suicide clearly and concisely, without a wasted moment. It links disparate events and locations by making transitions between similar images (from stump to stump, from hand to hand) and, by keeping physically close to Landor, creates empathy for a character we have known for only a few minutes. Even more impressively, Francis depicts the man's thoughts and feelings visually: The perfectly chosen images of the first shot convey the emptiness of Landor's ruined life. If this isn't "art," it misses only because the sequence does not exist solely for the sake of the character but is needed to set the viewer up for the thrills to come. It is, at any rate, as good a bit of cinema as one is likely to find.

The rest of the episode depicts Marsh's excruciating attempts to rid himself of the implacable hand. He throws it through the car window, thrusts it into a blazing fireplace, stabs it with a letter opener, and wraps it in a box that he tosses in a river. No

Franklyn Marsh (Christopher Lee) recoils from the disembodied hand in *Dr. Terror's House of Horrors* (1965).

matter what Marsh does, the hand keeps reappearing—without the writer or director attempting an explanation, a wise decision that eliminates potential distractions and makes the hand's presence more disturbing. Finally, the hand grasps Marsh's windshield wiper during a rainstorm, causing an accident that blinds the critic, depriving him of his life's work just as Landor had been deprived of his.

Dr. Terror's other segments are almost as well directed as this one, but their plots offer less support, especially the thin creeping vine and vampire stories. In the werewolf tale, Francis's elaborate camerawork and lighting build tense anticipation as the hero enters a cellar and examines an old sarcophagus, but this story tries to be tricky and ends up making little sense. "Voodoo," the middle segment, offers a change of pace with some unfunny comedy and prolonged musical numbers. A flippant musician (Roy Castle) steals the music of a West Indies voodoo ceremony and, despite warnings, adapts it into a London nightclub act; his performance literally blows up a storm, as a wind rises and drives the customers out. This story only comes to life after the comedy and music fade, when the musician walks along a dimly lit street, pursued by threatening gusts of wind, and then trembles in his apartment while the windows and doors slam shut and the lights go out. In an anticlimax, a tall native enters, takes the sheets of music, and departs.

Before his next episode film, Francis directed four other features for Amicus—*The Skull* (1965), *The Psychopath* (1966), *The Deadly Bees* (1967), and *They Came from Beyond Space* (1967)—the first two of which are almost-flawless thrillers. *The Skull,* in particular, is a horror classic, drawing more completely than any other film on the director's strong points. Adapted from Robert Bloch's 1945 short story "The Skull of the Marquis de Sade," it stars Peter Cushing as Christopher Maitland, a researcher into the occult who adds de Sade's skull to his collection of black magic objects and is destroyed by the demonic spirits that inhabit it. Milton Subotsky's screenplay elaborates effectively on Bloch's plot, and Francis deftly employs visual style to evoke unseen, nameless powers, using mood and suggestion to escalate the viewer's dread. In the film's second half, as Maitland's environment becomes his antagonist, *The Skull's* subtle, atmospheric images vividly convey the plot—indeed, they virtually become the plot—to create a truly cinematic whole that taps into our fears of the unknown.

Bloch's story begins as a shady dealer named Marco arrives at Maitland's house to sell the exotic relic. With the plot instantly set in motion, Bloch has little room for characterization, so Maitland starts out as an irritable and impatient collector whose obsession already almost controls him. Bloch's Maitland is never sympathetic because he has nothing to change from or to lose; the arrival of the skull merely exaggerates his prior condition. The film, however, gives Maitland a wife (Jill Bennett), and, as he initially interacts with her and others, we discover a stable man convinced of his own rationality and self-control. This quality is implied by the dialogue and reinforced by Peter Cushing, who readily conveys inherent decency. The film thus adds subtlety and conflict, turning Maitland into a battlefield, the site of an intense struggle against corrupt, destructive forces that seek to dominate his moral nature—a struggle that, despite his ultimate death, Maitland does in fact win.

In the story, Marco mentions that a phrenologist originally exhumed and examined the skull, which then passed into the hands of a Dr. Londe. This prompted the filmmakers to add a prologue depicting the phrenologist's actions, which grabs the viewer's interest and hints at the skull's powers right away. As a result, fearful anticipation permeates the air, even though the skull does not return until several scenes later. Also in the story, Maitland once discusses the skull with a previous owner, his friend and fellow collector Sir Fitzhugh Kissroy. Subotsky renames this man Sir Matthew Phillips and gives him three additional scenes (which makes the role large enough to accommodate Christopher Lee as a guest star).

After the prologue, *The Skull* shifts to the present day, introducing its three main characters at an auction as Sir Matthew examines some books, which the camera follows until it reaches Maitland, while Marco (Patrick Wymark) hovers nearby, keeping a careful watch. When bidding starts on four statuettes of demons and Sir Matthew compulsively offers more than they are worth, Francis places Sir Matthew in very tight close-up as he stares intently, oblivious of the others clearly visible in the background. Here, and throughout the film, the director makes thorough use of his wide anamorphic image, filling the screen with important figures or objects, setting up relationships within a single composition, leaving no space unused. Francis's adaptability to this sometimes awkward screen shape may explain why *The Skull* is not as generally admired as it should be, for the virtues of this and certain other Francis films are less evident in their panned-and-scanned video versions.

Soon after the auction, Marco pays one of his frequent visits to Maitland's study. Maitland's wife, who obviously dislikes Marco, enters the room first to announce his arrival, and the way Francis handles her entrance and Marco's is worth noting. After the wife steps into the room, Francis cuts directly to a long shot of Maitland; the woman then walks into view, and their conversation begins. This simple, efficient presentation contrasts sharply with Marco's entrance shortly after. When he comes in, the camera moves across the room with him, as statuettes and the contents of a glass display case pass in the foreground. This establishes a new mood and creates a subtle link between the visitor and the black magic paraphernalia that is his stock-in-trade. With these two entrances, Francis visually contrasts the normal, everyday world of Maitland and his wife with the more exotic one associated with Marco.

Subotsky takes Bloch's brief reference to a book bound in human skin, already owned by Maitland, and creates a scene in which Marco sells it to him. This gives the film a chance to develop the characters and their situation before plunging ahead with the main plot: We learn about Maitland's researches, about the objects and layout of the room, and about Marco's function. Because the book is a biography of de Sade, Marco also offers some facts about the man, facts that Bloch had provided in the form of Maitland's thoughts. Later, the book will figure in the climax.

Finally, Marco returns with the skull and the film picks up the beginning of the short story. As Marco explains the object's history, we return to the prologue's events, which had been left tantalizingly incomplete: The phrenologist has been found dead, and the executor of his estate, Dr. Londe (George Coulouris), is forced by the skull to stab the man's mistress. At this point, Francis films a shot from the skull's point of view, so that we see the characters through its eye sockets. This is an understandable attempt to give the inert object an aura of awareness, but it feels contrived and obvious. However, Francis then employs the device as a transition by changing what is seen through the sockets from the woman's body and Dr. Londe to Marco and Maitland. This smoothly establishes a continuity between past and present and makes viewers feel the undiminished strength of the forces residing within the skull. Later, Francis uses this camera position again. "Because it was my idea and because it was a peculiar personal thing," he explains, "I in fact operated the camera on those shots,"[66] using a handheld camera with a large skull mock-up mounted on the front. At times the skull had to follow the characters' movements, so Francis wore roller skates and had himself pushed around.

Much of the dialogue during Marco's second visit, in which we learn of his willingness to lower his price and Maitland's decision not to buy the skull, derives directly from Bloch's story. Bloch then has Maitland suffer a paranoid dream, but the film saves that for later and moves directly to Maitland's conversation with Sir Matthew. Francis begins this scene with a medium long shot of Maitland standing in a room decorated with strange objects. He stares forward intently. The image is bathed in an eerie glare that creates a peculiar, unsettling effect. Maitland appears to be in another reality, one linked with the power of the book and the skull. Still concentrating, he bends forward and the camera retreats. This shift removes the glare, which we now realize came from some overhanging lamps, and we see that Maitland is merely playing a game of billiards. This shot is much more than a cheap attempt to trick the viewer. It is, in fact, a brilliant way of bypassing explicit external reality to depict the supernatural aura that surrounds the unsuspecting character.

During the conversation of Maitland and Sir Matthew, Subotsky makes a significant change from Bloch's dialogue: Sir Fitzhugh's claim that human members of secret cults had broken into his home to worship the skull has become Sir Matthew's assertion that "spirits from a strange, evil world" had made use of it. This feeds directly into the film's climax, which emphasizes unseen supernatural forces. Because the skull and those spirits needed one of the demon statuettes, they compelled Sir Matthew to buy it at the auction. Sir Matthew also says that he felt a call to join the ceremonies. Maitland responds that *he* wouldn't resist. "Make a good chapter for one of my books," he declares, with glib confidence.

Now the exposition has ended, and the rest of the film, fully half of it, develops the basic situation: Maitland's growing loss of self-control. While he sits in his study reading the de Sade biography, spectral forces assert themselves through the objects that fill the room. In a series of splendidly conceived shots, these occult artifacts hover large in the foreground, while Maitland, oblivious, remains a smaller, helpless background figure. Francis isolates him in the precarious security of a tiny pool of light, while masks and blades loom authoritatively in the surrounding gloom. Some shots begin with a close view of an object, then shift horizontally or vertically to bring Maitland into view. These compositions and movements, and the overall rhythm as each shot dissolves into the next, impart a throbbing sentience to the inanimate decor, as if the forms were joining in a massed infusion of power.

This scene, with its full-bodied relish of dream-like images, was something that Francis "thoroughly enjoyed" making, "because it was truly a visual telling of a story." The excellent results were obtained partially by selecting the right person (Scott Slimon) to dress the set and "then letting him run riot. I always like to have my sets, when I go onto them, mildly overdressed so I can pick out the best prop to use to make a particular point. On this occasion, we had somebody who could understand everything there was to know about black magic and we were inundated with various objects which we were able to use. In fact, I could have gone on creating various scenes within Peter Cushing's study for the rest of my life and enjoying it. It was one of the things that works out just right on a picture!"[67] The shooting script had merely called for a close shot "of pages turning, CLOSE UPS of the engravings in the book, and shots from various angles of MAITLAND as he reads and turns pages." Thanks to Francis's creative improvisation on the set, Subotsky's desired effect of Maitland's "almost hypnotic absorption in the reading" is fully achieved, and much more besides.

The footage of Maitland in his study leads unobtrusively into his dream (if dream it is), so that we never actually see him fall asleep. In Bloch's story, the dream involved two masked and black-robed men who whip Maitland, then place him in an iron maiden; as the torture chamber's lid closes on his face, Maitland realizes that it contains not the usual spikes but the demonic skull. Revived after this ordeal, he looks in a mirror and sees, reflected back at him, the skull where his own head should be. The film retains the idea of such a dream, but discards Bloch's details. Seemingly influenced by Alfred Hitchcock's *The Wrong Man* (1956), and possibly Orson Welles's *The Trial* (1963), Subotsky and Francis have two trench-coated, taciturn "policemen" invade the security of Maitland's home, declare that he is under arrest, and escort him to a large, bare hall, where a judge makes him play Russian roulette three times. Surviving, he is locked in a small room. Smoke enters, then the walls start to press together. About to be crushed, Maitland sees the skull float toward him and awakens standing in the hallway near Marco's room.

This dream begins with matter-of-fact realism, so one is not at first certain that it *is* a dream, and it successfully evokes the terror of irrational events. When he wakes, Maitland does not know how he got to Marco's building, a situation not present in Bloch's story and one that adds an eerie, disturbing overtone. Evidently, Maitland has been summoned by the skull, but the dream events themselves relate vaguely to the rest of the film, embodying in only a general way the fear and guilt aroused by contact with supernatural evil. In fact, the film's dream events feel arbitrary and familiar, whereas Bloch's dream has Maitland merge with the skull, creating an apt image of its powers entering the man.

Maitland returns home. Deciding to buy the skull, he goes back to the building, only to find Marco dead. Bloch had given Marco a guard dog, which Maitland shoots and which he assumes killed its master, but the film omits that detail and offers no explanation for the death. Maitland hides the skull in a hall closet, then notifies the police. During a short scene with two added characters, a police inspector (Nigel

Green) and a doctor (Patrick Magee), we learn that Marco's jugular vein, like that of the phrenologist, was "bitten clean through." After another short scene, this one with Sir Matthew, Maitland tries to retrieve the skull. Confronted by the building's caretaker, also an added character, Maitland pushes the man through a railing and he falls to his death. Francis follows this with a close-up of the skull, cinematically implying a connection between it and Maitland's action. Until now, Maitland was only a thief, but in an instant he has entered another level of evil.

When Maitland takes possession of the skull, Bloch's story is almost over. As the character starts to fall asleep, he realizes that Marco's dog had no blood on its muzzle, so it probably hadn't killed its owner. The skull then rolls along the floor, grasps the bedsheet with its teeth, swings up, rolls onto Maitland's chest, and bites his throat. The film wisely drops Bloch's surprise about the dog not killing Marco, which wasn't much of a surprise, and discards the absurd image of the rolling, swinging skull. Instead, it develops Maitland's struggle with the skull's power into a prolonged, highly visual sequence of intense, atmospheric scenes.

As Maitland locks the skull in a glass display case, a close-up of this new possession includes his own reflection, which indelibly links the two and depicts the man ensnared by the object's power. Still unaware of his own vulnerability, Maitland sits down to observe. The window curtains blow inward. Items on a small table fall to the floor. The key in the display case turns, and the skull floats across the room, settling onto the table, next to the book about de Sade. (The sight of the skull floating through the air is probably too literal—Francis felt compelled by commercial pressures to show it—but it is far less awkward than the movements described in the story.)

In a trance, Maitland leaves the room to steal the statuette from Sir Matthew. Interrupted, he kills his friend, using as his weapon the figure of a demon who, in the auctioneer's words, "tempts men to be quarrelsome and contentious and to commit murder." Back in his study, Maitland completes the table setting with the statuette. The skull then impels him to pick up a knife that had once belonged to Gilles de Rais, the wife-murderer. Still dazed, Maitland enters his wife's bedroom and raises the knife above her sleeping body, presumably to sacrifice her as part of the skull's ritual. Here, Francis dramatizes the struggle within Maitland by intercutting close-ups of the skull (in the next room), the woman's face, the cross around her neck, and Maitland himself. Finally, Maitland shakes off the skull's control. Having won the battle, he returns the skull to the case, hangs a cross from the key, and goes to his bedroom, but as he does so, his mirrored reflection shatters, presaging his doom.

The forces of evil mass again, and the empty study comes to life. The windows blow open, candles light on their own, the skull crashes out through the glass (this time we do not see it move), and Maitland is drawn back to the room. When he reenters, we see him through the shattered glass of the case, and, in one of the director's many fine, graphic images, a knife-sharp piece of splintered glass hovers at the top of the frame, then falls. Again Maitland grasps the knife, but again he wins the struggle, thrusting the blade through the eye of the skull and into the table.

The skull now takes control of the house and sets about punishing its rebellious victim. As Maitland returns to his bedroom, an hourglass inverts, setting the time of his death. He finds the knife in his pillow; the door refuses to open, trapping him within; the walls begin to vibrate. Terrified, Maitland screams and bangs on the door, but outside the room all appears normal and nothing can be heard. As the sand in the hourglass runs out, the skull floats toward him and the scene ends. The next morning, Maitland's wife discovers his body. In the final scene, the inspector and doctor remark that his throat had been torn out, like Marco's. Could there be a connection, such as

Freddie Francis (center) relaxes between takes on his atmospheric masterpiece, *The Skull* (1965). With him, from left to right, are cast members Patrick Wymark, Peter Cushing, Patrick Magee, and (standing) Nigel Green.

witchcraft, one of them wonders. "Not in this day and age," the other replies—in a shot filmed through the skull's eye sockets. This irony may be familiar, but Francis serves it up in a neatly cinematic form, with the image contradicting the dialogue.

In almost all respects, Milton Subotsky's script takes Bloch's brief tale and extends it with skill and integrity. It also transforms Bloch's comparatively abrupt finale into a progression that is subtler and more meaningful in its relationship to the central character. Still, the script was an unusually short one, but thanks to Francis's ability to create atmosphere visually, an 83-page screenplay became an 82-minute feature. (By way of contrast, the screenplay of Terence Fisher's 82-minute *Dracula* [1958] was 106 pages long.) "The script needed a good deal of bolstering," Francis recalls, "and I put a lot of that material about black magic into it on the set." In the process, he "got terribly involved" in his work. "I had a tremendous amount of freedom and it gave me something I really love, and that's lots of nice camera moves, because so much of the picture was purely and simply atmosphere."[68]

Strangely, Milton Subotsky has claimed that his reediting rescued the film after it was shot. "The plot, for some reason, didn't work," he said. "so we began to put it together in a different way and the whole last part of it, from the time Cushing gets the skull, is now made up of little bits and pieces of film that were shot for a different reason. . . . We actually reconstructed the whole last four reels out of teeny trims and bits and pieces of film."[69] The part of the film Subotsky refers to is twenty-two minutes long—only about two reels—but, even so, it is hard to imagine where he found so many "bits and pieces."

Subotsky's claim may, however, have a factual basis. In the shooting script, after Maitland resists killing his wife, the skull has him go to the maid's room, knock her unconscious, and bring her to his study. Then, he picks up the knife again and is about to sacrifice the woman when "the realization of what he is doing comes into his mind. He tries to fight the evil power of the SKULL. The MAID's eyes open. She sees the knife poised above her. She starts to scream. MAITLAND plunges the knife down—into the eye of the SKULL! He lets go of the MAID, who runs out of the room, too frightened to scream." It is probable that Francis filmed this action, which for some reason proved unsatisfactory. Subotsky then restructured the episode by intercutting some of that footage with shots of Maitland's wife and her cross which had been intended for use in the earlier scene. If so, this 75-second alteration became, in Subotsky's memory, the entire climax.

Overall, *The Skull* can be faulted only in a few minor details, and perhaps in the fact that it does not go beyond entertainment to make an implied statement about human nature, to function simultaneously as event and as metaphor. True, Marco once describes de Sade as a "symbol of the cruelty and savagery that is in all of us," and Maitland asks his friend, "How can a mere skull be dangerous, unless your *mind* makes it so?" But these hints stand alone and undeveloped. Ultimately, *The Skull's* merit lies in its creation of a very real sense of terror at losing control of the body and the mind, with Francis's visuals gripping the viewer in a manner quite beyond the power of simple synopsis. *The Skull* is a key work in the directorial career of Freddie Francis and a high point in the history of horror films.

For *The Psychopath,* Milton Subotsky commissioned an original script by Robert Bloch about the murders of four men who, after World War II, had unjustly accused a German industrialist of using slave labor, confiscated his estate, and caused his suicide. As a Scotland Yard inspector (Patrick Wymark) investigates the first murder, someone eliminates the remaining three men and attempts to kill the inspector. Although several characters have suspicion cast their way, the viewer assumes—rightly—that the guilty party must be either the industrialist's widow, Mrs. von Sturm (Margaret Johnston), or her soft-spoken son, Mark (John Standing). In its overall effect, *The Psychopath* is more a suspense thriller than a mystery, with clues and plot twists replaced with situations that permit the director to develop tension.

Besides providing a narrative on which Francis could elaborate, Bloch contributed an image that unifies the entire film—dolls. After each killing, the murderer leaves near the body a doll that resembles that victim; Mrs. von Sturm, confined to a wheelchair with "hysterical paralysis," has fled to a world inhabited only by her son and an elaborate collection of dolls; Mark von Sturm, himself paralyzed at the film's end, finally becomes his mother's complete possession, "my *real* doll!" Francis was thoroughly receptive to this element of the story, for the dolls gave him a visual surrogate for the victims during the murder scenes, their discovery by an intended victim permits a buildup of suspense, their presence in the woman's home encourages highly atmospheric compositions, and the mother's relationship to what she calls "my children" conveys character and leads to an ending the grotesque pathos of which transcends thriller melodramatics.

During the shooting, the producers decided to lengthen the film's running time. Over lunch, Francis suggested adding a scene in which the son, attempting to cover up his mother's purchase of several incriminating doll bodies, talks with a girl who works in a doll shop and was present in an earlier scene. "So we had a scene which ran for two or three minutes between this boy and girl in a nightclub, and we had a semi-naked girl so that we could have a bit of atmosphere which would give us a few more

Mrs. von Sturm (Margaret Johnston) with her dolls in *The Psychopath* (1966).

minutes."[70] This scene and a few related ones, including the girl's murder, add about five minutes to *The Psychopath*'s length. Surprisingly, this material doesn't feel like last-minute padding, because it adds to our knowledge of the young man's character. In the genteelly seedy nightclub, frustrated males ogle the female form by ostensibly sketching a bikini-clad model, and when the current center of attention greets Mark by name we realize that he is a regular patron. Although the shop girl's death is not directly related to the basic plot, audiences are unlikely to suspect that these scenes were not originally planned.

As he had with *The Skull,* Milton Subotsky later claimed that he saved *The Psychopath* at the last minute. "I wrote in four murders," he said, "and they turned out to be the most exciting parts of the film."[71] Because *The Psychopath* contains only five murders, with four of them integral to the plot, this statement must be regarded as a flight of the producer's fancy. In addition, Subotsky said that he decided, during editing, that the murderer's identity was too obvious, so "every time Patrick Wymark opens his mouth in the next to last scene we cut away from him and overlaid his dialogue [with new dialogue], and every time someone replied we cut away from them and overlaid their dialogue . . . and that way we changed the murderer!"[72] Actually, in that scene both the inspector and the people he talks to remain on screen as they speak, which refutes Subotsky's claim. The scene may have been reshot after Subotsky tried to alter the dialogue; more likely, it was created to pad the film, because it contains no information unavailable elsewhere. As the film now stands, it is not entirely clear whether Mark or his mother is the killer, and even Francis himself isn't certain.

The Psychopath contains a profusion of visual and atmospheric opportunities for Francis. One of the victims, a sculptor, has a studio filled with abstract metal structures, and the killer stalks him in a cluttered junkyard. Another man awakens from a

The murdered shop girl, with a doll in her likeness, in *The Psychopath* (1966).

nap to find himself alone in his home, with Francis building tension from the stillness and a few stark sounds. Near the end, Mark stalks the inspector in a deserted boathouse, while a classical recording plays in the background, its beauty contrasting with this life-and-death struggle and its rhythm reinforcing that of the grim cat-and-mouse game. Francis relishes these opportunities when they appear, but, unlike many thriller directors, he handles the other scenes equally well. As the inspector talks to suspects, Francis cuts between questions and answers; he also conveys the antagonism between the inspector and the others within a single wide-screen composition, framing the policeman in a tight close-up and arranging the suspects in the middle ground.

Especially satisfying is Francis's visual handling of Mrs. von Sturm, who shares a real-life dollhouse with her "friends" and "children." Shots of the woman in her wheelchair, talking to the dolls, involve us in her fantasy; Francis films them from a low level, and the foreground figures appear equal to her in size. When the inspector first enters the house, he and the viewer hear a voice but at first cannot locate its source among the myriad dolls positioned on the floor. Later, as the two converse, shots of the seated woman place her in her world, among the dolls, while the still-standing inspector towers above and apart from it. In Mrs. von Sturm's workroom, naked doll bodies hang in the foreground, insidiously reminiscent of mangled human forms. Another scene ends with a striking long shot of Mrs. von Sturm embracing her grown son, who crouches before her like a small child, in the middle of the roomful of dolls. Even more emotionally evocative is the film's final image, a close-up of Mark's face as he sits, paralyzed, his face pasty with makeup and lined by dark, mascara tears.

Francis's next Amicus film, *The Deadly Bees,* was adapted by Robert Bloch from H. F. Heard's 1941 novel, *A Taste for Honey.* The book, although sometimes termed a "classic" of its type, contains little mystery and not much suspense, but it does offer a distinctive narrative device: The endangered hero who tells the story—Sydney Silchester—is recognized by the reader, but not by himself, as a shallow, somewhat dense, and not very likeable fellow. This man, however, is not the central character. His rescuer, Mr. Mycroft, serves that function, and, although the narrator considers Mycroft an irritating bore, the reader soon identifies him as Sherlock Holmes, in rural retirement as a beekeeper.

Because Silchester stumbles into the story near its climax, most of the plot's events are reported to him after the fact, and their implications are explained by Mycroft, who already knows that a neighbor, Mr. Heregrove, has bred an unusually fierce and poisonous bee, with which he has killed a dog and his wife. Mycroft has repelled the bees with a recording of the sound of a death's-head moth. Later, Heregrove contaminates Silchester's jacket with a liquid that attracts the bees, but the man survives the attack by taking refuge in his bathroom. In the climax, Mycroft retaliates by placing some of the liquid on Heregrove's clothes, and the madman is later killed by his own swarm.

This novel offered a major challenge to its adapter. First, the contrast between what the narrator understands and what the reader concludes could not be transposed to the screen. In addition, the main character had to become more directly involved in the action, because, according to Bloch, Amicus wanted the "Holmesian angle . . . eliminated."[73] *A Taste for Honey* had never questioned Heregrove's guilt, but Bloch created a second suspect by turning Mycroft into a rival beekeeper. Francis was "extremely unhappy" with Bloch's screenplay and wanted it rewritten, but Milton Subotsky resisted. "To make matters worse," adds Francis, "Milton was taken ill and was in hospital. The other producer, Max Rosenberg, was on his way over from America and we were virtually unable to move until we could confer with him."[74] When Rosenberg arrived, Subotsky told him "to get another director and shoot the Bloch script, but he said that Paramount wanted Freddie and we'd have to let him rewrite."[75] Then, with the studio deadline near, Francis and playwright Anthony Marriott revised the script under tremendous pressure. Francis also made changes on the set—his usual practice, but in this case also a necessity.

Not surprisingly, Bloch resented having his script changed; like many screenwriters, he resisted *any* alteration a director might make in his work. "I write my scripts in detail," he once declared, "setting up every shot and camera angle and describing action and attitude minutely."[76] In contrast, Francis feels that scriptwriters "are usually frustrated directors" who "devote most of their time to forgetting about the plot and the dialogue and such things as are really their province" and instead "put great, great masses of stage directions in the script, which I completely ignore." The director certainly holds no brief for the superiority of his version of *The Deadly Bees:* "Bloch wrote a script which I thought was awful and we wrote a script which was also awful, and then one loses sight about which was the more awful."[77]

Without a copy of Bloch's script to examine, it is impossible to say what changes were made, but the final film is a reasonable—if not quite successful—attempt to solve the adaptation problems, while retaining many of the novel's plot details. Sydney Silchester has become Vicki Robbins (Suzanna Leigh), a more traditional heroine, although making her a pop singer adds freshness. After she collapses during a performance, a doctor sends her for a rest on Seagull Island, where she stays with Hargrove (Guy Doleman), a beekeeper whose surly manner and abrasive relationship with his wife make her uncomfortable. When a swarm of bees kills first a pet dog, then Mrs. Hargrove, Vicki confides her suspicions to Manfred (Frank Finlay), a quiet, scholarly neighbor. It is Manfred who—like Mycroft in the novel—explains about the killer bees and the death's-head moth. Ultimately, because Hargrove seems so guilty, it comes as little surprise that the mild-mannered Manfred is the real killer. His motive, however, remains vague (but so, too, was Heregrove's motive in the novel).

Despite the conclusion's predictability, the filmmakers' biggest misjudgment is starting with a superfluous, satiric scene in which two lazy civil servants receive, and ignore, a letter from a man on Seagull Island who claims to have developed a strain of killer bees and threatens to kill someone. By announcing this situation at the start, the film prevents viewers from sharing Vicki's gradual development of suspicion and fear. Nevertheless, *The Deadly Bees*—while lacking the elegance and intensity of *The Skull* or *The Psychopath*—turns out to be a fairly controlled and civilized thriller, thanks to solid acting and some intelligent directorial choices.

To explain Vicki's initial collapse, Francis creates a claustrophobic feeling through subjective shots of the multilensed television cameras hovering close (and vaguely suggesting insect eyes). He also makes good use of the fact that she lip-synchs the song, so that after the overworked performer faints we continue to hear her singing the words, "stop the music." Mrs. Hargrove's resentment of her husband is efficiently established when, after he enters the house to answer the telephone, we realize that she was sitting in the room all the time. Also, when Hargrove hires a local girl to help out, it is their manner, not the dialogue, that reveals a prior romantic involvement. During the inquest into Mrs. Hargrove's death, Francis carefully arranges his characters in the frame, using composition to suggest relationships and attitudes. The bee attacks are acceptably convincing, but the only memorable one juxtaposes their menace with the bright, white, antiseptic bathroom in which Vicki takes refuge.

For Francis, the actual filming of *The Deadly Bees* offered "no enjoyment at all," for a variety of reasons. "For instance," he explains, "we made it in the winter, and winter is no time to be in England. The bees had to be flown in from Australia and their life span was very short. The list of disasters could go on and on forever. At the end of the shooting, for the first time in my life I began to think, 'I don't care if I ever make another picture.' It was that sort of experience!"[78]

According to Subotsky, a rough assembly of the film ran just over two hours (although the director does not recall shooting that much footage), and it "made no sense. I asked Francis for an outline of the plot. His outline made no sense. I then set to work in the editing room to create a playable film out of the footage" by cutting it down to about seventy minutes.[79] That, however, was too short, so Subotsky "added a dream sequence and a flashback sequence in which all of the murders were explained."[80] These scenes contribute nothing to the film but padding: The heroine's dream summarizes events that already occurred, and the flashbacks merely illustrate Manfred's off-screen explanation, much of which is unnecessary. The film's plot is so simple, and so similar to the novel's, that it is hard to believe Subotsky actually changed it after shooting ended. (Some sources, notably a review in *Variety*, state that Amicus initially released the film at 123 minutes, but that must be an error.[81])

Despite his criticisms, Subotsky at the time couldn't have been too unhappy with Francis, because the director's next two films also were made for Amicus. The first, *They Came from Beyond Space*, is a science-fiction story outside the range of his interests and strengths. "That was when I was Max and Milton's blue-eyed boy at Amicus," recalls Francis, chuckling. "I suppose in those days they thought I could do *any-thing*."[82]

After several "meteors" crash in a V formation, a team of scientists studying the possibility of extraterrestrial life is sent to the site. Most of the film follows the group's leader, Dr. Curtis Temple (Robert Hutton), as he notices changes in his associates' manner and they prevent him from entering the fenced-off, guarded site. His investigation climaxes when he learns that aliens control the humans' minds and bodies. Unfortunately, an early scene shows the scientists being taken over by invisible forces from the "meteors," and this, like the first scene in *The Deadly Bees,* undermines audience involvement, for Temple spends nearly an hour of film time trying to learn what the audience already knows. Nevertheless, this portion—although familiar from numerous 1950s American films—works fairly well, because Francis maintains an atmosphere of dangerous uncertainty.

This part of the film also has the advantage of offbeat casting. The leading actors (Hutton, Jennifer Jayne) are not the usual picture-perfect types, and a tough but likeable gas station attendant is unexpectedly played by a woman (Luanshya Greer). Other minor charms include handsome Cornwall scenery, the hero's vintage car, and occasional details such as the dust left on a mantelpiece after some trophies are removed. Also worth noting is the graceful shot that introduces Temple and his two associates. First, the camera tracks across a painting of the solar system, which we only realize is a design on the floor when it reaches a doorway, whereupon Lee Mason (Jayne) steps into medium shot, looks off-screen, and says, "Good morning." As Temple's voice greets her, we follow Lee into the room until she stops and, over her shoulder, see Temple. Then, we move with Temple until he joins their partner, Mullane (Geoffrey [Hedger] Wallace).

Once Temple learns the truth about the alien presence, however, *They Came from Beyond Space* grows silly. Realizing that he is immune to the aliens' power because he has a silver plate in his skull, Temple quickly constructs a skull cap, which looks like an inverted kitchen colander, for a friend (Zia Mohyeddin) to wear. The two also build giant-lensed goggles that reveal the creatures and a ray gun that destroys them. Thus equipped, they stow away on the aliens' rocket to the moon. On arrival, they meet the leaders, who wear pastel-colored cloaks, and learn that the aliens' disembodied intellects have merely borrowed human bodies in order to repair their mother ship. When Temple says, "You need only to have asked" for help, the surprised aliens release the humans and the film ends happily for all. It is difficult to believe that anyone expected this conclusion to be taken seriously, but nothing indicates otherwise; Milton Subotsky, who wrote the script, even called it "a good science-fiction film that lacked only one ingredient for box office success—a star!"[83]

Milton Subotsky had written his first anthology film, *Dr. Terror's House of Horrors,* but for *Torture Garden* Robert Bloch adapted four of his own short stories, which kept this script thoroughly original. In Bloch's case, however, originality is not entirely a virtue. Too often, his stories seem contrived to lead to a final, self-conscious play on words that leaves the reader (or viewer) feeling shortchanged. For example, one segment of *Torture Garden* has a Hollywood starlet join the "immortals of the screen" who "never age" by adopting their method of preserving the brain in a synthetic body. This idea, which fails as a metaphor for stardom, slips down a few more notches when, at the end, two female fans cry out, "Isn't she a doll?" "A living doll!" Similarly, a story about a collector of Edgar Allan Poe memorabilia who owns the writer's reanimated corpse exists almost solely for the double meaning in its title, "The Man Who Collected Poe." The film's two other tales skip the verbal jokes, settling instead for ideas that are farfetched and arbitrary (a Satanic cat that, for no particular reason, eats human heads) or just plain silly (a piano, possessed by the spirit of its owner's mother, jealously murders his girlfriend). But these stories do touch on unfamiliar topics, in contrast to those in *Dr. Terror.*

Despite the simplistic conception of the characters in *Torture Garden,* most of the acting is quite convincing. The cat episode requires an almost solitary tour de force from Michael Bryant, who evolves from controlled ruthlessness when he withholds medicine from his dying uncle to pain and helplessness as the cat scratches and claws inside his head until he obeys its order to commit murder. Also effective is John Standing, whose baby-faced vulnerability and sophisticated bearing as the mother-dominated pianist help distract from that story's foolishness. Peter Cushing makes a believably urbane Poe collector, but Jack Palance is hard to accept as his breathless rival. Burgess Meredith, as the framing story's carnival showman, Dr. Diabolo, acts more impish than diabolical.

Torture Garden fully illustrates Francis's desire to give the episodes separate styles. These range from the cat story's shadowy basement to the bright California apartments in the Hollywood episode, from the overstuffed, semi-Victorian ambiance of the Poe segment to the elegant austerity of the piano's room. In the last case, Francis "insisted upon" a stylized black-and-white motif that permeates every element of the decor (including a black floor with white lines) and the costumes (the heroine wears a black skirt with a white blouse and white boots). This design creates a sense of richness and formality, of tight control and artificiality, that fits the story's social milieu and helps counterbalance the plot's absurdity.

At the end of this episode, the jealous piano attacks the trapped heroine by rolling aggressively across the room. Although the sight of an adult being chased by a grand piano is more ludicrous than horrifying, Francis almost makes it work by using mostly close shots of the woman and the musical instrument, much as he had done during Kieron Moore's fight with a Triffid. Another example of Francis's directorial intelligence appears in the cat episode. As Bryant searches the uncle's room for money, Francis places his camera close to the floor and has the bed dominate the compositions; thus, when Bryant finds a trapdoor beneath the bed, it feels like an inevitable discovery.

Once more, Milton Subotsky claimed credit for part of *Torture Garden'*s success. Francis, he said, had "changed the ending" of the Poe story during shooting. "Freddie's version left us with no motivation for the whole place burning up," declared Subotsky. "We had to do something before Palance went back to the States so that he could post-synch it, so I wrote a whole new ending in the cutting room, basing it on the footage we had." As a result, "every time that Palance starts talking we cut away from him and changed all the dialogue."[84] The actual scene, however, reveals that the fire is explained not by Palance's character but by the resurrected Edgar Allan Poe, and he does so in full view, not in a voice-over.

Despite Subotsky's dubious claim, *Torture Garden'*s four episodes constitute a directorial success, with Francis's stylistic control turning indifferent material into something well worth viewing. This is especially true of the cat and piano segments, which involve intangible influences over the characters and include extended periods of wordless action. But *Torture Garden* remained Francis's final Amicus film until *Tales from the Crypt,* four years later, and his next film, *Dracula Has Risen from the Grave* (1968), became his last for Hammer.

The studio had originally assigned the Dracula screenplay, written by John Elder, to Terence Fisher, but when Fisher suffered one of his auto accidents, the studio hired Francis. *Dracula Has Risen* deviates from traditional vampire lore by establishing that even after Dracula has been staked, he will not die unless a prayer is said. But the film's hero is an atheist and cannot pray, so the vampire wrenches the stake from his chest and carries on. "It was all wrong that Dracula should have been able to remove the stake," asserts Christopher Lee, who played the role. "I objected at the time but it was overruled."[85] Francis disagreed with the actor because this was Hammer's fifth vampire film (its third to feature Dracula), and, he felt, the plots had already "been done to death." As a result, "one has to play about with the legend, because if one sticks rigidly to the legend, then in no time at all . . . each [film] is going to be a remake of a remake of a remake."[86] Actually, the scene works quite well as drama, but many viewers resented such a radical break from tradition.

In the film's plot, Dracula forces a priest (Ewan Hooper) to do his bidding. He also interacts sensually with two females, Zena (Barbara Ewing), a down-to-earth barmaid, and the wholesome, if not quite pure, Maria (Veronica Carlson). With symbolic appropriateness, Maria's uncle and guardian is a Monsignor (Rupert Davies), whereas her lover, Paul (Barry Andrews), is an atheist. Given this strongly sexual and religious material, Terence Fisher probably would have constructed a solidly ethical conflict between the forces of good and evil. Francis, however, went in a different direction. "I was more interested in the love affair between the boy and the girl," he explains, and he viewed Dracula as "just a fly in the ointment."[87]

Although the studio omitted some of Francis's boy-girl footage from the final version of *Dracula Has Risen,* the scenes depicting the characters' everyday lives still stand out. Maria and Paul convey a natural sincerity, Paul and his employer banter good-naturedly, and the family relations between Maria, her mother, and her surrogate father reveal a comfortable affection. Certain situations could easily have become familiar complications, but Francis sidesteps them through his guidance of the actors. By rejecting the easy good girl/bad girl contrast of Maria and Zena, he adroitly avoids the obvious misunderstanding that could have arisen when Maria finds Zena in Paul's room. These people, we discover with some relief, actually like and understand each other. The characters may be one-dimensional, but they come to believable life nonetheless.

Because Dracula himself is just a malevolent force, the tainted priest becomes the central tragic figure of *Dracula Has Risen,* but Francis fails to elicit from his actor any sense of inner conflict. This man is a weakling before he becomes Dracula's cringing slave, so the change hardly matters and his scenes lack impact. Without emotional or psychological complexity, the character inspires no pity or even interest. Christopher Lee, as Dracula, appears on screen for only short periods, but his facial expressions are imposingly malevolent, and, impaled on the upper point of a cross in the climax, he writhes in furious agony until the priest redeems himself by praying.

Francis handles two of the scenes between Dracula and Maria with cinematic skill. When the vampire first attacks the girl in her bedroom, the slow movements of the characters and the long duration of the shots develop a floating grace that turns the attack into a romance. Francis builds the same quiet mood during Dracula's later visit, then shatters it with rapidly edited close shots of the Monsignor, of Dracula as he turns toward the camera, of the Monsignor's crucifix, and of Dracula as he raises his hands in front of his face and turns to run. After this, though, the director relinquishes his tight control, depicting the chase that follows in a series of long shots that dissipate the tension.

When he finished *Dracula Has Risen,* Francis had directed all or part of thirteen horror films and his frustration at being unable to branch out had built to the breaking point. Hitherto, he had functioned mainly as a storyteller who adapts to each individual script, depicting events and evoking an appropriate mood with dedicated professionalism. The results reveal a consistent level of talent and craftsmanship that became true artistry when the elements came together properly. In 1969, however, Francis's strongly negative feeling about his status led him into a period of highly varied, even erratic, filmmaking. For the next five years, he accepted projects solely to keep working, while resenting the nature of the jobs being offered. At the same time, he sought to break free of the limitations imposed on him by setting up productions more to his own taste. Four of the eight films he made during this period were artistic, financial, and critical failures, but even they sometimes reveal an attempt to do something out of the ordinary; two others are quite substantial works; and the remaining two stand out as among his most interesting and individualistic films.

Francis's first feature of the 1970s is also the first film that was truly his own in conception and execution. As such, *Mumsy, Nanny, Sonny, and Girly* (1970) set free the idiosyncratic humor, the thematic tendencies, and the stress on visuals already glimpsed in his earlier films. Francis has an unabashed enthusiasm for *Mumsy*. "I love the film! I bought the original play from which I took the idea. I had the script written and I chose the locations and chose the artists. I like everything about it and I enjoyed making the film."[88] For a change, he had a two-week period of rehearsal before shooting began.

"I looked upon it as a black comedy," says Francis, adding, "slightly more black than comedy."[89] *Mumsy*'s blending of horror and humor, done without a wink or other

A family portrait from what Freddie Francis called his "black comedy," *Mumsy, Nanny, Sonny, and Girly* (1970). Pictured from left to right are Sonny (Howard Trevor), Mumsy (Ursula Howells), Girly (Vanessa Howard), and Nanny (Pat Heywood).

clue about intention, kept the film from fitting neatly into any category, so the distributor didn't know how to market it. "From a financial point of view it was all right," admits Francis, "because we sold it outright to Cinerama and, because we made it reasonably cheaply, we made quite a lot of money out of it."[90] But Cinerama tried to hard-sell the film as a horror movie, so both audiences and critics were confused and, perhaps unconsciously, disturbed by it. Although *Mumsy* wasn't the career breakthrough Francis had wanted, it stands as proof of the director's individuality and ability.

The story takes place in the present, but its characters exist in an abstract world isolated from normal "reality." Two teenagers who dress and act like children (Vanessa Howard, Howard Trevor), an elegant and primly proper mother (Ursula Howells), and a solicitous nanny (Pat Heywood) form a parody of a sweetly happy semi-Victorian family. They inhabit an old country mansion with overgrown gardens and a decaying greenhouse. Here they play "games" with "friends" lured to the house and imprisoned there. These games, which range from innocent to suggestive and violent, usually end in death for the "friends."

Mumsy aroused extreme and contradictory responses. The *Independent Film Journal* described the film as "a visual knockout," containing "some of the finest cinematography of the year. . . . Francis, who seems to regard reality as something to be transformed into a hallucination by his camera, handles his material with his accustomed sardonic, if detached, campy touch." However, Roger Greenspun of the *New York Times* called it "poison treacle" that belongs "among the really rotten movies of 1970." Peter Buckley, in the British magazine *Films and Filming,* also turned his review into an offended tirade, calling *Mumsy* "a film with a complete and utter lack of taste," adding that "the basic immorality of the film sticks to one like slime."[91]

When a picture drives otherwise reasonable critics into vituperative hyperbole, one might assume it to be viciously violent and crudely manufactured. In this case, it most assuredly is not. In fact, Greenspun even complained that, "given a house presumably full of terrifying dead men, he keeps trying to shock us with, literally, jack-in-the-box heads." Greenspun refers to such moments as "teases,"[92] as if he would prefer explicit views of decomposing corpses and brutal killings to Francis's more involving and sophisticated use of implication.

When Girly kills her brother by slamming him on the head with a mirror, the impact is blocked from our sight by the weapon itself, and its effect is shown not by the body but by her headless drummer-boy figurine. This choice creates the scene's main point—the family chides her for breaking the toy, but no one mentions the murder—and the use of a mirror as the weapon is apt because appearances are everything to this happy family. In another scene, Girly is chopping wood and singing a rather violent rhyme. After she enters the house, the camera pans down to reveal Nanny's feet protruding from the bushes. In the kitchen, a large pot sits on the stove and a line of the rhyme suggests to "New Friend" (Michael Bryant) that the boiling liquid contains a human head. As the man starts to rise from his chair, Francis cuts to a subjective view of the uncovered pot, which lets us see more and more into it. But New Friend's courage fails him, so he and the camera back down. There is a head in the pot, but we never see it, just as the character doesn't. Sometimes discretion is the better part of horror.

Another side of Francis's cinematic skill can be seen when New Friend first enters the house. The camera observes from a distance as the man, drunk, staggers through the doorway. His breath drifts tangibly in the cold air and a golden glow sifts through a high, tinted window as the camera tracks past green palm leaves. These colors and textures and movements marvelously evoke the character's perception of a place, a mood, and an event. Later, in a billiard table scene, the wide overhead lights weigh heavily above New Friend in emphatic compositions. As Girly threatens him, she stuffs the table's pockets with little dolls, then strikes a ball against each of them. The editing here is excellent, with each billiard shot visually and dramatically punctuating the girl's dialogue. The scene ends with a doll's head shattering.

Much of *Mumsy* contrasts the neat, attractive, and innocently good-natured family with its dilapidated but still impressive environment and its emotionless manipulation of the guests/victims. One Friend is killed by an arrow during a Humpty-Dumpty game that lets him think he has a chance to escape, while Sonny diligently films the entire event. Later, the family sits and watches his movie. Eventually, New Friend, who has more animal cunning than the other "guests," turns the tables by seducing the three women and using jealousy to sow discord among them. The film ends with Sonny and Nanny dead and Girly taking over Mumsy's chair, while New Friend plots to gain complete control through murder.

"Maybe I've got a peculiar sense of humor," speculates Francis when considering the fact that audiences didn't know they should laugh during *Mumsy*.[93] Actually, the film is not a laughing matter, although it should elicit wry smiles. It is, instead, a painful satire. Its main weakness—possibly a pivotal one—is that it seems to lack a single, ultimate target. Throughout, various themes and aims are indicated, but a viewer will feel disturbed without quite knowing why he is disturbed. It may be that Francis himself did not fully recognize the completeness with which this story, to which he felt so strongly attracted, undermines the very foundations of civilized society. Himself a loving family man, a polite and dignified and even courtly man, a man who loves the look of beauty, Francis here provides the most explicit example of his tendency to link evil with childhood, with families, and with the appearance of neatness, cleanliness, politeness, beauty, and dignity.

Within its narrow, almost allegorical boundaries, *Mumsy* touches on class conflict, sibling rivalry, and a spectrum of unpleasant sexual tensions that rarely come this close to the surface. It also diagrams society's blatant hypocrisy, as well as the emptiness and artificiality of order, of stability. The characters, convinced that they form a placid, healthy family, are in fact more concerned with artifacts than people; they have reduced human beings to playthings, to dolls.

Mottos, such as "Cleanliness is next to Godliness," pepper this happy family's conversation and the rules must always be obeyed. "If you don't have rules," we are told, "where are you?" and rule number one is, "Play the game!" The purposes or morality of these rules and games can never be questioned, for that would bring disaster through the loss of ruthless innocence. Death is the punishment for the worst crime this society can conceive—disobeying the rules. Extreme indulgences can be accepted, decay can be ignored, as long as the game of purity is played and appearances remain above reproach.

This type of society is criticized in *Mumsy*, but its replacement appears even less appealing. New Friend is a gigolo from the outside world whose own unpleasant manipulations become the most destructive game, one that shatters the family's immaculate protective shell and arouses the characters' extreme emotions. Their hypocrisy disappears, but their ruthlessness doesn't. It merely floods out into the open.

Because *Mumsy* offers nothing positive, only futility and a bleak conception of human nature, audiences could hardly be expected to respond with pleasure, and because the film exists in the abstract, without a grounding in the everyday world, viewers had difficulty identifying what they were reacting to or against. This abstract quality makes a variety of interpretations possible: *Mumsy* could be about close personal interactions or wider social intercourse; it could even be a parable about Britain, the Britain of the Empire, blinded to its own immorality by tradition and finally "freed" into a condition that is more open, but less appealing. *Mumsy* is all of these things, but none of them exclusively.

The seeds of *Mumsy*'s elegant anarchy lie scattered throughout Francis's previous horror films. Only two of these had period or Gothic settings; the rest take place in the present, often in settings bright with the colors and sheen of the modern world. Cleanliness frequently cloaks perversity, especially in Francis's Amicus films, where the abnormal and irrational breed beneath the surface of everyday order and innocent wholesomeness. *Hysteria* had offered an early instance of Francis's response to such settings, for much of its eerie action occurs not in an isolated manor house but in a new apartment building, unfinished and unfurnished except for the main character's flat. The very emptiness of the building, like the bare walls of his psychiatrist's office, remove it from the realm of the securely familiar. In *Dr. Terror*, the crawling vine disrupts a perfect family by first killing their pet dog, vampires exist in a calm New England town, and the werewolf played by Ursula Howells (later cast as Mumsy) epitomizes icy gentility. Classical music is juxtaposed with violence in *The Psychopath* and *Torture Garden,* and in the latter a piano commits murder in its expensively stark room.

Families, in Francis's films, often cultivate misleading surfaces. As early as *Paranoiac,* Jimmy Sangster's screenplay stressed this. "Your only concern," Simon tells the Mumsy-like Aunt Harriet, "is to keep alive . . . the good name of the family." Simon bluntly calls Eleanor "insane," but Aunt Harriet prefers the word "disturbed." Shortly after, she lectures Simon about his behavior, saying, "There are certain standards, you know." Although this contrast forms the heart of Sangster's screenplay, Francis makes the most of the situation, relishing each revelation of duplicity and manipulation.

Beneath these surfaces, the relationships between close family members tend to take uncomfortable twists. Mother and son pairs are especially bizarre, with the man treated—and often acting—like a child. In *Hysteria,* the mature Chris Smith, manipulated in ways he doesn't understand, is haunted by a male voice yelling at a woman, "stop treating me like a child!" and eventually he repeats those words to his elegant female "protector," who had earlier assured him, "I'm here to look after you." Mark von Sturm, in *The Psychopath,* says of his mother, "she was the one who always protected me," but now that she is ostensibly helpless, "I have to take care of her." In that film's finale, Mrs. von Sturm declares, "He's mine now. . . . No one can take him away." Even after death, the mother of *Torture Garden*'s pianist (played, like Mark von Sturm, by John Standing) jealously protects him from romance, and his manager (Ursula Howells, again) is an equally possessive mother surrogate. Later, the man's girlfriend herself declares, "Leo belongs to *me,* now." *The Psychopath* also provides an unusual bonus, for in it a father resists his daughter's desire to marry, saying, "I need you here. . . . I need attention," which prompts her fiancée to declare, "He's your father—he's not your *lover!*"

Actually, all of this goes back to *The Innocents* and *Night Must Fall,* both of which stress surrogate mothers and sons. In *The Innocents,* Miss Giddens (Deborah Kerr) could be speaking of the *Mumsy* family when she says that her two young charges are "playing, or being made to play, some monstrous game!" She discovers, or thinks she discovers, corruption within the two beautiful children, who inhabit a lush and lovely world of flowing white dresses and broad-brimmed hats, of stately gazebos and quiet lakes, of swans and butterflies, blossoms and doves. Miss Giddens's motherly protectiveness soon grows into paranoia, as she perceives mature, knowing threats in her charges' giggles and glances. Miles's show of affection to her becomes a perverse sexual seductiveness, and she suspects possible incest between the "possessed" brother and sister. A music box, a toy clown, and a doll take on unhealthy connotations, as does a game of hide-and-seek between the governess and the children.

Night Must Fall also depicts the thin line between the normal and the perverse, and does so with unacknowledged brilliance. Danny (Albert Finney) is a charming scoundrel who, the viewer knows, is also an insane murderer. He fits neatly into a settled household, which he then disrupts by satisfying the needs of its three women: Having gotten his girlfriend, a servant, pregnant, he seduces the sophisticated daughter and becomes a "son" to the wheelchair-ridden Mrs. Bramson (Mona Washbourne). A seemingly happy family, charming characters, and essentially normal romantic complications slip subtly out of joint as an aged gardener laughs toothlessly, the daughter enters Danny's room to sit on his bed and handle his possessions, and the old woman grows jealous of her daughter. In Danny's relationship with Mrs. Bramson, maternal affection is tinged with sexual flirtation and physical danger. Once again, games take a threatening turn, as the two play hide-and-seek, she moving about in her wheelchair and he crawling along the floor, then crouching behind a chair or leaping from behind a curtain. Ultimately, Danny regresses completely to childhood.

It is but a short step from Danny's hatbox, containing a never-seen severed head, to *Mumsy*'s boiling stewpot and from this peculiar mother-and-son pair to the families in the films Francis directed. For instance, in *Paranoiac* Eleanor believes she has fallen in love with her own brother, while Aunt Harriet reveals an unhealthy solicitude for her nephew; the film ends with the demented Simon cradling in his arms the skeletal body of the brother he long ago had killed. In *Nightmare*, Janet is driven insane by Uncle Henry and murders his wife. Taken away, she leaves a doll behind. Much later, the villainess unconsciously squeezes this doll's rubber face into a warped caricature. The doll, still disfigured, lies on her bed, and the camera tracks from it to a knife, then up to the woman who picks up both the doll and the weapon; after the woman stabs Henry, the camera moves past the man's body to include the doll. Thus, through his staging of the scenes, Francis uses the doll to link innocence with menace and the illusion of vulnerability with the unexpected ugliness of guilt. In *Dracula Has Risen from the Grave*, the vampire's wholesome victim cuddles in bed with her doll, but when Dracula despoils the girl, her hand (in close-up) first clutches the doll's arm, then abruptly thrusts the toy away; the shooting script contains no mention of a doll, so this was Francis's addition.

Certainly the fact that both *The Psychopath* and *Torture Garden* (in its Hollywood sequence) feature "living dolls" derives from Robert Bloch's scripts, but that does not explain why the sight of Mark von Sturm with his invalid mother evokes *Night Must Fall* or Mrs. von Sturm's satisfaction at finally possessing her now-helpless and childlike son ("I have my boy again—my *real* doll") suggests Aunt Harriet's protectiveness of her surrogate son in *Paranoiac* ("Simon belongs to me—no one shall hurt him"). These films have no common denominator other than the involvement of Freddie Francis.

One cannot reasonably claim that the concept of perverse family relationships and the use of dolls to unite innocence and menace are a concerted attempt by Francis to express a personal outlook. The exigencies of film production—the chance allotment of projects and plots—preclude that possibility. Yet Francis's track record of success with particular types of films, his evident empathy for certain kinds of material, would tend to keep such stories coming his way. He himself, improvising his visual approach on the set and using the script only as an overall guide, would probably add such references unconsciously, thinking he was merely expanding on the characterizations and telling the story visually. In fact, he was also making the films his own by incorporating, and evolving, a personal perspective.

In the case of *Mumsy*, however, that connection was deliberate. As Francis explains, the idea of having the film's characters be like living dolls "came almost subconsciously out of *The Psychopath*. I had decided when I bought the play . . . that it needed opening out with a different approach because it was far too trivial. I was planning to film it in Oakley Court from the start, and while I was thinking about that house, I suddenly remembered the big dollhouse in *The Psychopath*. Out of that came an idea that the story should be told through the eyes of a girl who has gotten mixed up between the real characters and her dolls."[94] Although that specific device was discarded, the implied perspective—and the use of dolls in the action—remained.

From the extremely satisfying experience of directing *Mumsy*, Francis shifted to *Trog* (1970), which he accepted mainly to work with Joan Crawford, an actress he admired. In this film, a troglodyte—or prehistoric cave dweller—is discovered and captured near a small English village. An anthropologist, Dr. Brockton (Crawford), makes progress in educating him, as Trog responds to music, colors, and textures and learns how to wind up a mechanical doll and roll a ball. From the start, however, a local businessman, Sam Murdock (Michael Gough), claims that Trog is a menace and should be killed. To prove his case, Murdock sneaks into the laboratory and releases Trog, who then kills Murdock as well as a butcher who attacks him with a cleaver. Trog is drawn to a playground, but when the children scream and flee, he picks up a small girl and carries her to his cave. Dr. Brockton enters alone and convinces him to release the girl, whereupon the military kill this missing link.

The plight of Trog could have made a moving film, but this script reduces character conflicts and ethical debates to clichés and stereotypes. Sam Murdock is so irrational and obsessive that his determination to have Trog destroyed lacks even a token justification. The anthropologist, on the other hand, has too many self-righteous speeches about the virtue of science, which Joan Crawford delivers in a stiff, unconvincing manner. This gives Murdock the edge, owing to the invigoratingly enthusiastic overacting of Michael Gough, whose lines are at least short and lively: He calls Trog a "slimy beast," claims that the discovery is "ruining my plans for a housing project," and, glaring at a crowd of sightseers, announces, "All this riffraff gives our town a bad name."

Trog disappointed Francis, but less because of the script than because of Miss Crawford. Her unwillingness or inability to convey any personality undermines the scenes of Trog's education, while her reliance on cue cards forced the director to relinquish his usual camera style and use frequent static shots instead. Another problem was the absurd appearance of Trog himself, who is thickly coated with hair, but only down to the shoulders, his head stiff and inexpressive. Unable to develop a sensitive scene under such conditions, Francis settles for the bluntly obvious and semicomic: Trog rages at the color red and at rock music, but a classical record calms him.

The fact that Dr. Brockton treats her prehistoric man like an overgrown child, even giving him a doll to play with, places *Trog* in line with many other Francis films. Also, the director includes a bit of characteristic visual humor when Trog, during his rampage through the village, impales the butcher on his own hanging meathook, in a shot composed so that an actual slab of meat blocks our view of the newly hung human slab. Nevertheless, the film hardly reveals either Francis's personality or his skill. In fact, Trog's supposed memories of dinosaurs, which were drawn (without credit) from *The Animal World* (1956), provide this otherwise slowly paced and talkative film with its most dynamic four minutes.

The Vampire Happening (1971) came about because Francis, expecting to make a film in America, turned down all other jobs. Then, after the Hollywood project collapsed, he found himself at loose ends. When *Vampire Happening* was offered, he read the script. "It warranted a lot of work," Francis recalls, "but I liked the idea. I agreed to do it, but then it started going rotten from the start."[95] *Vampire Happening* turned out to be, in the director's words, "a sort of home movie"[96] produced by a German millionaire and starring his wife, actress Pia Degermark. Although Degermark had received good notices for *Elvira Madigan* (Sweden, 1967), in this case she and most of the other performers were, in Francis's opinion, "wrongly cast."[97] The film was shot in Austria, with Francis the only crew member who spoke English. During the first two days of production, he used up three assistant directors; in desperation, he contacted Peter Saunders, a director of documentaries whom he had met on an earlier, unproduced project. "I said, 'Come over and help me, for God's sake!' He was a tower of strength and has been ever since."[98] (Saunders was assistant director on Francis's next seven features.)

In *Vampire Happening*, Degermark portrays both Betty Williams, a Hollywood actress who inherits a Transylvanian castle, and her great-grandmother, a vampire. Thomas Hunter costars as a teacher at the girls' school nearby. "I made it an absolute farce," explains Francis, "because if you're going to do a horror film with comedy, you've got to go madly overboard. Some of the dialogue that I gave to Dracula was in the old music hall style" of the 1930s. In one skit that he recalled, the man played a Russian cossack "and the payoff line came when the woman was lounging on a bed and said to him, 'Amuse me!' and just as the lights go out he pulls out a harmonica and starts playing."[99] In *Vampire Happening*'s version of that gag, Dracula (Ferdy Mayne) lounges on a bed with four beauties, declares "Let us play," then pulls out a large hunting horn.

Knowing that the dialogue delivery would be especially important, Francis insisted that the producer let him supervise an English-dubbed version. "Then, when it came to it, they didn't want to spend the money. I think they've done a cheap English version in Germany. I don't imagine it's very funny. I shouldn't think this film will ever be seen. I *hope* it will never be seen. But I would still be quite happy for people to see it if I were given the opportunity to dub it myself."[100] Although eventually released on videotape in America, *Vampire Happening* still languishes in deserved obscurity.

The film has no real plot, only a series of events that feel as if they were made up from day to day, and characters pop in and out arbitrarily. Much footage is expended on scenes that, if removed, would not be missed; they do not so much pad the story as replace it, and although they seem intended to be funny, they aren't. For instance, as Betty tours the castle's torture chamber, she pauses to imagine each device in use. For the most part, the humor occurs in undeveloped fragments, as when a servant wears a knight's helmet to protect his neck, a vampire punctures tires by biting them, or Dracula tells a sexy woman, "something's come up," then bites a banana.

Sex and nudity are at least as important to *Vampire Happening* as comedy, with Ms. Degermark going topless at every opportunity. Shortly after her arrival, Betty decides to seduce a none-too-appealing monk from the monastery next door. Subtlety is not her strong point, so she bares her breasts at her window. After seeing this, the man struggles briefly against temptation: When he glances at trees, their shapes do not just suggest crotches and penises—they look exactly like crotches and penises. The film also includes a horny abbot, a horny teacher, and horny schoolgirls in sexy uniforms.

Vampire Happening devotes its last half-hour to the vampires' annual convention, a costume ball that Betty attends dressed as the vampire and the vampire attends dressed as Betty. Count Dracula, the guest of honor, arrives by helicopter and tells his host, "Call me Christopher—I'm sure he won't mind." After much aimless (and topless) milling around, the teacher has the clock stopped and dawn sneaks up on the vampires. "One of the shots," recalls Francis, "is of Dracula rushing out of the castle with his trousers falling down, so it's really a mad film—nothing to do with horror at all!"[101] Quite true, but also very little to do with comedy.

The failure of *Mumsy* disappointed Francis, the awkwardness of *Trog* illustrated the depth of his fall, and the "home movie" nature of *Vampire Happening* dramatized the uselessness of trying to do something different in the genre. In this context, Francis surely viewed *Tales from the Crypt* (1972) as just another job. For this Amicus anthology film, Milton Subotsky adapted five stories from the E. C. horror comics of the 1950s. True to their source, the plots make no claim to subtlety. Rather, they exist only for the heavily ironic, gruesome punishments imposed on the characters. Yet Francis, fueled by frustration about his career, somehow elevated these superficial tales through a fresh empathy for people trapped by circumstances.

In the first tale, "All through the House," a woman (Joan Collins) murders her husband on Christmas Eve, then is herself killed by a maniac dressed as Santa Claus. The second, "Reflection of Death," is a brief anecdote about a man (Ian Hendry) who leaves his family for another woman and, after an auto accident, staggers home only to discover that two years have passed and he is now a decaying corpse. In "Poetic Justice" (a title that could apply to most of these stories), an old man (Peter Cushing) is driven to suicide by a neighbor. A year later, on Valentine's Day, he returns from the grave to tear out the heart of his heartless nemesis. "Wish You Were Here" tells how an avid art collector and ruthless businessman (Richard Greene) gains eternal life, which turns to eternal agony because he has embalming fluid in his veins. His wife tries to help by chopping him into pieces, but the pieces continue to live and suffer. In the final tale, "Blind Alleys," a group of indigent blind men, mistreated by the administrator of their home, place him in a narrow passage studded with razor blades, release his ravenous dog, and turn out the lights.

The physical horror and blunt morality of these stories encourage characterizations of comic-book simplicity, and because in each case the early scenes simply set up the climax, the director might have been tempted to dismiss them as quickly as possible. Francis had in fact handled *Torture Garden* that way, but with *Tales from the Crypt* he goes in the opposite direction, for he invariably finds, evokes, and stresses the characters' emotions. In "Reflection of Death," more memorable than the ultimate horror is an early moment when the man, about to desert his family, kisses his two sleeping children; one looks up and says, "Goodnight, Daddy," and he responds, "Good-bye, darling." Here, Francis provides a close-up in which actor Ian Hendry touchingly conveys the father's regret at what he has chosen to do.

Francis seems particularly responsive to characters who are the helpless victims of fates they do not deserve, such as the blind men in the final story. "Wish You Were Here" serves as an interesting illustration, for Milton Subotsky reportedly disliked a change that Francis made in the story, so he added new dialogue over a cutaway shot to reestablish the initial plot point.[102] This can be detected during the episode's first scene, where words spoken by the businessman during a shot of the listener have a different timbre than the rest of his speech. The line Francis shot—"I had to fight my way up the hard way, but I always paid my debts"—stresses the man's sincerity, so in the middle of the sentence Subotsky inserted "and if people got hurt, they got hurt," which establishes a ruthlessness not otherwise evident. Francis may well have identified with this man's later victimization by his own well-intentioned but misjudged decisions and therefore made him so sympathetic that, unlike the characters in the other stories, he doesn't deserve the terrible punishment he receives.

Even in "All through the House," Francis paid attention to the plot's victim. In the script, the segment opens with the camera discovering a seated man reading a newspaper, whereupon the man's wife hits him from behind with a fireplace poker. As a result, the viewer would have no idea what the man is like or how he treats his wife, and therefore would not know how to react to his death. "So, what we'll probably do," Francis confided shortly before production began, "is have the husband played by a fat, jolly actor and maybe show him looking happily at a present he bought for his wife."[103] In the final film, after a slow tracking shot around the room that lets the decor add to the characterizations, Francis essentially follows his plan (although the actor, Martin Boddey, is more cheerful than fat).

"Poetic Justice" stands out as the most emotional segment, and this was the result of a spontaneous collaboration between Francis and Peter Cushing, who chose to play Grimsdyke even though the script gave the victimized old man no dialogue. Together, Francis and Cushing built up Grimsdyke's scenes, constructing a personality and background for this poor but kindly junkman. In a classic case of an actor bringing his personal experience to a role, Cushing—whose wife, Helen, had recently died—suggested that Grimsdyke, left alone after the loss of his wife, receive satisfaction from working for others, by repairing broken toys and giving them to the neighborhood children. Cushing also suggested that the wife's name be changed from "Mary" to "Helen," "so that I could relate this to my own feelings." Because Grimsdyke lives alone, Francis and Cushing had him talk to a photo of his wife. "I talk all the time to

Peter Cushing as Grimsdyke, a poor old man driven to suicide, in *Tales from the Crypt* (1972).

Helen," explained Cushing. "I get no reply, I do know she's dead, but this is what lonely people do."[104] Cushing even provided a picture of his own wife to use in the scene (as he did again, three years later, in *The Ghoul*). Ultimately, Grimsdyke drew tears of sympathy from viewers totally unaware of the situation's basis in reality.

Although Francis's fondness for tracking shots does not reproduce the traditional "editing" of a comic's panel drawings, the director did modify his use of complex, textured images, relying instead on primary colors and immediate impact. Nonetheless, one still finds instances of the director's preoccupations. In "All through the House," the woman smashes her husband's skull in a bright, pristine living room (even the fireplace is white). Afterward, she scrubs the red blood out of her plush, pure-white rug. Later, in "Poetic Justice," Grimsdyke hangs himself near a discarded doll body. The *Tales from the Crypt* television series that premiered on Home Box Office in 1989 may, in visual terms, be more faithful to its source material, but in its own way Francis's film is unexpectedly satisfying.

Midway through the filming of *Tales from the Crypt,* producer Bernard Gordon asked Francis to go to Spain and direct *Horror Express.* Milton Subotsky, however, offered him a film that would star Rex Harrison, so Francis turned Gordon down. Then, the Harrison project fell through, which left Francis without a job—or even a "sorry" from Subotsky. As a result, Francis directed *The Creeping Flesh* (1973) for producer Norman Priggen and World Film Services. The screenplay, written by two novices, offers a clear potential for disaster: Onto a premise that is, at best, farfetched, it loads an excess of superficially unrelated plot elements. Luckily for the production, Francis at this time had a psychological affinity for the plot's implications, and he created a work that is both brutally unpleasant and subtly insightful. In the finished film, one finds the sensitivity and professionalism of *Tales from the Crypt* overlaid with a new layer of bitter, humorless disillusionment.

Peter Cushing stars as Emmanuel Hildern, a scientist who returns from New Guinea, where he excavated a large, humanoid skeleton. When he starts washing the skeleton, flesh develops around one finger, which Hildern then cuts off to study. Relating this discovery to a local myth, he concludes that this is a member of a race of giants that once waged a titanic war between good and evil. According to the myth, erosion will eventually expose the figures, rainfall will reconstitute their bodies, and pure evil will again walk the earth. In the blood of the finger's flesh, Hildern finds distinctive cells that he calls the essence of evil. Theorizing that evil is a kind of disease, he sets about preparing a serum with which he hopes to immunize humanity. Inevitably, his experiment backfires, the skeleton gets caught in a rainstorm, and the force of evil is prematurely unleashed on an unsuspecting world.

This situation would be enough for most horror films, but *The Creeping Flesh* includes much more. Hildern's relationship with his daughter, Penelope (Lorna Heilbron), is strained by his immersion in his work. Also, he fears that she may inherit her mother's insanity and withholds from her the truth about his wife's fate. Meanwhile, Hildern's half-brother, James (Christopher Lee), runs the asylum where Hildern's wife had been secretly held until her recent death. There, he conducts cruel experiments on his patients in an attempt to determine the nature of insanity. Although James has subsidized Hildern's expeditions, he reveals a cold resentment toward his kinder, gentler sibling and scientific rival. At the same time, a hunt is on for a mute, murderous lunatic who escaped from the asylum.

Somehow, all of these plot strands develop and converge in (usually) meaningful ways. When Penelope discovers the truth about her mad, promiscuous mother, Hildern uses his serum to inoculate her against "contamination by the evils of this world." Instead, the girl turns into a hoyden and, wearing her mother's dress, wanders into a tavern, is nearly raped, deliberately causes the lunatic's death, and is taken to the asylum. At this point, the plot's emphasis shifts to James Hildern, who jealously steals the skeleton, but his carriage overturns during a storm and the rain revives the creature, which heads for Emmanuel's house. Thanks to some visually stunning, emotionally chilling images, this climax is quite frightening: The hooded figure stands silhouetted among distant trees; the figure's shadow is cast against Cushing's house, swelling in size until it engulfs the building; and that same shadow flows up a flight of stairs, while Emmanuel cowers above. Such shots make the creature's approach both intimidating and severely beautiful. The final confrontation with Emmanuel, though, is anticlimactic, because the creature simply seeks his finger to replace the one the scientist had severed.

All of this has been placed in the context of a flashback, with Emmanuel telling the story to a visitor. At the film's end, it returns to this frame and only now—in a revelation borrowed from *The Cabinet of Dr. Caligari*—do we learn that Emmanuel is an inmate of the asylum and, as James Hildern tells the visitor, has the delusion that the two are brothers and that a woman in a nearby cell is his daughter. Did Emmanuel create the entire story out of his paranoia, "casting" it with the people around him, or has James triumphed over his rival by making him seem crazy? The final image stresses Emmanuel's missing finger, but that evidence also permits ambiguous interpretations.

The film's basic premise about the embodiment of evil has mythic power, but what holds the film together is Francis's clear, efficient storytelling, which conveys the com-

The reconstituted humanoid skeleton in *The Creeping Flesh* (1973).

plex plot (plus a flashback summary of Mrs. Hildern's decline and fall) in little more than ninety minutes and does so without sacrificing mood or visual style. The film's opening scene takes place in a totally white, sterile, anonymous room and in a single, highly varied moving camera shot. Similarly, the first scene in the main body— Emmanuel's return home—has the camera unobtrusively turn more than 360 degrees. Later, when the daughter breaks into her mother's room, which remains as she left it, the camera tracks with her from object to object, creating the needed tone of nostalgia and discovery as we deduce the woman's personality from the props.

Francis's professionalism gives this story dramatic force, but what heightens its power is an unstated set of implications that Francis elicits from his material. The initial contrast between Emmanuel's idealism and James's ruthlessness rapidly fades, as we realize that—on an emotional level—Emmanuel manipulates his daughter just as cruelly as James does his patients. However, Emmanuel does not understand this. Instead, he typifies the controlling parent who so often haunts Francis's films.

Emmanuel not only lies to Penelope about her mother; he is so protective of her that even during his lengthy expedition she obediently stayed at home, never leaving the security of their house. Emmanuel treats the fully grown Penelope like a helpless child, saying, "I've tried to keep from you anything which might cause you distress" and "You must trust me. I do know what is best—for both of us." Emmanuel's possessiveness even hints at a semi–incestuous affection: Calling her "my beloved responsibility," he declares, "You are everything to me, and . . . I've tried to be everything to you." When he injects her with the serum, it is only the latest stage of an ongoing "experiment," dating back to Penelope's childhood, in which he has controlled her environment and experiences. With the serum, he hopes to protect all of humanity from "contamination by the evils of this world," but on a small scale he has always done that with his daughter.

When Penelope leaves the protective prison, or asylum, of her house, we indeed find the outside world to be an "evil" place or, at any rate, a place without goodness. This world is summed up not by a convivial pub but by a sleazy tavern filled with boisterous drunks and prostitutes. As Penelope takes her place in this world, she becomes sexually provocative and/or cruel, mad and/or evil. The film presents these options as virtually interchangeable, although a more encompassing term might be *corrupt*. Finally, she murders a family servant and, like the little girl in "All through the House," opens the door to admit evil into her parent's home.

According to the script, Emmanuel's misjudged injection corrupts Penelope, but Francis's film suggests a series of more profound questions: Was it her father's protectiveness that corrupted her? Was it her discovery of the truth about her mother, or perhaps the illness inherited from her? Was it society's misinterpretation of both women's natural sexuality? Or was Emmanuel right all along—did Penelope's contact with the outside world in fact cause her downfall? Ultimately, the film implies that the answer to all these questions is, "Yes." In the process, it offers no possibility of innocence and no protection from corruption, for that protection is itself a form of corruption.

The Creeping Flesh is far from a typical monster film, for its creature appears only at the end and is not a menace in and of itself. It is not the essence of evil, released to infect an innocent world. Rather, it embodies all the corruption that already pervades existence. Five years earlier, in *Dracula Has Risen from the Grave,* a more optimistic Francis was determined to create characters who truly liked each other. *The Creeping Flesh* offers the other side of the coin, for it contains no truly sympathetic people and its final, cynical irony is the fact that the escaped lunatic comes closest to being an innocent. With *The Creeping Flesh,* Francis once more demonstrated his ability to make a film that is visual without being self-indulgent. At the same time, he revealed that his own frustration and disillusionment could elevate rough-hewn material by turning it into a disturbing, but possibly profound, view of life. All of the film's loose ends may not be firmly tied together, but the result is far more intriguing than many a more neatly packaged work.

Francis followed this impressive film with *Son of Dracula* (1973), which, like *Vampire Happening,* blends fantasy, horror, and broad comedy. Also like its predecessor, it may have seemed like an attractive change of pace, but it became an emotional and physical disaster. *Son of Dracula* began life as *Count Downe,* a story and screenplay written by Ben Carruthers as a satire of horror films. (Carruthers later had his name removed from the credits.) When the film's producer, former Beatle Ringo Starr, asked Francis to direct, he found the script incomprehensible. "I said, 'There's only one incident in the script that could be anything at all, and that is the one little scene where this guy, who is a vampire, has to come to London to be devampirized.' "[105] Ringo agreed to let him rewrite the script, based on this idea, so Francis took the job and set to work with writers Brian Comport (who had adapted *Mumsy*) and Jay Fairbank (the pen name of Jennifer Jayne, who had acted in several of Francis's films).

David Bowie declined the leading role of Count Downe, a young vampire who wishes to become human, so Ringo at the last minute cast Harry Nilsson. At an even later date, he decided to change the film into a musical by making the vampire a pop singer. Unfortunately for Francis, the budget remained low and the shooting schedule short. Nilsson selected several of his already-familiar songs ("Jump into the Fire," "Remember Christmas," "The Moonbeam Song") and Ringo brought in some of his friends (George Harrison, Peter Frampton, Jim Webb, Klaus Voorman) as performers. One of the production's problems involved these high-powered, financially independent musicians, who were not used to arriving for work at eight in the morning.

Francis managed to finish the picture on schedule, but only by pushing everyone—especially himself—very hard. Then, while editing the footage, he became the victim of exhaustion and severe tonsillitis. He told Ringo that because he would no doubt fiddle with the editing himself anyhow, he might as well start immediately. Francis then moved from the movieola to a sickbed. Frustratingly, the final product was not worth the effort or the illness. The story—barely more than a situation—hinges on a gathering of monsters to crown Count Downe as King of the Netherworld, but he falls in love with a human, interacts with Dr. van Helsing and Baron Frankenstein, becomes mortal, and abdicates the throne. Nothing works well in this film, which has the dubious distinction of placing one poor actor (Ringo, as Merlin the Magician), one beginner with never-fulfilled promise (Nilsson), and several experienced performers (Suzanna Leigh, Dennis Price, Freddie Jones) on the same embarrassingly low level. *Son of Dracula* received mercifully few theatrical bookings.

The financial success of *The Creeping Flesh* prompted World Film Services to invite Francis to direct another film. Grasping the opportunity, he and Jay Fairbank devised four stories in the Roald Dahl style of whimsically grotesque fantasy, which became *Tales That Witness Madness.* World liked the script and set the film up with Paramount Pictures. Production went smoothly, except for one major difficulty: The star of the final story, Rita Hayworth, disappeared after about a week's work and filming was delayed until Kim Novak arrived to replace her.

The framing story has a professor (Donald Pleasence) attempt to convince a visitor (Jack Hawkins) of his theory about the relativity and tangibility of truth. As evidence, he tells the stories of four patients, all of which he believes to be true. In the first tale, a quiet child (Russell Lewis) eliminates his forever-bickering parents (Georgia Brown, Donald Houston) with the aid of his fantasy friend, a tiger. "He hated them and then he went away," explains the now totally alone boy. The next story involves an antique dealer (Peter McEnery) with a photograph of his late relative, Uncle Albert, and with Albert's high-wheeler bicycle. Forced to mount the bicycle, the man is transported into the past, where he becomes Albert and courts a young woman (Suzy Kendall). To escape Albert's control, he burns the picture, which also kills Albert in the past. Now, he dwells on the fact that the unattainable woman is waiting for him. Next, a man (Michael Jayston) brings home a shapely tree trunk with which he has become infatuated. When his jealous wife (Joan Collins) confronts her rival, she is killed, and the tree takes her place in his bed. Finally, Kimo (Michael Petrovitch), a handsome Hawaiian visiting England, carries out a ritual in which he serves a virgin's cooked flesh to her mother (Kim Novak). The framing story then ends with a variation on *Creeping Flesh's* conclusion. The visitor, convinced that the professor is mad, is himself attacked by the boy's "imaginary" tiger.

These four tales, relatively insubstantial as narratives, depend almost entirely on style to keep them from becoming gross or absurd, to maintain a tone of fantasy, to create humor without farce, and above all to add charm and elegance. "This is the sort of thing that I like," said Francis of *Tales That Witness Madness,* adding that it was never intended to be a straight horror film. "It won't stand up as I want it to," he explained, "unless you do giggle. When we finished the film, I absolutely loved it." Then, a Paramount executive screened the picture. "That morning," recalls Francis, "he had cancelled the John Schlesinger stage musical about Albert and Victoria. Then he saw *Hitler: The Last Ten Days,* which I don't think he liked. Then he saw our film. He watched it and then was very quiet. Finally, he said, " 'It's not a horror film!' I said, 'But, it never *was* a horror film. The script wasn't a horror script.' 'Jesus—I didn't read the script!' he said."[106]

Because Paramount expected another *Tales from the Crypt,* Francis had to go back and "put a certain amount of terror" in the film, "things like seeing the mother and father killed by the tiger." The original version had shown only the boy seated at his toy piano, "with a tremendous amount of blood all over the place." Francis and his assistant director, Peter Saunders, obtained an old tiger skin rug and a kind of glove with claws. "I held the tiger's head and Peter held the tiger's claw and we put about twenty-eight pounds of old steak around the place and shot some quick flashes of this." They also added close-ups of metal spikes bristling on the possessive tree and a nightmare sequence in which the doomed wife is attacked in the woods, by the woods.[107] Not surprisingly, these additions failed to turn the film into a horror feature, but neither did they completely ruin the original product. Conceived as a droll black comedy, the film simply became blacker and a little less droll.

In fact, *Tales That Witness Madness* is a remarkable example of Francis's style of comedy—his straight-faced, oddly charming treatment of absurd and perverse premises. The tree tale illustrates this best, with the characters taking events very seriously in typical romantic-triangle fashion. The arboreal intruder subtly provokes the wife by dropping leaves onto her nice, clean floor and, when the husband defends it as "a perfectly delightful little tree," she describes it as "sawn-off and upside down and ugly." After she throws a drink into the "face" of her rival, he gently daubs the liquid away, while romantic music plays in the background. The tree itself is so perfectly designed that although it fits the woman's description, a viewer can also understand the husband's infatuation.

In the film's last episode, the virgin's mother plans a surprise luau for her guest. The kitchen table is covered with fruit, and when Kimo's associate, Keoki (Leon Lissek),

Joan Collins, as a jealous wife, cleans up the mess made by a provocative tree, the new object of her husband's affections. From *Tales That Witness Madness* (1973).

enters unexpectedly, the woman leans across the table, somehow hoping to block his view of the vast spread, while trying to be casual about nearly lying on the table and holding two pineapples at her chest. The moment is pleasingly absurd, especially because no one in the scene seems aware of the fact. A more uncomfortable example of Francis's humor occurs after the girl's death, as Keoki, chopping up her body, is intercut with the mother and Kimo in a romantic scene. The woman fingers the man's hair, followed by a shot of Keoki holding the girl's head by the hair and raising his knife. As the mother kisses Kimo's hand, Keoki lifts one of the girl's hands and hacks away. The shots of Keoki at work, stabbing and carving, make the viewer wince, but because Francis places his gory action just below the frame edge, the viewer's attention is directed to Keoki's facial expressions. His enthusiastic involvement in his work is amusingly, disturbingly incongruous.

Francis, explaining his approach to "Luau," says, "I thought that it was a story of not suspense, but inevitability, because quite early on in the piece you realize that the young Hawaiian has got to sacrifice this girl. . . . To my mind, you've got to get the audience thinking, 'Oh, this is ridiculous—they're not going to do *that*,' and then keep playing it out, until finally they think, 'The rotten swine, they *did* do it after all!' I think it's funny in *that* context."[108] This scene expresses, as well as any, Francis's type of humor.

The "Luau" segment might also be considered Francis's ultimate destruction of the modern "happy family," in which a mother and daughter who have everything, materially, compete for the same man. This mother literally devours her virginal, but far-from-innocent, offspring and ends up clinging to a makeshift doll she received as a substitute. In addition, Kimo performs the ritual because of a promise he made to *his* dying mother. Earlier, in "Mr. Tiger," the boy is kept at home by his overly protective mother. "You pamper him like a hothouse flower," accuses her husband. "You've tried everything you know how to keep him to yourself." Although the man is no pleasure to be around, either, the film stresses this mother's compulsion to control others.

Tales That Witness Madness is also typical of Francis in the way it uses misleadingly innocent and ordered appearances. Various kinds of danger emerge from a well-behaved child, a quaint photo and bicycle, a "delightful" piece of wood, and an equally delightful Hawaiian. The hallways in the framing scenes are totally white and completely bare, and the child in "Mr. Tiger" sits in his toy-filled room as its white rug and doors are splattered with his parents' blood. The other stories also play off their richly modern, brightly colored, and thoroughly clean settings in similar ways, except for "Penny Farthing," part of which lovingly evokes a leisurely era of afternoon strolls in the park.

Not surprisingly, this film encountered the same problem as *Mumsy:* Audiences did not know how to take it. Critics, too, were divided in their responses, although they stopped short of the virulence that greeted *Mumsy. Variety* evidently understood the film's tone, describing it as "deliberately comedic. . . . a dead-pan rendition of non-sequiturs and improbabilities. Thus, the audience's sense of humor is being tested, not that of the film-makers." The *New York Times*'s Vincent Canby must have failed this test, because he seemed confused by the film's "grotesque effects, some of which are comic without being especially funny." He added, "Considering the generally depressed state of horror films these days, it takes a special kind of optimism to continue seeing them, especially when they are directed by Freddie Francis." In contrast, *Variety* asserted, "Fortunately for macabre chiller fans, former cinematographer Freddie Francis keeps directing such films."[109]

As he had with *Mumsy, Nanny, Sonny, and Girly,* Francis hoped that *Tales That Witness Madness* would "get me out of this rut" of making horror films,[110] but Paramount's disenchantment, the public's confusion, and the film's rather subtle merits kept it from financial success. So Francis, still in the "rut," directed *Craze* (1974), another low-budget, poorly scripted horror film produced by Herman Cohen, who had given the world *Trog.* By no means a good film, *Craze* is nonetheless an unconsciously personal one, for its nihilism sums up Francis's private frustration over his position in the film industry.

Although based on a novel, the script reveals similarities to parts of *Tales That Witness Madness:* This time, it is the antique dealer who makes human sacrifices to a primitive god. If *Craze* had been a film about black magic, like *The Skull,* Francis could have made atmosphere the star. Instead, Cohen—perhaps taking his cue from *The Abominable Dr. Phibes* (1971) and *Theatre of Blood* (1973), in which the main character murders a series of guest stars—decided to stress the killings. Although improvisation from a general script idea had worked with *The Skull,* "You can't shoot an ordinary thriller that way," Francis noted. "You've got to have a better script."[111]

The result is a strangely pointless and emotionally confused film. It contains no mystery, for the viewer knows all along that Neal Mottram (Jack Palance) kills women for the idol, Chuku. Nor does Mottram have interesting characteristics. He is not an insane serial killer, because Chuku really does reward him. He is not a semisympathetic victim, for he acts voluntarily and endures no internal struggle. He is not even a sincere worshipper of Chuku, for his motive is purely monetary. It is hard to know what to make of Neal Mottram, as *Craze* moves from murder to murder without any dramatic progression or complication, inspiring neither suspense nor uncertainty. The resulting emphasis on Mottram's actions—his preparations and methods—creates only a feeling of tedious inevitability, mixed with morbid curiosity. Without even attempting to understand its central character, *Craze* resembles one of the splatter films of the 1980s, only without their elaborate gore.

The film boasts a large supporting cast of good performers, many of whom (Edith Evans, Hugh Griffith, Trevor Howard) are helpless in small, underwritten roles. Michael Jayston receives more screen time, but his character is not clearly conceived. More satisfying are Diana Dors as Mottram's overweight former girlfriend, with a crude but open acceptance of her appetites, and Suzy Kendall as a cheerfully enthusiastic prostitute. Yet even these two characters leave the viewer with a distasteful impression.

Craze also has implications of homosexuality and examples of outright misogyny that may have been intended to add substance, but have little to do with the basic plot. Mottram shares his business and living quarters with Ronnie (Martin Potter), a former male hustler, and his victims are all women. He burns one alive and, while telephoning the prostitute, sets fire to a *Playboy* centerfold photo. Later, he strangles the prostitute while kissing her. The policeman who investigates the killings (Michael Jayston) abruptly reveals his own nasty side when he slaps the vulnerable Ronnie and makes caustic remarks about the appearance of Diana Dors's character (homophobia and homosexual denial?).

Francis seems unsure how to handle this material. The film's details are not novel enough, its characters not intriguing enough, to justify its leisurely pace, and only one scene reveals the director's visual imagination. Mottram has just picked up a woman, and the viewer knows he intends to kill her. Next, we see a close shot of her legs on a bed. The camera tilts up, discovering Mottram standing against a wall in the background. He walks into close-up, then sits, blocking our view of the woman. He lies back, his head resting on her stomach, and only now do we realize that we have been fooled—she is still alive. This is a satisfying bit of filmmaking, the only one in the film.

Actually, the first cut of *Craze* created a slightly novel tone, because the editor occasionally cut in brief shots of the idol to keep the viewer aware of its influence; he also cut in shots of future victims before they entered the plot. Producer Cohen, however, had the film reedited to a standard pattern, although a scene in which Chuku is briefly superimposed over Mottram's face could be a remnant of the first approach. The earlier version might not have been better than the one finally used, but it would have been more unusual.

How, then, to explain *Craze* in the context of Francis's career? At one point in *The Psychopath,* a sculptor notices another character looking at his constructions. "You don't like my work?" he asks, and then adds, "Neither do I, but it *sells."* In 1966, this may have been just a passing comment, but the idea of an artist forced to compromise his commitment to art—to "sell out"—epitomizes Francis's view of his status during the 1970s.

In the episode "Wish You Were Here" in *Tales from the Crypt,* Francis, as mentioned earlier, attempted to increase sympathy for the main character, an art collector-businessman in need of funds. On the verge of selling "all the beautiful things" he's acquired over the years, the man makes a series of carefully considered decisions that seem to lead to a solution. Instead, they plunge him into a life of perpetual agony. One imagines that Francis could not allow himself to depict this character as a villain who deserves such punishment, for his predicament came uncomfortably close to Francis's own, at least on a metaphorical level: The cinematic artist who thought he was making a wise decision by becoming a director instead found himself trapped and suffering in a compromised netherworld. Francis's response to *Son of Dracula* reveals a similar instinctive attraction to an uncomfortably familiar situation: A character enduring a living death who hopes to become "normal" evokes the director caught in a professional limbo but working to escape from its grip.

Like the *Crypt* episode, *Craze* centers on a man with an appreciation of art, but one whom success eludes. In a sense, Mottram sells his soul for financial reward. He gets to keep his beautiful objects and his way of life, but for that he must pay by killing people—or, in Francis's case, by making films in which people are killed. Mottram accepts his situation just as Francis accepted his, an acceptance revealed by the fact that he directed *Craze*. But the distastefulness that hovers over this film very likely matches Francis's feeling about the compromise of his art that he had permitted, about the living death and suffering he was enduring.

Craze both illustrates the low status of Francis's career at the time and indirectly expresses his reaction to it. One would expect, considering the bitterness it reveals, that he would then have taken steps to change his situation. Instead, he made a final attempt to accept the state of his career. At that time, he "got to thinking" that "people literally come from all over the world to interview me. . . . I suddenly discover that here I am a cult figure, all right, a small cult, I know, but quite a big cult in a small industry. And I thought, well, what am I doing being so unhappy? My bank manager's happy, I like making films, I keep on making films, why should I get myself all knotted up over this?"[112]

Previously, Francis admitted, he had felt "almost ashamed" to mention his movies to those of his friends who, working in the industry's mainstream, disdained horror films.[113] Eventually, these individuals stumbled across some of Francis's pictures on television. "They'd ring me and say how amazed they were. They'd seen this film, and it's a proper film—and they were amazed. Now, these are the people who knock horror films. And they knock horror films never having seen them."[114] This realization, Francis claimed, helped him relax about the merits of his own work.

Francis also tried to alter his attitude toward the traditional Gothic horror film. "Because I have not been entirely sold on this genre," he said in 1974, "I have tried to put a more down-to-earth, everyday logic into it. And the two things don't go together. I mean, one knows how a wolfman would bite somebody's throat or tear the liver out, but not how he would sit down in the morning and eat his eggs and bacon. So, one might be spending so much time figuring out how a wolfman *would* eat eggs and bacon that you forget about the excitement of the film. A lot of my films have suffered from my trying to apply the wrong sort of logic to them."[115]

Francis voiced this fresh perspective just before making *The Ghoul* (1975) and *Legend of the Werewolf* (1975) for Tyburn Films, a company newly formed by his ambitious but none-too-diplomatic son, Kevin. About *The Ghoul*, the director admitted, "I decided I wasn't going to worry about it being a horror film, I was just going to enjoy it—which I did. So I'm just starting a second career really."[116] In retrospect, however, this comment sounds like wishful thinking, for after *Werewolf* Francis gave up directing for nearly ten years, and in 1988 he admitted that he couldn't judge these two works fairly: "I was really so bored with those sort of films."[117]

The Ghoul and *Werewolf* offered Francis little to work with, for their plots are thin and their characters undeveloped. In the past, Francis had struggled to bolster those elements during shooting, but here he seems not to have tried very hard. Anthony Hinds, retired from his position at Hammer, wrote the screenplays for both films under his pseudonym, John Elder, but from the beginning he worked closely with

Freddie Francis (center) with his son, Kevin (left), and John Wilcox. Kevin Francis produced *The Ghoul* and *Legend of the Werewolf* (both 1975), while Wilcox served as director of photography for both films.

both director Freddie Francis and producer Kevin Francis. *The Ghoul,* like so many Freddie Francis films, centers on a perverse parent-child relationship, but here—for the first and only time—that relationship involves a father and son. This may not be a coincidence, for, as Hinds commented some years later, Freddie Francis and Kevin Francis "don't get on too well."[118]

Dr. Lawrence (Peter Cushing) lives in an isolated house, where, after returning from India, he fulfills a vow to his late wife by tending his fully grown but immature and cannibalistic offspring. The script makes only one, vague attempt to explain this problem, when Lawrence mentions a Maharajah's son who was "perverted and depraved. He corrupted my loved ones, first my wife and then my son, and afterward she took her own life." Another insufficiently explained aspect of Lawrence's background is a conflict between his Western religious beliefs (he is a clergyman who lost his faith) and those he encountered in India.

The Ghoul begins well, with Daphne (Veronica Carlson) prowling a darkened corridor with a candle, drawn by a voice that calls her name. She ascends a flight of stairs and, entering a room, discovers a man hanging with a hook through his neck. This tense and atmospheric sequence—which self-consciously evokes such early Francis films as *Nightmare*—turns out to be a party game, staged with Daphne's knowledge by her friends to see whether or not she would scream. Thus, Francis has simultaneously tricked the audience, defined the jaded boredom of his characters, made a joke about his association with horror films, and visually defined his view of such films as a game, in which Daphne represents the film's viewers.

At the end of *The Ghoul* (1975), Dr. Lawrence (Peter Cushing) commits suicide near a photo of his late wife. The woman in the photograph is actually Cushing's late wife, Helen, who died several years before the film was made. (Helen Cushing's photograph is also used in conjunction with the actor in *Tales from the Crypt*. See page 275.)

As the party continues, two young couples race their cars along rural roads. Stranded on the foggy, midnight moors, Daphne is imprisoned by a demented gardener (John Hurt), then taken in by Dr. Lawrence. The gardener kills her teammate, and, after Lawrence's son murders Daphne, his Indian nurse cuts up her body and packs the pieces in salt to provide her charge with future meals. Having unexpectedly disposed of its heroine, the film continues to follow the model of *Psycho* by shifting to Angela (Alexandra Bastedo), the sister of one of the victims, who investigates, along with Billy (Stewart Bevan), her partner from the auto race. In the climax, the son kills both Billy and the gardener, after which Lawrence shoots his offspring and then commits suicide.

The Ghoul offers a series of situations, not a fully developed plot, so scenes that should have explored events and relationships become filler. The gardener, for instance, is often inexplicable in his actions and, despite his extensive involvement, serves only as a red herring to mark time before the real menace is revealed. Of the four outsiders, only the impulsive and self-confident Daphne possesses any individuality. Also, aside from the opening, only the nearly seven-minute sequence that precedes Daphne's death fully reveals the director's skill. As Daphne sleeps, Lawrence plays his violin and the nurse prays before an idol. Then the nurse unlocks the son's door and sits nearby, chanting. Here, Francis summarizes events while depicting a conflict of cultures, as Lawrence's Western melody is juxtaposed with the nurse's voice. We realize that Lawrence has lost the struggle when he shifts to playing Indian music. This elegantly evocative blend of image and sound recalls Michael Powell's ideal of the "composed film" and is something few directors would have thought of, much less achieved.

According to Kevin Francis, *Legend of the Werewolf* combined separate stories written by himself and John Elder. "His beginning was great and his middle was rubbish and his end was great; my end was all right and my middle was great and my beginning was weak. . . . So we put it together, literally cutting up pages and stapling them together."[119] Both stories have been published, however, and Kevin Francis's in no way resembles the film, while Elder's contains most of its basic elements. The final script, credited to Elder, includes a number of plot ideas that could have made an interesting film, but all are undeveloped and lack interconnections, as if an early draft, not a finished version had been filmed.

Legend of the Werewolf opens in Central Europe, where wolves kill an émigré couple and raise the couple's newborn son. Some years later, this wolf-boy is captured by a traveling showman (Hugh Griffith), who declares, "He's gonna be our star attraction," and names him Etoile ("star"). Grown to adulthood, Etoile (David Rintoul) changes into wolf form and, after committing a murder, flees. Because John Elder depicts his main character's childhood, as he did in his script for Hammer's *Curse of the Werewolf* (1961), the film has to cover too great a period of time. The result is ultimately uninformative, and the cause of Etoile's problem remains vague. The film even resorts to the crutch of narration to convey information that ought to have been dramatized, as when the narrator states, "Aware of his terrible legacy, the boy fled. He traveled for days, sheltering under trees, feeding from the land, until he found himself on the outskirts of a great city."

Once in Paris, Etoile accepts a job assisting a drunken, decrepit zoo keeper (Ron Moody). There he meets and falls in love with Christine (Lynn Dalby), who works in a nearby bordello. Jealous of her customers, Etoile changes into wolf form and murders them as they leave. Paul Cataflanque (Peter Cushing), the medical pathologist who investigates these deaths, eventually confronts Etoile in the Paris sewers. As he begins to communicate with the wolf-man, a policeman shoots this young victim of his own nature, who dies as Christine offers comfort.

Legend of the Werewolf fails to achieve any of its situations' dramatic or emotional potential. It is unclear why Etoile is attracted to Christine and not to either of her companions, and we never see their relationship evolve. To justify casting Peter Cushing as Cataflanque, considerable time is spent on his activities, which are interesting in themselves, but the film is about a werewolf, not a detective. Because Cataflanque hardly ever encounters Etoile, there is little support for the sympathetic interaction between the two at the end. All other aspects aside, said producer Kevin Francis, with such a film "you've got millions of people sitting there waiting for this bloke to turn into a werewolf. So we spent a lot of time and money developing a new photographic technique that can do this absolutely marvelously."[120] If so, the money was not well spent, for the transitions rely on a familiar combination of editing between different stages of makeup and dissolving on a stationary shot of the actor.

The director, on the other hand, was more interested in the film's visual style. "The moment I read it was France," he said at the time, "and there were these girls in the bordello I just saw it as Toulouse-Lautrec. Probably I was pushed this way because I'm a great fan of Lautrec and having been camera operator on *Moulin Rouge* I liked the whole style."[121] Little of that affection shows in the film, however, aside from the Madame's hairstyle and a few images of her ladies poised for work. In addition, the

script's underdeveloped plot and characters prompt Francis to encourage broad cari-
catures from Hugh Griffith, Ron Moody, and Roy Castle, but the general lack of
energy defeats any ambitions its makers may have had.

On a personal level, Francis includes two inside jokes. At one point, when
Cataflanque has pictures taken of some corpses, he stands next to the camera like a
director, and the photographer says, "I'm just focusing the lens—a technical expression, you understand." More revealing, perhaps, is a moment when Christine makes a
feeble joke and her Madame responds, "I'm in no mood for your warped sense of
humor"—a phrase that Francis has sometimes applied to his own humor, so its use
here suggests that he may have identified with the status of prostitute. It is not surprising that the monsters in both *The Ghoul* and *Legend of the Werewolf* are, in their final
scenes, pathetic victims who plead for help but are not rescued from their fates.

The plots of these two films are not of the type that elicits Francis's best work, but
Tyburn's intention to follow *Legend of the Werewolf* with a black magic film called *The
Satanists,* to be shot during the summer of 1975, seemed encouraging. Then, the bottom fell out of the market for low-budget horror films. *The Ghoul* and *Legend* were
shown in Europe but never reached theaters in the United States, and Tyburn never
made *The Satanists.* What happened? It appears that *The Exorcist* (1973) is the culprit.
That film brought horror to the major studios, with big budgets and mainstream
directors, but it also drove Hammer, Amicus, and Tyburn out of the horror business.
Director William Friedkin spent almost a year and about $10 million making *The
Exorcist,* whereas most Amicus films cost as little as $500,000 and were shot in around
five weeks. Amicus's biggest hit, *Tales from the Crypt,* grossed in the vicinity of $3 mil-
lion, while in three years *The Exorcist* passed the $78 million mark. Inevitably, the
smaller companies couldn't compete with an expensive film's special effects, and
financiers lost interest in minor profits when a bonanza was obviously possible.

In the early 1970s, horror films were just about keeping the British film industry
afloat, but by 1975 the era that had begun in 1957 with Hammer's *The Curse of
Frankenstein* had ended. With depressing irony, Francis had accepted his ability to work
regularly by making small horror films just as that kind of work disappeared. The next
few years found the director trying in vain to set up his own projects. For example,
producer Don Getz announced a July 1978 starting date for *Dreams and Mrs. Ainsley,*
based on a script by Francis and Maisie Mosco (who had written the play on which
Mumsy was based). Lili Palmer expected to star in the occult drama, but the project
never materialized. During this period, Francis returned to television for employment, having contributed episodes in 1967–68 to *The Saint, Man in a Suitcase,* and
The Champions. In 1973, he directed five episodes of *Black Beauty;* he also worked on
Star Maidens, a British-German series syndicated to American stations in 1977. For
theaters, he did a "salvage job" on *Golden Rendezvous* (1977) by providing a precredits
sequence to explain the loose ends of this adventure film, which starred Richard Harris and David Janssen.

Then, in 1979 and at the age of sixty-one, Freddie Francis found his career come
full circle, when director David Lynch and producer Jonathan Sanger asked him to
photograph *The Elephant Man* (1980) for Mel Brooks's company, Brooksfilms. The
success of this picture led to his filming *The French Lieutenant's Woman* (1981) for
director Karel Reisz, and Francis won the British Society of Cinematographers' award
two years in a row. Finally emerging from the netherworld of horror films, he was
back in the mainstream and in demand—but as a photographer, not a director. Ironically, *The Elephant Man,* which centers on a sympathetic "monster," would have been
an ideal project for Francis himself to direct as his long-sought transition between

horror and respectability. In fact, its Victorian setting, atmospheric visuals, sleazy showman with a human oddity (*The Evil of Frankenstein* and *Legend of the Werewolf*), and familiar cast members (John Hurt, Freddie Jones, John Standing) give it the look and feel of some Francis films. *The Elephant Man* is, ultimately, the perfect combination of talents and sensibilities. The result is pure Lynch, of course, but it also seems to be pure Francis.

A cinematographer, Francis believes, should be able understand what style a director wants and then find ways to create it. This empathy and adaptability led him, in 1980–84, to such varied works as the realistic *The Executioner's Song* (1982), filmed on location in Utah, and the fantastic *Dune* (1984), filmed entirely on sets. At the same time, Francis's background made him an ideal choice to support directors with little or no experience making theatrical features. In this capacity, he helped David Lynch move from the semiamateur *Eraserhead* (1978) to *The Elephant Man* and *Dune*. Lawrence J. Schiller had directed two feature-length documentaries and two television movies, but nothing on the scale of *The Executioner's Song*. Editor Walter Murch found himself out of his depth directing *Return to Oz* (1985), but Francis could not establish a rapport with him and left the production after shooting the opening scenes.

When Jonathan Sanger, producer of *The Elephant Man,* turned director (*Code Name: Emerald,* 1984), it was natural that Francis should back him up as photographer. Perhaps in exchange, Sanger then produced Francis's first film as director in ten years, *The Doctor and the Devils* (1985), inspired by the true story of Dr. Knox, the Edinburgh teacher of anatomy, and the grave robbers-turned-murderers Burke and Hare. The 1953 screenplay by Welsh poet Dylan Thomas first hooked Francis's imagination in 1973 when Dr. Barrington Cooper, who owned the rights, contacted John Hayman, the head of World Film Services. Hayman, in turn, showed it to Francis during the shooting of *Tales That Witness Madness.* An agreement was reached, and Francis planned to follow *Craze* with a return to World for *The Doctor and the Devils.* However, the failure of *Witness Madness* cancelled that project.

Later, during the production of *The Executioner's Song,* Cooper again approached Francis, who this time considered mounting it as a television movie, but financing remained elusive. Finally, perhaps because *The Elephant Man* had a similar setting and also was based on fact, Dr. Cooper approached Mel Brooks, which led to Jonathan Sanger setting the production up for Francis. Shooting started in January 1985 with a budget of about $5 million and a nine-week schedule, both well above the director's usual. "The film," Francis said just before its release, "was a very happy experience—the whole thing."[122]

There were, however, some frustrations. When playwright Ronald Harwood adapted the script for Brooksfilms, he lost some of the qualities of Dylan Thomas's original, so at the last minute Francis "had to practically rewrite it."[123] The finished product is quite faithful to its source, which centers on Dr. Thomas Rock and his open disregard for the hypocritical laws that allow doctors access only to the bodies of executed criminals. As there are not enough of these, Rock buys "material" for dissection in his classes from grave robbers like Fallon and Broom. His resentment of respectable society is heightened by the fact that his peers snub his wife, Elizabeth, and even his sister, Annabella, feels he married beneath him.

The scenes alternate between Rock's world and the poverty-ridden slum world of Fallon and Broom, with Rock's assistant Murray linking the two, when he falls in love with a prostitute, Jenny Bailey. To date, Rock's arrogance has been balanced by his ability, but events undermine his security when Fallon and Broom start to bring him the bodies of people they have killed. Rock ignores indications of this and continues to make his purchases, but when Jenny is one of the corpses, Murray confronts his mentor. Later, after some lodgers report another killing to the police, Fallon and Broom are arrested. Broom soon turns King's evidence and Fallon is executed, but the doctors close ranks to protect Rock.

The film restructures and modifies these events somewhat. For example, in the original script Fallon and Broom gradually develop into murderers: When a lodger dies in Broom's house, they take the opportunity to sell a fresh corpse to the doctor, which then leads to them to kill people themselves. The film simplifies this evolution, so that the men (Jonathan Pryce and Stephen Rea) are aggressively violent from the outset and don't wait for the lodger to die. It also plays down the social stigma of Rock (Timothy Dalton) marrying beneath him, while adding the fact that Elizabeth makes anatomical drawings, which the repressed, puritanical Annabella considers "filthy" and "disgusting." The film creates the character of Alice, Jenny's friend, and it has Rock operate on Billy Bedlam's leg after he is run over by a cart, which reveals his skill and provides one of his few moments of gentleness. At the end, instead of having Fallon and Broom kill Jenny (Twiggy), the film sacrifices Alice instead and has Murray (Julian Sands) rescue Jenny at the last moment.

The central theme of Thomas's script and the film is the question of whether the end justifies the means, whether the breaking of laws is counterbalanced by Rock's goal of education and healing. "The science of anatomy," Rock announces to his students in the film's first scene, "contributes to the great sum of all knowledge, and I believe that all men must work towards that end. And I believe that that end justifies any means." As a result, Rock knowingly and without qualms supports grave robbing, arguing that it is essentially harmless. But does the moral relativism of this position prepare him to ignore the evidence of murder? If the end justifies the means in one case, does it in the other? "We are anatomists, not policemen," Rock argues, with defensive, hair-splitting logic. "We're scientists, not moralists. I need bodies. They brought bodies. I pay for what I need. I do *not* hire murderers."

Proud of his emotionlessness, Rock sees himself as "a material man" to whom the heart "is an elaborate physical organ and not the 'seat of love.' " He may claim that "mankind is worth fighting for," but in reality he feels superior to both the pompous hypocrites on his social level and the poor. He notes the existence of "the homeless and the hopeless and the insane and the wretchedly drunken lying in their rags on the stinking cobbles," but describes them as "depraved things that prowl in the alleys" and coolly adds, "They were men and women once." Rarely does he have a sympathetic moment—notably, when Alice offers her ring as thanks for operating on her brother, Billy Bedlam, and Rock thinks aloud, "Aren't people extraordinary."

The irony of Rock's position is conveyed by the film's very structure, in which his idealistic pronouncements about his "duty to improve the quality of human life" are juxtaposed with scenes in which his attempt to do that—by acquiring specimens— causes lives to be extinguished. Is he responsible for these indirect results of his mission? The film (in an addition to Thomas's script) implies as much by having Fallon recall his wartime service as a hospital orderly, when surgeons would order him to put the severely wounded "out of their misery" as "an act of kindness." At the same time, these juxtapositions also serve as a contrast, with the coldly intellectual Rock set against the chaotic world of brothels and taverns, where physical indulgence reigns. As Jenny, the prostitute, says, "No dead bodies here!"

Does Rock change by the film's end? Does he learn anything about himself? Even when Fallon and Broom are arrested, he resists acknowledging his own involvement.

"Out of the mud of the darkness come two ignorant animals and quite slowly they set about the task of bringing my life and my work down—down into the slime that bred them." At this late date, he still rationalizes the situation by claiming that his downfall was caused by others, something done *to* him. Only at the very end does he think, "Did I set myself up as a god over death? Did I set myself over pity? Oh, my God—I knew what I was doing!" This conclusion feels abrupt and unsupported by the preceding action, at least in the film as released. "We needed," explains Francis, "about five minutes at the end that Mel [Brooks] cut out, which is the sort of 'the doctor's remorse.' Mel wouldn't have that," and also was "insistent on overplaying the horror."[124] As a result, "The way it was edited, it comes over as more of a horror film than I would have liked."[125]

Whatever changes were made, they probably didn't alter the film's ambivalence toward Rock, which is reflected in contrasting comments by its producer and director. "I think Dylan Thomas intended it as a moral fable," said Jonathan Sanger during production, "the component of that being, human life is more important than the search for knowledge."[126] Francis, however, said at the time of the film's release, "I think in this case, the ends justified the means. Not murdering people certainly, but had Dr. Knox not bought those bodies, medical research may not have proceeded at the pace it did."[127]

Ambivalence pervades *The Doctor and the Devils.* Although Francis seems to offer Jenny's world as a semipositive alternative to upper-class pomposity, it comes across as gin-soaked and sleazy. Neither world is even slightly appealing, but Rock—who places himself apart from both—does not provide a viable alternative. Even a viewer eager to side with him against his narrow-minded peers finds it hard to do so, because of the doctor's arrogance and self-deception. Elizabeth Rock is a fairly positive character, but she defends her husband and intimidates Murray into keeping quiet about his suspicions. Murray, himself, is impulsive, shallow, and easily intimidated by Elizabeth. The prostitutes, Jenny and Alice, at least accept who they are, but one questions their contentment with such corrupt lives and decrepit surroundings. Thus, the realism with which Francis depicts the era produces a harrowing, desperate mood, one totally consistent with that of *The Creeping Flesh* and other late Francis films.

What is it about *The Doctor and the Devils* that so appealed to Francis that he retained the desire to make it for so long? Certainly, from the start he viewed it as "a great opportunity" to get out of the horror film "rut."[128] He also said that he liked "the beauty of Thomas's writing" and the "chance to create wonderful atmospheres."[129] Two years later, he revealed a personal link when he said that in staging the slum scenes he drew on his childhood memories of "dirty, filthy London."[130] *The Doctor and the Devils* may also have appealed to him because, like many earlier Francis films, it criticizes society's obsession with appearance. One character even voices the familiar fear, "Our name will be dragged in the mud." In addition, the film's theme is linked to the start of Francis's directorial career: At the end of *Vengeance,* more than twenty years before, the woman who killed her father to put a wonder drug on the market asks Dr. Corrie, "Do you think the end justifies the means?"

But might there not have been more to the appeal of *The Doctor and the Devils* than that? When he first read Thomas's script in 1973, Francis was deeply questioning his career, his accomplishments, and his status among industry colleagues, so he probably felt an instant kinship with Dr. Rock. In Rock's first class lecture, to which the film gives added prominence by moving it to the first scene, Rock could almost be speaking for Francis, the photographer-director, the technician-artist: "It is," he declares, "in my dual capacity of . . . anatomist [that is, technician] and artist that I intend to conduct my lectures [that is, make my films]—to expound, inform, illustrate, entertain, and edify."

Rock, like Francis, is a kind of outcast; his smugly superior peers, who work in the profession's mainstream, treat him with condescension. In reaction, he stubbornly takes the offensive and asserts, with a force that hints at inner uncertainty, "Mine is the *right* direction. The fact that the majority would consider it to be the wrong direction only substantiates my opinion that *I am right*." The image of Rock is of someone "performing" in a theater-like lecture hall, a man whose emotionally detached but useful efforts are misjudged by others as corrupting. This is supplemented by the addition to Thomas's script of Elizabeth's drawings, visual images perceived by society as "vile" and "obscene." Determined to go his own way and to defend his wife, Rock uses the force of his will to stand apart from accusations that he brings the entire profession "into disrepute."

Right to the end, Rock insists that he is working to improve the quality of human life while blinding himself to the fact that in some cases his work indirectly undermines that quality of life. The film's ambivalent view of Rock reflects Francis's ambivalence toward his career, as he tries to stay aloof from what he half-believes is the less-than-salutary effect of his horror films on their audiences. Several times, Francis has reported his distress when, conversing with horror film fans, he realized that they had less interest in film than in horror. So, Rock's contradictory comments about the public—"pay no attention to the mob," even though "mankind is worth fighting for"—reflect Francis's uncertain view of his audience.

Rock's lecture-performances have their unpleasant counterpart in a scene added to Thomas's script, a cockfight, which stirs its audience's blood-lust. Later, Francis stages Fallon's murder of Alice and his attack on Jenny in the cock pit, suggesting that this is an extension of the same human flaw seen there earlier. It is also in the cock pit that Murray, not content with rescuing Jenny, indulges his own cruelty by deliberately cracking Fallon's arm. Francis dissolves from this event and setting to a shot of Rock in his lecture hall, which links the actions in the cock pit with Rock's callously witty showmanship as he dissects bodies before an appreciative, amused audience. The clear implication is that Francis questions Rock's view of himself, with the cock pit less a contrast with than a parallel to Rock's supposedly idealistic activities.

Other characters, such as Fallon and Broom, also reveal aspects of Francis's self-criticism. Although they rationalize a bit about putting people "out of their misery," these murderers are basically more realistic and self-aware than Rock. At least initially, they see themselves as practical businessmen who, responding to the demands of the marketplace, provide a desired product. If fresh bodies are what sells, they'll supply fresh bodies, and if horror movies—which involve the planning and staging of murders—are wanted, Francis will oblige. In another addition to Thomas's script, however, the film complicates this "honest" commerce by having Fallon start to enjoy killing, while still claiming that he does it for the money. Until this point, Fallon and Broom had acted as a single entity, but now Broom becomes that entity's voice of conscience: "There's a madness in you," he tells Fallon. Thus the practical businessman has been corrupted by what he had done strictly for money. Fallon—like Rock—is unaware of his inner corruption, but the film is aware of it, as is Francis.

Just as Francis appears to have identified with the prostitutes in *Legend of the Werewolf,* Jenny in *The Doctor and the Devils* is the film's most self-aware character. She knows what she is and accepts it, but even she has difficulty when faced with Murray's love. Initially, she urges him to come to her room, but he refuses unless she stops selling herself, which she will not do because she knows she doesn't belong in Murray's world. Later, however, she tells him, "I'm a whore, but I don't want to be *your* whore." After Murray rescues her, the two drop out of the film, so Jenny's status remains as unresolved as Francis's own "prostitution." Certainly the best the pair can hope for is indicated by Rock's marriage to Elizabeth, a marriage haunted by his sister's claim that he should have kept her as his mistress, instead of "legalizing" his "shabby amours."

Francis may not have realized it, but *The Doctor and the Devils* turned into an extreme example of self-criticism by a man who felt he had tried to ignore the compromise of his principles, a man who, in truth, accused himself more harshly than necessary. It is this harshness, as seen in the film's thoroughly bleak world, that probably kept it from becoming popular with audiences. Having invested so much of himself in *The Doctor and the Devils*—more, perhaps, than he realized—Francis says he was "slightly shattered" when it failed at the box office, adding, "I had high hopes for the film. I liked it."[131]

"I *don't* want to go back to making cheap horror pictures," said Francis, after *The Doctor and the Devils* disappeared from the few theaters where it had played. "Financially, I don't have to do that. I can make far more photographing a big feature like *Dune,* and it's also more enjoyable."[132] However, after stepping in as a photographer in an attempt to rescue the floundering *Brenda Starr* (shot in 1986, but not released until 1992), Francis *did* direct a cheap horror picture, *The Dark Tower* (1987), and he immediately rediscovered the frustrations associated with international coproductions.

"I was called in by [producer] Sandy Howard, with whom I've had an off-and-on relationship for some time. When he's called in the past, I've usually had other commitments." *The Dark Tower* was three weeks away from its shooting date in Spain, and director Ken Wiederhorn had "dropped out" because of "personal problems. I read the script, which I thought was good, and agreed. But I came on the project with very little preparation. . . . When we got to Spain, we found certain problems," which "pushed back the start date by a few weeks."[133] For unknown reasons, stars Roger Daltry and Lucy Gutteridge were replaced at the last minute. Then, about two weeks after production began, Sandy Howard "sued a trio of film companies for allegedly breaching an agreement to provide financing" for the film.[134] As a result, Francis had to cut corners even more sharply than he had expected. In one scene, he even made a cameo appearance in an elevator because, he says half-jokingly, "we couldn't afford anyone else."[135]

Further complications arose because the film was made in Barcelona with a less-than-expert crew, so Francis served as his own photographer (with his frequent camera operator, Gordon Hayman, receiving the official credit). Although he finished the film on schedule, Francis found the process "maddening. . . . I usually have lots of fun on pictures, but this was really heavy going."[136] The following August, the producer took the film to Los Angeles, where he had several new scenes shot and added some replacement special effects of a rotting corpse and an exploding wall. *The Dark Tower* was released to European theaters in 1987, but in the United States it turned up on video two years later. In the credits, Francis used the pseudonym Ken Barnett.

Like *Hysteria,* this film deals with a newly constructed building that appears to be haunted; this time, it really *is* possessed by a murderous spirit, which security officer Dennis Randall (Michael Moriarty) investigates. The actual deaths are mundane. An unseen force hurls a window washer from his platform, a guard is killed when an elevator crashes, and Randall's partner suddenly shoots several people in the building's lobby. Even the scenes in which the building itself menaces someone fail to create much atmosphere, as lamps and plaster drop to the floor. Only a few shots reveal Francis's visual sense: the outline of the window washer's figure is seen through half-closed blinds; when a woman touches a foreground window, blood emerges from her fingertips and drips down the glass; and (in what could be considered a trademark image) blood spatters on the elevator's bare wall.

Prior to the film's release, Francis told an interviewer, "The element of evil in the story, for me, was secondary to the psychology of Michael Moriarty's character. He's a man who has this recurring nightmare of being pushed from a high building, and once the events start, he is convinced nothing will stop this from becoming a reality. So the question the audience will ask is, 'How's he going to stop it from happening?' "[137] This aspect may have attracted Francis because of its similarity to the situation in his unrealized project *Dreams and Mrs. Ainsley,* in which the main character has periodic dreams of future events, dreams that ultimately reveal her true character.

As it turned out, this entire—and significant—plot element disappeared from the final version of *The Dark Tower,* in which the character merely has a degree of precognition, through which he briefly experiences future events. Evidently, after Francis completed the film, the producer modified the central characterization and, with it, much of the film's potential interest. This change could also explain Moriarty's rather distracted performance, which might have been appropriate to a character in fear of his death.

Probably for the same reason, the plot's resolution remains ambiguous. In a climax evoking *Vengeance,* Randall is possessed by the late husband of Carolyn Page (Jenny Agutter), the building's architect, and accuses her of killing him. "He had to die!" she argues. "He was evil! I tried to leave him, but he wouldn't let me." Because she had pushed him into the structure's foundation and buried him alive under a load of concrete, at the film's end his rotting corpse emerges and pulls her into the wall with him. This and an earlier scene suggest that the husband was—like Max Holt—a "monster," but the film nonetheless allows him to gain revenge, as if he were only an innocent victim. (This climax differs in several respects from the summary in the film's press-book, which includes a final encounter between Randall and Carolyn on the building's roof, one that evidently relates to Randall's fear of falling.[138])

As it stands, *The Dark Tower* is full of scenes that lead nowhere, and its protagonists seldom hold the viewer's attention. Only once does the action relate in an intriguing way to a character's personality and feelings. Carolyn, the workaholic architect, wants her building "to be perfect" because, she says, "I put my whole life into this project," which leads to some emotional resonance when her creation starts falling apart around her. Perhaps, in this situation, Francis found a metaphor that unconsciously expressed his own feelings about the "collapse" of *The Doctor and the Devils.* Similarly, only one character has a sympathetic human dimension. Dr. Max Gold (Theodore Bikel), a parapsychologist, reveals a professional frustration much like Francis's when he says, "My colleagues seem to be getting most of the limelight. . . . Of course, there's no shame in not getting recognition, even if you deserve it as much as I do," but it would be nice, "especially after you had to endure insults." Later, he declares, "I'm only a man trying to do his job." In an epilogue, Randall visits this man's grave and notes that he "finally made contact" with a spirit. "What good did it do him?" his companion asks. "Not a hell of a lot," replies Randall.

"I consider myself a successful cameraman, but I'm still a *struggling* director,"[139] commented Francis in 1986, and so after *The Dark Tower* he returned to the still-satisfying world of photography. Averaging more than one feature per year, he revealed an energy and vitality that belied the fact that he had entered his seventies. These films included such varied works as two sensitive character studies by veteran Robert Mulligan (*Clara's Heart,* 1988; *The Man in the Moon,* 1991); Martin Scorsese's frightening, hyperbolic *Cape Fear* (1991); and director Ed Zwick's powerful segment of Civil War history, *Glory* (1989). In addition, as an affectionate gesture toward his friend and frequent collaborator, Francis shot the documentary *Peter Cushing: A One-Way Ticket to Hollywood,* shown on British television in 1989.

On the set, Francis conveys a thoroughly relaxed professionalism, while using his ironic sense of humor to keep the mood light. "I believe movies have to be fun to make," he explains, "because once I undertake to do a movie they own me body and soul for that period and it becomes my whole life; so if you don't have fun while you're making the movie you don't have any fun at all."[140] Interestingly, Francis's joking has its serious function, for—with his tongue only partly in his cheek—he defuses tension by saying things that less secure members of the crew might not dare say. Often, this involves a barb aimed at the generally sacrosanct director.

At one point, on the set of *Dune,* David Lynch asked a trainee to beat a drum as accompaniment for a shot. When Lynch, caught up in his staging, kept demanding more complex rhythms from the beleaguered young man, Francis interrupted. "David," he said, "for the amount of money we're paying the poor boy, don't expect Buddy Rich."[141] On *Clara's Heart,* Francis noticed that the director had left his copy of the script in the camera's view, so just before a take he walked over, picked it up, and asked ostentatiously, "What idiot left this script here?" In both cases, the cast and crew enjoyed this teasing of a director by someone who could get away with it.

In 1990, after winning his second Academy Award (for *Glory*) at the age of seventy-two, Freddie Francis said, "When people ask me when I'm going to retire, I tell them probably never. You retire so you can spend your time doing what you love. For me, that's making movies."[142] Therefore, Francis has continued making major contributions to new films as a photographer, while looking forward to directing again. Whether or not he will direct other features remains an open question. In 1993, he thought that Martin Scorsese would be able to arrange production of *Death Masque,* a script about the life of Edgar Allan Poe that Francis had received while working on *Cape Fear,* but that has not yet come to pass. He did, however, direct a segment of HBO's *Tales from the Crypt;* entitled "Last Respects," it was broadcast in 1996.

Whatever happens or fails to happen in the future, Francis can look back with satisfaction on three thoroughly admirable careers: as a photographer, as a director, and again as a photographer. During all three, he consistently maintained a high standard of artistic integrity and professionalism. From the start, he believed that the only approach to any film, even one that appears hopeless, is "to make it as well as you can,"[143] and he maintained this outlook in the face of conditions more conducive to commercial compromise than to creative cinema. "One works very hard on a film," he declares, adding, "It's very distressing to know that your work is being reviewed by people who really don't know what you're getting at. However, one has to learn to live with this. It's something that comes with the job."[144]

While working for Tyburn, Francis described his then-current status. "I'm happy with life," he said. "At the moment it looks as though I'll go on doing horror films as long as people keep offering them to me, and I just hope that before I can't do any more work, before I'm too old, I will be able to do something different. But if not I've spent my life making films, which I love doing. I mean, how many people go through their lives always doing things they've wanted to do?"[145] Still, despite this realistic perspective, his ambivalence remained. In 1991, Francis wrote, "My main regret, I think, is that I have not achieved the same sort of status as a director that I have as a director of photography." Then, almost immediately, he expressed surprise that "I seem to get more satisfaction from the small films I've directed than from the big films I've pho-tographed."[146] It is exactly this division in his feelings about his achievements, this mixture of regret and satisfaction, that frequently fueled his creativity. In person, how-ever, Freddie Francis is far from a bitter or cynical man, so it seems that the films themselves provided a useful means of releasing such negative feelings.

Many of Francis's twenty-six complete features stand securely as fine examples of popular storytelling. Many are also highly individualistic in mood and content. A clas-sical stylist, Francis stressed form and suggestion and complex emotional overtones, while other directors recklessly escalated their films' overt violence and sexuality. Even as he depicted some of the worst excesses of human nature, Francis retained a con-trolled aesthetic sense and an overall dignity that transcend flashy sensationalism. He may have sought only to be a skilled and sensitive craftsman, but almost despite him-self he evolved into a personal filmmaker whose works—their weaknesses as well as their strengths—cannot be separated from his outlook and state of mind. As both entertainer and artist, Freddie Francis possesses an established place in film history.

NOTES AND REFERENCES

Chapter I

1. Ted Kent, interview with the author, 9 August 1973.
2. Elsa Lanchester, interview with the author, 3 May 1974.
3. Kent interview.
4. Gloria Stuart, letter to the author, 20 July 1993.
5. Kent interview.
6. Gregory Mank, "Mae Clarke Remembers James Whale," *Films in Review,* May 1985, 298.
7. James Curtis, *James Whale* (Metuchen and London: Scarecrow Press, 1982), 67.
8. Ibid., 95.
9. Gregory Mank, "*The Old Dark House:* Elegant Gothic Comedy," *American Cinematographer,* October 1988, 43–44.
10. Curtis, *James Whale,* 81.
11. Ibid., 95–96.
12. Tom Weaver, "Dark Houses and Invisible Men," *Bloody Best of Fangoria* 13 (September 1994): 72.
13. Gregory Mank, "Introduction: An Interview with Valerie Hobson," in *The Bride of Frankenstein,* ed. Philip J. Riley (Absecon: MagicImage Filmbooks, 1989), 22.
14. Weaver, "Dark Houses," 71.
15. Mank, "Elegant Gothic Comedy," 43.
16. Curtis, *James Whale,* 95.
17. Dennis Fischer, *Horror Film Directors, 1931–1990* (Jefferson and London: McFarland, 1991), 719.
18. Gregory Mank, "Production Background," in *Frankenstein,* ed. Philip J. Riley (Absecon: MagicImage Filmbooks, 1989), 26.
19. R. C. Sherriff, interview with the author, 27 August 1971.
20. Mank, "Production Background," 27.
21. Ernest Thesiger, "Recollection," *Times* (London), 31 May 1957, 12.
22. John Gielgud, *Early Stages* (London: Falcon Press, 1953), 64.
23. Curtis, *James Whale,* 9–10.
24. Gregory Mank, *It's Alive* (San Diego and New York: A. S. Barnes, 1981), 55.
25. Lanchester interview.
26. "*The Cherry Orchard,*" *Stage,* 28 May 1925, 16.
27. "*The Cherry Orchard,*" *Era,* 30 May 1925, 1.
28. James Agate, *The Contemporary Theatre, 1925* (London: Chapman and Hall, 1926), 80–81.
29. Giles Playfair, *My Father's Son* (London: Geoffrey Bles, 1937), 120.
30. Irene Thirer, "Director James Whale Here En Route to Europe," *New York Post,* 4 June 1936.
31. David Lewis, interview with the author, 9 August 1973.
32. Thirer, "Director James Whale."
33. C. H. B., "*A Man with Red Hair,*" *Theatre World,* April 1928, 12.
34. "*A Man with Red Hair,*" *Era,* 29 February 1928, 4.
35. James Agate, "*A Man with Red Hair,*" *Sunday Times* (London), 4 March 1928, 6.
36. "*A Man with Red Hair,*" *Stage,* 1 March 1928, 18.
37. "*A Revival of London's Grand Guignol,*" *Stage,* 17 May 1928, 16–17.

38. *"Mr. Godly beside Himself,"* *Era,* 10 March 1926, 8.

39. G.W. B., *"Fortunato," Era,* 24 October 1928, 1.

40. Richard Koszarski, unpublished interview with Paul Ivano, 26 May 1973.

41. "James Whale and *Frankenstein," New York Times,* 20 December 1931, sec. 8, p. 4.

42. Ibid.

43. "To Film War Play," *New York Times,* 8 September 1929, sec. 9, p. 5.

44. *"Frankenstein* Finished," *New York Times,* 11 October 1931, sec. 8, p. 5.

45. Mordaunt Hall, *"Frankenstein," New York Times,* 5 December 1931, 21.

46. "James Whale and *Frankenstein."*

47. *"Frankenstein* Finished."

48. Ibid.

49. "James Whale and *Frankenstein."*

50. Tom Hutchinson, *Horror and Fantasy in the Movies* (New York: Crescent Books, 1974), 132.

51. Ibid., 42.

52. "James Whale and *Frankenstein."*

53. Cecelia Ager, "Going Places," *Variety,* 8 December 1931, 47.

54. "Inside Stuff—Pictures," *Variety,* 14 July 1931, 43.

55. *"Frankenstein* Finished."

56. "James Whale and *Frankenstein."*

57. Lewis interview, 9 August 1973.

58. *Motion Picture Herald,* 6 February 1932, 59.

59. *"The Devil," Stage,* 16 January 1930, 16.

60. *"The Old Dark House," Motion Picture Herald,* 16 July 1932, 52.

61. Sherriff interview.

62. R. C. Sherriff, *No Leading Lady* (London: Victor Gollancz, 1968), 241.

63. *Variety,* 27 June 1933, 21.

64. Colin Clive, "The Woman Who Thrilled Me," *Picturegoer,* 29 July 1933, 11.

65. David Lewis, interview with the author, 30 April 1974.

66. John P. Fulton, "How We Made the Invisible Man," *American Cinematographer,* September 1934, 201.

67. Sherriff, *No Leading Lady,* 260.

68. Ibid., 263.

69. Ibid., 267.

70. Char., *"The Invisible Man," Variety,* 21 November 1933, 14, 20.

71. Richard Watts, Jr., *"The Invisible Man," New York Herald-Tribune,* 20 November 1933.

72. Mordaunt Hall, *"The Invisible Man," New York Times,* 26 November 1933, sec. 9, p. 5.

73. "Words on Music by James Whale: *Invisible Man* Director Debates a Topical Problem with *Film Weekly," Film Weekly,* 2 February 1934, 5.

74. Lewis interview, 30 April 1974.

75. Ibid., 9 August 1973.

76. Sherriff, *No Leading Lady,* 269.

77. The script's title page cites both Hurlbut and Balderston as authors, but on the film itself Hurlbut receives sole screenplay credit. Universal's records also list Josef Berne, R. C. Sherriff, Edmund Pearson, and Morton Covan among the original authors, without indicating the dates or nature of their contributions.

78. Gerald Gardner, *The Censorship Papers* (New York: Dodd, Mead and Co., 1987), 67.

79. Ibid., 69.

80. Ibid., 66.

81. Lewis interview, 9 August 1973.

82. "James Whale and *Frankenstein."*

83. Lanchester interview.

84. Gardner, *Censorship Papers,* 67.

85. Ibid.

86. Kent interview.

87. "James Whale and *Frankenstein.*"

88. Lanchester interview.

89. Curtis Harrington, interview with the author, 10 August 1973.

90. Mank, "Elegant Gothic Comedy," 43.

91. Mank, *It's Alive,* 57.

92. Lanchester interview.

93. Mank, *It's Alive,* 59.

94. Mank, "Interview with Valerie Hobson," 23.

95. Lewis interview, 9 August 1973.

96. Ibid.

97. Lanchester interview.

98. Stuart letter.

99. Ernest Thesiger, *Practically True* (London: Wm. Heinemann, 1927), 3.

100. Ibid., 4.

101. Ibid., 87.

102. Ibid., 112.

103. Obituary of Ernest Thesiger, *Observer,* 15 January 1961.

104. Lewis interview, 9 August 1973.

105. Ibid.

106. Ibid.

107. Harrington interview.

108. Curtis, *James Whale,* 201–2.

109. Ted Kent, letter to Peter Barnsley, quoted in Curtis, *James Whale,* 122.

Chapter 2

1. John Brosnan, *Movie Magic: The Story of Special Effects in the Cinema* (New York: St. Martin's Press, 1974), 166.

2. "Interview with Darlyne O'Brien," *Classic Images* 131 (May 1986): 10.

3. Ibid., 11.

4. *Closeup* 3 (1977): 5.

5. Ibid., 11; paraphrased by Turner.

6. "Dinosaurs Cavort in Film for Doyle," *New York Times,* 3 June 1922, sec. 1, p. 4.

7. "His Dinosaur Film a Hoax, Says Doyle," *New York Times,* 4 June 1922, 18.

8. Steve Archer, *Willis O'Brien: Special Effects Genius* (Jefferson and London: McFarland & Co., 1993), 13; from a 1965 interview with Don Shay.

9. *Closeup,* 5.

10. Rudy Behlmer, "Foreword," in *The Girl in the Hairy Paw,* ed. Ronald Gottesman and Harry Geduld (New York: Avon, 1976), 10. From a letter to W. Douglas Burden, 22 June 1964.

11. Reginald Taviner, "A Pipe Is His Scepter," *Photoplay,* July 1933, 42.

12. Ibid., 42, 113.

13. Behlmer, "Foreword," 12. From a memo to David O. Selznick, 19 December 1931. Memo also quoted, with slightly different phrasing and given as 18 December 1931, in Ronald Haver, *David O. Selznick's Hollywood* (New York: Alfred A. Knopf, 1980), 81.

14. Behlmer, "Foreword," 10; from letter to Burden.

15. Orville Goldner and George E. Turner, *The Making of King Kong* (New York and South Brunswick: A. S. Barnes, 1975), 38. From a 1933 press release.

16. Ibid.

17. Ibid.

18. Edgar Wallace, *My Hollywood Diary* (London: Hutchinson, n.d.), 141.

19. Ibid., 93.

20. Ibid., 143–44.

21. Goldner and Turner, *Making of King Kong,* 37.

22. "The Secret Is Out," *Picturegoer Weekly,* 15 April 1933, 14.

23. Haver, *Selznick's Hollywood,* 104.

24. Rudy Behlmer, ed., *Memo from David O. Selznick* (New York: Viking Press, 1972), 44.

25. Fay Wray, "How Fay Met Kong, or The Scream That Shook the World," *New York Times,* 21 September 1969, sec. 2, p. 17.

26. Ibid.

27. "Rango, a Tiger Film," *New York Times,* 4 January 1931, sec. 8, p. 6. Shoedsack said almost the same thing in a prior interview, *New York Times,* 17 March 1929, sec. 10, p. 8.

28. Ibid.

29. Goldner and Turner, *Making of King Kong,* 173.

30. Ibid., 73.

31. Paul Mandell, "Untold Horrors of Skull Island," *Cinemagic* 30 (Summer 1985): 36.

32. Haver, *Selznick's Hollywood,* 113.

33. *Closeup,* 5.

34. Archie Marshek, "King Kong . . . 1933; Memories of Kong," *American Cinemeditor,* Winter 1976–77, 12.

35. Paul Mandell, "The Great Animated Apes: Part I, *King Kong,*" *Fangoria* 4 (February 1980): 66.

36. Behlmer, "Foreword," 13.

37. *Motion Picture Herald,* 18 March 1993, 33.

38. Goldner and Turner, *Making of King Kong,* 197.

39. *Closeup,* 5.

40. Marshek, "Memories," 13.

41. Don Shay, "Willis O'Brien: Creator of the Impossible," *Cinefex* 7 (January 1982): 42.

42. *Closeup,* 13.

43. Paul Mandell, "The Great Animated Apes: Part II, *Son of Kong,*" *Fangoria* 5 (April 1980): 21.

44. *Variety,* 6 June 1933, 49.

45. *New York Evening Post,* 7 October 1933.

46. Ray Harryhausen, *Film Fantasy Scrapbook* (New York and South Brunswick: A. S. Barnes, 1972), 18.

47. Archer, *Willis O'Brien,* 43–44.

48. Elliott Stein, "The Thirteen Voyages of Ray Harryhausen," *Film Comment,* November–December 1977, 27.

49. Brosnan, *Movie Magic,* 161.

50. Paul Mandell, "Pete Peterson: Working against All Odds," *Cinemagic* 28 (Winter 1984): 30.

51. Shay, "Willis O'Brien," 53.

52. Larry French, "The Harryhausen Interview," *Fangoria* 16 (1981): 36.

53. Ibid., 37.

54. "Interview with Darlyne O'Brien," 11.

55. Archer, *Willis O'Brien,* 52; from an interview with Kevin Brownlow.

56. Ibid., 44.

57. Steve Archer and Mike Hankin, "An Interview with Ray Harryhausen about *One Million Years B.C.,*" *Little Shoppe of Horrors* 10–11 (July 1990): 135.

58. Mandell, "Pete Peterson," 31.

59. "Interview with Darlyne O'Brien," 11.

60. Ezra Goodman, *The Fifty-Year Decline and Fall of Hollywood* (New York: MacFadden Books, 1962), 310.

61. Ibid.

62. Published in Archer, *Willis O'Brien.* Quotations in the text are from this volume.

63. Paul Mandell, "Of Beasts and Behemoths," *Fantastic Films,* March 1980, 38.

64. Archer, *Willis O'Brien,* 129; from a letter to Mike Hankin, 16 March 1982.

Chapter 3

1. Ray Bradbury, introduction to *Film Fantasy Scrapbook,* by Ray Harryhausen (New York and South Brunswick: A. S. Barnes, 1972), 11.

2. "Ray Harryhausen and Charles Schneer at the National Film Theatre, Part II," *Special Visual Effects Created by Ray Harryhausen,* Spring 1974, 12.

3. Ray Harryhausen, interview with the author, 1 June 1974.

4. Harryhausen, *Scrapbook,* 117.

5. Ted Newsom, "The Ray Harryhausen Story: Part One, The Early Years, 1920–1958," *Cinefantastique,* December 1981, 26.

6. Ibid.

7. Larry French, "The Harryhausen Interview," *Fangoria* 16 (1981): 36.

8. Newsom, "Harryhausen Story," 27.

9. Harryhausen, *Scrapbook,* 19.

10. Newsom, "Harryhausen Story," 29.

11. Steve Swires, "Ray Harryhausen: The Man Who Can Work Miracles," *Starlog* 100 (November 1985): 35.

12. Newsom, "Harryhausen Story," 30.

13. Ibid., 27.

14. Ibid., 32.

15. Ibid., 36.

16. Ibid., 29.

17. Harryhausen, *Scrapbook,* 25.

18. Ibid., 19.

19. Newsom, "Harryhausen Story," 33.

20. Harry Nadler and Dave Trengove, "Ray Harryhausen, Part I," *Castle of Frankenstein* 19 (n.d.): 10.

21. John Brosnan, *Movie Magic: The Story of Special Effects in the Cinema* (New York: St. Martin's Press, 1974), 167.

22. Nadler and Trengove, "Harryhausen, Part I," 10.

23. Brosnan, *Movie Magic,* 173.

24. Harryhausen interview.

25. Nadler and Trengove, "Harryhausen, Part I," 14.

26. Don McGregor, "An Interview with Ray Harryhausen," *Starlog* 51 (October 1981): 26.

27. French, "Interview," 35.

28. Paul Mandell, "Careers: Ray Harryhausen," *Cinemagic* 37 (Winter 1987): 55.

29. Ann Tasker, "Ray Harryhausen Talks about His Cinematic Magic," *American Cinematographer,* June 1981, 607.

30. Blake Mitchell and James Ferguson, "*Clash of the Titans,*" *Fantastic Films* 25 (August 1981): 75.

31. Mandell, "Careers," 57.

32. "Ray Harryhausen and Charles Schneer," 10.

33. Harryhausen, *Scrapbook,* 19.

34. Dan Scapperotti, "Ray Harryhausen's *Clash of the Titans,*" *Cinefantastique,* Winter 1980, 45.

35. Steve Swires, "The Fantasy Voyages of Jerry the Giant Killer [Part 1]," *Starlog,* April 1989, 61.

36. Swires, "Miracles," 36.

37. Brosnan, *Movie Magic,* 167.

38. Harryhausen, *Scrapbook,* 41.

39. Brosnan, *Movie Magic,* 167.

40. Jeff Rovin, *From the Land beyond Beyond: The Films of Willis O'Brien and Ray Harryhausen* (New York: Berkley Windhover, 1977), 101.

41. Harryhausen, *Scrapbook,* 50.

42. Nadler and Trengove, "Harryhausen, Part I," 13.

43. Harryhausen, *Scrapbook,* 50.

44. Nadler and Trengove, "Harryhausen, Part I," 13.

45. Harryhausen, *Scrapbook,* 50.

46. Swires, "Fantasy Voyages," 57.
47. Ibid., 61.
48. Mandell, "Careers," 55.
49. Mark Carducci, "Ray Harryhausen," *Millimeter,* April 1975, 23.
50. Harryhausen, *Scrapbook,* 53.
51. Nadler and Trengove, "Harryhausen, Part I," 12.
52. Harryhausen, *Scrapbook,* 64.
53. Newsom, "Harryhausen Story," 45.
54. "Exclusive Interview with Ray Harryhausen and Charles Schneer: Part I," *Special Visual Effects Created by Ray Harryhausen* 3 (Summer 1972): 9.
55. Rovin, *Land beyond Beyond,* 150.
56. Ibid., 156.
57. Ibid., 161.
58. Harryhausen, *Scrapbook,* 81.
59. Scapperotti, "*Clash of the Titans,*" 9.
60. Rovin, *Land beyond Beyond,* 185.
61. Harryhausen, *Scrapbook,* 85.
62. Mandell, "Careers," 58.
63. Elliott Stein, "The Thirteen Voyages of Ray Harryhausen," *Film Comment,* November–December 1977, 28.
64. Swires, "Miracles," 35.
65. Ray Harryhausen, on the alternative soundtrack of the *Jason and the Argonauts* laser disc (Criterion Collection, 1992).
66. Mandell, "Careers," 56.
67. Harryhausen interview.
68. Harryhausen, *Scrapbook,* 94.
69. Brosnan, *Movie Magic,* 169.
70. Harryhausen, *Scrapbook,* 106.
71. Ibid., 108. This volume reproduces five of Harryhausen's drawings for the unfilmed sequence.
72. Ibid., 114.
73. Ibid., 111.
74. Harryhausen interview.
75. Harry Nadler and Dave Trengove, "Ray Harryhausen, Part II," *Castle of Frankenstein* 20 (Summer 1973): 8.
76. Mandell, "Careers," 55.
77. Brosnan, *Movie Magic,* 172.
78. Nadler and Trengove, "Harryhausen, Part I," 14.
79. Mandell, "Careers," 55.
80. Rovin, *Land beyond Beyond,* 234.
81. Roy Kinnard, *Beasts and Behemoths: Prehistoric Creatures in the Movies* (Metuchen: Scarecrow Press, 1988), 138.
82. Harryhausen interview.
83. Dan Scapperotti and David Bartholomew, "The Golden Voyage of Sinbad," *Cinefantastique* 3, no. 2 (1974): 43.
84. Harryhausen, *Scrapbook,* 88.
85. Brosnan, *Movie Magic,* 176.
86. Don Shay, "*Clash of the* (Foot-Tall) *Titans,*" *Cinefex* 5 (July 1981): 38.
87. Steve Swires, "Merchant of the Magicks," *Starlog* 152 (March 1990): 71.
88. James H. Burns, "Burgess Meredith: Multidimensional Man," *Rod Serling's The Twilight Zone Magazine* (March–April 1984): 31.
89. Berg., "*Clash of the Titans,*" *Variety,* 10 June 1981, 18.
90. Burns, "Burgess Meredith," 31.

91. Steve Swires, "Ray Harryhausen: Farewell to Fantasy Films," *Starlog* 127 (February 1988): 67.

92. McGregor, "Interview," 28.

93. Swires, "Farewell," 63–65.

94. Ibid., 65–67.

95. Mandell, "Careers," 58.

96. Bradbury, "Introduction," 11.

Chapter 4

1. Quoted in John Brosnan, *The Horror People* (New York: St. Martin's Press, 1976), 105.

2. Terence Fisher, interview with the author, 4 June 1974.

3. Michel Caen, "Entretien avec Terence Fisher," *Midi-Minuit Fantastique* 10–11 (Winter 1964–65): 2; my translation.

4. Harry Ringel, "Terence Fisher: Underlining," *Cinefantastique,* Fall 1975, 22.

5. Terence Fisher, "Horror Is My Business," *Films and Filming,* July 1964, 7.

6. Ringel, "Underlining," 24.

7. Fisher interview.

8. Ibid.

9. Ringel, "Underlining," 20.

10. Allen Eyles and Robert Adkinson, Nicholas Fry, eds., *The House of Horror: The Story of Hammer Films* (London: Lorrimer, 1973), 15.

11. Fisher interview.

12. Ibid.

13. Ibid.

14. Fisher, "Horror Is My Business," 8.

15. Fisher interview.

16. Ibid.

17. Ibid.

18. Robin Bean, "Dracula and the Mad Monk," *Films and Filming,* August 1965, 55–56.

19. Fisher interview.

20. Ringel, "Underlining," 20.

21. Brosnan, *Horror People,* 116.

22. Fisher interview.

23. Ibid.

24. Caen, "Entretien," 4; my translation.

25. Gary Parfitt, "The Fruitation of Terence Fisher," *Little Shoppe of Horrors,* February 1974, 62.

26. S[ue] and C[olin] Cowie, "The Terence Fisher Interview," *Horror Elite* 2 (September 1975): 40.

27. Fisher interview.

28. "Charles Gray—'Mocata,' " *Little Shoppe of Horrors,* April 1994, 47.

29. Bruce G. Hallenbeck, "Madeleine [*sic*] Smith," *Little Shoppe of Horrors,* May 1984, 68.

30. Quoted in Mark A. Miller, *Christopher Lee and Peter Cushing and Horror Cinema: A Filmography of Their 22 Collaborations* (Jefferson and London: McFarland & Co, 1995), 138.

31. Al Taylor, "Barbara Shelley," *Little Shoppe of Horrors,* December 1982, 45.

32. "Yvonne Monlaur," *Little Shoppe of Horrors,* March 1986, 84.

33. Tom Weaver, *Science Fiction Stars and Horror Heroes: Interviews with Actors, Directors, Producers, and Writers of the 1940s through 1960s* (Jefferson and London: McFarland & Co., 1991), 43.

34. Dennis Lynch, "Hugh and Pauline Harlow Interview," *Little Shoppe of Horrors,* April 1994, 114.

35. "Terence Fisher," *Little Shoppe of Horrors,* July 1981, 15.

36. Ibid., 16.

37. Al Taylor, "Hammer's Old Guard: Bill Lenny," *Little Shoppe of Horrors,* March 1986, 106.

38. "Terence Fisher," 14.

39. Al Taylor, "Hammer's Old Guard: Len Harris," *Little Shoppe of Horrors,* March 1986, 103.

40. Steve Swires, "Michael Carreras: Inside the House of Hammer," *Fangoria* 63 (May 1987): 60.

41. "Terence Fisher," 16.

42. Taylor, "Hammer's Old Guard: Bill Lenny," 105.

43. Bruce G. Hallenbeck, "Veronica Has Risen from the Grave: An Interview with Veronica Carlson," *Scarlet Street* 9 (Winter 1993): 67.

44. Quoted in Wheeler Winston Dixon, *The Charm of Evil: The Life and Films of Terence Fisher* (Metuchen and London: Scarecrow Press, 1991), 35.

45. Cowie, "Fisher Interview," 37.

46. *Dracula—Prince of Darkness* pressbook. Quoted in Dixon, *Charm of Evil,* 185–86.

47. Cowie, "Fisher Interview," 35.

48. Quoted in Dixon, *Charm of Evil,* 77.

49. Ibid.

50. "Terence Fisher," 14.

51. Quoted in Dixon, *Charm of Evil,* 444.

52. Ibid., 146.

53. Cowie, "Fisher Interview," 26.

54. Quoted in Dixon, *Charm of Evil,* 77.

55. Ringel, "Underlining," 22.

56. "Terence Fisher," 14.

57. Fisher interview.

58. Caen, "Entretien," 10; my translation.

59. Mark A. Miller, "Britain's Duchess of Dark Cinema: Hazel Court," *Filmfax* 20 (May 1990): 74.

60. Hallenbeck, "Madeleine [*sic*] Smith," 68.

61. James Kravaal, "Peter Cushing," *Little Shoppe of Horrors,* May 1984, 61.

62. Ton Paans and Colin Cowie, "Hammer's Old Guard: Tilly Day and Len Harris," *Little Shoppe of Horrors,* March 1986, 101.

63. Oscar Martinez, "The Vampire Woman and the Hunchback—An Interview with Andree Melly and Oscar Quitak," *Little Shoppe of Horrors,* July 1990, 140.

64. Ibid., 147.

65. Bertrand Tavernier, "Entretien avec Terence Fisher," *Midi-Minuit Fantastique* 7 (September 1963): 10; my translation.

66. Bill Kelley, "Christopher Lee: King of the Counts," *Dracula: The Complete Vampire* (Starlog Movie Magazines 6, 1992): 46.

67. Taylor, "Barbara Shelley," 47.

68. "Yvonne Monlaur," 85.

69. Stephen Laws, "Andrew Keir," *Little Shoppe of Horrors,* April 1994, 109.

70. Quoted in Miller, *Christopher Lee and Peter Cushing,* 138.

71. Fisher interview.

72. Fisher, "Horror Is My Business," 7–8.

73. Ibid., 8.

74. Fisher interview.

75. Ibid.

76. Ibid.

77. Ibid.

78. Ibid.

79. Ibid.

80. Cowie, "Fisher Interview," 38.

81. Parfitt, "Fruitation of Terence Fisher," 50.

82. Cowie, "Fisher Interview," 33.

83. Ibid., 38.

84. Parfitt, "Fruitation of Terence Fisher," 50.

85. Eyles et al., *House of Horror,* 13.
86. Parfitt, "Fruitation of Terence Fisher," 50.
87. Ringel, "Underlining," 19.
88. Cowie, "Fisher Interview," 38.
89. Parfitt, "Fruitation of Terence Fisher," 50.
90. Ibid.
91. Eyles et al., *House of Horror,* 13.
92. Parfitt, "Fruitation of Terence Fisher," 50.
93. Caen, "Entretien," 2; my translation.
94. Brosnan, *Horror People,* 112.
95. Fisher, "Horror Is My Business," 8.
96. Parfitt, "Fruitation of Terence Fisher," 51.
97. Brosnan, *Horror People,* 112.
98. Quoted in Dixon, *Charm of Evil,* 11.
99. Brosnan, *Horror People,* 112.
100. Eyles et al., *House of Horror,* 13.
101. Brosnan, *Horror People,* 109.
102. Caen, "Entretien," 10; my translation.
103. Brosnan, *Horror People,* 116.
104. Quoted in Dixon, *Charm of Evil,* 21.
105. Parfitt, "Fruitation of Terence Fisher," 53.
106. Brosnan, *Horror People,* 112.
107. Robert W. Pohle, Jr., and Douglas C. Hart, *The Films of Christopher Lee* (Metuchen and London: Scarecrow Press, 1983), 8–9.
108. Paans and Cowie, "Tilly Day and Len Harris," 100.
109. Fisher interview.
110. Quoted in Dixon, *Charm of Evil,* 446.
111. Ringel, "Underlining," 20.
112. Caen, "Entretien," 14; my translation.
113. Colin Heard, "Hammering the Box Office," *Films and Filming,* June 1969, 17.
114. Kravaal, "Peter Cushing," 61.
115. "Anthony Hinds," *Hammer Journal,* August 1989, 19.
116. Eyles et al., *House of Horror,* 14.
117. Steve Swires, "Hammer's Michael Carreras: Horror as a Family Business," *Fangoria* 61 (February 1987): 57.
118. Anthony Hinds, "Letter," *Little Shoppe of Horrors,* March 1986, 19.
119. Fisher interview.
120. Brosnan, *Horror People,* 113.
121. Eyles et al., *House of Horror,* 14.
122. Fisher, "Horror Is My Business," 8.
123. Fisher interview.
124. Brosnan, *Horror People,* 190.
125. Ringel, "Underlining," 26.
126. Richard Klemensen, Colin Cowie, and Keith Dudley, "Hammer's Old Guard: Len Harris—Part 2," *Little Shoppe of Horrors,* March 1986, 103.
127. Fisher, "Horror Is My Business," 8.
128. Ibid.
129. "Christopher Lee Enters the House of Hammer," *Scarlet Street* 8 (Fall 1992): 44.
130. Bean, "Dracula and the Mad Monk," 56.
131. Christopher Lee, *Tall, Dark, and Gruesome* (London: W. H. Allen, 1977), 197.
132. Randy Palmer, "Reluctant Monster Maker," *Fangoria* 50 (January 1986): 48.
133. "Ask Roy Ashton," *Little Shoppe of Horrors,* July 1981, 36.
134. "Ask Roy Ashton," *Hammer Journal,* August 1980, 9.
135. Fisher interview.

136. Fisher, "Horror Is My Business," 8.
137. Ibid.
138. Eyles et al., *House of Horror,* 14.
139. Fisher interview.
140. Ringel, "Underlining," 26.
141. Brosnan, *Horror People,* 113.
142. Fisher interview.
143. Ibid.
144. Brosnan, *Horror People,* 22.
145. Quoted in Dixon, *Charm of Evil,* 319.
146. Bruce G. Hallenbeck, "Anthony Hinds/John Elder—Producer/Screenwriter," *Little Shoppe of Horrors,* July 1990, 56.
147. Fisher interview.
148. "Anthony Hinds," 19.
149. Bob Sheridan, "Letter," *Little Shoppe of Horrors,* April 1994, 10.
150. Fisher interview.
151. Ringel, "Underlining," 24.
152. Fisher, "Horror Is My Business," 8.
153. Richard Klemensen, "Hammer's Old Guard: Jack Asher," *Little Shoppe of Horrors,* March 1986, 94.
154. Caen, "Entretien," 4; my translation.
155. Ibid., 4–5.
156. Klemensen et al., "Len Harris—Part 2," 103.
157. Ibid.
158. Caen, "Entretien," 4–5; my translation.
159. Tavernier, "Entretien," 12; my translation.
160. "Anthony Hinds—Executive Producer," *Little Shoppe of Horrors,* April 1994, 48.
161. Brosnan, *Horror People,* 115.
162. Ibid., 115–16.
163. Fisher interview.
164. Fisher, "Horror Is My Business," 7.
165. Cowie, "Fisher Interview," 39.
166. Tavernier, "Entretien," 11; my translation.
167. Ringel, "Underlining," 24.
168. Caen, "Entretien," 16; my translation.
169. Ibid.
170. Roy Ashton, "Letter," *Little Shoppe of Horrors,* December 1982, 6.
171. Hallenbeck, "Son of Hammer, Part One," 54.
172. Caen, "Entretien," 16; my translation.
173. Parfitt, "Fruitation of Terence Fisher," 52.
174. Edward de Souza, "Letter," *Little Shoppe of Horrors,* July 1990, 62.
175. Parfitt, "Fruitation of Terence Fisher," 52.
176. "An Interview with Thorley Walters," *Little Shoppe of Horrors,* July 1990, 155.
177. Quoted in Dixon, *Charm of Evil,* 364.
178. Martinez, "Vampire Woman," 141.
179. Caen, "Entretien," 4; my translation.
180. Fisher interview.
181. Caen, "Entretien," 4; my translation.
182. Ringel, "Underlining," 22.
183. Brosnan, *Horror People,* 116.
184. "Terence Fisher," 17.
185. Ton Paans, "Philip Martell," *Little Shoppe of Horrors,* July 1990, 95.
186. Caen, "Entretien," 4; my translation.
187. Ibid., 13.

188. "John Gilling," *Little Shoppe of Horrors,* April 1978, 57.

189. Ringel, "Underlining," 24.

190. Quoted in Miller, *Christopher Lee and Peter Cushing,* 129.

191. Gary Parfitt, *The Films of Peter Cushing* (United Kingdom: An HFCGB Publication, 1975), 52; as quoted in Miller, *Christopher Lee and Peter Cushing,* 133.

192. Kravaal, "Peter Cushing," 56.

193. "Jimmy Sangster," *Little Shoppe of Horrors,* April 1978, 82.

194. "Anthony Hinds," 20.

195. Bruce G. Hallenbeck, "Anthony Hinds, Prince of Hammer," *Fangoria* 75 (July 1988): 54.

196. Pohle and Hart, *Films of Christopher Lee,* 107.

197. Brosnan, *Horror People,* 115.

198. Taylor, "Barbara Shelley," 47.

199. Stephen Laws, "Francis Matthews," *Little Shoppe of Horrors,* April 1994, 118.

200. Quoted in Miller, *Christopher Lee and Peter Cushing,* 196.

201. Ibid., 202.

202. Cowie, "Fisher Interview," 41.

203. Brosnan, *Horror People,* 114.

204. Weaver, *Science Fiction Stars,* 314.

205. Fisher interview.

206. Ibid.

207. Hallenbeck, "Veronica Has Risen," 68.

208. Fisher interview.

209. Ibid.

210. Mark A. Miller, "Veronica Carlson: A Lady and Her Monsters," *Filmfax* 14 (March–April 1989): 72.

211. Swires, "Inside the House of Hammer," 60.

212. Quoted in Dixon, *Charm of Evil,* 288.

213. Ringel, "Underlining," 20.

214. Cowie, "Fisher Interview," 27.

215. Fisher interview.

216. Eyles et al., *House of Horror,* 15.

217. Cowie, "Fisher Interview," 40.

Chapter 5

1. Edward Buscombe, *Making "Legend of the Werewolf"* (London: British Film Institute, 1976), 9.

2. Ibid., 55.

3. Freddie Francis, interview with the author, 9 September 1967.

4. Reynold Humphries and Chris Knight, "Tyburn," *Cinefastastique,* Winter 1976–77, 40.

5. Francis interview, 9 September 1967.

6. Susan Munshower, "Freddie Francis," *Monsters of the Movies,* Summer 1975, 80.

7. "Amicus: Two's a Company," *Little Shoppe of Horrors,* March 1973, 30.

8. Francis interview, 9 September 1967.

9. Ibid.

10. Ibid.

11. Munshower, "Freddie Francis," 80.

12. Francis interview, 9 September 1967.

13. Wheeler Winston Dixon, *The Films of Freddie Francis* (Metuchen and London: Scarecrow Press, 1991), 126.

14. John Brosnan, *The Horror People* (New York: St. Martin's Press, 1976), 231.

15. Francis, 9 September 1967.

16. Ibid.

17. Dixon, *Films of Freddie Francis,* 46.

18. Kevin Jackson, "Gothic Shadows," *Sight and Sound,* November 1992, 19.

19. Michael Powell, *A Life in Movies* (New York: Alfred A. Knopf, 1987), 242.

20. Ibid., 168.

21. Ibid., 583.

22. Michael Powell, *Million-Dollar Movie* (London: Mandarin, 1993), 316.

23. Francis interview, 9 September 1967.

24. Brosnan, *Horror People,* 226.

25. Freddie Francis, interview with the author, 6 June 1974.

26. Brosnan, *Horror People,* 226.

27. Ibid., 226–27.

28. Francis interview, 6 June 1974.

29. Stephen Rebello, "Jack Clayton's *The Innocents,*" *Cinefantastique,* June–July 1983, 54.

30. Freddie Francis, introduction to Dixon, *Films of Freddie Francis,* x.

31. Francis interview, 9 September 1967.

32. Ibid.

33. Brosnan, *Horror People,* 228.

34. Hammer Films press release biography of Freddie Francis, c. 1963.

35. Francis interview, 6 June 1974.

36. Francis interview, 9 September 1967.

37. Ibid.

38. Freddie Francis, interview with the author, 31 August 1971.

39. Ibid.

40. Francis interview, 9 September 1967.

41. Al Taylor, "Veronica Carlson," *Little Shoppe of Horrors,* May 1984, 90.

42. Mark A. Miller, "Veronica Carlson: A Lady and Her Monsters," *Filmfax* 14 (March–April 1989): 70.

43. Buscombe, *Making,* 57.

44. Ibid., 24.

45. Gary Parfitt and Ian Yeoman, "An Informal Conversation with Freddie Francis," *Famous Film Stars* 1, no. 2 (1974): 8.

46. Francis interview, 9 September 1967.

47. Buscombe, *Making,* 55.

48. Francis interview, 6 June 1974.

49. Buscombe, *Making,* 28–30.

50. Brosnan, *Horror People,* 228.

51. Francis interview, 31 August 1971.

52. Francis interview, 6 June 1974.

53. Tom Weaver, *Science Fiction Stars and Horror Heroes: Interviews with Actors, Directors, Producers, and Writers of the 1940s through 1960s* (Jefferson and London: McFarland & Co., 1991), 120–21.

54. Francis interview, 6 June 1974.

55. Ibid.

56. Ibid.

57. Howard Thompson, "*Paranoiac,*" *New York Times,* 23 May 1963, 31.

58. Francis interview, 6 June 1974.

59. "Amicus: Two's a Company," 29.

60. A version of *The Evil of Frankenstein* released to network television in 1968 contains more than seven minutes of additional footage shot later, by another director. The new scenes involve a newspaper reporter and an elderly doctor; also, the film's flashback includes a new scene in which the monster (we see only his legs) frightens a child into muteness. This added footage is so poorly written and acted, and so flatly lit and directed, that the rest of the film looks remarkably good by comparison. The videocassette release of the film, however, is the original version.

61. Francis interview, 6 June 1974.

62. "Amicus: Two's a Company," 34a.

63. Brian McFadden, "The Studio That Dripped Blood," *Monster Times,* May 1973, 12.

64. "Amicus: Two's a Company," 30.

65. Francis interview, 6 June 1974.

66. "Amicus: Two's a Company," 30.

67. Francis interview, 9 September 1967.

68. Francis interview, 6 June 1974.

69. Brosnan, *Horror People,* 239.

70. Francis interview, 6 June 1974.

71. "Amicus: Two's a Company," 34a.

72. Brosnan, *Horror People,* 239.

73. "Amicus: Two's a Company," 27.

74. Francis interview, 9 September 1967.

75. "Amicus: Two's a Company," 34b.

76. Ibid.

77. Francis interview, 9 September 1967.

78. Ibid., 26.

79. "Amicus: Two's a Company," 34b.

80. Ibid., 22.

81. Dool., "*The Deadly Bees,*" *Variety,* 25 January 1967, 6.

82. Francis interview, 6 June 1974.

83. "Amicus: Two's a Company," 34b.

84. Brosnan, *Horror People,* 239.

85. Supernatural 1, quoted in Brosnan, *Horror People,* 169.

86. "Amicus: Two's a Company," 31–32.

87. Brosnan, *Horror People,* 229.

88. "Amicus: Two's a Company," 32.

89. Brosnan, *Horror People,* 231.

90. Francis interview, 6 June 1974.

91. "*Mumsy, Nanny, Sonny, and Girly,*" *Independent Film Journal,* 18 February 1970; Roger Greenspun, "*Mumsy, Nanny, Sonny, and Girly,*" *New York Times,* 13 February 1970, 24; Peter Buckley, "*Mumsy, Nanny, Sonny, and Girly,*" *Films and Filming,* June 1970, 82.

92. Greenspun, "*Mumsy, Nanny, Sonny, and Girly,*" 24.

93. Francis interview, 6 June 1974.

94. Ibid.

95. Dixon, *Films of Freddie Francis,* 124.

96. Brosnan, *Horror People,* 231.

97. "Amicus: Two's a Company," 32.

98. Francis interview, 6 June 1974.

99. Ibid.

100. Ibid.

101. Ibid.

102. Dennis Fischer, *Horror Film Directors, 1931–1990* (Jefferson and London: McFarland & Co., 1991), 421.

103. Francis interview, 31 August 1971.

104. R. Allen Leider, "A Tale from behind the Crypt," *Monster Times,* 31 July 1972, 11.

105. Dixon, *Films of Freddie Francis,* 136.

106. Francis interview, 6 June 1974.

107. Ibid.

108. Ibid.

109. Vincent Canby, "*Tales That Witness Madness,*" *New York Times,* 1 November 1973, 48; Murf., "*Tales That Witness Madness,*" *Variety,* 31 October 1973, 26.

110. "Amicus: Two's a Company," 33.

111. Francis interview, 6 June 1974.

112. Buscombe, *Making*, 9.

113. Brosnan, *Horror People*, 228.

114. Munshower, "Freddie Francis," 79.

115. Francis interview, 6 June 1974.

116. Brosnan, *Horror People*, 229.

117. Dixon, *Films of Freddie Francis*, 139.

118. Bruce G. Hallenbeck, "Anthony Hinds, Prince of Hammer," *Fangoria* 75 (July 1988): 54.

119. Buscombe, 10–11. This volume includes the two original stories on which the script was based.

120. Brosnan, *Horror People*, 247.

121. Buscombe, *Making*, 13.

122. Janrae Frank, "The Director and the Devils: A Talk with Freddie Francis," *Monsterland* 6 (December 1985): 59.

123. Dixon, *Films of Freddie Francis*, 18.

124. Ibid., 152–53.

125. Philip Nutman, "An Autopsy of Movie Horror," *Fangoria* 54 (June 1986): 53.

126. Fabienne Marsh, "Grim Doings in Victorian Britain," *New York Times*, 4 August 1985, sec. 3, p. 8.

127. Frank, "The Director and the Devils," 58.

128. "Amicus: Two's a Company," 31.

129. Nutman, "Autopsy," 53.

130. Dixon, *Films of Freddie Francis*, 147.

131. Ibid., 153.

132. Nutman, "Autopsy," 54.

133. Philip Nutman, "*Dark Tower:* How Not to Make a Horror Film?" *Fangoria* 71 (February 1988): 23.

134. "Howard Sues Re: *Tower*," *Variety*, 28 January 1987, 7.

135. Freddie Francis, letter to the author, 7 February 1995.

136. Nutman, "*Dark Tower*," 24–25.

137. Ibid., 23.

138. Dixon, *Films of Freddie Francis*, 280–81.

139. Nutman, "Autopsy," 54.

140. Brosnan, *Horror People*, 230.

141. Ed Naha, *The Making of Dune* (New York: Berkley, 1984), 106.

142. Bob Fisher, "Moving Portrait of War," *American Cinematographer*, November 1990, 64.

143. "Amicus: Two's a Company," 32.

144. Francis interview, 9 September 1967.

145. Buscombe, *Making*, 9.

146. Francis, introduction to Dixon, *Films of Freddie Francis*, x.

SELECTED BIBLIOGRAPHY

James Whale

Primary Sources

The Invisible Man. A film treatment, dated 3 January 1932, included as an appendix in *James Whale: A Biography; or, The Would-be Gentleman,* by Mark Gatiss, 172–77. London and New York: Cassell, 1995.

Secondary Sources

BOOKS AND PARTS OF BOOKS

Agate, James. *The Contemporary Theatre, 1925.* London: Chapman and Hall, 1926.

Anobile, Richard J., ed. *James Whale's Frankenstein.* New York: Universe Books, 1974. A recreation of the film using frame enlargements and dialogue. Anobile's introduction praises Robert Florey over Whale.

Balderston, John L. *Frankenstein: An Adventure in the Macabre.* The 1930 adaptation of Peggy Webling's play, reprinted in *Hideous Progenies: Dramatizations of "Frankenstein" from Mary Shelley to the Present,* by Steven Earl Forry, 251–86. Philadelphia: University of Pennsylvania Press, 1990.

Bram, Christopher. *Father of Frankenstein.* New York: Dutton, 1995. A novel depicting Whale's state of mind during the last weeks of his life.

Brunas, Michael, John Brunas, and Tom Weaver. *Universal Horrors: The Studio's Classic Films, 1931–1946.* Jefferson and London: McFarland, 1990.

Curtis, James. *James Whale.* Metuchen, N.J., and London: Scarecrow Press, 1982.

Denton, Clive. *James Whale, Ace Director: A Career Study.* Ontario: Ontario Film Institute, 1979. An eighteen-page monograph.

"Director of *The Bride of Frankenstein* Tells All." Interview included in the *Bride of Frankenstein* pressbook. In *The Bride of Frankenstein,* by Philip J. Riley, ed., 50. Absecon, N.J.: MagicImage Filmbooks, 1989.

Egremont, Michael. *The Bride of Frankenstein.* London: Queensway Press, n.d. Novelization of the film, published around 1936.

Ellis, Reed. *A Journey into Darkness: The Art of James Whale's Horror Films.* New York: Arno Press, 1980. Typescript reproduction of a 1979 doctoral thesis.

Everson, William K. *Classics of the Horror Film.* Secaucus, N.J.: Citadel Press, 1974.

Fischer, Dennis. *Horror Film Directors, 1931–1990.* Jefferson, N.C., and London: McFarland, 1991. Includes a career profile of Whale.

Florey, Robert. *Hollywood: d'hier et d'aujourd'hui.* Paris: Editions Prisma, 1948.

Forry, Steven Earl. *Hideous Progenies: Dramatizations of "Frankenstein" from Mary Shelley to the Present.* Philadelphia: University of Pennsylvania Press, 1990.

Gardner, Gerald. *The Censorship Papers.* New York: Dodd, Mead and Co., 1987. Quotes from Hays Office correspondence about *Bride of Frankenstein.*

Gatiss, Mark. *James Whale: A Biography; or, The Would-be Gentleman.* London and New York: Cassell, 1995. A volume in the Cassell Lesbian and Gay Studies series.

Gielgud, John. *Early Stages.* London: Falcon Press, 1953. Reprint of the 1939 memoir.

Glut, Donald F. *The Frankenstein Legend: A Tribute to Mary Shelley and Boris Karloff.* Metuchen, N.J.: Scarecrow Press, 1973.

Halliwell, Leslie. *The Dead That Walk.* New York: Continuum, 1988. U.S. edition of a 1986 British publication. Reprints from the shooting script a sequence cut from *Bride of Frankenstein* (138–44).

Hanke, Ken. "James Whale." In *The Fearmakers: The Screen's Directorial Masters of Suspense and Terror,* edited by John McCarty, 29–35. New York: St. Martin's Press, 1994.

Hutchinson, Tom. *Horror and Fantasy in the Movies.* New York: Crescent Books, 1974. Quotes from an interview with Boris Karloff.

Jensen, Paul M. *Boris Karloff and His Films.* South Brunswick, N.J., and New York: A. S. Barnes, 1974.

Lanchester, Elsa. *Elsa Lanchester Herself.* New York: St. Martin's Press, 1983.

Mank, Gregory. *Hollywood Cauldron.* Jefferson, N.C., and London: McFarland, 1994. Includes a revision of Mank's article on *The Old Dark House.*

———. "Introduction: An Interview with Valerie Hobson." In *The Bride of Frankenstein,* edited by Philip J. Riley, 20–24. Absecon, N.J.: MagicImage Filmbooks, 1989.

———. *It's Alive!* San Diego and New York: A. S. Barnes, 1981. A survey of Universal's Frankenstein film series.

———. *Karloff and Lugosi: The Story of a Haunting Collaboration.* Jefferson, N.C., and London: McFarland, 1990.

———. "Production Background." In *The Bride of Frankenstein,* edited by Philip J. Riley, 9–42. Absecon, N.J.: MagicImage Filmbooks, 1989.

———. "Production Background." In *The Bride of Frankenstein,* edited by Philip J. Riley, 25–36. Absecon, N.J.: MagicImage Filmbooks, 1989.

Playfair, Giles. *My Father's Son.* London: Geoffrey Bles, 1937.

Priestley, J. B. *The Old Dark House.* New York: Harper and Brothers, 1928. American edition of *Benighted.*

Sevastakis, Michael. *Songs of Love and Death: The Classical American Horror Film of the 1930s.* Westport, Conn., and London: Greenwood Press, 1993. A condensed version of the author's doctoral thesis, which was published in facsimile form as *Death's Love Songs: The American Horror Film (1931–1936) and Its Embodiment of Romantic Gothic Conventions.* 2 vols. Ann Arbor and London: University Microfilms International, 1981.

Sherriff, R. C. *Journey's End.* New York: Coward-McCann, 1929.

———. *No Leading Lady.* London: Victor Gollancz, 1968. Autobiography.

Skal, David J. *The Monster Show: A Cultural History of Horror.* New York and London: W. W. Norton and Co., 1993. Includes comments on Whale's Frankenstein films.

Taves, Brian. *Robert Florey: The French Expressionist.* Metuchen, N.J., and London: Scarecrow Press, 1987. Includes a revision of Taves's magazine article.

Thesiger, Ernest. *Practically True.* London: Wm. Heinemann, 1927. Memoir.

Turner, George E. "*Frankenstein:* The Monster Classic." In *The Cinema of Adventure, Romance, and Terror,* edited by George E. Turner, 86–101. Hollywood: ASC Press, 1989.

Walpole, Hugh. *Portrait of a Man with Red Hair: A Romantic Macabre.* New York: George H. Doran Co., 1925.

Wells, H. G. *The Invisible Man.* New York: Pocket Books, 1957. Paperback edition of the 1898 novel.

Welsch, Janice R., and Syndy M. Conger. "The Comic and the Grotesque in James Whale's Frankenstein Films." In *Planks of Reason: Essays on the Horror Film,* edited by Barry Keith Grant, 290–306. Metuchen, N.J., and London: Scarecrow Press, 1984.

Whittemore, Don, and Philip Alan Cecchettini. *Passport to Hollywood.* New York: McGraw-Hill Book Co., 1976. The authors' essay on Whale (270–78) introduces relevant reprinted works by Roy Edwards, William K. Everson, and Mordaunt Hall, as well as material on horror films in general.

Wylie, Philip. *The Murderer Invisible.* New York: Popular Library, n.d. Paperback edition of the 1931 novel.

ARTICLES

Abel. "*Old Dark House.*" *Variety,* 1 November 1932, 12. Review.

Agate, James. "*A Man with Red Hair.*" *Sunday Times* (London), 4 March 1928, 6. Review of the London theatrical production.

Ager, Cecilia. "Going Places." *Variety,* 8 December 1931, 47.

B., C. H. "*A Man with Red Hair.*" *Theatre World,* April 1928, 12, 14. Review of the London theatrical production.

Behlmer, Rudy. "Letter to the Editor." *American Cinematographer,* June 1987, 10. Identifies drafts of *Frankenstein*'s script in the Universal Studios files.

B., G. W. "*Fortunato.*" *Era,* 24 October 1928, 1. Review of the London theatrical production.

———. "Grand Guignol Again." *Era,* 23 May 1928, 6. Review of the London theatrical production.

Boehnel, William. "English Director Emerges as King of Horror Films." *New York World-Telegram.* Interview with Whale, circa 1933.

"British Director's Views." *New York Times,* 13 April 1930, sec. 10, p. 6. Interview with Whale.

Char. "*The Invisible Man.*" *Variety,* 21 November 1933, 14, 20. Review.

"*The Cherry Orchard.*" *Stage,* 28 May 1925, 16. Review of the London theatrical production.

———. *Era,* 30 May 1925, 1. Review of the London production.

Clive, Colin. "The Woman Who Thrilled Me." *Picturegoer,* 29 July 1933, 10–11. Interview conducted by John Gliddon.

"Clive of *Frankenstein.*" *New York Times,* 15 November 1931, sec. 8, p. 6. Interview with Colin Clive.

Collura, Joe. "Gloria Stuart: A Bright but Fleeting Star." *Classic Images* 219 (September 1993): Center 12, 14, 16. Interview.

Cunningham, James. "Asides and Interludes." *Motion Picture Herald,* 28 November 1931, 19. Information on showings of *Frankenstein.*

Del Valle, David. "Curtis Harrington on James Whale." *Films in Review,* January–February 1996, 2–17.

"*The Devil.*" *Stage,* 16 January 1930, 16. Review of the London theatrical production.

Edwards, Roy. "Movie Gothick: A Tribute to James Whale." *Sight and Sound,* Autumn 1957, 95–98. Pioneer discussion of Whale's career.

"Films Cast Up James Whale after 15 Years." *New York Herald-Tribune,* 3 December 1944. Interview.

Florey, Robert. "The Monster Lives!" Eight-page typescript of the plot for a proposed sequel to *Frankenstein,* dated 20 December 1931.

"*Frankenstein* Finished." *New York Times,* 11 October 1931, sec. 8, p. 5. Includes excerpts from a letter sent by Whale to Colin Clive.

"*Frankenstein* Refund Gag Added to Picture." *Variety,* 10 November 1931, 4. News item about last-minute changes to the film.

Fulton, John P. "How We Made the Invisible Man." *American Cinematographer,* September 1934, 200–201, 214. Describes the film's special effects.

Hall, Mordaunt. "*Frankenstein.*" *New York Times,* 5 December 1931, 21. Review.

———. "*The Invisible Man.*" *New York Times,* 26 November 1933, sec. 9, p. 5. Reviewer's Sunday column.

———. "*The Old Dark House.*" *New York Times,* 28 October 1932, 22. Review.

"Inside Stuff—Pictures." *Variety,* 14 July 1931, 43. Item about Whale screening *The Cabinet of Dr. Caligari.*

———. *Variety,* 8 December 1931, 48. Report on *Frankenstein*'s preview.

"James Whale and *Frankenstein.*" *New York Times,* 20 December 1931, sec. 8, p. 4. Interview.

Jensen, Paul M. "The Great *Frankenstein* Debate: Whale vs. Florey." *Phantasma* 2 (Winter 1988): 36–50.

———. "*The Invisible Man:* A Retrospective." *Photon* 23 (1973): 10–23, 35.

———. "James Whale." *Film Comment,* Spring 1971, 52–57.

———. "A Visit to *The Old Dark House.*" *Phantasma* 1 (Spring 1988): 32–45.

Kauf. "*Bride of Frankenstein.*" *Variety,* 15 May 1935, 19. Review.

Kent, Ted. Letters to Peter Barnsley. Extensive excerpts, without citation, appear in James Curtis, *James Whale.* Metuchen, N.J., and London: Scarecrow Press, 1982.

Kinnard, Roy. "Gloria Stuart Remembers *The Old Dark House.*" *Filmfax* 3 (June 1986): 42–45. Includes an interview by Tom Weaver and John Brunas.

McCarthy. "*Bride of Frankenstein.*" *Motion Picture Herald,* 20 April 1935, 34. Review.

McManus, John T. "Interview with a Passing Whale." *New York Times,* 7 June 1936, sec. 9, p. 4.

"*A Man with Red Hair.*" *Era,* 29 February 1928, 4. Review of the London theatrical production.

———. *Stage,* 1 March 1928, 18. Review of the London theatrical production.

Mank, Gregory. "Little Maria Remembers." *Films in Review,* October 1992, 329-31. Interview with Marilyn Harris.

———. "Mae Clarke Remembers James Whale." *Films in Review,* May 1985, 298–303. Interview.

———. "*The Old Dark House:* Elegant Gothic Comedy." *American Cinematographer,* October 1988, 42–48. Includes quotations from an interview with Gloria Stuart.

Meehan, Leo. "*Frankenstein.*" *Motion Picture Herald,* 14 November 1931, 40, 42. Review.

Milne, Tom. "One Man Crazy." *Sight and Sound,* Summer 1973, 166–70. Discussion of Whale's films.

Motion Picture Herald, 21 November 1931, 40–41. Ad for *Frankenstein.*

———, 5 December 1931, 48–49. Ad for *Frankenstein.*

———, 19 December 1931, 35. Box-office statistics for *Frankenstein.*

———, 19 December 1931, 67. Reprints six sample ads for *Frankenstein.*

———, 6 February 1932, 59. Item about *Frankenstein*'s success in Iowa.

"Mr. Godly beside Himself." *Era,* 10 March 1926, 8. Review of the London theatrical production.

New York Times, 28 February 1932, sec. 8, p. 5. Item about *The Invisible Man.*

Nielsen, Ray. "Ray's Way." *Classic Images* 172 (October 1989). Interview with Gloria Stuart.

Norwine, Doug. "Remembering Mae Clarke." *Autograph Collector,* August 1992, 32–37.

Nugent, Frank S. "*Bride of Frankenstein.*" *New York Times,* 11 May 1935, 21. Review.

Obituary of Ernest Thesiger. *Observer,* 15 January 1961.

"*The Old Dark House.*" *Motion Picture Herald,* 16 July 1932, 52. Review.

Pierce, Jack. "Character Make-Up." *American Cinematographer,* May 1932, 8–9, 43.

Rascoe, Burton. "Directing a Movie versus Directing a Play." *New York World-Telegram,* 2 December 1944, 6. Interview with Whale.

"*A Revival of London's Grand Guignol.*" *Stage,* 17 May 1928, 16–17. Review of the London theatrical production.

Rush. "*Frankenstein.*" *Variety,* 8 December 1931, 14. Review.

Scheuer, Philip K. "*The Old Dark House.*" *Los Angeles Times,* 18 November 1932. Review.

Sennwald, Andre. "That Invisible Actor." *New York Times,* 3 December 1933, sec. 9, p. 8. Interview with Claude Rains.

Server, Lee. "Gloria Stuart." *Films in Review,* February 1988, 66–75. Interview.

Taves, Brian. "Universal's Horror Tradition." *American Cinematographer,* April 1987, 36–48. Includes comments on Florey's *Frankenstein* script, supplemented by a letter, August 1987, 26.

Taylor, Al. "The Forgotten Frankenstein." *Fangoria,* October 1979, 39–42. Interview with Robert Florey.

Thesiger, Ernest. "Recollection." *Times* (London), 31 May 1957, 12. Included with Whale's obituary.

Thirer, Irene. "Director James Whale Here En Route to Europe." *New York Post,* 4 June 1936. Interview.

Thomaier, William. "James Whale." *Films in Review,* May 1962, 277–90. Addenda and filmography by Robert F. Fink. A pioneer career article; contains some factual errors.

"To Film War Play." *New York Times,* 8 September 1929, sec. 9, p. 5. Interview with Whale.

Troy, William. "Films." *Nation,* 13 December 1933, 688. Review of *The Invisible Man.*

Variety, 8 December 1931, 6. Item about *The Invisible Man* and Robert Florey.

————, 8 December 1931, 9. Box-office figures for *Frankenstein.*

————, 15 December 1931, 9. Box-office figures for *Frankenstein.*

————, 5 January 1932, 6. Item about *The Invisible Man,* Robert Florey, and Garrett Fort.

————, 1 November 1932, 9. Box-office figures for *The Old Dark House.*

————, 8 November 1932, 9. Box-office figures for *The Old Dark House.*

————, 15 November 1932, 9. Box-office figures for *The Old Dark House.*

————, 22 November 1932, 9. Box-office figures for *The Old Dark House.*

————, 20 June 1933, 6. Item about *The Invisible Man* and Una O'Connor.

————, 27 June 1933, 16. Item about *The Invisible Man* and Chester Morris.

————, 27 June 1933, 21. Item about *The Invisible Man* script.

————, 3 August 1933, 31. Item about *The Invisible Man* and technicians' strike.

————, 29 August 1933, 3. Item about *The Invisible Man* and Claude Rains.

Watts, Richard, Jr. "*The Invisible Man.*" *New York Herald-Tribune,* 20 November 1933. Review.

Weaver, Tom. "Dark Houses and Invisible Men." *Bloody Best of Fangoria* 13 (September 1994): 68–74. Interview with Gloria Stuart.

"Words on Music by James Whale: *Invisible Man* Director Debates a Topical Problem with *Film Weekly.*" *Film Weekly,* 2 February 1934, 4–6. Reports on a luncheon Universal gave for H. G. Wells.

INTERVIEWS

Florey, Robert. Interview with the author, 2 May 1974.

Harrington, Curtis. Interview with the author, 10 August 1973,

Kent, Ted. Interview with the author, 9 August 1973.

Lanchester, Elsa. Interview with the author, 3 May 1974.

Lewis, David. Interviews with the author, 9 August 1973, 30 April 1974.

Sherriff, R. C. Interview with the author, 27 August 1971.

Stuart, Gloria. Letter to the author, 20 July 1993.

SCREENPLAYS

Florey, Robert, and Garrett Fort. *Frankenstein.* Unpublished screenplay, dated 15 May–20 June 1931. Florey is credited with the original story and adaptation, both Florey and Fort with the continuity.

Fort, Garrett, and Francis Edwards Faragoh. *Frankenstein.* Shooting script, dated 12 August 1931. Absecon, N.J.: MagicImage Filmbooks, 1989 (Philip J. Riley, editor).

————. *Frankenstein.* Unpublished "Continuity and Dialogue" of the finished film. Undated.

Hurlbut, William, and John L. Balderston. *The Return of Frankenstein.* Shooting script of *Bride of Frankenstein,* dated 1 December 1934. Published as *The Bride of Frankenstein,* edited by Philip J. Riley. Absecon, N.J.: MagicImage Filmbooks, 1989.

Sherriff, R. C. *The Invisible Man.* Unpublished shooting script, dated 12 June 1933.

Willis O'Brien

Primary Sources

"Miniature Effect Shots." *International Photographer,* April 1933 (unpaginated). Reprinted, without acknowledgment, as "Miniature Effects Shots," in *The Girl in the Hairy Paw,* edited by Ronald Gottesman and Harry Geduld, 183–84. New York: Avon, 1976.

Secondary Sources

BOOKS AND PARTS OF BOOKS

Archer, Steve. *Willis O'Brien: Special Effects Genius.* Jefferson, N.C., and London: McFarland, 1993. Reprints stories and illustrations for many of O'Brien's unproduced projects.

Behlmer, Rudy. Foreword to *The Girl in the Hairy Paw*, edited by Ronald Gottesman and Harry Geduld, 9–13. New York: Avon, 1976. Contains information about *King Kong*'s origin.

———, ed. *Memo from David O. Selznick*. New York: Viking Pess, 1972.

Bezanson, Mark. "Edgar Wallace and Kong." In *The Girl in the Hairy Paw*, edited by Ronald Gottesman and Harry Geduld, 45–47. New York: Avon, 1976. A description, with excerpts, of Wallace's script.

Brosnan, John. *Movie Magic: The Story of Special Effects in the Cinema*. New York: St. Martin's Press, 1974. Includes a discussion of O'Brien's work.

Carroll, Noel. "King Kong: Ape and Essence." In *Planks of Reason*, edited by Barry Keith Grant, 215–44. Metuchen and London: Scarecrow Press, 1984.

Cooper, Merian C. *Grass*. New York and London: G. P. Putnam's Sons, 1925. Illustrated with photographs by Ernest Beaumont Schoedsack.

Doyle, Arthur Conan. *The Lost World*. In *The Professor Challenger Stories*. London: John Murray, 1952.

Goldner, Orville, and George E. Turner. *The Making of King Kong*. New York and South Brunswick: A. S. Barnes, 1975.

Goodman, Ezra. *The Fifty-Year Decline and Fall of Hollywood*. New York: MacFadden Books, 1962. Paperback edition of the 1961 original; includes two pages on O'Brien, with interview quotations.

Harryhausen, Ray. *Film Fantasy Scrapbook*. New York and South Brunswick: A. S. Barnes, 1972.

Haver, Ronald. *David O. Selznick's Hollywood*. New York: Alfred A. Knopf, 1980. Includes extensive coverage of *King Kong*, but rarely cites sources.

Kinnard, Roy, ed. *"The Lost World" of Willis O'Brien: The Original Shooting Script of the 1925 Landmark Special Effects Dinosaur Film, with Photographs*. Jefferson, N.C., and London: McFarland, 1993. Reprints the scenario written by Marion Fairfax.

Lovelace, Delos W. *King Kong*. New York: Ace Books, 1976. Reprint of the screenplay's 1932 novelization.

Rovin, Jeff. *From the Land beyond Beyond: The Films of Willis O'Brien and Ray Harryhausen*. New York: Berkley Windhover, 1977.

Turner, George E. "*Creation:* The Lost Epic." In *The Cinema of Adventure, Romance, and Terror*, edited by George E. Turner, 102–13. Hollywood: ASC Press, 1989. A well-illustrated, slightly expanded version of an article in *American Cinematographer*, March 1987, 34–40.

Wallace, Edgar. *My Hollywood Diary*. London: Hutchinson, n.d. Wallace's letters to his wife, published after his death, with several references to *King Kong*.

Warren, Bill. *Keep Watching the Skies; American Science Fiction Movies of the Fifties: Volume I, 1950–1957*. Jefferson, N.C., and London: McFarland, 1982. Contains analyses of *The Black Scorpion* and *The Beast of Hollow Mountain*.

———. *Keep Watching the Skies; American Science Fiction Movies of the Fifties: Volume II, 1958–1962*. Jefferson, N.C., and London: McFarland, 1986. Contains analyses of *The Giant Behemoth* and *The Lost World*.

Wray, Fay. *On the Other Hand: A Life Story*. New York: St. Martin's Press, 1989.

ARTICLES

Archer, Steve, and Mike Hankin. "An Interview with Ray Harryhausen about *One Million Years B.C.*" *Little Shoppe of Horrors* 10–11 (July 1990): 132–35.

Closeup 3 (1977). Special issue devoted to *King Kong* and its 1976 remake. Contains extensive excerpts from letters by George E. Turner and his conversations with people who worked on *Kong*.

Crnkovich, Tony. "King Kong's Hidden Appeal." *Classic Images* 155 (May 1988): C20–21.

"Dinosaurs Cavort in Film for Doyle." *New York Times*, 3 June 1922, 1, 4.

French, Larry. "The Harryhausen Interview." *Fangoria* 16 (1981): 35–39.

Goodman, Ezra. "Master Monster Maker: Willis O'Brien." *New York Times*, 25 June 1950, sec. 2, p. 4.

"His Dinosaur Film a Hoax, Says Doyle." *New York Times*, 4 June 1922, 18.

"Interview with Darlyne O'Brien." *Classic Images* 131 (May 1986): 10–11. Combines interviews conducted by Kevin Brownlow and Mike Hankin.

King, Vance. "From a 'Missing Link' to Tyrannosaurus Rex." *New York Times,* 26 June 1955, sec. 2, p. 5. Much of this article is devoted to an interview with O'Brien.

MacQueen, Scott. "*The Lost World*—Merely Misplaced?" *American Cinematographer,* June 1992, 37–44.

———. "*The Lost World*—1925's Motion-Picture Miracle." Liner notes for Lumivision's 1991 laser disc of the film.

Mandell, Paul. "The Brothers Delgado: The Titans of Miniatures." *Cinemagic* 29 (Spring 1985): 26–31.

———. "The Great Animated Apes: Part I, *King Kong.*" *Fangoria* 4 (February 1980): 52–56, 66.

———. "The Great Animated Apes: Part II, *Son of Kong.*" *Fangoria* 5 (April 1980): 20–22.

———. "The Great Animated Apes: Part III, *Mighty Joe Young.*" *Fangoria* 10 (January 1981): 30–32, 66.

———. "Of Beasts and Behemoths: Part II, *The Giant Behemoth.*" *Fantastic Films* 15 (March 1980): 34–38, 55, 57, 60, 62. Background on the film's production.

———. "Pete Peterson: Working against All Odds." *Cinemagic* 28 (Winter 1984): 30–32.

———. "Untold Horrors of Skull Island." *Cinemagic* 30 (Summer 1985): 34–37. Reprints the script's description of *Kong*'s ravine sequence, with a few transcription errors.

Marshek, Archie. "*King Kong* . . . 1933; Memories of Kong." *American Cinemeditor,* Winter 1976–77, 10–13.

New York Evening Post, 7 October 1933. News item.

"*Rango,* a Tiger Film." *New York Times,* 4 January 1931, sec. 8, p. 6. Interview with Ernest B. Schoedsack.

"The Secret Is Out." *Picturegoer Weekly,* 15 April 1933, 14–15. Interview with Merian C. Cooper.

Shay, Don. "Willis O'Brien: Creator of the Impossible." *Cinefex* 7 (January 1982): 4–71. Contains important biographical and technical information, derived from interviews, but does not cite sources. A shorter version, under the same title, appeared in *Focus on Film* 16 (Autumn 1973): 18–48.

Stein, Elliott. "The Thirteen Voyages of Ray Harryhausen." *Film Comment,* November–December 1977, 24–28. Interview.

Taviner, Reginald. "A Pipe Is His Scepter." *Photoplay,* July 1933, 42, 113. Interview with Merian C. Cooper.

Turner, George. "Sailing Back to Skull Island: *The Son of Kong.*" *American Cinematographer,* August 1992, 67–71.

Weaver, Tom. "Director of Dinosaurs." *Starlog* 193 (August 1993): 63–68. Interview with Eugene Lourie.

———. "Monkey Business." *Starlog* 220 (November 1995): 59–63. Interview with actress Terry Moore.

Wray, Fay. "How Fay Met Kong, or The Scream That Shook the World." *New York Times,* 21 September 1969, sec. 2, p. 17.

SCREENPLAYS

Kong. Unpublished shooting script of *King Kong.* Title page missing. Includes revisions dated through 6 September 1932.

Rose, Ruth. *Mr. Joseph Young of Africa.* Unpublished shooting script of *Mighty Joe Young.* No date listed. Includes revisions dated from 30 September 1947 through 3 February 1948.

Ray Harryhausen

Primary Sources

Aliens, Dragons, Monsters, and Me. Midwich Entertainment, 1990. A forty-five-minute documentary about Harryhausen, written and produced by Richard Jones.

Film Fantasy Scrapbook. New York and South Brunswick: A. S. Barnes, 1972. The second edition (1974) adds a section on *The Golden Voyage of Sinbad* and the third (1981) also includes *Sinbad and the Eye of the Tiger* and *Clash of the Titans*.

Interview conducted by Terence Kelly for BBC radio, late 1960s (five minutes).

Interview included in the motion picture *The Fantasy Film World of George Pal*.

Interview included in the "Special Effects" segment of *The Moviemakers*. Atlantis Films, 1983.

Interview segments are included on the following laser discs: *Earth vs. the Flying Saucers,* Columbia TriStar Home Video, 1995; *Jason and the Argonauts,* Criterion Collection, 1992 (Harryhausen provides commentary on an alternative soundtrack of this laser disc); *Jason and the Argonauts,* Encore Entertainment (Britain), 1994; *Jason and the Argonauts,* Columbia TriStar Home Video, 1995; *Mysterious Island,* Columbia TriStar Home Video, 1995; *The Sinbad Collection,* liner notes for boxed set of laser discs, Columbia TriStar Home Video, 1995 (one disc includes Harryhausen's acceptance of the 1991 Gordon E. Sawyer Academy Award and a documentary featuring interviews with Harryhausen, Charles Schneer, and Kerwin Mathews); and *The 3 Worlds of Gulliver,* Columbia TriStar Home Video, 1995.

Interview with the author, 1 June 1974.

Introduction to *The Illustrated Dinosaur Movie Guide,* by Stephen Jones, 7–9. London: Titan, 1993.

Secondary Sources

BOOKS AND PARTS OF BOOKS

Apollonius Rhodius. *The Argonautica.* Cambridge: Harvard University Press, 1961. Translated by R. C. Seaton. First printed in 1912. Part of the Loeb Classical Library Series.

Arabian Nights: The Marvels and Wonders of the Thousand and One Nights. New York: New American Library, 1991. Adapted from Richard F. Burton's unexpurgated translation by Jack Zipes. A Signet Classic.

Bradbury, Ray. Introduction to *Film Fantasy Scrapbook,* by Ray Harryhausen, 11. New York and South Brunswick: A. S. Barnes, 1972.

Brosnan, John. *Movie Magic: The Story of Special Effects in the Cinema.* New York: St. Martin's Press, 1974. Discusses Harryhausen's work, with interview material.

Gods and Heroes of the Greeks: The "Library" of Apollodorus. Amherst: University of Massachusetts Press, 1976. Translated and with introduction and notes by Michael Simpson.

Graves, Robert. *The Greek Myths.* New York: George Braziller, 1955.

Homer. *The Odyssey: The Story of Ulysses.* New York: New American Library, 1949. Translated by W. H. D. Rouse. A Mentor Book. Reprint of the 1937 edition.

Keyhoe, Major Donald E. *Flying Saucers from Outer Space.* New York: Henry Holt and Co., 1953.

Kinnard, Roy. *Beasts and Behemoths: Prehistoric Creatures in the Movies.* Metuchen and London: Scarecrow Press, 1988.

Lourie, Eugene. *My Work in Films.* San Diego, New York, and London: Harcourt, Brace, Jovanovich, 1985. Contains production information on *The Beast from 20,000 Fathoms.*

Rovin, Jeff. *From the Land beyond Beyond: The Films of Willis O'Brien and Ray Harryhausen.* New York: Berkley Windhover, 1977. Contains interview material.

Swift, Jonathan. *Gulliver's Travels.* New York: Random House, n.d. Modern Library edition, with an introduction dated 1931.

Verne, Jules. *The Mysterious Island.* New York: Charles Scribner's Sons, n.d. Reprint of a 1920 edition, illustrated by N. C. Wyeth; part of The Scribner Illustrated Classics series.

Warren, Bill. *Keep Watching the Skies; American Science Fiction Movies of the Fifties: Volume I, 1950–1957.* Jefferson, N.C., and London: McFarland, 1982. Includes analyses of *The Beast from 20,000 Fathoms, It Came from Beneath the Sea, Earth vs. the Flying Saucers,* and *20 Million Miles to Earth.*

———. *Keep Watching the Skies; American Science Fiction Movies of the Fifties: Volume II, 1958–1962.* Jefferson, N.C., and London: McFarland, 1986. Contains an analysis of *Mysterious Island.*

Wells, H. G. *The First Men on the Moon.* In *The Collector's Book of Science Fiction by H. G. Wells,* edited by Alan K. Russell. Secaucus: Castle, 1978. Reprint, with original illustrations, from *Strand Magazine,* December 1900–August 1901.

ARTICLES

Archer, Steve. "Two Titans of Animation and Their Work for Hammer: Ray Harryhausen and Jim Danforth." *Little Shoppe of Horrors,* July 1990, 130–38.

Berg. "*Clash of the Titans.*" *Variety,* 10 June 1981, 18. Review.

Bradbury, Ray. "*The Beast from 20,000 Fathoms.*" *Saturday Evening Post,* 23 June 1951, 28–29, 117. Reprinted as "The Fog Horn," in *The Golden Apples of the Sun.* New York: Doubleday and Co., 1953.

Bradley, Matthew R. "Ray Harryhausen: Now and Then." *Filmfax* 52 (September–October 1995): 50–57, 74, 80. Interview.

Burns, James H. "Burgess Meredith: Multidimensional Man." *Rod Serling's The Twilight Zone Magazine,* March–April 1984, 26–31, 80.

Carducci, Mark. "Ray Harryhausen." *Millimeter,* April 1975, 20–24. Interview.

Childs, Mike and Alan Jones. "*Clash of the Titans.*" *Cinefantastique* vol. 9, no. 2 (1979): 22–27. Interview with Harryhausen.

"Exclusive Interview with Ray Harryhausen and Charles Schneer: Part I." *Special Visual Effects Created by Ray Harryhausen* 3 (Summer 1972): 8–19. Transcript of a John Player Lecture at London's National Film Theatre.

French, Larry. "The Harryhausen Interview." *Fangoria* 16 (1981): 35–39. Third part of interview.

———. "The Harryhausen Story." *Fangoria* 15 (1981): 48–52. Second part of interview.

———. "Ray Harryhausen Speaks." *Fangoria* 14 (1981): 49–53. First part of interview.

Greenberger, Robert. "*Clash of the Titans.*" *Fangoria,* April 1981, 56–57.

Hamill, Mark, and Anne Wyndham. "Interview with Kerwin Mathews." *Special Visual Effects Created by Ray Harryhausen* 4 (Spring 1974): 38–45. Combines the transcript of an interview at Westercon 26—SFCON '73 in San Francisco (3 July 1973) and a personal interview.

Jensen, Paul M. "Ray Harryhausen: Cinemagician as Filmmaker." *Phantasma* 4 (Spring 1990): 6–53.

Mandell, Paul. "Careers: Ray Harryhausen." *Cinemagic* 37 (Winter 1987): 48–58. Career profile, with interview material.

———. "Harryhausen Animates Annual Sci-Tech Awards." *American Cinematographer,* May 1992, 73–74.

———. "Of Beasts and Behemoths; Part 1: *The Beast from 20,000 Fathoms.*" *Fantastic Films* 14 (February 1980): 34–38, 58–60, 62. Background on the film's production. A revised version of this article appeared in *Cinemagic* 36 (Fall 1987).

McGregor, Don. "An Interview with Ray Harryhausen." *Starlog* 51 (October 1981): 24–28, 60–61.

Mitchell, Blake, and James Ferguson. "*Clash of the Titans.*" *Fantastic Films* 25 (August 1981): 72–78. Interview with Harryhausen.

Mitchell, Steve. "Ray Harryhausen Discusses *Sinbad and the Eye of the Tiger.*" *Filmmakers Newsletter,* September 1977, 20–24.

Nadler, Harry, and Dave Trengove. "Ray Harryhausen, Part I." *Castle of Frankenstein* 19 (n.d.): 6–17. Interview, circa 1972.

———. "Ray Harryhausen, Part II." *Castle of Frankenstein* 20 (Summer 1973): 6–18. Interview.

Naha, Ed. "It's Sinbad Taste." *Crawdaddy,* July 1977, 33–35. Includes interview material.

Newsom, Ted. "King of Dynamation—Ray Harryhausen." *Imagi-Movies,* Spring 1995, 14–28, 61. Second part of career profile, covers Harryhausen's films from *Gulliver* to *Gwangi.*

———. "The Ray Harryhausen Story: Part One, The Early Years, 1920–1958." *Cinefantastique,* December 1981, 24–45. Contains much original research.

"Ray Harryhausen and Charles Schneer at the National Film Theatre, Part II." *Special Visual Effects Created by Ray Harryhausen.* Spring 1974, 3–14. Interview.

Scapperotti, Dan. "Ray Harryhausen's *Clash of the Titans.*" *Cinefantastique,* Winter 1980, 4–11, 38–45. Article, with interview material.

———. "*Sinbad and the Eye of the Tiger:* Ray Harryhausen Interview." *Cinefantastique* vol. 6, no. 2 (1977): 4–16.

———, and David Bartholomew. "*The Golden Voyage of Sinbad.*" *Cinefantastique* vol. 3, no. 2 (1974): 4–5, 42–45. Interview with Charles Schneer.

Shay, Don. "*Clash of the* (Foot-Tall) *Titans.*" *Cinefex* 5 (July 1981): 20–41. Thorough account of *Titans*' production history.

Stein, Elliott. "The Thirteen Voyages of Ray Harryhausen." *Film Comment,* November–December 1977, 24–28. Interview.

Stevenson, C. M. "*Clash of the Titans.*" *Starlog,* September 1980, 59–60, 70. Article, with interview material.

Swires, Steve. "The Fantasy Voyages of Jerry the Giant Killer." *Starlog,* April 1989, 57–62. Part I of a career profile of Nathan Juran, with interview material.

———. "The Fantastic Film Voyages of Jerry the Giant Killer." *Starlog,* May 1989, 55–59, 62. Conclusion of career profile of Nathan Juran, with interview material.

———. "Kerwin Mathews: Confessions of a Giant Killer." *Starlog* 120 (July 1987): 67–71, 95. Part two of interview.

———. "Kerwin Mathews: The Perilous Voyages of Sinbad." *Starlog* 119 (June 1987): 28–31, 64. Part one of interview.

———. "Maestro of the Magicks." *Starlog* 151 (February 1990): 65–68, 70. Part two of Schneer interview.

———. "Mentor to the Magicks." *Starlog* 150 (January 1990): 57–62. Part one of interview with Charles Schneer.

———. "Merchant of the Magicks." *Starlog* 152 (March 1990): 65–68, 71. Part three of Schneer interview.

———. "Ray Harryhausen: Farewell to Fantasy Films." *Starlog* 127 (February 1988): 63–67. Interview.

———. "Ray Harryhausen: The Man Who Can Work Miracles." *Starlog* 100 (November 1985): 34–37. Interview.

Tasker, Ann. "Ray Harryhausen Talks about His Cinematic Magic." *American Cinematographer,* June 1981, 556–58, 600–615. Interview.

Weaver, Tom. "Director of Dinosaurs." *Starlog* 193 (August 1993): 63–68. Interview with Eugene Lourie.

Wolf, Mark. "*Sinbad and the Eye of the Tiger:* The Special Visual Effects." *Cinefantastique* vol. 6, no. 2 (1977): 40–47.

SCREENPLAYS

Clemens, Brian. *Sinbad's Golden Voyage.* Unpublished shooting script of *The Golden Voyage of Sinbad,* dated April 1972, with revisions through 5 July 1972.

Cross, Beverley. *Clash of the Titans.* Unpublished shooting script. "Final Draft," n.d. Includes storyboard drawings.

The Giant Ymir. Unpublished shooting script of *20 Million Miles to Earth.* Missing title page, so no author(s) or dates listed.

Kneale, Nigel, and Jan Read. *First Men in the Moon.* Unpublished shooting script. "Estimating Draft," revised 8 June 1963.

Prebble, John, Danial [sic] Ullman, and Crane Wilbur. *Mysterious Island.* Unpublished shooting script. Dated 27 May 1960; revised 30 May 1960.

Read, Jan, Ray Bowers, and Beverly [sic] Cross. *Jason and the Golden Fleece.* Unpublished shooting script of *Jason and the Argonauts,* dated 6 August 1961; revised 11 August 1961.

Smith, Robert, and Louis Morheim. *The Monster from Beneath the Sea.* Unpublished shooting script of *The Beast from 20,000 Fathoms,* revised 25 July 1952.

Yates, George Worthing, and R. T. Marcus. *Attack of the Flying Saucers.* Unpublished shooting script of *Earth vs. the Flying Saucers,* dated 7 June 1955.

Terence Fisher

Primary Sources

"Horror Is My Business." *Films and Filming,* July 1964, 7–8. Interview conducted by Raymond Durgnat and John Cutts, written as a first-person article.
Interview with the author, 4 June 1974.

Secondary Sources

BOOKS AND PARTS OF BOOKS

Brosnan, John. *The Horror People.* New York: St. Martin's Press, 1976. Draws on interviews with Fisher, Peter Cushing, and Christopher Lee.
Cushing, Peter. *Past Forgetting: Memoirs of the Hammer Years.* London: Weidenfeld and Nicolson, 1988.
———. *Peter Cushing: An Autobiography.* London: Weidenfeld and Nicolson, 1986.
Del Vecchio, Deborah, and Tom Johnson. *Peter Cushing: The Gentle Man of Horror and His Ninety-one Films.* Jefferson, N.C., and London: McFarland, 1992.
———. *Hammer Films: An Exhaustive Filmography.* Jefferson, N.C., and London: McFarland, 1996.
Dixon, Wheeler Winston. *The Charm of Evil: The Life and Films of Terence Fisher.* Metuchen and London: Scarecrow Press, 1991.
Eyles, Allen, Robert Adkinson, and Nicholas Fry, eds. *The House of Horror: The Story of Hammer Films.* London: Lorrimer, 1973. Includes interviews with Fisher and others.
Fischer, Dennis. *Horror Film Directors, 1931–1990.* Jefferson, N.C., and London: McFarland, 1991.
Hallenbeck, Bruce G. "Terence Fisher." In *The Fearmakers: The Screen's Directorial Masters of Suspense and Terror,* edited by John McCarty, 85–93. New York: St. Martin's Press, 1994.
Hutchings, Peter. *Hammer and Beyond: The British Horror Film.* Manchester and New York: Manchester University Press, 1993.
Lee, Christopher. *Tall, Dark, and Gruesome.* London: W. H. Allen, 1977. Autobiography.
Leroux, Gaston. *The Phantom of the Opera.* New York: Popular Library, 1962. Paperback edition of the 1911 novel.
Lyndon, Barre, and Jimmy Sangster. *The Man Who Could Cheat Death.* New York: Avon Books, 1959. Paperback novelization of the film's screenplay.
McCarty, John. *The Modern Horror Film: 50 Contemporary Classics.* New York: Citadel Press, 1990.
Miller, Mark A. *Christopher Lee and Peter Cushing and Horror Cinema: A Filmography of Their Twenty-Two Collaborations.* Jefferson, N.C., and London: McFarland & Co., 1995.
Owen, Dean. *The Brides of Dracula.* Derby, Conn.: Monarch Books, 1960. Paperback novelization of the film's screenplay.
Pirie, David. *A Heritage of Horror: The English Gothic Cinema, 1946–1972.* London: Gordon Fraser, 1973.
Pohle, Robert W., Jr., and Douglas C. Hart. *The Films of Christopher Lee.* Metuchen and London: Scarecrow Press, 1983.
Ringel, Harry. "Hammer Horror: The World of Terence Fisher." In *Graphic Violence on the Screen,* edited by Thomas R. Atkins, 35–45. New York: Monarch Press, 1976.
Weaver, Tom. *Science Fiction Stars and Horror Heroes: Interviews with Actors, Directors, Producers, and Writers of the 1940s through 1960s.* Jefferson, N.C., and London: McFarland & Co., 1991. Includes interviews with Hazel Court and Richard Matheson.
Wheatley, Dennis. *The Devil Rides Out.* London: Arrow Books, 1969. Paperback edition of the 1934 novel.

ARTICLES

"Anthony Hinds." *Hammer Journal,* August 1980, 16–20. Interview.

"Anthony Hinds—Executive Producer." *Little Shoppe of Horrors,* April 1994, 47–49. Interview.

Ashton, Roy. "Letter." *Little Shoppe of Horrors,* December 1982, 6.

"Ask Roy Ashton." *Little Shoppe of Horrors,* July 1981, 35–36. Phil Leakey's response to a reader's question.

"Ask Roy Ashton." *Hammer Journal,* August 1980, 9.

Barbano, Nicolas. "Yutte Stensgaard: A Collage." *Little Shoppe of Horrors,* April 1994, 89–97.

Bean, Robin. "Dracula and the Mad Monk." *Films and Filming,* August 1965, 55–57. Quotes from an interview with Christopher Lee.

Borst, Ronald V. "*Horror of Dracula:* An Analysis of the Hammer Film Classic." *Photon* 27 (1977): 23–35. Includes interview quotations.

Burns, James H. "The Horror of Sangster." *Fangoria* 10 (January 1981): 37–39. Interview with Jimmy Sangster.

Caen, Michel. "Entretien avec Terence Fisher." *Midi-Minuit Fantastique* 10–11 (Winter 1964–65): 1–16, 20–21. Interview. An inconsistent translation by Ton Paans appeared as "Hammer's Old Guard: Terence Fisher," *Little Shoppe of Horrors,* March 1986, 87–91.

"Charles Gray—'Mocata.' " *Little Shoppe of Horrors,* April 1994, 47. Interview.

"Christopher Lee Enters the House of Hammer." *Scarlet Street* 8 (Fall 1992): 43–47. Transcription of an interview conducted for Cinemax.

Cowie, S[ue] and C[olin]. "The Terence Fisher Interview." *Horror Elite* 2 (September 1975): 24–42.

Cowie, Sue, Colin Cowie, Jan Van Genechten, and Gilbert Verschooten. "Hammer's Old Guard: Michael Ripper." *Little Shoppe of Horrors,* March 1986, 106–7. Interview reprinted from *Fantoom* 6 (Winter 1979–80).

Del Vecchio, Carl. "I Met David Peel." *Little Shoppe of Horrors,* April 1994, 77–79, 83.

de Souza, Edward. "Letter." *Little Shoppe of Horrors,* July 1990, 49.

Devine, J. Llewellyn. "The Gorgon." *Little Shoppe of Horrors,* July 1990, 34–35. The story on which the film's script was based.

Hallenbeck, Bruce G. "Anthony Hinds/John Elder—Producer/Screenwriter," *Little Shoppe of Horrors,* July 1990, 56–58. Interview.

———. "Anthony Hinds, Prince of Hammer." *Fangoria* 75 (July 1988): 53–56. Part two of interview.

———. "Dennis Wheatley at Hammer." *Little Shoppe of Horrors,* April 1994, 38–40.

———. "James Bernard—Composer." *Little Shoppe of Horrors,* April 1994, 50–52. Interview.

———. "Madeleine [*sic*] Smith." *Little Shoppe of Horrors,* May 1984, 67–69. Interview.

———. "Rosalyn Landor—'Little Peggy.' " *Little Shoppe of Horrors,* April 1994, 49–50. Interview.

———. "Son of Hammer, Part One." *Fangoria* 74 (June 1988): 52–56. Interview with Anthony Hinds.

———. "Veronica Has Risen from the Grave: An Interview with Veronica Carlson." *Scarlet Street* 9 (Winter 1993): 64–68.

Heard, Colin. "Hammering the Box Office." *Films and Filming,* June 1969, 17–18. Quotes from an interview with James Carreras.

Hinds, Anthony. "Letter." *Little Shoppe of Horrors,* March 1986, 19.

Humphreys, Fred. "Margaret Robinson." *Little Shoppe of Horrors,* July 1990, 162–66. Interview.

"Interview with Edward de Souza." *Little Shoppe of Horrors,* July 1990, 62–64.

"An Interview with Thorley Walters." *Little Shoppe of Horrors,* July 1990, 154–56.

Irvin, Sam. "Malcolm Williamson." *Little Shoppe of Horrors,* July 1990, 102–4. Interview.

"Jimmy Sangster." *Little Shoppe of Horrors,* April 1978, 81–83. Interview and profile.

"John Gilling." *Little Shoppe of Horrors,* April 1978, 56–58. Interview.

Johnson, Tom. "*Brides of Dracula:* Hammer Horror's Second Vampire Classic." *Midnight Marquee* 49 (Summer 1995): 36–39.

———. "*The Curse of the Werewolf.*" *Fangoria* 134 (July 1994), 72–77.

"The Keith Dudley Report." *Little Shoppe of Horrors,* March 1986, 35–44.

Kelley, Bill. "Christopher Lee: King of the Counts." *Dracula: The Complete Vampire* (Starlog Movie Magazines 6, 1992): 44–53. Contains interview material.

————. "Christopher Lee on *The Devil Rides Out.*" *Little Shoppe of Horrors,* April 1994, 44–47. Interview.

Klemensen, Richard. "Hammer Films Unearth the Mummy." *Midnight Marquee* 47 (Summer 1994): 74–87.

————. "Hammer's Old Guard: Harry Oakes." *Little Shoppe of Horrors,* March 1986, 97–98. Interview. Transcribed by Dennis Lynch.

————. "Hammer's Old Guard: Jack Asher." *Little Shoppe of Horrors,* March 1986, 92–97. Interview. Transcribed by Dennis Lynch.

————, Colin Cowie, and Keith Dudley. "Hammer's Old Guard: Len Harris—Part 2." *Little Shoppe of Horrors,* March 1986, 103–4. Interview.

Kravaal, James. "Peter Cushing." *Little Shoppe of Horrors,* May 1984, 56–62. Interview.

Laws, Stephen. "Andrew Keir." *Little Shoppe of Horrors,* April 1994, 107–10. Interview.

————. "Francis Matthews." *Little Shoppe of Horrors,* April 1994, 117–19. Interview.

Leakey, Phil. "Letter." *Little Shoppe of Horrors,* July 1990, 9.

Lee, Christopher. *Hammer—The Studio That Dripped Blood.* Fifty-minute documentary shown on BBC2, 26 June 1987.

"The Loneliness of Evil." *Shriek* 3 (Summer 1966): 4–13. Interview with Christopher Lee.

Lucas, Tim. "Remembering Terence Fisher." *Gorezone* 16 (Winter 1990): 52–55. Comments on video versions of Fisher's films.

Lynch, Dennis. "Hugh and Pauline Harlow Interview." *Little Shoppe of Horrors,* April 1994, 112–17.

Mank, Gregory William. "Hazel Court." *Films in Review,* September–October 1993, 319–24. Interview.

Martinez, Oscar. "The Vampire Woman and the Hunchback—An Interview with Andree Melly and Oscar Quitak." *Little Shoppe of Horrors,* July 1990, 139–47.

————, and Bob Sheridan. "The Evolution of *The Brides of Dracula.*" *Little Shoppe of Horrors,* July 1981, 18–14.

Midi-Minuit Fantastique 1 (May–June 1962). Issue devoted to Fisher's career. Articles, in French, emphasize the films' "erotisme et sadisme."

Miller, Mark A. "Britain's Duchess of Dark Drama: Hazel Court." *Filmfax* 20 (May 1990): 72–75. Interview. Reprinted, with slight revisions, in *Filmfax* 51 (July–August 1995): 73–76.

————. "Veronica Carlson: A Lady and Her Monsters." *Filmfax* 14 (March–April 1989): 68–72, 95. Interview. Reprinted in *Filmfax* 46 (August–September 1994): 31–37, 97.

Nutman, Philip. "Hammer's Monster Man." *Fangoria* 35 (April 1984): 32–35. Interview with Roy Ashton.

Paans, Ton. "Philip Martell." *Little Shoppe of Horrors,* July 1990, 92–100. Interview.

————, and Colin Cowie. "Hammer's Old Guard: Tilly Day and Len Harris." *Little Shoppe of Horrors,* March 1986, 98–102. Interview.

Palmer, Randy. "Fisher Fantastica." *Fangoria* 11 (February 1981): 34–37. Article with interview material.

————. "Reluctant Monster Maker." *Fangoria* 50 (January 1986): 46–49. Interview with Phil Leakey.

Parfitt, Gary. "The Fruitation of Terence Fisher." *Little Shoppe of Horrors,* February 1974, 49–62. Interview.

"Peter Cushing on Frankenstein and Others." *Castle of Frankenstein* 22 (1974): 16–21. Interview.

Ringel, Harry. "The Horrible Hammer Films of Terence Fisher." *Take One* vol. 3, no. 9 (January–February 1972 [published May 14, 1973]): 8–12.

————. "Terence Fisher: The Human Side." *Cinefantastique,* Fall 1975, 5–16. Analysis of Fisher's films.

————. "Terence Fisher: Underlining." *Cinefantastique,* Fall 1975, 19–28. Interview, conducted by Peter Nicholson from questions by Ringel and Richard Hogan; includes material from a 1973 interview by Chris Knight.

Sheridan, Bob. "Letter." *Little Shoppe of Horrors,* March 1986, 8–9.

————. "Letter." *Little Shoppe of Horrors,* April 1994, 10.

Soren, David. "Dracula Speaks: An Interview with Christopher Lee." *Gore Creatures* 17 (February 1970): 13.

Svehla, Gary J. "Evolving Worlds of Hammer's Baron Frankenstein." *Midnight Marquee* 47 (Summer 1994): 6–19.

Swires, Steve. "Hammer's Michael Carreras: Horror as a Family Business." *Fangoria* 61 (February 1987): 54–59. Interview.

————. "Michael Carreras: Inside the House of Hammer." *Fangoria* 63 (May 1987): 58–63, 68. Part two of interview.

————. "Peter Cushing: Stitcher of Limbs, Staker of Hearts, Part Two." *Starlog* 100 (November 1985): 89–92. Article with interview material.

Tavernier, Bertrand. "Entretien avec Terence Fisher." *Midi-Minuit Fantastique* 7 (September 1963): 9–12. Interview.

Taylor, Al. "Barbara Shelley." *Little Shoppe of Horrors,* December 1982, 43–49. Interview. A condensed, slightly modified version reprinted in *Little Shoppe of Horrors,* April 1994, 101–7.

————. "Hammer's Old Guard: Bill Lenny." *Little Shoppe of Horrors,* March 1986, 105–6. Interview.

————. "Hammer's Old Guard: Len Harris." *Little Shoppe of Horrors,* March 1986, 102–3. Interview.

————, and Dick Klemensen. "Terence Fisher: The Gentleman Genius of Hammer Horror Films Takes a Last Bow." *Fantastic Films,* April 1981, 24–31. Career profile, plus tributes from five coworkers.

"Terence Fisher." *Little Shoppe of Horrors,* July 1981, 12–17. A collection of testimonials.

Valley, Richard. "Mornings with Peter Cushing." *Scarlet Street* 8 (Fall 1992): 34–38, 101. Interview.

"Yvonne Monlaur." *Little Shoppe of Horrors,* March 1986, 83–85. Interview, probably by Alain Schlockoff; translated by Safi Farrah.

SCREENPLAYS

Bryan, Peter, and Jimmy Sangster. *The Brides of Dracula.* Unpublished shooting script, dated 19 November 1959.

The Curse of the Werewolf. Unpublished shooting script, dated August 1960, with undated revisions; includes two lists of scenes still to be shot as of 25 October 1960. No author identified.

The Devil Rides Out. Unpublished shooting script, no title page.

Elder, John. *The Phantom of the Opera.* Unpublished shooting script, dated 8 September 1961.

Frankenstein Created Woman. Unpublished shooting script, no title page.

Frankenstein Must Be Destroyed. Unpublished shooting script, dated 9 December 1968, with revisions dated through 11 February 1969. No author listed.

Gilling, John. *The Gorgon.* Unpublished shooting script, dated November 1963, with a list of amendments dated 2 December 1963.

Sangster, Jimmy. *Dracula.* Unpublished shooting script, undated.

Sansom, John. *Dracula—Prince of Darkness.* Unpublished shooting script, dated 4 March 1965. Includes extensive, undated revisions in a different typescript.

Freddie Francis

Primary Sources

Interview about *Dracula Has Risen from the Grave,* conducted by Terence Kelly for BBC radio, circa 1968 (three minutes).

Interviews with the author, 9 September 1967, 31 August 1971, 6 June 1974.

Letter to the author, 7 February 1995.

Introduction to *The Films of Freddie Francis,* by Wheeler Winston Dixon, ix–xi. Metuchen and
    London: Scarecrow Press, 1991.
"New Trends in Black and White Cinematography: On Shooting *The Elephant Man.*" *Millimeter,*
    March 1981, 139–51.

Secondary Sources

BOOKS AND PARTS OF BOOKS

Bloch, Robert. *Bogey Men.* New York: Pyramid, 1963. Contains the stories "The Skull of the
    Marquis De Sade" and "The Man Who Collected Poe."
———. *Horror-7.* New York: Belmont, 1963. Contains the story "Enoch."
———. *Nightmares.* New York: Belmont, 1961. Contains the story "Mr. Steinway."
———. *Once around the Bloch: An Unauthorized Autobiography.* New York: Tom Doherty Associ-
    ates, 1993.
———. *Tales in a Jugular Vein.* New York: Pyramid, 1965. Contains the story "Terror over
    Hollywood."
Brosnan, John. *The Horror People.* New York: St. Martin's Press, 1976. Profiles of Francis, Milton
    Subotsky, Kevin Francis, and Christopher Lee include interview quotations.
Buscombe, Edward. *Making "Legend of the Werewolf."* London: British Film Institute, 1976.
    Includes interviews with Francis and others.
Comport, Brian. *Mumsy, Nanny, Sonny, and Girly.* New York: Lancer, 1970. Novelization of the
    author's screenplay.
Dixon, Wheeler Winston. *The Films of Freddie Francis.* Metuchen and London: Scarecrow Press,
    1991. A book-length interview.
Fischer, Dennis. *Horror Film Directors, 1931–1990.* Jefferson, N.C., and London: McFarland,
    1991. Includes an unsympathetic career profile of Francis.
Hallenbeck, Bruce G. "Freddie Francis." In *The Fearmakers: The Screen's Directorial Masters of Sus-
    pense and Terror,* edited by John McCarty, 95–103. New York: St. Martin's Press, 1994.
Heard, H. F. *A Taste for Honey.* New York: Lancer, 1967. Paperback edition of the 1941 novel on
    which *The Deadly Bees* was based.
Miller, Mark A. *Christopher Lee and Peter Cushing and Horror Cinema: A Filmography of Their
    Twenty-two Collaborations.* Jefferson, N.C., and London: McFarland, 1995.
Naha, Ed. *The Making of Dune.* New York: Berkley, 1984. Includes a chapter on Francis and
    other references to his involvement.
Powell, Michael. *A Life in Movies.* New York: Alfred A. Knopf, 1987. First volume of the writer-
    director's autobiography.
———. *Million-Dollar Movie.* London: Mandarin, 1993. Paperback edition of the 1992 work.
    Second volume of Powell's autobiography.
Siodmak, Curt. *Donovan's Brain.* New York: Berkley Medallion, 1969. Paperback edition of the
    1942 novel.
Tales from the Crypt. New York: Ballantine, 1964. Paperback reprint of stories from William
    Gaines's horror comics.
Weaver, Tom. *Science Fiction Stars and Horror Heroes: Interviews with Actors, Directors, Producers, and
    Writers of the 1940s through 1960s.* Jefferson, N.C., and London: McFarland, 1991. Pro-
    ducer Bernard Glasser discusses *Day of the Triffids.*
Wyndham, John. *The Day of the Triffids.* New York: Carroll & Graf, 1993. Paperback edition of
    the 1951 novel.

ARTICLES

"Amicus: Two's a Company." *Little Shoppe of Horrors,* March 1973, 12–36. Survey of Amicus
    Films, containing interviews with Francis, Milton Subotsky, and Robert Bloch. Includes
    additional comments by Subotsky in an unpaginated insert between pages 34 and 35
    (referred to in notes as 34a and 34b).
Buckley, Peter. "*Mumsy, Nanny, Sonny, and Girly.*" *Films and Filming,* June 1970, 82. Review.
Canby, Vincent. "*Tales That Witness Madness.*" *New York Times,* 1 November 1973, 48. Review.
Dool., "*The Deadly Bees.*" *Variety,* 25 January 1967, 6.

Fisher, Bob. "Moving Portrait of War." *American Cinematographer,* November 1990, 63–64. Interview with Francis about *Glory.*

Frank, Janrae. "The Director and the Devils: A Talk with Freddie Francis." *Monsterland* 6 (December 1985): 57–59. Interview.

Greenspun, Roger. "*Mumsy, Nanny, Sonny, and Girly.*" *New York Times,* 13 February 1970, 24. Review.

Haigh, Peter. "Francis for Fright." *Film Review,* August 1975, 26, 28. Interview.

Hallenbeck, Bruce G. "Anthony Hinds, Prince of Hammer." *Fangoria* 75 (July 1988): 53–56. Interview.

Hammer Films press release biography of Freddie Francis (circa 1963).

Hans. "Gebissen wird nur nachts—Happening der Vampire." *Variety,* 4 August 1971, 27. Review of *Vampire Happening* from Berlin.

"Hayworth Takes Powder." *Variety,* 20 December 1972, 7. News article about *Tales That Witness Madness.*

"Howard Sues Re: *Tower,*" *Variety,* 28 January 1987, 7.

Humphries, Reynold, and Chris Knight. "Tyburn." *Cinefantastique,* Winter 1976–77, 40–44. Includes interview quotations.

Jackson, Kevin. "Gothic Shadows." *Sight and Sound,* November 1992, 16–19. Includes interview material.

Jensen, Paul M. "Freddie Francis." *Photon* 22 (1972): 32–34. Report on preparations for filming *Tales from the Crypt,* with interview quotations.

———. "*Mumsy, Nanny, Sonny, and Girly.*" *Inter/View* 1, no. 7 (1970). Review, with interview quotations.

———. "The Land That Time Forgot." *Photon* 25 (1974): 41–43. Includes a brief account of a visit to the Tyburn Films offices during preproduction of *Legend of the Werewolf.*

Jones, Alan. "The Bloody Best of Freddie Francis." *Shivers,* June 1995, 32–35. Interview.

Leider, R. Allen. "A Tale from behind the Crypt." *Monster Times,* 31 July 1972, 10–11. Interview with Peter Cushing.

Mandell, Paul. "Photography and Visual Effects for *Dune.*" *American Cinematographer,* December 1984, 50–61.

Marsh, Fabienne. "Grim Doings in Victorian Britain." *New York Times,* 4 August 1985, sec. 3, p. 8. Discusses production of *The Doctor and the Devils.*

McFadden, Brian. "The Studio That Dripped Blood." *Monster Times,* May 1973, 10–12. Includes an interview with Milton Subotsky.

Miller, Mark A. "Veronica Carlson: A Lady and Her Monsters." *Filmfax* 14 (March–April 1989): 68–72, 95. Interview. Reprinted in *Filmfax* 46 (August–September 1994): 31–37, 97.

Morgan, David. "A Remake That Can't Miss: *Cape Fear.*" *American Cinematographer,* October 1991, 34–40. Interview with Francis.

"*Mumsy, Nanny, Sonny, and Girly.*" *Independent Film Journal,* 18 February 1970. Review.

Munshower, Susan. "Freddie Francis." *Monsters of the Movies,* Summer 1975, 77–80. Interview with Francis between the filming of *The Ghoul* and *Legend of the Werewolf.*

Murf. "*Tales That Witness Madness.*" *Variety,* 31 October 1973, 26. Review.

"The Newest *Evil:* Shoot Scenes to Pad Pic for TV." *Variety,* 17 January 1968, 1, 62. News article about *The Evil of Frankenstein.*

Nolan, Jack Edmund. "Films on TV." *Films in Review,* August–September 1974, 431–34. Unsympathetic career profile of Francis.

Nutman, Philip. "An Autopsy of Movie Horror." *Fangoria* 54 (June 1986): 51–54. Interview with Francis about *The Doctor and the Devils.*

———. "*Dark Tower:* How Not to Make a Horror Film?" *Fangoria* 71 (February 1988): 22–25. Includes interview material.

Palmer, Randy. "The British Terror of Freddie Francis." *Fangoria* 30 (October 1983): 12–16. Unacknowledged reworking of the anonymous interview in *Little Shoppe of Horrors,* March 1973.

Parfitt, Gary, and Ian Yeoman. "An Informal Conversation with Freddie Francis." *Famous Film Stars* vol. 1, no. 2 (1974): 2–14.

Rebello, Stephen. "Jack Clayton's *The Innocents.*" *Cinefantastique,* June–July 1983, 51–55.

Taylor, Al. "Veronica Carlson." *Little Shoppe of Horrors,* May 1984, 89–91, Supplement A-B. Interview.

Thompson, Howard. "*Paranoiac.*" *New York Times,* 23 May 1963, 31. Review.

"Tips from the Top." *Film Making* vol. 9, no. 9 (September 1971): 33. Interview with Francis.

Wordsworth, Chris. "Freddie Francis." *Film Making* vol. 16, no. 8 (August 1978): 35–39. Part one of interview.

———. "Freddie Francis." *Film Making* vol. 16, no. 9 (September 1978): 30–31. Part two of interview.

SCREENPLAYS

Elder, John. *Dracula Has Risen from the Grave.* Unpublished shooting script, dated March 1968.

Subotsky, Milton. *The Skull.* Unpublished shooting script, undated. Revisions dated 20 January 1965.

Thomas, Dylan. *The Doctor and the Devils, and Other Scripts.* New York: New Directions, 1966.

FILMOGRAPHY

For most of the entries below, credits were transcribed from the film itself, then supplemented by consulting *The Film Daily Yearbook* (various editions), Denis Gifford's *The British Film Catalogue, 1895–1985,* and reviews in *Variety,* the *New York Times,* and the *Monthly Film Bulletin.* Additional information was derived from *Little Shoppe of Horrors* magazine; *Universal Horrors,* by Michael Brunas, John Brunas, and Tom Weaver; *Hammer Films,* by Tom Johnson and Deborah Del Vecchio; the two volumes of *Keep Watching the Skies!* by Bill Warren; and various other works, listed in the bibliography, by Gregory Mank and George Turner.

Some inconsistencies from film to film have been left as they appear in a given film. Examples include the names Elizabeth (Elisabeth) Lutyens and Anthony Nelson-Keys, which is sometimes hyphenated and sometimes not. Occasional misspellings of a name on a film's opening or closing credits have been corrected, if discovered. Otherwise, variations of names have been placed in brackets, as have uncredited contributions.

Exact running times are always problematic. Whenever possible, I have timed the films myself and used that measurement (rounded off to the nearest minute) if the prints are known to be complete. Occasionally, I have rejected the timing of a print that appears to be "time compressed," as in the case of a Cinemax broadcast of *Dracula Has Risen from the Grave.*

Films have been listed by their years of release, not production. For films made in other countries, if their American titles, distributors, or release dates differ, they are provided after the initial information.

James Whale

The Love Doctor (Paramount, 1929)
Director: Melville Brown.
Dialogue director: James Whale.
Dialogue: Guy Bolton.
Adaptation: Guy Bolton, J. Walter Ruben.
Based on the play *The Boomerang* by Winchell Smith, Victor Mapes.
Photography: Edward Cronjager.
Cast: Richard Dix (Dr. Gerald Sumner), June Collyer (Virginia Moore), Morgan Farley (Bud Woodbridge), Miriam Seegar [Segar] (Grace Tyler), Winifred Harris (Mrs. Woodbridge), Lawford Davidson (Preston DeWitt), Gale Henry (Lucy).
Running time: 6 reels (5503 feet; 60 minutes).

Hell's Angels (United Artists, 1930)
A Caddo Production.
Presented by Howard Hughes.
Director: Howard Hughes.
Dialogue staged by James Whale.

Dialogue: Joseph Moncure March.
Adaptation and continuity: Howard Estabrook, Harry Behn.
Based on a story by Marshall Neilan, Joseph Moncure March.
Photography: Gaetano [Antonio] Gaudio, Harry Perry, others (part-Technicolor).
Settings: Julian Boone-Fleming, Carroll Clark.
Editors: Frank Lawrence, Douglass Biggs, Perry Hollingsworth.
Musical arrangement: Hugo Riesenfeld.
Sound: Lodge Cunningham.
Chief pilot: Frank Clarke.
Chief of aeronautics: J. B. Alexander.
Assistant directors: Reginald Callow, William J. Scully, Fred A. Fleck.
Cast: Ben Lyon (Monte Rutledge), James Hall (Roy Rutledge), Jean Harlow (Helen), John
    Darrow (Karl Arnstedt), Lucien Prival (Baron von Kranz), Frank Clarke (Lieutenant von
    Bruen), Roy Wilson (Baldy), Douglas Gilmore (Captain Redfield), Jane Winton (Baroness
    von Kranz), Evelyn Hall (Lady Randolph), William B. Davidson (Staff Major), Wyndham
    Standing (Squadron Commander), Lena Malena (Gretchen), Marilyn Morgan (Girl Selling
    Kisses), Carl von Haartman (Zeppelin Commander), F. Schumann-Heink (1st Officer of
    Zeppelin), Stephen Carr (Elliott), Pat Somerset (Marryat), William von Brinken (Von
    Richter), Hans Joby (Von Schlieben), Thomas Carr, J. Granville-Davis, Larford Davidson,
    Joan Standing.
Running time: 129 minutes [UCLA restoration] (135, 119 minutes).

Journey's End (Tiffany-Gainsborough, 1930)

A Gainsborough Welsh-Pearson Production.
Supervisor: George Pearson.
Assistant supervisor: Gerald L. G. Samson.
Director: James Whale.
Adaptation: Joseph Moncure March.
Based on the play by R. C. Sherriff.
Photography: Benjamin Kline.
Art director: Hervey Libbert.
Editor: Claude Berkeley.
Sound: Buddy Myers.
Assistant director: M. K. Wilson.
Cast: Colin Clive (Captain Stanhope), Ian MacLaren (Lieutenant Osborne), David Manners
    (2nd Lieutenant Raleigh), Billy Bevan (2nd Lieutenant Trotter), Anthony Bushell (2nd
    Lieutenant Hibbert), Robert A'Dair (Captain Hardy), Charles Gerrard (Private Mason),
    Tom Whiteley (The Sergeant Major), Jack Pitcairn (The Colonel), Warner Klinger (German Soldier).
Running time: 130 minutes (117, 110 minutes).

Waterloo Bridge (Universal, 1931)

Producer: Carl Laemmle, Jr.
Director: James Whale.
Screenplay: Benn W. Levy.
Continuity: Tom Reed.
Based on the play by Robert E. Sherwood.
Photography: Arthur Edeson.
Art director: Charles D. Hall.
Editor: Maurice Pivar.
Makeup: Jack P. Pierce.
Sound: William Hedgecock.
Assistant director: Joseph A. McDonough.
Cast: Mae Clarke (Myra), Kent Douglass (Roy), Doris Lloyd (Kitty), Ethel Griffies (Mrs. Hob-

ley), Enid Bennett (Mrs. Wetherby), Frederick Kerr (Major Wetherby), Bette Davis (Janet), Rita Carlisle (Old Woman).
Running time: 81 minutes (72 minutes).

Frankenstein (Universal, 1931)
Presented by Carl Laemmle.
Producer: Carl Laemmle, Jr.
Associate producer: E. M. Asher.
Director: James Whale.
Screenplay: Garrett Fort, Francis Edwards Faragoh [Robert Florey, John Russell, uncredited].
Based on the composition by John L. Balderston.
Adapted from the play by Peggy Webling.
From the novel by Mrs. Percy B. Shelley.
Scenario editor: Richard Schayer.
Photography: Arthur Edeson.
Art director: Charles D. Hall.
Set design: Herman Rosse.
Supervising film editor: Maurice Pivar.
Editor: Clarence Kolster.
Musical director: David Broekman.
Dance arranger: C. Baier.
Costumes: Ed Ware, Vera West.
Makeup: Jack Pierce.
Recording supervision: C. Roy Hunter.
Sound: William Hedgecock.
Special effects: John P. Fulton.
Electrical properties: Kenneth Strickfaden.
Technical advisor: Dr. Cecil Reynolds.
Assistant director: Joseph A. McDonough.
Cast: Colin Clive (Henry Frankenstein), Mae Clarke (Elizabeth), John Boles (Victor Moritz), Boris Karloff (The Monster), Edward van Sloan (Doctor Waldman), Frederick Kerr (Baron Frankenstein), Dwight Frye (Fritz), Lionel Belmore (The Burgomaster), Michael Mark (Ludwig, Maria's Father), Marilyn Harris (Little Maria), Arletta Duncan (Bridesmaid), Pauline Moore (Bridesmaid), Francis Ford (Villager), Joseph North (Butler), Maidel Turner (Housekeeper), Cecilia Parker (Maid), Paul Panzer, Ines Palange, Ted Billings, Harry Tenbrook (Villagers), Mary Sherman.
Running time: 70 minutes.

Impatient Maiden (Universal, 1932)
Producer: Carl Laemmle, Jr.
Director: James Whale.
Screenplay: Richard Schayer, Winnifred Dunn.
Dialogue: Donald Henderson Clarke.
Based on the novel *Impatient Virgin* by Donald Henderson Clarke.
Photography: Arthur Edeson.
Art director: Charles D. Hall.
Editor: Clarence Kolster.
Sound: C. Roy Hunter.
Assistant director: Joseph A. McDonough.
Cast: Lew Ayres (Dr. Myron Brown), Mae Clarke (Ruth Robbins), Una Merkel (Betty Merrick), John Halliday (Albert Hartman), Andy Devine (Clarence Howe), Oscar Apfel (Dr. Wilcox), Ethel Griffies (Nurse Lovett), Helen Jerome Eddy (Mrs. Gilman), Bert Roach

(Mr. Gilman), Cecil Cunningham (Mrs. Rosy), Berton Churchill, Monty Montague, Lorin Baker, Arthur Hoyt, Blanche Payson.
Running time: 78 minutes (72 minutes).

The Old Dark House (Universal, 1932)

Presented by Carl Laemmle.
Producer: Carl Laemmle, Jr.
Director: James Whale.
Screenplay: Benn W. Levy.
Additional dialogue: R. C. Sherriff.
Based on the novel *Benighted* by J. B. Priestley.
Photography: Arthur Edeson.
Art director: Charles D. Hall.
Editorial supervision: Maurice Pivar.
Editor: Clarence Kolster.
Music: David Broekman, Heinz Roemheld.
Makeup: Jack Pierce.
Special effects: John P. Fulton.
Recording supervision: C. Roy Hunter.
Sound: William Hedgecock.
Assistant director: Joseph A. McDonough.
Cast: Boris Karloff (Morgan), Melvyn Douglas (Roger Penderel), Charles Laughton (Sir William Porterhouse), Gloria Stuart (Margaret Waverton), Lillian Bond (Gladys DuCane), Ernest Thesiger (Horace Femm), Eva Moore (Rebecca Femm), Raymond Massey (Philip Waverton), Brember Wills (Saul Femm), John [Elspeth] Dudgeon (Sir Roderick Femm).
Running time: 72 minutes.

The Kiss before the Mirror (Universal, 1933)

Presented by Carl Laemmle.
Producer: Carl Laemmle, Jr.
Director: James Whale.
Screenplay: William Anthony McGuire.
Based on the play [*Kuss vor dem Spiegel*] by Ladislaus Fodor.
Photography: Karl Freund.
Art director: Charles D. Hall.
Editor: Ted Kent.
Composer: W. Franke Harling.
Sound: Gilbert Kurland.
Assistant director: M. Mancke.
Cast: Nancy Carroll (Maria), Frank Morgan (Dr. Paul Held), Paul Lukas (Dr. Walter Bernsdorf), Gloria Stuart (Frau Bernsdorf), Jean Dixon (Hilda), Donald Cook (Maria's Lover), Charles Grapewin (Schultz), Walter Pidgeon (Bachelor), Wallis Clark (Prosecutor), Allen Connor (Hilda's Lover), May Boley, Christian Rub, Reginald Mason.
Running time: 67 minutes.

The Invisible Man (Universal, 1933)

Presented by Carl Laemmle.
Producer: Carl Laemmle, Jr.
Director: James Whale.
Screenplay: R. C. Sherriff.
Based on the novel by H. G. Wells.
Photography: Arthur Edeson.
Re-take photography and lighting of miniatures: John Mescall.
Art Director: Charles D. Hall.

Editor: Ted Kent.
Composer: W. Franke Harling.
Makeup: Jack Pierce.
Sound: William Hedgecock.
Special effects: John P. Fulton.
Assistant director: Joseph A. McDonough.
Cast: Claude Rains (Jack Griffin), Gloria Stuart (Flora Cranley), William Harrigan (Dr. Kemp),
    Henry Travers (Dr. Cranley), Una O'Connor (Mrs. Hall), Forrester Harvey (Mr. Hall),
    Holmes Herbert (Chief of Police), E. E. Clive (Jaffers), Dudley Digges (Chief of Detec-
    tives), Harry Stubbs (Inspector Bird), Donald Stuart (Inspector Lane), Merle Tottenham
    (Milly), Dwight Frye (Reporter), Walter Brennan (Man with Bicycle), John Carradine
    (Informer), D'Arcy Corrigan (Villager), Robert Brower (Farmer), Jameson Thomas (Doc-
    tor), Ted Billings (Villager), Mary Gordon (Villager), John Merivale (Newsboy), Violet
    Kemble Cooper (Woman), Bob Reeves (Official), Jack Richardson (Official), Robert Adair
    [A'Dair] (Official), Craufurd Kent (Doctor), Monte Montague (Policeman).
Running time: 71 minutes.

By Candlelight (Universal, 1933)

Presented by Carl Laemmle.
Producer: Carl Laemmle, Jr.
Director: James Whale.
Screenplay: Hans Kraly, Karen De Wolf, F. Hugh Herbert, Ruth Cummings.
Based on a play by Siegfried Geyer.
Photography: John J. Mescall.
Art director: Charles D. Hall.
Editor: Ted Kent.
Composer: W. Franke Harling.
Makeup: Jack P. Pierce.
Sound: Gilbert Kurland.
Assistant director William Reith.
Cast: Elissa Landi (Marie), Paul Lukas (Josef), Nils Asther (Count Von Bommer), Dorothy
    Revier (Countess Von Rischenheim), Lawrence Grant (Count Von Rischenheim), Esther
    Ralston (Louise, Baroness Von Ballin), Warburton Gamble (Baron Von Ballin), Lois January
    (Ann).
Running time: 70 minutes.

One More River (Universal, 1934)

A James Whale Production.
Presented by Carl Laemmle.
Producer: Carl Laemmle, Jr.
Director: James Whale.
Screenplay: R. C. Sherriff.
Based on the novel Over the River by John Galsworthy.
Photography: John J. Mescall.
Art director: Charles D. Hall.
Editor: Ted Kent.
Musical director: W. Franke Harling.
Makeup: Jack P. Pierce.
Special effects: John P. Fulton.
Assistant director Joseph A. McDonough.
Cast: Diana Wynyard (Lady Clare Corven), Frank Lawton (Tony Croom), Colin Clive (Sir Ger-
    ald Corven), Mrs. Patrick Campbell (Lady Mont), Jane Wyatt (Dinny), Lionel Atwill (Mr.
    Brough), Alan Mowbray (Mr. Forsyte), Reginald Denny (David Dornford), C. Aubrey
    Smith (General Charwell), Henry Stephenson (Sir Lawrence Mont), Gilbert Emery (The

Judge), Kathleen Howard (Lady Charwell), E. E. Clive (Chayne), Robert Greig (Blore), Gunnis Davis (Benjy), Tempe Piggott (Mrs. Purdy), "Snub" Pollard (George), Billy Bevan (Cloakroom Attendant), Reginald Sheffield (Tommy), Doris Llewelyn (Vi), Arthur Hoyt, Gino Corrado, Montague Shaw, Tom Ricketts.
Running time: 87 minutes.

Bride of Frankenstein (Universal, 1935)

A James Whale Production.
Presented by Carl Laemmle.
Producer: Carl Laemmle, Jr.
Director: James Whale.
Screenplay: William Hurlbut.
Adaptation: William Hurlbut, John L. Balderston.
Suggested by the novel *Frankenstein* by Mary Wollstonecraft Shelley.
Photography: John J. Mescall.
Art director: Charles D. Hall.
Editor: Ted Kent.
Composer: Franz Waxman.
Conductor: Bakaleinikoff.
Makeup: Jack P. Pierce.
Sound supervisor: Gilbert Kurland.
Photographic effects: John P. Fulton.
Electrical properties: Kenneth Strickfaden.
Assistant directors: Harry Mancke, Joseph McDonough, Fred Frank.
Cast: Boris Karloff (The Monster), Colin Clive (Henry Frankenstein), Valerie Hobson (Elizabeth), Ernest Thesiger (Dr. Pretorius), Elsa Lanchester (The Monster's Mate, Mary Shelley), Gavin Gordon (Lord Byron), Douglas Walton (Percy Bysshe Shelley), Una O'Connor (Minnie), E. E. Clive (Burgomaster), Lucien Prival (Butler), O. P. Heggie (Hermit), Dwight Frye (Karl), Reginald Barlow (Hans), Mary Gordon (Hans's Wife), Ann Darling (Shepherdess), Ted Billings (Ludwig), Neil Fitzgerald (Rudy), John Carradine (Hunter), Grace Cunard (Villager), Rollo Lloyd (Neighbor), Walter Brennan (Neighbor), Joan Woodbury (Queen), Arthur S. Byron (King), Josephine McKim (Mermaid), Norman Ainsley (Archbishop), Peter Shaw (Devil), Kansas DeForrest (Ballerina), Edward Piel, Sr. (Villager), Frank Benson (Villager), Anders Van Haden (Villager), John George (Villager), Maurice Black (Villager), Peter Shaw (Villager), D'Arcy Corrigan (Villager), Brenda Fowler (A Mother), Robert A'Dair [Adair] (A Hunter), Sarah Schwartz (Marta), Mary Stewart (A Neighbor), John Curtis (A Hunter), Helen Gibson (Woman), Frank Terry (A Hunter), Murdock MacQuarrie (Sympathetic Villager), Harry Northrup, Joseph North, Helen Parrish.
[In cut scenes: Gunnis Davis (Uncle Glutz), Tempe Piggott (Auntie Glutz), Billy Barty (Baby), Edwin Mordant (Coroner), Lucio Villegas (Priest).]
Running time: 75 minutes.

Remember Last Night? (Universal, 1935)

A James Whale Production.
Presented by Carl Laemmle.
Producer: Carl Laemmle, Jr.
Director: James Whale.
Screenplay: Harry Clork, Doris Malloy, Dan Totheroh.
Based on the novel *Hangover Murders* by Adam Hobhouse.
Photography: Joseph Valentine.
Art director: Charles D. Hall.
Editor: Ted Kent.
Composer: Franz Waxman.
Makeup: Jack P. Pierce.

Sound supervisor: Gilbert Kurland.
Photographic effects: John P. Fulton.
Assistant director: Scott Beal.
Cast: Edward Arnold (Danny Harrison), Constance Cummings (Carlotta Milburn), Sally Eilers
(Bette Huling), Robert Young (Tony Milburn), Robert Armstrong (Fred Flannagan), Regi-
nald Denny (Jake Whitridge), Monroe Owsley (Billy Arliss), George Meeker (Vic Huling),
Ed Brophy (Maxie), Jack LaRue (Baptiste), Louise Henry (Penny Whitridge), Gustav von
Seyffertitz (Professor Jones), Gregory Ratoff (Faronea), Arthur Treacher (Phelps), Rafaela
Ottiano (Mme. Bouclier), Alice Ardell (Florabelle), E. E. Clive, Frank Reicher, Dewey
Robinson, Harry Woods, Ed Gargan, Kate Price, Warner Richmond, Wade Boteler.
Running time: 81 minutes.

Show Boat (Universal, 1936)

A James Whale Production.
Presented by Carl Laemmle.
Producer: Carl Laemmle, Jr.
Director: James Whale.
Screenplay: Oscar Hammerstein II.
Based on the play by Hammerstein, derived from the novel by Edna Ferber.
Photography: John J. Mescall.
Art director: Charles D. Hall.
Editors: Ted Kent, Bernard W. Burton.
Musical director: Victor Baravalle.
Dances: LeRoy Prinz.
Music: Jerome Kern.
Lyrics: Oscar Hammerstein II.
Makeup: Jack P. Pierce.
Costume design: Doris Zinkeisen.
Sound supervisor: Gilbert Kurland.
Special cinematographer: John P. Fulton.
Assistant director: Joseph A. McDonough.
Cast: Irene Dunne (Magnolia Hawks), Allan Jones (Gaylord Ravenal), Charles Winninger
(Cap'n Andy Hawks), Paul Robeson (Joe), Helen Morgan (Julie), Helen Westley (Parthy),
Queenie Smith (Elly), Sammy White (Frank), Donald Cook (Steve), Hattie McDaniel
(Queenie), Francis X. Mahoney (Rubber Face), Arthur Hohl (Pete), Charles Middleton
(Sheriff Vallon), J. Farrell MacDonald (Windy), Marilyn Knowlden (Kim, as a child), Sunnie
O'Dea (Kim), Clarence Muse (Janitor), Charles Wilson (Green), Patricia Barry (Kim, as a
baby), Mae Beatty (Landlady), Barbara Pepper, Dorothy Granger, Harry Harris, Flora
Finch, Tiny Stafford.
Running time: 113 minutes.

The Road Back (Universal, 1937)

A James Whale Production.
Executive producer: Charles R. Rogers.
Associate producer: Edmund Grainger.
Director: James Whale [and Ted Sloman, uncredited].
Screenplay: R. C. Sherriff, Charles Kenyon.
Based on the novel by Erich Maria Remarque.
Photography: John J. Mescall, George H. Robinson.
Art director: Charles D. Hall.
Editors: Ted Kent, Charles Maynard.
Composer: Dimitri Tiomkin.
Musical director: Charles Previn.
Makeup: Jack P. Pierce.

Sound: William Hedgcock, Bernard B. Brown.

Assistant director: Joseph A. McDonough.

Cast: John King (Ernst), Richard Cromwell (Ludwig), "Slim" Summerville (Tjaden), Andy
Devine (Willy), Barbara Read (Lucy), Louise Fazenda (Angelina), Noah Beery, Jr.
(Wessling), Maurice Murphy (Albert), John Emery (Von Hagen), Etienne Girardot
(Mayor), Lionel Atwill (Prosecutor), Henry Hunter (Bethke), Larry Blake (Weil), Gene
Garrick (Giesicke), Jean Rouverol (Elsa), Hedwig Ibsen [Greta Gynte] (Maria), Spring
Byington (Ernst's Mother), Frank Reicher (Ernst's Father), Arthur Hohl (Heinrich),
William B. Davidson (Bartscher), Al Shean (Mr. Markheim), Edwin Maxwell (Principal),
Samuel S. Hinds (Defense Attorney), Robert Warwick (Judge), Clara Blandick (Willy's
Mother), Laura Hope Crews (Ernst's Aunt), Charles Holton [Halton] (Uncle Rudolph),
Jonathan Hale, Buddy Roosevelt, Lane Chandler, Tom Steele, Paul Panzer, William Bene-
dict, Edward van Sloan, Dwight Frye, Francis Ford, Eddie Phillips.

Running time: 105 minutes.

The Great Garrick (Warner Bros., 1937)

A James Whale Production.

Personally supervised by Mervyn LeRoy.

Director: James Whale.

Screenplay: Ernest Vajda.

Photography: Ernest Haller.

Art director: Anton Grot.

Editor: Warren Low.

Composer: Adolph Deutsch.

Music director: Leo F. Forbstein.

Cosmetician: Perc Westmore.

Costumes: Milo Anderson.

Sound: C. A. Riggs.

Assistant director: Sherry Shrourds.

Cast: Brian Aherne (David Garrick), Olivia de Havilland (Germaine), Edward Everett Horton
(Tubby), Melville Cooper (M. Picard), Lionel Atwill (Beaumarchais), Luis Alberni (Basset),
Lana Turner (Auber), Marie Wilson (Nicolle), Linda Perry (Molee), Fritz Leiber (Horatio),
Etienne Girardot (Jean Cabot), Dorothy Tree (Mme. Moreau), Craig Reynolds (M. Janin),
Paul Everton (Innkeeper of Adam and Eve), Trevor Bardette (M. Noverre), Milton Owen
(Thierre), Albert van Dekker (LeBrun), Chester Clute (M. Moreau), Henry O'Neill (Sir
Joshua Reynolds).

Running time: 89 minutes.

Sinners in Paradise (Universal, 1938)

A James Whale Production.

Associate producer: Ken Goldsmith.

Director: James Whale.

Screenplay: Lester Cole, Harold Buckley, Louis Stevens.

Based on a story by Harold Buckley.

Photography: George Robinson.

Art director: Jack Otterson.

Associate: Richard H. Riedel.

Editor: Maurice Wright.

Musical director: Charles Previn.

Makeup: Jack P. Pierce.

Sound: William R. Fox, Edwin Wetzel.

Assistant director: Fred Frank.

Cast: Madge Evans (Anne Wesson), John Boles (Jim Taylor), Bruce Cabot (Robert Malone),
Marion Martin (Iris Compton), Gene Lockhart (Senator Corey), Charlotte Wynters

(Thelma Chase), Nana Bryant (Mrs. Franklin Sydney), Milburn Stone (Honeyman), Donald Barry (Jessup), Morgan Conway (Harrison Brand), Willie Fung (Ping).
Running time: 64 minutes.

Wives under Suspicion (Universal, 1938)

A James Whale Production.
Associate producer: Edmund Grainger.
Director: James Whale.
Original screenplay: Myles Connolly.
Suggested by a play [*The Kiss before the Mirror*] by Ladislaus Fodor.
Photography: George Robinson.
Art director: Jack Otterson.
Editor: Charles Maynard.
Musical director: Charles Previn.
Makeup: Jack P. Pierce.
Sound: Robert Pritchard, Edwin Wetzel.
Assistant director: Fred Frank.
Cast: Warren William (District Attorney Jim Stowell), Gail Patrick (Lucy Stowell), Constance Moore (Elizabeth), William Lundigan (Phil), Ralph Morgan (Shaw MacAllen), Cecil Cunningham ("Sharpy"), Samuel S. Hinds (David Marrow), Milburn Stone (Kirk), Lillian Yarbo (Creola), Jonathan Hale (Allison), Anthony Hughes (Murphy), Edward Stanley (The Judge), James Flavin (Jenks), Edward LeSaint, William Ruhl, William Gould, Minerva Urecal, Jim Harmon, William Bakewell.
Running time: 69 minutes.

Port of Seven Seas (MGM, 1938)

Producer: Henry Henigson.
Director: James Whale.
Screenplay: Preston Sturges.
Based on the play *Fanny* by Marcel Pagnol.
Photography: Karl Freund.
Art director: Cedric Gibbons.
Editor: Frederick Y. Smith.
Montage: Slavko Vorkapich.
Composer: Franz Waxman.
Makeup: Jack Dawn.
Assistant director: Joseph A. McDonough.
Cast: Wallace Beery (Cesar), Frank Morgan (Panisse), Maureen O'Sullivan (Madelon), John Beal (Marius), Jessie Ralph (Honorine), Cora Witherspoon (Claudine), Etienne Girardot (Bruneau), E. Allyn Warren (Captain Escartefigue).
Running time: 81 minutes.

The Man in the Iron Mask (United Artists, 1939)

Edward Small presents.
A James Whale Production.
Director: James Whale.
Screenplay: George Bruce.
Based on the novel by Alexander Dumas.
Photography: Robert Planck.
Art director: John DuCasse Schulze.
Editor: Grant Whytock.
Composer: Lucien Moraweck.
Musical director: Lud Gluskin.
Makeup director: Paul A. Stanhope.

Costumes: Bridgehouse.
Sound: W. H. Wilmarth.
Second unit director: Cullen Tate.
Assistant director: Edgar Anderson.
Cast: Louis Hayward (Louis XIV/Philippe of Gascony), Joan Bennett (Maria Theresa), Warren
    William (D'Artagnan), Joseph Schildkraut (Fouquet), Alan Hale (Porthos), Walter Kings-
    ford (Colbert), Miles Mander (Aramis), Bert Roach (Athos), Montagu Love (Spanish
    Ambassador), Doris Kenyon (Queen Anne), Marian Martin (Mlle. de la Valliere), Albert
    Dekker (Louis XIII), Nigel de Brulier (Cardinal Richelieu), William Royle (Commandant
    of Bastille), Boyd Irwin (Lord High Constable of France), Howard Brooks (Cardinal),
    Reginald Barlowe [Barlow] (Jean Paul), Lane Chandler (Captain of Fouquet's Guards),
    Wyndham Standing (Doctor), Dorothy Vaughan (Midwife), Sheila Darcy (Maria Theresa's
    Maid), Robert Milasch (Torturer), D'Arcy Corrigan (Tortured Prisoner), Harry Woods
    (First Officer), Peter Cushing (Second Officer), Emmett King (King's Chamberlain), The
    St. Brenden Choir.
Running time: 110 minutes.

Green Hell (Universal, 1940)

A James Whale Production.
Producer: Harry Edington.
Director: James Whale.
Screenplay: Frances Marion.
Based on a story by Frances Marion.
Photography: Karl Freund.
Art director: Jack Otterson.
Editor: Ted Kent.
Musical director: Charles Previn.
Makeup: Jack P. Pierce.
Sound supervisor: Bernard B. Brown.
Sound technician: Charles Carroll.
Assistant director: Joseph A. McDonough.
Cast: Douglas Fairbanks, Jr. (Keith Brandon), Joan Bennett (Stephanie Richardson), John
    Howard (Hal Scott), George Sanders (Forrester), Alan Hale (Doctor Loren), George Ban-
    croft ("Tex" Morgan), Vincent Price (David Richardson), Gene Garrick (Graham), Francis
    McDonald (Gracco), Ray Mala (Mala), Peter Bronte (Santos), Lupita Tovar (Native Girl).
Running time: 87 minutes.

They Dare Not Love (Columbia, 1941)

Producer: Samuel Bischoff.
Director: James Whale [and Charles Vidor, uncredited].
Screenplay: Charles Bennett, Ernest Vajda.
Based on a story by James Edward Grant.
Photography: Franz F. Planer.
Art director: Lionel Banks.
Editor: Al Clark.
Musical director: M. W. Stoloff.
Makeup: Clay Campbell.
Assistant director: William Mull.
Cast: George Brent (Prince Kurt von Rotenberg), Martha Scott (Marta Keller), Paul Lukas
    (Baron von Helsing), Egon Brecher (Professor Keller), Roman Bohnen (Baron Shafter),
    Edgar Barrier (Captain Wilhelm Ehrhardt), Kay Linaker (Barbara Murdock), Frank
    Reicher (Captain), Peter Cushing.
Running time: 76 minutes.

Personnel Placement in the Army (1942)

U.S. Army training film.
Cast: Preston Foster, Gordon Jones, Frank Coughlin, Peter Michael, Alan Hale, Jr.

Hello Out There (unreleased, 1948)

Huntington Hartford Productions.
Producer: Huntington Hartford.
Director: James Whale.
Screenplay: George Tobin.
Based on the play by William Saroyan.
Photography: Karl Struss.
Art director: Edward Ilou.
Editor: Otto Mayer.
Makeup: Gustav Norin.
Cast: Harry Morgan (The Roustabout), Lee Patrick (The Woman), Marjorie Steele (The Sheriff's Wife).
Running time: 33 minutes.

Willis O'Brien

The Dinosaur and the Missing Link (Edison, 1917)

[May have been reissued as *The Dinosaur and the Baboon*].
Producer: Herman Wobber.
Direction, story, photography, special effects: Willis O'Brien.
Running time: 1 reel [5.5 minutes].

Morpheus Mike (Edison, 1917)

Direction, story, photography, special effects: Willis O'Brien.
Running time: 1 reel [3 minutes].

The Birth of a Flivver (Edison, 1917)

Direction, story, photography, special effects: Willis O'Brien.
Running time: 1 reel.

R. F. D., 10,000 B. C.; A Mannikin Comedy (Edison, 1917)

Direction, story, photography, special effects: Willis O'Brien.
Running time: 2 reels [9 minutes].

Prehistoric Poultry; The Dinornis or Great Roaring Whiffenpoof (Edison, 1917)

Direction, story, photography, special effects: Willis O'Brien.
Running time: 1 reel [4 minutes].

Curious Pets of Our Ancestors (Edison, 1917)

Direction, story, photography, special effects: Willis O'Brien.
Running time: 1 reel.

In the Villain's Power (Edison, 1917)

Direction, story, photography, special effects: Willis O'Brien.
Running time: 2 reels.
[Information on this title is tenuous.]

Sam Loyd's Famous Puzzles; The Puzzling Billboard (Edison, 1917)
Running time: 1 reel.
[Information on this title is tenuous.]

Mickey's Naughty Nightmares (Edison, 1917)
Direction, story, photography, special effects: Willis O'Brien.
Running time: 1 reel.
[Information on this title is tenuous.]

The Ghost of Slumber Mountain (World, 1919)
Producer: Herbert M. Dawley.
Direction, story, photography, special effects: Willis O'Brien.
Cast: Herbert M. Dawley. [O'Brien may have played "Mad Dick."]
Running time: 2 reels [12 minutes].

The Lost World (First National, 1925)
Produced by arrangement with Watterson R. Rothacker.
Producer: Earl J. Hudson.
Director: Harry O. Hoyt.
Additional direction: William Dowling.
Scenario: Marion Fairfax.
Based on the novel by Sir Arthur Conan Doyle.
Photography: Arthur Edeson.
Additional photography: Homer Scott, J. Devereaux Jennings.
Art direction: Milton Menasco.
Editorial direction: Marion Fairfax.
Editor: George McGuire.
Original music compilation: James C. Bradford.
Song "The Lost World" ("inspired by" the film), Rudolph Friml, Harry B. Smith.
Ape man makeup: Cecil Holland.
Research and technical direction: Willis H. O'Brien.
Chief technician: Fred W. Jackman.
Special effects technicians: Marcel Delgado, Ralph Hammeras, Hans Koenekamp, Vernon L. Walker.
Cast: Bessie Love (Paula White), Lloyd Hughes (Ed Malone), Lewis Stone (Sir John Roxton), Wallace Beery (Professor Challenger), Arthur Hoyt (Professor Summerlee), Margaret McWade (Mrs. Challenger), Finch Smiles (Austin, Challenger's Butler), Jules Cowles (Zambo), Bull Montana (Apeman), George Bunny (Colin McArdle), Charles Wellsley (Major Hibbard), Alma Bennett (Gladys Hungerford), Virginia Browne Faire (Marquette), Nelson MacDowell (*Gazette* Attorney), Mary (Female Ape), Jocko (Monkey).
Running time: 10 reels, 104 minutes [Abridged version: 57 minutes].

King Kong (RKO Radio, 1933)
Executive producer: David O. Selznick.
A Merian C. Cooper and Ernest B. Schoedsack Production.
Directors [not listed on film]: Merian C. Cooper, Ernest B. Schoedsack.
Screenplay: James Creelman, Ruth Rose.
From an idea conceived by Merian C. Cooper, Edgar Wallace.
Photography: Eddie Linden, Vernon Walker, J. O. Taylor.
Art direction: Carroll Clark, Al Herman.
Editor: Ted Cheesman.
Composer: Max Steiner.
Sound recording: Earl A. Wolcott.

Sound effects: Murray Spivack.

Chief technician: Willis H. O'Brien.

Art technicians: Mario Larrinaga, Byron L. Crabbe.

Technical staff: E. B. Gibson, Marcel Delgado, Fred Reese, Orville Goldner, Carroll Shepphird.

Production assistants: Archie F. Marshek, Walter Daniels.

Cast: Fay Wray (Ann Darrow), Robert Armstrong (Carl Denham), Bruce Cabot (Jack Driscoll), Frank Reicher (Captain Englehorn), Sam Hardy (Charles Weston), Noble Johnson (Native Chief), James Flavin (Second Mate), Steve Clemento (Witch King), Victor Wong (Charley [Lumpy]), Paul Porcasi (Socrates), Russ Powell (Dock Watchman), Ethan Laidlaw, Blackie Whiteford, Dick Curtis, Charles Sullivan, Harry Tenbrook, Gil Perkins (Sailors), Vera Lewis, Leroy Mason (Theater Patrons), Frank Mills, Lynton Brent (Reporters), Jim Thorpe (Native Dancer), George MacQuarrie (Police Captain), Madame Sul-te-wan (Hand-maiden), Etta MacDaniel (Native Woman), Ray Turner (Native), Dorothy Gulliver (Girl), Carlotta Monti (Girl), Barney Capehart, Bob Galloway, Eric Wood, Dusty Mitchell, Russ Rodgers (Navy Pilots), Reginald Barlow (Engineer), Merian C. Cooper (Flight Commander), Ernest B. Schoedsack (Chief Observer).

Running time: 100 minutes.

The Son of Kong (RKO Radio, 1933)

Executive producer: Merian C. Cooper.

Associate producer: Archie Marshek.

Director: Ernest B. Schoedsack.

Story: Ruth Rose.

Photographers: Eddie Linden, Vernon Walker, J. O. Taylor.

Settings: Van Nest Polglase, Al Herman.

Editor: Ted Cheesman.

Composer: Max Steiner.

Song "Runaway Blues," lyrics by Edward Eliscu.

Sound recording: Earl A. Wolcott.

Sound effects: Murray Spivack.

Chief technician: Willis O'Brien.

Art technicians: Mario Larrinaga, Byron L. Crabbe.

Technical staff: E. B. Gibson, Marcel Delgado, Fred Reese, Carroll Shepphird, W. G. White.

Cast: Robert Armstrong (Carl Denham), Helen Mack (Hilda Petersen [Peterson]), Frank Reicher (Captain Englehorn), John Marston (Helstrom), Victor Wong (Charley), Ed Brady (Red), Lee Kohlmar (Mickey), Clarence Wilson (Petersen [Peterson]), Katherine Ward (Mrs. Hudson), Gertrude Short (Girl Reporter), Gertrude Sutton (Servant Girl), Noble Johnson (Native Chief), James B. Leong (Chinese Trader), Steve Clemento (Witch King), Frank O'Conner (Process Server), Bud Geary (Cop), D. G. Del Valle (Singer), Constantine Romanoff, Bill Williams, Harry Tenbrook, Dutch Hendrian, William Lally, Frank Mills, Harry Cornbleth, Tex Higginson, John Gough, Claude Payton, Jack Richardson, Cy Clegg, Frank Garrity (Crew Members).

Running time: 69 minutes.

The Last Days of Pompeii (RKO Radio, 1935)

A Merian C. Cooper Production.

Production associate: John Speaks.

Director: Ernest B. Schoedsack.

Screenplay: Ruth Rose.

Collaboration on adaptation: Boris Ingster.

Original story: James Ashmore Creelman, Melville Baker.

Photography: J. Roy Hunt.

Art direction: Van Nest Polglase.

Associate: Al Herman.

Set dressing: Thomas Little.
Editor: Archie F. Marshek.
Composer: Roy Webb.
Costumes: Aline Bernstein.
Recording: Clem Portman.
Music recording: P. J. Faulkner, Jr.
Chief technician: Willis O'Brien.
Art technician: Byron Crabbe.
Photographic technician: Eddie Linden.
Photographic effects: Vernon Walker.
Special effects: Harry Redmond.
Sound effects: Walter Elliott.
Cast: Preston Foster (Marcus), Alan Hale (Burbix), Basil Rathbone (Pontius Pilate), John Wood (Flavius, as a man), Louis Calhern (Prefect), David Holt (Flavius, as a boy), Dorothy Wilson (Clodia), Wyrley Birch (Leaster), Gloria Shea (Julia), Frank Conroy (Gaius), William V. Mong (Cleon), Murray Kinnell (Judean Peasant), Henry Kolker (Warder), Edward Van Sloan (Calvus), Zeffie Tilbury (The Wise Woman), John Davidson (Slave).
Running time: 96 minutes.

Dancing Pirate (RKO Radio, 1936)

A Pioneer Pictures Production.
Executive producer: Merian C. Cooper.
Producer: John Speaks.
Director: Lloyd Corrigan.
Screenplay: Ray Harris, Francis Edwards Faragoh.
Adaptation: Jack Wagner, Boris Ingster.
Based on a story by Emma Lindsay Squier.
Photography: William V. Skall (Technicolor).
Designed in color by Robert Edmond Jones.
Art direction: W. B. Ihnen.
Editor: Archie F. Marshek.
Musical direction: Alfred Newman.
Songs "When You're Dancing the Waltz" and "Are You My Love" by Richard Rodgers, Lorenz Hart.
Dance direction: Russell Lewis.
Sound recording: Oscar Lagerstrom.
Photographic effects: Willis H. O'Brien.
Cast: Charles Collins (Jonathan Pride), Frank Morgan (Alcalde), Steffi Duna (Serafina), Luis Alberni (Pamfilo), Victor Varconi (Don Baltazar), Jack La Rue (Chago), Alma Real (Blanca), William V. Mong (Tecolote), Mitchell Lewis (Pirate Chief), Julian Rivero (Shepherd), John Eberts (Mozo), Cansino Family (Royal Cansinos), Cy Kendall (Pirate Cook), Harold Waldridge (Orville), Vera Lewis (Orville's Mother), Nora Cecil (Landlady), Ellen Lowe (Miss Ponsonby), Max Wagner (Pirate Mate), James Farley (Sailor).
Running time: 85 minutes.

Mighty Joe Young (RKO Radio, 1949)

An ARKO Production.
Presented by John Ford and Merian C. Cooper.
Director: Ernest B. Schoedsack.
Screenplay: Ruth Rose.
Based on an original story by Merian C. Cooper.
Photography: J. Roy Hunt.
Art direction: James Basevi.
Assistant: Howard Richmond.

Set dressing: George Altwils.
Editor: Ted Cheesman.
Composer: Roy Webb.
Musical direction: C. Bakaleinikoff.
Costumes: Adele Balkan.
Sound: John L. Cass, Clem Portman.
Sound editor: Walter Elliott.
Technical creator: Willis O'Brien.
First technician: Ray Harryhausen.
Second technician: Peter Peterson.
Technical staff: Marcel Delgado, George Lofgren, Fitch Fulton.
Photographic effects: Harold Stine, Bert Willis.
Optical photography: Linwood Dunn.
Production effects: Jack Lannon.
Unit production manager: Lloyd Richards.
Assistant director: Samuel Ruman.
Cast: Terry Moore (Jill Young), Ben Johnson (Gregg Johnson), Robert Armstrong (Max
     O'Hara), Frank McHugh (Windy), Douglas Fowley (Jones), Denis Green (Crawford), Paul
     Guilfoyle (Smith), Nestor Paiva (Brown), Regis Toomey (Mr. Young), Lora Lee Michel
     (Jill, as a girl), James Flavin (Schultz), Primo Carnera, Man Mountain Dean, The Swedish
     Angel (Themselves).
Running time: 94 minutes.

The Animal World (Warner Bros., 1956)

A Windsor Production.
Producer-director: Irwin Allen.
Screenplay: Irwin Allen.
Photography: Harold Wellman and naturalist photographers throughout the world (Techni-
     color).
Art direction: Bert Tuttle.
Editors: Gene Palmer, Robert A. Belcher.
Composer/conductor: Paul Sawtell.
Sound effects editors: Henry L. DeMond, Walter Elliott, Bert Schoenfeld.
Music editor: Richard Harris.
Supervising animator: Willis O'Brien.
Animation: Ray Harryhausen.
Special effects: Arthur S. Rhoades.
Production associate: George E. Swink.
Narrators: Theodore Von Eltz, John Storm.
Running time: 82 minutes.

The Beast of Hollow Mountain (United Artists, 1956)

A Nassour Studios-Peliculas Rodriguez Production.
Producers: William Nassour, Edward Nassour.
Directors: Edward Nassour, Ismael Rodriquez.
Screenplay: Robert Hill.
Additional dialogue: Jack DeWitt.
From an idea by Willis O'Brien.
Photography: Jorge Stahl, Jr. (DeLuxe color, CinemaScope).
Editors: Holbrook Todd, Maury Wright.
Composer: Raul Lavista.
Sound director: James L. Fields.
Sound dialogue: Nick Rosa.
Photographic effects: Jack Rabin, Louis DeWitt.

Assistant to the producer: Henry Sharp.

Assistant director: Gene Anderson, Jr.

Cast: Guy Madison (Jimmy), Patricia Medina (Sarita), Carlos Rivas (Felipe), Edward Noriega (Enrique Rios), Julio Villarreal (Don Pedro), Mario Navarro (Panchito), Pasquel Garcia Pena (Pancho), Lupe Carriles (Margarita), Manuel Arvide (Martinez), Jose Chavez (Manuel), Margarito Luna (Jose), Roberto Contreras (Carlos), Lobo Negro [Guillermo Hernandez] (Jorge), Jorge Trevino (Shopkeeper).

Running time: 82 minutes.

The Black Scorpion (Warner Bros., 1957)

Producers: Frank Melford, Jack Dietz.

Director: Edward Ludwig.

Screenplay: David Duncan, Robert Blees.

Based on a story by Paul Yawitz.

Photography: Lionel Lindon.

Art direction: Edward Fitzgerald.

Supervising editor: Richard L. Van Enger.

Composer-conductor: Paul Sawtell.

Electronic music: Jack Cookerly.

Sound: Rafael L. Esparza.

Sound effects: Mandine Rogne.

Supervisor of special effects: Willis O'Brien.

Animation: Peter Peterson.

Assistant directors: Ray Heinze, Jaime Contreras.

Cast: Richard Denning (Henry Scott), Mara Corday (Teresa Alvarez), Carlos Rivas (Arturo Ramos), Mario Navarro (Juanito), Carlos Muzquiz (Dr. Velazco), Pascual [Pasquel] Pena (Jose de la Cruz), Fanny Schiller (Florentina), Pedro Galvan (Father Delgado), Arturo Martinez (Major Cosio).

Running time: 88 minutes.

Behemoth the Sea Monster (U.K.; Eros, 1959) [U.S.: The Giant Behemoth (Allied Artists)]

A David Diamond Production.

Associate producer: Ted Lloyd.

Directors: Eugene Lourie, Douglas Hickox [U.S.: just Lourie].

Screenplay: Eugene Lourie.

Photography: Ken Hodges.

Art direction: Harry White.

Supervising editor: Lee Doig.

Composer-conductor: Edwin Astley.

Makeup: Jimmy Evans.

Sound: Sid Wiles.

Sound editor: Richard Marden.

Special effects designers and creators: Jack Rabin, Irving Block, Louis DeWitt, Willis O'Brien, Pete Peterson.

Assistant director: Kim Mills.

Cast: Gene Evans (Steve Karnes), Andre Morell (Professor Bickford), John Turner (John), Leigh Madison (Jean Trevethan), Jack McGowran [MacGowran] (Dr. Sampson), Maurice Kaufmann (Submarine Commander), Henry Vidon (Tom Trevethan), Leonard Sachs (Scientist), Neal Arden (Announcer).

Running time: 72 minutes [U.S.: 80 minutes].

The Lost World (20th Century–Fox, 1960)

Producer-director: Irwin Allen.

Screenplay: Charles Bennett, Irwin Allen.

Based on the novel by Sir Arthur Conan Doyle.
Photography: Winton Hoch (DeLuxe color, CinemaScope)
Art direction: Duncan Cramer, Walter M. Simonds.
Set decoration: Walter M. Scott, Joseph Kish, John Sturtevant.
Editor: Hugh S. Fowler.
Composers: Paul Sawtell, Bert Shefter.
Makeup: Ben Nye.
Costume designer: Paul Zastupnevich.
Hairstyles: Helen Turpin.
Sound: E. Clayton Ward, Harry M. Leonard.
Special photographic effects: L. B. Abbott, James B. Gordon, Emil Kosa, Jr.
Effects technician: Willis O'Brien.
Production illustrator: Maurice Zuberano.
Technical adviser: Henry E. Lester.
Assistant director: Ad Schaumer.
Cast: Michael Rennie (Lord John Roxton), Jill St. John (Jennifer Holmes), David Hedison (Ed Malone), Claude Rains (Prof. Challenger), Fernando Lamas (Gomez), Richard Haydn (Prof. Summerlee), Ray Stricklyn (David Holmes), Jay Novello (Costa), Vitina Marcus (Native Girl), Ian Wolfe (Burton White).
Running time: 96 minutes.

Ray Harryhausen

Mother Goose Stories (Bailey, 1946)
Producer-director-animator: Ray Harryhausen.
Associate: Fred Blasauf [Fred Harryhausen].
Costumes: Martha Reske [Martha Harryhausen].
Running time: 11 minutes.

Mighty Joe Young (RKO Radio, 1949)
[See under Willis O'Brien.]

Little Red Riding Hood (Bailey, 1949)
Producer-director-animator: Ray Harryhausen.
Associate: Fred Blasauf [Fred Harryhausen].
Writer: Charlott Knight.
Photography: Jerome Wray [Ray Harryhausen].
Costumes: Martha Reske [Martha Harryhausen].
Narrator: James Matthews.
Running time: 9 minutes.

Hansel and Gretel (Bailey, 1951)
Producer-director-animator: Ray Harryhausen.
Associate: Fred Blasauf [Fred Harryhausen].
Adaptation: Charlott Knight.
Costumes: Martha Reske [Martha Harryhausen].
Narrator: Hugh Douglas.
Running time: 10 minutes.

Rapunzel (Bailey, 1951)
Producer-director-animator: Ray Harryhausen.
Associate: Fred Blasauf [Fred Harryhausen].

Adaptation: Charlott Knight.
Costumes: Martha Reske [Martha Harryhausen].
Narrator: Del Moore.
Running time: 11 minutes.

The Beast from 20,000 Fathoms (Warner Bros., 1953)

Producers: Hal Chester, Jack Dietz.
Associate producer: Bernard W. Burton.
Director: Eugene Lourie.
Screenplay: Lou Morheim, Fred Freiberger [shooting script lists Morheim and Robert Smith].
Suggested by the story by Ray Bradbury.
Photography: Jack Russell.
Art direction: Eugene Lourie [uncredited].
Assistant: Hal Waller.
Set decoration: Edward Boyle.
Editor: Bernard W. Burton.
Composer: David Buttolph.
Orchestrator: Maurice de Packh.
Makeup: Louis Phillippi.
Costumes: Berman's of Hollywood.
Sound: Max Hutchinson.
Technical effects creator: Ray Harryhausen.
Special effects: Willis Cook.
Dialogue director: Michael Fox.
Assistant director: Horace Hough.
Cast: Paul Christian (Prof. Tom Nesbitt), Paula Raymond (Lee Hunter), Cecil Kellaway (Professor Elson), Kenneth Tobey (Colonel Evans), Donald Woods (Captain Jackson), Lee Van Cleef (Corporal Stone), Steve Brodie (Sgt. Loomis), Ross Elliott (George Ritchie), Jack Pennick (Jacob), Ray Hyke (Sgt. Willistead), Mary Hill (Nesbitt's Secretary), Michael Fox (Doctor), Alvin Greenman (First Radar Man), Frank Ferguson (Dr. Morton), King Donovan (Dr. Ingersoll), James Best (Radar Man).
Running time: 80 minutes.

The Story of King Midas (Bailey, 1953)

Producer-director-animator: Ray Harryhausen.
Associate: Fred Blasauf [Fred Harryhausen].
Adaptation: Charlott Knight.
Costumes: Martha Reske [Martha Harryhausen].
Music editor: Walter Soul.
Narrator: Del Moore.
Running time: 10 minutes.

It Came from Beneath the Sea (Columbia, 1955)

Executive producer: Sam Katzman.
Producer: Charles H. Schneer.
Director: Robert Gordon.
Screenplay: George Worthing Yates, Hal Smith.
Based on a story by Yates.
Photography: Henry Freulich.
Art direction: Paul Palmentola.
Set decoration: Sidney Clifford.
Editor: Jerome Thoms.
Music conductor: Mischa Bakaleinikoff.
Sound: Josh Westmoreland.

Technical effects creator: Ray Harryhausen.

Special effects: Jack Erickson.

Assistant director: Leonard Katzman.

Cast: Kenneth Tobey (Pete Mathews), Faith Domergue (Lesley Joyce), Donald Curtis (John Carter), Ian Keith (Admiral Burns), Dean Maddox, Jr. (Admiral Norman), Chuck Griffiths (Griff), Harry Lauter (Bill Nash), Richard W. Peterson (Captain Stacy), Del Courtney (Assistant Secretary Robert Chase), Tol Avery (Navy Intern), Ray Storey (Reporter), Rudy Puteska (Hall), Jack Littlefield (Aston), Ed Fisher (McLeod), Jules Irving (King).

Running time: 79 minutes.

Earth vs. the Flying Saucers (Columbia, 1956)

Executive producer: Sam Katzman.

Producer: Charles H. Schneer.

Director: Fred F. Sears.

Screenplay: George Worthing Yates, Raymond T. Marcus.

Screen story: Curt Siodmak.

Suggested by the book *Flying Saucers from Outer Space* by Major Donald E. Keyhoe.

Photography: Fred Jackman, Jr.

Art direction: Paul Palmentola.

Set decoration: Sidney Clifford.

Editor: Danny D. Landres.

Music conductor: Mischa Bakaleinikoff.

Sound: Josh Westmoreland.

Technical effects creator: Ray Harryhausen.

Special effects: Russ Kelley.

Assistant director: Gene Anderson, Jr.

Cast: Hugh Marlowe (Dr. Russell Marvin), Joan Taylor (Carol Marvin), Donald Curtis (Major Huglin), Morris Ankrum (General Hanley), John Zaremba (Professor Kanter), Tom Browne Henry (Admiral Enright), Grandon Rhodes (General Edmunds), Larry Blake (Motorcycle Officer), Harry Lauter (Cutting), Charles Evans (Dr. Alberts), Clark Howatt (Sgt. Nash), Frank Wilcox (Alfred Cassidy), Alan Reynolds (Maj. Kimberly).

Running time: 83 minutes.

The Animal World (Warner Bros., 1956)

[See under Willis O'Brien.]

20 Million Miles to Earth (Columbia, 1957)

A Morningside Production.

Producer: Charles H. Schneer.

Director: Nathan Juran.

Screenplay: Bob Williams, Christopher Knopf.

Based on a story by Charlott Knight.

Photographer: Irving Lippman, Carlos Ventigmilia.

Art director: Cary Odell.

Set decorator: Robert Priestley.

Editor: Edwin Bryant.

Music conductor: Mischa Bakaleinikoff.

Sound: Lambert Day.

Technical effects creator: Ray Harryhausen.

Assistant directors: Eddie Saeta, Octavio Oppo.

Cast: William Hopper (Colonel Calder), Joan Taylor (Marisa), Frank Puglia (Dr. Leonardo), John Zaremba (Dr. Judson Uhl), Thomas B. Henry (Gen. MacIntosh [McIntosh]), Tito Vuolo (Comissario of Police), Jan Arvan (Signore Contino), Arthur Space (Dr. Sharman), Bart Bradley (Pepe), George Khoury (Verrico), Don Orlando (Mondello), Rollin Moriyama

(Dr. Koroku), George Pelling (Mr. Maples), Ray Harryhausen (Man Feeding Elephants in Zoo).

Running time: 82 minutes.

The 7th Voyage of Sinbad (Columbia, 1958)

A Morningside Production.
Producer: Charles H. Schneer.
Director: Nathan Juran.
Screenplay: Kenneth Kolb.
Photography: Wilkie Cooper (Technicolor).
Art direction: Gil Parrendo.
Editors: Edwin Bryant, Jerome Thoms.
Composer: Bernard Herrmann.
Recording supervisor: John Livadary.
Special visual effects creator: Ray Harryhausen.
Technical assistant: George Lofgren.
Stunt supervisor: Enzo Musumeci-Greco.
Assistant directors: Eugenio Martin, Pedro de Juan.
Cast: Kerwin Mathews (Sinbad), Kathryn Grant (Princess Parisa), Richard Eyer (The Genie), Torin Thatcher (Sokurah), Alec Mango (Caliph), Danny Green (Karim), Harold Kasket (Sultan), Alfred Brown (Harufa), Nana de Herrera (Sadi), Nino Falanga (Gaunt Sailor), Luis Guedes (Crewman), Virgilio Teixeira (Ali).
Running time: 88 minutes.

The 3 Worlds of Gulliver (U.K.; Columbia, 1960)

A Morningside-Worldwide Production.
Producer: Charles H. Schneer.
Director: Jack Sher.
Screenplay: Arthur Ross, Jack Sher.
Based on the novel *Gulliver's Travels* by Jonathan Swift.
Photography: Wilkie Cooper (Eastman color by Pathé).
Art direction: Gil Parrendo, Derek Barrington.
Editor: Raymond Poulton.
Composer-conductor: Bernard Herrmann.
Songs "Gentle Love" and "What a Wonderful, Wonderful Fellow Is Gulliver," lyrics by Ned Washington, music by George Duning.
Costume designer: Eleanor Abbey.
Special visual effects creator: Ray Harryhausen.
Stunt supervisor: Enzo Mucimeci Greco [Musumeci-Greco].
Assistant directors: Eugenio Martin, Paul Ganapoler.
Cast: Kerwin Mathews (Dr. Lemuel Gulliver), Jo Morrow (Gwendolyn), June Thorburn (Elizabeth), Lee Patterson (Reldresal), Gregoire Aslan (King Brobdingnag), Basil Sydney (Emperor of Lilliput), Sherri Alberoni (Glumdalclitch), Charles Lloyd Pack (Makovan), Martin Benson (Flimnap), Peter Bull (Lord Bermogg), Mary Ellis (Queen Brobdingnag), Alec Mango (Galbet), Marian Spencer.
Running time: 98 minutes.

Mysterious Island (U.K.; Columbia, 1961)

A Charles H. Schneer Production.
Producer: Charles H. Schneer.
Director: Cy Endfield.
Screenplay: John Prebble, Daniel Ullman, Crane Wilbur.
Based on the novel *The Mysterious Island* by Jules Verne.
Photography: Wilkie Cooper (Eastman color by Pathé).

Underwater photography: Egil Woxholt.
Art direction: Bill Andrews.
Editor: Frederick Wilson.
Composer-conductor: Bernard Herrmann.
Sound supervisor: John Cox.
Sound recording: Peter Handford, Bob Jones.
Special visual effects creator: Ray Harryhausen.
Assistant director: Rene Dupont.
Cast: Michael Craig (Capt. Cyrus Harding), Joan Greenwood (Lady Mary Fairchild), Michael Callan (Herbert Brown), Gary Merrill (Gideon Spilett), Herbert Lom (Captain Nemo), Beth Rogan (Elena), Dan Jackson (Neb), Percy Herbert (Sgt. Pencroft). [Nigel Green is sometimes listed, but his scenes were never shot.]
Running time: 101 minutes.

Jason and the Argonauts (U.K.; Columbia, 1963)

A Charles H. Schneer Production.
Producer: Charles H. Schneer.
Associate producer: Ray Harryhausen.
Director: Don Chaffey.
Screenplay: Jan Read, Beverley Cross [shooting script also lists Ray Bowers].
Photography: Wilkie Cooper (Eastman color by Pathé).
Production design: Geoffrey Drake.
Art direction: Herbert Smith, Jack Maxsted, Tony Sarzi Braga.
Editor: Maurice Rootes.
Composer-conductor: Bernard Herrmann.
Sound recording: Cyril Collick, Red Law.
Sound editor: Alfred Cox.
Special visual effects creator: Ray Harryhausen.
Assistant director: Dennis Bertera.
Cast: Todd Armstrong (Jason), Nancy Kovack (Medea), Gary Raymond (Acastus), Laurence Naismith (Argus), Niall MacGinnis (Zeus), Douglas Wilmer (Pelias), Jack Gwillim (King Aeetes), Honor Blackman (Hera), Nigel Green (Hercules), John Crawford (Polydeuces), Michael Gwynn (Hermes), John Cairney (Hylas), Patrick Troughton (Phineas), Andrew Faulds (Phalerus), Douglas Robinson (Euphemus), Fernando Poggi (Castor).
Running time: 104 minutes.

First Men in the Moon (U.K.; Columbia, 1964)

A Charles H. Schneer Production.
Producer: Charles H. Schneer.
Associate producer: Ray Harryhausen.
Director: Nathan Juran.
Screenplay: Nigel Kneale, Jan Read.
Based on the novel The First Men in the Moon by H. G. Wells.
Photography: Wilkie Cooper (Lunacolor by Pathé, Panavision).
Art direction: John Blezard.
Editor: Maurice Rootes.
Composer: Laurie Johnson.
Makeup: Colin Garde.
Sound recording: Buster Ambler, Red Law.
Special visual effects creator: Ray Harryhausen.
Technical staff: Les Bowie, Kit West.
Technical adviser: Arthur Garratt.
Assistant director: George Pollard.
Cast: Edward Judd (Arnold Bedford), Lionel Jeffries (Cavor), Martha Hyer (Kate Callender),

Erik Chitty (Gibbs), Betty McDowall (Maggie), Miles Malleson (The Registrar), Lawrence Herder (Glushkov), Hugh McDermott (Challis), Paul Carpenter (Announcer), Huw Thomas (Announcer), Marne Maitland (Dr. Tok), Gladys Henson (The Matron), Peter Finch (Bailiff's Man), Gordon Robinson (UN Astronaut Martin), Sean Kelly (UN Astronaut Colonel Rice), John Murray Scott (UN Astronaut Nevsky).
Running time: 103 minutes.

One Million Years B.C. (U.K.; Warner-Pathe, 1966) [U.S.: 20th Century–Fox, 1967]

A Hammer Film Production for Associated British-Pathe [U.S.: A Seven Arts-Hammer Film Production].
Producer: Michael Carreras.
Associate producer: Aida Young [U.S.: Young, Hal E. Roach, Sr.].
Director: Don Chaffey.
Screenplay: Michael Carreras.
Adapted from an original screenplay by Mickell Novak, George Baker, Joseph Frickert.
Photography: Wilkie Cooper (Technicolor; US: Deluxe color).
Second unit cameraman: Jack Mills.
Art direction: Robert Jones.
Supervising editor: James Needs.
Editor: Tom Simpson.
Music and special musical effects: Mario Nascimbene.
Musical supervisor: Philip Martell.
Makeup supervisor: Wally Schneiderman.
Costume design: Carl Toms.
Recording director: A. W. Lumkin.
Sound editors: Roy Baker, Alfred Cox.
Sound mixers: Len Shilton, Bill Rowe.
Special visual effects creator: Ray Harryhausen.
Special effects: George Blackwell.
Prologue designer: Les Bowie.
Assistant director: Denis [Dennis] Bertera.
Cast: Raquel Welch (Loana), John Richardson (Tumak), Percy Herbert (Sakana), Robert Brown (Akhoba), Martine Beswick (Nupondi), Jean Wladon (Ahot), Lisa Thomas (Sura), Malya Nappi (Tohana), Richard James (Young Rock Man), William Lyon Brown (Payto), Frank Hayden (1st Rock Man), Terence Maidment (1st Shell Man), Micky De Rauch (1st Shell Girl), Yvonne Horner (Ullah).
Running time: 100 minutes [U.S.: 91 minutes].

The Valley of Gwangi (Warner Bros.-Seven Arts, 1969)

A Charles H. Schneer Production.
Producer: Charles H. Schneer.
Associate producer: Ray Harryhausen.
Director: James O'Connolly.
Screenplay: William E. Bast.
Additional material: Julian More.
Based on a story by Willis O'Brien [uncredited].
Photography: Erwin Hillier (Technicolor).
Art direction: Gil Parrondo [Parrendo].
Editor: Henry Richardson.
Composer-conductor: Jerome Moross.
Wardrobe designer: John Furness.
Sound: Malcolm Steward.
Creator of special visual effects: Ray Harryhausen.
Assistant director: Pedro Vidal.

Cast: James Franciscus (Tuck Kirby), Gila Golan (T. J. Breckenridge), Richard Carlson (Champ Connors), Laurence Naismith (Prof. Horace Bromley), Curtis Arden (Lope). Freda Jackson (Tia Zorina), Gustavo Rojo (Carlos), Dennis Kilbane (Rowdy), Mario de Barros (Bean), Jose Burgos (Dwarf).
Running time: 94 minutes.

The Golden Voyage of Sinbad (U.K.; Columbia, 1974)

A Charles H. Schneer Production.
Producers: Charles H. Schneer, Ray Harryhausen.
Director: Gordon Hessler.
Screenplay: Brian Clemens.
Based on a story by Brian Clemens, Ray Harryhausen.
Photography: Ted Moore (color)
Production design: John Stoll.
Art direction: Fernando Gonzalez.
Set dressing: Julian Mateos.
Editor: Roy Watts.
Composer: Miklos Rozsa.
Makeup: Jose Antonio Sanchez.
Costume design: Verena Coleman, Gabriella Falk.
Special Masks: Colin Arthur.
Sound recording: George Stephenson, Doug Turner.
Dubbing editor: Peter Elliott.
Creator of special visual effects: Ray Harryhausen.
Assistant director: Miguel A. Gil, Jr.
Cast: John Phillip Law (Sinbad), Caroline Munro (Margiana), Tom Baker (Koura), Douglas Wilmer (Vizier), Martin Shaw (Rachid), Gregoire Aslan (Hakim), Kurt Christian (Haroun), Takis Emmanuel (Achmed), John D. Garfield (Abdul), Aldo Sambrell (Omar), Fernando Poggi.
Running time: 105 minutes.

Sinbad and the Eye of the Tiger (U.K.; Columbia, 1977)

A Charles H. Schneer Production.
Producers: Charles H. Schneer, Ray Harryhausen.
Director: Sam Wanamaker.
Screenplay: Beverley Cross.
Based on a story by Beverley Cross, Ray Harryhausen.
Photography: Ted Moore (Metrocolor).
Production design: Geoffrey Drake.
Art direction: Fernando Gonzales, Fred Carter.
Editor: Roy Watts.
Composer: Roy Budd.
Makeup: Colin Arthur.
Costume design: Cynthia Tingey.
Sound recording: George Stephenson.
Dubbing editors: Philip Bothamley, Terry Poulton.
Dubbing mixer: Douglas Turner.
Creator of special visual effects: Ray Harryhausen.
Technical assistant: John Beach.
Assistant director: Miguel A. Gil, Jr.
Cast: Patrick Wayne (Sinbad), Taryn Power (Dione), Margaret Whiting (Zenobia), Jane Seymour (Farah), Patrick Troughton (Melanthius), Kurt Christian (Rafi), Nadim Sawaiha (Hassan), Damien Thomas (Kassim), Bruno Barnabe (Balsora), Bernard Kay (Zabid), Salami Coker (Maroof), David Sterne (Aboo-Seer), Peter Mayhew (Minaton).
Running time: 113 minutes.

Clash of the Titans (U.K.; MGM, 1981)
A Charles H. Schneer Production.
Producers: Charles H. Schneer, Ray Harryhausen.
Associate producer: John Palmer.
Director: Desmond Davis.
Screenplay: Beverley Cross.
Photography: Ted Moore (Prints in Metrocolor)
Underwater and aerial cameraman: Egil S. Woxholt.
Production design: Frank White.
Art direction: Don Picton, Peter Howitt, Giorgio Desideri, Fernando Gonzalez.
Set dressing: Harry Cordwell.
Editor: Timothy Gee.
Composer: Laurence Rosenthal.
Makeup: Basil Newall, Connie Reeve.
Masks: Colin Arthur.
Costume design: Emma Porteous.
Sound mixer: Robin Gregory.
Creator of special visual effects: Ray Harryhausen.
Assistants: Jim Danforth, Steven Archer.
Floor-physical effects: Brian Smithies.
Assistant director: Anthony Waye.
Cast: Harry Hamlin (Perseus), Judi Bowker (Andromeda), Burgess Meredith (Ammon), Lau-
    rence Olivier (Zeus), Maggie Smith (Thetis), Ursula Andress (Aphrodite), Claire Bloom
    (Hera), Sian Phillips (Cassiopeia), Tim Pigott-Smith (Thallo), Neil McCarthy (Calibos),
    Susan Fleetwood (Athena), Flora Robson (Stygian Witch), Anna Manahan (Stygian Witch),
    Freda Jackson (Stygian Witch), Donald Houston (Acrisius), Jack Gwillim (Poseidon), Pat
    Roach (Hephaestus), Vida Taylor (Danae), Harry Jones (Huntsman).
Running time: 118 minutes.

Terence Fisher

A Song for Tomorrow (U.K.; General Film Distributors, 1948)
A Highbury Production.
Producer: Ralph Nunn-May.
Director: Terence Fisher.
Screenplay: W. E. C. Fairchild.
Photography: Walter Harvey.
Art direction: Don Russell.
Editor: Gordon Pilkington.
Composer: William Blezaid [Blezard].
Cast: Evelyn McCabe (Helen Maxwell), Ralph Michael (Roger Stanton), Shaun Noble (Derek
    Wardwell [Wardell]), Valentine Dunn (Mrs. Wardwell [Wardell]), James Hayter (Klause-
    mann), Christopher Lee (Auguste), Conrad Phillips (Lt. Fenton), Yvonne Forster (Nurse),
    Carleen Lord (Helen's Dresser), Ethel Coleridge (Woman in Cinema), Martin Boddey
    (Major), Sam Kydd (Sergeant), Lockwood West (Mr. Stokes).
Running time: 62 minutes.

Colonel Bogey (U.K.; General Film Distributors, 1948)
A Highbury Production.
Producer: John Croydon.
Director: Terence Fisher.
Screenplay: John Baines, W. E. C. Fairchild.
Based on an original story by John Baines.

Photography: Gordon Lang.
Art direction: Don Russell.
Editor: Gordon Pilkington.
Composer: Norman Fulton.
Sound supervisor: W. Anson Howell.
Assistant director: Philip Horne.
Cast: Mary Jerrold (Aunt Mabel), Jack Train (Voice of Uncle James), Jane Barrett (Alice Graham), John Stone (Wilfred Barriteau), Ethel Coleridge (Emily), Hedli Anderson (Millicent), Bertram Shuttleworth (Cabby), Sam Kydd (Soldier), Charles Rolfe (Soldier), Dennis Woodford (Chemist).
Running time: 51 minutes.

To the Public Danger (U.K.; General Film Distributors, 1948)

A Highbury Production.
Producer: John Croydon.
Director: Terence Fisher.
Screenplay: T. J. Morrison, Arthur Reid.
Based on a play by Patrick Hamilton.
Photography: Harry Waxman, Roy Fogwell.
Art direction: Don Russell.
Editor: Graeme Hamilton.
Composer: Doreen Carwithen.
Sound supervisor: W. Anson Howell.
Assistant director: Philip Horne.
Cast: Dermot Walsh (Captain Cole), Susan Shaw (Nancy Bedford), Barry Letts (Fred Lane), Roy Plomley (Reggie), Betty Ann Davies (Barmaid), Sidney Bromley (Man at Bar), Cliff Weir (Landlord), Patricia Hayes (Postmistress), John Lorrell (Police Sergeant), Sam Kydd (Police Driver), Frederick Piper (Labourer), Patience Rentoul (Labourer's Wife).
Running time: 44 minutes.

Portrait from Life (U.K.; General Film Distributors, 1948) [U.S.: *The Girl in the Painting* (Universal, 1949)]

A Gainsborough Film.
Producer: Antony Darnborough.
Director: Terence Fisher.
Screenplay: Frank Harvey, Jr., Muriel Box, Sydney Box.
Based on an original story by David Evans.
Photography: Jack Asher.
Supervising art director: George Provis.
Art direction: John Elphick.
Editor: V. Sagovsky.
Composer: Benjamin Frankel.
Makeup: W. T. Partleton.
Dress design: Joan Ellacott.
Director of sound: Brian Sewell.
Sound recording: Al Rhind, W. Salter.
Assistant director: Ernie Morris.
Cast: Mai Zetterling (Hildegard), Robert Beatty (Campbell Reid [Duncan Reid]), Guy Rolfe (Major Lawrence), Herbert Lom (Hendlmann), Patrick Holt (Ferguson), Arnold Marle (Professor Menzel), Sybilla Binder (Eitel), George Thorpe (Brigadier), Gerard Heinz (Heine), Philo Hauser (Hans), Thora Hird (Mrs. Skinner), Peter Murray (Lieutenant Keith), Eric Messiter (Coroner), Cyril Chamberlain (Supervisor), Betty Lynne (Woman Interpreter), Dorothea Glade (Hildegard Schmidt), Nellie Arno (Anna Skutetsky), Richard Molinas (Man in Crowd, with Anna), Hugo Schuster (Interpreter), Gordon Bell (Captain

Roberts), Sam Kydd (Army Truck Driver), Eric Pohlmann (Leader of Search Party), Yvonne Owen (Helen).
Running time: 90 minutes.

Marry Me! (U.K.; General Film Distributors, 1949) [U.S.; Ellis, 1952]
A Gainsborough Film.
Producer: Betty Box.
Director: Terence Fisher.
Screenplay: Lewis Gilbert, Denis Waldock.
Photography: Ray Elton.
Art direction: George Provis.
Editor: Gordon Pilkington.
Composer: Clifton Parker.
Makeup: W. T. Partleton.
Sound: Brian C. Sewell.
Sound recording: Al Rhind, M. Hobbs, H. L. Bird.
Assistant director: Ernie Morris.
Cast: Derek Bond (Andrew), Susan Shaw (Pat), Patrick Holt (Martin), Carol Marsh (Doris), David Tomlinson (David), Zena Marshall (Marcelle), Guy Middleton (Sir Gordon), Nora Swinburne (Enid), Brenda Bruce (Brenda), Denis O'Dea (Sanders), Jean Cadell (Hestor Parsons), Mary Jerrold (Emily Parsons), Yvonne Owen (Sue Carson), Alison Leggatt (Miss Beamish), Beatrice Varley (Mrs. Perrins), Anthony Steel (Jack Harris), Anthony Neville, George Merritt, Sandra Dorne, Judith Furze, Tamara Lees, Esma Cannon, Mary [Marianne] Stone, Everley Gregg, J. H. Roberts, Lyn Evans, Hal Osmond, Cyril Chamberlain, John Warren, Ann Valery, John Boxer, Herbert C. Walton, Don Yarranton, Jill Allen.
Running time: 97 minutes.

The Astonished Heart (U.K.; General Film Distributors, 1950) [U.S.: Universal]
A Gainsborough Film.
A Sydney Box Production.
Producer: Antony Darnborough.
Directors: Terence Fisher, Antony Darnborough.
Screenplay: Noel Coward.
Based on the play by Noel Coward.
Photography: Jack Asher.
Supervising art director: George Provis.
Art direction: Maurice Carter.
Editor: V. Sagovsky.
Composer: Noel Coward.
Makeup: W. T. Partleton.
Assistant director: Ernie Morris.
Cast: Noel Coward (Dr. Christian Faber), Celia Johnson (Barbara Faber), Margaret Leighton (Leonora Vail), Joyce Carey (Susan Birch), Graham Payn (Tim Verney), Amy Veness (Alice Smith), Ralph Michael (Philip Lucas), Michael Hordern (Ernest), Patricia Glyn (Helen), Everley Gregg (Miss Harper), Alan Webb, John Salew, Gerald Anderson, John Warren.
Running time: 89 minutes [U.S.: 92 minutes].

So Long at the Fair (U.K.; General Film Distributors, 1950) [U.S.: Eagle-Lion Classics, 1951]
A Gainsborough Film.
A Sydney Box Production.
Producer: Betty E. Box.
Associate producer: Vivian Cox.
Directors: Terence Fisher, Antony Darnborough.

Screenplay: Hugh Mills, Anthony Thorne.
Dialogue: Hugh Mills.
Based on the novel by Anthony Thorne.
Photography: Reginald Wyer.
Supervising art director: George Provis.
Art direction: Cedric Dawe.
Editor: Gordon Hales.
Composer-conductor: Benjamin Frankel.
Makeup: George Blackler.
Dress design: Elizabeth Haffenden.
Sound recording: S. Lambourne, Gordon McCallum.
Special effects: Bill Warrington, Leslie Bowie.
Assistant director: Gerald O'Hara.
Cast: Jean Simmons (Vicky Barton), Dirk Bogarde (George Hathaway), David Tomlinson (John Barton), Honor Blackman (Rhoda O'Donovan), Cathleen Nesbitt (Madame Herve), Felix Aylmer (British Consul), Betty Warren (Mrs. O'Donovan), Marcel Poncin (Narcisse), Austin Trevor (Police Commissaire), Andre Morell (Dr. Hart), Zena Marshall (Nina), Eugene Deckers (Day Porter), Natasha Sokolova (Charlotte), Nelly Arno (Madame Verni).
Running time: 85 minutes.

Home to Danger (U.K.; Eros, 1951)

A New World Film.
Producer: Lance Comfort.
Director: Terence Fisher.
Screenplay: John Temple-Smith, Francis Edge.
Photography: Reg Wyer.
Art direction: Cedric Dawe.
Editor: Francis Edge.
Composer: M. Arnold.
Cast: Guy Rolfe (Robert), Rona Anderson (Barbara), Francis Lister (Wainwright), Alan Wheatley (Hughes), Bruce Belfrage (Solicitor), Stanley Baker (Willie Dougan), Dennis Harkin (Jimmy-the-one), Peter Jones (Lips Leonard), Betty Henderson, Cyril Conway, Amy Dalby, Christopher Hodge, Joe Stern, Glyn Houston, Toni Frost, Frederick Buckland.
Running time: 66 minutes.

The Last Page (U.K.; Exclusive, 1952) [U.S.: Man Bait (Lippert)]

A Hammer-Lippert Film.
Producer: Anthony Hinds.
Director: Terence Fisher.
Screenplay: Fredrick Knott.
Based on a story by James Hadley Chase.
Photography: Walter Harvey.
Art direction: Andrew Mazzei.
Editor: Maurice Rootes.
Composer: Frank Spencer.
Makeup: Phil Leakey.
Sound engineer: Bill Salter.
Casting: Michael Carreras.
Assistant director: Jimmy Sangster.
Cast: George Brent (John Harman), Marguerite Chapman (Stella), Raymond Huntley (Clive), Peter Reynolds (Jeff), Diana Dors (Ruby), Eleanor Summerfield (Vi), Meredith Edwards (Dave [Dale]), Harry Fowler (Joe), Conrad Phillips (Todd), Isabel Dean (May), Lawrence Ward (Lang), Nelly Arno (Miss Rossetti), David Keir (Quince), Eleanor Brown [Bryan]

(Mary Lewis), Jack Faint (Blue Club Receptionist), John Mann (Jack), Harold Goodwin (Frank), Archie Duncan (Police Constable), Cyril [Sybil] Saxon (Bank Clerk), Leslie Weston (Mr. Bruce), Lawrence O'Madden (First Customer), Ian Wilson (Second Customer).
Running time: 84 minutes [U.S.: 78 minutes].

Wings of Danger (U.K.; Exclusive, 1952) [U.S.: Dead on Course (Lippert)]

A Hammer–Lippert Film.
Producer: Anthony Hinds.
Director: Terence Fisher.
Screenplay: John Gilling.
Based on the novel Dead on Course by Elleston Trevor, Packham Webb.
Photography: Walter Harvey.
Art direction: Andrew Mazzei.
Editor: James Needs.
Composer: Malcolm Arnold.
Makeup: Phil Leakey.
Wardrobe: Ellen Trussler.
Sound engineer: Bill Salter.
Casting: Michael Carreras.
Assistant director: Jimmy Sangster.
Cast: Zachary Scott (Van), Robert Beatty (Nick Talbot), Naomi Chance (Avril), Kay Kendall (Alexia), Colin Tapley (Maxwell), Arthur Lane (Boyd Spencer), Harold Lang (Snell), Diane Cilento (Jeannette), Jack Allen (Truscott), Sheila Raynor (Nurse), Courtney Hope (Mrs. Clarence-Smith), June Ashley (First Blonde), Natasha Sokolova (Second Blonde), June Mitchell (Third Blonde), James Steel (First Flying Officer), Russ Allen (Second Flying Officer), Darcy Conyers (Signals Officer).
Running time: 72 minutes.

Stolen Face (U.K.; Exclusive, 1952) [U.S.: Lippert]

A Hammer–Lippert Film.
Producer: Anthony Hinds.
Director: Terence Fisher.
Screenplay: Martin Berkeley, Richard Landau.
Based on an original story by Alexander Paal, Steven Vas.
Photography: Walter Harvey.
Art direction: Wilfred Arnold.
Editor: Maurice Rootes.
Composer: Malcolm Arnold.
Solo piano: Miss Bronwyn Jones.
Specialty numbers: Jack Parnell.
Makeup: Philip Leakey.
Lizabeth Scott's gowns: Edith Head.
Furs by Deanfield of London and Paris.
Sound recording: Bill Salter.
Assistant director: Jimmy Sangster.
Cast: Paul Henreid (Dr. Philip Ritter), Lizabeth Scott (Alice Brent/Lily), Andre Morell (David), Mary Mackenzie (Lily Conover), John Wood (Dr. Jack Wilson), Arnold Ridley (Dr. Russell), Susan Stephen (Betty), Diana Beaumont (May), Terence O'Regan (Peter Snipe), Everley Gregg (Lady Harringay), Cyril Smith (Alf), Janet Burnell (Maggie), Grace Gavin (Nurse), Alexis France (Mrs. Emmett), John Bull (Charles Emmett), Dorothy Bramhall (Miss Simpson), Ambrosine Phillpotts (Miss Patten), Russell Napier (Cutler), Hal Osmond (Photographer), William Murray (Floorwalker), Howard Douglas (Farmer), James Valentine (Soldier), John Warren (First Commercial Traveler), Frank Hawkins (Second Commercial

Traveler), Richard Wattis (Wentworth), Brookes Turner, Bartlett Mullins, Philip Viccars, Ben Williams.
Running time: 71 minutes.

Distant Trumpet (U.K.; Apex, 1952)
A Meridian Film.
Producers: Harold Richmond, Derek Elphinstone.
Director: Terence Fisher.
Screenplay: Derek Elphinstone.
Photography: Gordon Lang.
Art direction: George Jones.
Editor: John Seabourne.
Music: David Jenkins.
Cast: Derek Bond (David Anthony), Jean Patterson (Valerie Maitland), Derek Elphinstone (Richard Anthony), Anne Brooke (Beryl Jeffries), Grace Gavin (Mrs. Phillips ["Flips"]), Keith Pyott (Sir Rudolph Gettins), Jean Webster-Brough (Mrs. Waterhouse), Grace Denbigh-Russell (Mrs. Hallett), Constance Fraser, Alban Blakelock, John Howlett, Peter Fontaine, Gwynne Whitby, Anne Hunter.
Running time: 63 minutes.

Mantrap (U.K.; Exclusive, 1953) [U.S.: *Man in Hiding* (United Artists)] [Alternate U.S. title: *Woman in Hiding*]
A Hammer Film.
Producers: Michael Carreras, Alexander Paal.
Director: Terence Fisher.
Screenplay: Paul Tabori, Terence Fisher.
Adaptation: Paul Tabori.
Based on the novel *Queen in Danger* by Elleston Trevor.
Photography: Reginald Wyer.
Art direction: J. Elder Wills.
Editor: James Needs.
Composer: Doreen Carwithen.
Makeup: D. Bonnor-Moris.
Miss Maxwell's wardrobe: Jane Ironside.
Model gowns: Rick Michaels, Ltd.
Sound recording: Jack Miller.
Dialogue director: Nora Roberts.
Assistant director: Bill Shore.
Cast: Paul Henreid (Hugo Bishop), Lois Maxwell (Thelma Tasman), Kieron Moore (Mervyn Speight), Hugh Sinclair (Maurice Jerrard), Kay Kendall (Vera), Anthony Forwood (Rex), Lloyd Lamble (Frisnay), Liam Gaffney (Douval), Mary Laura Wood (Susie), Bill Travers (Victor Tasman), John Penrose (Du Vancet), Conrad Phillips (Barker), John Stuart (Doctor), Anna Turner (Marjorie), Christina Forrest (Joanna), Arnold Diamond (Alphonse), Jane Welsh (Laura), Geoffrey Murphy (Plainclothesman), Terry Carney (Detective), Sally Newland (Receptionist), Barbara Kowin [Shelley] (Fashion Commere).
Running time: 78 minutes.

Four–Sided Triangle (U.K.; Exclusive, 1953) [U.S.: Astor] [Alternate U.S. title: *The Monster and the Woman*]
A Hammer Film.
Presented by Alexander Paal.
Producer: Alexander Paal.
Director: Terence Fisher.
Screenplay: Paul Tabori, Terence Fisher.

Adaptation: Paul Tabori.
Based on the novel by William F. Temple.
Photography: Reginald Wyer.
Art direction: J. Elder Wills.
Editor: Maurice Rootes.
Composer: Malcolm Arnold.
Conductor: Muir Mathieson.
Makeup: D. Bonnor-Moris.
Wedding scene dressed by Young's Dress Hire, London.
Sound recording: Bill Salter.
Dialogue director: Nora Roberts.
Assistant director: Bill Shore.
Cast: Barbara Payton (Lena/Helen), James Hayter (Dr. Harvey), Stephen Murray (Bill Leggatt), John Van Eyssen (Robin Grant), Percy Marmont (Sir Walter Grant), Glyn Dearman (Bill, as a child), Sean Barrett (Robin, as a child), Jennifer Dearman (Lena, as a child), Kynaston Reeves (Lord Grant), John Stuart (Solicitor), Edith Saville (Lady Grant).
Running time: 81 minutes [U.S.: 74 minutes].

Spaceways (U.K.; Exclusive, 1953) [U.S.: Lippert]
A Hammer-Lippert Film.
Producer: Michael Carreras.
Director: Terence Fisher.
Screenplay: Paul Tabori, Richard Landau.
Adaptation: Paul Tabori.
Based on the radio play by Charles Eric Maine.
Photography: Reginald Wyer.
Art direction: J. Elder Wills.
Editor: Maurice Rootes.
Music director: Ivor Slaney.
Makeup: D. Bonnor-Moris.
Sound recording: Bill Salter.
Special effects: Trading Post
Process shots: Bowie, Margutti and Company.
Dialogue director: Nora Roberts.
Assistant director: Jimmy Sangster.
Cast: Howard Duff (Dr. Steve Mitchell), Eva Bartok (Dr. Lisa Frank), Alan Wheatley (Smith), Philip Leaver (Dr. Keppler), Michael Medwin (Toby Andrews), Andrew Osborn (Philip Crenshaw), Cecile Chevreau (Vanessa Mitchell), Anthony Ireland (General Hays [Hayes]), Hugh Moxey (Colonel Daniels), David Horne (Minister), Jean Webster-Brough (Mrs. Daniels), Leo Phillips (Sgt. Peterson), Marianne Stone (Mrs. Rogers).
Running time: 76 minutes.

Blood Orange (U.K.; Exclusive, 1953) [U.S.: *Three Stops to Murder* (Astor)]
A Hammer Film.
Producer: Michael Carreras.
Director: Terence Fisher.
Original screenplay: Jan Read.
Photography: Jimmy Harvey.
Art direction: J. Elder Wills.
Editor: Maurice Rootes.
Music director: Ivor Slaney.
Makeup: Philip Leakey.
Special gowns created by Ben Pearson.
Production facilities kindly granted by Worth (London).

Fur models by Molho.
Sound recording: Bill Salter, George Burgess.
Dialogue director: Molly Terraine.
Assistant director: Jimmy Sangster.
Cast: Tom Conway (Tom Conway), Mila Parely (Helen Pascall), Naomi Chance (Gina), Eric
Pohlmann (Mercedes), Andrew Osborn (Capt. Colin Simpson), Richard Wattis (Inspector
Macleod), Margaret Halstan (Lady Marchant), Eileen Way (Mme. Fernande), Delphi
Lawrence (Chelsea), Michael Ripper (Eddie), Thomas Heathcote (Jessop), Betty Cooper
(Miss Betty), Alan Rolfe (Inspector), Roger Delgado (Morrow), Reed de Rouen (Heath),
Christina Forrest (Blonde), Ann Hanslip (Jane), Leon Davey (George), Leo Phillips
(Harry), Dorothy Robson (Fitter), Robert Moore (Stevenson), Dennis Cowles (Commis-
sionaire), John Watson (Chauffeur), Cleo Rose (Vivian).
Running time: 76 minutes.

Three's Company (U.K.; 1953)

Feature compiled from episodes of TV's *Douglas Fairbanks Presents*. Fisher directed two of the
three segments.

Face the Music (U.K.; Exclusive, 1954) [U.S.: The Black Glove (Lippert)]

A Hammer Film.
Producer: Michael Carreras.
Director: Terence Fisher.
Screenplay: Ernest Borneman.
Based on the novel *Face the Music* by Ernest Borneman.
Photography: Jimmy Harvey.
Art direction: J. Elder Wills.
Editor: Maurice Rootes.
Music direction: Ivor Slaney, Kenny Baker.
Trumpet theme and special arragements: Kenny Baker.
Makeup: Philip Leakey.
Sound recording: Bill Salter, George Burgess.
Assistant director: Jimmy Sangster.
Cast: Alex Nicol (James Bradley), Eleanor Summerfield (Barbara Quigley), John Salew (Max
Margulis), Paul Carpenter (John Sutherland), Geoffrey Keen (Maurice Green), Ann
Hanslip (Maxine), Fred Johnson (Inspector Mackenzie), Arthur Lane (Jeff Colt), Martin
Boddey (Sgt. Mulrooney), Paula Byrne (Gloria Colt), Gordon Crier (Vic Parsons), Leo
Phillips (Dresser), Fred Tripp (Stage Manager), Ben Williams (Gatekeeper), Frank Birch
(Trumpet Salesman), Jeremy Hawk (Recording Engineer), James Carney (Barman),
Melvyn Hayes (Page Boy), Mark Singleton (Waiter), Tony Hilton (Call Boy), Robert San-
som (Doctor), Pat Jorden (First Policeman), Frank Pettitt (Second Policeman), Kenny
Baker's Dozen.
Running time: 84 minutes.

Murder by Proxy (U.K.; Exclusive, 1955) [U.S.: Blackout (Lippert, 1954)]

A Hammer Film.
Producer: Michael Carreras.
Director: Terence Fisher.
Screenplay: Richard Landau.
Based on the novel *Murder by Proxy* by Helen Nielsen.
Photography: Jimmy Harvey.
Art direction: J. Elder Wills.
Editor: Maurice Rootes.
Music direction: Ivor Slaney.
Makeup: Philip Leakey.

Miss Lee's gowns by Ben Pearson.
Furs by Malho.
Sound recording: Bill Salter, George Burgess.
Dialogue director: Andrew Osborn.
Assistant director: Jimmy Sangster.
Cast: Dane Clark (Casey Morrow), Belinda Lee (Phyllis Brunner), Betty Ann Davies (Alicia Brunner), Eleanor Summerfield (Maggie Doone), Andrew Osborn (Lance Gordon), Harold Lang (Travis), Jill Melford (Miss Nardis), Alvis Maben (Lita Huntley), Michael Golden (Inspector Johnson), Alfie Bass (Ernie), Delphi Lawrence (Linda), Cleo Laine (Singer), Nora Gordon, Martin Lawrence, Arnold Diamond, Verne Morgan, Charles Stanley, Arthur Lovegrove, Mark Singleton, Stafford Byrne, Alfred March, Ann Gow, Kim Mills, Frank Singuineau, Harry Brunning.
Running time: 87 minutes.

The Stranger Came Home (U.K.; Exclusive, 1954) [U.S.: *The Unholy Four* (Lippert)]
A Hammer Film.
Producer: Michael Carreras.
Director: Terence Fisher.
Screenplay: Michael Carreras.
Based on the novel *Stranger at Home* by George Sanders.
Photography: James Harvey.
Art direction: J. Elder Wills.
Editor: Bill Lenny.
Composer: Leonard Salzedo.
Music director: John Hollingsworth.
Makeup: Philip Leakey.
Furs by Molho.
Sound recording: Sid Wiles, Ken Cameron.
Production manager: Jimmy Sangster.
Assistant director: Jack Causey.
Cast: Paulette Goddard (Angie Vickers), William Sylvester (Philip Vickers), Patrick Holt (Job Crandall), Paul Carpenter (Bill Saul), Alvys Maben (Joan Merrill), Russell Napier (Inspector Treherne), Kay Callard (Jenny), David King Wood (Sessions), Jeremy Hawk (Sgt. Johnson), Pat Owens (Blonde), Jack Taylor (Brownie), Kim Mills (Roddy), Owen Evans (Redhead), Philip Lennard (Medical Examiner).
Running time: 80 minutes.

Final Appointment (U.K.; Monarch, 1954)
A Unit-A. C. T. Film.
Producer: Francis Searle.
Director: Terence Fisher.
Screenplay: Kenneth R. Hayles.
Based on the play *Death Keeps a Date* by Sidney Nelson, Maurice Harrison.
Photography: Jonah Jones.
Art direction: C. P. Norman.
Editor: John Ferris.
Cast: John Bentley (Mike Billings), Eleanor Summerfield (Jenny Drew), Hubert Gregg (Hartnell), Jean Lodge (Laura Robens), Sam Kydd (Vickery), Meredith Edwards (Tom Martin), Liam Redmond (Inspector Corcoran), Charles Farrell (Percy), Peter Bathurst, Arthur Lowe.
Running time: 69 minutes (61 minutes).

Mask of Dust (U.K; Exclusive, 1954) [U.S.: *Race for Life* (Lippert, 1955)]
A Hammer Film.
Executive producer: Michael Carreras.

Producer: Mickey Delamar.
Director: Terence Fisher.
Screenplay: Richard Landau.
Based on the novel *Last Race* by Jon Manchip White.
Photography: Jimmy Harvey.
Art direction: J. Elder Wills.
Editor: Bill Lenny.
Composer: Leonard Salzedo.
Music director: John Hollingsworth.
Makeup: Phil Leakey.
Sound recording: Sid Wiles, Ken Cameron.
Production manager: Jimmy Sangster.
Assistant director: Jack Causey.
Cast: Richard Conte (Peter Wells), Mari Aldon (Pat Wells), George Coulouris (Dallapiccola), Peter Illing (Bellario), Alec Mango (Guido Rizetti), Meredith Edwards (Lawrence), James Copeland (Johnny), Edwin Richfield (Gibson), Richard Marner (Brecht), Tim Turner (Alverez), Jeremy Hawk (Martin), Stirling Moss, Reg Parnell, John Cooper, Alan Brown, Geoffrey Taylor, Leslie Marr (Themselves).
Running time: 79 minutes [U.S.: 68 minutes].

Children Galore (U.K.; General Film Distributors, 1954)

A Grendon Film.
Producer: Henry Passmore.
Director: Terence Fisher.
Screenplay: John Bonnett, Emery Bonnett, Peter Plaskitt.
Photography: Jonah Jones.
Art direction: John Elphick.
Editor: Inman Hunter.
Makeup: D. Bonnor Moris.
Sound recording: Sid Squires.
Assistant director: Eric Pavitt.
Cast: Eddie Byrne (Zacky Jones), Marjorie Rhodes (Ada Jones), June Thorburn (Milly Ark), Richard Leach (Harry Bunnion), Betty Ann Davies (Mrs. Ark), Jack McNaughton (Pat Ark), Peter Evan Thomas (Lord Redscarfe), Marjorie Hume (Lady Redscarfe), Lucy Griffiths (Miss Prescott), Henry Caine (Bert Bunnion), Violet Gould (Mrs. Bunnion), Grace Arnold (Mrs. Gedge), Olive Milbourne, Anna Turner, John Peters, Jack Hartman, John Lothar, David Ludlow.
Running time: 60 minutes.

Stolen Assignment (U.K.; British Lion, 1955)

An A. C. T.-Unit Film.
Producer: Francis Searle.
Director: Terence Fisher.
Screenplay: Kenneth Hayles.
Based on the original story "Involuntary Confession" by Sidney Nelson, Maurice Harrison.
Photography: James Harvey.
Art direction: William Kellner.
Editor: John Pomeroy.
Makeup: Phil Leakey.
Sound recording: L. B. Bulkley.
Assistant director: William Shore.
Cast: John Bentley (Mike Billings), Hy Hazell (Jenny Drew), Eddie Byrne (Inspector Corcoran), Patrick Holt (Henry Crossley), Joyce Carey (Ida Garnett), Kay Callard (Stella Watson), Jessica Cairns (Marilyn Dawn), Charles Farrell (Percy Simpson), Violet Gould (Mrs. Hud-

son), Michael Ellison (Danny Hudson), Desmond Rayner (John Smith), Graham Stuart (Coroner), Frank Forsyth (Dr. Roberts), Clement Hamelin (Seth Makepeace), John H. Watson (Plain Clothes Detective Sergeant), Raymond Rollett (Desk Sergeant).
Running time: 62 minutes.

The Flaw (U.K.; Renown, 1955)

A Cybex Film.
Producer: Geoffrey Goodheart, Brandon Fleming.
Director: Terence Fisher.
Screenplay: Brandon Fleming.
Photography: Cedric Williams.
Editor: Carmen Belaieff.
Song "Getting Away with Murder" by Gene Crowley.
Sound: S. Squires.
Assistant director: George Pollard.
Cast: John Bentley (Paul Oliveri), Donald Houston (John Millway), Rona Anderson (Monica Oliveri), Tonia Bern (Vera), Doris Yorke (Mrs. Bower), J. Trevor Davis (Sir George Bentham), Cecilia Cavendish (Lady Bentham), Vera Mechechnie, Ann Sullivan, June Dawson, Langley Howard, Gerry Levey, Herbert St. John, Christine Bocca, Derek Barnard, Andrew Leigh, Eric Aubrey.
Running time: 61 minutes.

The Gelignite Gang (U.K.; Renown, 1956) [U.S.: The Dynamiters (Astor)]

A Cybex Film.
Producer: Geoffrey Goodheart, Brandon Fleming.
Director: Terence Fisher [or Francis Searle].
Screenplay: Brandon Fleming.
Photography: Cedric Williams.
Art direction: John Elphick.
Editor: Douglas Myers.
Song "Soho Mambo" by Gene Crowley.
Cast: Wayne Morris (Jimmy Baxter), James Kenney (Chapman), Patrick Holt (Rutherford), Sandra Dorne (Sally Morton), Simone Silva (Simone), Arthur Young (Scobie), Eric Pohlmann (Popoulos), Lloyd Lamble (Inspector Felby), Hugh Miller (Crosby), Ossie Waller, Bertha Russell, Leigh Crutchley, Monti de Lyle, Bernadette Milnes, Mark Daly, Tony Doonan.
Running time: 75 minutes [U.S: 71 minutes].

The Last Man to Hang? (U.K./U.S.; Columbia, 1956)

An A. C. T.-Warwick Film.
Producer: John W. Gossage.
Director: Terence Fisher.
Screenplay: Ivor Montagu, Max Trell.
Adaptation: Gerald Bullett, Maurice Elvey.
Based on the novel The Jury by Gerald Bullett.
Photography: Desmond Dickinson.
Art direction: Allan Harris.
Editor: Peter Taylor.
Composer-conductor: John Wooldridge.
Sound: Wally Day.
Assistant director: Rene Dupont.
Cast: Tom Conway (Sir Roderick Strood), Elizabeth Sellars (Daphne Strood), Eunice Gayson (Elizabeth Anders), Freda Jackson (Mrs. Tucker), Hugh Latimer (Mark Perryman), Ronald Simpson (Dr. Cartwright), Victor Maddern (Bonaker), Anthony Newley (Cyril Gaskin), Margaretta Scott (Mrs. Cranshaw), Leslie Weston (Mayfield), Bill Shine (Underhay), Anna

Turner (Lucy Prynne), Jack Lambert (Major Forth), Harold Goodwin (Cheed), Joan Newell (Mrs. Iseley), Thomas Heathcote (Bracket), Tony Quinn (Nywood), Hal Osmond (Coates), Joan Hickson (Mrs. Prynne), Gillian Lynne (Gaskin's Girl), Shelagh Fraser (Mrs. Bracket), Olive Sloane (Mrs. Bayfield), Michael McKeag (Ernie Bayfield), Harold Siddons (Cheed's Doctor), Maya Koumani (Cheed's Nurse), Walter Hudd (The Judge), Raymond Huntley (Attorney General), David Horne (Anthony Harcombe, Q.C.), Dan Cunningham (Clerk of the Court), Russell Napier (Det. Sgt. Bolton), Martin Boddey (Det. Sgt. Horne), John Schlessinger (Dr. Goldfinger), Conrad Phillips (Dr. Mason), Sheila Manahan (Senior Sister), Rosamund Waring (Nurse Tomkins), John Stuart, John Warren, Charles Lloyd Pack.

Running time: 75 minutes.

Kill Me Tomorrow (U.K.; Renown, 1957) [U.S.: Tudor, 1958]

A Delta Film.
Producer: Francis Searle.
Director: Terence Fisher.
Screenplay: Robert Falconer, Manning O'Brine.
Photography: Geoffrey Faithfull.
Editor: Ann Chegwidden.
Music: Temple Abady.
Sound: Richard Smith.
Cast: Pat O'Brien (Bart Crosbie), Lois Maxwell (Jill Brook), George Coulouris (Heinz Webber), Wensley Pithey (Inspector Lane), Freddie Mills (Waxy), Ronald Adam (Brook), Robert Brown (Steve), Richard Pasco (Dr. Fisher), April Olrich (Bella Braganza), Tommy Steele (Himself), Claude Kingston, Peter Swanick, Al Mulock, Stuart Nichol, Georg Eugeniou, Vic Wise.

Running time: 80 minutes.

The Curse of Frankenstein (U.K./U.S.; Warner Bros., 1957)

A Hammer Film.
Executive producer: Michael Carreras.
Producer: Anthony Hinds.
Associate producer: Anthony Nelson-Keys.
Director: Terence Fisher.
Screenplay: Jimmy Sangster.
Based on the novel *Frankenstein* by Mary W. Shelley.
Photography: Jack Asher (Eastmancolor) [U.S.: Warnercolor].
Production design: Bernard Robinson.
Art direction: Ted Marshall.
Editor: James Needs.
Composer: James Bernard.
Makeup: Phil Leakey.
Sound recording: Jock May.
Assistant director: Derek Whitehurst.
Cast: Peter Cushing (Baron Victor Frankenstein), Hazel Court (Elizabeth), Robert Urquhart (Paul Krempe), Christopher Lee (The Creature), Melvyn Hayes (The Young Victor), Valerie Gaunt (Justine), Paul Hardtmuth (Professor Bernstein), Noel Hood (Aunt Sophia), Fred Johnson (Grandpa), Claude Kingston (Little Boy), Alex Gallier (Priest), Michael Mulcaster (Warder), Andrew Leigh (Burgomaster), Ann Blake (Burgomaster's Wife), Sally Walsh (Young Elizabeth), Middleton Woods (Lecturer), Raymond Ray [Rollett] (Uncle), Bartlett Mullins (Tramp), Patrick Troughton (Kurt), Joseph Behrman (Fritz), Ernest Jay (Undertaker), Eugene Leahy (Priest).
[In cut scenes: Marjorie Hume (Mother), Henry Caine (Schoolmaster).]
Running time: 83 minutes.

Dracula (U.K.; Universal, 1958) [U.S.: *Horror of Dracula*]

A Hammer Film.
Executive producer: Michael Carreras.
Producer: Anthony Hinds.
Associate producer: Anthony Nelson-Keys.
Director: Terence Fisher.
Screenplay: Jimmy Sangster.
Based on the novel by Bram Stoker.
Photography: Jack Asher (Eastman color processed by Technicolor).
Production design: Bernard Robinson.
Supervising editor: James Needs.
Editor: Bill Lenny.
Composer: James Bernard.
Makeup: Phil Leakey.
Sound recording: Jock May.
Special effects: Sydney Pearson.
Assistant director: Bob Lynn.
Cast: Peter Cushing (Dr. Van Helsing), Michael Gough (Arthur Holmwood), Melissa Stribling (Mina Holmwood), Christopher Lee (Count Dracula), Carol Marsh (Lucy Holmwood), John Van Eyssen (Jonathan Harker), Olga Dickie (Gerda), Valerie Gaunt (Vampire Woman), Janine [Janina] Faye (Tania), Barbara Archer (Inga), Charles Lloyd Pack (Dr. Seward), George Merritt (Policeman), George Woodbridge (Landlord), George Benson (Frontier Official), Miles Malleson (Marx, The Undertaker), Geoffrey Bayldon (Porter), Paul Cole (Lad), John Mossman (Hearse Driver).
[In cut scene: Guy Mills (Coach Driver), Dick Morgan (Driver's Companion), Judith Nelmes (Woman in Coach), William Sherwood (Priest), Stedwell Fletcher (Man in Coach), Humphrey Kent (Fat Merchant).]
Running time: 81 minutes.

The Revenge of Frankenstein (U.K./U.S.; Columbia, 1958)

A Hammer Film.
Executive producer: Michael Carreras.
Producer: Anthony Hinds.
Associate producer: Anthony Nelson Keys.
Director: Terence Fisher.
Screenplay: Jimmy Sangster.
Additional dialogue: Hurford Janes.
Photography: Jack Asher ([Eastman color processed by] Technicolor).
Production design: Bernard Robinson.
Supervising editor: James Needs.
Editor: Alfred Cox.
Composer: Leonard Salzedo.
Makeup: Phil Leakey.
Sound recording: Jock May.
Assistant director: Robert Lynn.
Cast: Peter Cushing (Dr. Victor Stein), Francis Matthews (Dr. Hans Kleve), Eunice Gayson (Margaret), Michael Gwynn (Karl), John Welsh (Bergman), Lionel Jeffries (Fritz), Oscar Quitak (Dwarf), Richard Wordsworth (Up Patient), Charles Lloyd Pack (President), John Stuart (Inspector), Arnold Diamond (Molke), Margery Gresley (Countess Barscynska), Anna Walmsley (Vera Barscynska), George Woodbridge (Janitor), Michael Ripper (Kurt), Ian Whittaker (Boy), Avril Leslie (Girl), Michael Mulcaster (Tattoo).
Running time: 90 minutes.

The Hound of the Baskervilles (U.K./U.S.; United Artists, 1959)

A Hammer Film [U.S.: in association with Kenneth Hyman].
Executive producer: Michael Carreras.
Producer: Anthony Hinds.
Associate producer: Anthony Nelson Keys.
Director: Terence Fisher.
Screenplay: Peter Bryan.
Based on the novel by Sir Arthur Conan Doyle.
Photography: Jack Asher ([Eastman color processed by] Technicolor).
Production design: Bernard Robinson.
Supervising editor: James Needs.
Editor: Alfred Cox.
Composer: James Bernard.
Makeup: Roy Ashton.
Sound recording: Jock May.
Special effects: Sydney Pearson.
Assistant director: John Peverall.
Production supervisor for the Doyle Estate: Henry E. Lester.
Cast: Peter Cushing (Sherlock Holmes), Andre Morell (Dr. Watson), Christopher Lee (Sir Henry Baskerville), Marla Landi (Cecile), David Oxley (Sir Hugo Baskerville), Francis De Wolff (Dr. Mortimer), Miles Malleson (Bishop Frankland), Ewen Solon (Stapleton), John Le Mesurier (Barrymore), Helen Goss (Mrs. Barrymore), Sam Kydd (Perkins), Michael Hawkins (Lord Caphill), Judi Moyens (Servant Girl), Michael Mulcaster (Convict), David Birks (Servant), Ian Hewitson (Lord Kingsblood), Elizabeth Dott (Mrs. Goodlippe).
Running time: 86 minutes.

The Man Who Could Cheat Death (U.K./U.S.; Paramount, 1959)

A Hammer Film.
Producer: Michael Carreras.
Associate producer: Anthony Nelson-Keys.
Director: Terence Fisher.
Screenplay: Jimmy Sangster.
Based on the play *The Man in Half Moon Street* by Barre Lyndon.
Photography: Jack Asher ([Eastman color processed by] Technicolor).
Production design: Bernard Robinson.
Supervising editor: James Needs.
Editor: John Dunsford.
Composer: Richard Bennett.
Music supervisor: John Hollingsworth.
Makeup: Roy Ashton.
Sound recording: Jock May.
Assistant director: John Peverall.
Cast: Anton Diffring (Dr. Georges Bonner), Hazel Court (Janine Dubois), Christopher Lee (Dr. Pierre Gerard), Arnold Marle (Dr. Ludwig Weisz), Delphi Lawrence (Margo Philippe), Francis De Wolff (Inspector Legris), Gerda Larsen (Street Girl), Michael Ripper (Morgue Attendant), Denis Shaw (Tavern Customer), Ian Hewitson (Roget), Frederick Rawlings (Footman), Marie Burke (Woman), Charles Lloyd-Pack (Man at Exhibit), John Harrison (Servant), Lockwood West (First Doctor), Ronald Adam (Second Doctor), Barry Shawzin (Third Doctor).
Running time: 83 minutes.

The Mummy (U.K./U.S.; Universal, 1959)

A Hammer Film.
Producer: Michael Carreras.

Associate producer: Anthony Nelson-Keys.
Director: Terence Fisher.
Screenplay: Jimmy Sangster.
Photography: Jack Asher (Eastman color processed by Technicolor).
Production design: Bernard Robinson.
Supervising editor: James Needs.
Editor: Alfred Cox.
Composer: Frank Reizenstein.
Music supervisor: John Hollingsworth.
Makeup: Roy Ashton.
Sound recording: Jock May.
Special effects: Bill Warrington.
Technical advisor: Andrew Low.
Assistant director: John Peverall.
Cast: Peter Cushing (John Banning), Christopher Lee (The Mummy/Kharis), Yvonne Furneaux (Isobel/Ananka), Eddie Byrne (Inspector Mulrooney), Felix Aylmer (Stephen Banning), Raymond Huntley (Joseph Whemple), George Pastell (Mehemet Bey), Michael Ripper (Poacher), George Woodbridge (Police Constable), Harold Goodwin (Pat), Denis Shaw (Mike), Gerald Lawson (Irish Customer), Willoughby Gray (Dr. Reilly), John Stuart (Coroner), David Browning (Police Sergeant), Frank Sieman (Bill), Stanley Meadows (Attendant), Frank Singuineau (Head Porter), Frederick Rawlings, John Harrison, James Clarke.
Running time: 88 minutes.

The Stranglers of Bombay (U.K.; Columbia, 1959) [U.S.: 1960]

A Hammer Film [U.S.: In association with Kenneth Hyman].
Executive producer: Michael Carreras.
Producer: Anthony Hinds.
Associate producer: Anthony Nelson-Keys.
Director: Terence Fisher.
Screenplay: David Z. Goodman.
Photography: Arthur Grant (MegaScope)
Production design: Bernard Robinson.
Supervising editor: James Needs.
Editor: Alfred Cox.
Composer: James Bernard.
Music supervisor: John Hollingsworth.
Makeup: Roy Ashton.
Sound recording: Jock May.
Sound editor: Arthur Cox.
Historical advisor: Michael Edwards.
Assistant director: John Peverall.
Cast: Guy Rolfe (Captain Lewis), Allan Cuthbertson (Captain Connaught-Smith), Andrew Cruickshank (Colonel Henderson), Marne Maitland (Patel Shari), George Pastell (High Priest), Jan Holden (Mary), Paul Stassino (Silver), Tutte Lemkow (Ram Das), David Spenser (Gopali), Marie Devereaux [Devereux] (Karim), Michael Nightingale (Flood), Margaret Gordon (Mrs. Flood), Ewen Solon (Camel Vendor), John Harvey (Burns), Roger Delgado (Bundar), Steven Scott (Walters), Jack McNaughton (Corporal Roberts).
Running time: 80 minutes.

The Brides of Dracula (U.K./U.S.; Universal, 1960)

A Hammer Film.
Executive producer: Michael Carreras.
Producer: Anthony Hinds.
Associate producer: Anthony Nelson-Keys.

Director: Terence Fisher.
Screenplay: Jimmy Sangster, Peter Bryan, Edward Percy.
Photography: Jack Asher ([Eastman color processed by] Technicolor).
Production design: Bernard Robinson.
Art direction: Thomas Goswell.
Supervising editor: James Needs.
Editor: Alfred Cox.
Composer: Malcolm Williamson.
Music supervisor: John Hollingsworth.
Makeup: Roy Ashton.
Sound recording: Jock May.
Sound editor: James Groom.
Special effects: Sydney Pearson.
Assistant director: John Peverall.
Cast: Peter Cushing (Dr. Van Helsing), Martita Hunt (Baroness Meinster), Yvonne Monlaur (Marianne), Freda Jackson (Greta), David Peel (Baron Meinster), Miles Malleson (Dr. Tobler), Henry Oscar (Herr Lang), Mona Washbourne (Frau Lang), Andree Melly (Gina), Victor Brooks (Hans), Fred Johnson (Cure), Norman Pierce (Landlord), Vera Cook (Landlord's Wife), Marie Devereux [Devereaux] (Village Girl), Michael Ripper (Coachman), Michael Mulcaster (Latour), Harold Scott (Severin).
Running time: 85 minutes.

The Two Faces of Dr. Jekyll (U.K.; Columbia, 1960) [U.S.: *House of Fright* (American-International, 1961)]

A Hammer Film.
Producer: Michael Carreras.
Associate producer: Anthony Nelson Keys.
Director: Terence Fisher.
Screenplay: Wolf Mankowitz.
Based on *The Strange Case of Dr. Jekyll and Mr. Hyde* by Robert Louis Stevenson.
Photography: Jack Asher ([Eastman color] Print by Technicolor, MegaScope).
Production design: Bernard Robinson.
Supervising editor: James Needs.
Editor: Eric Boyd-Perkins.
Composers: Monty Norman, David Heneker.
Music supervisor: John Hollingsworth.
Dance direction: Julie Mendez.
Makeup: Roy Ashton.
Costume designer: Mayo.
Sound recording: Jock May.
Sound editor: Archie Ludski.
Assistant director: John Peverall.
Cast: Paul Massie (Dr. Henry Jekyll/Edward Hyde), Dawn Addams (Kitty Jekyll), Christopher Lee (Paul Allen), David Kossoff (Ernest Litauer), Norma Marla (Maria), Francis De Wolff (Inspector), Joy Webster (Sphinx Girl), Magda Miller (Sphinx Girl), Oliver Reed (Man in Nightclub), Joe Robinson (Corinthian), William Kendall (Clubman), Helen Goss (Nannie), Pauline Shepherd (Girl in Gin Shop), Percy Cartwright (Coroner), Arthur Lovegrove (Cabby).
Running time: 88 minutes [U.S.: 80 minutes].

Sword of Sherwood Forest (U.K.; Columbia, 1960) [U.S.: 1961]

A Hammer Film, in association with Yeoman Films.
Executive producer: Michael Carreras.
Producers: Sidney Cole, Richard Greene.

Director: Terence Fisher.
Screenplay: Alan Hackney.
Photography: Ken Hodges (Eastman color by Pathé, MegaScope).
Art direction: John Stoll.
Supervising editor: James Needs.
Editor: Lee Doig.
Composer: Alun Hoddinott.
Music supervisor: John Hollingsworth.
Songs: Stanley Black.
Makeup: Gerald Fletcher.
Sound editor: Alban Streeter.
Sound mixers: John Mitchell, Harry Tate.
Master of horse: Ivor Collin.
Master of arms: Patrick Crean.
Master of archery: Jack Cooper.
Assistant director: Bob Porter.
Cast: Richard Greene (Robin Hood), Peter Cushing (The Sheriff of Nottingham), Richard Pasco (Earl of Newark), Jack Gwillim (Hubert Walter, Archbishop of Canterbury), Sarah Branch (Marian Fitzwalter), Niall MacGinnis (Friar Tuck), Dennis Lotis (Alan-a-Dale), Derren Nesbitt (Martin), Vanda Godsell (Prioress), Oliver Reed (Melton), Nigel Green (Little John), Edwin Richfield (Sheriff's Lieutenant), Patrick Crean (Ollerton), Adam Kean (Retford), Charles Lamb (Old Bowyer), James Neylin (Roger), Brian Rawlinson (Falconer), Reginald Hearne (Man at Arms), Jack Cooper (Archer), Desmond Llewellyn (Traveler), Aiden Grennell (Outlaw).
Running time: 80 minutes.

The Curse of the Werewolf (U.K./U.S.; Universal, 1961)

A Hammer Film.
Executive producer: Michael Carreras.
Producer: Anthony Hinds.
Associate producer: Anthony Nelson-Keys.
Director: Terence Fisher.
Screenplay: John Elder [Anthony Hinds].
Based on the novel *The Werewolf of Paris* by Guy Endore.
Photography: Arthur Grant ([Eastman color processed by] Technicolor).
Production design: Bernard Robinson.
Art direction: Don Mingaye.
Supervising editor: James Needs.
Editor: Alfred Cox.
Composer-conductor: Benjamin Frankel.
Makeup: Roy Ashton.
Sound recording: Jock May.
Sound editor: Alban Streeter.
Special effects: Les Bowie.
Assistant director: John Peverall.
Cast: Clifford Evans (Don Alfredo Carido), Oliver Reed (Leon), Yvonne Romain (Servant Girl), Catherine Feller (Cristina), Anthony Dawson (The Marques Siniestro), Josephine Llewellyn (The Marquesa), Richard Wordsworth (The Beggar), Hira Talfrey (Teresa), Justin Walters (Young Leon), John Gabriel (The Priest), Warren Mitchell (Pepe Valiente), Anne Blake (Rosa Valiente), George Woodbridge (Dominique), Michael Ripper (Old Soak), Ewen Solon (Don Fernando), Peter Sallis (Don Enrique), Martin Matthews (Jose), David Conville (Rico Gomez), Denis Shaw (Gaoler), Charles Lamb (Chef), Serafina Di Leo (Senora Zumara), Sheila Brennan (Vera), Joy Webster (Isabel), Renny Lister (Yvonne).
Running time: 93 minutes.

The Phantom of the Opera (U.K./U.S.; Universal, 1962)

A Hammer Film.
Producer: Anthony Hinds.
Associate producer: Basil Keys.
Director: Terence Fisher.
Screenplay: John Elder [Anthony Hinds].
Based on the novel by Gaston Leroux.
Photography: Arthur Grant (Eastman color by Pathé)
Production design: Bernard Robinson.
Art direction: Don Mingaye.
Supervising editor: James Needs.
Editor: Alfred Cox.
Composer-conductor: Edwin Astley.
Opera scenes staged by Dennis Maunder, by permission of the General Administrator, Royal
    Opera House, Covent Garden.
Makeup: Roy Ashton.
Sound recording: Jock May.
Sound editor: James Groom.
Assistant director: John Peverall.
Cast: Herbert Lom (The Phantom [Prof. Petrie]), Heather Sears (Christine Charles), Edward de
    Souza (Harry Hunter), Thorley Walters (Lattimer), Michael Gough (Lord Ambrose
    d'Arcy), Harold Goodwin (Bill), Martin Miller (Rossi), Liane Aukin (Maria), Sonya
    Cordeau (Yvonne), Marne Maitland (Xavier), Miriam Karlin (Charwoman), Patrick
    Troughton (Ratcatcher), Renee Houston (Mrs. Tucker), Keith Pyott (Weaver), John Har-
    vey (Sergeant Vickers), Michael Ripper (First Cabby), Miles Malleson (Second Cabby), Ian
    Wilson (The Dwarf).
Running time: 84 minutes.

Sherlock Holmes und das Halsband des Todes [Sherlock Holmes and the Deadly Neck-
lace] (West Germany/France/Italy; Omnia, 1962)

A CCC (Berlin)/Criterion (Paris)/INCEI (Rome) Film.
Producer: Artur Brauner.
Directors: Terence Fisher, Frank Winterstein.
Screenplay: Curt Siodmak.
English version: Peter Riethof.
Photography: Richard Angst.
Set design: Paul Markwitz.
Editor: Ira Oberberg.
Composer: Martin Slavin.
Costume design: Vera Mugge.
Sound engineer: Gerhard Muller.
Cast: Christopher Lee (Sherlock Holmes), Thorley Walters (Dr. Watson), Hans Sohnker (Professor
    Moriarty), Hans Nielsen (Inspector Cooper), Senta Berger (Ellen Blackburn), Ivan Desny
    (Paul King), Wolfgang Lukschy (Peter Blackburn), Leon Askin (Charles, Chauffeur), Edith
    Schultze-Westrum (Mrs. Hudson), Bernard Lajarrige (Inspector French), Bruno Panthel
    [Pantel] (Williams, Auctioneer), Heinrich Gies (Texan), Linda Sini (Small Girl), Roland
    Armontel (The Doctor), Danielle Argence (Librarian), Franco Giacobini (Jenkins), Walde-
    mar Frahm (Butler), Renate Hutter (Barmaid), Max Strassberg [Straasberg] (Johnny), Cor-
    rado Anicelli (Samuels), Kurt Hain (Post Office Clerk), Pierre Gualdi (Innkeeper).
Running time: 86 minutes.

The Horror of It All (U.K./U.S.; 20th Century-Fox, 1964)

A Lippert Film.
Executive producer: Robert L. Lippert.

Associate producer: Margia Dean.
Director: Terence Fisher.
Screenplay: Ray Russell.
Photography: Arthur Lavis.
Art direction: Harry White.
Editor: Robert Winter.
Assistant editor: Clive Smith.
Composer: Douglas Gamley.
Makeup: Bill Lodge.
Sound recording: "Steve" Stephenson.
Assistant director: Frank Nesbitt.
Cast: Pat Boone (Jack Robinson), Erica Rogers (Cynthia Marley), Dennis Price (Cornwallis Marley), Andree Melly (Natalia Marley), Valentine Dyall (Reginald Marley), Jack Bligh (Percival Marley), Archie Duncan (Muldoon Marley), Eric Chitty (Grandpa Marley), Oswald Laurence (Doctor).
Running time: 75 minutes.

The Earth Dies Screaming (U.K./U.S.; 20th Century-Fox, 1964)

A Lippert Film.
Producers: Robert L. Lippert, Jack Parsons.
Director: Terence Fisher.
Screenplay: Henry Cross.
Photography: Arthur Lavis.
Art direction: George Provis.
Supervising film editor: Robert Winter.
Assistant editor: Clive Smith.
Composer: Elisabeth Lutyens.
Makeup: Harold Fletcher.
Sound recording: Buster Ambler.
Sound editor: Spencer Reeve.
Assistant director: Gordon Gilbert.
Cast: Willard Parker (Jeff Nolan), Virginia Field (Peggy), Dennis Price (Taggart), Vanda Godsell (Violet Courtland), Thorley Walters (Edgar Otis), David Spenser (Mel), Anna Palk (Lorna).
Running time: 62 minutes.

The Gorgon (U.K.; Columbia, 1964) [U.S.: 1965]

A Hammer Film.
Producer: Anthony Nelson Keys.
Director: Terence Fisher.
Screenplay: John Gilling.
Based on an original story by J. Llewellyn Devine.
Photography: Michael Reed (Eastman color by Pathé).
Production design: Bernard Robinson.
Art direction: Don Mingaye.
Editing supervisor: James Needs.
Editor: Eric Boyd Perkins.
Composer: James Bernard.
Music supervisor: Marcus Dods.
Makeup: Roy Ashton.
Sound recording: Ken Rawkins.
Sound editor: Roy Hyde.
Special effects: Syd Pearson.
Fight arranger: Peter Diamond.
Assistant director: Bert Batt.

Cast: Peter Cushing (Dr. Namaroff), Christopher Lee (Prof. Carl Meister), Richard Pasco (Paul Heitz), Barbara Shelley (Carla Hoffman), Michael Goodliffe (Prof. Heitz), Patrick Troughton (Kanof), Jack Watson (Ratoff), Jeremy Longhurst (Bruno Heitz), Toni Gilpin (Sascha Cass), Redmond Phillips (Hans), Alister Williamson (Janus Cass), Joyce Hemson (Martha), Joseph O'Conor (Coroner), Michael Peake (Policeman), Prudence Hyman (Chatelaine), Sally Nesbitt (Nurse).
Running time: 83 minutes.

Dracula—Prince of Darkness (U.K.; Warner-Pathe, 1966) [U.S.: 20th Century–Fox]
A Hammer Film [U.S.: A Seven Arts–Hammer Film]
Producer: Anthony Nelson Keys.
Director: Terence Fisher.
Screenplay: John Sansom [Jimmy Sangster].
From an idea by John Elder [Anthony Hinds].
Based on characters created by Bram Stoker.
Photography: Michael Reed (Technicolor, Techniscope) [U.S.: DeLuxe color].
Production design: Bernard Robinson.
Art direction: Don Mingaye.
Supervising editor: James Needs.
Editor: Chris Barnes.
Composer: James Bernard.
Music supervisor: Philip Martell.
Makeup: Roy Ashton.
Sound recording: Ken Rawkins.
Sound editor: Roy Baker.
Special effects: Bowie Films Ltd.
Assistant director: Bert Batt.
Cast: Christopher Lee (Dracula), Barbara Shelley (Helen Kent), Andrew Keir (Father Sandor), Francis Matthews (Charles Kent), Suzan Farmer (Diana Kent), Charles Tingwell (Alan Kent), Thorley Walters (Ludwig), Walter Brown (Brother Mark), Philip Latham (Klove), George Woodbridge (Landlord), Jack Lambert (Brother Peter), Philip Ray (Priest), Joyce Hemson (Mother), John Maxim (Coach Driver).
Running time: 90 minutes.

Island of Terror (U.K.; 1966) [U.S.: Universal, 1967] [Alternate titles: *Night of the Silicates, The Night the Silicates Came*]
A Protelco-Planet Film.
Executive producers: Richard Gordon, Gerald A. Fernback.
Producer: Tom Blakeley.
Director: Terence Fisher.
Screenplay: Edward Andrew Mann, Allan Ramsen.
Based on an original story by Mann, Ramsen.
Photography: Reg Wyer (Eastman color).
Art direction: John St. John Earl.
Assistant: Fred Hole.
Editor: Thelma Connell.
Composer-conductor: Malcolm Lockyer.
Electronic effects: Barry Gray.
Makeup: Bunty Phillips.
Sound recording–dubbing mixer: Bob McPhee.
Special effects: John St. John Earl.
Assistant: Michael Albrechtson.
Special-effects makeup: Billy Partleton.
Assistant director: Don Weeks.

Cast: Peter Cushing (Dr. Brian Stanley), Edward Judd (Dr. David West), Carole Gray (Toni Merrill), Eddie Byrne (Dr. Landers), Sam Kydd (Constable Harris), Niall MacGinnis (Mr. Campbell), James Caffrey (Peter Argyle), Liam Gaffney [Caffney] (Bellows), Roger Heathcote [Heathcott] (Dunley), Keith Bell (Halsey), Shay Gorman (Morton), Peter Forbes Robertson (Dr. Phillips), Richard Bidlake (Carson), Joyce Hemson (Mrs. Bellows), Edward Ogden (Helicopter Pilot), Margaret Lacy.
Running time: 87 minutes.

Frankenstein Created Woman (U.K.; Warner-Pathe, 1967) [U.S.: 20th Century–Fox]
A Hammer Film [U.S.: A Seven Arts–Hammer Film].
Producer: Anthony Nelson Keys.
Director: Terence Fisher.
Screenplay: John Elder [Anthony Hinds].
Photography: Arthur Grant (Technicolor) [U.S.: DeLuxe color].
Production design: Bernard Robinson.
Art direction: Don Mingaye.
Editing supervisor: James Needs.
Editor: Spencer Reeve.
Composer: James Bernard.
Music supervisor: Philip Martell.
Makeup: George Partleton.
Sound recording: Ken Rawkins.
Sound editor: Roy Hyde.
Special effects: Les Bowie.
Assistant director: Douglas Hermes.
Cast: Peter Cushing (Baron Frankenstein), Susan Denberg (Christina Kleve), Thorley Walters (Dr. Hertz), Robert Morris (Hans), Duncan Lamont (The Prisoner), Peter Blythe (Anton), Barry Warren (Karl), Derek Fowlds (Johann), Alan MacNaughtan [MacNaughton] (Kleve), Peter Madden (Chief of Police), Philip Ray (Mayor), Ivan Beavis (Landlord), Colin Jeavons (Priest), Bartlett Mullins (Bystander), Alec Mango (Spokesman), Kevin Flood (Jailer), John Maxim (Police Sergeant), Stuart Middleton (Hans, as a boy).
Running time: 92 minutes.

Night of the Big Heat (U.K.; Maron, 1967) [Alternate titles: *Island of the Burning Damned, Island of the Burning Doomed*]
A Planet Film.
Producer: Tom Blakeley.
Associate producer: Ronald Liles.
Director: Terence Fisher.
Screenplay: Ronald Liles.
Additional scenes and dialogue: Pip Baker, Jane Baker.
Based on a novel by John Lymington.
Photography: Reg Wyer (Eastman color).
Art direction: Alex Vetchinsky.
Editor: Rod Keys.
Composer-conductor: Malcolm Lockyer.
Makeup: Geoffrey Rodway.
Sound recording: Dudley Messenger, E. Kannon.
Dubbing editor: Norman A. Cole.
Assistant director: Ray Frift.
Cast: Christopher Lee (Godfrey Hanson), Patrick Allen (Jeff Callum), Peter Cushing (Dr. Vernon Stone), Jane Merrow (Angela Roberts), Sarah Lawson (Frankie Callum), William Lucas (Ken Stanley), Kenneth Cope (Tinker Mason), Percy Herbert (Gerald Foster), Tom

Heathcote (Bob Hayward), Anna Turner (Stella Hayward), Jack Bligh (Ben Siddle), Sidney Bromley (Old Tramp), Barry Halliday (Radar Operator).

Running time: 93 minutes.

The Devil Rides Out (U.K.; Warner-Pathe, 1968) [U.S.: *The Devil's Bride* (20th Century–Fox)]

A Hammer Film [U.S.: A Seven Arts-Hammer Film].
Producer: Anthony Nelson Keys.
Director: Terence Fisher.
Screenplay: Richard Matheson.
Based on the novel by Dennis Wheatley.
Photography: Arthur Grant (DeLuxe color).
Supervising art director: Bernard Robinson.
Supervising editor: James Needs.
Editor: Spencer Reeve.
Composer: James Bernard.
Music supervisor: Philip Martell.
Choreography: David Toguri.
Makeup: Eddie Knight.
Sound recording: Ken Rawkins.
Sound editor: Arthur Cox.
Special effects: Michael Stainer-Hutchins.
Assistant director: Bert Batt.
Cast: Christopher Lee (Duc Nicholas de Richleau), Charles Gray (Mocata), Nike Arrighi (Tanith Carlisle), Leon Greene (Rex Van Ryn), Patrick Mower (Simon Aron), Gwen Ffrangcon-Davies (Countess D'Urfe), Sarah Lawson (Marie Eaton), Paul Eddington (Richard Eaton), Rosalyn Landor (Peggy Eaton), Russell Waters (Malin).

Running time: 96 minutes.

Frankenstein Must Be Destroyed (U.K.; Warner-Pathe, 1969) [U.S.: Warner Bros.-Seven Arts, 1970]

A Hammer Film.
Producer: Anthony Nelson Keys.
Director: Terence Fisher.
Screenplay: Bert Batt.
Based on an original story by Bert Batt, Anthony Nelson Keys [and Fisher, uncredited].
Photography: Arthur Grant (Technicolor)
Supervising art director: Bernard Robinson.
Editing supervisor: James Needs.
Editor: Gordon Hales.
Composer: James Bernard.
Music supervisor: Philip Martell.
Makeup: Eddie Knight.
Sound supervisor: Tony Lumkin.
Sound recording: Ken Rawkins.
Sound editor: Don Ranasinghe.
Special effects: Studio Locations.
Assistant director: Bert Batt.
Cast: Peter Cushing (Baron Frankenstein), Veronica Carlson (Anna Spengler), Simon Ward (Dr. Karl Holst), Freddie Jones (Professor Richter), Thorley Walters (Inspector Frisch), Maxine Audley (Ella Brandt), George Pravda (Dr. Brandt), Geoffrey Bayldon (Police Doctor), Colette O'Neil (Mad Woman), Harold Goodwin (Burglar), Frank Middlemass (Guest), Norman Shelley (Guest), Michael Gover (Guest), George Belbin (Guest), Peter Copley

(Principal), Jim Collier (Dr. Heidecke), Allan Surtees (Police Sergeant), Windsor Davies (Police Sergeant).
Running time: 97 minutes [complete version: 101 minutes].

Frankenstein and the Monster from Hell (U.K.; Avco-Embassy, 1974) [U.S.: Paramount] [Made in 1972]
A Hammer Film.
Producer: Roy Skeggs.
Director: Terence Fisher.
Screenplay: John Elder [Anthony Hinds].
Photography: Brian Probyn (Technicolor).
Art direction: Scott MacGregor.
Assistant art director: Don Picton.
Editor: James Needs.
Composer: James Bernard.
Music supervisor: Philip Martell.
Makeup: Eddie Knight.
Sound recording: Les Hammond.
Sound editor: Roy Hyde.
Dubbing mixer: Maurice Askew.
Assistant director: Derek Whitehurst.
Cast: Peter Cushing (Baron Frankenstein), Shane Briant (Dr. Simon Helder), Madeline Smith (Sarah), John Stratton (Adolph Klauss, Asylum Director), Dave Prowse (Monster), Michael Ward (Transvest), Elsie Wagstaff (Wild One), Norman Mitchell (Police Sergeant), Clifford Mollison (Judge), Patrick Troughton (Body Snatcher), Philip Voss (Ernst), Chris Cunningham (Hans), Charles Lloyd Pack (Professor Durendel), Lucy Griffiths (Old Hag), Bernard Lee (Tarmut), Sydney Bromley (Muller), Andrea Lawrence (Brassy Girl), Jerold Wells (Landlord), Sheila Dunion [D'Union] (Gerda), Mischa De La Motte (Twitch), Norman Atkyns (Smiler), Victor Woolf (Letch), Winifred Sabine (Mouse), Janet Hargreaves (Chatter), Peter Madden (Coach Driver).
Running time: 93 minutes.

Freddie Francis

Two and Two Make Six (U.K.: British Lion-Bryanston, 1962)
A Prometheus Film.
A Monja Danischewsky Production.
Executive producer: Norman Priggen.
Producer: Monja Danischewsky.
Director: Freddie Francis.
Screenplay: Monja Danischewsky.
Photography: Desmond Dickinson, Ronnie Taylor.
Second unit photography: Denys Coop.
Art direction: Ted Marshall.
Editor: Peter Taylor.
Composer-conductor: Norrie Paramor.
Makeup: Harold Fletcher.
Costumes by Nathans.
Sound: John Cox, Teddy Mason.
Sound recording: Dickie Bird, Edgar Law.
Assistant director: Jim Brennan.
Cast: George Chakiris (Larry Curado), Janette Scott (Irene), Alfred Lynch (Tom), Jackie Lane (Julie), Athene Seyler (Aunt Phoebe), Malcolm Keen (Harry Stoneham), Ambrosine

Phillpotts (Lady Smith-Adams), Jack MacGowran (Night Porter), Robert Ayres (Colonel Thompson), Edward Evans (Mack), Gary Cockrill (Leo Kober), Bernard Braden (Sergeant Sokolow), Harry Locke (Ted), Jeremy Lloyd (Young Man), Marianne Stone (Hotel Receptionist), Nina Parry (Prudence), Ken Wayne (Major Calhoun), Bill Mitchell (Bob Young), Eric Woodburn (Dresser), Bob Kantor, John Gardner, Bill Edwards, George Sperdakos (Air Policemen), Patricia English (Club Stewardess).
Running time: 89 minutes.

The Day of the Triffids (U.K.: Rank, 1962) [U.S.: Allied Artists, 1963]
A Security Film.
A Philip Yordan Production.
Executive producer: Philip Yordan.
Producer: George Pitcher [Bernard Glasser, uncredited].
Director: Steve Sekely [lighthouse scenes directed by Francis, uncredited].
Screenplay: Philip Yordan [lighthouse scenes by Bernard Gordon, uncredited].
Based on the novel by John Wyndham.
Photography: Ted Moore (Eastman color, CinemaScope) [lighthouse scenes by Arthur Grant, uncredited].
Art direction: Cedric Dawe.
Supervising editor: Spencer Reeve.
Composer-conductor: Ron Goodwin.
Additional music: Johnny Douglas.
Makeup: Paul Rabiger.
Sound recording: Bert Ross, Maurice Askew.
Sound editor: Matt McCarthy.
Special effects photography: Wally Veevers.
Assistant director: Douglas Hermes.
Main Cast: Howard Keel (Bill Masen), Nicole Maurey (Christine Durrant), Mervyn Johns (Coker), Ewan Roberts (Dr. Soames), Alison Leggatt (Miss Coker), Janina [Janine] Faye (Susan), Geoffrey Matthews (Luis de la Vega), Gilgi Hauser (Teresa de la Vega), Carol Ann Ford (Bettina), Collette Wilde (Nurse Jamison), Victor Brooks (Poiret), Katya Douglas (Mary), Thomas Gallagher (Burly Man), Sidney Vivian (Ticket Agent), Gary Hope (Pilot), John Simpson (Blind Man).
Cast for lighthouse scenes: Janette Scott (Karen Goodwin), Kieron Moore (Tom Goodwin).
Running time: 94 minutes.

Ein Toter sucht seinen Morder [A Dead Man Seeks His Murderer] (West Germany, 1962) [U.K.: *Vengeance* (Garrick-British Lion, 1963); U.S.: *The Brain* (Governor, 1965)]
A Raymond Stross–C. C. C. Film.
Executive producer: Artur Brauner.
Producer: Raymond Stross.
Director: Freddie Francis.
Screenplay: Robert Stewart, Philip Mackie.
Based on the novel *Donovan's Brain* by Curt Siodmak.
Photography: Bob Huke.
Art direction: Arthur Lawson.
Editor: Oswald Hafenrichter.
Composer-conductor: Kenneth V. Jones.
Makeup: George Frost.
Director of sound: Stephen Dalby.
Sound mixer: Bill Bulkley.
Assistant director: Buddy Booth.
Cast: Anne Heywood (Anna Holt), Peter Van Eyck (Dr. Peter Corrie), Cecil Parker (Stevenson), Bernard Lee (Frank Shears), Ellen Schwiers (Ella), Maxine Audley (Marion Fane), Jeremy

Spenser (Martin Holt), Siegfried Lowitz (Walters), Hans Nielsen (Immerman), Miles Malleson (Dr. Miller), Jack MacGowran (Furber), George A. Cooper (Gabler), Irene Richmond (Mrs. Gabler), Ann Sears (Secretary), Victor Brooks (Farmer), Alistair Williams (Inspector Pike), Kenneth Kendall (Newscaster), John Junkin (Frederick), Frank Forsyth (Francis), Bandana Das Gupta (Miss Soong), Allan Cuthbertson (Dr. Silva), Richard McNeff (Parkin), John Watson (Priest), Patsy Rowlands (Dancehall Girl), Brian Pringle (Master of Ceremonies).
Running time: 83 minutes.

Paranoiac (U.K./U.S.; Universal, 1963)

A Hammer Film.
Producer: Anthony Hinds.
Associate producer: Basil Keys.
Director: Freddie Francis.
Screenplay: Jimmy Sangster.
Photography: Arthur Grant (widescreen).
Production design: Bernard Robinson.
Art direction: Don Mingaye.
Supervising editor: James Needs.
Composer: Elisabeth Lutyens.
Music supervisor: John Hollingsworth.
Makeup: Roy Ashton.
Sound recording: Ken Rawkins.
Sound editor: James Groom.
Special effects: Les Bowie.
Assistant director: Ross Mackenzie.
Cast: Janette Scott (Eleanor Ashby), Oliver Reed (Simon Ashby), Sheila Burrell (Aunt Harriet Ashby), Maurice Denham (John Kosset [Kossett]), Alexander Davion (Tony Ashby), Liliane Brousse (Francoise), John Bonney (Keith Kosset [Kossett]), John Stuart (Williams), Colin Tapley (Vicar), Harold Lang (RAF Type), Laurie Leigh (First Woman), Marianne Stone (Second Woman), Sydney Bromley (Tramp), Jack Taylor (Sailor), Arnold Diamond.
Running time: 80 minutes.

Nightmare (U.K./U.S.; Universal, 1964)

A Hammer Film.
Producer: Jimmy Sangster.
Director: Freddie Francis.
Screenplay: Jimmy Sangster.
Photography: John Wilcox (Hammerscope).
Production design: Bernard Robinson.
Art direction: Don Mingaye.
Supervising editor: James Needs.
Composer: Don Banks.
Music supervisor: John Hollingsworth.
Makeup: Roy Ashton.
Sound recording: Ken Rawkins.
Sound editor: James Groom.
Assistant director: Douglas Hermes.
Cast: David Knight (Henry Baxter), Moira Redmond (Grace Maddox), Jennie Linden (Janet), Brenda Bruce (Mary Lewis), George A. Cooper (John), Irene Richmond (Mrs. Gibbs), Timothy Bateson (Barman), John Welsh (Doctor), Clytie Jessop (Woman in White), Elizabeth Dear (Janet, as a child), Hedger [Geoffrey] Wallace (Sir Dudley), Julie Samuel (Maid), Isla Cameron (Janet's Mother).
Running time: 82 minutes.

The Evil of Frankenstein (U.K./U.S.; Universal, 1964)

A Hammer Film.
Producer: Anthony Hinds.
Director: Freddie Francis.
Screenplay: John Elder [Anthony Hinds].
Photography: John Wilcox (Eastman color).
Art direction: Don Mingaye.
Supervising editor: James Needs.
Composer: Don Banks.
Music supervisor: Philip Martell.
Makeup: Roy Ashton.
Sound recording: Ken Rawkins.
Sound editor: Roy Hyde.
Special effects: Les Bowie.
Assistant director: Bill Cartlidge.
Cast: Peter Cushing (Baron Frankenstein), Peter Woodthorpe (Zoltan), Duncan Lamont (Chief
     of Police), Sandor Eles (Hans), Katy Wild (Beggar Girl), David Hutcheson (Burgomaster),
     James Maxwell (Priest), Howard Goorney (Drunk), Anthony Blackshaw (Policeman),
     David Conville (Policeman), Caron Gardner (Burgomaster's Wife), Kiwi Kingston (The
     Creature), Tony Arpino (Body Snatcher), Alister Williamson (Landlord), Frank Forsyth
     (Manservant), Kenneth Cove (Cure), Michele Scott (Little Girl), Timothy Bateson (Hyp-
     notized Man), Derek Martin, Robert Flynn, Anthony Poole, James Garfield (Roustabouts).
Running time: 86 minutes.

Hysteria (U.K./U.S.; MGM, 1965)

A Hammer Film.
Producer: Jimmy Sangster.
Director: Freddie Francis.
Screenplay: Jimmy Sangster.
Photography: John Wilcox.
Production design: Edward Carrick.
Supervising editor: James Needs.
Composer: Don Banks.
Music supervisor: Philip Martell.
Makeup: Alec Garfath.
Sound recording: Cyril Swern.
Sound editor: Roy Hyde.
Assistant director: Basil Rayburn.
Cast: Robert Webber (Smith), Lelia Goldoni (Denise), Anthony Newlands (Dr. Keller), Jennifer
     Jayne (Gina), Maurice Denham (Hemmings), Sandra Boize (English Girl), Peter
     Woodthorpe (Marcus Allan), Sue Lloyd (French Girl), John Arnatt, Marianne Stone, Irene
     Richmond, Kiwi Kingston.
Running time: 85 minutes.

Traitor's Gate [*Das Verratertor*] (West Germany-U.K.; Columbia, 1964)

A Summit Film.
Producer: Ted Lloyd.
Director: Freddie Francis.
Screenplay: John Sansom [Jimmy Sangster].
Based on the novel by Edgar Wallace.
Photography: Denys Coop.
Art direction: Tony Inglis.
Editor: Oswald Hafenrichter.
Makeup: Jill Carpenter.

Sound recording: Bill Bulkley.
Sound editor: John S. Smith.
Assistant director: Claude Hudson.
Cast: Gary Raymond (Arthur Graham/Lt. Lee-Carnaby), Albert Lieven (Trayne), Margot Trooger
(Dinah Pauling), Catherina von Schell (Hope Joyner), Edward Underdown (Inspector
Adam), Eddi Arent (Hector Ollarby), Klaus Kinski (Kinski), Anthony James (John, the chauf-
feur), Heinz Bernard (Martin), Peter Porteous (Kelly), Maurice Good (King), Alec Ross (Sgt.
Carter), Robert Hunter (Captain), Harry Baird (Mate), Dave Birks (Spider), Tim Barrett
(Lieut. Lloyd), Alan Rolfe (Yeoman Warder), Beresford Williams (Warder), [Geoffrey] Hedger
Wallace (Det. Sgt. Alexander), Marianne Stone (Cashier at Dandy Club), Julie Mendez (Strip-
per), Joe Ritchie (News Vendor), Katy Wild (Mary), Frank Forsyth (Chief Yeoman Warder),
Karen [Caron] Gardner (Blonde), Frank Seaman (Yeoman Warder Guide).
Running time: 80 minutes.

Dr. Terror's House of Horrors (U.K.; Regal, 1965) [U.S.: Paramount]

An Amicus Film.
Producers: Milton Subotsky, Max J. Rosenberg.
Director: Freddie Francis.
Screenplay: Milton Subotsky.
Photography: Alan Hume (Technicolor, Techniscope).
Art direction: Bill Constable.
Editor: Thelma Connell.
Composer: Elizabeth Lutyens.
Songs: Kenny Lynch.
Jazz music: Tubby Hayes.
Choreography: Boscoe Holder.
Makeup: Roy Ashton.
Director of sound: John Cox.
Sound recording: Buster Ambler.
Dubbing editor: Roy Hyde.
Special effects: Ted Samuels.
Assistant director: Bert Batt.
Cast: Peter Cushing (Dr. Terror [Dr. Sandor Schreck]).
["Werewolf"] Neil McCallum (Jim Dawson), Ursula Howells (Deirdre Biddulph), Katy
Wild (Valda), Peter Madden (Caleb), Edward Underdown (Tod), George Mossman (Pony
and Trap Driver).
["Creeping Vine"] Alan Freeman (Bill Rogers), Ann Bell (Ann Rogers), Sarah Nicholls
(Carol Rogers), Bernard Lee (Hopkins), Jeremy Kemp (Drake), Tauros (dog).
["Voodoo"] Roy Castle (Biff Bailey), Kenny Lynch (Sammy Coin), Christopher Carlos
(Vrim), Thomas Baptiste (Dambala), Harold Lang (Shine), The Tubby Hayes Quintet, Russ
Henderson Steel Band.
["Disembodied Hand"] Christopher Lee (Franklyn Marsh), Michael Gough (Eric Landor),
Hedger [Geoffrey] Wallace (Surgeon), Judy Cornwell (Nurse), Frank Forsyth (Toastmaster),
James (chimpanzee).
["Vampire"] Donald Sutherland (Bob Carroll), Jennifer Jayne (Nicolle), Max Adrian (Dr.
Blake), Irene Richmond (Mrs. Ellis), Frank Barry (Johnny), Laurie Leigh (Nurse), Al
Mulock (Detective).
Also: Isla Blair, Brian Hawkins, Faith Kent, John Martin, Kenneth Kove, Walter Sparrow,
Valerie St. Clair.
Running time: 98 minutes.

The Skull (U.K./U.S.; Paramount, 1965)

An Amicus Film.
Producers: Milton Subotsky, Max J. Rosenberg.

Director: Freddie Francis.
Screenplay: Milton Subotsky.
Based on the story "The Skull of the Marquis de Sade" by Robert Bloch.
Photography: John Wilcox (Technicolor, Techniscope)
Art direction: Bill Constable.
Set decoration: Scott Slimon.
Editor: Oswald Hafenrichter.
Composer: Elisabeth Lutyens.
Makeup: Jill Carpenter.
Sound supervisor: John Cox.
Sound recording: Buster Ambler.
Sound editor: Tom Priestley.
Special effects: Ted Samuels.
Assistant director: Anthony Waye.
Cast: Peter Cushing (Christopher Maitland), Patrick Wymark (Marco), Christopher Lee (Sir
    Matthew Phillips), Jill Bennett (Jane Maitland), Nigel Green (Inspector Wilson), Patrick
    Magee (Police Surgeon), Peter Woodthorpe (Bert Travers), Michael Gough (Auctioneer),
    George Coulouris (Dr. Londe), April Olrich (French Girl), Maurice Good (Phrenologist),
    Anna Palk (Maid), Frank Forsyth (Judge), Paul Stockman (First Guard), Geoffrey Cheshire
    (Second Guard), George Hilsdon (Policeman), Jack Silk (Driver).
Running time: 83 minutes.

The Psychopath (U.K./U.S.; Paramount, 1966)

An Amicus Film.
Producers: Max J. Rosenberg, Milton Subotsky.
Director: Freddie Francis.
Screenplay: Robert Bloch.
Photography: John Wilcox (Technicolor, Techniscope).
Art direction: Bill Constable.
Set decoration: Scott Slimon.
Editor: Oswald Hafenrichter.
Composer: Elisabeth Lutyens.
Makeup: Jill Carpenter.
Dolls supplied by Doll Industries and Irene Blair Hickman.
Miss Huxtable's wardrobe by Carnegie.
Sound supervisor: John Cox.
Sound recording: Baron Mason.
Sound editor: Janet Davidson.
Special effects: Ted Samuels.
Assistant director: Peter Price.
Cast: Patrick Wymark (Inspector Holloway), Margaret Johnston (Mrs. von Sturm), John Stand-
    ing (Mark von Sturm), Alexander Knox (Frank Saville), Judy Huxtable (Louise Saville),
    Don Borisenko (Donald Loftis), Thorley Walters (Martin Roth), Robert Crewdson (Victor
    Ledoux), Colin Gordon (Dr. Glyn), Tim Barrett (Morgan), Frank Forsyth (Tucker), Olive
    Gregg (Mary), Harold Lang (Briggs), Gina Gianelli (Gina), Peter Diamond (Junk Yard
    Man), John Harvey (Reinhardt Klermer), Greta Farrer (Cigarette Girl), Caron Gardner
    (Model in Nightclub).
Running time: 82 minutes.

The Deadly Bees (U.K./U.S.; Paramount, 1967)

An Amicus Film.
Producers: Max J. Rosenberg, Milton Subotsky.
Director: Freddie Francis.
Screenplay: Robert Bloch, Anthony Marriott.

Based on the novel *A Taste for Honey* by H. F. Heard.
Photography: John Wilcox (Technicolor)
Art direction: Bill Constable.
Set decoration: Andrew Low.
Editor: Oswald Hafenrichter.
Composer: Wilfred Josephs.
Songs: "It's Not What I Need You For" sung by The Birds, "Baby, Let Me Love You" sung by Elkie Brooks.
Makeup: Jill Carpenter.
Furs by Deanfield Models.
Sound recording: Ken Rawkins.
Sound editor: Michael Pidcock.
Special effects: Michael Collins.
Special effects cameraman: John Mackey.
Assistant director: Anthony Waye.
Cast: Suzanna Leigh (Vicki Robbins), Frank Finlay (Manfred), Guy Doleman (Hargrove), Catherine Finn (Mrs. Hargrove), John Harvey (Thompson), Michael Ripper (Hawkins), Anthony Bailey (Compere), Tim Barrett (Harcourt), James Cossins (Coroner), Frank Forsyth (Doctor), Katy Wild (Doris Hawkins), Greta Farrer (Sister), Gina Gianelli (Secretary), Michael Gwynn (Doctor Lang), Maurice Good (Agent), Alister Williamson (Inspector).
Running time: 84 minutes.

They Came from beyond Space (U.K.; Planet, 1967) [U.S.: Embassy]
An Amicus Film.
Producers: Max J. Rosenberg, Milton Subotsky.
Director: Freddie Francis.
Screenplay: Milton Subotsky.
Based on the novel *The Gods Hate Kansas* by Joseph Millard.
Photography: Norman Warwick (Eastman color, prints by Pathé).
Production design: Bill Constable.
Art direction: Don Mingaye, Scott Slimon.
Editor: Peter Musgrave.
Composer: James Stevens.
Makeup: Bunty Phillips.
Sound recording: George Stephenson.
Sound editor: Clive Smith.
Models made and photographed at Bowie Films.
Assistant director: Ray Corbett.
Cast: Robert Hutton (Dr. Curtis Temple), Jennifer Jayne (Lee Mason), Zia Mohyeddin (Farge), Bernard Kay (Richard Arden), Michael Gough (Master of the Moon), Geoffrey [Hedger] Wallace (Allan Mullane), Maurice Good (Stilwell), Luanshya Greer (Girl Attendant), John Harvey (Bill Trethowan), Diana King (Mrs. Trethowan), Paul Bacon (Rogers), Christopher Banks (Doctor—Street), Dermot Cathie (Peterson), Norman Claridge (Dr. Andrews), James Donnelly (Guard), Frank Forsyth (Blake), Leonard Grahame (McCabe), Michael Hawkins (Williams), Jack Lambert (Doctor—Office), Robin Parkinson (Maitland), Edward Rees (Bank Manager), Katy Wild (Girl in Street), Kenneth Kendall (Commentator).
Running time: 85 minutes.

Torture Garden (U.K./U.S.; Columbia, 1968)
An Amicus Film.
Producers: Max J. Rosenberg, Milton Subotsky.
Director: Freddie Francis.
Screenplay: Robert Bloch.
[Based on short stories by Robert Bloch, uncredited.]

Photography: Norman Warwick (Technicolor).
Production design: Bill Constable.
Art direction: Don Mingaye, Scott Slimon.
Set dressing: Andrew Low.
Editor: Peter Elliott.
Composers: Don Banks, James Bernard.
Piano solo played by Martino Tirimo.
Makeup: Jill Carpenter.
Sound recording: Ken Rawkins.
Sound editor: Ken Rolls.
Assistant director: Derrick Parr.
Cast: Burgess Meredith (Dr. Diabolo), Michael Ripper (Gordon Roberts), Timothy Bateson
   (Fairground Barker), Clytie Jessop (Atropos).
   ["Enoch"] Michael Bryant (Colin Williams), Maurice Denham (Uncle Roger), Niall
   MacGinnis (Doctor), Catherine Finn (Nurse Parker), Michael Hawkins (Constable).
   ["Terror over Hollywood"] Beverly Adams (Carla Hayes), Robert Hutton (Bruce Benton),
   David Bauer (Mike Charles), Bernard Kay (Dr. Heim), Nicole Shelby (Millie), John Phillips
   (Eddie Storm).
   ["Mr. Steinway"] John Standing (Leo Winston), Barbara Ewing (Dorothy Endicott), Ursula
   Howells (Maxine Chambers).
   ["The Man Who Collected Poe"] Jack Palance (Ronald Wyatt), Peter Cushing (Lancelot
   Canning), Geoffrey [Hedger] Wallace (Edgar Allan Poe).
   Also: Roy Stevens, James Copeland, Norman Claridge, Roy Godfrey, Barry Low.
Running time: 93 minutes.

Dracula Has Risen from the Grave (U.K.; Warner Pathe, 1968) [U.S.: Warner Bros.-Seven Arts, 1969]

A Hammer Film.
Producer: Aida Young.
Director: Freddie Francis.
Screenplay: John Elder [Anthony Hinds].
Based on the character created by Bram Stoker.
Photography: Arthur Grant (Technicolor)
Supervising art director: Bernard Robinson.
Supervising editor: James Needs.
Editor: Spencer Reeve.
Composer: James Bernard.
Music supervisor: Philip Martell.
Makeup: Heather Nurse, Rosemarie McDonald-Peattie.
Sound recording: Ken Rawkins.
Sound editor: Wilfred Thompson.
Special effects: Frank George.
Matte artist: Peter Melrose.
Assistant director: Dennis Robertson.
Cast: Christopher Lee (Dracula), Rupert Davies (Monsignor), Veronica Carlson (Maria), Bar-
   bara Ewing (Zena), Barry Andrews (Paul), Ewan Hooper (Priest), Marion Mathie (Anna),
   Michael Ripper (Max), John D. Collins (Student), George A. Cooper (Landlord), Chris
   Cunningham (Farmer), Norman Bacon (Boy), Carrie Baker (Victim in Bell).
Running time: 92 minutes.

The Intrepid Mr. Twigg (U.K.; British Lion, 1969)

A Talus International Film.
Producers: Alistair Foot, Anthony Marriott.
Director: Freddie Francis.

Screenplay: Robert W. O'Brien, Keith Williams.
Based on an original story by Keith Williams.
Photography: Aubrey Dewar (color).
Editor: Peter Mayhew.
Composer–conductor: Max Harris.
Song lyrics: Roy Castle.
Makeup: Audrey Clegg.
Special effects: Gordon Straithairn.
Assistant director: Gary White.
Cast: Roy Castle (Mr. Twigg), Clovissa Newcombe (Girl), Jack Haig (Garage Owner), Clayton and Walker (Crooks), Peter Frazer (Young Sports Car Driver), Peter Elliott (Chemist), Dennis Ramsden (Policeman), Jackie Toye (Nurse), Arthur Watson, Stephen Campbell (Ambulance Men).
Running time: 36 minutes.

Mumsy, Nanny, Sonny, and Girly (U.K./U.S.; Cinerama, 1970)

A Fitzroy-Francis Film.
Producer: Ronald J. Kahn.
Associate producer: Peter J. Thompson.
Director: Freddie Francis.
Screenplay: Brian Comport.
Based on the play *Happy Family* by Maisie Mosco.
Photography: David Muir (Eastman color)
Art direction: Maggie Pinhorn.
Set decoration: Dimity Collins.
Editor: Tristam Cones.
Composer–conductor: Bernard Ebbinghouse.
Makeup: Phil Leakey.
Sound mixer: John Brommage.
Assistant director: John Stoneman.
Cast: Michael Bryant (New Friend), Ursula Howells (Mumsy), Pat Heywood (Nanny), Howard Trevor (Sonny), Vanessa Howard (Girly), Robert Swann (Soldier), Imogen Hassall (Girl Friend), Michael Ripper (Zoo Attendant), Hugh Armstrong (Friend #5).
Running time: 102 minutes.

Trog (U.K./U.S.; Warner Bros., 1970)

A Herman Cohen Film.
Producer: Herman Cohen.
Associate producer: Harry Woolveridge.
Director: Freddie Francis.
Screenplay: Aben Kandel.
Based on an original story by Peter Bryan, John Gilling.
Photography: Desmond Dickinson (Technicolor)
Art direction: Geoffrey Tozer.
Set dressing: Helen Thomas.
Editor: Oswald Hafenrichter.
Composer: John Scott.
Makeup: Jim Evans.
Trog designer: Charles Parker.
Sound mixers: Tony Dawe, Maurice Askew.
Sound editor: Michael Redbourn.
Assistant director: Douglas Hermes.
Cast: Joan Crawford (Dr. Brockton), Michael Gough (Sam Murdock), Bernard Kay (Inspector Greenham), Kim Braden (Anne Brockton), David Griffin (Malcolm Travers), John Hamill

(Cliff), Thorley Walters (Magistrate), Jack May (Dr. Selbourne), Geoffrey Case (Bill), Robert Hutton (Dr. Richard Warren), Simon Lack (Colonel Vickers), David Warbeck (Alan Davis), Chloe Franks (Little Girl), Maurice Good (Reporter), Joe Cornelius (Trog), Rona Newton-John (Second Reporter), Robert Crewdson (Dr. Pierre Duval), Paul Hansard (Dr. Kurtlimer), Golda Casimir (Prof. Manoskiensky), Brian Grellis (John Dennis), Cleo Sylvestre (Nurse), John Baker (Anaesthetist), Bartlett Mullins (Butcher), Shirley Cooklin (Little Girl's Mother).

Running time: 91 minutes.

Gebissen wird nur nachts—Happening der Vampire [The Vampire Happening] (West Germany; Constantin-Film, 1971)

An Aquila Film.
Producer: Pier A. Caminneci.
Director: Freddie Francis.
Screenplay: August Rieger.
Based on an idea by Karl Heinz Hummel.
Photography: Gerard Vandenberg (Eastman color)
Art direction: Hans Zehetner.
Editor: Fred Srp.
Composer: Jerry van Rooyen.
Makeup: Jupp Paschke, Helmut Kraft.
Costume design: Lambert Hofer, Jr., Klara Zichy-Kiss.
Miss Degermark's dresses: Uli Richter, Berlin.
Sound: Erwin Tews, Kurt Dau.
Assistant director: Peter Saunders.
Cast: Pia Degermark (Betty Williams), Thomas Hunter, Ivor Murillo, Ingrid van Bergen, Joachim Kemmer, Lyvia Bauer, Daria Damar, Ferdie [Ferdy] Mayne (Dracula), Oskar Wegrostek, Michael Janisch, Toni Wagner, Raoul Retzer, Kay Williams.
Running time: 97 minutes [U.S. video version: 101 minutes].

Tales from the Crypt (U.K./U.S.; Cinerama, 1972)

Presented by Metromedia Producers Corporation.
An Amicus Film.
Executive producer: Charles Fries.
Production executive: Paul Thompson.
Producers: Max J. Rosenberg, Milton Subotsky.
Director: Freddie Francis.
Screenplay: Milton Subotsky.
Based on stories by William Gaines, Al Feldstein, Johnny Craig.
Photography: Norman Warwick (Eastman color)
Art direction: Tony Curtis.
Set dressing: Helen Thomas.
Editor: Teddy Darvas.
Composer-conductor: Douglas Gamley.
Bach's Toccata and Fugue in D Minor played by Nicolas Kynaston.
Chief makeup: Roy Ashton.
Sound mixer: Norman Bolland.
Sound editor: Pat Foster.
Dubbing mixer: Nolan Roberts.
Assistant director: Peter Saunders.
Cast: Ralph Richardson (The Crypt Keeper), Geoffrey Bayldon (Guide).
["And All through the House"] Joan Collins (Joanne Clayton), Martin Boddey (Richard Clayton), Chloe Franks (Carol), Oliver MacGreevy (Maniac).
["Reflection of Death"] Ian Hendry (Carl Maitland), Susan Denny (Mrs. Maitland), Angie

Grant (Susan), Frank Forsyth (Tramp), Paul Clere (Maitland's son), Sharon Clere (Maitland's daughter).

["Poetic Justice"] Peter Cushing (Grimsdyke), Robin Phillips (James Elliot), David Markham (Edward Elliot), Robert Hutton (Neighbor), Manning Wilson (Vicar), Dan Caulfield (Postman), Edward Evans (Mr. Ramsay), Ann Sears (Mrs. Carter), Kay Adrian (Mrs. Davies), Carlos Baker (Mrs. Davies's Son), Melinda Clancy (Mrs. Carter's Daughter), Clifford Earl (Police Sergeant), Irene Gawne (Mrs. Phelps), Stafford Medhurst (Mrs. Phelps's Son).

["Wish You Were Here"] Richard Greene (Ralph Jason), Barbara Murray (Enid Jason), Roy Dotrice (Gregory), Hedger [Geoffrey] Wallace (Detective), Peter Thomas (Undertaker).

["Blind Alleys"] Nigel Patrick (William Rogers), Patrick Magee (George Carter), Harry Locke (Cook), Bartlett Mullins, Carl Bernard, Bert Palmer, Louis Mansi, Ernest C. Jennings, John Barrard, Chris Cannon, Hugo de Vernier, George Herbert (Blind Men).

Also: Peter Frazer, Jayne Sofiano, Tony Wall.

Running time: 92 minutes.

The Creeping Flesh (U.K.; Tigon, 1973) [U.S.: Columbia]

A World Film Services Film.
Executive producer: Norman Priggen.
Producer: Michael Redbourn.
Director: Freddie Francis.
Original screenplay: Peter Spenceley, Jonathan Rumbold.
Photography: Norman Warwick (Eastman color).
Art direction: George Provis.
Set dressing: Peter James.
Editor: Oswald Hafenrichter.
Composer-conductor: Paul Ferris.
Makeup: Roy Ashton.
Sound recording: Norman Bolland, Nolan Roberts.
Dubbing editor: Colin Miller.
Assistant director: Peter Saunders.
Cast: Christopher Lee (James Hildern), Peter Cushing (Emmanuel Hildern), Lorna Heilbron (Penelope Hildern), George Benson (Waterlow), Kenneth J. Warren (Lenny), Duncan Lamont (Inspector), Harry Locke (Barman), Hedger [Geoffrey] Wallace (Dr. Perry), Michael Ripper (Carter), Catherine Finn (Emily), Robert Swann (Young Aristocrat), David Bailie (Young Doctor), Maurice Bush (Karl), Tony Wright (Sailor), Marianne Stone (Female Assistant), Alexandra Dane (Whore), Jenny Runacre (Emmanuel's Wife), Larry Taylor (1st Warder), Martin Carroll (2nd Warder), Dan Meaden (Lunatic).
Running time: 92 minutes.

Son of Dracula (U.K.; 1973?) [U.S.: Cinemation, 1974]

An Apple Film.
Producer: Ringo Starr.
Director: Freddie Francis.
Screenplay: Jay Fairbank [Jennifer Jayne].
Photography: Norman Warwick (color)
Art direction: Andrew Sanders.
Set decoration: Tessa Davies.
Consultant editor: Derek York.
Music editor: Paul Davies.
Composer: Paul Buckmaster.
Songs: Harry Nilsson, T. Rex, Abner-Moore, Ham-Evans.
Makeup: Jill Carpenter.

Sound mixer: Tony Jackson.
Dubbing editor: Mike Redbourn.
Dubbing mixer: Hugh Strain.
Motorcycle sequences: White Helmets, Royal Signals Display Team.
Assistant director: Peter Saunders.
Cast: Harry Nilsson (Count Downe), Ringo Starr (Merlin), Suzanna Leigh (Amber), Dennis Price (Van Helsing), Freddie Jones (The Baron), David Bailie (Chauffeur), Shakira Baksh (Housekeeper), Morris Bush (Monster), John Coleclaugh (Bill), Nita Lorraine (Gorgon Woman), Skip Martin (Igor), Dan Meaden (Count Dracula), Rachelle Miller (Club Hostess), Beth Morris (Wendy), Jenny Runacre (Woman in Black), Hedger [Geoffrey] Wallace (Vampire), Lorna Wilde (Countess Dracula), Derek Woodward (Werewolf), John Bonham, Peter Frampton, Ricki Farr, Bobby Keyes, Keith Moon, Jim Price, Klaus Voormann (The Count Downes).
Running time: 91 minutes.

Tales That Witness Madness (U.K.; World, 1973) [U.S.: Paramount]
A World Film Services Film.
Producer: Norman Priggen.
Director: Freddie Francis.
Original screenplay: Jay Fairbank [Jennifer Jayne].
Photography: Norman Warwick (Eastman color).
Art direction: Roy Walker.
Set dressing: Michael Lamont.
Editor: Bernard Gribble.
Composer-conductor: Bernard Ebbinghouse.
Makeup: Eric Allwright.
Sound recording: Ken Ritchie, Nolan Roberts.
Dubbing editor: Allan Sones.
Assistant director: Peter Saunders.
Cast: Jack Hawkins (Nicholas), Donald Pleasence (Tremayne).
["Mr. Tiger"] Georgia Brown (Fay), Donald Houston (Sam), Russell Lewis (Paul), David Wood (Tutor).
["Penny Farthing"] Suzy Kendall (Ann/Beatrice), Peter McEnery (Timothy), Neil Kennedy (1st Removal Man), Richard Connaught (2nd Removal Man), Beth Morris (Polly), Frank Forsyth (Uncle Albert).
["Mel"] Joan Collins (Bella), Michael Jayston (Brian).
["Luau"] Kim Novak (Auriol), Michael Petrovitch (Kimo), Mary Tamm (Ginny), Lesley Nunnerley (Vera), Leon Lissek (Keoki), Zohra Segal (Malia).
Running time: 90 minutes.

Craze (U.K.; EMI, 1974) [U.S.: Warner Bros.]
A Herman Cohen Film.
Executive producer: Gustave Berne.
Producer: Herman Cohen.
Director: Freddie Francis.
Screenplay: Aben Kandel, Herman Cohen.
Based on the novel *Infernal Idol* by Henry Seymour.
Photography: John Wilcox (Technicolor).
Art direction: George Provis.
Set dressing: Helen Thomas.
Editor: Henry Richardson.
Composer-conductor: John Scott.
Makeup: Bill Lodge.
Sound editor: Mike LeMare.

Sound mixer: Ken Ritchie.

Assistant director: Peter Saunders.

Cast: Jack Palance (Neal Mottram), Diana Dors (Dolly Newman), Julie Ege (Helena), Edith Evans (Aunt Louise), Hugh Griffith (Solicitor), Trevor Howard (Supt. Bellamy), Michael Jayston (Sgt. Wall), Suzy Kendall (Sally), Martin Potter (Ronnie), Percy Herbert (Detective Russet), David Warbeck (Detective Wilson), Kathleen Byron (Muriel Sharp), Venecia Day (Girl Dancer), Marianne Stone (Barmaid), Dean Harris (Ronnie's Friend).

Running time: 96 minutes.

The Ghoul (U.K.; Rank, 1975)

A Tyburn Film.

Producer: Kevin Francis.

Director: Freddie Francis.

Screenplay: John Elder [Anthony Hinds].

Photography: John Wilcox (Eastman color).

Art direction: Jack Shampan.

Editor: Henry Richardson.

Composer: Harry Robinson.

Music supervisor: Philip Martell.

Makeup created by Roy Ashton.

Makeup: Jimmy Evans.

Costume design: Anthony Mendleson.

Costumes executed by Bermans & Nathans of London.

Sound recording: John Brommage, Ken Barker.

Sound editor: Roy Baker.

Process photography: Charles Staffell.

Assistant director: Peter Saunders.

Cast: Peter Cushing (Doctor Lawrence), John Hurt (Tom Rawlings), Alexandra Bastedo (Angela), Gwen Watford (Ayah), Veronica Carlson (Daphne), Stewart Bevan (Billy), Ian McCulloch (Geoffrey), Don Henderson (The Ghoul), John D. Collins (Young Man), Dan Meaden (Police Sergeant).

Running time: 84 minutes [British videotape: 90 minutes].

Legend of the Werewolf (U.K.; Rank, 1975)

A Tyburn Film.

Producer: Kevin Francis.

Director: Freddie Francis.

Screenplay: John Elder [Anthony Hinds].

Photography: John Wilcox (Eastman color).

Art direction: Jack Shampan.

Editor: Henry Richardson.

Composer: Harry Robinson.

Music supervisor: Philip Martell.

Makeup: Jimmy Evans, Graham Freeborn.

Sound recording: John Brommage, Ken Barker.

Sound editor: Roy Baker.

Special photographic effects: Charles Staffell.

Assistant director: Peter Saunders.

Cast: Peter Cushing (Professor Paul Cataflanque), Ron Moody (Zoo Keeper), Hugh Griffith (Maestro Pamponi), Roy Castle (Photographer), David Rintoul (Etoile), Lynn Dalby (Christine), Stefan Gryff (Max Gerard), Mark Weavers (Young Etoile), Renée Houston (Chou-Chou), Norman Mitchell (Tiny), Marjorie Yates (Madame Tellier), Patrick Holt (Dignitary), John Harvey (Prefect), David Bailie (Boulon), Michael Ripper (Sewerman),

Pamela Green (Anne-Marie), Elaine Baillie (Annabelle), Hilary Labow (Zoe), Sue Bishop (Tania), James McManus (Emigre Husband), Jane Cussons (Emigre Wife).
Running time: 86 minutes.

Golden Rendezvous (U.K.; Rank, 1977) [TV: Nuclear Terror]

A Film Trust-Milton Okun Productions/Golden Rendezvous Productions Film.
Executive producer: Murray Frank.
Producer: André Pieters.
Associate producer: Robert Porter.
Director: Ashley Lazarus.
[Precredits sequence directed by Freddie Francis, uncredited].
Screenplay: Stanley Price.
Adaptation: John Gay.
Based on the novel by Alistair MacLean.
Photography: Ken Higgins (color).
[Precredits sequence photographed by Arthur Grant, uncredited].
Art direction: Frank White.
Editor: Ralph Kemplen.
Composer-conductor: Jeff Wayne.
Makeup: Richard Mills, Wally Schneiderman, George Frost.
Sound recording: John Bramall.
Sound editor: Nick Stevenson.
Cast: Richard Harris, David Janssen, Ann Turkel, Burgess Meredith, John Verson, Gordon Jackson, Keith Baxter, Dorothy Malone, John Carradine.
Running time: 103 minutes.

The Doctor and the Devils (U.K.; Brooksfilms, 1985) [U.S.: 20th Century–Fox]

A Brooksfilms Film, in association with Dr. Babbington Cooper and Burton Gintell.
A Jonathan Sanger Production.
Executive producer: Mel Brooks.
Associate producer: Geoffrey Helman.
Associate producers for Brooksfilms: Jo Lustig, Barbara Stone, David C. Stone.
Producer: Jonathan Sanger.
Director: Freddie Francis.
Screenplay: Ronald Harwood.
Based on an original screenplay by Dylan Thomas.
Photography: Gerry Turpin, Norman Warwick (J-D-C Widescreen, Rank color).
Production design: Robert Laing.
Art direction: Brian Ackland-Snow.
Set decoration: Peter James.
Editor: Laurence Mery-Clark.
Composer-conductor: John Morris.
"Tainted Hands" and other incidental music written and performed by In Tua Nua.
"Whisper and I Shall Hear" sung by Twiggy; music by M. Piccolomini, words by C. Hubi Newcombe.
Makeup designer: Naomi Donne.
Costumes: Imogen Richardson.
Hair design: Sally Sutton.
Sound mixer: Ken Weston.
Sound editor: Alan Paley.
Dubbing mixer: John Iles.
Special effects: Alan Bryce.
Assistant director: Peter Bennett.
Cast: Timothy Dalton (Dr. Thomas Rock), Jonathan Pryce (Robert Fallon), Twiggy (Jenny Bai-

ley), Julian Sands (Dr. Murray), Stephen Rea (Timothy Broom), Beryl Reid (Mrs. Flynn), Phyllis Logan (Elizabeth Rock), Lewis Fiander (Dr. Thornton), T. P. McKenna (O'Connor), Patrick Stewart (Prof. Macklin), Sian Phillips (Annabella Rock), Philip Davis (Billy Bedlam), Philip Jackson (Andrew Merry-Lees), Danny Schiller (Praying Howard), Bruce Green (Mole), Toni Palmer (Rosie), David Bamber (Cronin), Nichola McAuliffe (Alice), Deidre Costello (Nelly), Terry Neason (Kate), Paul Curran (Tom the Porter), Merelina Kendall (Mrs. Webb), Dermot Crowley (Mr. Webb), Sarah Melia (Nora Webb), Stephen Yardley (Joseph), John Horsley (Dr. Mackendrick), Jack May (Dr. Stevens), Rachel Herbert (Mrs. Stevens), Simon Shepherd (Harding), David Parfitt (Billings), Simon Adams (Green), Jeff Rawle (Lambert), Morgan Sheppard (Landlord), Jennifer Jayne (Barmaid), Moira Brooker (Molly the Maid), P. G. Stevens (Priest), Roy Evans (Sewerman), Peter Burton (Customer), Leonard Maguire (Nightwatchman), Hedger [Geoffrey] Wallace (Doctor), Ray Dunbobbin (Tinker), Martin Herring (Messenger), Shaun Curry (Policeman), David Grahame (Old Man), Kevin Duffield (Daniel), Ray Armstrong (Prison Guard), Sam Bartlett (Prison Guard).
Running time: 93 minutes.

The Dark Tower (Fries, 1987)

A Testzone Film.
Presented by Sandy Howard.
Executive producers: Tom Fox, Ken Wiederhorn.
Producers: John R. Bowey, David M. Witz.
Coproducer: Paco Poch.
Associate producers: Tom Merchant, Michael Masciarelli.
Director: Ken Barnett [Freddie Francis].
Screenplay: Robert J. Averech, Ken Blackwell, Ken Wiederhorn.
Based on a story by Robert J. Avreck [Averech].
Photography: Gordon Hayman (color).
Art direction: Jose Maria Espada.
Art director for U.S. scenes: Jimmy Williams.
Set decoration: Juan Alberto, Jr.
Editor: Tom Merchant.
Associate editor: Timothy Fletcher.
Composer: Stacy Widelitz.
Special effects makeup: Steve Neill.
Makeup: Caitlin Acheson.
Costume designer: Josefa Sentier.
Sound mixers: Jaume Puig [Spanish crew], Margaret Duke [U.S. crew].
Special visual effects: Quicksilver Studio.
Special effects: Enrique Jorba, Paco Teres.
Second unit director: Dan Bradley.
Second unit photography: Chris Tufty.
Cast: Michael Moriarty (Dennis Randall), Jenny Agutter (Carolyn Page), Carol Lynley (Tilly), Theodore Bikel (Max Gold), Anne Lockhart (Elaine), Kevin McCarthy (Sergie), Patch Mackenzie (Maria), Robert Sherman (Williams), Rick Azulay (Charlie), Radmiro Oliveros (Joseph), Jordi Batalla (Mueller), Juame Ross (Beck), Monica Fatjo (Rebecca), Juan Ramon Romani (Philip Page), Mara Bador (Rebecca's Mother), Freddie Francis (Man in Elevator).
Running time: 91 minutes

INDEX

THE AUTHOR

Paul M. Jensen is an Associate Professor at the State University of New York at Oneonta. A member of the Speech Communication and Theatre Department, he teaches courses in film history and appreciation. After graduating from SUNY-Albany, Mr. Jensen received his M.F.A. in Film, Radio, and Television from Columbia University. He is the author of two books, *The Cinema of Fritz Lang* and *Boris Karloff and His Films*, and has contributed articles to various magazines, including *Film Comment, Films in Review, Video Watchdog,* and *Scarlet Street.*

THE EDITOR

Frank E. Beaver, General Editor of Twayne's Filmmakers Series, was born in Cleveland, North Carolina, in 1938. He was educated at the University of North Carolina, Chapel Hill (B.A., M.A.), and at the University of Michigan (Ph.D.), where he chairs the Department of Communication. He has authored three books on the art and history of the motion picture as well as *Oliver Stone: Wakeup Cinema* (1993) and the *Dictionary of Film Terms* (1994), both published in Twayne's Filmmakers Series. For twenty years he has served as media commentator for National Public Radio stations WUOM-WVGR-WFUM.